THE INTERNATIONAL SURVEY OF FAMILY LAW

2006 EDITION

Published on behalf of the
International Society of Family Law

THE INTERNATIONAL SURVEY OF FAMILY LAW

2006 Edition

General Editor

Andrew Bainham

Fellow of Christ's College, Cambridge
Reader in Family Law and Policy, University of Cambridge, UK

Associate Editor (Africa)

Bart Rwezaura

Associate Professor of Law
University of Hong Kong
Hong Kong

Family Law

Published by

Jordan Publishing Limited
21 St Thomas Street
Bristol BS1 6JS

British Library Cataloguing-in-Publication Data

A catalogue record for this book is available from the British Library.

ISBN 1 84661 017 6

Typeset by Etica Press Ltd, Malvern, Worcestershire

Printed and bound in Great Britain by Antony Rowe Limited, Chippenham, Wiltshire

THE INTERNATIONAL SOCIETY OF FAMILY LAW

ASSOCIATION INTERNATIONALE DE DROIT DE LA FAMILLE

INTERNATIONALE GESELLSCHAFT FÜR FAMILIENRECHT

PUBLISHED ON BEHALF OF THE INTERNATIONAL SOCIETY OF FAMILY LAW

Website: www.law2.byu.edu/ISFL

OFFICERS AND COUNCIL MEMBERS 2005–2008

PRESIDENT
Professor Paul Vlaardingerbroek
Faculty of Law
Tilburg University
PO Box 90153
5000 LE Tilburg
THE NETHERLANDS
Tel: 013-466-2032/2281
Fax: 013-466-2323
E-mail: p.vlaardingerbroek@uvt.nl

SECRETARY-GENERAL
Professor Marsha Garrison
Brooklyn Law School
250 Joralemon Street
Brooklyn, NY 11201
USA
Tel: 1-718-780-7947
Fax: 1-718-780-0375
E-mail:
marsha.garrison@brooklaw.edu

EDITOR OF THE NEWSLETTER
Professor Margaret F Brinig
College of Law
University of Iowa
Boyd Law Building
Iowa City, IA 52242
USA
Tel: 1-319-335-6811
Fax: 1-319-335-9098
E-mail: margaret-brinig@uiowa.edu

EDITOR OF THE INTERNATIONAL SURVEY
Professor Bill Atkin
Faculty of Law
Victoria University of Wellington
PO Box 600
Wellington
NEW ZEALAND
Tel: (04) 463 6343
Fax: (04) 463 6366
E-mail: bill.atkin@vuw.ac.nz

IMMEDIATE PAST PRESIDENT

Professor Peter Lødrup
Institute of Private Law
Faculty of Law, University of Oslo
PB 6706 St Olavs pl
0130 Oslo
NORWAY
Tel: 47 22 85 97 26
Fax: 47 22 85 97 20
E-mail: peter.lodrup@jus.uio.no

VICE PRESIDENTS

Professor Olga Dyuzheva
Law Faculty
Vorobiovy Gory
Moscow State University
119992 Moscow
RUSSIA
Tel: 095-290-1697
Fax: 095- 939-5195
E-mail: odyuzheva@mtu-net.ru

Professor Dominique Goubau
Faculté de droit
Université Laval
Québec (QUE)
CANADA
G1K 7P4
Tel: 418-656-2131 (poste 2384)
Fax: 418-656-7714
E-mail:
dominique.goubau@fd.ulaval.ca

Professor Nigel Lowe
Cardiff Law School
University of Wales
PO Box 427
Cardiff CF10 3XJ
UK
Tel: 44 029 20 874365
Fax: 44 029 20 874097
E-mail: lowe@cardiff.ac.uk

Professor Dr Miquel Martin-Casals
Facultat de Dret
Universitat de Girona
Campus de Montilivi
17071 Girona
SPAIN
Tel: 34 972 41 81 39
Fax: 34 972 41 81 46
E-mail: martin@elaw.udg.es

Professor June D Sinclair
Pro Vice Chancellor
College of Humanities and Social
Sciences,
Old Teachers College Room U201
University of Sydney
Sydney, New South Wales 2006
AUSTRALIA
Tel: 61 2 93516366, 62 402 285
645
Fax: 61 2 93516368
E-mail:
j.sinclair@chass.usyd.edu.au

Professor Bea Verschraegen
Universitat Wien, Institut fur
Rechtsvergleichung
Juridicum, Schottenbastei 10-16
A-1010 Wien
AUSTRIA
Tel: 43-1-4277-3510
Fax: 43-1-4277-9351
E-mail:
bea.verschraegen@univie.ac.at

EXECUTIVE COUNCIL

Professor Dr M V Antokolskaia
Vrije Universiteit
Faculty of Law
De Boelelaan 1105
1081 HV Amsterdam
THE NETHERLANDS
Tel: 31 20 5986294
Fax: 31 20 5986280
E-mail:
m.v.antokolskaia@rechten.vu.nl

Professor Carol Bruch
School of Law
University of California, Davis
400 Mark Hall Drive
Davis, CA 95616-5201
USA
Tel: 1-530-752-0243
Fax: 1-530-752-2535

Dr Mi-Kyung Cho
Emeritus Professor
College of Law
Ajou University
Hanyang Apt. 25-705
Abguchung-Dong, Kangnam-Ku
Seoul 135-906
KOREA
E-mail: mkcho@ajou.ac.kr

The Rt Hon the Baroness Deech
St Anne's College
Oxford OX2 6HS
UK
Tel: 44-1865-274820
Fax: 44-1865-274895
E-mail: ruth.deech@st-
annes.ox.ac.uk

Professor Dr Nina Dethloff, LLM
Institut für Deutsches, Europäisches
und Internationales Familienrecht
Universität Bonn
Adenauerallee 8a
D 53113 Bonn
GERMANY
Tel: 49 228 739290
Fax: 49 228 733909
E-mail: www.nina-dethloff.de

**Professor Giselle Groeninga de
Almeida**
Rua das Jaboticabeiras, 420
Cidade Jardim
Sao Paolo - SP. 05674-010
BRAZIL
E-mail: giselle@attglobal.net

Professor Sanford N Katz
Boston College Law School
885 Centre Street
Newton Centre, Mass 02459
USA
Tel: 1-617-552-437
Fax: 1-617-552-2615
E-mail: sanford.katz@bc.edu

**Professor Marie-Thérèse
Meulders**
29, Chaussee de la verte voie
1300 Wavre
BELGIUM
Tel: 32.10.24.78.92
Fax: 32.10.22.91.60
E-mail : meulders@cfap.ucl.ac.be

Professor Hugues Fulchiron
Faculte de Droit
Universite Jean Moulin
Lyon 3, 15 quai Claude-Bernard
F-69007 Lyon
FRANCE
Tel: 00 33 4 72 41 05 54
Fax: 00 33 4 78 78 71 31
E-mail: hugues.fulchiron@online.fr

Professor Urpo Kangas
Faculty of Law
Institute of Private Law
University of Helsinki
SF - 000140 University of Helsinki
Helsinki
FINLAND
Tel: 358 0 1912 2918
Fax: 358 0 1912 3108
E-mail: urpo.kangas@helsinki.fi

Professor Olga A Khazova
Institute of State and Law
Russian Academy of Sciences
Znamenka Str. 10
119992 Moscow
RUSSIA
E-mail: olga@khazova.msk.ru

Professor Satoshi Minimakata
Faculty of Law
Niigata University
8050 Ikarashi-ninocho
Niigata
JAPAN 950-2181
Tel/Fax: 81-25-262-6478
E-mail: satoshi@jura.niigata-u.ac.jp

Professor Linda Nielsen
Rector /Vice Chancellor
University of Copenhagen
Nørregade 10
P.O.B. 2177
K-1017 Copenhagen K
DENMARK
Tel: 45 35 32 26 26
Fax: 45 35 32 26 28
E-mail: rektor@adm.ku.dk

Professor Patrick Parkinson
Head of School
Faculty of Law
University of Sydney
173-175 Phillip Street
Sydney, New South Wales 2006
AUSTRALIA
E-mail:
familylaw@law.usyd.edu.au

Professor Bart Rwezaura
Dept of Law
University of Hong Kong
Pokfulam Road
Hong Kong
CHINA
Tel: 852- 2859-2936
Fax: 852- 2857-3146
E-mail: rwezaura@hkucc.hku.hk

Professor Avv Maria Donata Panforti
Dipartimento di Scienze del linguaggio e della cultura
Largo Sant'Eufemia 19
I-41100 Modena
ITALY
Tel: 39 059 205 5916
Fax: 39 059 205 5933
E-mail:
panforti.mariadonata@unimore.it

Professor J A Robinson
Faculty of Law
Potchefstroom Campus of the North West University
North West University
Potchefstroom 2520
SOUTH AFRICA
Tel: 27 18 299 1940
Fax: 27 18 299 1933
E-mail: pvjar@puknet.puk.ac.za

Professor Anna Singer
Uppsala University
Faculty of Law
PO Box 512
SE-751 20 Uppsala
SWEDEN
Tel: 46 18 471 20 35
Fax: 46 18 15 27 14
E-mail: anna.singer@jur.uu.se

Professor dr. juris Tone Sverdrup
Department of Private Law
Faculty of Law, University of Oslo
PO Box 6706 St. Olavs plass
NO-0130 Oslo
NORWAY
Tel: 47 22859781
Fax: 47 22859620
E-mail: tone.sverdrup@jus.uio.no

Professor Lynn D Wardle
518 J Reuben Clark Law School
Brigham Young University
Provo, UT 84602
USA
Tel: 1-801-422-2617
Fax: 1-801-422-0391
E-mail: Wardlel@lawgate.byu.edu

Professor Xia Yinlan
Dean of School of International
Studies
China University of Political
Science & Law
No 25 Xitucheng Road
Beijing
PR CHINA 100088
Tel: 0086-10-82650072
Fax: 0086-10-82650072
E-mail: yinlan112@sina.com

Professor Hazel Thompson-Ahye
Eugene Dupuch Law School
Farrington Road
PO Box SS-6394
Nassau, NP
THE BAHAMAS
Tel: 242- 326-8507/8
Fax: 242-326-8504
E-mail: thomahye2000@yahoo.com

Professor Barbara Bennett Woodhouse
Director, Center on Children and
Families
Frederic G Levin College of Law
Spessard L Holland Law Center
PO. Box 117625
Gainesville, FL 32611-7625
USA
Tel: 1-352-273-0969
Fax: 1-352-392-3005
E-mail: woodhouse@law.ufl.edu

A THE HISTORY OF THE SOCIETY

On the initiative of Professor Zeev Falk, the Society was launched at the University of Birmingham, UK, in April 1973. The Society's first international conference was held in West Berlin in April 1975 on the theme *The Child and the Law*. There were over 200 participants, including representatives of governments and international organisations. The second international conference was held in Montreal in June 1977 on the subject *Violence in the Family*. There were over 300 participants from over 20 countries. A third world conference on the theme *Family Living in a Changing Society* was held in Uppsala, Sweden in June 1979. There were over 270 participants from 26 countries. The fourth world conference was held in June 1982 at Harvard Law School, USA. There were over 180 participants from 23 countries. The fifth world conference was held in July 1985 in Brussels, Belgium on the theme *The Family, The State and Individual Security*, under the patronage of Her Majesty Queen Fabiola of Belgium, the Director-General of UNESCO, the Secretary-General of the Council of Europe and the President of the Commission of the European Communities. The sixth world conference on *Issues of the Ageing in Modern Society* was held in 1988 in Tokyo, Japan, under the patronage of HIH Takahito Mikasa. There were over 450 participants. The seventh world conference was held in May 1991 in Croatia on the theme, *Parenthood: The Legal Significance of Motherhood and Fatherhood in a Changing Society*. There were 187 participants from 37 countries. The eighth world conference took place in Cardiff, Wales in June/July 1994 on the theme *Families Across Frontiers*. The ninth world conference of the Society was held in July 1997 in Durban, South Africa on the theme *Changing Family Forms: World Themes and African Issues*. The Society's tenth world conference was held in July 2000 in Queensland, Australia on the theme *Family Law: Processes, Practices and Pressures*. The eleventh world conference was held in August 2002 in Copenhagen and Oslo on the theme *Family Life and Human Rights*. The Society's twelfth world conference was held in Salt Lake City, Utah in July 2005 on the theme *Family Law: Balancing Interests and Pursuing Priorities*. The Society's thirteenth world conference is to be held in Vienna in 2008. The Society has also increasingly held regional conferences including those in Lyon, France (1995); Quebec City, Canada (1996); Seoul, South Korea (1996); Prague, Czech Republic (1998); Albuquerque, New Mexico, USA (June 1999); Oxford, UK (August 1999); and Kingston, Ontario (2001). In 2003, regional conferences took place in Oregon, USA; Tossa de Mar, Spain; and Lyon, France and, in July 2004, in Beijing, China, on the theme 'Divorce and its Consequences'. In 2005, a regional conference took place in the Netherlands and dealt with the centennial anniversary of the establishment of juvenile courts.

B   ITS NATURE AND OBJECTIVES

The following principles were adopted at the first Annual General Meeting
of the Society held in the Kongresshalle of West Berlin on the afternoon of
Saturday 12 April 1975.

(1) The Society's objectives are the study and discussion of problems of
     family law. To this end the Society sponsors and promotes:
     (a)   International co-operation in research on family law subjects of
            world-wide interest.
     (b)   Periodic international conferences on family law subjects of
            world-wide interest.
     (c)   Collection and dissemination of information in the field of family
            law by the publication of a survey concerning developments in
            family law throughout the world, and by publication of relevant
            materials in family law, including papers presented at
            conferences of the Society.
     (d)   Co-operation with other international, regional or national
            associations having the same or similar objectives.
     (e)   Interdisciplinary contact and research.
     (f)   The advancement of legal education in family law by all practical
            means including furtherance of exchanges of teachers, students,
            judges and practising lawyers.
     (g)   Other objectives in furtherance of or connected with the above
            objectives.

C   MEMBERSHIP AND DUES

In 2005 the Society had approximately 570 members.

(a) Membership:
     •   Ordinary Membership, which is open to any member of the legal
            or a related profession. The Council may defer or decline any
            application for membership.
     •   Institutional Membership, which is open to interested
            organisations at the discretion of, and on terms approved by, the
            Council.
     •   Student Membership, which is open to interested students of law
            and related disciplines at the discretion of, and on terms approved
            by, the Council.
     •   Honorary Membership, which may be offered to distinguished
            persons by decision of the Executive Council.
(b) Each member shall pay such annual dues as may be established from
     time to time by the Council. At present, dues for ordinary membership
     are €41 (or equivalent) for one year, €100 (or equivalent) for three years
     and €155 (or equivalent) for five years, plus €7 (or equivalent) if cheque
     is in another currency.

D   DIRECTORY OF MEMBERS

A Directory of Members of the Society is available to all members.

E   BOOKS

The proceedings of the first world conference were published as *The Child and the Law* (F Bates, ed, Oceana, 1976); the proceedings of the second as *Family Violence* (J Eekelaar and S Katz, eds, Butterworths, Canada, 1978); the proceedings of the third as *Marriage and Cohabitation* (J Eekelaar and S Katz, eds, Butterworths, Canada, 1980); the fourth, *The Resolution of Family Conflict* (J Eekelaar and S Katz, eds, Butterworths, Canada, 1984); the fifth, *Family, State and Individual Economic Security (Vols I & II)* (MT Meulders-Klein and J Eekelaar, eds, Story Scientia and Kluwer, 1988); the sixth, *An Ageing World: Dilemmas and Challenges for Law and Social Policy* (J Eekelaar and D Pearl, eds, Clarendon Press, 1989); the seventh *Parenthood in Modern Society* (J Eekelaar and P Sarcevic, eds, Martinus Nijhoff, 1993); the eighth *Families Across Frontiers* (N Lowe and G Douglas, eds, Martinus Nijhoff, 1996) and the ninth *The Changing Family: Family Forms and Family Law* (J Eekelaar and T Nhlapo, eds, Hart Publishing, 1998). The proceedings of the tenth world conference in Australia were published as *Family Law, Processes, Practices and Pressures* (J Dewar and S Parker, eds, Hart Publishing, 2003). The proceedings of the eleventh world conference in Denmark and Norway were published as *Family Life and Human Rights* (P Lødrup and E Modvar, eds, Gyldendal Akademisk, 2004). These proceedings are commercially marketed but are available to Society members at reduced prices.

F   THE SOCIETY'S PUBLICATIONS

The Society regularly publishes a newsletter, *The Family Letter*, which appears twice a year and which is circulated to the members of the Society and reports on its activities and other matters of interest. *The International Survey of Family Law* provides information on current developments in family law throughout the world and is received free of charge by members of the Society. The editor is Professor Bill Atkin, Faculty of Law, Victoria University of Wellington, PO Box 600, Wellington, New Zealand. The Survey is circulated to members or may be obtained on application to the Editor.

PREFACE

The 2006 *International Survey of Family Law* begins with the Annual Review of International Family Law and this is followed by articles from 27 jurisdictions worldwide. There are 11 contributions from Europe, five each from Africa and the Americas and three each from Asia and Australasia. The British Virgin Islands is appearing for the first time. As in previous years each article is preceded by a French abstract for the benefit of French-speaking readers.

In relation to this edition, I would like to thank again Dominique Goubau and Hugues Fulchiron for their work on translation of the English abstracts into French and Peter Schofield for his translation of the French and Spanish articles. Bart Rwezaura has once again ensured that the continent of Africa is well represented in the Survey. And again the publishers have patiently managed to deal with my editorial scrawls. On this occasion I would like to thank in particular Greg Woodgate of Jordans and Cheryl Prophett.

This is my last Survey as editor, having served in this capacity since 1994. It has been a considerable privilege to act for the International Society of Family Law in this way and I am grateful to the Society for having placed its confidence in me more than a decade ago. It is right that I should also thank again those who I believe have contributed to the development of the International Survey in my period as editor. Michael Freeman, my predecessor as editor, did the pioneering work which established the Survey and, importantly, also established a wide range of contacts which he generously passed on to me. Carol Dowling, then of the Cambridge Law Faculty, provided an enormous amount of secretarial support in the early years when my competence on the PC left something to be desired. Ed Carter and Jo Morton, both then of Jordans, also contributed greatly to the quality of the finished product through their work on the manuscripts. I have been overwhelmed by the commitment which has been shown to the Survey by a number of people over very many years – Peter Schofield who has been translating articles since long before I became editor, Bart Rwezaura who has been tireless in his work on commissioning in Africa and several authors who have written on their respective jurisdictions every year without fail. I will not mention them by name but they know who they are. Lynn Wardle, then Secretary-General of the Society, gave me valuable support during the transition between publishers of the Survey. And of course the Survey could not survive at all without the willingness of those who contribute to each volume. I thank them all. The Survey has always been a collaborative venture and its continued success depends on the willingness, primarily of members of the Society, to assist the editor both by writing themselves and by helping with the commissioning of others.

In my period as editor I have tried to push back the frontiers of the Survey and to extend its coverage so that it may truly be regarded as a *world* Survey. During my editorship some 92 jurisdictions worldwide have been covered in the Survey. Much work remains to be done in increasing coverage in Asia and Latin America in particular. There have been the occasional irritations. Despite efforts over many years, I never managed to press anyone into writing an article on Luxembourg. It remains the only significant country in western Europe not to have appeared and a tantalising challenge for my successor. The Society is fortunate indeed to have been able to appoint Bill Atkin as editor. He will be known to readers of the Survey as the regular contributor on New Zealand. I know that I am leaving the editorship in very capable hands and I wish him every success in his period as editor. The editorship is an onerous, and at times a lonely, occupation, but I have always felt that the benefits, especially in relation to the editor's own intellectual development, far outweigh the burdens. I am confident that with Bill Atkin at the helm the Survey will go on from strength to strength.

Andrew Bainham

Christ's College Cambridge

May 2006

INTERNATIONAL SOCIETY OF FAMILY LAW
SUBSCRIPTION FORM

☐ I prefer to communicate in ☐ English ☐ French

☐ Please charge my credit card ☐ **MASTERCARD or EUROCARD** ☐ **VISA or JCB**

☐
☐ Subscription for 1 year €41 (Euros)

☐ Subscription for 3 years €100 (Euros)

Subscription for 5 years €155 (Euros)

Name of Card Holder: _____

Card no. | | | | | | | | | | | | | | | | | | | | |

CVC-code (three figures at the back of your card behind the 16 figures): | | | |

Expiry date: ———/———

Address of Card Holder: _____

_____

☐ I pay by *postgiro* to **63.18.019** €155[1] for 5 years, €100 for 3 years or €41 for one year,

plus €7 if cheque in another currency (from)

The International Society of Family Law,
Den Hooiberg 17
4891 NM Rijsbergen
The Netherlands

(We have a bank account at the Postbank, Amsterdam, The Netherlands.)

☐ Payment enclosed *by cheque* to the amount of €155[1] for 5 years, €100 for 3 years or €41

for one year, plus €7 if cheque in another currency

Date: _____ Signature: _____

☐ *New member, or*

☐ *(Change of) name/address:* _____

_____

Tel: _____

Fax: _____

E-mail: _____

Comments: _____

To be sent to the treasurer of the ISFL:
Prof. Dr. Paul Vlaardingerbroek, International Society of Family Law
Den Hooiberg 17
4891 NM Rijsbergen
THE NETHERLANDS (or by fax: +31-13-4662323;
E-mail address P.Vlaardingerbroek@uvt.nl)
Website ISFL: http://www.law2.byu.edu/isfl

[1] Or its *counter*value in US dollars.

ASSOCIATION INTERNATIONALE DE DROIT DE LA FAMILLE FORMULAIRE DE COTISATION

☐ Je désire de communiquer　　　☐ en français　　☐ en anglais

☐ Je vous prie de charger ma carte de crédit: ☐ **MASTERCARD/EUROCARD** ☐ **VISA/JCB**

☐ Souscription pour une année　　　€41 (Euros)

☐ Souscription pour trois années　　€100 (Euros)

☐ Souscription pour cinq années　　€155 (Euros)

Le nom du possesseur de la carte de crédit: _____

Carte no　│ │ │ │ │　│ │ │ │ │ │　│ │ │ │ │　│ │ │ │ │

CVC-code (trois numéros sur l'arrière-coté de votre carte)　│ │ │ │

Date d'expiration: _____ / _____

L'adresse du possesseur de la carte de crédit: _____

_____

☐ Je payerai par postgiro à *63.18.019* €155[1] pour 5 ans ou €100 pour 3 ans ou €41 pour 1

an, *plus* €7 surcharge si paiement est un autre cours,

(du) International Society of Family Law
Den Hooiberg 17
4891 NM Rijsbergen
Les Pays-Bas
(Nous avons un crédit au Postbank, Amsterdam, les Pays-Bas)

☐　Paiement est inclus avec un chèque de €155[1] pour 5 ans ou €100 pour 3 ans ou €41 pour

1 an, *plus* €7 surcharge si paiement est un autre cours.

La date: _____　Souscription: _____

☐ *Nouveau membre, ou*

☐ *(Changement de) nom/adresse:* _____

_____

Tel:　_____

Fax:　_____

E-mail:　_____

Remarques: _____

_____

Veuillez envoyer ce formulaire au trésorier de l'Association:
Prof. Paul Vlaardingerbroek
International Society of Family Law
Den Hooiberg 17
4891 NM Rijsbergen
LES PAYS BAS (ou par fax: +31-13-466 2323; e-mail address
P.Vlaardingerbroek@uvt.nl)

[1] Ou la contrevaleur en US dollars.

CONTENTS

ANNUAL REVIEW OF
INTERNATIONAL FAMILY LAW

Ursula Kilkelly[*]

Résumé

Ce chapitre présente une revue des développements en droit international de l'enfance et de la famille en 2004, en mettant l'accent sur les Nations Unies et le Conseil de l'Europe. En ce qui a trait à la *Convention sur les droits de l'enfant* (CDE), nous traiterons essentiellement des *Observations générales sur l'application des droits de l'enfant dans la petite enfance*, formulées par le Comité des droits de l'enfant et nous analyserons la situation de certains états ayant ratifié les protocoles facultatifs de la CDE. Ce chapitre fait également le point sur *l'Étude du Secrétaire général de l'Organisation des Nations Unies sur la violence contre les enfants*, qui devrait normalement arriver à un terme en 2006.

En ce qui concerne le Conseil de l'Europe, ce chapitre s'intéresse à deux domaines particuliers: d'une part la ratification de différents traités du Conseil, incluant la *Convention sur les relations personnelles concernant les enfants,* la *Convention en matière de garde des enfants* et la *Convention sur l'exercice des droits des enfants* et, d'autre part, la jurisprudence de la Cour européenne des droits de l'homme dans le domaine du droit de la famille et du droit de l'enfance. Nous nous pencherons en particulier sur les plus importants jugements concernant les pères non mariés (*Görgülü c. Allemagne* et *Lebbink c. Pays-Bas*), le droit de l'adoption (*Pla* et *Puncernau c. Andorre* et *Pini et Autres c. Roumanie*), la justice juvénile (*SC c. Royaume-Uni*) et la déchéance de droits parentaux à titre de sanction pénale (*Sabou et Pircalab c. Roumanie).*

I   INTRODUCTION

This chapter sets out a review of developments in international law for the year 2004.[1] It concentrates on developments in two principal areas: the UK and the Council of Europe including the case-law of the European Court of Human Rights.

---

[*]   Senior Lecturer, Faculty of Law, University College Cork.
[1]   Where appropriate, developments in 2005 are also taken into account.

II UNITED NATIONS

(a) Convention on the Rights of the Child (CRC)

The Committee on the Rights of the Child continued its work monitoring implementation of the CRC although no General Comments on the implementation or interpretation of the CRC were adopted in 2004. However, in September, the Committee held its annual Day of Discussion on the subject of implementing children's rights in early childhood. The recommendation adopted by the committee following this discussion highlighted the fact that early childhood years are critical for laying a solid foundation for the sound development of the child's personality, talents, mental and physical abilities.[2] In guaranteeing rights to the youngest children, it urges states to develop rights-based, multidimensional and multisectoral strategies that promote a systematic and integrated approach to law and policy development, and provide comprehensive and continuous programmes in early childhood development, taking into consideration children's evolving capacity in light of Art 5 of the Convention.[3] In light of the importance of early childhood development services and programmes for the short- and long-term cognitive and social development of children, the Committee urges states to adopt comprehensive and strategic plans on early childhood development within the rights-based framework, and accordingly, to increase their human and financial resource allocations for early childhood development services and programmes.[4] It then went on to highlight the relevance of specific CRC provisions to early childhood as follows:

- the best interests of the child (Art 3);

- the right to life, survival and development and the right to health and education (Arts 6, 25, 28, 29);

- the right to rest, leisure and play (Art 31); and

- the right to participate (Art 12).

The Committee recommended that states adopt community-based programmes of childhood development, invest in systematic training and research in the field of early childhood development from a rights-based perspective, and provide appropriate assistance to parents, legal guardians and extended families in the performance of their child-rearing responsibilities, inter alia, by providing parenting education.[5] It also recommended that human rights education be incorporated in pre- and primary school programmes with such education being participatory and

---

[2]   United Nations Committee on the Rights of Child *Day of Discussion: Implementing Child Rights in Early Childhood,* 17 September 2004, Palais Wilson. See also UN Doc CRC/C/SR.979, the Summary Record of the Meeting.

[3]   *Ibid,* para 3.

[4]   *Ibid,* para 4.

[5]   *Ibid,* paras 11–13.

adapted to the ages and evolving capacities of young children. Bearing in mind the role of the non-governmental sector as a channel for programme implementation, it called on all non- state service providers to respect the principles and provisions of the Convention. From an international perspective, it recommended that donor institutions, including the World Bank, other United Nations institutions and bi-lateral donors, support early childhood development programmes financially and technically with a view to assisting sustainable development in countries benefiting from international assistance. It ended its recommendation by urging states' inter-governmental organisations, NGOs, academics, professional groups and grass-root communities to foster continuous high-level dialogues and research on the crucial importance of quality in early childhood development, including at the regional and local levels. It concluded with a commitment to draft a General Comment on children's rights in early childhood.[6]

(b) Optional Protocols to the CRC

No further instruments of ratification to the CRC were received in 2004. However, both Optional Protocols, which came into force in 2002, received several ratifications in 2004. In particular, Austria, Brazil, Ecuador, El Salvador, Estonia, Lebanon, Madagascar, Niger, Republic of Korea, Slovakia, Slovenia and Togo ratified the Optional Protocol to the CRC on the sale of children, child prostitution and child pornography and there were a further seven accessions to the Protocol.[7] The following states ratified the Optional Protocol to the CRC on the involvement of children in armed conflict in 2004: Botswana, Brazil, Cambodia, Ecuador, Germany, Japan, Luxembourg, Madagascar, Mongolia, Republic of Korea, Senegal, Slovenia, Former Yugoslav Republic of Macedonia and Turkey. There were a further eight accessions to the Protocol.[8] In 2005, the Optional Protocol on the sale of children received a further seven ratifications[9] and a further eight states ratified[10] the Optional Protocol on armed conflict.

Clearly, the growth in the ratifications of the Optional Protocols is steady rather than dramatic; the total number of parties to the Optional Protocol on armed conflict now stands at 102 whereas there are 101 parties to the Optional Protocol on the sale of children. Not all the same states have ratified both Protocols suggesting, in theory at least, that some consideration is being given to what is required to implement the Protocols prior to their ratification by states. Importantly, the number of reservations entered to both Protocols is very low and in the case of Qatar, for example, which reserved

---

[6] This was adopted by the Committee in 2005. See further www.ohchr.org (5 December 2005).

[7] The current state of ratifications can be found at www.ohchr.org (10 December 2005).

[8] *Ibid.*

[9] In 2005, it was ratified by Armenia, Benin, Canada, India, Japan, the Netherlands and Poland, with five accessions.

[10] In 2005, it was ratified by Armenia, Benin, Columbia, Israel, Liechtenstein, Poland, Sudan and Ukraine, with a further three accessions.

the rights not to apply the Protocol where it conflicts with Islamic law, prompted the lodgement of objections by a number of states in response.[11]

(c) Children in armed conflict

With respect to the Optional Protocol on armed conflict, there are virtually no reservations but a wide range and large number of declarations have been entered by states of ratification. For the most part, these are of a positive nature: for example, some states have clarified that admission to the armed forces is reserved for those over 18 years (for example, Argentina, Belgium, Bosnia and Herzegovina, Finland, Jamaica, Peru), that admission is voluntary only (no conscription) or that those who enter below that age do not take part in military activity (for example, Ireland, Bulgaria, Canada and Lithuania). However, the ratification of this Optional Protocol (and the entry of such positive declarations) by states in which involvement of children in armed conflict is a known reality serves to highlight the shortcomings of the Protocol.[12] The extent of the problem of children's involvement in armed conflict worldwide was highlighted in the report of the Secretary General to the Security Council in February 2005 in which the following countries were identified as permitting directly or indirectly the involvement of children in armed conflict in their countries: Burundi, Colombia, Democratic Republic of Congo, Ivory Coast, Myanmar, Nepal, Philippines, Somalia, Sri Lanka, Sudan and Uganda.[13] The fact that many of these states have signed and ratified the Convention and its Optional Protocol on children in armed conflict[14] (Somalia signed the Protocol in September 2005, Colombia and Sudan ratified the Protocol in 2005, whereas the Democratic Republic of Congo ratified in 2001) raises serious questions about both the ratification process and the integrity of the Convention and the Optional Protocol in this area.[15]

The response of the Security Council to the Secretary General's report and plan of action was to establish a working group on children in armed conflict which began work in November 2005. This group, set up pursuant to Security Council resolution 1612 adopted on 26 July 2005, has been given the task of reviewing monitoring reports and progress on the implementation of Security Council mandated action plans to promote the protection of

---

[11]   For example, objections to the reservation entered by Qatar were lodged by Austria, France, Germany, Norway and Spain to the effect that the reservation was so broad as to interfere with the object and purpose of the Optional Protocol.

[12]   See further 'Child Soldiers: No Longer a Minor Incident' (2004) 12 *Williamette Journal of International Law and Dispute Resolution* 124.

[13]   UN Doc A/59/695-S/2005/72, 9 February 2005. This can be found at www.un.org/special-rep/children-armed-conflict/English/index.html.

[14]   With the exception of Somalia which has neither signed nor ratified the Convention, all these states have either ratified or acceded to the CRC, Art 38 of which prohibits the involvement of children below 15 years in armed conflict and requires states to provide such children with care and protection.

[15]   See also Abraham 'Child soldiers and the Capacity of the Optional Protocol to Protect Children in Conflict' (2003) 10 *Human Rights Brief* 15.

children affected by armed conflict. The fact that the Security Council has decided finally to act on this problem is a measure of its gravity and of the effectiveness of the work carried out by the Special Rapporteur on Children in Armed Conflict, Olara A Otunnu, whose office expired in July 2005, in raising its profile.[16] Moreover, the Security Council's decision to establish a monitoring process rather than to improve the admittedly weak standards in the area is a welcome focus on action. At the same time, the slow nature of the Security Council's response must be criticised, especially given the fact that many of the world's children are involved in armed conflict, which means that they continue to suffer egregious violations of their rights under international law.[17] In this regard, it is notable that the Security Council's action had come 7 years after the issue of children in armed conflict was first placed on its agenda in 1998 and following five Security Council resolutions.[18]

(d) Secretary-General's Study on Violence against Children

A further area of attention in the United Nations in recent years has been the issue of violence against children. As reported in last year's Survey, in 2001 the General Assembly requested the Secretary-General to conduct an in-depth international study on violence against children,[19] and in 2003, following the suggestion of the Commission on Human Rights in 2002,[20] Mr Paulo Sergio Pinheiro was appointed to direct the Study. There followed the publication of a concept paper for the study in July 2003 in which it was explained that the purpose of the Study was to provide an in-depth global picture of violence against children and to propose clear recommendations for the improvement of legislation, policy and programmes relating to the prevention of and responses to violence against children. Since that time, the study has been in consultation mode with governments, non-governmental organisations and the public being given the opportunity to participate. In March 2004, the Study issued all governments with a questionnaire designed to gather material on the laws, policies and programmes in place to address violence against children.[21] To date, almost 120 governments have

---

[16] Mr Otunnu first made the recommendation for an independent watchdog in this area in 2001. While he has not yet been replaced, the Secretary-General appointed Norwegian Karin Sham Poo, a former Deputy Executive Director of UNICEF, as officer in charge pending this appointment.

[17] For more information see Watchlist on Children in Armed Conflict, a global network on HGOs dedicated to monitoring and reporting on violations in the area at www.watchlist.org (9 December 2005) and the *children and armed conflict unit* at the University of Essex at www.essex.ac.uk/armedcon (10 December 2005). The latest report of the Special Representative of the Secretary-General for Children and Armed Conflict to the General Assembly was made in September 2005: UN Doc A/60/335. The submission of this report was delayed due to serious staff shortages in the Special Representative's office.

[18] See Report of the Secretary-General to the Security Council *Children and Armed Conflict* UN Doc A/58/546-S/2003/1053 (October 2003).

[19] Resolution 56/138.

[20] Resolution 2002/92.

[21] See the Report of the Independent Expert for the United Nations Study on Violence against Children to the General Assembly, UN Doc A/60/282, 19 August 2005, paras 7–9.

responded. In addition, nine regional consultations were carried out by Mr Pinheiro, his partners in the Study UNICEF, WHO and the Office of the High Commissioner for Human Rights – and other non-governmental and state partners.[22] Consultations in individual countries were then used to supplement the regional consultations and in particular to undertake field research on particular problems of violence against children. [23] Also in 2004–2005, public submissions on the issue of violence against children were invited, a number of expert thematic meetings were held and the Expert participated in a number of academic meetings, colloquiums, workshops and seminars related to the topic of violence against children. He has also considered the issues raised by the Committee on the Rights of the Child in its Concluding Observations. The participation of children and young people in the Study is also a priority and the Expert's website had a child-friendly section as well as a toolkit to facilitate this participation. For example, children and young people were involved in the regional consultations and published statements at the end of the consultation.[24]

In his report to the General Assembly in 2005, the Expert highlighted the key areas identified through the consultation processes regarding violence against children, which will be the focus of his work in the coming year. These include the continued legality and prevalence of corporal punishment against children in the home, schools, alternative care institutions and the juvenile justice system, the vulnerability of children in conflict with the law, as well as street children, to violence; and the persuasiveness of harmful traditional practices. He has also become very aware of the underlying conditions, such as community attitudes to violence, discrimination, poverty, the unequal status of women and girls, lack of access to quality education and denial of human rights generally, which exacerbate children's vulnerability to violence. Lack of systematic and quality data and the importance of capacity building for those working with children have also become clear.[25] His final report to the Secretary-General is expected to be presented in the spring of 2006.

III COUNCIL OF EUROPE

In the Council of Europe developments took place in two areas: a small number of countries ratified the Convention on Contact concerning Children and the Convention on Custody and the European Court of Human Rights

---

22   *Ibid,* paras 10–24. Further details of what happened at these consultations are also available on the
       Study's website at www.violencestudy.org (10 December 2005).
23   For example, the Expert visited Israel and the Occupied Territories, Brazil and South Africa. *Ibid,*
       paras 29–36.
24   The statements of the consultations on the Caribbean Region, East Asia and Pacific Region,
       Middle East and North Africa Region, North America Region and South Asia Region can all be
       downloaded from the Study's website.
25   Report of the Expert to the General Assembly, above n 21, para 62.

handed down relevant judgments in a variety of areas relevant to child and family law.

(a) Convention on Contact concerning Children

As reported in last year's Survey, the Convention on Contact concerning Children,[26] which was opened for signature on 15 May 2003, received only two ratifications in 2004: San Marino ratified on 13 September 2004 and the Czech Republic ratified on 27 September 2004. Albania ratified the Convention on 27 May 2005 providing the three ratifications required for it to come into force on 1 September 2005. The slow pace of ratifications must, however, be a cause of concern questioning in particular the relevance of the Convention and, more importantly, states' commitment to implementing its provisions.

(b) Convention on Custody

The European Convention on Recognition and Enforcement of Decisions concerning Custody of Children and on Restoration of Custody of Children[27] is the most widely ratified children's Convention in the Council of Europe framework and has now been ratified by a total of 34 states. This number includes Hungary which ratified on 4 February 2004, Moldova which ratified on 14 January 2004 and Romania which ratified on 12 May 2004.

(c) Convention on the Exercise of Children's Rights

Albania also ratified the Council of Europe Convention on the Exercise of Children's Rights (CECR)[28] on 25 October 2005 bringing the total number of states which have ratified this Convention to ten. Fourteen states have signed the Convention but have so far chosen not to ratify it. Just one state has ratified the Convention since 2003, undoubtedly heightening concern about the viability of the Convention and states' commitment to the principle that it attempts to implement, namely the child's right to participate in family law proceedings. The CECR was intended by the Council of Europe, which drafted it in the mid 1990s, as a supplement to the CRC, particularly Art 12(2), which requires states to provide children involved in judicial and administrative proceedings with the right to be heard, directly or indirectly. In this way, the CECR aims to provide a mechanism for the further implementation of Art 12 in family proceedings, inter alia, by providing procedural mechanisms by which the voice of the child can be heard. In particular, it takes a novel and practical approach to the implementation of Art 12 by requiring states, under Art 1(4) of the CECR, to identify three

---

26   ETS 192.
27   ETS 105.
28   ETS 160.

categories of family cases before a judicial authority on which the CECR is to apply. The detail as to what states must provide in these proceedings is contained in Art 3, which provides that a child considered by internal law as having sufficient understanding shall be entitled to request the right:

(a) to receive all relevant information;

(b) to be consulted and express his or her views; and

(c) to be informed of the possible consequences of compliance with these views and the possible consequences of any decision.

Further rights which may be granted on application are set out in Art 4 (the appointment of a special representative) and Art 5 (the right to be assisted by an appropriate person of their choice in order to help them express their views; the right to a separate representative, in appropriate cases a lawyer; the right to appoint their own representative; and the right to exercise some or all of the rights of parties to such proceedings).

While, on the one hand, the Convention's pragmatic approach can be said to have real potential to ensure that theory is translated into reality with respect to the child's right to participate in family law proceedings which concern him or her, this novel approach is also problematic insofar as it requires states to take positive and precise steps to implement the Convention prior to ratification. Thus, despite states' apparent commitment to the principle of Art 12, it is clear that many are unwilling to accept a legal duty, such as that in the CECR, which requires them to translate this principle into practice.[29] The requirement that states implement the provisions of the CECR prior to ratifying it may be the reason why so few states have ratified the CECR at all, despite ratifying the CRC (which requires no such pre-emptory action).

(d) Convention on the Adoption of Children

Also of questionable relevance is the outdated Convention on the Adoption of Children adopted by the Council of Europe in 1967.[30] Last year's Survey reported on proposals to revise the Convention and noted that despite some reservations, the revision of the treaty was to be welcomed. Since that time, however, the work of the body given responsibility for updating the Convention – the Committee of Experts in Family Law – appears to have stalled. As a result, it is regrettable that no further development has occurred in this area.

---

[29]   See a brief survey of the legal position in a number of European jurisdictions in this area in Stalford 'The Rights of the Child in International Family Law Proceedings – an EU Perspective (2003) *International Family Law Journal* 68. For other issues in this area see Murch 'The Voice of the Child in Private Family Law Proceedings in England and Wales' (2005) *International Family Law Journal* 8.

[30]   ETS 58.

IV CASE-LAW OF THE EUROPEAN COURT OF HUMAN RIGHTS

Notable case-law was handed down by the European Court of Human Rights in 2004 in several important family and child law cases. It is presented below in relation to the rights of unmarried fathers, adoption, juvenile justice and deprivation of parental rights as a penal sanction.

(a) The rights of unmarried fathers

Following on from the German cases concerning unmarried fathers discussed in last year's Survey,[31] the European Court decided two further cases on this issue in 2004. In *Görgülü v Germany*,[32] the applicant was an unmarried father who complained that he was denied access to his child who was then placed with foster parents who eventually adopted him. He complained in particular that the decision of the courts to refuse him access to his son was incompatible with Art 8 of the European Convention of Human Rights (ECHR), inter alia, because it did not take his son's right to know his real family into account and was thus not in the child's best interests. Before deciding the merits of the case, the European Court reiterated its approach to such cases: it reminded that its role was to consider whether in the light of the case as a whole, the reasons adduced to justify this measure were relevant and sufficient for the purposes of Art 8(2). Recognising that it was not its role to second guess the domestic authorities which have the benefit of direct contact with all the persons concerned it held that its task was to review, in the light of the Convention, the decisions taken by those authorities in the exercise of their power of appreciation. While a wide margin of appreciation was enjoyed by states in relation to matters of custody, the Court noted that a stricter scrutiny is called for as regards any further limitations, such as restrictions placed by those authorities on parental rights of access, and as regards any legal safeguards designed to secure an effective protection of the right of parents and children to respect for the their family life as such further limitations entail the danger that the family relations between a young child and one or both parents would be effectively curtailed. The Court reiterated that Art 8 requires that the domestic authorities strike a fair balance between the interests of the child and those of the parents and that, in the balancing process, particular importance should be attached to the best interests of the child which, depending on their nature and seriousness, may override those of the parents. In particular, a parent cannot be entitled under Art 8 of the Convention to have such measures taken as would harm the child's health and development.

---

[31] *Sahin v Germany* [GC], no 30943/96, para 12, ECHR 2003-VIII and *Sommerfield v Germany* [GC], no 31871/96, paras 11–12, ECHR 2003-VIII. See Kilkelly 'Annual Review of International Family Law' in A Bainham (ed) *The International Survey of Family Law 2004 Edition* (Jordans, Family Law, 2004).

[32] Judgment of 26 May 2004.

With regard to the issue of custody, the Court noted that although the applicant was in a position to care for his son, the domestic appeal court had concluded that granting him custody would not be in the child's best interest given the deep social and emotional bond that had evolved between the child and his foster family, separation from which would lead to severe and irreparable psychological damage for the child. The Court also noted that 3 months earlier, a lower court had reached the contrary conclusion, namely that it *was* in the child's best interests that his father obtain custody of him.

When striking a balance between the conflicting rights and interests of the applicant, his son and his foster parents, the Court noted that it may be relevant that father and son had never lived together. In this regard, it recalled its consistent case-law that where the existence of a family tie with a child has been established, the state must act in a manner calculated to enable that tie to develop. Moreover, the Court highlighted the positive obligation that Art 8 imposes on the state to aim at reuniting a natural parent with his or her child and, in this context, noted that effective respect for family life requires that future relations between parent and child not be determined by the mere passage of time. In this regard, the Court conceded that an instant separation from this foster family might have had negative effects on the child's physical and mental condition. However, bearing in mind that his biological parent was undisputedly willing and able to care for him, the Court was not convinced that the German Court of Appeal had examined all possible solutions to the problem. In particular, it held that:

> 'That court does not appear to have examined whether it would be viable to unify father and son under circumstances that would minimise the strain put on [the child].'[33]

It concluded that the Court of Appeal had apparently only focused on the 'imminent effects' which a separation from his foster parents would have on the child, and failed to consider the long-term effects which a permanent separation from his natural father might have on him. The solution envisaged by the District Court, namely to increase and facilitate contact between father and son, who would at an initial stage continue to live with his foster family, was seemingly not taken into account. The Court recalled in this respect that the possibilities of reunification will be progressively diminished and eventually destroyed if the biological father and the child are not allowed to meet each other at all, or only so rarely that no natural bonding between them is likely to occur. Accordingly, it held that a violation of Art 8 had occurred.

With regard to the suspension of the applicant's access rights, the Court noted that the appeal court had based its decision on the physical and psychological strain for the child that any contact with his natural father would involve. It thereby had regard to the unrest and insecurity occasioned by the unresolved legal dispute and concluded that suspending access for a

---

[33]   *Ibid*, para 46.

certain time would allow the boy to regain the necessary inner repose and emotional balance. However, it noted that prior to the decision of the appeal court, the applicant was able to see his child on only six occasions for several hours at a time, and that the decision rendered any form of family reunion and the establishment of any kind of further family life impossible. According to the Court, it is in a child's interest for its family ties to be maintained, as severing such ties means cutting a child off from its roots; this, the Court said, could only be justified in very exceptional circumstances which did not exist in this case. Thus, by revoking all decisions that would have granted the applicant access to his son, the appeal court did not fulfil the positive obligation imposed by Art 8 to unite the family. Accordingly, the Court found that the reasons relied on by the appeal court to suspend the applicant's access to his child for one year were insufficient to justify such a serious interference with his family life. Notwithstanding the domestic authorities' margin of appreciation, therefore, the interference was disproportionate to the legitimate aims pursued and violated Art 8.[34]

Despite the unanimous nature of its conclusions in *Görgülü*, a judgment of the European Court which finds a violation based on the decision of a national court is always going to be accused of second guessing the domestic authorities. In such cases, the distinction between supervisory and appeal jurisdiction can become blurred. On the merits of the case, however, the Court's judgment is a welcome restatement of the importance of the biological link between unmarried fathers and their children and the need to focus on both long-term and short-term consequences for the child and his or her biological parents of severing ties with the latter in favour of the adoptive family. The judgment is welcome from the perspective of the child also whose rights, particularly the right to identify and to know his/her parents, can be relegated to the background in disputes of this nature. In future cases, the Court is encouraged to appoint independent representation for the child to ensure full and objective consideration is given to his or her rights.

The rights of the unmarried father were also the subject of the dispute in *Lebbink v the Netherlands*.[35] Here, the applicant complained that he was denied access to his daughter in breach of his rights under Art 8. His complaint had failed before the domestic courts on the basis that their relationship did not amount to family life within the meaning of that provision. This was the question before the European Court of Human Rights also. The Court reminded that marriage is not a pre-requisite for the establishment of a family life relationship; nor is cohabitation always required for family life to exist. Accordingly, the existence of family life is essentially a 'question of fact depending upon the real existence in practice of close personal ties'. Where the case concerns a potential relationship which could develop between a child and her unmarried father, relevant

---

34   The applicant was awarded €15,000 in pecuniary damages. However, the Court found no violation to have occurred with respect to the applicant's procedural rights under Art 8 and 6.
35   1 June 2004.

factors include the nature of the relationship between the natural parents and the demonstrable interest in and commitment by the father to the child both before and after birth. In the present case, the Court noted that, unlike the German cases of *Sahin* and *Sommerfeld*,[36] the applicant had never sought to recognise his daughter (this being open to him), nor had he formed a family unit with her mother. In the absence of these factors, the question was whether other factors demonstrated that the applicant's relationship with his daughter had sufficient 'constancy and substance' to create *de facto* family ties. The Court did not agree with the applicant that:

> 'A mere biological kinship, without any further legal or factual elements indicating the existence of a close personal relationship, should be regarded as sufficient to attract the protection of Article 8.'[37]

It went on to note that his daughter was born from her parents' genuine relationship, which lasted for about 3 years and that, until the function was abolished when she was 7 months old, the applicant was her 'auxiliary guardian'. The Court also noted that the parents' relationship ended when the child was about 16 months old, and that, although the applicant never cohabited with his daughter and her mother, he was present at his daughter's birth and after their relationship ended, he visited her regularly. In these circumstances, the Court concluded that when the applicant's relationship with the child's mother ended, there existed – in addition to the biological link – certain ties between the applicant and his daughter which were sufficient to attract the protection of Art 8 of the Convention. As the domestic courts had refused to consider the merits of the applicant's claim for access and had dismissed it on the basis that family life did not exist, the Court held that there had been a violation of Art 8 of the Convention.

While the Court's further clarification on the definition of family life is welcome, the specific nature of the judgment raises an interesting question as to its consistency with earlier case-law particularly the case of *Keegan v Ireland*.[38] In this case, the Court held that although family life between the applicant and his daughter did not exist, potential family life could be shown to be present by virtue of the fact that the parents cohabited, had planned the pregnancy and intended to marry. In *Keegan*, however, the applicant had met his daughter only once after which time his requests to see her were turned down by the mother. In *Lebbink*, on the other hand, the applicant had seen a lot of his daughter, babysitting on occasion and providing support to her mother regarding her welfare. While it is inconceivable that family life would not be found to exist in either case, prima facie, *Lebbink* appears to make a more persuasive case for the existence of family life with his daughter on its own merits and not with reference to the parents' relationship particularly given the Court's long-established test of family life as the 'existence in fact of close personal ties'. It is to be welcomed in this respect.

---

[36]   See above n 31.

[37]   Above n 31, para 37.

[38]   *Keegan v Ireland*, judgment of 26 May 1994, Series A no 290.

However, the Court's rejection that a 'mere biological' link is sufficient to amount to family life appears at odds with the case-law which offered strong support for this view.[39] For example, in *Boughanemi v France* in 1996, the Court noted that:

> 'The concept of family life on which Article 8 is based embraces, even when there is no cohabitation, the tie between a parent and his or her child, regardless of whether or not the latter is legitimate. Although that tie may be broken by subsequent events, this can only happen in exceptional circumstances.[40]

This appeared to establish a presumption in favour of family life between parents and their biological children which could only be subsequently broken by, it is submitted, damaging or negative action on the part of the parent. The Court's position on the application of Art 8 to this important category of persons is a little uncertain after all.

(b) Adoption

The European Court considered two different human rights dimensions on adoption in 2004. The case of *Pla and Puncernau v Andorra*[41] concerned the inheritance rights of an adopted person whereas *Pini and Others v Romania*[42] concerned the compatibility with the Convention of the international adoption of two Romanian children.

Pla and Puncernau concerned the following slightly complicated facts: in 1949 Carolina Pujol Oller died leaving three children – Francesc-Xavier and two sisters. Carolina's will, drawn up in 1939, had settled her estate on Francesc-Xavier, as tenant for life. Should he be unable to inherit, the estate was to pass to his first sister and if she was also unable to inherit, it was to pass to his second sister's son. Clause 7 of the will indicated that Francesc-Xavier was to transfer the estate to 'a son or grandson of a lawful and canonical marriage'. However, while Francesc-Xavier had married, his only son was adopted; in his will, he left his estate to his wife and the remainder to his son. After his death in 1995, a dispute arose between his widow and son, and Carolina's other great-grandchildren, who claimed that adherence to Clause 7 of Carolina's will required the estate to rest with them. Interpretation of domestic law by the courts in these proceedings resulted in Francesc-Xavier's wife and son's challenge being dismissed and the

---

39   See *C v Belgium*, no 21794/93, Reports 1996-III, no 12, p 915 and *Ahmut v Netherlands*, no 21702/93, Reports 1996-VI, no 24, p 2017, 24 EHRR 62. See also *Söderbäck v Sweden*, no 24484/94, Reports 1998-VII, no 94. However, purely genetic relationships – such as the relationship between a sperm donor and the child born as a result – are unlikely to constitute family life. See *G v Netherlands*, no 16944/90, Dec 8.2.93, 16 EHRR 38. See further Kilkelly 'Child and Family Law' in Kilkelly (ed) *ECHR and Irish Law* (Jordans, 2004) pp 111–149 at 112–114.

40   *Boughanemi v France*, Reports 1996-II no 8, p 593, 22 EHRR 228, para 35.

41   13 July 2004.

42   22 June 2004.

applicants thus complained to the European Court of Human Rights that this violated Art 8 read together with Art 14.

According to the Court, it is in the first place for the national courts to construe and apply domestic law; this was even more pertinent when interpreting an eminently private instrument such as a clause in a person's will. As the domestic courts are evidently better placed than an international court to evaluate the particular context of the legal dispute and the various competing rights and interests, a wide margin of appreciation applies in such cases. This means that an issue of interference with private and family life could only arise under the Convention if the national court's assessment of the facts or domestic law were 'manifestly unreasonable or arbitrary or blatantly inconsistent with the fundamental principles of the Convention'.

According to the Court as it was indisputable that the marriage in question was legitimate, the remaining question was whether the notion of 'son' in Carolina's will included only biological sons or whether it also included the applicant who was adopted. By inferring a negative intention on the part of the testatrix, the Andorran High Court had found that as she did not expressly state that she was not including adopted sons this meant that she did intend to exclude them. However, the European Court took the opposite view noting that as the testatrix could have excluded adopted grandsons expressly but chose not to, the only possible and logical conclusion was that this was not her intention. It referred to the reasoning of the Andorran court as 'over contrived and contrary to the general legal principle that where a statement is unambiguous there is no need to examine the intention of the person who made it'.[43] The Court was not unaware that is was interfering in the determination by a domestic court of a private law dispute, and in this respect noted that:

> 'In exercising the European supervision incumbent on it, it cannot remain passive where a national court's interpretation of a legal act, be it a testamentary disposition, a private contract, a public document, a statutory provision or an administrative practice appears unreasonable, arbitrary or, as in the present case, blatantly inconsistent with the prohibition of discrimination established by Article 14 and more broadly with the principles underlying the Convention.'[44]

According to the Court, the domestic court's interpretation of the will had the effect of depriving the first applicant of the right to inherit under his grandmother's estate thereby amounting to the judicial deprivation of an adopted child's inheritance rights. It reminded that only very weighty reasons can justify a difference in treatment on the ground of birth out of wedlock.

---

[43]   *Ibid*, para 58.
[44]   *Ibid*, para 59.

The Court reminded that the Convention is a living instrument to be interpreted in the light of present-day conditions and noted that great importance is attached today in the member states of the Council of Europe to the question of equality between children born in and outside marriage as regards their civil rights. The Court went on to note that the interpretation of the will by domestic courts could not be made exclusively in the light of the social conditions existing when the will was made (in 1939) or at the time of the testatrix's death (in 1949), particularly where a period of 57 years had elapsed between the date when the will was made and the date on which the estate passed to the heirs. According to the Court:

> '[w]here such a long period has elapsed, during which profound social, economic and legal changes have occurred, the courts cannot ignore these new realities. The same is true with regard to wills: any interpretation, if interpretation there must be, should endeavour to ascertain the testator's intention and render the will effective, while bearing in mind that "the testator cannot be presumed to have meant what he did not say" and without overlooking the importance of interpreting the testamentary disposition in the manner that most closely corresponds to domestic law and to the Convention as interpreted in the Court's case-law.'[45]

Accordingly, a violation of Art 8, read together with Art 14 was found to have occurred.

The dissenting view of Judge Bratza highlights a clear difficulty with this judgment which can be summarised as follows: in the Court's previous case-law[46] it was the domestic legislation at issue which gave rise to the difference of treatment of which complaint was made under the Convention. A clear connection exists therefore between the state's duty to implement and abide by the Convention and the responsibility for the resulting violation. In the instant case, however, it was accepted that domestic law was compatible with the Convention but the violation was brought about as a result of the judicial interpretation of a private will. As Judge Bratza explained, the Convention cannot and should not prevent individuals from leaving their estate to whomever they please. In extreme form, this view might support the proposition that judicial acts cannot result in breaches of the Convention. However, as Judge Bratza pointed out, a distinction can be made between this case, where the court was merely interpreting and applying the will of the testatrix, and others in which the court itself was interfering with the rights of the applicant. However, it is clearly a thin line between a judgment which directly interferes with the applicant's Convention rights and one which does so indirectly and in defence of the majority judgment; it highlights that the Court had two interpretations of the will open to it – one which interfered with the applicant's rights and could be said to be discriminatory the other which did not. However, consistent with

---

[45] *Ibid*, para 62.

[46] See, for example, *Marckx v Belgium*, judgment of 13 June 1979, Series A no 31, p 24, *Vermeire v Belgium*, judgment of 29 November 1991, Series A no 214-C, p 83 and *Inze v Austria*, judgment of 28 October 1987, Series A no 126, p 18.

the assertion made above in respect of both the *Görgülü* and *Lebbink* cases, the difficulty with the judgment is that despite insisting that it is not its role to substitute its opinion for that of the domestic courts, that is precisely what the European Court has done here.

One point was not considered expressly in the judgment: the testatrix was clearly making a value judgment about who she wanted to inherit her estate – her express preference was in favour of children born inside marriage distinguishing them from those born outside wedlock. No view was being expressed as to her preference for biological over adopted children. In this regard, the Court's conclusion would seem to be correct, ie that opposition to children born outside marriage could not be said to include opposition to adopted children also. The alternative view is also possible but surely the lack of express provision cannot make that definitive. Even if it had, is this exercise of free will in a discriminatory manner to be held to be compatible with the Convention? According to the Court's controversial judgment, that question would appear to have a negative answer; even if that exercise of free will is lawful it may be contrary to the Convention.

Pini and Others v Romania[47] was an adoption case of a very different kind insofar as it concerned the adoption of two Romanian children by two Italian couples. According to the facts, both adoptions had been carried out in compliance with Romanian law (and the Hague Convention on the Protection of Children and Cooperation in respect of Intercountry Adoption, 1993) but difficulties arose with regard to their enforcement. In particular the Educational Centre, where the children resided and who opposed the adoptions, took various measures to frustrate the adoption process. The applicants, the prospective adopters, complained to the European Court that the failure of the Romanian authorities to execute the adoption orders violated their rights under both Art 8 and Art 6 (right to a fair trial) of the Convention.

With respect to their claim under Art 8, the Court first considered the disputed matter of whether the ties between the applicants and their respective adoptive daughters amounted to ties of family life. Guided by the relevant international law, namely the Hague Convention on Intercountry Adoption, the Convention on the Rights of the Child and the European Convention on Adoption, older case-law of the European Commission and domestic law, the Court found that as the relationship arose from a lawful and genuine adoption it was sufficient to attract the respect due to family life within the meaning of Art 8. While it recognised that the children's consent was not obtained by the courts that made the adoption orders, the Court did not consider this an omission given that they had not yet reached the age at which their consent must be obtained, set at 10 years under the domestic legislation. Nor did the Court find this threshold to be unreasonable[48] given

---

[47]   22 June 2004.
[48]   However, see Stalford, above n 29, who discusses research from the European Forum for Child Welfare in 2001–2002 that using age 12 as a cut off in this context is based on 'old psychology'

that the relevant international treaties leave the national authorities some discretion as to the age from which children are to be regarded as sufficiently mature for their wishes to be taken into account.[49] With respect to the fact that the applicants had not lived with the children, or developed sufficiently close de facto ties with them, the Court noted that they simply followed the procedure put in place by the state in such matters.[50]

With regard to compliance with Art 8, the Court reiterated its consistent case-law that the state has a duty to take positive measures to reunite parents and their children where they have been separated. Although it noted that this obligation is not absolute, especially where parent and child are still strangers to one another, the nature and extent of such measures will depend on the circumstances of each case, but the understanding and co-operation of all concerned will always be an important ingredient. While the national authorities must do their utmost to facilitate such co-operation, any obligation to apply coercion must be limited since the interests and the rights and freedoms of all concerned, including the child, must be taken into account. Where contact with the parent might appear to threaten those interests, it is for the national authorities to strike a fair balance between them. What was decisive in this case, therefore, was whether the national authorities took the necessary steps to enable the applicants to establish family relations with each of the children they had adopted. As the government stated, at issue here were the competing interests of the applicants and of the adopted children.

According to the Court, there are no grounds, from the children's perspective, for creating emotional ties against their will between them and people to whom they are not biologically related and whom they view as strangers. The Court thus found it clear from the facts of the case that at the time of the judgment, the children preferred to remain in the Educational Centre in which they had grown up, were fully integrated and which was conducive to their physical, emotional, educational and social development, than be transferred to different surroundings abroad. On the other hand, the adoptive parents' interest derived from their desire to create a new family relationship by forging ties with the children they had adopted. Although it noted the legitimate nature of this desire, the Court considered that it could not enjoy absolute protection under Art 8 insofar as it conflicts with the

---

'   and that a more modern understanding of the area requires the conclusion that a child's capacity to express his or her views is frequently determined by the adult's competence in eliciting those views.

49   Here it referred to Art 4(1)(d) of the Hague Convention which requires that an adoption shall only take place where the domestic authorities have ensured, having regard to the age and degree of maturity of the child, that: (i) he or she has been counselled and duly informed of the effects of the adoption and of his or her consent to the adoption, where such consent is required; (ii) consideration has been given to the child's wishes and opinions; (iii) the child's consent to the adoption, where such consent is required, has been given freely, in the required legal form, and expressed or evidenced in writing; and (iv) such consent has not been induced by payment or compensation of any kind.

50   This conclusion presents an interesting conclusion to the judgment discussed above in the *Lebbink* case.

children's refusal to be adopted by a foreign family. The Court has consistently held that particular importance must be attached to the best interests of the child in ascertaining whether the national authorities have taken all the necessary steps that can reasonably be demanded to facilitate the reunion of the child and his or her parents. In particular, it has held in such matters that the child's interests may, depending on their nature and seriousness, override those of the parent. The Court considered that it is even more important that the child's interests should prevail over those of the parents in the case of a relationship based on adoption, since adoption means 'providing a child with a family, not a family with a child'.[51] Moreover, it considered it important that in the instant case the children rejected the idea of joining their adoptive parents in Italy once they had attained the necessary maturity to express their opinion as to the surroundings in which they wished to be brought up, provision for which was made in domestic law. According to the Court, then, it was not in doubt that the children's interests were assessed by the relevant authorities in the course of the adoption proceedings. However, that did not rule out the possibility of a fresh examination of all the relevant evidence at a later stage where this was required by specific circumstances and where the child's best interests are at stake.

On the facts, the Court noted that at the time that the adoption orders were made, the applicants' relationship with the girls was purely formal and was not accompanied by any real ties. Indeed, the girls were opposed to the relationship and had lodged applications in their own name to have the adoption orders revoked; one such application was successful. The Court also noted that for a number of years after the adoption orders were made, various other sets of proceedings were pending in the national courts to have the adoption orders declared void on the ground that, inter alia, provisions of relevant international treaties had been infringed. The Court did not find it unreasonable that the authorities should await the conclusion of those proceedings, whose outcome could not have been foreseen, before taking measures of a permanent nature that were likely to create a new family life for the applicants. Indeed, insofar as allegations of irregularities in adoption procedures were the subject of proceedings before the competent courts, the authorities had a duty to ensure that any uncertainty as to the lawfulness of the adoption was dispelled. That conclusion is particularly valid in the present case as the enforcement of the decisions in the applicants' favour, with the children moving to Italy, would have made it difficult for the children and harmful to their interests to return to Romania in the event of a subsequent court decision setting aside or revoking the adoption orders.

In its judgment, the European Court deplored the manner in which the adoption proceedings were conducted, in particular, the lack of real, effective contact between the interested parties before the adoption and found it particularly regrettable that the children did not receive any psychological support capable of preparing them for their imminent

---

[51]   *Fretté v France*, no 36515/97, ECHR 2002-I.

departure from the Centre which had been their home for several years and in which they had strong social and emotional ties. Such measures would probably have made it possible for the applicants' interests to converge with those of their adopted children, instead of competing with them as occurred in the present case. Nevertheless, in the circumstances of the case, given that the applicants' interests were weaker as they had been acknowledged as the adoptive parents of children aged almost 10 without having any genuine pre-existing ties with them, there could be no justification for imposing on the Romanian authorities an absolute obligation to ensure that the children went to Italy against their will and irrespective of the pending judicial proceedings instituted with a view to challenging the lawfulness and well-founded nature of the initial adoption orders. The children's interests dictated that their opinions on the subject should have been taken into account once they had attained the necessary maturity to express them. According to the Court, their consistent refusal, after they had reached the age of 10, to travel to Italy and join their adoptive parents carried a certain weight in this regard not least given that their conscious opposition would make their harmonious integration into their new adoptive family unlikely. According to the Court, therefore, the national authorities were legitimately and reasonably entitled to consider that the applicants' right to develop ties with their adopted children was circumscribed by the children's interests, notwithstanding the applicants' legitimate aspirations to found a family. It found, accordingly, that there had been no violation of Art 8.

However, the Court reached the opposite conclusion with respect to Art 6 noting that the adoption orders, which were lawfully made by a domestic court as final and irrevocable, remained unenforced despite the irremediable consequences that the passing of time can have on relations between children and parents who do not live with them. Reiterating its settled case-law to the effect that Art 6 protects the implementation of final, binding judicial decisions, which cannot remain inoperative to the detriment of one party, the Court noted that the execution of a judicial decision cannot be prevented, invalidated or unduly delayed. On the facts, the failure to execute the decisions ordering the adoption was due solely to the actions of the Educational Centre, who consistently opposed the children's departure to Italy by lodging various objections to enforcement or by thwarting the steps taken by the bailiffs with impunity. Therefore, by refraining for more than 3 years from taking the effective measures required to comply with final, enforceable judicial decisions, the Court held that the national authorities had deprived the provisions of Art 6(1) of the Convention of all useful effect. This conclusion was all the more necessary given the probably irreversible consequences of the passage of time for the potential relationship between the applicants and their adopted daughters. With regret, therefore, the Court noted that the prospects of that relationship flourishing now appeared if not seriously jeopardised, then at least highly unlikely, particularly as the children, now aged 13, recently indicated that they were strongly opposed to being adopted and moving to Italy. Accordingly, these circumstances gave rise to a violation of Art 6.

This is the first case concerning international adoption from Romania to be considered by the European Court of Human Rights and while the historical and modern contexts, social, legal and political, add to the complexity and difficulty of this decision,[52] it is important nonetheless to consider the judgment on its merits. There are a number of points to be made: the first question that arises relates to the consistency of the Court's approach in finding the failure to enforce an order for adoption to violate Art 6 of the Convention, but not Art 8. In particular, it would appear logical to argue that either the adoption order was valid and lawful and should have been enforced, or it was not. This view that the circumstances were worthy of a finding of a violation in respect of both Convention provisions, or neither, appears to find some support among the judges who dissented from all or part of the majority judgment. For example, Judge Loucaides found it more rational to find a breach of both Art 6 and Art 8 insofar as the failure to prepare the children for their adoption violated both provisions, whereas two other judges – Judge Thomassen joined by Judge Jungwiert – found a violation of neither provision. As Judge Birsan noted, the conclusion of the Court that Art 6 had been violated by the failure of the authorities to take effective measures to implement a final, enforceable judicial decision was 'difficult to reconcile with that reached by the majority under Article 8 of the Convention'. Although for other reasons, the Judge voted with the majority in finding a violation of Art 6, he had clear difficulty with the formalistic approach taken by the Court to the enforcement of court orders without reference to the particularly sensitive and difficult circumstances involved here.

Aside from Judge Birsan's warning to the Court to take into account the difficult and sensitive issues involved in enforcing court orders in the family law area, it is difficult to agree with the judgment of the Court under Art 6. Once the order had lawfully been made and all legitimate appeals and objections to it had been dealt with by the appellate courts, then respect for the rule of law required that the appropriate measures be put in place effectively to implement the order. However, some elements of the procedure raise concerns about its compatibility with Art 6, and perhaps also Art 8. One of the difficulties, for example, seems to relate to the fact that at the time the adoption order was made, the children were close to the age at which their views must be taken into account. In other words, had they been 6 months older it would have been compulsory under domestic law for their views to be taken into account. Apart from the failure to prepare the children for adoption, it would appear that the procedure enshrined in Romanian legislation does not, prima facie at least, comply with Art 12 of the Convention on the Rights of the Child. In particular, the fact that the law requires children above a certain age to have their views heard and taken into account but makes no provision at all for children below that age seems arbitrary and a failure to take into account the requirement that all children have the right to be heard, those views being given due weight in accordance

---

[52]   See Bainham 'International Adoption from Romania – why the moratorium should not be ended' (2003) 15(3) *Child and Family Law Quarterly* 223.

with the child's age and maturity. For example, had the views of the children in these cases been heard – despite their age of 9½ – their strong opposition might have become clear thereby avoiding the debacle that followed. In the light of the perceived advantage of adoption – that it creates a final, irrevocable tie with the merits of certainty and finality for all the parties – it is difficult to marry this with a procedure which allows the child's views to trigger a review of the legality of the process once he/she has reached the age of 10. In this context, a programme of long-term fostering is clearly preferable.

The other question that the case raises, however, is the success or otherwise of the Romanian system at identifying the extent to which the order of adoption is in the child's best interest. This case clearly witnessed a conflict between the Child Welfare Board, who supported the adoption, and the staff of the Education Centre who cared for and raised the children but who were violently opposed to it. A procedure which ignores the views and opinions of those working and living so closely with the children concerned would seem to be fatally flawed not only for the practical reasons encountered here but also more generally as it suggests that the process was not informed by the relevant considerations.

A further issue here relates to the basis for the distinction between the Court's conclusion on Arts 8 and 6, namely the emphasis placed in the judgment on the views and wishes of the children concerned. The judgment is overall reminiscent of the view, expressed in some Strasbourg case-law on contact and custody matters,[53] that a decision requires the child to undertake personal relations and contact with people whom he/she does not know or with whom he/she has a negative relationship. It clearly demands greater weight to be attached to eliciting the views of children of all ages with a view to building a process of informed consent into the adoption process. In this regard, it is important that the children were themselves represented at the European Court, a very positive practice which should be encouraged in all such cases.

Finally, it is necessary to comment on the manner in which the adoption was organised, which attracted strong criticism from the Court, and the impact that this had on its overall conclusion. Clearly, the Romanian process has several serious flaws – the first, discussed above, is the fact that the adoption can be approved without first seeking the consent and opinion of those with intimate knowledge and understanding of the child and his or her rights and interests. The second point, also heavily criticised by the Court, is the use of a process by which a child is matched with prospective adopters in a foreign country by photograph. Regardless of the adoption laws, regulations and procedures to ensure that adoption is in the child's best interests and compatibly with domestic law, no modern concept of adoption, particularly

---

[53] Kilkelly *The Child and the ECHR* (Aldershot, Ashgate, 1999) pp 257–258.

in the case of international adoption, which seeks to protect the rights of the children involved, can allow the use of this practice to continue.[54]

It is well known that in 1999, the European Court considered for the first time the compatibility with Art 6 of the Convention of trying children in an adult court. The seminal cases of *T v UK* and *V v UK*[55] concerned the trial of two 11-year-old boys in public in the Crown Court among high levels of media and public interest. The Court noted that although measures were taken in view of their young age and to promote their understanding of the proceedings, the formality and ritual of the Crown Court must, at times, have seemed 'incomprehensible' to a child of 11. Overall, the Court held that it was insufficient for the purposes of Art 6 that the boys were represented by skilled and experienced lawyers because it was highly unlikely that they would have felt sufficiently uninhibited, in the tense courtroom and in the glare of public scrutiny, to have consulted with them during the trial. Indeed, given their immaturity and disturbed emotional state, it considered it unlikely that they were capable of co-operating with their lawyers even outside the courtroom in order to give them information for their defence. These factors, the Court concluded, meant that neither applicant was able to participate effectively in the criminal proceedings against him and both boys were, as a consequence, denied a fair hearing.

It is clear that the failure to take effective measures to reduce or eliminate both the publicity and the formality of the proceedings was the principal factor in the Court's conclusion that Art 6 had been violated in this case. The impact on the judgment of the children's mental state during their trial is not clear; nor is the significance of the Court's conclusion that the decision to allow them to stand trial in the first place was not contrary to the Convention.[56] What is important, however, is the Court's clear requirement that:

'... a child charged with an offence (must be) dealt with in a manner which takes full account of his age, level of maturity and intellectual and emotional capacities, and that steps are taken to promote his ability to understand and participate in the proceedings.'[57]

This strongly worded principle requires, therefore, that the ability of children to understand and participate in their own criminal proceedings be facilitated. The principle is not confined to children charged with murder or serious crime or even those tried in an adult court, but is intended to govern in a general way how the criminal justice system deals with all child defendants. In 2004, the Court elaborated further on the state's duty to facilitate the child's right to participate and understand their criminal

---

[54] In this regard, see the concerns of Bainham, above n 52. See also the views of Baroness Nicholson of Winterbourne, Rapporteur to the European Parliament, who was joined as a third party to the proceedings, para 96 of the judgment.
[55] *T v UK* and *V v UK* (2000) 30 EHRR 121.
[56] *T v UK, ibid,* paras 68–78.
[57] *Ibid,* para 84.

proceedings. *SC v UK*[58] concerned the compatibility with Art 6 of the trial in the Crown Court of an 11-year-old boy who had a very low intellectual level for his age meaning that he could not, it was argued, fully comprehend or participate in the trial process or give adequate instructions. Considering the case, the Court accepted that Art 6 does not require that a child on trial should understand or indeed be capable of understanding every point of law or evidential detail, not least because given the sophistication of modern legal systems many adults of normal intelligence are unable fully to comprehend all the intricacies and exchanges which take place in the courtroom. However, 'effective participation' in this context presupposes that the accused has a broad understanding of the nature of the trial process and of what is at stake for him or her, including the significance of any penalty which may be imposed.[59]

Thus, the Court said, the defendant should be able to follow what is said by the prosecution witness, to explain to his own lawyers his version of events, point out any statements with which he disagrees and make them aware of any facts which should be put forward in his defence.

On the facts, the Court noted that although the applicant was tried in public, steps were taken to ensure that the procedure was as informal as possible and many of the intimidating features of the trial in *T* and *V* cases were absent. Notwithstanding that the Recorder had the judgment in these cases in mind when exercising his discretion to allow the trial to proceed, the Court noted that the two experts who assessed the applicant before the hearing concluded that he had a low intellectual level for his age. One concluded that while he had probably been aware that is actions were wrong, 'his understanding of their consequences may have been adversely affected by his learning difficulties and impaired reasoning skills'.[60] Despite the recommendation that the process be explained carefully to him in a manner commensurate with his learning difficulties, and the efforts to that end by the social worker, the Court noted that the applicant seemed to have little comprehension of the role of the jury in the proceedings or the importance of making a good impression on them. 'Even more strikingly', the Court said:

> 'he does not seem to have grasped the fact that he risked a custodial sentence and once sentence had passed and he was taken to the holding cells he appeared confused and expected to go home with his foster father.'

In the light of this evidence, the Court found that the applicant was not capable of participating effectively in his trial and there was, accordingly, a violation of Art 6.[61]

---

58   15 June 2004.
59   *Ibid*, para 29.
60   *Ibid*, para 32.
61   Judge Pelonpaa joined by Judge Bratza expressed the dissenting view that the domestic court's assessment of the applicant's ability to proceed and be tried in the Crown Court should have prevailed, inter alia, due to the absence of the aggravating factors present in the cases of *T* and *V*,

According to the Court, when the decision is taken to deal with a child who risks not being able to participate effectively because of his young age and limited intellectual capacity, by way of criminal proceedings (rather than some form of disposal directed primarily at his best interests and those of the community), 'it is essential that he be tried in a specialist tribunal which is able to give full consideration to and make proper allowance for the handicaps under which he labours and adapt its procedure accordingly'.[62]

The Court did not see any conflict with this position and the failure on the part of the applicant to argue that he was unfit to plead. It noted, in particular, that it does not follow from a child being fit to plead that he is capable of participating effectively in this trial to the extent required by Art 6. Again, the wide application of this principle is clear.

The right to a fair trial under Art 6 thus requires that steps be taken to ensure the participation and understanding of children in criminal proceedings. According to the Court, this requires that criminal proceedings in which children are involved are adapted to take into account any possible learning, intellectual or developmental difficulty which might hinder the child's effective participation in the process. While no preference is shown for an adult or a youth court, what is clear is that the tribunal in which this hearing takes place must be a 'specialist' one, which is sufficiently flexible to allow child's circumstances to be fully considered and whose procedures have been modified accordingly.

(c) Denying parental rights as a penal sanction

The case of *Sabou and Pircalab v Romania*[63] was not a matter of family law; rather it concerned the denial of parental rights imposed as a penal sanction. Following a criminal conviction for defamation, the applicant, who was a journalist, was sentenced to 10 months' imprisonment, he was banned from exercising his profession and his parental and electoral rights were suspended for the duration of his imprisonment. In addition to violating Art 10 of the Convention, the Court also concluded that Art 8 had been violated. In particular, it pointed out that the child's interest had to take precedence over all other considerations and that only particularly unworthy behaviour could justify a person being deprived of his or her parental rights in the child's best interests. According to the Court, the offence for which the applicant had been convicted was completely unrelated to questions of parental responsibility and at no time had any allegation been made concerning a lack of care on his part or ill treatment of his children. Under Romanian law, the ban on exercising parental rights was an ancillary penalty which was imposed automatically on any person who served a prison

---

the lack of evidence that the applicant was unfit to plead, and the fact that the domestic judge, who made the assessment which was upheld on appeal, had personal contact with the young defendant.

62   *Ibid*, para 35.
63   28 September 2004.

sentence, without the supervision of the courts and without taking account of the type of offence and the child's interests. Accordingly, the ban represented a moral reprimand aimed at punishing the convicted person rather than a child-protection measure. Accordingly, the Court concluded that there had been a violation of Art 8.

V   CONCLUSION

While the remit of this review is necessarily narrow in scope, nonetheless a number of important conclusions can be drawn from the developments noted. In particular, it is important that the serious issues of violence against children and the not unrelated issue of children and armed conflict are finally receiving strategic and concerted attention at the United Nations. The success of the processes now underway will continue to be monitored by academic and non-governmental bodies alike. From the judgments of the European Court of Human Rights discussed here, the most important legal question to emerge is undoubtedly whether the Court is continuing to prefer an appellate to its traditional supervisory role notwithstanding that the line between the two has always been a little blurred. On the merits of the cases above, the definition of family life continues to loom large in cases of unmarried and adopted families; the flexibility of the concept, once its most positive characteristic, may yet prove to be its downfall as the Court struggles to find a consistent line other than one which is determined exclusively by the facts of each case. While the Court's judgments in the cases above make important, if indirect, contributions to the development of children's rights in Strasbourg law, it is blatant criticism of the Romanian system of international adoption that highlights the fact that, as in Africa, Asia and the Americas, Europe has much to learn about protecting the rights of children and promoting their right to be heard.

Angola

THE NEW ANGOLAN LAW ON CHILDREN'S AND JUVENILE JUSTICE

Maria Do Carmo Medina[*]

Résumé

L'entrée en vigueur de la loi 9/96 du 19 de avril, la Loi du Jugée des Mineurs et du Code du Procès du Jugée des Mineurs approuvé par le Décret 6/03, du 28 Janvier, a cause de la longue guerre subi par Angola, a seulement être mise en vigueur, avec l'ouverture a Luanda du premier tribunal pour les mineurs, en juin de 2003.

Comme État part de la Convention de Droits de L'Enfant et d'autres conventions internationales concernant les droits de l'enfant, Angola devait introduire dans son système judiciaire, en tribunal spécifiquement ouvert pour les questions des mineurs.

Le Jugée des Mineurs fait part du Tribunal Provincial comme une Salle de compétence spécialisée et sa finalité légale c'est la protection juridictionnelle et la défense des droits et des intérêts des mineures par l'application des mesures soit de protection social soit de prévention criminelle. Ces mesures prises pour le tribunal peut être révisées et changées d'accord le déroulement de la situation du mineur.

Sur sa juridiction sont inclus tout les mineurs jusqu'à 18 ans qui ont besoin de protection social et les jeunes de 12 années a moins de 16, accusées de avoir commis un délit. Les parents ou qui a la garde du mineur, aussi bien ceux que violent le devoir constitutionnelle de protection social au mineur, sont aussi sujets a la compétence du tribunal.

Le Code du Procès des Mineurs a adopté comme ses principes, la confidentialité du procès, la flexibilité et la célérité. Seulement le juge a le pouvoir d'interroger le mineur. Au jugement, au delà du juge, prendre part 2 pérîtes assesseurs que donnent son avis sur la décision a prendre par le tribunal.

Prés de chaque Jugée des Mineurs, et aussi avec compétence provinciale, est instituée la Commission Tutélaire des Mineurs a qui sont attribuées larges fonctions sociales préventives d'information et dénonce des cas sujets á la compétence du Jugée des Mineurs, mais aussi quand tel est décidé, le devoir de

---

[*] Professor of Family Law at the Faculty of Law of Agostinho Neto University.

contrôler l'exécution des mesures décrétées par le juge, proposer son changement et promouvoir l'intégration sociale des jeunes.

Un Centre d'Observation fonctionne prés du Jugée des Mineurs qui accueille provisoirement les mineurs qui y sont apportées pour des raisons de nécessité de protection sociale ou des infractions de la loi. Quatre Centres de Référence ont étés ouverts aux Municipalités de Luanda, qui sont en contact direct avec la population et réceptionnent la plupart des cas qui doivent être apportées au Jugée des Mineurs.

Les chiffres des cas attendues par le Jugée des Mineurs est bien aussi la gravité des délits subies aux jugements, démontrent comme il était nécessaire et urgent sont fonctionnement.

I   INTRODUCTION

In Angola the end of the long war at the beginning of 2002, allowed the implementation of new Law no 9/96 of 19 April, the Children's and Juvenile Court Act, and subsequently the approval by Decree no 6/03 of 28 January, of the Proceedings Code of the Children's Court.

The impact of decades of war on the civilian population and foremost on children had been extremely severe: a quarter of the population has been dislocated from its homeland, there has been a collapse of most of the family structure, forced separation of thousands of children from their families, increasing the number of street children in seaside Angolan towns.[1]

Before the opening of the Children's and Juvenile Court, it was necessary to inform, and train magistrates, Judges and Public Ministry, social technicians and specialized police, and during 2002 and 2003, intensive courses took place for this purpose. The support of UNICRI (United Nations Interregional Crime and Justice Institute) was very important for launching this new project, from the beginning up to the present day.

On 16 June 2003, the African Child's Day, the Children's and Juvenile Court integrated at the Provincial Court of Luanda was officially opened. At the same time in five districts of Luanda, social centres were opened, called 'Social Reference Centres'. The increasing demand of cases, both in Centres and in Court, is evidence of the urgency of their functions.

But this urgency is also extensive in other Angolan Provinces that suffered the war's effects, such as Uíge, Moxico, Huambo, Benguela and Huíla, and

---

[1]   An inquiry made in 1995, by the Christian Children's Foundation in Angola, on the impact of war
       on children showed these statistics:
       –   27% have lost one or both parents;
       –   82% have supported bomb attacks or artillery fire;
       –   66% assisted mines explosion;
       –   33% were wounded and 24% suffered physical or mental illness;
       –   65% were said have to escaped death or to have seen people dying; and
       –   10% have participated in fighting.

continuing efforts are going on to open other new Children's and Juvenile Courts all over the country, as soon as possible.

II INTERNATIONAL AND CONSTITUTIONAL FRAMEWORK

Angola ratified the UN Convention on the Rights of the Child of 1989 by the People's Assembly Resolution no 20/90 of 10 November. More recently, on 13 August 2002, the National Assembly of Angola approved by Resolution no 21/02 the Optional Protocol of the UN Convention on the Rights of the Child, concerning Children in Armed Conflicts, and by Resolution no 22/02, the Optional Protocol concerning the sale of children, prostitution and pornography.

Also the African Charter on the Rights and Welfare of the African Child, of the Organization of African Unity, was ratified by an earlier Angolan Parliament, in April 1992.

Several other international conventions specifically concerned with children's rights have also been introduced in the Angolan legal system: the UN Convention on the worst forms of child labour and immediate action in order to secure its elimination, by National Assembly Resolution no 5/01, and the ILO Minimum Age Convention for Employment by the National Assembly Resolution no 8/01, both of 16 February 2001.

All these children's human rights enshrined in international instruments, according to Art 21 of Constitutional Law no 23/92 of 16 September, are considered as internal law and mandatory for courts to apply.

The United Nations Standard Minimum Rules for Administration of Juvenile Justice – 'The Beijing Rules' approved in 1985 – had already recommended that there must be 'in each national jurisdiction, a set of laws rules and provisions specifically applicable to juvenile offenders and institutions and bodies entrusted with functions of administration of juvenile justice' (2.3).

This recommendation has been incorporated in the UN Convention on the Rights of the Child at Art 40, no 3, which states:

> 'States Parties shall seek to promote the establishment of laws, procedures, authorities and institutions specifically applicable to children alleged as, accused of, or recognized as having infringed the penal law ...'

Angolan judicial organisation, the Unified Justice System, approved by Law no 18/88 of 31 December had not provided a specific court for children's trials and had given transitory competence to the Provincial Court's President for those cases.

Constitutional Law no 23/92 has important provisions on children's rights and emphasizes that uppermost consideration must be given to them.

Article 30 rules that:

'Children must been given paramount priority, and the family, the society and the State shall undertake special protection to ensure them their integral development.'

And Art 31 ensures that:

'The State with family and society support must promote youth personality and harmonious development and must create the conditions to guarantee effectiveness of their economic, social and cultural rights ...'

So, it was necessary to put the internal judicial system in line with international and regional standards, by the enactment of a new law which creates a special body for the administration of child and juvenile justice.

III THE CHILDREN'S AND JUVENILE COURT ACT

Article 1 of Law 9/96, the Children's and Juvenile Court Act, created a new specialized court designated as 'Sala do Julgado de Menores' which is named as a judicatory organ and not as a court in order to avoid an intimidatory labelling. Its competence and fundamental purposes are enacted in Art 2:

'To ensure to minors subject to this jurisdiction, judiciary protection, defence of their rights and interests and legal protection given by Constitutional Law, by application of tutoring measures of vigilance, assistance and education.'

Under its jurisdiction are:

–   minors under 18 years, in need of social protection measures; and
–   minors of 12 years and minors of 16 years who must be the object of criminal prevention measures.

The Court has complementary jurisdiction as Art 3 states, over parents, tutors or anyone who is in charge of the child, and whoever violates their duty of social protection to children. The jurisdiction of the court extends to those who are not fulfilling their duties to the child, court injunctions and also whoever commits offences against a child by behaviours specified in Art 18, 1(a)–(h).

The judicial procedure is a function of the minor's Prosecutor but whoever in exercising their professional work takes notice of any situation concerned with the Court's jurisdiction may report the situation. This is the case of doctors, nurses, medical assistants, teachers and those responsible for care institutes, psychologists, etc. Action can also be initiated by associations which defend children's rights or their social protection or any citizen who takes notice of the situation.

Due to the very difficult situation faced by the great proportion of children in Angola, it was necessary to put under the Court's protection children in social danger and not to leave them only in public care institutions, as other laws actually do.

Otherwise, according to the Angolan judicial system, every case related to family affairs, such as the establishment and contesting of affiliation, parents' guardianship and child support, maintenance, adoption and tutelage are under the jurisdiction of the 'Sala de Família' (the Family Court), which was created by Law no 18/88.

IV SOCIAL PROTECTION MEASURES

Principally, orders for child welfare and social protection must be made where the child's psychological and moral well-being is in danger, in cases such as:

- physical or moral ill-treatment, by his/her guardian;
- neglect or abandonment;
- anti-social behaviour of the child in the family and the community;
- when the child is subjected to compulsory labour or compelled to perform dangerous, harmful or hazardous work which puts at risk his/her well-being; and
- using the child in activities such as begging, vagrancy, prostitution or alcohol/drug addiction.

The social situation of children in Angola is truly very difficult. General family dysfunction, loss of their economic resources, destruction of the main infrastructures such as schools, hospitals and also the danger of mines in rural areas do not allow normal agriculture, etc. Basic education is free and compulsory till the sixth degree of school attendance (Act no 13/01, the Bases of Education System Act) as a socio-economic right. But there is a lack of schools all over the country, in spite of many efforts that have been made to rebuild them. More than a million children are estimated to be outside the education system and those children who do enter school, for the most part, do not achieve basic education. Lack of normal school attendance is due mainly to economic difficulties and lack of parental supervision.

The health situation is also very critical, not only because of war destruction but also because medical care, in most cases, cannot be afforded by the population in general.

With no skills for specific jobs and in many cases refusing land labour, which is less well paid and gives no immediate return, most of the young people prefer to come in to towns and engage in informal trade in the streets.

Recently a hideous phenomenon has appeared which is directly affecting children and putting them in great danger. Belief in witchcraft has increased in the country as a consequence of isolation and cultural backwardness. Obscurantism and superstition have spread underground. Before, it was the old people in the community that were generally regarded as witches. It must be explained that the family member who is identified by the 'kimbanda' (fortune teller) as the 'witch' is considered responsible for all evil things that are taking place in the family group, such as deaths, diseases, loss of good employment or political function. This deep feeling of anger against the 'bad' member of the family unfortunately results mainly in the physical elimination of this person by his/her own family.

During the war period things have changed in the Northern Provinces of Angola, such as Uíge, Zaire and Cabinda, where children, most of them of tender age, have begun to be appointed as witches. That kind of suspicion puts at great risk the physical integrity and even the life of the child whose family thinks that he/she must be eliminated to put an end to all evils suffered by the family.

Heavily abused children have been saved by authorities and put under protection of public care institutions. For instance, in Cabinda at the end of 2004, with great public protest, the press had announced that two children, named as witches, had been delivered by their own family to a religious sect who made them fast for nearly a fortnight.

The social protection measures applied by the Children's and Juvenile Court, depending on the gravity of case, are namely: allowing the child to remain at the parents' or family home, under vigilance of the social assistant and the Court; placement in a foster family; ordering medical treatment or psychiatric examinations; compulsory attendance at school or professional centres; or being put in care in public or private institutions. These measures can be taken simultaneously according to the particular situation.

Most cases going to the Luanda Children's Court are related to maltreatment, abandonment and sexual abuse. In such cases the child is taken out of their family and put under care and protection. Nevertheless lack of enough institutions provides an inadequate solution for all of them.

Truly, the fight against sexual abuse of children and youth prostitution has not yet started, in spite of being a widespread phenomenon.

The Children's and Juvenile Court may coordinate its functioning with the Criminal Court whenever any act or crime against a child is alleged in order to prosecute those involved. Where, however, the court's decision may interfere with parental authority, the case must be sent to a Family Court.

V   CRIMINAL PREVENTION MEASURES

Law no 9/96, the Children's and Juvenile Court Act, did not change the age of criminal responsibility as it is stated in the Penal Code, which came from the colonial period, because this Code is now the object of complete revision. So, the age of criminal responsibility had not been changed and remained at less than 16 years. Those who are above 16 years must be tried by the Criminal Court, but with a large restriction on the penalties which may be imposed. A child under 12 years cannot suffer criminal prevention measures, but only social protection measures.

A young person who commits a criminal offence is said to be in a 'pre-delinquency' situation. All judicial proceedings must respect the principles stated in international instruments: including the right to a fair trial, access to legal assistance, appealing to the Supreme Court, and other rights generally in Arts 37 and 40 of the UN Convention on the Rights of the Child.

Criminal prevention measures are prescribed by statute. They are: reprimand, behaviour orders in the family and in the community; financial penalties; compensation and restitution; community service orders; court supervision; and semi- institutional or institutional treatment.

Most criminal prevention orders are not enforced, due to lack of appropriate institutions to accommodate juvenile offenders.

There are a few that belong to churches and private NGOs, and are not specifically concerned with reintegration of young people in society, but rather for care and social protection.

A general programme of preparing community service orders is now beginning with the approval of a new Executive Decree and by training social workers with UNICEF support.

Programmes of Community Services must be agreed between each Provincial Court, Provincial Government and private care institution. Community Services must be free, be an activity of public utility, with a social or environmental impact, or on behalf of disabled people. Community Service orders must be prescribed by the Court, after due trial and only in relation to young people convicted of a criminal offence. It must be determined in hours and weeks, from a minimum of 2 weeks and not more than 52 weeks, and must not interfere with school attendance or professional training.

Nevertheless, experience shows that frequently those who are convicted of a criminal offence need social protection also and so the Court must also apply a social measure to them.

VI CHILDREN'S TUTORIAL COMMITTEE AND CARE UNITS

Alongside the above measures, the new law created in each Province, the Children's Tutorial Committee is a structural complement to the Court's activity with mainly care and social functions. Principally, this Committee is deeply linked to social reality and must be in permanent communication with the Court presenting cases under its jurisdiction, giving information about social circumstances, availability of foster families, professional training centres, community-based services or programmes, specialized units available for housing children or young people subjected to half-accommodation or accommodation measures. According to the Court, the decision can be made by a social worker, but is compulsory when accommodation measures have been applied. It is always the Children's Tutorial Committee which is charged to go along with measures' execution, visiting children and young persons regularly, making periodic reports, proposing changes for Court decision according to circumstances envisaged in law, and promoting their socialization and integration.

The Children's Tutorial Committee is composed of five members, chosen by public services concerned with children's care: three of them by the Ministry of Welfare and Social Reintegration and two by the Children's National Institute.

In the future, when municipalities are settled in Angola, this important care committee must be established in the community and it is expected that its members must be elected.

The Children's Tutorial Committee is intended to deal directly with children's problems in its own Province, must also make preventive claims to the Court, and ask for the registration of children.

The Court has an Observation Centre where children and young people can stay temporarily, and they are attended there by psychologists and by social workers.

In Luanda Province in four Municipalities, Social Reference Centres have been created which have direct contact with the population and receive claims of children in a dangerous situation, victims of ill-treatment, family abandonment, family conflicts, misconduct, theft or prostitution.

VII THE CODE OF PROCEDURE IN THE CHILDREN'S COURT

Decree no 6/03 of 28 January approved the Code of Procedure of the Children's Court which completes the legal system of children's specialized jurisdictions.

The main rules of this code can be summarised as follows:

- a unified code for each child or young person must extend to adulthood;
- confidentiality and protection of privacy;
- speed and informality in order to handle each case expeditiously. Nevertheless the Judge of the Children's Court has exclusive competence to examine the minor about the facts of the case.

A social inquiry report must be presented by the Court's Social Assistant relating to the minor's personality, family, economic and social conditions of life, his/her social behaviour, etc. The minor's Prosecutor leads the preliminary part of the proceedings and may propose that a trial must be held. After receiving the case it is for the Judge to determine whether or not to conduct a trial. If the Judge so decides, the trial will be held by the Judge and two 'Peritos Assessores' (Expert Advisers) designated by the Ministry of Justice and chosen from a list of specially qualified persons on children's affairs.

The trial is not in public, but the press can be present whilst protecting the minor's identity. The solicitor chosen by the minor's representative or by the child him/herself after 16 years of age, must be present at the trial.

The sentence must contain essential elements such as the minor's personal details, the facts of the case, measures adopted, or reasons why it is not necessary to adopt any measures, appointment of the body or person responsible for carrying out the measures, and whether this should be the Children's Tutorial Committee or the Court's Social Assistant.

The sentence is subject to appeal to the Chambers of the Supreme Court by the minor, by the Prosecutor and by the third person who is supposed to have suffered damage.

The Court must supervise how its decisions are being carried out, receiving regular reports and evaluating the child's progress. It can propose revision and when long-term measures have been applied, a sentence revision is compulsory every 2 years.

Statistics about cases before the Courts show that juvenile delinquency cases have changed since the beginning of the Court's activity in 2003 and 2005.

In the two months of 2003, 125 proceedings against young persons, presented to the Court, were distributed as follows:

Murder – 19% and 20%

Rape – 26% and 40%

Physical assault – 14% and 40%

Damage to property – 2% and 40%

Infanticide – 1% and 60%

In the three months of 2005, 149 proceedings were presented to the Court, concerning these crimes:

Theft, robbery, and qualified robbery – 45%

Participating in a criminal gang – 16%

Murder with a firearm – 10%

Possession and drug trafficking, psychological aggression, damage to property and rape – about 5% each.

So it must be concluded that juvenile delinquency has diminished as regards crimes against the person and increased in relation to crimes against property.

VIII   CONCLUSION

This new jurisdiction for the Children's Court implies a strong contribution from both central and provincial Government and Community and citizens' structures which need to accord with social reality. The Angolan judicial system and welfare institutions must adapt themselves to today's social reality, and first and foremost the protection, socialization and integration of children and young people. The consequences of war, great disparity between rich and poor, lack of professional skill, family disruption, increasing and uncontrolled urbanization are all promoting juvenile delinquency.

Nevertheless a positive role can be played by this new judicial entity expressly created for children and juvenile justice.

The new jurisdiction of the Children's Court with both welfare and socialization measures must be spread all over the country in order to promote Angolan children's human rights and their social integration in this promising country.

Argentina

THE NEW LAW FOR THE INTEGRAL PROTECTION OF CHILDHOOD AND ITS IMPACT ON FAMILY LAW

Cecilia P Grosman[*] and Marisa Herrera[**]

Résumé

I. Une nouvelle loi, celle du 28 août 2005 (No 26.061), établit un système de protection intégrale pour l'enfance et l'adolescence en conformité avec la Convention Internationale. II. Elle dispose des nouveaux droits sociaux, comprenant prestations et services. Mais puisqu'une loi n'arrive pas à atteindre son objet toute seule il faut que l'État trouve aussi les resources, financières, autant qu'en termes de l'équipe spécialisée pour opérer le système. Ou le législateur a habilité les juges, pour obliger le pouvoir administratif à le faire. III. Droits devant les tribunaux, représentation par des avocats spécialisés, et droit de faire écouter la voix de l'enfant intéressé. IV, Droit à l'identité, mais incertitude lorsqu'il s'agit de l'interprétation de ce droit, et surtout s'il y a un conflit entre la verité et la stabilité de la filiation. V. Droits et obligations des grandparents et autres membres de la famille rélatives à la garde et à la visite; y compris le droit de la mère abandonnée par le père de ses enfants à une pension alimentaire payée par son beau-père.

I INTRODUCTION

'There is no sense in sending a space probe to Mars to discover what Martian rocks are like while millions die of hunger in Africa. Nor in building a motorway between two cities to arrive fifteen minutes earlier, while lost villages have nothing. There is wealth in the world. How is it distributed? How can it be that some have it all, and so easily, and others get nothing or next to nothing?'

José Saramago

---

[*] Titular Consultant Professor of Family and Succession Law, Faculty of Law, University of Buenos Aires; Investigadora Superior of the Consejo Nacional de Investigaciones Científicas y Técnicas; Director of the Carrera de Especialización en Derecho de Familia and of the Maestría en Derecho de Familia, Infancia y Adolescencia of the Faculty of Law, Universidad de Buenos Aires.

[**] Lecturer in the Faculty of Law, University of Buenos Aires; Coordinator of the Carrera de Especialización en Derecho de Familia y la Maestría en Derecho de Familia, Infancia y Adolescencia de la Faculty of Law, University of Buenos Aires; Coordinator of postgraduate Family Law courses in other universities in the interior of the country. Translated by Peter Schofield.

On this occasion, it has seemed to us to be of general interest to point to some aspects of the recent Law for the Integral Protection of Children and Adolescents (law 26.061) passed by the National Congress on 28 August 2005.[1]

The first thing to note is that this new legal tool forms part of a process now being pursued in Latin American countries,[2] to bring internal law into line with the terms of the Convention on the Rights of the Child.[3]

The Convention on the Rights of the Child (along with the so-called 'doctrine of integral protection') was ratified in 1990 by law 23.849, and put on the level of constitutional law along with other treaties on human rights, by the reform of the Magna Carta that took place in 1994. Likewise, a number of Argentine provinces, in a particularly fruitful spell of work,[4] have passed local laws in conformity with international minimum standards in relation to the rights of children and adolescents.[5]

We have, in earlier articles in recent editions of this survey, given an account of the legislative changes and the various developments in case-law. On this occasion we shall delve more deeply into the theme of the rights of the child in Argentine law, but focusing on the latest law, which is national in character, directed at consolidating the advances that have been in the process of being made along these lines.

---

[1]	Published in the *Boletín Oficial*, 26 October 2005.

[2]	By way of examples, the first in the region was Brazil, in its 'Statute of Child Rearing and Adolescence' on 13 July 1990. Followed in various countries such as the 'Code of Childhood and Adolescence' of Honduras (1996); the 'Code of Childhood and Adolescence' of Nicaragua (1998); the 'Code of the Child and Adolescent' of Bolivia (1999); the 'Peruvian Code of Children and Adolescents' (2000); the 'Organic Law for the Protection of the Child and Adolescent' of Venezuela (2000); the 'Code of Childhood and Adolescence' of Paraguay (2001); the 'Law of Integral Protection of Childhood and Adolescence' of Ecuador (2003); the 'Law of Integral Protection of Childhood and Adolescence' of Guatemala (2003); and the 'Code for the System of Protection and Fundamental Rights of Children and Adolescents' of the Dominican Republic (2003). Most recently, we can look to the 'Code of Childhood and Adolescence' of Uruguay, passed in 2004 and the Argentine law we are now considering.

[3]	Consultative Opinion 17/2003 on the 'Legal Position of the Child' issued by the Corte Interamericana de Derechos Humanos (CIDH) which affirmed the 'need for a further examination of the process of bringing the legislation of American States into line with the principles of the Convention on the Rights of the Child and the American Convention', made '*aggiornamiento legislativo*' imperative for Argentina, on pain of international responsibility.

[4]	Mary Beloff 'Constitución y derechos del Niño'; David Baigún et al *Estudios sobre Justicia Penal. Homenaje al Profesor Julio B Maier* (Editores del Puerto, Buenos Aires, 2005) p 766.

[5]	For an overview of provincial progress in the field of childhood and adolescence we note the provinces that have so far produced legislation to satisfy the Convention on the Rights of the Child: Mendoza; Chubut; Chaco; Río Negro; Ciudad Autónoma de Buenos Aires; Neuquén; Salta; Tierra del Fuego; Misiones; Jujuy; San Juan; and the Province of Buenos Aires.

By way of clarification, we note that, at the time of writing, the law we are considering still awaits the corresponding regulations, which must be brought forward within 90 days from the passing of the law, in conformity with art 77 of law 26.061.

Our approach, in commenting on the new rules, will be to analyse the following central themes:

(a) the social rights of children, adolescents and their families (II);

(b) the notion of gradual progress towards legal capacity, and its impact on judicial proceedings (III);

(c) the right to one's identity (IV); and

(d) the wider family's responsibility (V).

Within this plan, we examine the chosen themes incorporating into our study some of the judgments handed down in 2005, which, on the one hand, provide interesting precedents for the protection of childhood and, on the other, give evidence of the continuing fierce debates about the extent of some of the rights of children and adolescents.

II SOCIAL RIGHTS AND THE RIGHTS OF THE CHILD

1. Law and reality: poverty of countries – wealth of rights

Argentina, like all underdeveloped countries, of the 'third world' or 'peripheral', is unavoidably conditioned by certain traits or characteristics. Poverty, exclusion, unfair distribution of wealth and external debt are among the principal elements of this, entailing the consistent, firm application of frankly neoliberal economic policies.[6]

As the heading of this section indicates, the law does not exist independently of reality. Hence it is easy to recognise how that basic fact affects, in a general way, the effective protection of the human rights of children, adolescents and their families. On this point, it has been clearly and concisely stated that: 'Poverty restricts the ability of families and communities to take care of their children.'[7]

---

[6] On this, a review note on the poverty and unemployment indices for the first half of 2005 points out that 'levels of poverty and destitution continued to fall in the first half of 2005, but more slowly than in earlier periods. Poverty increased in some cities, including Buenos Aires and continues to be very high in the North of the country. 38.5% of the urban population is poor and 13.6% indigent' (see www.cambiocultural.com.ar/actualidad/pobreza.htm).

[7] 'Estado Mundial de la Infancia 2005. La infancia amenazada' (Childhood at risk) (UNICEF, New York, 2004) p 25.

The adverse effects on children of this aspect of the current situation in Argentina are taken into account in the text of the new national law on the protection of childhood.

In the first place, law 26.061 on the protection of childhood and adolescence, in common with similar laws in the Latin American region, gives priority to the action of social services rather than judicial intervention where there are social conflicts or deficiencies. Thus it is affirmed that:

> 'Family problems involving social or economic needs should be resolved by universal public policies, in an administrative context, with the judicial system becoming involved as a last resort and only to resolve questions or disputes of a legal nature.'[8]

In this connection, various provisions of the law recognise, directly or indirectly, the importance of action taken by the State in drawing up and giving effect to public policies, whether universal in nature (directed at meeting the basic needs of all children and adolescents and their families), or specific (directed at a particular sector of childhood or adolescence, with a view to countering particular basic inequalities, for example, children with special needs or with health problems).

The central aim of public policies for satisfying and/or restoring violated rights of children and adolescents, enshrined in the new law, is a reassertion of the importance of the family.[9] The law establishes a network of measures and/or actions, varying in nature (administrative, legislative, judicial) directed at the family (in the wide sense, not confined to parents, but covering any affective relation of the child), to be used to fight for and support the ability of families to perform their primary function in raising and educating children.

Thus we find a series of measures of integral protection that must be employed when the rights of children are threatened or violated (art 37), giving priority to those enabling children to 'remain living with their family group' (cl a); the provision of bursaries for study, or of day nurseries and nursery schools (cl b); their inclusion in programmes of family support (cl d); the care of children and/or adolescents in their own homes and at the same time programmes for educating parents, and others responsible, in the performance of their duties and in the practical functioning of the family (cl e); medical, psychological or psychiatric treatment of the child or of any of his/her parents or others responsible (cl f); and economic support (cl g).

---

8   CELS and Fundación Sur 'El proyecto de Ley de Protección Integral: la posición del CELS de la Fundación Sur – Argentina' Emilio García Méndez (compiler), *Infancia y Democracia en la Argentina. La cuestión de la responsabilidad penal de los adolescentes* (Fundación Sur – Editores del Puerto y Ediciones del Signo, Buenos Aires, 2004) p 146.

9   Thus art 7 starts by affirming: 'The family is primarily responsible for ensuring the full and effective enjoyment of their rights and guarantees by children and adolescents.'

Indeed, if the State does not provide the means for the responsible adults to perform their obligations in relation to the welfare of their children, and fails to implement the provisions of the law, the responsibility for that failure lies with the State itself, not the family.

Hitherto, the tendency has been to penalise the parents (and in our view, clearly also the children) for their physical or psychological inability to meet the demands of raising children, and on that basis to remove the children from the family group to which they belong. To counter this obvious violation of the right of children to live/remain with their family of origin, the law provides in the final paragraph of art 33 that:

> 'Lack of material resources on the part of the parents, the family or the legal representatives or persons responsible for the children or adolescents, whether this be circumstantial, transitory or permanent, is not a ground for separating [children] from their nuclear or extended family or from those with whom they have emotional bonds, or for institutionalising them.'

From a different point of view, but on a similar conceptual basis, the final paragraph of art 11 rules that:

> 'Only in cases where [remaining in the same family] is impossible will they have to live, be cared for and develop in an alternative family or to have an adoptive family in accordance with the law.'[10]

To summarise, the new law adjusts the balance of the system of integral protection so that its twin pillars now concern, first, strongly family-oriented public policies valuing and supporting children's families and/or affective bonds, and, secondly, giving greater weight to administrative, rather than judicial intervention.

2. The enforceability of social rights

From what we have said so far, the importance of the role of public policies in relation to the rights of children and adolescents is obvious. So far, in theory, it all seems simple.

The principal concern the law raises is its practical application. Reference to public policies, by implication, means considering the material resources with which to meet the cost or requirements of acting on them.

---

[10] On the other hand, conforming to the principle of not separating children and of keeping them in their family of origin, art 41 provides, among other factors to be considered when, as a last resort, it is a matter of separation of a child, that 'the measures consist of seeking and identifying persons bonded to them by relationship by consanguinity or affinity, or other members of their wider family or of their community ...' (cl a). That 'only by way of exception can recourse be made to a pattern of living away from their family group, and efforts should be made, by quick and flexible means, to ensure the return of children to their family or community group or surroundings ...' (cl b). And (in cl c) that 'measures are to be put into effect by way of forms of intervention which do not involve substitutes for the family of origin, with the aim of preserving the child's or adolescent's family identity'.

Thus, placing administrative intervention above judicial action means a major commitment (both in human and material terms) on the part of the administrative authority to realise bigger and better public policies coordinated and constructed within the doctrine of integral protection.

In this context, it has been said that:

> 'For the doctrine of human rights and of integral protection to give satisfactory results requires not only the provision of high quality professional attention, which respects the guarantees and rights of the children and their families, but also an inclusive social policy and a State with enough resources to respond to the needs of families.'[11]

Achieving this goal raises two questions. The first refers to the machinery the law provides to achieve its effects. The second (and related to the first), to the measures and/or actions available to deal with failure to fulfil obligations leading to violation of the social rights of children and adolescents.

On the first point, it is interesting to note that the law creates the office of *Defensor del Niño* (arts 47–68), endowed with wide powers, including: promoting collective actions to protect general rights of children or adolescents; suing to protect rights of children and adolescents in any field; and overseeing effective respect for the rights and guarantees of children, promoting any necessary judicial and extrajudicial measures (art 55). Control of public and private institutions forming part of the system of protection of rights created by the law is explicitly provided for (art 48).

Our concern over this relates to the manner of appointment. As we can see, the law provides that nominating the *Defensor* is the responsibility of the National Congress (art 49). If, as is normally the case, this body has a majority of members belonging to the governing party, this control function could be weakened. The fact is that it is precisely the executive that, through a variety of organs, is responsible for carrying forward public policies. This makes it hard for the *Defensor,* faced with non-performance of such positive actions, to take the necessary administrative and/or judicial steps, if he is answerable to, or is of the same political persuasion as the ruling party.

A second question relates to the need to push ahead with the judicial enforcement of violated social rights, by means of actions, such as the *acción de amparo*, which Argentine law has shown to be quick and effective. Here, in our view, the law reinforces a trend in decided cases that has developed in recent years, whereby, when the administrative power does not satisfy basic social rights (to health, maintenance, education, etc), the courts constitute the relevant organ for vindicating those rights.

---

[11]   María Federica Otero (coordinator) *Infancia. Vulneración de derechos e intervenciones en la urgencia* (Editorial Espacio, Buenos Aires, 2004) p 8.

It is worth noting here that, in countries like ours, subject to a variety of deficiencies, judicial activism has a vital role in giving effect to the social rights of children and adolescents. It would be beneficial, in the application of this law, if the executive or administrative authority itself were to take account of the duties placed upon it, so that recourse to the courts would not have to be used to compel fulfilment of the law, to say what should be done.

III CHILDREN AND ADOLESCENTS IN THE JUDICIAL PROCESS

1. The concept of progress towards full capacity as the governing principle

We recall that the Convention on the Rights of the Child introduces indeterminate concepts which we find particularly useful, such as maturity, development and autonomy. Law 26.061 carries on this line, in art 3, calling for respect for 'their condition as subjects of law' (cl a) their right to 'be heard and for their views to be taken into account' (cl b), as well as for consideration to be given to 'their age, level of maturity, power of discernment and other personal conditions' (cl d).

This shows that this law reaffirms the concept of 'progressive capacity' whereby it is necessary to think about how the law should respond or adapt in conformity with the 'evolution of faculties' that are an integral part of 'growing up'. In this way the notion of respect for the principle of autonomy referred to in the Convention on the Rights of the Child is clarified and fleshed out.

It is certain that this radical change of thinking about the legal condition of childhood has an impact on the legal regime of the capacity of minors established in the Civil Code. First, and as a preliminary, we note that the governing principle of that regime is that all children and adolescents are incapable until they reach the age of 21 – the age of majority in Argentina. They only have capacity for such acts as the law expressly specifies.[12]

In our view, this system was already in conflict with the incorporation of the Convention on the Rights of the Child, the latter having constitutional status, but the recent law 26.061 makes the contradiction even sharper.

We consider that the regulation now under way will not totally resolve this tension, but that it must now form part of a thorough revision of the Civil Code, covering all the rules directly or indirectly governing the rights of children and adolescents which concern family law. This would have to begin with a discussion of whether fixed and determined ages should be laid down for particular acts, or whether, as the Convention and the present law propose, it is

---

[12]   Civil Code, art 55 provides that 'Adult minors only have capacity for acts which the laws authorise them to perform'.

better to accept open and indeterminate concepts. Also of whether it is necessary to distinguish between proprietary and non-proprietary transactions, and within the latter, acts of a particularly personal nature.

It can readily be appreciated that the question of progressive capacity continues to raise issues as to its practical effect, but at least law 26.061 strengthens the recognition of this ruling principle as the basis on which the regime of the capacity of minors and adolescents must be built.

As the topic of progressive capacity is so wide, we confine ourselves in the next section to some contradictions presented by one of the many sub-topics, the participation of children in the judicial process.

2.   The right to be heard and of defence before the court

The right to be heard and to express one's own opinion has also been one of the 'star' rights introduced by the Convention on the Rights of the Child. This is one of the basic rights, thanks to which the key concept of the doctrine of integral protection is taking shape: that of children as 'subjects' of the law. Thus the participation, advocacy, and self-expression of children and adolescents in cases that affect them becomes a fundamental element, reflecting the autonomy we pointed to in the preceding section.

So much so that the Law of Protection of Childhood (law 26.061) does not just accept it, but goes so far as to make it explicit that this right must be respected in all matters involving children 'including those related to status, family, community, social, educational, scientific, cultural, sportive and recreational matters' (art 24).

The law gives directions as to how this right operates in court proceedings in art 27. It establishes that organs of the State should guarantee the following rights for children and adolescents:

(a) to be heard by the competent authority whenever a child or adolescent so requests;

(b) to have their views taken into account primordially at the time of taking any decision that affects them;

(c) to be assisted by a lawyer, preferably one specialising in children and adolescents, from the start of any judicial or administrative proceedings in which they are involved. In case of lack of economic resources, the State should *ex officio* assign a lawyer to protect them;

(d) to take an active part in any proceedings; and

(e) to take any decision affecting them to the appellate level.

Argentine doctrine considers that this guarantee for children and adolescents to take part in proceedings is not restricted to those in which they are 'parties', but extends to all cases in which they could be 'affected' without the need to specify the capacity in which they would take part.[13]

A further problem, or at least concern, raised by the law in connection with the right to be heard, relates to the possibility that children could initiate proceedings with the assistance of a lawyer of their own choosing. On this, the law for the protection of childhood on which we are commenting (art 27, cl c) accepts the notion of the child's advocate. In our view, this provision deserves special caution when regulations are drawn up, not only to deal with possible conflicts of interest with the parents, holders of the misnamed *patria potestas*, in relation to representation, but also – and for the first time – with practical aspects, since the obligation is placed on the State to designate for the child or adolescent a lawyer or advocate specialising in children and adolescents.

3.   The right to be heard in current decisions of Argentine courts

In closing this section devoted to the principle of progressive capacity and its impact on the judicial process we wish to refer to three earlier decided cases which have shaped this right to be heard. After this brief account of the rules of the law we are studying as to the child's right to be heard, we underline some aspects of the theme of the child's voice in judicial proceedings in the light of some current judicial precedents.

3.1. A decision on the international return of minors[14]

The first of these decisions relates to a case of the international return of a minor. In summary terms, the facts of the case were as follows.

A girl of Argentine nationality lived with her parents in Brazil. After the breakdown of the marriage, the mother took her back to Argentina without authorisation or warning. The father brought proceedings against this impetuous transfer.

The Argentine Court of First Instance rejected the order for return made by the Brazilian court. On appeal the request for return was granted on the ground that the girl's habitual residence was Brazil, so that the courts of that country had competence to deal with the dispute before them. On 9 February 2005, the Buenos Aires Supreme Court revoked the order for return made in the lower court, and restored the decision at first instance. Effect was not given to the order for return made by the court of the country of the girl's habitual residence.

---

13   Jorge L Kielmanovich 'Reflexiones procesales sobre la ley 26.061 (ley de Protección Integral de los Derechos de los Niños, Niñas y Adolescentes)' *La Ley* review, 17/11/2005, p 1.
14   SCBA, 09/02/2005, 'B d S D c/ T, E s/ exhorto', Ac 87.754 in www.scba.gov.ar.

In relation to the right to be heard, the dispute turned on whether the decision of the appellate court was vitiated by failure to hear the girl, so that there was non-compliance with a rule of provincial law (art 50 of law 10.067, under which the court was, in all cases, required to hear the child). Some members of the Supreme Court were for rejecting the appeal for nullification, saying she had been heard at least once (at first instance or originally), so the requirement to hear her was satisfied. However, other members held that, bearing in mind the relevance of the right involved, and the gravity of the omission, nullity was the unavoidable consequence. But, so as not to drag out the proceedings, the court ordered that facilities be provided there (in the highest provincial court) for compliance with the right to be heard, and that a final order be made. Among the reasons for the decision, it was said that:

> 'The right to be heard is of a highly personal character, so that it was not admissible to cut out its exercise on the basis of the general representation of the child – by the Asesor de Menores – or the tutor ad litem, because his intervention defeated the object of the law.'

Put in the form of a question:

> 'Does the right to live in one or the other country affect her? We answer in the affirmative. Consequently the girl must be allowed freely to express her opinion, giving her the opportunity to be duly heard.'

Nonetheless, as a dictum in the opinion of another judge put it, the debate on the nullity or otherwise of the judgment of the lower court, for failing to hear the child, touches on an abstract question, of her being personally interviewed by the judges of the Supreme Court themselves, by the judges of the highest level in the provincial order.

3.2. A decision on child custody[15]

The conflict with which this decision deals arose from another divorce case where parents disputed the custody of their child. The core issue was that the mother, who had returned to a former partner, was working abroad (in Spain, in fact), and so was applying not only for custody of her daughter, but also for judicial approval for taking her out of the country. It is relevant that the parents had signed an agreement whereby custody went to the father while the mother was out of the country, with a liberal regime of access and visits for her maternal grandparents.

The appellate court of the city of Mar del Plata, on 9 June 2005, allowed an appeal of the defendant father, reversing the judgment of the court below, whereby the mother's application for custody and for authorisation to travel was rejected. In reaching this decision the judges of the appellate court laid stress on what the daughter, then nearly 12 years old, had said – that she wanted

---

[15]   Capel Civ y Com, Mar del Plata, Sala II, 09/06/2005, 'G L E c/ C M s/ tenencia de hijo, régimen de comunicación y autorización judicial supletoria', Diario Jurídico on line El Dial, 06/07/2005.

to stay in her home town (Balcarce, Buenos Aires Province) 'near her father, her family, her friends, fellow pupils, neighbours'.

On the weight of children's expressed opinions in judicial proceedings affecting them, the judgment says that:

> 'while a minor's opinion cannot have binding force in deciding which of two parents should be given custody, it must be taken into account when the minor is twelve years old and has spoken freely.'

It adds that, among factors to be considered:

> 'to analyse and evaluate the opinion of the minor, we must include the minor's age, without strict limits, since it is known that an older child is presumed to have greater ability, objectivity and discretion, and the relationship between the paramount interest and the wishes of the minor, which can easily be at variance with the interests of the parents.'

In consequence, by application of one of the principles or guidelines for solving custody disputes, such as maintaining the status quo or the current factual position, where there are no grave reasons to the contrary, custody of the girl was given to her father, with a liberal regime of communication with the mother. Finally, it is interesting to note that, in conclusion, it was said:

> 'it must be added that it must be for the parents, in situations like this, to come forward with agreed solutions, with a view to the paramount objective of the welfare of the minor concerned, innocent victims of their parents' quarrels.'

3.3. An adoption case[16]

The last decision we have chosen, to give a brief glimpse of the evolution of the right to be heard in current judicial decisions, as well as to show how it is becoming established in the light of the recent national law for the integral protection of the rights of the child, is a case of adoption and restitution.

That is to say, a judicial conflict between those seeking to adopt and genetic parents (in this case, the father alone). It is a matter of a more complex precedent than we normally come across in such cases, because of the particular facts, which we shall now outline.

On 23 April 1997, a girl was born in the city of Posadas, Misiones Province, in Northwest Argentina. Two days later, the mother entrusted her daughter to a married couple living in Esquel, Chubut Province, in the South. Straight away the couple applied to the court for judicial custody of the girl. At the same time, the maternal grandmother told the putative father the girl had died. Soon after – precisely 6 days after the birth – he learned the truth and tried to recognise his daughter. The Civil Register Officer, in breach of Argentine law, which allows

---

[16] TSJ, Chubut, 14/09/2005, 'V, F M s/ Adopción Simple', Boletín electrónico de la Revista de Derecho de Familia, www.lexisnexis.com.ar.

anyone to recognise his extramarital child, without the mother's prior consent, refused to allow the unilateral act. This situation forced the putative father to start judicial proceedings to claim paternity. After 2 years of litigation, he obtained an order establishing him as the father. During this time, the daughter remained in the couple's custody, consolidating the affective bond between them.

Armed with the certification of his status as such, the father entered the couple's proceedings for custody with a view to adoption, claiming the return of his daughter. In the meantime, he had also moved from Posadas to live in Esquel.

The dispute between the custodians – would-be adopters – and the father grew deeper and more acute as the years passed. Finally it came before the Tribunal Superior de Chubut for a decision as to whether to return the girl to her father or to allow the adoption and, in the latter case, whether as a full or a simple adoption, for Argentine law recognises both forms (Civil Code, arts 323 ff).

The Superior Tribunal de Justicia of Chubut gave its ruling on 14 September 2005. It was in a somewhat novel form. Before examining the judgment itself, we note that the court had made use of its powers under the procedural codes to appoint an advocate specialising in mediation, to try to find an agreed solution. This turned out to be impossible, so the court eventually had to decide.

In a long judgment, the highest provincial court rejected both petitions – that for adoption and that for return – granting simple (not adoptive) custody to the couple, on the grounds that the girl had lived with them for 8 years. It ordered a pattern of gradual contact, under professional supervision in favour of the father.

However, the most interesting aspect of this decision is in relation to the right to be heard. The fundamental basis of this decision, which was to be considered provisional and temporary, was the need to hear the girl's own view of her future, whether to be adopted or to return to her father, at a time when she had enough maturity and understanding to give an autonomous opinion.

The relevant section of the judgment reads:

> '... when the girl is between thirteen and fourteen years old, the First Instance court is to hear her (see second paragraph of art. 14 of law 4347[17] and CDN art. 12), with a view to deciding whether to make any change. Naturally, at this stage, the situation will be reassessed not only in the light of her opinion, but taking account of all the evidence available to the First Instance Court, as a Family Court, directing the course of the proceedings.'

To complete this section, we note this judgment is subject to appeal before the Alto Tribunal Federal, and thus not final.

---

[17]   Ley de Protección Integral de la Niñez, la Adolescencia y la Familia de Chubut.

IV THE CHILD'S RIGHT TO IDENTITY

The law of integral protection we are considering here emphasises the child or adolescent's right to identity, establishing that children and adolescents have a right to a family name, nationality, a native language and the knowledge of who their parents are, to preservation of their family relationships and the culture of their home locality. The rule includes and even broadens the content of that right as set out in the Convention on the Rights of the Child (arts 7 and 8).

In this connection, we think it interesting to note two judgments made in 2005, in which we see differing doctrinal positions in relation to the extent, meaning, and direction of the child or adolescent's right to identity, indicating the differing views taken, at the time of deciding a particular case, of the issues involved.

1. Putative father challenging paternity

In one case, the biological putative father of a girl brought an action to challenge the paternity of the mother's husband, and called for art 259 of the Civil Code, which makes this action only available to the husband, the child and the husband's heirs if he dies during the period of caducity, to be declared unconstitutional. He argued that that rule infringed several provisions of international treaties, which enjoy constitutional status in our country (art 75, cl 22 of the Constitution), which provide for the child's right to identity. These high order norms are infringed, because they make it impossible for the child or the biological father to establish the legal bonds arising from the blood tie. Thus, he maintained, the rights of the child are ignored, along with those of the biological father, and the guarantees of due process and of natural justice.

The facts of the case were that the putative father and the mother had an intimate relationship, resulting in the girl's birth. The husband forgave the mother's infidelity and the marital relationship continued, with the husband assuming responsibility for the child's care and upbringing as if she were his own. The applicant also related that, in conversation with the husband, the latter had asked him to drop any idea of recognition.

The opinion of judge Aída Kemelmajer de Carlucci, member of the Supreme Court of Mendoza Province, Argentina, takes us through an extensive review of all relevant precedents. We only mention that, in one earlier decision, the National Superior Tribunal, by majority, rejected a claim for the unconstitutionality of the said art 259 of the Civil Code on the ground that it denied the mother the means of challenging the paternity of a matrimonial child.[18] The minority (Drs Petracchi, Bossert and Vásquez) considered, among other grounds, that the provision of the Civil Code did infringe the Convention on Elimination of all Forms of Discrimination against Women. They also

---

[18]   C S, 1/11/99, LL, 1999-F-670, E D 185–451.

pointed out that allowing the action to be brought by a child on reaching majority, by implication, left children below that age unprotected when they most needed it. We must note that the question of failing to allow the mother to challenge her husband's paternity opened a broad and heated debate, with divided doctrinal opinions, which still continues.

The decision we are now considering opens up another dispute in doctrine and case-law as to whether to allow or deny the putative father the right to bring the action to challenge the husband's paternity. Argentine courts have, in general, rejected this possibility. However, in some other provinces, first instance courts faced with particular facts have begun to open the way to the idea of the unconstitutionality of the rule denying the action to the putative father. Thus the decision of one provincial court[19] declared the article unconstitutional and allowed an action to challenge matrimonial paternity to be brought by a putative biological father. It was held that the rule, by not including the mother or third parties among those entitled to challenge paternity, showed a discriminatory attitude against persons with a legal interest in arriving at the true filiation of the child and towards the child's right to identity recognised in rules ranking at constitutional level.

While some doctrinal writers affirm that the restriction imposed on biological fathers is unconstitutional, others justify it. However, there is also an eclectic or intermediate position, holding that, although it is generally right for legal and biological filiation to coincide, there must be certain limits, justified by, among other things, the maintenance of social or family peace. So the distinction is made according to the facts of the particular case; if the child's *possessión de estado* (ostensible status, in terms of practical living arrangements) is with the biological father, it is right to allow him a filiation that gives effect to his true parenthood. On the other hand, if he is treated as the child of the mother's husband, such legitimation should be denied. So this tendency does not reject the right to know the biological reality, but places obstacles in the way of that right where it is not justified by social reality.

The principles of this eclectic position are applied in this decision, so that the opinion of Dr Aída Kemelmajer de Carlucci, with which the other judges concurred, confirms the decision rejecting the putative father's claim to bring the action to challenge the mother's husband's paternity. Among the circumstances she cites to justify that decision, are the following:

(a) The girl is hardly 3 years old and is with her mother who lives with her husband and who loves and cares for her. That is, in favour of the husband, he has *de facto* parental status, having assumed each and all of the responsibilities of legal filiation.

(b) The proposed filiation, if the application succeeds, would remove her from that situation of legitimacy and place her in an extramarital situation, in

---

[19] Juzg Civ Com, N 4, Paraná, 15/9/2003, 'Zalazar, Horacio Miguel c/Correa, Jorge Rosa y ots. p/Impugnación de la paternidad', J A 2004-III-402, con nota aprobatoria de Solari, Néstor.

which she would lose legal ties not only with those who care for her and love her as their child, but with her entire family group.

(c) The State, in the shape of the judicial power, would be interfering in the intimacy of the family, in the right to family life of the respondents, with no certainty that the change would be in the paramount interest of the child.

(d) Even if – runs the judgment – one agrees with the applicant and the doctrine he cites, that true family peace is based on truth, in this case, the husband and wife are not living a lie, and they are the ones who, with such scientific assistance as they think necessary, can best disclose to the child the facts that let her know her biological origin at a time when, in the exercise of their *patria potestas*, they think she has enough maturity for this.

The proposed solution, the judge said, does not penalise someone who wants to assume his responsibilities as a father, nor deny the production of scientific evidence, nor the new social concepts. It is simply a matter of the State not intruding into the intimate family life of a developing person, giving primacy to her true paramount interest, not as an abstraction, the determining of which is for the persons to whom the law attributes the character of parents, not for the judges.

It is clear from the terms of this and the earlier decisions of our courts, that there is a need to reform the law, defining with greater precision the extent and content of the right to identity set out in the legislation.

2. Res judicata in face of the progress of science

In a case[20] in which the applicant sought a fresh decision on the same facts as those of a filiation decision in 1982, on the basis of new genetic evidence (from DNA), the application was rejected on the grounds of *res judicata*. By a majority, the court recognised that in the state of science at that time it was not possible to determine paternal filiation with certainty and that today the situation has changed and reliable proof of whether there is a biological link is now possible. Despite the fact that the right to identity has constitutional rank, the filiation action was rejected, because the case had been properly decided, according to the evidence then available, for which reason it was not admissible to reopen a case that had been concluded, which would be contrary to the principle of judicial certainty.

Nonetheless, this was not a unanimous decision. One judge, dissenting, held that even if the principle of judicial certainty is based on immutable judgments, in filiation cases there was a social interest in verifying the truth, since it was in the interest of the community to ascertain responsibility for procreation and of the child to obtain his filial status, which was a right of personality. He argued that the immutability of judicial decisions was not an absolute principle, since

---

[20] CNCiv, Sala: B Expte N1: B404595, 21/03/05, 'G, RM c/ E, JM s/ filiación'.

the law, in regulating the dynamics of human relations, could not stand aside from reality: however much one would like a judgment to be immutable for reasons of legal policy and certainty, it was no less a cultural product and, for that reason, not exempt from change. In the face of a conflict between a fundamental right like juridical certainty and the most personal right of the applicant to know his/her identity, it was the latter that must prevail. We see this as a conflict of rights, in the words of the German constitutionalist Robert Alexis, where one has to weigh up which of the two takes precedence in this case in accordance with the factual circumstances.

V   PERSONAL RELATIONS AND REGIME OF CONTACT WITH GRANDPARENTS, RELATIVES AND OTHERS: DELEGATION OF PARENTAL AUTHORITY TO GRANDPARENTS

The Convention on the Rights of the Child guarantees the integral protection of children and adolescents and, to that end, various provisions make reference to the wider family and its responsibilities and resulting faculties. In the same direction, the law for the protection of childhood emphasises the importance that relations with their wider family can have in the life of children and adolescents. In this context, the legislature has understood and assumed that grandparents and other relatives play a fundamental role in the protection of childhood, in what they can do as well as in the values they pass on. Current legislation shows a steadily growing emphasis on the relations of grandchildren with grandparents for a variety of biological and social reasons. First, because greater life expectancy enables adults to play a useful part in the development of their grandchildren. Also relevant is the increase in the rates of separation and divorce, which make work for grandparents in maintaining some stability in the children's affective relationships, by being a necessary and secure point of reference in their environment. Further, the professional activity of both parents often results in grandparents taking charge of their grandchildren during the absence of the parents.[21]

The Law of Integral Protection gives effect to the obligation imposed on States by art 2 of the Convention on the Rights of the Child, to respect the duties, rights and responsibilities not only of parents, but also of members of the wider family. Moreover, in cases where exceptional measures are necessary to protect children and adolescents who are separated from their familiar surroundings, or who, in their own interest, have to be removed from there, there is a preference for placement with relatives by blood or marriage and other members of the wider family, subject to the child's or adolescent's views (art 41).

---

[21]   Ana María Colas Escandon *Relaciones familiares de los nietos con sus abuelos: derecho de visita, estancia, comunicación y atribución de la Guarda y custodia (ley 42/2003 de 21 de noviembre)* (Thomson-Aranzadi, Navarra, 2005) p 34 y ss.

We should like to comment briefly on various judicial pronouncements providing interesting precedents in relation to the recognition of personal relationships of the child with the wider family that we have just emphasised.

1. Placing children in the care of grandparents

It often happens in our country that when the mother of children born out of wedlock is unable to look after them, she leaves them with her own parents. This is a regular practice not normally made into a court order. It is, however, worth citing a decision that arose from the mother's and maternal grandparents' application for custody to be granted to the latter, as without this they did not qualify for social benefits which would come to them if they had custody. It was a case of giving the force of a judicial order to a *de facto* situation. From her birth to the age of 8 the child had lived with her grandparents, because her mother could not maintain her or have the child with her. The decision follows the doctrine by which the parent with *patria potestas* has the right to place the child in another household and in the care of other persons if the circumstances make this desirable. Judicial confirmation of delegation of care – according to the judgment – is the right way to give effect to this with regard to third parties, and recognises the paramount interest of the child, where the mother is not in a position to provide for her maintenance.[22] In another judgment, the court held that it was right that, on a temporary basis, the child should be put in the care of third parties, aunts and uncles or grandparents, if conflict between the parents posed a risk to the child's physical safety.[23]

2. Granting custody and care of a grandchild to grandparents[24]

In another case, a father claimed custody of his daughter who had been placed by a court order in the care of her maternal grandparents after the mother's death. The court rejected the application, and granted custody to the grandparents. The grounds for the judgment included the argument that, with her grandparents, the girl had an experience of well-being and stability and that 'at this stage of her chronological age it would be highly damaging to bring about an interruption of this process, which would be retrograde in effect'. So the decision not to change the current situation was based on the principle of the status quo and of the child's paramount interest. However, the judgment added that this did not imply 'displacement of the paternal figure' and his role must be respected, but his inclusion must be gradual. For these reasons he was accorded generous facilities for communication with the girl.

---

[22] CNCiv, Sala H, 31/3/98, Revista El Derecho, 14/12/98.
[23] CNCiv, Sala H, 31/3/98, Revista El Derecho, 14/12/98.
[24] Cámara de Apelación en lo Civil y Comercial de Mercedes, Sala 2ª, FCCv F, HL y otras s/ tenencia, 3/6/2005.

In another recent decision,[25] the appellate court confirmed a decision at first instance granting the grandparents' application for care and control of a girl, arguing that this did not deprive the father of his *patria potestas* as it only affected one element of this, and that it was best for the child to live with her grandparents. The judgment held that living with them, with their devotion, love, care and attention – particularly after the loss of her mother at a young age – made it essential to leave her with them.

3. The right of grandparents, relatives and others to maintain personal relationships with children and adolescents

In Argentine legislation, children are given the right to have communication with those relatives to whom, under the Civil Code (art 376 bis), they are under a reciprocal duty of maintenance: ascendants, descendants, brothers and sisters, half-brothers and half-sisters (art 367); relatives by affinity in the first grade – son-in-law, daughter-in-law, parents-in-law, step-parents, step-children (arts 363 and 368).

Various decisions affirm the importance of grandchildren maintaining their relationship with grandparents, and its formative benefits. Often, in separation or divorce, one parent, through animosity, bitterness or resentment against the other, opposes contact between children and members of the other's family. On this question, courts have refused to let parents abusively obstruct contact that is for the child's benefit[26] and have affirmed the advantages of maintaining family solidarity, affective bonds and family traditions, all of which benefit the child, unless in the circumstances this involves risk to their physical or mental health.[27]

On the same basis of the child's paramount interest, this contact has been extended to others, wherever it is beneficial for the child. In any case, parents can object to such contact on the ground that it would harm the child's health, physical or mental. The court decides in summary form and can lay down the modalities of such contact (art 376 bis, final part).[28]

4. Grandparents' maintenance obligation

As we know, when parents do not live together, or have separated or divorced, when, as in most cases, the mother remains in charge of the children, the father often stops performing his maintenance responsibility, in part or entirely. The

---

25   CNCiv, Sala K, 31/3/2005, LL, 27/6/2005.
26   CNCiv, Sala E, 7/8/1987, La Ley, 1988-A, p 391; Cciv, com Trab y Familia Cruz del Eje, 16/6/2000, LLC, 2000, p 1349.
27   Cciv y Com. Moron, Sala II, 19/6/97, LLBA, 1998, p 401.
28   Di Lella Pedro 'La legitimación en los denominados "regímenes de visitas"' *Revista Jurisprudencia Argentina*, 2/7/2003.

mother, in this position, if she is not in a position to maintain the children, makes a claim against their paternal grandparents.

The current tendency in decided cases holds that, to make grandparents liable for maintenance, it must be shown that the father is in default of his obligations, and that the mother neither has nor is capable of obtaining sufficient resources, since their liability is subsidiary in nature. However, another decision has held that 'it is not enough merely to show default on the father's part, if compulsory measures have not been sought to obtain the enforced satisfaction of the judgment that held him liable'.[29] These might involve garnishee proceedings against the father's assets, or attachment of his earnings, to compel payment.[30]

This line of strict decisions is contrary to the ideology of the Convention on the Rights of the Child, which requires signatory States to take all measures necessary to ensure payment of maintenance by parents and others with financial responsibility for the child (art 27, cl 4).

The new approach, based on the interest of the child, had already weakened the strictness of the rule. The result of this is that non-payment of maintenance on the part of the liable parent enables a claim to be made against grandparents for the maintenance of their grandchildren on the basis of subsidiary liability.[31]

Another decision affirmed that 'it is not appropriate to require one claiming maintenance to exhaust a series of formalities if circumstances demonstrate that they would be of no use. All that should be required is the production of evidence that there is no other remedy short of pursuing the more distant relative'.[32] It has also been said that 'it has been the mother whose sacrifices have advanced the raising of her daughter, so it is not fair that the grandfather should be exonerated unless he can show that the mother's income is sufficient to meet all the expenses required by the minor'.[33] Similarly, a grandfather has been held liable to pay a share of the maintenance amount when what the father paid was not enough,[34] applying art 27 of the Convention on the Rights of the Child.

In this development towards reinforcing the responsibility of the wider family, we pick out a recent decision of the National Supreme Court of Justice, allowing the extraordinary appeal against an appellate court decision which, reversing a first instance judgment, had rejected a mother's claim for maintenance, in the name of her three minor children, against their paternal

---

[29] CNCiv, Sala H, 7/3/97, 'D de P, G M c P, Me N', LL, t 1997-D, 110. CNCiv, Sala H, 31/12/97, 'B C, G E c C, J E y otro', LL, 1999-C, p 802.

[30] Trib Col Fam Formosa, 1/8/96, 'P, L C c C, C A', LL Litoral, 1997, p 626.

[31] CNCiv, Sala G, 7/11/95, 'M de V, M c S de V, M', LL, 1996-B, 202; CNCiv, Sala G, 24/9/97, 'S, S c D N, A', LL, 1998-B, 916.

[32] CNCiv, Sala G, 7/11/95, 'M de V, M c S de V, M, LL, t 1996-B, 202; Trib Col Fam Formosa, 1/8/96, 'P, L C c C, C A y otra', LL Litoral, 1997, p 626; CNCiv, Sala I, 7/7/00, 'Q M B y otro c C, A', LL, 2001-A, 168 y CNCiv, Sala E, 14/5/01, 'M L, K c N, J A', Revista El Derecho, 17/10/01, p 8.

[33] CNCiv, Sala E, 14/5/01, El Derecho, 17/10/01.

[34] CNCiv, Sala B, 15/3/88,LL t1998-D, p 397; CNCiv, Sala A, 1/7/91, El Derecho, t 143, p 235.

grandfather. The court found that, not only was there an inadequate assessment of the evidence, but also a failure to consider the directives of the Convention on the Rights of the Child, which had constitutional status (art 27, cl 4 of the Convention), and rules of internal law (Civil Code, art 367), placing the grandchildren in grave danger of it being impossible to cover their most basic needs. The highest federal court, in the same judgment, laid down the amount of maintenance the defendant had to provide.

It is interesting to note that the decision at first instance took a wide view of the grandparents' maintenance obligations. While the majority of decided cases hold that their liability only extended to the basic necessities of the child or adolescent, that judgment took the more modern approach, considering that it should provide for necessities 'of a moral and cultural order, including what was indispensable for a reasonable life, not that the payment should be limited to mere physical subsistence'.[35]

To complete this section, we must point out that current doctrine opens the way to the idea that the interests of the child, and the need to fix the maintenance in proper time, requires the law to permit action against the grandparent directly, not successively, by virtue of the right of access to justice. Some decisions show movement in this direction. Thus, where it was shown that a father had failed to meet his liability, it has been held that, to make grandparents liable, it is not necessary to bring a separate action, but that a demand against them can be made in the proceedings to obtain maintenance from the father.[36] In accord with the trend, already established in some countries in Europe and America, the project for the reform of the Civil Code provides that 'where there is more than one obligee, each and any of them can be sued for the whole sum' (art 621). Another rule would reverse the burden of proof, requiring the person against whom maintenance is claimed to prove that there is 'another closer or equally close relative capable of making the payments' (art 623).

VI CLOSING REMARKS

Our overview of some relevant rights taken up in the new rules of integral protection of childhood, and of judicial precedents relating to their extent and interpretation, shows a serious progression towards treating the child as a subject of law. Likewise, we can conclude that, even if the interest of the child – the essential paradigm in the field of child law – is respected in relation to fundamental rights, at the same time that notion requires in every case an assessment of the factual circumstances, to determine how best those rights, representing the necessities of childhood, can be protected.

---

[35] First instance decision, 6/3/2002.

[36] María Victoria Famá 'Obligación alimentaria de los abuelos' en *Alimentos a los hijos y derechos humanos* (dir Cecilia P Grosman) (Editorial Universidad, Buenos Aires, 2004) p 279 y sgtes; CNCiv, Sala H, 7/3/97, LL, 1997-D-112.

And in this aspect, the truths that emerge are not absolute, they depend on the ideas of whoever predicates them, and on changes in society and in its values. All the same, there is a truth that perhaps does rank as absolute: deprived of their social rights, subject to poverty and abandonment, all their civil rights, so energetically written into international treaties, will only with difficulty be realised, and may only remain an empty dream.

In short, the law we are considering travels this path. It now remains to watch carefully how this new normative tool will operate in Argentine court decisions. Once again, law and reality flow together. This time, in pursuit of an effective defence and protection of the rights of childhood, in a country where social deficiencies and inequality rule.

Australia

THERE WAS MOVEMENT AT THE [FAMILY LAW] STATION[1] – AUSTRALIAN FAMILY LAW IN 2004

Frank Bates[*]

Résumé

Comme le laisse à penser le titre, des bouleversements considérables ont marqué l'année 2004 à tous les niveaux – législatif, jurisprudentiel, et gouvernemental – dans les domaines essentiels du droit de la famille. Ainsi, des évolutions significatives ont été observées en matière de mariage (création et reconnaissance du lien matrimonial), de relations entre parents et enfants, de relations patrimoniales et d'administration des biens, de pratique et de procédure en droit de la famille. L'ampleur de ces évolutions incline à penser que les années 2005 et suivantes verront de nouveaux changements, dans un secteur du droit australien qui n'a jamais été véritablement statique depuis la loi sur le droit de la famille de 1975 (*Family Law Act* 1975), une législation, révolutionnaire pour son époque, mais qui, aujourd'hui, serait en grande partie méconnaissable, pour le meilleur ou pour le pire, pour ceux qui ont été à l'origine de sa conception, de sa naissance et de ses premiers développements.

I INTRODUCTION

As the chapter title suggests, 2004 was a year in which there was considerable activity at all levels – statutory, case-law and governmental report – in significant areas of family law. Thus, there were, as will be seen, significant developments in the areas of marriage (its creation and recognition), parent and child, finance and property and the administration of, and practice and procedure in, family law generally. The totality of these developments strongly suggests that the years 2005 and following will see yet further changes in a part of Australian law which has never been in any way static since the Family Law Act 1975, a revolutionary item of legislation at the time of its inception, but which, today, would largely be

---

[1]   With apologies to the Australian poet A B ('Banjo') Patterson 'The Man from Snowy River' (1896).

[*]   Professor of Law, University of Newcastle (NSW).

unrecognisable, for better or worse, to those responsible for its conception, birth and initial growth.[2]

II MARRIAGE: CREATION AND CAPACITY

The developments in the area of marriage law during 2004 have attracted considerable public attention, whether for good or ill or for good or dubious reason.

First of all, the Marriage Act Amendment Act 2004 sought to remove the possibility that same-sex marriages entered into overseas might be recognised, in Australian law, as being valid. To that end, a new definition was inserted in s 5 of the Marriage Act 1961 that 'marriage' meant the union of a *man and a woman*[3] to the exclusion of all others voluntarily entered into for life. In addition, a new s 88EA provided that a union solemnised in a foreign country between a man and another man or a woman and another woman 'must not be recognised as a marriage in Australia'. Since the same result would have been achieved, though albeit in a slightly more convoluted way, through existing law especially s 43(a) of the Family Law Act 1975, the need for it seems questionable, the more so as there seems to be no legislative attempt to negate the recent decisions at first instance[4] and on appeal[5] in *Re Kevin*. It is, though, certainly true that the change was a significant plank in the coalition parties' election platform prior to their re-election in 2004.

Another instance which has been productive of public comment in the area has been the decision of Nicholson CJ[6] in *Re Alex: Hormonal Treatment for Gender Identity Dysphoria*.[7] This case concerned a 13-year-old child who, both anatomically and in the eyes of the law, was female but who had been diagnosed as having gender identity dysphoria. This is a condition in which the person regards her/his physical sex as wrong. Indeed, Alex was referred to as male throughout the proceedings. The application, made by a government department which had care of Alex, asked the Court to authorise medical treatment which involved the administration of hormonal therapy as part of a 'sex change' procedure. The first stage was reversible, though a further stage would have particular irreversible effects. No surgical intervention was contemplated before Alex reached the age of 18.

Alex was under the Department's legal guardianship in consequence of care proceedings which had taken place a number of years earlier. The Department had made the application to the Family Court because the proposed treatment was of such a kind that the Court's consent was required, as had been specified by the High Court of Australia in the leading case of

---

2   For a general comment, see L Star *Counsel of Perfection: The Family Court of Australia* (1996).
3   Author's emphasis.
4   (2001) FLC 93-087.
5   (2003) FLC 93-127.
6   For comment on Nicholson CJ's contribution, see below.
7   (2004) FLC 93-175.

Secretary, Department of Health and Community Services v JWB and SMB.[8]
At the hearing, a Child Representative was appointed[9] and the Human Rights
and Equal Opportunity Commission intervened[10] for the purpose of making
submissions regarding matters of law and principle. The respondents were
Alex's estranged mother, whose whereabouts were unknown, and who did
not take part in the proceedings, and Alex's aunt, with whom Alex lived, and
who supported the application. The hearing was conducted in an
inquisitional, rather than adversarial, format and the judge met with Alex in
private.

In essence, the evidence which was available to Court was as follows: first,
that, during his early years, Alex was treated as if he was a boy and spent
effectively all of his time with his father until his father's death when Alex
was about 6 years old. Alex was much hurt by his father's death and felt
rejected by his mother from an early age. That rejection apparently continued
after Alex and his mother came to Australia subsequent to his mother
marrying a man who had sponsored them. The rejection by his mother and
step-father continued and led to a child protection investigation where it was
found that Alex was depressed and attention to Alex's identification as a
male was also recommended.

Second, the outcome of that investigation was that Alex went to live with an
aunt and her daughter, the applicant Department assuming the decision-
making responsibilities of a guardian. Third, however, during the following
year, the principal of Alex's primary school as well as a case worker became
concerned regarding Alex's level of stress and talk of suicide because of
Alex's body and male gender identity not being congruent. As a result, Alex
was assessed by experts in psychiatry and endocrinology who proposed the
treatment under consideration in the case and gave evidence in the
proceeding. Another psychiatric expert, who had not previously been
involved with Alex's medical management, provided a further report which
agreed with the proposed treatment. In further addition, the director of an
English clinic, which specialised in children and adolescents with gender
dysphoria, had reviewed the Australian doctors' recommendations. He was
in general agreement that Alex should receive hormonal treatment with
ongoing support, but suggested a slightly different course and timing of
treatment from those earlier made. Alex's school had also taken steps to
accommodate special needs and had prepared strategies to meet possible
adverse reactions were Alex to disclose any transition to being male.

Nicholson CJ was of the view that it was in Alex's best interests that both
the reversible and irreversible hormonal therapies should be carried out, their
administration being authorised as from time to time determined by the
attending physicians.

---

[8]   (1992) 175 CLR 218.
[9]   See Family Law Act 1975, ss 68L, 68M.
[10]   See Family Law Act 1975, Part XI.

Most importantly on the substantive issue, Nicholson CJ first turned his mind[11] to the factors which he himself had set out in *Re Marion (No 2)*[12] and their relevance to the present case. The first was the particular condition of the young person which required the treatment. In the Chief Justice's *ipsissima verba* it was stated:

> 'It is common ground that Alex has a gender identity dysphoria which compels him to want to present as a male. That desire is longstanding and most unlikely to change. It has its most likely origins in Alex's biological and psychosocial developmental features.'

Second, Nicholson CJ referred to the nature of the procedure or treatment proposed. In that regard, he accepted a submission to the effect that he should view the instant application as the question of authorising a single package of reversible and irreversible treatment which Alex could elect to cease at any time.[13] Third, Nicholson CJ examined the reasons for which it was proposed that the procedure or treatment be carried out. The evidence, he considered:

> '... spoke with one voice as to the distress which Alex is genuinely suffering in a body which feels alien to him and disgusts him, particularly due to menstruation. It is also consistent as to his unwavering and profound wish to present as the male he feels himself to be.'

The Chief Justice also noted the possibility that Alex was an emerging lesbian had been considered by the expert psychiatric witnesses who had examined him but had not been accepted. The fourth issue enunciated in *Marion (No 2)* was the alternative courses of treatment which might be available in relation to the condition. In that respect, Nicholson CJ commented that the prognosis for behavioural intervention to change Alex's self-image and behaviour was poor. Hormonal intervention was the agreed expert view.

Fifth, Nicholson CJ then considered the desirability and effect of authorising the procedure for the treatment proposed rather than available alternatives. The Chief Justice's view was that the proposed treatment was uniformly recommended by the expert witness and was in keeping with Alex's wishes[14] and would facilitate his socialisation into his chosen identity from the onset of his secondary schooling.[15] Sixth, the physical effects on the child or

---

11   (2004) FLC 93-175 at 78,979.

12   (1994) FLC 92-448.

13   As Nicholson CJ described the issue, (2004) FLC 93-175 at 78,979:

> 'The two stages of hormonal intervention as contemplated by the initial application or with a period of analogue alone will be a matter for clinical advice by the treating physicians for so long as Alex wishes to pursue his transition. The hormonal treatment will be accompanied by on-going psychological and psychiatric support to Alex, in the context of the guardianship and educational supports ...'

14   For comment on the relevance of Alex's wishes, see below.

15   The Chief Justice went on to say that:

> 'In the past Alex has been depressed and self-harming when he thought that his deep wish to present as a male has not been taken seriously. Those who know him well are supportive of

young person and the psychological and social implications for the child or young person of authorising the proposed procedure or treatment or not authorising the proposed procedure or treatment were considered. In that regard, the Chief Justice stated that he had canvassed the physical consequences arising from each stage of the treatment.[16] He was satisfied that Alex had the capacity to know and, indeed, did know the side effects which might arise and desired the proposed treatment, with knowledge of those risks. The Chief Justice also referred to the social implications of the proposed treatment which were that Alex would:

'... face challenges in respect of his chosen identity in respect of peer relationships, possible bullying and ostracism, but [he was] satisfied that impressive steps have been taken to anticipate such risks.'

On the other side, he noted[17] that, if the treatment were not permitted, there was consistent concern that Alex would revert to the unhappiness, behavioural difficulties and self-harming behaviour. The Chief Justice went on to say:

'Socially he will be significantly ill at ease with body and self-image during his period of adolescent development until he is competent to make his own treatment decision. Transition into a male public identity will be more difficult than if it occurs at the commencement of secondary school.'

Seventh, the issue of the nature and degree of any risk to the child or young person of authorising or not authorising the proposed procedure was considered. In addition to those matters which he had considered earlier, Nicholson CJ was also concerned that Alex's residential and educational arrangements together with developmental socialisation would be adversely affected to his long-term detriment were authorisation to be refused. In that context, one particular risk was noted which related to the need for Alex to continue with the hormonal treatment and, when an adult, to have further interventions, all of which have financial implications. The Chief Justice was satisfied that the medical management of the case was inappropriate and that Alex would have access to moneys which his aunt had set aside for him to meet the cost of continuing treatment after the Department's guardianship function came to an end. Finally, the Chief Justice considered the views, if any, expressed by the guardians of the child or young person or those entitled to the custody or day-to-day care of the child or young person to the procedure and any alternatives. As will be clear, the aunt and the Department[18] all fully supported the proposed treatment. The mother's views were not known but the Chief Justice emphasised that, even if she were opposed to the treatment, he would give her views little weight, owing to the contrary evidence and her withdrawal from Alex's life.

---

the treatment that is proposed and concerned about self-harming conduct if he is unable to embark on the proposed treatment.'

[16] (2004) FLC 93-175 at 78,966*ff*.

[17] Ibid at 78,980.

[18] Together with Alex's cousin.

After his consideration of the application of *Re Marion (No 2)*, the Chief Justice then sought to examine the relevance of s 68F(2) of the Family Law Act 1975, as amended in 1995, which sets out the matters to be taken into account by courts in determining what is in the best interests of children. First, Nicholson CJ, agreeing with the submission of the child representative, stated[19] that he should place considerable weight on the realistic wishes expressed by Alex as well as the concerns which had been expressed about the risks which might occur if the treatment was not authorised.

In addition, the Chief Justice agreed[20] with submissions made by the Human Rights and Equal Opportunity Commission on the rights of a transgender child as a matter of general principle and concluded that they supported the application. In particular, he referred to those which stated that, first, a child has a right to live with a transgender identity, free from discrimination, under international human rights law. Second, it is in that child's best interests to have that right respected. Third, 'a child's right to live with a transgender identity should not be limited by a narrow definition of "transgender identity" that relies on medical or surgical intervention. There is a right to choose how that identity is expressed'. Fourth, '[i]t follows that respecting a child's right to live with a transgender identity does not, of itself, decide the issue, one way or the other, of whether the authorisation of a medical procedure is in the child's best interests. The latter is a separate yet contextually related question to be decided by the Court, based on its assessment of the child's best interests, and taking into account the right of a child to express their wishes [*sic*] and to be heard ...'.

Whilst so accepting those submissions, Nicholson CJ added a proviso[21] to the effect that it was necessary in every case (not merely medical procedure cases), where the wishes of children were seen to be significant, to take into account the evidence and opinions concerning the bases for such wishes and the weight they should be accorded as enunciated by the Full Court of the Family Court of Australia in *R and R: Children's Wishes*[22] and *R v R (Children's Wishes)*.[23]

The last, and probably tangential point, raised[24] by the Chief Justice was the matter of Australian birth certificates and he urged the various State and Territory legislatures which make surgery a prerequisite for a change in birth certificates to reconsider their position. His basis[25] for that view was that a scheme for a change of birth certificates which requires a Magistrate or Board to make a finding of fact but which does not make surgery a prerequisite was, in his view, more consistent with human rights and, therefore, preferable to an administrative scheme wherein the applicant must

---

19   (2004) FLC 93-175 at 78,980.
20   Ibid at 78,981.
21   Ibid at 78,982.
22   (2000) FLC 93-000.
23   (2002) FLC 93-108. For general comment on the issue, see F Bates '"Completing the Charm" – The Relevance of Children's Wishes in Contested Cases' (2004) 5 (2) *Newcastle LR* 97.
24   (2004) FLC 93-175 at 78,982.
25   Ibid at 78,983.

have had surgery to be eligible for the changed birth certificate. In that broad context, Nicholson CJ also suggested[26] that the requirement for surgery was:

'... more disadvantageous and burdensome for people seeking legal recognition of their transfer from female to male than male to female. Expressed in this way, there is an additional objection to surgery as a prerequisite; the requirement of surgery is a form of indirect discrimination.'

It is clear that *Re Alex* is a case which goes rather further than anything hitherto in Australia and, as such, its journalistic critics may have found themselves a little out of their depth. At the same time, the strength of Nicholson CJ's argument when taken together with the totality of the evidence, both medical and personal, means that it is hard for the ultimate decision to be effectively disputed. One hopes that it will help, as *Re Kevin*, make the lot of the transgender person less ambiguous and unhappy than it has been hitherto.

The decision of Chisholm J, who, it may be remembered, was the judge at first instance in *Re Kevin*,[27] in *AK and NC*[28] presents, especially given the ageing population throughout the western world, a number of interesting features and does suggest that care has to be taken in an area which might have reasonably been regarded as settled law.

The case involved an application for nullity on the grounds that the wife (Mrs AK) was incapable of giving an effective consent at the time of her purported marriage in October 2001 to the husband (Mr NC). The application was brought on behalf of the wife by her next friend. At the time of the purported marriage, the wife who was aged over 80 was in a nursing home suffering from dementia and under guardianship. The husband was of a similar age.

The parties had been previously married to one another (the ceremony having taken place in 1947) but had divorced in 1993. However, after that, they continued to live in adjoining houses, though the circumstances of that arrangement were unclear and in dispute. The wife became ill and was admitted to a nursing home in January 2000. Proceedings were then taken under State law whereby a guardian was appointed in respect of her. The husband was a frequent visitor to the wife whilst she was in the nursing home. The marriage ceremony in question had taken place after the husband had taken the wife away from the nursing home during one of his visits to her.

When the matter first came on for hearing, the respondent husband, who was somewhat deaf and spoke little English, was unrepresented. An attempt to arrange representation for him was unsuccessful. He had no witnesses available and was treated as having applied for an adjournment, which was opposed. At that point, Chisholm J reserved his decision both on the adjournment application and on the merits of the application. The application

---

26   Ibid at 78,984.
27   Above note 4.
28   (2004) FLC 93-178.

was largely based on the evidence of a psychiatrist, Dr C, who was of the view that the wife lacked the necessary capacity. However, one of the attachments to that report was a further report by a Dr R, who took the contrary view that the wife did have the requisite capacity.

In early 2003, Chisholm J delivered a judgment which, in effect, would have dismissed the application, but was prevailed upon to allow the applicant to re-open. At a subsequent hearing some months later, when the husband was represented, Dr R gave further evidence and further submissions were made on behalf of both parties. In final submissions, counsel for the applicant submitted that, on the evidence, the wife believed, at the time of the ceremony, that she was still married to the respondent and did not understand that the ceremony changed her status and, in any event, that she had not given a valid consent.

A number of issues arose out of Chisholm J's dismissal of the application for nullity: the first of these being the question of the admissibility of Dr R's report, in the strange circumstances in which it made its initial appearance. In dealing with that issue,[29] Chisholm J commented that the reports had been tendered for a limited basis – that was to enable the Court to appreciate the basis of Dr C's submissions. However, as the judge appropriately pointed out, the effect of s 60 of the Commonwealth Evidence Act 1995 is that, once the material had been admitted for one purpose, the hearsay rule did not apply and, hence, the material was in evidence for all purposes, including *as evidence of the truth of what was asserted in the reports*.[30] That was the more so as counsel for the applicant had not sought an order under s 136 of the Act to the effect that the judge should limit the use of the evidence. Hence, the reports were in evidence for all purposes.

The judge then turned his attention to the legal principles which governed the proceeding. First, the relevant statutory provision, which was contained in s 23B(1)(d)(iii) of the Marriage Act 1961 which provided that a marriage would be void where the relevant party was 'mentally incapable of understanding the nature and effect of the marriage ceremony'. Chisholm J, after having noted the existence of prior authority,[31] stated[32] that:

> 'It is clear from the authorities that the law does not require the person to have such a detailed and specific understanding of the legal consequences. Of course if there were such a requirement, few if any marriages would be valid.'

Nonetheless, the judge went on to say that, despite the view that the contract was simple and easy to understand,[33] there were, he said, some problems in applying the standard especially in cases such as the present, where both the parties were elderly and one required some kind of institutional care. The

---

[29]   (2004) FLC 93-178 at 79,020.
[30]   Author's emphasis.
[31]   *In the Estate of Park dec'd* [1954] P89; *Durham v Durham* (1885) PD 80; *Foster v Foster* (1923) 39 TLR 658.
[32]   (2004) FLC 93-178 at 79,020.
[33]   Expressed by Sir James Hannen P in *Durham*, above note 31.

judge then, properly, asked himself what a marriage meant in such circumstances.

After having noted the cases which had been cited to him,[34] Chisholm J agreed[35] with Dickey, who had written[36] that:

'... mere awareness of going through a marriage ceremony is not enough: a person must understand the nature and effect of the ceremony involved.'

After having considered the decision of McCall J of the Family Court of Western Australia in *Brown and Brown*[37] in some detail, Chisholm J was of the view that:

'... a valid consent involves either a general understanding of marriage and its consequences or an understanding of the specific consequences of marriage for the person whose consent is in issue.'

It was not, he thought,[38] necessary at that stage in his judgment, to rule on whether there was an inconsistency between those approaches.

All of this led to the judge's ultimate decision: first, he emphasised[39] that he could not, and nor, in all probability, could anyone else, answer the question as to whether the wife was capable of consenting to the marriage on the date in question. The case turned, in reality, on the issue of whether the applicant had proved on the balance of probabilities that the wife lacked the capacity to give such consent. *In fine*, the judge was of the view that the evidence was consistent both with the wife's having an understanding of marriage in general and its consequences for her. Accordingly, the application for a decree of nullity was dismissed.

All in all, *AK and NC* represents an interesting step in the continuum described by the judge and one which must, as I suggested[40] earlier, not be put to one side as a quaint archaism. One peripheral matter, too, should be borne in mind: it is provided in s 42(1) of the Marriage Act 1961 that:

'... a marriage shall not be solemnised unless – (a) notice in writing has been given in accordance with this section and has been received by the authorised celebrant solemnising the marriage not earlier than 18 months before the date of the marriage and not later than 1 month before the date of the marriage.'

There is no suggestion that that requirement had been complied with and it does not seem to have been brought to the attention of the judge. Hence, the issue of formality, as well as capacity, ought to have been relevant.

---

34   *Mathieson v Perry* (1939) 56 WN (NSW) 89; *Faull v Reilly* [1971] ALR 157; *Evans v Brenton* (1887) 3 WN (NSW) 129; *Brown and Brown* (1982) FLC 91-232.
35   (2004) FLC 93-178 at 79,021.
36   A Dickey *Family Law* (4th edn, 2002) p 175.
37   (1982) FLC 91-232.
38   (2004) FLC 93-178 at 79,022.
39   Ibid at 79,034.
40   Above text at note 29.

III PARENT AND CHILD

From a conceptual standpoint, the major issue in the development of parent and child law is to be found in a government report – the House of Representatives' Standing Committee on Family and Community Affairs, *Every picture tells a story: Report of the inquiry into child custody arrangements in the event of family separation.*[41]

It is important to contextualise the findings of the Report[42] especially as they relate to the 1995 amendments to the Family Law Act 1975. A key issue in both was the role played by both parents, after separation, towards their children.[43] At an early stage, the Committee were critical of the 1995 amendments as having created expectations which were ultimately unmet. Thus, the amendments were said to have been intended to have created a rebuttable presumption of shared parenting, but evidence given to the Committee indicated that was not happening in the courts or community.[44] In a connected vein, the Committee noted[45] that s 61C of the Act, as amended, specifies that parental responsibility lies with each parent, but, in practice, they stated, that was:

> '... often ignored. The parent with residence usually assumes the power because this is the practical outcome of living arrangements rather than as the result of legal exclusion.'

In fact, the Committee went on, relying on a submission from the Family Court of Australia, to say that courts did not pay especial attention to shared responsibility as that was the 'ordinary position'; one might be forgiven for thinking that that paragraph was, on one level, tautologous, on another paradoxical and, on yet another, simply hard to comprehend. Nevertheless, the Committee went on[46] to state that it was committed to an approach based on the principle that both parents should remain involved in children's lives and which maximised the time children spent with each parent.

Inevitably, that view gave rise to an issue which, earlier, had troubled the Family Law Council in its deliberations which led to the report, *Patterns of Parenting After Separation*, which appeared in 1992 and which provided much of the impetus for the 1995 amendments. In that report, the Council

---

[41]   The Committee was asked to examine various issues which included whether a presumption should exist to the effect that children should spend equal time with each parent and, if so, in what circumstances that presumption should be rebutted. It was also asked to comment on whether the existing child support formula was appropriate in the sense that it worked fairly for both parents in relation to their care of, and contact with, relevant children. In the event, the Committee reported on 28 December 2003 (hardly to height of legal activity or interest) and, additionally, made important recommendations regarding the actual and potential administration of the law: see below.

    As regards the report itself, it was unanimous in its conclusions, having taken evidence throughout Australia and from all interested parties and received nearly 1,800 submissions.

[42]   Hereinafter referred to as *Picture*.

[43]   Above note 41.

[44]   *Picture* at para 1.20.

[45]   Ibid at para 2.33.

[46]   Ibid at para 2.34.

had considered the question of whether a joint custody presumption referred to an equal sharing of time and had rejected any presumption of equal time as being unworkable. In the event, the standing Committee, stated[47] that:

'... the goal for the majority of families should be one of equality of care and responsibility along with substantially shared parenting time. They should start with an expectation of equal care.'

Despite that statement the Committee continued by saying that they did not support 'forcing this outcome in potentially inappropriate circumstances by legislating a presumption (rebuttable or not) that children will spend equal time with each parent'. Instead, they took the view that 'all things considered each parent should have an equal say on where the children reside'.[48]

On the immediate issue of shared parenting – howsoever confused the Committee might initially appear to be – they were of the view that merely changing the Act, of itself, was not sufficient. They took the view[49] that:

'... community perception of legislation is as critical to its actual success as its actual content. Any legislative change which the government decides to implement may therefore need to be community and professional education.'

It may well be that any perceived failure of the 1995 amendments[50] might be attributed to such lack of awareness.

In that general context, the way in which courts deal with breach of orders which seek to involve parents in the lives of their children is both of interest and importance. The matter was considered by Kay J in *D and C (Imprisonment for Breach of Contact Orders)*.[51] The appellant was the mother of a female child born in 1998 and who was involved in a contact dispute with the child's father. The appellant had argued that the father should have no contact with the child as she was at risk of sexual abuse. That claim was rejected initially after a 7-day hearing. That judge then made orders for the father to have contact with the child, though those were then immediately breached by the appellant. The matter then came before a member of the Federal Magistracy who was of the view that it was necessary to impose a penalty on the appellant. In so doing, the Magistrate rejected a submission that that hearing be adjourned to permit the appellant to be psychiatrically examined and noted that the appellant had not expressed any remorse nor did she express any intent to comply with the original orders. On that basis, the Magistrate imposed a prison sentence of one month on the appellant.

In the event, the appellant served two periods of imprisonment. She was initially arrested on 19 May 2004, the day the sentence was imposed, and remained incarcerated until 26 May when she obtained a stay. Contact then

---

47   Ibid at para 2.35.
48   Yet, at the same time, the Committee urged still that, wherever possible, an equal amount of parenting time should, taking individual circumstances into account, be the desired objective.
49   *Picture* at para 2.77.
50   Above text at note 41.
51   (2004) FLC 93-193.

took place between the child and father on 29 and 30 May. The appellant was later arrested on 16 June when she failed to attend a Court hearing resulting in the lifting of the stay. She remained imprisoned until the 21 June when a further stay was obtained. Thus far, she had served 12 of the 30 days as at the date of the appeal's hearing.

At appeal, two submissions were made on behalf of the appellant: first, that the Magistrate was in error in failing to grant the adjournment for the purposes of obtaining a psychiatric examination to assist in deliberations regarding the penalty; and, second, that the Magistrate erred in failing to suspend the period imposed by him.

In allowing the appeal in part, Kay J first of all stated[52] that nothing had been demonstrated by the mother to indicate any error on behalf of the Magistrate, who appeared to have conscientiously and thoroughly investigated all of the options which were open to him. He also expressed sound reasons for the courses he had adopted. Second, Kay J was of the opinion that it would have been quite inappropriate for the Magistrate to have imposed a suspended sentence of imprisonment:

> '... on the basis that the mother was showing no capacity or willingness to comply with the orders. The Magistrate took the view that if the mother was given a chance to realise the seriousness of the event by serving a period of incarceration and that got the orders back on foot, then that was going to be the best thing for the child.'

Kay J further noted[53] that there were circumstances which did not represent punishment for its own sake but which were basically coercive in nature, there being circumstances where it was important to uphold the authority of the court and impose a penalty as a specific or general deterrent.[54]

However, third, the judge noted that, unlike the situation before the Magistrate, the mother was presently indicating that she would comply with the Court's orders.[55] At the same time, Kay J pointed out that the mother's basic attitude that contact was not in the child's best interests had not changed and the hostility between the mother and father was palpable. Finally, given the change in circumstances, Kay J regarded[56] the suspension of the remaining 18 days of the sentence as being warranted on the condition that the mother would comply with Court orders. If she should fail to comply, then it would be open to the Court to remove the suspension and require the mother to serve the remainder of the term. Given Kay J's proviso relating to the mother's apparently pervasive attitude, one can but await developments.

---

52   Ibid at 79,230.
53   Ibid at 79,230.
54   See *Tate and Tate (No 3)* (2003) FLC 93-138.
55   As Kay J put the matter, (2004) FLC 93-193 at 79,230:

> 'As the Magistrate optimistically put it, the term of imprisonment has given the mother a chance to "deeply reflect" upon the consequences of her non-compliance.'

56   (2004) FLC 93-193 at 79,231.

The issue of contravention of parenting orders was also considered, in rather less dramatic circumstances, by the Full Court of the Family Court of Australia in *Fooks and Clark*.[57] In that case, the parties were married in 1995 and had separated in 2001, there being one child, born in 1997. In late 2001, consent orders were made which provided for contact with the father on alternate weekends for a full weekend, alternate Friday nights, half of each school holiday and half of Christmas day. In February 2003, the father filed a contravention application in which he submitted that the order relating to school holidays should be interpreted literally, thus claiming that he was entitled to alternate weekend and Friday contact with the child during the whole of the school holiday periods even when the child was with the mother during that party's holiday entitlement. The application was dismissed at first instance, the trial judge finding that the mother had not contravened the order or, if she had, had provided a reasonable excuse. The father also alleged that the mother, and others, had prevented him from having contact on Christmas day. The mother argued that she had actively encouraged the child to go but that he had refused and had provided the trial judge with such evidence as had convinced her of that being so.[58] The Full Court[59] dismissed the father's appeal, including an application for the reception of additional evidence.[60]

As regards the major issue, the Full Court commented,[61] first, that adopting the interpretation sought by the father would mean that the mother would never enjoy a continuous week or more of school holidays with the child. More generally, the Court stated[62] that where there was an existing order for parents to share all school term and holiday periods equally:

'... it must be that, as a matter of common sense and practicability that, as well as being in the best interests of the child, the order is read as a whole and that daily and alternate weekend contact be suspended during all such school holiday periods. If parents wish to make other specific arrangements then they must ensure that they are properly identified and provided for in the order.'

As regards the Christmas Day application, the Court was of the view[63] that it was clearly open to the trial judge to conclude that if, at the relevant time, the child was so upset it would not have been reasonable for the mother to

---

57   (2004) FLC 93-83.

58   As the trial judge had put the matter:

> '[A]lthough a resident parent, as the mother is, had a positive obligation to provide contact for a child to the other parent, it is not reasonable that that parent put the child in a position where they [*sic*] are refusing.'

59   Elllis, Holden and Young JJ.

60   That being the tapes of a hearing before a Judicial Registrar in January 2003. The Full Court were of the view, (2004) FLC 93-183, that the father's application had been made during the course of submissions to the trial judge after all evidence had been received. The Full Court were not satisfied the demands of justice would be met by the making of the order, nor persuaded otherwise that the discretion under s 94A(2) of the Family Law Act should be exercised. See *CJD v VAJ* (1998) FLC 92-828; *T and S* (2001) FLC 93-086.

61   (2004) FLC 93-183 at 79,066.

62   Ibid at 79,067.

63   Ibid at 79,070.

have taken further steps to have ensured contact. *Fooks and Clark* is of interest in that it points to the kind of trivial issues which can be raised in cases of this nature, to the general advantage of no one (and, since both parties were unrepresented, that includes the legal profession too), both directly and those, indirectly, seeking explication of the issues.

Since the decision of the High Court of Australia in *M v M*,[64] much curial and critical time has inevitably been taken up with the issue of child sexual abuse as it relates to applications for residence and contact. The matter arose in 2004 in the decision of the Full Court of the Family Court in *Re W (Sex Abuse: Standard of Proof)*,[65] a case which has in no way clarified the legal situation at large.

In *Re W*, at first instance, Nicholson CJ had ordered that the appellant father be prohibited from having contact with either of the two children of the marriage, aged 10 and 7 years. The Chief Justice had found that it was probable that the younger had been sexually abused by the appellant. It had also been held that the benefits which that child might receive from supervised contact were outweighed by the detriments.

The evidence upon which the Chief Justice relied consisted, first, of evidence by the wife that she had been told by the elder child that the appellant had 'rubbed himself' against the younger when she was asleep. The wife had then contacted an officer of the Sexual Support Service who had conducted interviews with both children where the elder child had repeated her allegation. Later, the younger child was said to have informed that official that the appellant had touched her genitals and had put his penis in her mouth. She repeated those allegations in a subsequent police interview.

A medical examination of the child, though, disclosed no sign of sexual penetration. However, evidence was given by the wife as well as the younger child's grandparents and teacher that the child's behaviour had changed during the relevant period. Evidence was also given by a psychiatrist to the effect that, although he had not interviewed the children, other interviews suggested to him that the appellant had abused the younger child.

The appellant consistently denied the allegations. He referred to the fact that, during the police interviews, the elder child had not said that he had seen the appellant indulge in the conduct alleged. There was also evidence to the effect that the children had retracted their statements at different stages; in particular, the younger had told the wife and her teacher that she had lied regarding the appellant's conduct towards her.

Nicholson CJ rejected the appellant's denials on the grounds of credibility, especially because of an apparent attempt to suggest that the wife had induced the children to fabricate the allegations. Similarly, an attempt to suggest that the elder child had been the actual perpetrator caused his credibility to suffer.

---

[64]   (1988) 166 CLR 69.
[65]   (2004) FLC 93-912.

On appeal to the Full Court, it was argued that the positive finding of abuse was unsound and, hence, ought not to have been made. Regardless of that, he also argued that the Chief Justice's conclusion that supervised contact would be more detrimental than no contact was not reasonable.[66]

The Full Court of the Family Court of Australia[67] allowed the appeal, which had been contested by the wife and the court-appointed child representative. First, after having considered[68] various decisions[69] relating to the legal principles applicable to sex abuse allegations, the Full Court stated [70] that:

'... the grave consequences of a finding of sexual abuse cannot be overstated. Accordingly, before trial Judges find themselves impelled to make a positive finding of sexual abuse, as opposed to a finding of unacceptable risk, the standard of proof they are required to apply must be towards the strictest end of the civil spectrum ... Inexact proofs, indefinite testimony, or indirect inferences are insufficient to ground a finding of abuse.'[71]

It appeared, the Full Court noted[72], that Nicholson CJ had not paid appropriate attention to those established and strict principles.

The Court then went on to emphasise that:

'The termination of a worthwhile relationship between the parent and child ought in most cases to be the course of last resort.'

The Court, in that context were conscious of the problems attaching to the fact-finding process when they remarked that trial judges should be aware that both adversarial and inquisitional processes could produce artificial results or are not always productive of the truth. In consequence, the Court noted that a false negative finding which was accompanied by appropriate safeguards such as adequate supervision may be far less disastrous for the child than an erroneous finding which leads to a termination of the parent-child relationship. The Court, they stated:[73] 'needs to remain conscious of this imperfection at all times'. The Court's final comment on the issue at large reflects a view expressed elsewhere[74] by the present writer. 'The risk', it was said:

'... that the Court will find heinous behaviour where none has occurred needs to be borne in mind at all times. The harm and injustice that flows to both parent and child from an erroneous positive is almost too horrible to contemplate.'

---

[66] Nicholson CJ had rejected the appellant's proposal that an appropriate supervisor would be his brother's partner who was a teacher qualified in the area of early childhood education.

[67] Kay, Holden and O'Ryan JJ.

[68] (2004) FLC 93-192 at 79,214*ff.*

[69] *M v M*, above note 64; *B and B* (1988) FLC 91-978; *WK and SR* (1997) FLC 92-787.

[70] (2004) FLC 93-192 at 79,215. Adopting the views expressed in *WK and SR*, above.

[71] Put another way, at the strictest end of the spectrum set out in *Briginshaw v Briginshaw* (1938) 60 CLR 336 and, presently in s 140 of the Commonwealth Evidence Act 1995.

[72] (2004) FLC 93-192 at 79,217.

[73] Ibid at 79,218.

[74] See, F Bates 'Child Sexual Abuse, The Fact-Finding Process and Negligence: An Opportunity Lost' (1998) 6 *Tort Law Review* 125.

Further, the Court were critical[75] of the failure of Nicholson CJ to particularise of what precisely the abuse had consisted. 'Unless such findings were made', the Court said, 'it is impossible for the alleged perpetrator to challenge the findings or for an appellate Court to properly review the evidence to see if the findings are safe'. The fact that Nicholson CJ had failed to provide such particulars made his findings that abuse had occurred the more unnecessary and inappropriate in the particular case.

Yet the central problem still remains unresolved from the original decision in *M v M*:[76] although specifics and particularities are necessary for a finding that abuse had occurred, they seem not to be for findings of 'unacceptable risk' as that case laid down. However, 'unacceptable risk' is the test for deciding central issues regarding residence and contact rather than specific findings of abuse. Is this a naked paradox or rather an inadequate threshold test?

Finally as regards children, the High Court of Australia has finally pronounced on the question of children held in immigration detention; an issue which was discussed in some detail in the last commentary written on Australian developments. *Minister for Immigration and Multicultural and Indigenous Affairs and B (No 3)*[77] involved an appeal by the Minister against a decision of the Full Court of the Family Court of Australia which had ordered the release of five non-citizen children from detention pending a final hearing by the High Court.

The dispute involved two boys and three girls who were unlawful non-citizens within the meaning of ss 4 and 14 of the Migration Act 1958. In July 2002, the boys, through their mother as next friend, applied to the Family Court for orders for their release from immigration detention in South Australia. The application was for a mandatory order under s 67ZC of the Family Law Act 1975 that the Minister be required to release the children on the main ground that its continuance was contrary to their welfare. The father then intervened in the proceedings on behalf of all of the children seeking various orders, notably to protect the children whilst they remained in detention. In the October of that year, both applications were dismissed in the Family Court, a trial judge finding that the power contained in s 67ZC did not apply to the children in South Australia and, hence, that the Family Court did not have jurisdiction to make the orders.

The children appealed to the Full Court which, in July 2003, by a majority,[78] allowed the appeal and remitted the matter. The view of the majority was, in essence, that jurisdiction under s 67ZC was available in the instant case as it was based on the marriage power in the Australian Constitution and was not dependent on the referral of State powers. Hence, subject to the findings of a trial judge as to the children's ability to bring an end to their detention, the

---

75   (2004) FLC 93-132 at 79,226.
76   (1988) 166 CLR 69.
77   (2004) FLC 93-174. For more detailed comment, see R Chisholm 'Immigration and the Family
      Court: The High Court speaks' (2004) 18 *Aust J Fam L* 193.
78   Nicholson CJ and O'Ryan JJ, Ellis J dissenting.

majority considered that the continued detention of the children was unlawful.[79] The Minister then applied to the Full Court for a stay of the orders and filed an application for special leave to apply to the High Court of Australia. The Full Court refused the stay application and ordered that the children be released from immigration detention until the final hearing of the applications. The Full Court then granted a certificate which had the effect of transmitting the matter directly to the High Court.[80] The rehearing of the children's applications was heard in the Family Court prior to the High Court decision. At first instance, it was found that the detention was illegal but the judge was not persuaded that the orders which were sought were in the children's best interests. The Full Court upheld the appeal and orders were made that the children be released.

The High Court, though, unanimously upheld the Minister's appeal, although their reasons for so doing were not atypically these days consistent. Hence, the Full Court's orders were set aside and replaced by orders that the children's appeal to that Court be dismissed.

First, Gleeson CJ and McHugh J took the view that the Family Court, as a federal court could only be invested with jurisdiction[81] that Parliament has defined by a law with respect to one of the matters mentioned in s 75 or 76 of the Constitution. The 'welfare of children' was not a matter therein mentioned. Further, except where Part VII expressly imposed obligations on third parties, that part is concerned with the relationship between parents and children and, hence, the duties of parents in respect of their children. Nothing either in s 67ZC or Part VII requires third parties to act in the best interests, or to advance the interests, of any child.[82]

The next point made by Gleeson CJ and McHugh JJ related to the purpose of the orders which was to require the Minister to take or refrain from taking action in respect of the children. Nothing, the judges found,[83] in Part VII provided any support for the making of any such order against the Minister. Finally, the orders sought were not concerned with the relationship between the children's parents and, as such, were not analogous to the orders which

[79] See *B and B and Minister for Immigration and Multicultural and Indigenous Affairs* (2003) FLC 93-141.

[80] The Full Court certified that there were four important questions of law or public importance involved in the case, namely: first, whether there could be any 'matter' within the meaning of s 76 of the Constitution unless there was some immediate right, duty or liability to be established by the determination of the Court. Second, whether the provisions of Part VII of the Family Law Act were supported by s 51(xxix) of the Constitution as implementing the United Nations Convention on the Rights of the Child or only have a more limited application. Third, whether the detention of a child who is an 'unlawful non-citizen' within the Migration Act goes beyond the authority conferred by that Act when the detention extends over a lengthy period or its duration is indefinite. Finally, whether the detention of a child can be 'indefinite' if the child lacks the capacity to make a request under the Migration Act.

[81] (2004) FLC 93-174 at 78,905.

[82] Ibid at 78,910.

[83] Ibid at 78,913.

had been sought in the *JWB* case,[84] where no duty or liability was imposed on any third party.

Gummow, Hayne and Heydon JJ initially took the view that the analysis of statute law was not assisted[85] by the use of general expressions such as 'the welfare jurisdiction' or 'the *parens patriae* jurisdiction' in the interpretation of the Act. Whilst that comment might be apposite in the present context, it cannot be said to be of universal application, especially as regards the *JWB* decision. The judges continued[86] by noting that Division 12 of Part VII of the Family Law Act 1975 controlled the operation of the remainder of the past as regards the conferral of jurisdiction on the Court.

This meant that neither s 69ZE nor s 69ZH conferred jurisdiction to decide either of the applications which were involved in the instant appeal. The former provision conferred jurisdiction on the Court in matters limited to reference by the relevant State – in this case, South Australia. However, reference by that State was limited to matters of maintenance, custody, guardianship or access, none of which were presently involved.[87] As regards the second, it confirmed the operation of s 67ZC to disputes between the parental responsibilities of the parties to a child of the marriage.

Kirby J first commented[88] that the evidence disclosed that the Australian Parliament intended that a system of universal and mandatory detention of unlawful non-citizen arrivals would remain in force including in respect of children. In the face of that policy directive it was impossible, Kirby J said,[89] to construe the Migration Act 1958 otherwise than in accordance with its terms; it followed that it was impossible to accept that a significant alteration of that Act could have been effected 'by an undetected, unannounced, unnoticed side-wind such as the enactment of the [Family Law Reform Act 1995] or the amendment of the [Family Law Act 1975]'. Similarly, it was impossible[90] to interpret the *general* powers and jurisdiction of the Family Court as authorising intrusion into the clear and *specific*[91] obligations imposed on the Minister and other Federal officials by the Migration Act.

Still more emphatically, Kirby J stated[92] that the language of the Migration Act was *intractable*[93] and could not be 'read down' to avoid obligations created by international law, though the Court could note and call attention to the issue. However, it could not invoke international law to override clear and valid provisions of Australian national law.

---

84   (1992) 175 CLR 218.
85   (2004) FLC 93-1774 at 78,915.
86   Ibid at 78,919.
87   (2004) FLC 93-174 at 78,990.
88   Ibid at 78,924.
89   Ibid at 78,931.
90   Ibid at 78,932.
91   Kirby J's emphasis.
92   (2004) FLC 93-174 at 78,932.
93   Author's emphasis.

Finally, Kirby J was of the view[94] that the detention of the children under the Migration Act was neither permanent nor indefinite; although it was true that it had lasted for a considerable time prior to their release by the Full Court of the Family Court. However, under the Migration Act, there was a clear end to their detention: that is, until one of the conditions in s 196(1) of the Migration Act was fulfilled, ie until their removal or deportation from Australia or the grant of a visa.[95]

Callinan J was of the opinion[96] that s 67ZC of the Family Law Act did not, as a matter of statutory construction, extend to a jurisdiction to order the children to be released from detention. The only jurisdiction which the relevant States, including South Australia, transferred to the Family Court pursuant to that provision was parental responsibility for, and parental maintenance of, children. 'Clearly', he said, 'the orders sought by the respondents in this case are not orders with respect to any of those matters'. He further stated[97] that however extensive the powers conferred on the Family Court under s 51(xxi) and (xii) might be they:

> '... do not comprehend a general discretionary power over all children, whether of a marriage or not, exercisable in such a way as to override any or all other powers over children, such as to detain them in immigration detention, or rehabilitative, reformative, or penal institutions. The Family Court may no more do this than it would exercise a jurisdiction tort or contract in order to advance the welfare of a child.'

Thus, one thing, if one thing alone, is clear from *B (No 3)* and that is that it will be a disappointment to those who saw an opportunity for the High Court to clarify, if not actually extend, the relationship between family law and international law. Since only one member of the Court, Kirby J, touched on the issue at all, it may be, as Chisholm suggests,[98] that if any further dispute as to the relationship of domestic and international law, especially if – as was not the case in *B (No 3)* – the domestic law is unclear, arises, it may be that judgment which will repay the more avid reader.

IV FINANCE AND PROPERTY

Many of the problems which have affected the finance and property provisions of the Family Law Act have manifested themselves in the decision of the Full Court of the Family Court of Australia in *Coventry v Coventry and Smith*.[99] This is a complex case and, as such, a detailed commentary cannot be avoided.

---

[94] (2004) FLC 93-174 at 78,937.
[95] Gummow, Hayne and Heydon JJ and Kirby J also considered, *obiter*, the effect of a certificate under s 95(b) of the Family Law Act 1975 which enabled an appeal to be brought directly to the High Court.
[96] (2004) FLC 93-174 at 78,937.
[97] Ibid at 78,939.
[98] Above note 77 at 207.
[99] (2004) FLC 93-184.

Mr Coventry and Ms Smith married in 1991, the child of the marriage being born in 1992. During the marriage, the husband worked full time at various grazing properties owned by Lynoch Pty Ltd ('Lynoch'), a company which had been owned and operated by the husband's father. Although the wife was not employed for much of the marriage she was always responsible for the management of the child and household.

The parties separated in 2000, the child continuing to live with the wife in rented premises, with the husband making fortnightly payments to support him. Applications for parenting, property and spousal maintenance were also begun.

Identification of the property held by each of the parties required consideration because of the nature of the husband's interest in Lynoch, which had an agreed gross value of $30,000,000. The husband's interest arose because, in 1974, his father had established four trusts ('The McLean Settlements' Nos 1, 2, 3 and 4). These trusts were identical except that each named one of the four Coventry children as the principal beneficiary, the husband being the principal beneficiary of the McLean Settlement No 1, his three sisters being so of the others.

As regards the first settlement, other beneficiaries were described by reference to their relationship to the principal beneficiary, including spouses. The property held in the No 1 settlement included the full equity rights attached to shares in Selin Pty Ltd. All of Lynoch's equity and voting shares were held by Selin. When the husband's father died in June 1995 only the husband and his mother remained as directors of both Selin and Lynoch. Also in consequence of the death, the mother became sole trustee of all the McLean Settlements.

Clause 3(a) of the McLean Settlement No 1 specified a power of appointment of the trust's fund to all its beneficiaries. However, any such appointment had to have taken place before the husband's father's death and it was common ground that no appointment had been so made. In default of any such appointments, cl 3(b)(i) of the same settlement required that the trustees hold the trusts funds for the principal beneficiary (ie the husband) if he survived to the distribution date.[100] At the same time, cl 5(m)(i) provided the trustees with a general power to advance the whole or any part of the trust's funds for the maintenance, advancement, education or benefit of all or any of the beneficiaries. Clause 10 empowered the husband's father to appoint or remove a new trustee or trustees. Upon the death of the husband's father, that power vested in the husband.

At first instance, it was held that the property held by the McLean Settlement No 1 was to be regarded as the husband's property. In reaching that conclusion, the trial judge accepted an argument advanced by the wife that a deed of variation of the McLean Settlement No 1 should be set aside pursuant to s 106B of the Family Law Act 1975. That deed, which had been executed by the husband's mother in her capacity as trustee, was found to

---

[100]   Which was 31 January 2020.

have been motivated by considerations which were irrelevant to the proper execution of the trust, particularly by an attempt to keep the trust property away from the wife. In consequence, the property held by the McLean Settlement No 1 went into the pool of net assets to be assessed in the context of ss 75 and 79 of the Family Law Act.[101] On the basis of the parties' contributions, the trial judge held that the wife was entitled to 12.5% of the total net assets, that being $3,508,049. As regards the s 75(2) factors, she found the wife to be entitled to a further adjustment of 2.5%.[102] In the issue of spousal maintenance, the trial judge noted that, as the wife was, thus, to receive a substantial sum as property distribution, she could not be regarded as being unable to support herself. At the same time, as payment of those funds might take some months, the judge ordered an interim periodic payment by the husband to the wife of $1,200 per week.

Both the husband and his mother appealed against the trial judge's orders. The grounds related to

(1) the appropriate construction of the terms of the McLean Settlement No 1 and the evaluation of the effect of those terms;

(2) the deed of variation;

(3) the appropriate construction of the terms of the remaining settlements;

(4) the relevance of the husband's interests;

(5) the factors considered by the trial judge in relation to s 75(2) of the Family Law Act;

(6) the judge's application of s 106B of that Act to the deed of variation;

(7) the valuation by the trial judge of shares held by the husband in Lynoch and the property held by McLean Settlement No 1;

(8) the assessment made of the contributions of each of the parties;

(9) the additional adjustment made in favour of the wife; and

(10) the amount and duration of spousal maintenance awarded.

The Full Court[103] dismissed the appeals. As regards the construction of the terms of the McLean Settlement No 1 and their effect, the Court were of the view[104] that cl 3(b) created in the husband's favour a vested interest in the Trust Fund which was subject to being divested upon the occurrence of a condition subsequent, which was his death prior to the distribution date. From that it followed[105] that:

'... the gift over to other beneficiaries in the event of the husband's death prior to the distribution date does not ... materially affect the conclusion that his interest in the trust fund was a vested rather than a contingent interest.'

---

[101] The value of the property contributed to the pool by the husband was $27,732,396, of which $25,609,324 represented the value of the McLean Settlement No 1. The wife's contribution was valued at $332,000. Both spouses had superannuation entitlements to the respective values of $162,911 and $67,770.

[102] That amounting to $701,609.

[103] Ellis ACJ, Holden and Brown JJ.

[104] (2004) FLC 93-184 at 79,092.

[105] Ibid at 79,093.

On that question, it was further argued that, in interpreting the terms of the Settlement, the trial judge had erred in referring to extraneous material and by emphasising the perceived intention of the husband's father rather than the actual effect of the document. The Court refused to[106] accept that argument and, likewise, declined to accept an alternative argument that, even assuming that the judge was entitled to examine extrinsic evidence to determine the trust's terms, she ought to have had regard to the proposed reconstruction of Selin. However, it was equally clear, the Court thought[107] that the husband's parents had determined not to proceed with them and, in any event, the trial judge was not taking the wishes of the husband's late father into account.

As regards the matters arising from the Deed of Variation, the Court, first, were of the opinion[108] that cl 10 of the McLean Settlement No 1 was a power insulated from variation, thereby affording a balancing mechanism within the trust. Hence, the trial judge's view that the amendment made to the Deed purporting to revoke the husband's power to remove and appoint a trustee was *ultra vires*. Hence, the trial judge was correct in implicitly concluding that the husband's mother's attempt to remove cl 10 was made by reference to considerations which were irrelevant to the proper execution of the Settlement. It was similarly open, on the evidence, for the trial judge to conclude as she did that the Deed gave effect to advice given to the husband regarding putting property beyond the reach of the Family Court. Thus, she was correct in finding that the Deed was made on the husband's behalf, or at his direction, or was in his interest.[109] The Full Court were not persuaded either that the trial judge's valuation of either the relevant shares or the relevant trust was in error.

In addition, an examination of the trial judge's reasoning at large demonstrated, first, that she had identified the relevant contributions of both the husband and wife to the marriage and had weighed and addressed them.[110] She had also not taken account of any irrelevant circumstance or ignored any relevant circumstance or attached inappropriate weight to any factor.[111]

The Court then turned its attention[112] to the matter of the s 75 adjustment made in favour of the wife and particularly found that the trial judge had not failed to take account of the benefits that the wife had already been awarded and made a similar finding with regard to the level of spousal maintenance.

It will be apparent that the *Coventry* case is extremely complex and, though its ultimate adjudication may have depended very largely on the facts, the Court did refer to case-law, especially in relation to the construction of the relevant trust's terms and their effect. It does demonstrate, too, that the areas

---

106   Ibid at 79,094.
107   Ibid at 79,095.
108   Ibid at 79,102.
109   Ibid at 79,113.
110   Ibid at 79,119.
111   Ibid at 79,121.
112   Ibid at 79,122.

of trusts and family law, particularly when large amounts of money are involved, have not been explored either judicially or by academic commentators in sufficient depth. It may be hoped that *Coventry* represents something of a stimulus for that kind of relatively novel exploration.

A less noisomely complex issue, though one of seemingly increasing relevance, arose in the Full Court's decision in *Beck and Beck*.[113] There, the parties had separated in 1994 after approximately 25 years of marriage. The wife had filed an application for property settlement, but the husband did not file a statement of financial circumstances, or give discovery, despite having been ordered to do so. At a conciliation conference in 1996, the wife's solicitor was provided with a document which purported to set out the husband's understanding of the parties' financial position at that time. The parties then signed a minute of consent orders which were subsequently approved by the Court.

Over 5 years later, the wife filed an application under s 79A of the Family Law Act 1975, claiming, *inter alia*, that there had been a miscarriage of justice by reason of fraud and suppression of evidence. The husband applied for dismissal of the wife's application. In late 2002, it was ordered at first instance that the wife's application be summarily dismissed, the judge making reference to material which had been supplied by the husband.

The wife appealed submitting that, although the trial judge had used the correct test relating to applications for summary dismissal, he had failed to apply that test as he had relied on the husband's as well as the wife's material.

The Full Court[114] upheld the appeal and remitted the husband's application for rehearing. In so doing, they noted[115] the judgment of Kirby J in the High Court of Australia in *Lindon v The Commonwealth (No 2)*[116] where it was said that:

'To secure such relief, the party seeking it must show that it is clear, on the face of the opponent's documents, that the opponent lacks a clear cause of action.'

In addition, they also noted[117] the Full Court's earlier decision in *Bigg v Suzi*.[118] There, it had been said that in such cases, the applicant:

'... had no right to adduce *any* evidence at that summary hearing to contradict the evidence of the husband or to seek to contradict any inference which it might be submitted should be drawn from that evidence.'

---

[113] (2004) FLC 93-181.
[114] Ellis, Finn and Chisholm JJ.
[115] (2004) FLC 93-181 at 79,052.
[116] (1996) 70 ALJR 541 at 544.
[117] (2004) FLC 931-181 at 79,052.
[118] (1998) FLC 92-799 at 84,981.

It followed that, though the exact extent to which the trial judge had relied on the husband's material was unclear, there were a number of references to it and, for that reason, the judgment should not be permitted to stand.

Beck suggests, once more, that s 79A is altogether an unhappy provision and could do with the kind of extensive revision which other areas of Part VIII seem to be now undergoing. As an example of the last point, the decision of Emett J in *Daniel v Daniel and Jones*[119] provides an interesting introduction. The proceedings arose out of a dispute between the trustee in bankruptcy for the husband, and the bankrupt's former wife. In 2001, the bankrupt and his wife were registered as proprietors as joint tenants in respect of two properties. Two years later, a creditors' petition was presented, seeking a sequestration order in respect of the bankrupt's estate.

Shortly after, following contested proceedings for property division, the Family Court made orders that the bankrupt transfer to his wife, on or before 1 February 2004, the whole of his right, title and interest in the properties. The bankrupt then presented a debtor's petition and his property vested in the trustee. Thereupon, the trustee became registered with the wife as proprietor of both properties as tenants in common in equal shares and, after that, the bankrupt executed a deed whereby he purported to transfer to the wife the whole of his right, title and interest in the properties.

The wife then sought orders recognising her beneficial interest in the properties and for the transfer of the legal estate of both properties. The Court, she argued, had the power to make such orders by reason of the Bankruptcy Act 1966. This provided that, if any person was affected by any act, omission of a trustee in bankruptcy, that person may apply to the Court that it make such orders in the matter as it thinks are just and equitable.

In support of her case, the wife argued that the present Court was bound by the decision of the Full Court of the Federal Court of Australia in *Official Trustee in Bankruptcy v Mateo*.[120] In *Mateo*, the circumstances, the judge noted[121] in *Daniel* were similar, though not identical to those in the instant case. In *Mateo*, it had been held that the transfer to the wife was not void because the Family Court's order which was pursuant to s 79 of the Family Law Act vested in the wife all of the beneficial interest in the matrimonial home and, consequently, the transfer only served to put those orders into effect and was not 'a transfer of property by a person who later becomes a bankrupt' within the terms of ss 120 and 121 of the Bankruptcy Act. The trustee argued that *Mateo* should be distinguished from the present case.

Accordingly, Emmett J declared that the trustee in bankruptcy held on trust for the wife an undivided one half share in the properties. The basis of the judge's reasoning was that, in *Mateo*, all three judges of the Court had been of the view that the order of the Family Court had a dispositive effect. In *Daniel*, the order was not by its terms dispositive, but rather an order that the

---

[119]   (2004) FLC 93-187.
[120]   (2003) FLC 93-128.
[121]   (2004) FLC 93-187 at 79,160.

bankrupt transfer the property to his wife. Nonetheless, Emmett J stated,[122] the reasoning in the earlier case was such that the Court should treat it as favouring the wife. In that context, the judge made some interesting comments[123] on the nature of the structure and wording of s 79 of the Family Law Act which he described as 'curious in some respects'. In general terms, he said, it authorises the Court to make such orders as it considers appropriate *altering the interests*[124] of the parties in property. However, it then goes on to say such orders *might include*[125] an order requiring either of the parties *to make such transfer*[126] of property for the benefit of the parties. 'Thus', the judge stated:

> '... the language of s 79 appears to assume that an order requiring a party to make a transfer of property for the benefit of another party is itself an order altering the interests of the parties. Section 79 only authorises orders which work an alteration of the legal or equitable interests of the parties.'[127]

After having said that there was something to be said for treating the effect of an order under s 79 as analogous to a binding contract for sale, the judge then continued that there was a remedy available if there was a justifiable complaint by the trustee on behalf of unsecured creditors. That remedy existed under s 79A and could be invoked through the means of s 92 which permitted persons to apply for leave to intervene in the proceeding. That supported his more central view that the effect of an order under s 79 was to vest a beneficial interest in one party[128] or, at least an interest of a proprietary nature which could still be enforced by that party, notwithstanding the intervening bankruptcy of the other.

The decision in *Daniel*, when taken together with *Beck*, leads us properly to a discussion of statutory changes in the area of finance and property. On 17 December 2004, a new Part VIII AA entitled 'Orders and Injunctions Binding Third Parties' will be introduced into the Act.[129] The purpose of the Part is to empower the Courts in relation to the property of parties to a marriage to make orders and injunctions under ss 79 and 114 of the Family Law Act 1975 which are directed towards, or which may alter the rights, liabilities or interests of third parties. The purpose of the change is, initially at least, quite clear: it is to modify the effect of the High Court of Australia's fundamental decision in *Ascot Investments v Harper*[130] and the cases which followed on from it.

---

122   Ibid at 79,162.
123   Ibid at 79,163.
124   Emmett J's emphasis.
125   Ibid.
126   Ibid.
127   See *Mullane v Mullane* (1983) FLC 91-303.
128   (2004) FLC 93-187 at 79,164.
129   For more detailed comment see T Altobelli 'Third parties in family law: Recent legislative developments' (2004) 18 *Aust J Fam L* 114.
130   (1981) 148 CLR 337. In essence, that case decided that the courts had no power under even the widely drawn s 114 to affect an existing right enjoyed by a third party or impose a new duty on such a person. There were only two exceptions to the rule: sham transactions and the closely

In the new amendments, s 90AB defines 'third party' as meaning 'a person who is not a party to the marriage'. The breadth of this definition is immediately apparent and, most importantly, no legal, or other relationship between the third party and the parties to the marriage is required. Similarly, s 90AC seeks to give the new Part primacy over all other Australian laws or any provision in a deed or trust instrument.

The existing definition of 'matrimonial cause' in s 4(1)(ca) of the Family Law Act is extended to treat as property a debt owed by a party to a marriage and, in s 114(e) of the Act, 'property' includes a debt owed by a party to a marriage, by reason of s 90AD. Most immediately important, s 90AE permits courts to make particular orders under s 79 binding on third parties. This adds further to the discretion contained in the original provision but, nonetheless, that does not mean that the discretion is not without proper safeguards. Thus, it is specified in s 90AE(3)(a) that an order can only be made against a third party if it is reasonable, appropriate (whatever that may mean) and adapted to bring about a division between parties to a marriage. Hence, it will be interesting to see the number of cases and the types of situation where such orders are actually made.

Section 90AF is likewise broadly drafted and refers to the injunctive power to be found in s 114 of the Act. Thus s 90AF(a) restrains a person from repossessing a property of a party to a marriage. Further, s 90AF(b) empowers a court from restraining the commencement of legal proceedings against a party to a marriage.

There are clearly apparent implications in the new Part for commercial bodies involved in relations with parties, who, whilst welcoming the changes wrought by s 90AE, may be less enthused by those effected by s 90AF.

In addition to the new Part VIII AA, note should also be taken of the Family Law Amendment Bill 2004 which proposes the addition of a subsection to s 79 of the Family Law Act. Section 79(10) provided that any person whose interests may be affected by a s 89 order is entitled to be treated as a party to proceedings. One wonders why, given the broad nature of the new Part, the need for this amendment was perceived.

Finally, in May 2004, the Bankruptcy Legislation Amendment (Anti-Avoidance and Other Measures) Bill appeared. For the purposes of this commentary, the major interest lies in the fourth aim of the Bill which is to 'Address long standing issues concerning the interaction of Family Law and Bankruptcy'.

In that respect, a new s 59A of the Bankruptcy Act means that any vesting of property in the trustee in bankruptcy will be subject to an order under Part VIII of the Act. That, together with other provisions, means that where family law and bankruptcy matters coincide, jurisdiction will be vested in the Family Court.

---

related situation involving third party entities such as companies which are effectively controlled by a party to a marriage.

There are further changes proposed to s 79 of the Family Law Act: notably, s 79(1)(d) will specify that the trustee in bankruptcy, as well as the parties to the marriage, may be ordered to make settlement or transfer property for the benefit of a party to the marriage or a child of the marriage. Further, there is a proposed new s 79(4)(ea) which refers to the effect of any proposed order on the ability of a party to recover the creditor's debts. This introduces the interests of creditors additionally into the s 79 process of property adjustment. Some further subjections have also been added to s 79 aimed at facilitating a trustee's application to be joined in the proceedings. The threshold test appears to be whether the bankrupt's creditors are likely to be affected by a s 79 order. Hence, in these cases, the trustee will endeavour to be joined as a party because, otherwise, the trustee may run the risk that the vested bankruptcy property will diminish as the result of a s 79 order in favour of non-bankrupt claimants.

Finally, s 106A of the Family Law Act, a major anti-avoidance provision is to be amended so as to give standing to a trustee who is also a party. Section 114 is to be amended so as to enable a trustee to be restrained from declaring and distributing dividends among the bankrupt's creditors.

V PRACTICE, PROCEDURE AND ORGANISATION

A useful starting point to this part of the commentary is the decision of the Full Court of the Family Court of Australia in *Re B (Alleged Apprehension of Bias)*.[131] The topic of judicial bias in the Family Court has not, one fears, been one from which the Court has been immune in its relatively recent history.[132]

Re B involved an appeal by a husband against a refusal by a trial judge to disqualify himself from hearing further proceedings between the parties.[133] The parties had married in 1995 and separated 3 years later. There were two children of the marriage aged 8 and 6. Initially, orders were made that the children reside with the wife with contact with the husband. Shortly thereafter, the wife made the first of many notifications to the Department of Youth and Community Services making allegations regarding inappropriate sexual behaviour by the husband towards the children. The wife had to be restrained from leaving Australia with the children. At that point, the Department of Families began a full investigation which did not reveal any substantiation of the wife's continued allegations.

Final orders were made in early 2000 that the children reside with the husband and that the wife have contact with them. The orders further restrained the wife from taking the children for medical examinations or

---

131 (2004) FLC 93-185.

132 See F Bates 'Judicial Bias in the Family Court of Australia' (1997) 16 *Civil Justice Q* 334.

133 The grounds of the appeal were: first, '… that the trial judge as a consequence of comments made during the course of the hearing had prejudged the matter without hearing the totality of the evidence' and, second, '… that the conduct of the trial judge during the course of the hearing raised a reasonable apprehension of bias in that he may not bring an impartial or unprejudiced mind to the resolution of the issues between the parties'.

from making notifications of sexual abuse to government authorities. The wife's appeal against those orders was dismissed at the end of that year.

Despite all of that, the wife continued to make repeated notifications of abuse by the husband and there was an additional claim by her daughter from a previous relationship, which led to the husband's being charged with indecent dealing. However, that charge did not proceed owing to the Director of Public Prosecutions deciding that an indictment would not be presented.

In early 2002, the Department of Families made an application for a child protection order, the husband making a contrary application that there be no contact between the wife and children. The Court concluded that the wife was subjecting the children to continuing emotional harm and a child protection order was granted. Thereafter, supervised contact took place on a weekly basis until it was suspended in May 2002 until further order because of continuing concerns about the wife's behaviour.

The matter ultimately came on for final hearing before the judge, whose conduct was the subject of the present proceeding, in June 2003. The evidence included a psychiatrist's report dated as of September 2002. That report recommended that contact be suspended for at least another year, but which had not been updated at the time of the hearing. There was also a family report which recommended supervised contact on the basis of the expressed wishes of the children. The husband then argued that there should be no contact between the mother and the children. The mother proposed that the children live with the father and that she would have supervised contact which would be reviewed once she had attended counselling for 3 months.

Prior to proceeding with the full trial, the judge indicated that orders should be made as suggested by the mother. The judge had said that this was not because he had a predetermined view, but because it was in the children's best interests for temporary orders to be made and for the mother to be later reviewed with the benefit of up-to-date evidence. The judge had further stated that he would continue to manage the matter and that he was properly aware of, and had noted, the father's concerns, and was willing to make the orders sought by the father – if, and when, appropriate.

Nevertheless, the father had made an application that the judge disqualify himself. The judge rejected the application and had commented that it was common practice for judges to adjourn cases part heard when they were contemplating applications such as the present. At the same time, he had pointed out that that was done, at least in part, in an attempt to ensure that the best evidence was available with a view to ascertaining how the children would cope in the circumstances.

The Full Court dismissed the husband's appeal. First, the Court[134] commented[135] that the test to apply in determining whether a judge should be

---

[134] *Per* Nicholson CJ; Ellis and Young JJ concurring.
[135] (2004) FLC 93-185 at 79,135.

disqualified by a reason of bias was to be found in the decision of the High Court of Australia in *Johnson v Johnson (No 3)*[136] who had said that the test was:

> '... whether a fair minded lay observer might reasonably apprehend that the judge might not bring an impartial and unprejudiced mind to the resolution of the question the judge is required to decide.'

It was, the Chief Justice considered, apparent that the judge in *Re B* had not prejudged the issue, even though he was not prepared to proceed on the evidence before him and in the light of absence of contact between the children and mother for a considerable period.

All the trial judge had done, Nicholson CJ said,[137] was to foreshadow a temporary arrangement which might enable him better to judge the issue. Further, the case was not ready for trial when it came before the judge, which he had clearly recognised. In those circumstances it would have been a waste of time for him to have proceeded.

The matter was graphically encapsulated by Young J who stated[138] that:

> '... the trial Judge was both conscientiously and properly hearing and managing the issues in these somewhat bitter and protracted proceedings. I find his Honour's conduct vigilant, even-handed and in the best interests of both children.'

The multinational nature of Australian family law is emphasised by the decision of Kay J in *Dalrymple and Dalrymple*.[139] There, the applicant father lived in the US, two of the children of the marriage resided with the respondent mother in Australia and orders existed for the provision of holiday contact in the US. The father brought contravention proceedings in the Federal Magistrates' Court. He made application to hold those proceedings by audio link as provided in relevant legislation[140] and proposed that the audio link be his home telephone number.

The Federal Magistrate dismissed the application on the grounds that the father's proposal would not satisfy the legislation,[141] which required that the place at which the remote person was situated be equipped with facilities – such as loud speakers – so as to enable 'eligible persons' to hear the proceedings. The Magistrate had said that neither an audio link to the father's telephone nor a telephone equipped with a speaker would be sufficient. Kay J upheld the father's appeal.

In so doing, the judge noted[142] that the legislation required[143] that sufficient equipment to enable all 'eligible persons' to partake in the proceedings by

---

[136]   (2000) 201 CLR 488 at 492 *per* Gleeson CJ, Gandron, McHugh Gummow and Hayne JJ.
[137]   (2004) FLC 93-185 at 79,136.
[138]   Ibid.
[139]   (2004) FLC 93-179.
[140]   Federal Magistrates Act 1999, Pt 6, Div 5.
[141]   Ibid, s 69(3)(b).
[142]   (2004) FLC 93-179 at 79,038.
[143]   Above note 141.

being able sufficiently to hear what was occurring be provided. Since the father was the only person who was, within the Act, an 'eligible person',[144] the provision of a telephone was more than sufficient to meet the requirements. There was no necessity to have a speaker telephone or series of loud speakers to enable non-eligible persons to hear the proceedings. If the husband were to be represented or if there were witnesses, then it would be necessary to have some facilities to enable them to hear what was happening at the other end, but that was not happening in the present instance.

However, under the present head, there is no question but that the most important development lies elsewhere. The Family Law Rules 2004 began operation on 29 March 2004. As Altobelli, a leading commentator, has written:[145]

> 'Never in the history of contemporary family law have Rules been used as such overt instruments of cultural change.'

That same writer properly notes that the Woolf reforms to UK civil procedure have formed the basis for the changes wrought by the new rules and as Lord Woolf himself has stated:[146]

> 'We have largely ignored the way we go about reaching ... decisions, the financial cost of achieving those decisions and the delays and the demands on the litigants which they involve. In our search for perfect justice we have produced a system to which a substantial proportion of the population cannot obtain access.'

With that in mind, Altobelli further writes[147]:

> '... it is clearly a call to reconsider how family law has been practised in the past. It draws the distinction between *substantive* justice and *procedural* justice and arguably elevates both on to the same platform.'

As will be seen,[148] Chapter 1 of the new Rules represents the central thrust of the aims of the Rules. This is readily apparent from r 1.04 which states that:

> 'The main purpose of these Rules is to ensure that each case is resolved in a just and timely manner at a cost to the parties and the Court that is reasonable in the circumstances of the case.'

That rule is interrelated to other major rules in the first Chapter of Rules, which prevails where there is a conflict and over all other chapters.[149]

---

[144]   As defined, ibid:

> '... such persons as the Federal Magistrates Court or a Federal Magistrate considers should be treated as eligible persons for the purpose of that proceeding.'

[145]   T Altobelli 'Family Law Rules 2004' (2004) 18 *Aust J Fam L* 92 at 92.

[146]   Lord Woolf 'The Court's Role in Achieving Environmental Justice' (2002) 4 *Env L R* 79 at 79.

[147]   Above note 145 at 93.

[148]   Below text at note 150.

[149]   Rule 1.03.

Other important rules in that Chapter, hence, are: r 1.06 which is entitled 'Promoting the main purpose' and sets out ten means by which the rules are applied to promote the main purpose and actively to manage each case. That rule, hence, focuses on positive case management which, further, seeks to promote principles of just and prompt resolution at a cost reasonable both to the parties and the Court. Altobelli properly notes,[150] though, that:

> 'A notable omission, however, is express reference to issues of power imbalance and inequality between the parties to the litigation, [is] most often manifested in family violence.'

Procedural rules, he urges, should be part of the solution to this problem not part of the problem itself.

Rule 1.07 goes on to set out the manner in which the rules are to be applied and, once more, the aims of just and timely resolution at a reasonable cost are emphasised, although there is an additional emphasis on the cost to the community, which may be less easy to identify immediately and specifically. Indeed r 1.07(c) makes particular reference to the complexity of matters, so that may suggest that complex matters may be somehow differentiated. That may be of importance in the context of organisation of family law matters at large.[151]

In the end, as Altobelli states:[152]

> 'Cultural change is clearly on the agenda. The main purpose cannot be achieved without changing the behaviour of at least some family lawyers, their clients and self-represented litigants.'

But the aims of the Rules, as well as that last statement, must be viewed in the scenario at large that some reformers might seek to paint for us. Thus, in the report *Every picture tells a story*, to which reference has already been made,[153] a proposal is made for the establishment of a Families' Tribunal which would be established to replace the Family Court at least in areas which are regarded as proving less immediately difficult. Many of the Committee's recommendations,[154] it must be said, are predicated on the desirability of a system where the involvement of lawyers was the exception rather than the rule. As regards the body itself, the Report stated[155] that tribunal members would be drawn from the ranks of professionals working in the family relationships field. Thus:

> 'The Tribunal would attempt to conciliate the dispute. This could be undertaken by a single member. If this does not resolve it, the hearing of the dispute and the decision making function of the Tribunal could be performed by a panel of members comprising a mediator, a child psychologist/ other

---

[150] Above note 145 at 97.
[151] Below text at note 153.
[152] Above note 145 at 100.
[153] Above text at note 41.
[154] *Picture* at para 4.47.
[155] Ibid at para 4.113.

person able to address the child's needs and a third person with appropriate legal expertise.'

The Committee also emphasised[156] that legal representation for parties appearing in a Families Tribunal Application should be totally excluded.

There are, it is suggested simple and obvious flaws in the scheme which, at the time of writing,[157] seems to be in appropriate abeyance. First, drawing the members of the Tribunals from groups of other professionals is unlikely, it is submitted, after a period of initial euphoria, to prove any more popular or successful than a more traditionally constituted Tribunal. Second, the problems which are attached to the personnel of the Family Court[158] are likely simply to be transferred to the members of the Tribunal as the results of their adjudications will have the same effects as those of the Court. Third, the attempt to minimise legal involvement has, throughout, failed to take matters of procedure into proper account. Some of the other suggestions made in the Report, including a single entry point to the process together with mediation and counselling facilities[159] seems to have found political favour.

Since the original Family Law Act 1975, it seems impossible to dissociate the law from the individuals who have created it or carried its administration.[160] So it has been in recent time. But on 2 July 2004, Nicholson CJ, of the Family Court of Australia, whose recent contribution has been noted throughout this commentary, retired from office. His contribution has been appropriately chronicled by Kirby J of the High Court of Australia.[161] He himself has written[162] of his time in office that:

> 'I also believe that, despite the small number of vociferous critics of the Act and the Court, Australia has a better family law system than have most other western countries.'

Most commentators who have observed the system closely and dispassionately would not disagree too much with that statement.

Nicholson CJ's replacement is to be the Hon Diana Bryant, previously Senior Federal Magistrate. In recent times, the Federal Magistracy has taken over a deal of family law work at first instance. Bryant CJ's appointment may be perceived as neutral, in the sense that government was seeking a less interventionist Chief Justice than Alastair Nicholson proved to be. However, it seems to this writer that her broad and varied experience will stand her and the Family Court in good stead. To conclude this commentary, I should note that, at a conference which I attended in November 2004, she emphasised to members of the practising profession that, if they were not prepared to make

---

156   Ibid at para 4.115.
157   January 2005, though see below text at note 163.
158   See H A Finlay 'Fault and Violence in the Family Court of Australia' (1985) 5J *Aust L J* 559.
159   *Picture* para 4.100.
160   See above note 2.
161   M Kirby 'Family Law: The special contribution of Alastair Nicholson' (2004) 18 *Aust J Fam L* 125.
162   A Nicholson 'Sixteen years of Family Law – A retrospective' (2004) 18 *Aust J Fam L* 131 at 146.

the new rules,[163] and the philosophy behind them, work, then they would certainly be faced with a Tribunal. A development which, to this commentator at least, would not serve the interests of litigants, profession or anyone else. Thus, the future remains as intriguing for Australian family law as it has at any time since 1975.

---

[163] Above text at note 145*ff*.

Botswana

RECENT DEVELOPMENTS IN FAMILY LAW IN BOTSWANA: THE ABOLITION OF MARITAL POWER ACT

Tebogo Jobetta[*]

Résumé

Depuis plusieurs années, des femmes au Botswana réclament du gouvernement l'abolition de lois discriminatoires à leur égard. Parmi elles, un certain nombre de femmes mariées, victimes des règles défavorables aux épouses. Il aura fallu plusieurs années avant que ces revendications ne se concrétisent par des réformes législatives. Les efforts du gouvernement se faisaient au compte-goutte et arrivaient bien souvent trop tard. L'adoption de la Loi sur l'abolition du pouvoir marital imposa un nouveau régime en matière de mariage. L'objectif avoué de cette loi était de rendre désuète l'idée même de pouvoir marital. Ces changements ont permis aux épouses du Botswana d'atteindre un statut semblable à celui dont les femmes mariées jouissent ailleurs, particulièrement en Afrique du Sud et en Namibie. On considère généralement que cette loi répond aux objectifs de la Convention sur l'élimination de toutes les formes de discrimination à l'égard des femmes et qu'elle est conforme à l'image que la société du Botswana entend se donner d'ici 2016.

L'adoption de cette loi illustre l'engagement du gouvernement du Botswana dans le processus d'abolition des législations discriminatoires à l'égard des femmes. Cet article présente un exposé de la Loi sur l'abolition du pouvoir marital et rappelle les aspects principaux de la loi antérieure. Il souligne les changements apportés, tout en mettant en lumière leurs éventuelles limites.

I   INTRODUCTION

Women in Botswana have for years called on the Government of Botswana to amend certain laws which were discriminatory against women. At the centre of these calls were a number of married women who bore the brunt of these unfortunate laws as they were prejudiced against because of their gender and marital status. These calls were heeded albeit after years of delays before the changes could find their way into the statutes. The efforts made by the government were incremental and often came a little too late

---

[*]   Lecturer, Department of Law, University of Botswana.

when all the damage had been done. The enactment of the Abolition of Marital Power Act ushered in a new regime in the institution of marriage. The intended objective of the new law was to make marital power obsolete. These changes have synchronised the position of married women in Botswana with their counterparts elsewhere, particularly South Africa and Namibia.[1] It is perceived that this law meets the objectives of the Convention on the Elimination of all forms of Discrimination[2] against Women as well as the long-term vision for Botswana, 2016.[3] The enactment of the new law perhaps goes to show the level of commitment by the Government of Botswana in doing away with all laws which are discriminatory on the basis of gender.[4]

This paper presents an overview of the Abolition of Marital Power Act as well as highlighting the position of the law prior to the enactment of the Act, the changes brought about by the Act and the limitations of the Act, if any.

II   PRE-ABOLITION OF MARITAL POWER ACT POSITION

Upon conclusion of a civil marriage ceremony, certain consequences follow which could either be proprietary or personal in nature.[5] The personal consequences have a long-lasting effect insofar as the parties to the marriage cannot alter them prior to or during the subsistence of the marriage. A cursory perusal of the content and import of these consequences would reveal that they are heavily skewed in favour of the male spouse, leaving the female spouse with no choice but to conform with the dictates of these consequences. One such consequence, which is the pith and kernel of this discussion, is the acquisition and possession of marital power by the male

---

[1]   South Africa abolished marital power way back in 1984 through the enactment of the Matrimonial Property Act No 88 of 1984 which commenced on the 1 November 1984. The rationale for the enactment was that the notion of marital power was outmoded and anachronistic with the right to equality. Namibia, however, enacted the Married Persons Equality Act 1996 (Act 1 of 1996) with the main objective of abolishing the archaic concept of marital power in marriage. It is only last year that Botswana saw fit to put the local women folk on an equal footing with their sisters in Namibia and South Africa.

[2]   Botswana is a signatory to this Convention. The theme of the Convention is to enjoin state parties to protect women through legislation which does not discriminate against women in any way.

[3]   The vision envisages that by the year 2016, Botswana would be an open, democratic and accountable nation. The objective of this vision would be to make all laws consistent with the Constitution including those laws which discriminate against women.

[4]   Perhaps this was a follow-up to a statement by His Excellency when he said that the government is preparing a bill to amend all legislation that discriminates against women. See also, *The Botswana Daily News*, 18 May 2004, No 94 when His Excellency was addressing the Commonwealth Women Parliamentarians (Africa Region) at a workshop reviewing progress on the implementation of the Beijing Plan of Action at Gaborone Sun Conference Centre. It can safely be concluded that the enactment of the Abolition of Marital Power Act was a step in the right direction in doing away with laws which discriminate against women. Hopefully we will begin to see more pieces of legislation which have over the years been out of step with reality, particularly where gender equality is involved, repealed or amended. The best way to achieve this would be through legislative intervention in such areas as domestic violence and marital rape issues.

[5]   See H R Hahlo *The South African Law of Husband and Wife* (Juta, Cape Town, 5th edn).

spouse. This power can only be exercised by the male spouse irrespective of whether they are married in community of property.

Marital power is the multi-faceted authority that is male-centred in marriage. This power is exclusively exercised by men by virtue of the marriage and it designates them as heads of the family unit. It entitles or empowers the man to deal with the matrimonial property without the wife's consent, to be the head of the family and to have control over the wife.[6] These constituents will be dealt with shortly and most of them are found at Common Law.

III POSITION OF HUSBAND AS HEAD OF THE FAMILY

Upon conclusion of the marriage the husband automatically becomes head of the family. This means that he has exclusivity in the decision-making process within the home. With regard to the making of decisions fundamentally affecting the family or household, it is expected that the husband acts reasonably and that in exercising this power he decides where and how his family is going to live and many other attendant matters.

IV HUSBAND'S POWER OVER THE WIFE

The other dimension of marital power was that it gave the husband power over the person of his wife. This power disabled the wife from partaking in binding legal transactions. She did not have the power or the capacity to enter into legal transactions without the due assistance of her husband. In effect, her position was akin to that of a minor or an insane person.[7] The woman could not even defend actions against her by third parties save where the husband consented. Any transactions entered into by the wife without the requisite consent were null and void.[8] It can be seen from the foregoing that women's status was regarded as inferior to that of men and this can be said to be outright discriminatory as there is no logical or rational basis for this anomaly.[9] This state of affairs offends against women's rights to equality and protection before the law.[10]

In the event that the husband unreasonably and without just cause withholds his consent to bring or defend proceedings, the wife may apply for an order of *venia agendi* which when granted would allow her to bring or defend proceedings on her own. However, there are exceptions where the wife can

---

[6]   See *Prior v Battle* 1999 (2) SA 850 at 858 (Tk).

[7]   Although just like a minor the married woman has to act with the assistance of her husband who is her legal guardian, the acts done are not always in the interest of the married woman. Unlike a guardian who has to act with a view to advancing the interests of the minor, the married man is not enjoined so to act when acting for the wife.

[8]   See *National Development Bank v Mogatwane* [1996] BLR 755 and *Joina and Associates v Bakwena Modikwa* [1999] 1 BLR 475.

[9]   See *Human Rights Reference Handbook*, 2004 edn, p 319.

[10] It can thus be said that the common law legal notion of marital power is unconstitutional as it offends the equality before the law provision.

bring proceedings on her own but this is only possible where she is a public trader[11] or where she has contracted for household necessaries.[12]

Since capacity to act and litigate are regarded as some of the factors which determine a person's status at law,[13] it can be said that a woman married in community of property as a general rule is denied this and that therefore, when it comes to the said determinants of status, she does not have any standing.

V HUSBAND'S POWER OVER THE WIFE'S PROPERTY

In exercise of the marital power, the husband solely administers the property of the joint estate as well as that of his wife if they are married in community. This means that the husband could even deal with the wife's property as he pleased without her consent and the law would sanction this. He could sell, cede or even mortgage the joint property without the wife knowing about it. However, this position has been altered by the provisions of s 18(5) of the Deeds Registry Amendment Act of 1996. Under the terms of this provision, the husband could only deal with the joint estate with the consent of the wife. It appears that this provision only applied to immovable property so that with respect to other property the husband exercised all power without the wife even knowing about such transactions.

It could be seen that marital power was a powerful tool which undermined women in marriage and that if it fell into the wrong hands it could be employed as a tool for oppression. The woman had to bear the brunt of marital power throughout the marriage. Although there were certain safeguards which could be employed to alleviate the harshness of an improper exercise of marital power, some of them were either too inadequate or the remedy only became available when it was a too late.[14]

The other personal consequence of marriage, which undermined the independence of women, was the fact that the woman had to take the domicile of her husband. This is in line with the doctrine of unity of matrimonial domicile. Domicile is a legal concept, which seeks to attach an individual with a particular legal system for the determination of his or her rights.[15] In matrimony the wife is domiciled where the husband is and her domicile changes automatically when that of the husband changes regardless of whether she is physically present in a particular area or not. Women viewed the concept of domicile as a serious handicap in the enforcement of personal rights in that a matter would be dismissed without even hearing the merits if a woman failed to prove that she was domiciled within the court's jurisdiction.[16]

---

11   See *Grobler v Schmilg and Freeman* 1923 AD 496.
12   See *Reelomel v Ramsey* 1920 TPD 371.
13   D S P Cronjè and J Heaton *South African Law of Persons* (Butterworths, Durban, 1999).
14   See H R Hahlo *The South African Law of Husband and Wife* (Juta, Cape Town, 5th edn).
15   D S P Cronjé and J Heaton *South African Law of Persons* (Butterworths, Durban, 1999).
16   See *Egner v Egner* [1974] 2 BLR 5.

VI THE ABOLITION OF MARITAL POWER ACT

A significant change in marital relationships has been brought about by the enactment of the Abolition of Marital Power Act of 2004 (hereinafter referred to as the Act).[17] The principal aim of this Act is to make the common law rule of marital power obsolete. In so doing the objective was to put women in marriage on an equal footing with their male counterparts.[18] The Act perceives women as individuals with legal capacities enjoyed by any adult person before the law. The law no longer singles out married women for special treatment in the way it used to do.

The Act expressly abolishes the common law rule of marital power.[19] This was done with a view to removing the various impediments that the marital power placed on a married woman. This translates to liberation in the sense that a married woman is now at liberty to do what she was prohibited from doing before. The implication of the abolition is threefold. First, the husband is no longer the head of the household[20] as was the case before, thereby implying that the married couple are now equal partners in marriage. This perhaps marks the beginning of marriage being viewed as a partnership in which consensus is the order of the day. Secondly, the husband does not have authority over the property of his wife and, thirdly, the husband no longer has authority over the wife as an individual.[21] The Act also excludes customary and religious marriages from its purview.[22]

The Act deals with marriages in community of property and it applies with retrospective effect.[23] The Act, however, is inapplicable to a marriage in community of property where such property was donated to a spouse with the caveat that this property should not form part of the joint estate.[24]

---

[17] The Act commenced on 1 May 2005 by virtue of Statutory Instrument 30 of 2005.

[18] Perhaps the realisation that women in marriage have for decades been marginalised led to the introduction of this piece of legislation.

[19] See s 4(1)(a) and (b) of the Act.

[20] See s 5 of the Abolition of Marital Power Act. The Botswana Act provision on the effect of the abolition of marital power is too brief and not as detailed as the Namibian one. The latter removes all doubt as to the mischief which the Act sought to address. Section 3 of the Namibian Act expressly provides among other things that the effect of the abolition is to remove the restrictions which the marital power places on the legal capacity of a wife to contract and litigate, including restrictions on her capacity to act as director of a company, bind herself as surety, or register immovable property in her name.

[21] See s 4 of the Abolition of Marital Power Act. It should be noted that the husband has lost the power he had over the wife with retrospective effect. Whatever power he had prior to the commencement of the Act no longer holds. Perhaps this indicates the seriousness with which the powers that be wanted to weed the evil, namely marital power, from marital relationships.

[22] See s 3 of the Act which provides that the Act shall not apply to customary and religious marriages. It is not clear from the Act as to why the customary and religious marriages have been left out from the remit of the new Act. These marriages also have a system similar to marital power although it is not called such. It appears therefore that the abolition affects one section of the society while the other which is married according to customary or religious rites bear the brunt of marital power.

[23] See s 6. The new Act applies to all marriages irrespective of when such marriages were entered into. The general position of the law is that all laws enacted should have prospective effect. It should be noted, however, that the retrospective nature of the Act does not affect the validity or legal consequences of acts done, omissions, or facts existing before the enactment.

[24] See s 6 of the Act.

Spouses married in community of property have been equated to partners in that they have equal capacity to dispose of the assets of the joint estate and to contract debts, as well as to administer the joint estate.[25] Although the spouses have equal capacity, spouses are at liberty to perform juristic acts or legal transactions with regard to the joint estate without the consent of the other spouse.[26] Be that as it may, there are certain juristic acts or legal transactions which cannot be undertaken without the written consent of the other spouse.[27] Consent can be dispensed with by way of application to the court where such consent has been unreasonably withheld or there is sufficient reason to dispense with it.[28] Where such consent has been issued by the court, the spouse who made the application is at liberty to perform the acts which require the consent of the other spouse under s 9. In effect the powers that the other spouse had with respect to the issue of consent are suspended for a fixed period of time or indefinitely and the suspension may be generic or specific to a particular act if such would protect the interests of the aggrieved spouse.[29] The Act does not define what unreasonable refusal of consent is and it would appear that this is left to the discretion of the court and on the peculiar facts of the case before it.

The Act also deals with the consequences which follow performance of the specified acts under the Act without the required consent or leave of court.[30] This provision comes into play only where the joint estate suffers or sustains a loss as a result of actions performed without the requisite consent. Where the joint estate sustains loss consequent to the other spouse acting without the requisite consent, the other spouse has a right to seek an adjustment either upon division of the joint estate or upon demand by the other spouse at anytime during the subsistence of the marriage.[31] In determining whether an estate has suffered loss or not, not only would the economic value of the property be considered but also any sentimental value the aggrieved spouse attached to the said property.[32]

---

[25]   See s 7 of the Act.

[26]   See s 8. This provision is subject to s 9 of the Act which sets out those acts which can only be done with the consent of the other spouse. This therefore means that spouses can do any act which is not listed under s 9 without the consent of each other. Perhaps this is done for business efficacy and it is in line with the maxim *expressio unius est exclusio alterius*.

[27]   See s 9 of the Act. It would appear that consent of the other spouse is a condition precedent for the validity of any juristic act.

[28]   See s 12.

[29]   See s 12(2) and (3).

[30]   See s 10.

[31]   See s 10(2)(a)–(b).

[32]   See s 10(3). This is one of the rare instances where the law is used to compensate for sentimental loss. It perhaps marks a fundamental departure in the law of damages that damages should be paid for patrimonial loss. It is submitted that the courts would have difficulty in assessing such sentiments as no guidelines have been put in place as to what factors would be considered in arriving at an appropriate figure. The phraseology adopted by s 8(2) of the Namibian Married Persons Equality Act 1996 (Act 1 of 1996) is that the loss should be in respect of any sentimental replacement value of the property at the time of alienation. At least the Namibian Act specifically deals with the replacement value which the Botswana Act does not allude to.

There are certain acts which can be performed by a spouse without consent of the other.[33] These include transactions involving the stock exchange or acts required to be performed in the ordinary course of business of his or her profession, trade, occupation or business.[34]

In terms of the new law, spouses married in community of property do not have the capacity to institute or defend proceedings without the written consent of the other spouse.[35] Previously, it was the woman who had to do legal acts with the authority and consent of the husband. There are some exceptions where the consent would be waived and this is where the legal proceedings are in respect of the spouses' separate property.[36]

The Act also deals with provisions relating to marriages out of community of property. It provides that there will be joint and several liability of the spouses with respect to household necessaries.[37] Where one of the spouses contributed more to the purchase of necessaries he or she will have a right of recourse against the other spouse.[38] However, where the spouses acquire property jointly, Part III of the Act becomes operational as if the couple were married in community of property.[39]

The last section of the Act deals with issues pertaining to domicile of married women and domicile and guardianship of children. The common law doctrine of unity of matrimonial domicile has been done away with. This then means that a married woman can have her own domicile which can either be similar or different to that of her husband.[40] With respect to children, their domicile will be determined by the place with which they are mostly connected and it can either be that of the mother or the father.[41]

With the advent of the new law, both parents have equal rights, powers and duties of guardianship over their minor children.[42] It is apparent that the father of the child no longer has the final say as used to be the case.

---

[33] See s 11.

[34] See s 11(a)–(b).

[35] See s 13. This marks a departure from the common law rule that it was the female spouse who lacked capacity. It appears that the male spouse also needs the written consent of the female spouse if required to bring or defend proceedings. The only shortfall with this provision is that there is no form or guideline of consent which should be followed and whether the consent has to be done with respect to each transaction or whether it can be universal.

[36] See s 13(1)(a)–(c).

[37] See s 14(1).

[38] See s 14(2).

[39] See s 15.

[40] See s 16. In terms of this provision a married woman could actually acquire a domicile of her own choice by a combination of residence in a particular area and an intention so to reside for an indefinite period. See also Cronjé on acquisition of a domicile of choice. This is also echoed by s 7(1)(a) of the Matrimonial Causes Act 1973.

[41] See s 17(2) – the domicile of minor children whose parents are married is no longer that of the father.

[42] See s 18(1).

VII CONCLUSION

The enactment of the Abolition of Marital Power Act brought with it long-awaited changes for the women of Botswana. Although the Act saw the light of day after years of oppressive laws in our law of marriage, it is, however, a welcome development and it is hoped that other laws which are discriminatory against women will see their way into the statute book. The doctrine of marital power can at best be described as unconstitutional as such a doctrine is outmoded and anachronistic and clashes with the principle of equality of all before the law.[43] The shortcomings in the new law are that, to date, no regulations have been made as to how the various provisions of the Act should be given effect. The other factor is that the Act does not give spouses an alternative to opt out of the provisions of the new law. The Act does not adequately deal with the issue of written consent particularly where the said consent is forged.[44] There is no precedent or format to determine what the said consent should be like and whether it should be attested to by a commissioner of oaths or done by a notary public. A lot of public education campaigns are required to sensitise the women folk in the rural areas about the new regime. Otherwise it is too early to judge how the new regime has been received. One evident limitation is the exclusion of customary and religious marriages from the purview of the Act. Since these marriages are recognised under the laws of Botswana, it appears illogical to exclude them as they also have a similar principle in place which is akin to marital power although it is not called such. A woman married under customary or religious law is subordinate to her husband in all respects. In essence what the new regime on the law of marriage has done is to give with one hand and take away with the other. It has taken away marital power from the statutory marriage and left it intact in both customary and religious marriages.

---

[43] See *Prior v Battle and Others* 1999(2) SA 850 (Tk). See also ss 3 and 15 of the Constitution of Botswana.

[44] The issue arose in *Sekga v Pule* [2000] 1 BLR 17 where an ordinary letter was sufficient to constitute consent. The Act needs to be clear as to the form of consent to avoid situations where spouses claim that consent was given whereas in fact no such consent was given.

EXPLORING VIRGIN TERRITORY: FAMILY LAW IN THE BRITISH VIRGIN ISLANDS

Hazel Thompson-Ahye[*]

Résumé

Les Îles Vierges britanniques constituent un petit chapelet d'îles nichées dans la région nord-est de l'archipel des Caraïbes. Sur le plan politique, il s'agit d'un territoire britannique d'Outre-Mer autonome; sa population est d'approximativement 25,000 habitants; la langue officielle y est l'Anglais et la monnaie, le dollar Américain. L'économie des Îles Vierges britanniques repose sur deux piliers, le tourisme et les services financiers.

Comme c'est le cas pour toutes les colonies britanniques ainsi que pour les anciennes colonies, les lois des Îles Vierges britanniques tirent leur origine de la Grande-Bretagne, mais elles n'ont pas toujours suivi les changements subséquents du droit de la métropole. C'est ainsi que dans ce paradis touristique, le droit familial consacre encore et toujours un certain nombre d'injustices dont sont victimes les femmes et les enfants. Dans notre exploration de ce "terrain vierge", nous examinons le droit du mariage, les nullités du mariage, le divorce, l'obligation alimentaire, la filiation, l'adoption, les successions et la problématique de la violence domestique et nous découvrons de nombreux secteurs où des réformes s'imposent. Nous sommes cependant encouragés par quelques rares mais réels progrès, notamment par l'adoption de la loi de 1996 concernant les poursuites sommaires en matière de violence domestique, véritable rayon de soleil dans le paysage par ailleurs plutôt sombre du droit familial.

I INTRODUCTION

The British Virgin Islands consists of a small cluster of islands nestling within the northeastern region of the Caribbean archipelago. Politically, it is an internally self-governing British Overseas Territory with a population of approximately 25,000 people, whose official language is English and official currency, the US Dollar.

---

[*] Attorney-at-Law and Mediator, Senior Tutor, Eugene Dupuch Law School, Nassau, the Bahamas.

The economy of the British Virgin Islands rests on the twin pillars of tourism and financial services which ensure for the populace a very high standard of living.[1] As is the case with all British colonies and former colonies, the laws of the British Virgin Islands were derived from England, but in many instances lag behind subsequent legal change in that jurisdiction. The family law of the British Virgin Islands is no exception for in this tourist paradise can be viewed, still lingering within the law's embrace, some of family law's injustices to children and women, which characterised English laws until the latter half of the twentieth century. There have been a few bold forward strides, such as the enactment of the Domestic Violence (Summary Proceedings) Act 1996, which stands out as a ray of sunshine illuminating the somewhat dismal family law landscape.

II MARRIAGE

A Requirements for a valid marriage

The Marriage Ordinance[2] specifies that marriages may be performed only by a Marriage Officer who must be a 'Minister of a Christian Religion' or by the Registrar-General.[3] The marriage of persons who knowingly and willfully consent to or acquiesce in their marriage being performed by a person other than a Marriage Officer or the Registrar-General is null and void.[4]

The law further provides that where 'parties to any marriage are within the prohibited degrees of consanguinity or affinity according to the law of England the marriage of such persons shall be null and void'.[5] The Marriage (Prohibited Degrees of Relationship) Act, enacted subsequently, amended the law with respect to prohibited degrees of relationship and legalised marriages contracted between certain relatives by affinity, such as a man and his deceased wife's sister.[6]

The minimum age for marriage is 16 years.[7] The law specifies that where either of the parties, not being a widower or widow, is under the age of 18 years, the consent of the parent or guardian to the marriage must first be obtained.[8]

---

[1]   Webster, O'Neal *Guide to Doing Business in the Virgin Islands*.
[2]   Marriage Ordinance, Cap 272 of the Revised Laws of the Virgin Islands.
[3]   Sections 3 and 15 of the Marriage Ordinance, Cap 272 of the Revised Laws of the Virgin Islands.
[4]   Section 61(2).
[5]   Section 24.
[6]   Section 3, Marriage (Prohibited Degrees of Relationship) Act, Cap 274 of the Laws of the Virgin Islands.
[7]   Section 2, Marriage (Amendment) Act 1994.
[8]   Section 25 as amended by the Age of Majority Act, Act No 21 of 1994 of the Laws of the Virgin Islands.

B Consequences of non-compliance with the requirement for consent and due publication of banns

Whereas the law clearly states that a marriage solemnised by persons either of whom is under the age of 16 is null and void,[9] the law is a bit more complicated with regard to the ramifications of a marriage contracted by persons between the ages of 16 and 18 without the requisite parental consent. What is fundamental to the nullifying of the purported marriage is whether there was notice of the denial of consent. The law provides that in a case where parental consent to the marriage was not given and neither has the Governor dispensed with such consent, nor the High Court granted its consent, a Marriage Officer who performs the marriage after due publication of banns, incurs no liability or penalty, unless the person whose consent is required by law had given notice to the Marriage Officer that he had forbidden the marriage.[10] If, however, the person, whose consent was required had, before the marriage was solemnised, given notice in writing of his objection to the marriage to the Marriage Officer publishing the banns, then the publication of the banns would be void.[11] The marriage of persons who knowingly and willfully intermarry without due publication of banns is null and void.[12]

C Further consequences for non-compliance with Marriage Ordinance

Marriages which do not take place in designated buildings, or are performed without the requisite Governor's licence, or Registrar-General's certificate are also null and void.[13]

Penal consequences can also be visited upon the person solemnising a marriage without due publication of banns, as the law prescribes a penalty on conviction for so doing of imprisonment for a term not exceeding 2 years.[14]

Any person hoping to gain from marrying a minor will have his plan frustrated as persons marrying underage minors without the benefit of parental consent cannot acquire property from such minors.[15]

---

[9]   Section 24A.
[10]   See s 48.
[11]   Section 30.
[12]   Section 61(1)(b).
[13]   *Ibid.*
[14]   Section 51.
[15]   Section 62.

III NULLITY

A Void marriages

A marriage is deemed void where it is not valid under the Marriage Ordinance, in that the parties are within the prohibited degrees of relationship, are under age, or have not complied with the formal requirements of the law, or either party was at the time of the marriage already lawfully married, or the parties are not respectively male and female.[16]

B Voidable marriages

A marriage is voidable on the following grounds:

(a) the marriage has not been consummated owing to the incapacity of either party to consummate it;

(b) the marriage has not been consummated owing to the willful refusal of the respondent to consummate it;

(c) either party to the marriage did not validly consent to it, whether in consequence of duress, mistake, unsoundness of mind or otherwise;

(d) at the time of the marriage either party, though capable of giving a valid consent, was suffering (whether continuously or intermittently) from mental disorder of such a kind or to such an extent as to be unfit for marriage;

(e) at the time of the marriage the respondent was suffering from a venereal disease in a communicable form;

(f) at the time of the marriage the respondent was pregnant by some person other than the petitioner.[17]

C Bars to the decree of nullity

The law provides that the court shall not grant a decree of nullity if on the evidence it is satisfied that:

(a) the petitioner, with knowledge that it was open to him to have the marriage voided, so conducted himself in relation to the respondent as to lead the respondent reasonably to believe that he would not seek to do so, and it would be unjust to the respondent to grant the decree;

(b) in respect of proceedings brought under grounds (c) to (f) above proceedings are instituted within 3 years.

---

[16]	Section 13, Matrimonial Proceedings and Property Act 1995.
[17]	*Ibid*, s 13.

In cases where the petitioner is relying on grounds (e) and (f) above, that is, presence of venereal disease and pregnancy by another, the court will not grant the decree of nullity unless the petitioner, at the time of the marriage was ignorant of the facts alleged.[18]

D   Effect of decree of nullity

The decree of nullity operates as from the time it is granted, so the marriage is treated as subsisting up to that time. Children born before the decree of nullity is granted in respect of a voidable marriage are treated as legitimate unless the decree was granted on the basis that the respondent was at the time of the marriage pregnant by someone other than the petitioner.[19]

IV DIVORCE

A   Grounds for divorce

The divorce law is to be found in the Matrimonial Proceedings and Property Act 1995 ('the Act'). The sole ground for divorce is irretrievable breakdown of the marriage which can be proved by one or more of five facts:

(1) that the respondent has committed adultery and the petitioner finds it intolerable to live with the respondent;

(2) that the respondent has behaved in such a way that the petitioner cannot reasonably be expected to live with the respondent;

(3) that the respondent has deserted the petitioner for a continuous period of at least 2 years immediately preceding the presentation of the petition;

(4) that the parties to the marriage have lived apart for a continuous period of at least 2 years immediately preceding the presentation of the petition and the respondent consents to a decree being granted; and

(5) that the parties to the marriage have lived apart for a continuous period of at least 5 years immediately preceding the presentation of the petition.[20]

B   Reconciliation provisions

Although the divorce law is closely patterned on the UK Matrimonial Causes Act 1973, there are slight deviations. Unlike in the UK, where a divorce cannot be filed within the first year of the marriage, there is no absolute ban on divorce for any period of time in the British Virgin Islands. However,

---

[18]   Section 14.

[19]   Section 14(6).

[20]   Sections 3 and 4 of the Matrimonial Proceedings and Property Act 1995.

persons who wish to file a petition for divorce before the expiration of 2 years from the date of their marriage must first seek leave of the court by an application alleging that the case is one of exceptional hardship being suffered by the petitioner, or one of exceptional depravity on the part of the respondent. The court, in determining the application, must have regard to the interests of any child of the family and to whether there is any possibility of reconciliation between the parties.[21]

C   Further reconciliation provisions

The court's concern with reconciliation can be gleaned not only from its power to dismiss the application for leave to file the divorce petition within 2 years where there is hope for reconciliation, but also from the requirement for the 'Certificate With Regard to Reconciliation' to be filed with each divorce petition. This document certifies whether the petitioner's legal representative has discussed with the petitioner the possibility of reconciliation and given to the petitioner the addresses of persons qualified to help effect such reconciliation.[22] The court is also empowered to adjourn the proceedings for such period as it thinks fit, to enable attempts to be made to effect reconciliation, if at any stage it appears that there is a possibility of reconciliation between the parties to the marriage.[23] Other provisions facilitating reconciliation are the court's power to disregard periods of living together for more than 6 months, in circumstances which might otherwise give rise to the question of condonation of the alleged adultery or unreasonable behaviour, or might jeopardise the computation of the requisite period of continuous desertion or separation.[24]

D   Divorce by special procedure

The law provides for divorce petitions to be heard by the ordinary procedure of oral examination of witnesses, but where the petition is undefended there is provision in the matrimonial rules for a special procedure. This requires that, with the application for directions for trial, an affidavit of evidence be filed requesting that the petition be placed in a special procedure list. The form and content of the affidavit varies according to the fact being relied upon to prove irretrievable breakdown of the marriage. If there are children of the family, then the affidavit must verify, with amendments if necessary, the contents of the filed statement of arrangements. Soon after the cause has been entered in the special procedure list, the judge considers the evidence filed by the petitioner. If he considers the contents of the petition sufficiently proved, and the petitioner entitled to a decree, the judge will so certify. The parties are then notified by the certificate of the judge that he finds the

---

21   *Ibid*, s 5(1) and (2).
22   Section 8(1).
23   Section 8(2).
24   Section 8(4)–(6).

contents of the petition proved and of the date fixed for the pronouncement of the decree by the judge in open court. If the judge is not so satisfied, he may give time to file further evidence or remove the cause from the special procedure list, whereupon the cause will be heard by the ordinary procedure.[25] The parties are not required to attend the hearing, unless an order for costs is included in the certificate and the party wishes to be heard on his objection to the order.

V MAINTENANCE

Maintenance orders are made by both the magistrates' courts and the High Court.

A Maintenance of spouses in the magistrates' courts

In the magistrates' courts the application is brought under Part V of the Magistrate's Code of Procedure Act which is entitled: *Summary Jurisdiction (Quasi Criminal) Protection and Maintenance of Married Women and Affiliation Proceedings*.

Despite this misleading rubric, this section of the Act does purport to provide relief for married men, as well as married women, for it allows 'any married person' to apply for an order for maintenance whose husband or wife:

(a) has been guilty of adultery; or

(b) has deserted the applicant; or

(c) has been convicted summarily of an aggravated assault on the applicant within the meaning of s 41 of the Offences Against the Person Act; or

(d) has been convicted on indictment of an assault upon the applicant; or

(e) has been guilty of persistent cruelty to the applicant or the children of the applicant; or

(f) being under a duty to provide reasonable maintenance for the applicant and the children of the applicant, has willfully neglected or refused to do so; or

(g) is a habitual drunkard, or user of illegal drugs who at times is dangerous to himself or to others or incapable of managing himself or herself or his or her affairs; or

(h) is a married woman whose husband has compelled her to submit to prostitution; or

---

[25] Rules 25, 34, 37, Matrimonial Proceedings Rules 1997.

(i) is a married woman whose husband while suffering from a venereal disease and knowing that he was so suffering, has insisted on having sexual intercourse with her.

The wording of the law in (f), namely, 'being under a duty to provide maintenance' throws the entitlement of the husband to maintenance into doubt, which is soon removed as one delves further into the legislation. It is now clear that the law intends to and does, in fact, discriminate against men as the heading implies as it precludes an order being made against a wife, unless the magistrate 'is satisfied that the applicant is not possessed of sufficient means to provide reasonable maintenance for himself or that the applicant is by reason of old age, illness or physical or mental disability unable to provide for his own maintenance'.[26]

B   Maintenance of spouses in the High Court

In the High Court, a maintenance application may be brought as an application for ancillary relief on a petition for divorce, nullity or judicial separation,[27] or as originating proceedings on the ground of willful neglect to maintain.[28]

1   Wilful neglect to maintain

The law with respect to maintenance on the ground that the other spouse has willfully neglected to provide reasonable maintenance for the applicant or to provide or to make a proper contribution for any child of the family also discriminates against a male spouse. It provides for the order for maintenance to be made in favour of a male spouse only in cases where 'in all the circumstances, it is reasonable to expect the respondent to contribute, by reason of the impairment of the applicant's earning capacity through age, illness or disability of mind or body and having regard to the resources of the respective parties'. A wife's right to reasonable maintenance is not similarly circumscribed. On the determination of the application, the court can make a periodical payments order, a secured periodical payments order or may award a lump sum.

2   Ancillary relief orders

The court can make a variety of orders on ancillary relief applications, such as maintenance pending suit, periodical payments, secured periodical payments, a lump sum order, or a transfer or settlement of property order.[29]

---

26   Section 114, Magistrate's Code of Procedure Act, Cap 44.
27   Section 24(1), Matrimonial Proceedings and Property Act 1995.
28   Section 27.
29   Section 23.

In determining matters of financial provision, the court will consider factors such as:

(a) the income, earning capacity, property and other financial resources which each of the parties to the marriage has or is likely to have in the foreseeable future;

(b) the financial needs, obligations and responsibilities which each party has or is likely to have in the foreseeable future;

(c) the standard of living enjoyed by the family before the breakdown of the marriage;

(d) the age of each party to the marriage and the duration of the marriage;

(e) any physical or mental disability of either of the parties to the marriage;

(f) the contribution made by each of the parties to the welfare of the family, including any contribution made by looking after the home or caring for the family;

(g) in proceedings for divorce or nullity of marriage, the value to either of the parties to the marriage, of any benefit (eg a pension) which, by reason of the dissolution or annulment of the marriage, that party will lose the chance of acquiring.

The court exercises its powers so as to place the parties, so far as it is practicable and, having regard to their conduct, just to do so, in the financial position in which they would have been if the marriage had not broken down and each had properly discharged his or her financial obligations and responsibilities towards the other.[30]

3   Other orders that the court can make

In addition to the orders above, the court can also make the following orders on an application made by a spouse in addition to, or in lieu of, an order for financial provision or property adjustment:

(a) an order for the sale of the matrimonial home and the division of the proceeds of sale in cases where both parties have made a substantial contribution to the matrimonial home, whether financial or otherwise;[31]

(b) an order vesting the matrimonial home held by the parties as joint tenants, in the parties as owners in common, in such shares as the court thinks fit.[32]

---

[30]   Section 26.
[31]   Section 50.
[32]   Section 51.

C　Maintenance of children

Orders for maintenance of children can be made in a similar manner as for spouses on application for ancillary relief orders and wilful neglect applications. They can also be made in affiliation proceedings as discussed below and also on the award of custody in guardianship proceedings under the Guardianship of Infants Act.[33]

The provision, which stipulates that a decree may not be made in the case of judicial separation, or made final, in the case of divorce and nullity unless the court is satisfied as to the arrangements of the children[34] (which includes their maintenance) is one of the methods by which the court safeguards the welfare of children.

VI　AFFILIATION PROCEEDINGS

Available statistics reveal that about 60% of children are born out of wedlock in the British Virgin Islands. Yet, unlike in most Caribbean jurisdictions, there is no Status of Children legislation in the British Virgin Islands. Paternity may only be established under the affiliation provisions in the Magistrate's Code of Procedure Act. This Act provides for a single woman who is pregnant or has delivered a child to apply to a Magistrate for a summons to be served on the alleged father of the child to compel him to maintain the child. The application must be made within 12 months of the birth of the child, or at a subsequent time if it is proved that the alleged father within 12 months after the child's birth gave money or assisted in the child's support, or that that he left the Territory within 12 months of the child's birth, in which case, the application must be brought within 12 months after his return to the Territory.[35]

Once the Magistrate is satisfied on the evidence, he will adjudge the defendant, the putative father of the child, and will make an order for maintenance to the mother or the person having custody of the child. The magistrate can award a sum of not less than $25 a week for the maintenance and education of the child and can further make an award for the expenses incidental to the birth of the child. If the child has died before the making of the order, an award can be made for the funeral expenses of the child. The order of the Magistrate can be varied or discharged on proof of a change in the means of the putative father since the making of the order.[36]

Although just about all of the Commonwealth Caribbean had similar provisions in their affiliation law, having inherited the same from the UK,

---

33　　Section 5(2), Guardianship of Infants Act, Cap 270.
34　　Section 43, Matrimonial Proceedings and Property Act 1995.
35　　Section 118 of the Magistrate's Code of Procedure Act, Cap 44.
36　　Section 119.

the vast majority of them have made amendments to these laws to reflect the changing times. Thus, the 12-month limitation for bringing affiliation proceedings has been either increased, or better yet, has been totally removed. Further, the minimum payment in the legislation has frequently been interpreted by Magistrates as a benchmark from which they were slow to deviate. The present trend in more modern Caribbean legislation is to remove any stated figure from the legislation and opt instead for the inclusion of various criteria to guide the Magistrate in arriving at a reasonable quantum. The law requires that the mother's evidence be corroborated in some material particular.[37] Even this provision has been expunged from some Caribbean legislation. The impetus for the changes in the law have come largely from the United Nations Committee on the Rights of the Child, which has, painstakingly, been reminding countries that having ratified the United Nations Convention on the Rights of the Child, they have an obligation to implement the Convention. The Convention on the Rights of the Child was extended to the British Virgin Islands on 7 September 1994. A fundamental principle of the Convention is that of non-discrimination. Many of the provisions that have been expunged from Caribbean family law offend against this principle as there are no similar restrictions placed on the application made by the mother of a child born in wedlock.

VII THE ILLEGITIMATE CHILD: REGISTRATION AND LEGITIMATION

A   Registration of birth of the illegitimate child

It may be noted here that the father of a child born out of wedlock may not have his name entered on the register of births unless at the joint request of himself and the mother of the child and he signs the register together with the mother. If he resides outside the jurisdiction the mother may have his particulars included as father of her child on production to the Registrar of an affidavit or statutory declaration made by him in which he acknowledges himself to be the father of the child.[38]

B   Legitimation

The illegitimate child can only be legitimated under the Legitimacy Act which provides that where parents of an illegitimate child marry, the child would become legitimate from the date of the marriage or, if the marriage took place prior to the enactment of the legislation, from the date of the commencement of the legislation, provided the father was at the date of the marriage domiciled in the Territory.[39] This is a blatant example of the law

---

[37]   *Ibid.*
[38]   Section 18, Registration of Births and Deaths Ordinance, Cap 276.
[39]   Section 3, Legitimacy Act, Cap 271.

discriminating against not only children, but also women, whose domiciles should be taken into account as well as their husbands' in a determination of legitimation. This law, as well as some provisions of the Constitution, such as the one which states that a woman from the Virgin Islands who marries a person who does not belong to the Virgin Islands loses her status as a belonger of the Virgin Islands,[40] violates the provisions of the United Nations Convention on the Elimination of Discrimination Against Women to which the British Virgin Islands is a party. These laws also violate the Convention on the Rights of the Child, as the illegitimate child derives its status from its mother and would consequently suffer the same discriminatory fate as the mother.

The Act does not operate to legitimate a person if, when he was born, either of his parents was married to a third person.[41] A legitimated person assumes all the rights and obligations of a legitimate person as from the date of his legitimation.[42] An illegitimate person who dies after the commencement of the Act but before the marriage of his parents will be deemed to have acquired the same rights to property as a legitimated child as from the date of the marriage of his parents, which will be taken as the date of his legitimation.[43] An application must be made to the High Court by petition for a declaration of legitimacy.[44]

Since there are so many children being born out of wedlock, it is evident that many persons are having children together but are not getting married to each other. Legitimation is, therefore, not a viable route to the child's acquisition of inheritance rights as few will be able to take advantage of this law. There is urgent need for the British Virgin Islands to enact legislation to grant equality of rights to all children, such as the Status of Children legislation enacted in most other Caribbean jurisdictions.

VIII ADOPTION

A Requirements for adoption

The law of adoption is to be found in the Adoption of Children Act[45] which provides for adoption orders to be made by the High Court.[46] The adoptee must be a minor and resident in the Territory. The adopter may be a single person over the age of 25 years, unless it is the mother of the child who is the adoptee, or at least 21 years older than the child, save in cases where the adoptees are close relatives, including the mother or putative father of the

---

40 Section 2, the Virgin Islands (Constitution) Order 1976.
41 *Ibid.*
42 Section 8.
43 Section 7.
44 Section 4.
45 Cap 269 of the Laws of the Virgin Islands.
46 Section 9.

child. Save in exceptional circumstances, an adoption order will not be made in favour of a sole male applicant allowing him to adopt a female child. A spouse may not adopt without the consent of the other spouse unless the other spouse cannot be found, is incapable of consenting, or the spouses have permanently separated.[47] 'Spouse' means married spouses. Persons in common law relationships cannot adopt jointly, regardless of the duration and stability of the common law relationship.

B Consent to adoption

The parents or guardian or the persons having actual custody of the child must consent to the adoption unless the court dispenses with their consent. The court will not make an adoption order unless it is satisfied that all the required consents have been received, that the persons consenting understand the nature and effect of the adoption order, the order is for the welfare of the infant and that there has been no payment or promise of payment or other reward in respect of the adoption.[48]

C Effect of adoption order

The adoption order extinguishes all the rights and obligations of the parents or guardians of the adoptee which now vest in the adopters. The order does not, however, deprive an adopted child from inheriting from its natural parent on intestacy and does not entitle an adopted child to inherit from its adopted parents.[49]

IX INHERITANCE RIGHTS

Matters of inheritance are dealt with under a multiplicity of statutes.

A Adoption and inheritance

The Adoption Act provides that an adoption order does not confer on the adopted child any right or interest in property as a child of the adopter, and the expressions 'child', 'children' and 'issue' where used in a disposition whether made before or after the making of an adoption order, shall not, unless the contrary intention appears, include an adopted child or children or issue of an adopted child.[50]

---

[47] Section 3.
[48] Section 4.
[49] Section 6.
[50] Section 6(2), Adoption Act, Cap 269.

The fact that the adoption order does not deprive the adopted child from inheriting from its natural parent does not make the situation any more acceptable. It is contrary to the concept of the adoption order extinguishing the rights and obligations of the natural parents for the adopted child to be able automatically to inherit from its natural parents and be debarred from inheriting from its adoptive parents and most jurisdictions of the Commonwealth Caribbean have expunged this anomalous provision from their laws.

B   Legitimation and inheritance

Under the legitimacy laws, the legitimated child becomes entitled to succeed to its parents' estate only from the date of legitimation. If there are legitimate children surviving the parent, an illegitimate child cannot share in the parent's estate on intestacy.[51] A mother is entitled to inherit from her illegitimate child on intestacy. There is no similar right in a father who might have been maintaining the child under a court order or voluntarily. This is another case scenario for enacting Status of Children laws.

C   Intestacy laws

The inheritance laws provide that on intestacy the surviving spouse is entitled to the personal chattels absolutely and in addition the net sum of $240 or a sum equivalent to 10% of the net value of the estate (excluding the personal chattels) whichever may be greater, free of death duties and costs. If there are no issue, the surviving spouse gets a life interest in the residuary estate; and if there are issue, the spouse gets a life interest in one half of the estate, with the other half being held in trust for the issue.[52] These laws are very archaic and are in urgent need of reform. The modern trend is to give the surviving spouse the entire property where there are no children and where there are children to grant the spouse an absolute share in half of the property.

D   No laws to recognise cohabitation

There are no laws granting rights to inheritance or maintenance to persons in common law unions in the British Virgin Islands.

---

[51]   Section 11(1), Legitimacy Act, Cap 271.
[52]   Section 4, Intestates Estates Act, Cap 34.

X DOMESTIC VIOLENCE

A Definition of domestic violence

The Domestic Violence (Summary Proceedings) Act 1996 provides protection from domestic violence which it defines as 'any act of violence whether physical or verbal abuse perpetrated by a member of a household upon a member of the same household which causes or is likely to cause physical, mental or emotional injury or harm to the abused party or any other member of the household'.[53]

B Persons protected under the legislation

The Act offers protection from violence to a spouse, a former spouse, a common law spouse and former common law spouse; any member of the household; a parent, including parent or grandparent of the spouse or respondent either by consanguinity or affinity; a child under 18 years of the parties, including an adopted child, a child who has been living in the household residence as a member of the family, a child of a common law union, a child residing in the household on a regular basis and a child of whom either the man or woman is the guardian; and also, a dependant.[54]

C Orders that the court can make

The court is empowered to make a protection order prohibiting the respondent:

(a) from entering or remaining in the household of a specified person;

(b) from entering or remaining in a specified area where the household residence of a specified person is located;

(c) from entering the place of work or education of a specified person;

(d) from molesting a specified person by –

    (i) watching or besetting the specified person's household residence, place of work or education;

    (ii) following or waylaying the specified person in any place;

    (iii) making persistent telephone calls or sending in writing any form of correspondence, whether in handwriting or by mechanical or electronic means, to a specified person; or

---

[53] Section 2.
[54] Section 3.

(iv) using abusive language or behaving towards a specified person in any manner which is of such nature and degree as to cause annoyance to or result in ill-treatment of the specified person.[55]

The court may make the order if it is satisfied that the respondent has used or threatened to use violence against or caused physical or mental injury to a specified person, is likely to do so again and it is necessary for the protection of the person that the order should be made. If the court thinks it fit, the court may attach a power of arrest to the order.[56]

D   Additional orders that the court can make

In addition to the orders stated above, the court can also make:

(a) a tenancy order vesting a tenancy of a dwelling house in the applicant;[57]

(b) an order granting the applicant the use of furniture, household appliances and household effects in the residence to which the occupation or tenancy order relates;[58]

(c) an order discharging the tenancy order and re-vesting the tenancy;[59]

(d) recommend that either or both parties participate in counselling.[60]

E   Penalty for breach of the order

The penalty for contravention of an order is a maximum fine of $5,000, or imprisonment for 6 months, or both.[61] The Act provides for an appeal which does not suspend the operation of the order unless the court so directs.

F   Other important provisions in the Act

The Act also makes provision for *ex parte* orders and interim orders to be granted in situations of emergency[62] and provides for hearings in camera.[63] The Act makes it an offence punishable on conviction by a fine of $5,000, for persons to publish any report of proceedings (other than criminal proceedings) without leave of the court.[64]

---

[55]   Section 4.
[56]   Section 4(2).
[57]   Section 11.
[58]   Section 16.
[59]   Section 14.
[60]   Section 22.
[61]   Section 5.
[62]   Sections 4(3), 9 and 12.
[63]   Section 18.
[64]   Section 20.

XI CONCLUSION

The British Virgin Islands, as a British Overseas Territory, cannot of itself defend its human rights legislative record in the international arena. That is the preserve of its parent country who must report to the United Nations Committee on the Rights of the Child and similar Committees to give an account of its stewardship post ratification of the various human rights conventions. The Constitution, the law which sets the tone of discrimination against women and their illegitimate children, despite proposals for reform and a draft Bill, has not been amended.

Further, obligations under the United Nations Convention on the Elimination of Discrimination Against Women remain unfulfilled. Meanwhile, the rights of many women and children of the British Virgin Islands languish in the murky waters of discriminatory laws in a land to which many are lured with the promise of sparkling clear waters. Even the provisions which have been identified in this paper as being discriminatory towards men, such as their equal right to maintenance, are based on the underlying assumptions which have been conceived on the patriarchal bed of inequality and bear no semblance to the reality on the ground. Men are not always the breadwinners and the laws need to recognise this. Women do not all enter the holy state of matrimony. All children are not conceived in the marital bed or during a temporary pause in a procession to the altar so that they will not all benefit from either the matrimonial law or the legitimation laws. All are, however, entitled to be maintained and to share in their inheritance of their fathers, as well as mothers.

The United Nations Committee on the Rights of the Child in its Concluding Observations on the Report of (Overseas Territories): United Kingdom Great Britain and Northern Ireland on 16 October 2000, recommended that that State party 'undertake a legal compatibility review to ensure that domestic legislation in each of the Overseas Territories fully conforms with and positively reflects the principles and provisions of the Convention'. The Committee was 'concerned that insufficient efforts have (sic) been made to ensure the full implementation of article 2 of the Convention and that discrimination based on birth status remain apparent' and recommended 'a review of domestic legislation in the Overseas Territories to ensure full compliance with article 2 of the Convention to prevent and combat discrimination especially as regards gender, sexual orientation and birth status'.[65]

But there is hope. A legislature that could produce such an innovative piece of legislation as the Domestic Violence (Summary Proceedings) Act, which in so many ways is ahead of similar Caribbean regional and even international legislation, must have within its collective bosom the political

---

[65]   Concluding Observations/Comments of the Committee on the Rights of the Child CRC/C/15/Add 135.

will to repeal these archaic laws that perpetuate discrimination against its citizenry, both female and to a lesser extent, male, and most importantly, its children.

I remain hopeful that the recommendations of the Committee on the Rights of the Child have not fallen on barren ground and will bear fruit in the near future.

Cameroon

THE FAMILY CODE:
A SATISFACTORY GESTATION PERIOD

Ephraim Ngwafor[*]

Résumé

La nature bi-juridique du système légal du Cameroun, provenant de la cohabitation de juridictions de *common law* et de droit civil, a été une importante source de conflits juridiques. L'application du droit coutumier devant certaines instances, entraîne également son lot de difficultés. Les questions liées, et souvent débattues, du choix de la juridiction et de la détermination de la loi personnelle, renvoient constamment les Camerounais anglophones et francophones à leur passé colonial. Il n'est donc pas étonnant que les auteurs aient salué l'élaboration d'un projet de Code de la famille uniforme qui harmonisera ces systèmes juridiques, comblera des lacunes dans certains domaine, comme celui du divorce, des droits de propriété et de l'adoption et qui devrait nécessairement introduire plus d'uniformité dans la jurisprudence.

I INTRODUCTION

Cameroon's colonial past is similar to that of other African countries. It connotes the reception and implantation of European imposed legal systems. However, Cameroon's peculiarity stems from the fact that unlike in most African countries where either the received Civil Law or Common Law prevails, mindful of its colonial past, these two legal systems operate in well-defined areas of the national territory. English-speaking Cameroonians practise the Common Law while their Francophone counterparts practise Civil Law. It is also worth mentioning that in addition to these two systems of law there is the prevalence of customary law in well-defined jurisdictions throughout the national territory.[1]

Under statutory law, original jurisdiction to try and hear matrimonial matters is vested in the High Court.[2] However, customary law matters are dealt with

---

[*]   Professor of Law at the University of Yaoundé.

[1]   Ephraim N Ngwafor 'CAMEROON: The Law Across the Bridge: Twenty years (1972–1992) of confusion' (1995) 26 RGD at 69–77.

[2]   Section 16(1)(b) of the Judicial Organisation Ordinance No 72/4 of 26 August 1972, as modified by Law No 89/019 of 29 December 1989.

in customary courts and it has been emphatically stated in s 9(1)(b) of the Southern Cameroons High Court Law 1955 that:

> 'Subject to the provisions of the Land and Native Right Ordinance and any other written law, the High Court shall not exercise original jurisdiction in any suit or matter which is subject to the jurisdiction of a native court relating to marriage, family status, guardianship of children, inheritance or the disposition of property on death.'

It is only at the level of an Appeal Court that issues on statutory law and customary law can be canvassed coming in the form of appeals from the High Court and the customary court respectively. It is at this second level that a serious conflict has emerged. The result has been that on several occasions customary law finds itself on a collision course with the written law.[3]

II FIRST STEPS TOWARDS HARMONISATION

The first attempt by Parliament to harmonise Family Law in Cameroon was made in 1968, when Law No 68/LF/2 of 11 June 1968 organising Civil Status Registration was passed. Indeed in addition to carrying out birth and death registrations it also did so for marriages. However, the 1968 Law dealt exclusively with formalities to marry,[4] making no reference to capacity to marry. This lacuna was filled in former West Cameroon (English-speaking) by the Nigerian Marriage Ordinance,[5] while the relevant provisions of the 1968 Law and the French Civil Code applied in former East Cameroon (French-speaking). Received Nigerian Law is one of the sources of law in English-speaking Cameroon. In fact art 9 of the British Mandate Agreement on the Cameroons did give Britain the liberty, inter alia, to:

> '... Constitute the territory into a customs, fiscal and administrative union or federation with the adjacent territories under the sovereignty or control provided always that the measures adopted to that end do not infringe the provisions of this mandate.'

It is on the strength of this provision that Britain fused together the British Cameroons with its Nigerian Protectorate for administrative and judicial purposes.[6]

Following the shortcomings of the 1968 Law it was repealed and its provisions consolidated in a new ordinance in 1981, namely, Ordinance No 81/2 of 29 June 1981. A big step was made by the introduction of provisions

---

[3] See generally, E N Ngwafor 'Customary Law versus Statutory Law: An Unresolved Second Millennium Moral Quagmire' (2000) *Int Surv Fam L* P 55; E N Ngwafor 'NULLITY: The Squaring of a Questionable Dilemma' (1994) *Int Surv Fam L* 101.

[4] Sections 38–44.

[5] Chapter 115, Vol IV of the Revised Laws of the Federation of Nigeria.

[6] See the British Cameroon Order-in-Council No 1621 of June 1922 which ordered the fusion of British Cameroon to Eastern Cameroon.

concerning capacity to marry. But there was a total absence in the discussion of divorce property rights, guardianship, adoption, etc.

III CONFUSION IN CHOICE OF PERSONAL LAW

The passing of the 1981 Ordinance did not help the courts very much on the issue of harmonisation, although there was some form of a uniform legal thread underlying the national territory. But there still existed evident inconveniences. In 1972 there was the merger of the two Federated States of East Cameroon (former French colony) and West Cameroon (former British colony) into the United Republic of Cameroon.[7] The new Constitution,[8] guaranteed the preservation of the two legal systems in its art 38:

> 'The legislation resulting from the laws and regulations applicable in the Federal State of Cameroon and in the Federated States on the day of entry into force of this constitution shall remain in force in all their dispositions which are not contrary to the stipulation of this constitution, for as long as it is not amended by legislative or regulatory powers.'

IV THE DILEMMA

The new United Republic came along with many administrative innovations. Cameroonians were almost immediately transferred from one jurisdiction to another. Anglophones were transferred to former East Cameroon while Francophones were sent to take up duties in former West Cameroon. And that is how the conflict of laws problem was born. Francophone Cameroonians who were transferred, say to Bamenda (a city in the English Law jurisdiction), and who eventually had a matrimonial dispute, were now confronted with the question of whether the High Court in Bamenda had any jurisdiction to entertain the matter. It was the same dilemma with a couple from former West Cameroon (British Cameroon) who were sent to work in Yaounde (a city in former East Cameroon), for example. Would the High Court in Yaounde be competent to hear the matter? For convenience reasons, Cameroonians who were domiciled in the Common Law jurisdiction, for example, found themselves petitioning for divorce in a Civil Law jurisdiction and vice versa. There are many examples and the following cases have been chosen at random, *Mbiaffie v Mbiaffie*,[9] *Nseke v Nseke*,[10] *Moussi v Moussi*,[11] *Donfack Marie v Kouati Daniel*,[12] *Yamnose Née Ngounou Thérèse v Yamnose Dieudonné*,[13] *Lelpon née Ngessi Helene v*

---

[7] See generally C Anyangwe 'The Administration of Justice in a Bi-jurial country – The United Republic of Cameroon'. Thesis submitted for the degree of Doctor of Philosophy (unpublished), University of London, 1979.

[8] Constitution of 2 June 1972.

[9] Unreported judgment of 3 September 1985, Suit No HCSW/30mc/85.

[10] Unreported judgment of 6 June 1985, Suit No HCSW/108mc/84.

[11] Unreported judgment of 6 June 1988, Suit No HFC/115mc/87.

[12] Unreported judgment of 27 March 1985, Suit No HCSW/12mc/83.

[13] Unreported judgment of 9 October 1990, Suit No HCF/9mc/89.

Lelpon Daniel[14] and *Onana v Onana*.[15] The parties in these cases were domiciled in former East Cameroon (Civil Law jurisdiction), had lived all their lives there, and yet decided to petition for divorce in a Common Law jurisdiction where they had been sent to work. In fact in two of the above cases the parties were married in France, returned to Cameroon and lived in former East Cameroon (Civil Law jurisdiction) before being transferred to former West Cameroon,[16] while in one other case[17] not only were the parties domiciled in former East Cameroon (Civil Law), but all the events which led to the case occurred in East Cameroon, and the matter was brought in the High Court in a Common Law jurisdiction, following their transfer to Buea (a city in former British Cameroon).

Examples which spring to mind concern citizens in former British Cameroon and whose only reason for presenting their petition for divorce in the former French Cameroon is that they were either employed or transferred there: *Arrêt Lantum*,[18] *Arrêt Jua*,[19] *Arrêt Iketuonye*,[20] all of which suffered several appeals in the Court of Appeal in this Civil Law jurisdiction. In fact, *Arrêt Lantum* went right up to the Supreme Court, and has been a subject of heated debates for several years.

Undeniably, we have two systems of law in Cameroon, the Civil Law applicable in former East Cameroon and the Common Law applicable in former West Cameroon. Will it be proper for a judge who has been schooled in a Civil Law system to hear and try matters concerning English Law? Yet we are not unaware of the fact that conditions like capacity to marry and jurisdiction to grant divorce are governed by a person's domicile. In other words such problems can only be resolved by referring to the person's domicile. This problem, however, does not apply in the case where the parties have now acquired a domicile of choice. Indeed when the Court of Appeal in February 1991, heard and tried the case of *Biaka v Biaka*,[21] any reader of Private International Law would have raised no objection notwithstanding the fact that Dr Biaka's roots were found to be in French Cameroon, for the facts disclosed that he had acquired a domicile of choice in former British Cameroon.[22]

It is true that to choose one's personal law, there must exist a connecting factor. Ordinarily, a connecting factor establishes a natural connection between a factual situation before the court and a particular legal system. Two of such connecting factors are domicile and nationality.

From the decisions arrived at in the courts in the Civil Law jurisdiction, it is clear that nationality has been used as a connecting factor. But should this

---

[14]   Unreported judgment of 12 June 1989, Suit No HCSW/76mc/85.
[15]   Suit No HCSW/38mc/85.
[16]   Above note 9; above note 15.
[17]   *Ondoa v Ondoa*, Suit No HCSW/127mc/85.
[18]   CL Arrêt No 94 CC of 4 May 1977.
[19]   Arrêt No 636 CC of 10 June 1986.
[20]   Arrêt No 64 CC of 18 January 1988.
[21]   Unreported judgment of 28 February 1991. Appeal No CASWP/37/90.
[22]   See also *Ngengwe v Ngengwe*, Suit No HCSW/-/81.

practice kick against the law as it is? Why should an Anglophone Cameroonian who is domiciled in former British Cameroon have his matter heard by a judge who is exclusively specialised in Civil Law? An example of adversity can be seen in the provisions of s 49 of Ordinance No 81-02 of 29 June 1981,[23] which requires the spouses-to-be to mention in their marriage certificate if they opt for co-ownership or separation of property. Presuming two English-speaking Cameroonians contract a monogamous marriage in the Civil Law jurisdiction (eg in Yaounde), but, as is almost always the case, they fail to state in the marriage certificate any of the options found in s 49, in the event of any breakdown of the marriage what will be the Civil Law judge's guidelines? His training will oblige him to employ the mechanism of community of property, mindful of the fact that it is a monogamous marriage. But these are people who are domiciled in a Common Law jurisdiction wherein the principle as applied is that English law knows no community of property.[24]

This same problem of choice of law also exists when the parties opt for a customary law marriage. There are more than 200 ethnic groups in Cameroon and although there is some resemblance of their various laws each tribe has a unique set of customary laws. If a man from tribe A gets married to a woman from this same tribe, there will be no problem as to the choice of the native law and custom, should they eventually go to court. The customary law of A will apply. The matter becomes complicated if a man from tribe C gets married to a woman from tribe D. What determines whether it will be the customary law of tribe C or that of tribe D that will govern the parties in the event of any legal problem? This is a long-standing dispute.[25]

But a more far-reaching conflict could arise where spouses from one tribe travel to a completely different district having customary laws that are foreign to theirs. In the event of the breakdown of the marriage in this foreign jurisdiction, will the customary court have jurisdiction? In the case of *Theresia Ndamken v Martin Sab*,[26] the spouses were married according to the native laws and customs of the Akum or Bafang tribes. But because the respondent was working in Buea, and the parties lived there (where the Bakweri native laws and custom apply), the petitioner filed her suit in Buea. The respondent disputed the jurisdiction of the Buea Customary Court arguing that the matter ought to be heard either by the Akum or Bafang Customary Court. This argument was very well founded, but the court went

---

23   Which governs Civil Status Registration in Cameroon.

24   *Pettit v Pettit* (1970) AC 777 (HL). See also S Melone 'Le Droit civil contre la coutume, La fin d'une suprématie à propos des effets patrimoniaux du marriage', *Rev Cam De Droit*, No 1, p 12; and P G Pougoue 'La Famille et la terre, essai de contribution à la systematisation du droit privé au Cameroun', these de Doctorat d'Etat en Droit, Université de Bordeaux, 1977, p 117, which discuss the peculiarities of the case where the spouses in former East Cameroon fail to draw up a contract, before marriage, defining their respective rights to property before and after the marriage ceremony.

25   But the Manual of Practice and Procedure for Court Clerks provides that the applicable law will be that of the parents of the girl.

26   Case No 166/86-87 – CRB/3-86, p 81.

ahead with the case contending that the petitioner was born in Buea and had permanently lived there. In any case, even if the court in Buea had accepted that Akum and Bafang customary laws could apply, the tendency today would be to hear the matter in Buea presided over by judges versed in Akum and Bafang customary laws.

It could happen that a customary court would expressly refuse to hear a matter if there is a conflict of laws problem. In *Ayuk Etang Elias Bechem v Manyi Agbor Serah and Agbor Simon*,[27] the Kumba Customary Court disclaimed jurisdiction on the strength of the respondent's argument that, according to the *Manyu Native Law* (under which the marriage was contracted), dowry is not refunded until the divorced woman remarries. This principle, the court noted, was different from that of the Bafaw people and so the case was accordingly transferred to Manyu Division.

Such a matter also arose in the Court of Appeal in Bamenda in the case of *Onana v Onana*,[28] where the parties had been married according to the customary laws of the Beti people. In a petition for divorce filed in the Mankon Customary Court, a dissolution of the marriage was ordered. On appeal it was held that as the parties had got married in Yaounde according to the customs of the Beti tribe, the Mankon Customary Court had no jurisdiction to hear the matter.

V THE FAMILY CODE: NEW HORIZONS

For the past 5 years the Government of Cameroon has made known its intentions to present a modern and uniform Law on Family matters in Cameroon. Before the 2004 Presidential elections many opposition parties took the view that the promise was a mere political gimmick. However, at the beginning of the year 2004, a draft Family Code was presented to the public. As Cameroonians anxiously waited to see this document debated in Parliament and eventually promulgated into Law, suffice it to state here that, a large portion of the inconveniences so far experienced in our legal system, would soon be a forgotten past.

A The inroads

1 Marriage

It should be noted that today two types of marriages are recognised in Cameroon: statutory marriage otherwise known as monogamous marriage and customary law marriage otherwise known as polygamous marriage. As indicated earlier judges usually found themselves in troubled waters when called upon to determine what type of marriage the couple had opted for, with the inherent question of which court had jurisdiction, the High Court or

---

27 Case No 44/85-86 – CRB 2/85-86, p 37.
28 Appeal No BCA/13cc/89.

the Customary Court. In fact in the case of *Motanga v Motanga*,[29] the parties to a marriage contract had failed to mention the type of marriage opted for, that is, whether it was monogamous or polygamous. In a very stunning judgment the judge averred that:

'The spouses must specifically state and must mention in the marriage certificate that the marriage is monogamous, otherwise the presumption is that it is polygamous, because a Cameroonian is polygamous by birth.'

More confusion was experienced in the case of *Asa'ah v Asa'ah*,[30] where the parties opted for both a customary marriage and a statutory marriage as registered in their marriage certificate, namely:

'... married according to the native laws and customs of Nweh Mundani and by the Cameroon Civil Status and Regulations.'

With the coming into force of the Family Code this uncertainty will be laid to rest. Such a conclusion may, however, be difficult to arrive at. When the 1981 Ordinance was passed, parties to a monogamous marriage who had satisfied both the conditions of capacity and formalities could present themselves before a civil status registrar and be issued with a certificate at the end of the ceremony. But this was not the case with those who preferred to get married under customary law. In this respect what was of paramount relevance for its validity was the fact that traditions had not been breached. Once the gifts and the bride price had rightfully changed hands the parties were declared husband and wife by their parents and elders. There was nothing in the form of a document serving as public notice. The marriage was valid and could not be challenged. This was the peaceful manner in which things were arranged in the village.

The problem, however, arose in the case where the parties got married under customary law and had to show proof of their marriage in order to enjoy the benefits accruing to married people. What immediately springs to mind in Cameroon are tax rebates, travelling benefits and family allowances. The tendency, therefore, for this group of people, was to present themselves in a magistrates' court, praying to the court for a declaratory judgment, the purport of which was merely to state in written form the fact that the couple had some time ago (it could be as long ago as 15 years or more) been married according to their native laws and customs of a particular ethnic group. What is momentous here is the fact that this document had nothing to do with the validity of marriage. It merely proved to the administrators concerned that the couple could equally enjoy the benefits mentioned above. Indeed one can always cite scores of examples of those who had to visit the magistrates' courts for this purpose after 15 years or so of a very happy customary law marriage. This simply means that the customary law marriage was celebrated, independently of the requirements of the 1981 Ordinance. However, s 4 of the 1981 Ordinance does not only make the registration of

---

[29] Suit No HCB/2/76 (unreported).
[30] Unreported judgment of 21 December 1994, Suit No HCF/66/94.

both monogamous and polygamous marriages obligatory, but failure to do so will be met with a criminal charge preferred against the parties concerned.

If s 4 talks of registration of all marriages (whether monogamous or polygamous), s 48 stipulates that 'a marriage shall be celebrated by a civil status registrar'. Ordinarily, this could be interpreted to mean that all those who celebrated their marriages according to native law and custom are obliged, under penalty of a criminal charge, to register their marriage with a civil status registrar. Section 81(1) of the same 1981 Ordinance provides that 'customary marriages shall be recorded in the civil status register of the place of birth or residence of the spouses'. Such a registration (or recording) has nothing to do with its validity. The civil status registrar has no *locus standi* to start the ceremony all over again. His job is mainly to record the marriage in the civil status register. In pursuance of this purpose, he could ask the parents and the elders of the couple if the necessary customs of the ethnic group in question had been respected. This only goes to prove that the celebration did, in fact, take place.

On the contrary by s 48 of the 1981 Ordinance he is bound to celebrate a monogamous marriage, making sure that he puts across to the spouses-to-be all the necessary questions. So, in this second case, the civil status registrar celebrates before registering. Unfortunately our civil status registrars have misunderstood their role, and so have attempted on several occasions to celebrate a marriage which the parties maintain had already been celebrated according to the native laws and customs of their tribe.

It is imperative that we take cognisance of our present social reality. To this day, marriages in villages, for example, are celebrated according to the native laws and customs of the parties. The couples of these 'valid' marriages have been living their lives in their homes since celebrating their marriages after 1981, with every other member of that society accepting them as married people. Their children are taken to be legitimate. These people are self-employed and do not care much about the intricate facets of obtaining any documentary proof of their marriage. This is understandable since self-employed citizens are not entitled to the State benefits accruing to civil servants.

The inevitable question is, are these marriages invalid simply because they have not been registered? The new Family Code recognises only a statutory marriage although the men may opt for either one or more wives.[31] And even in the event of choosing more than one wife (polygamy) the parties must fulfil the statutory formalities to marry, for example, there must be publication of banns. In other words the new Code does not recognise customary law marriages. Indeed, the payment of bride price or award of gifts as required by custom shall have no legal effect on the marriage.[32] Such goods when received shall not be refundable under any circumstances.[33]

---

31   Section 154(f).
32   Section 232.
33   Section 233.

Another blow to the customary law structure comes from the express provision in the new Code that any petition for divorce can be entertained only by the High Court. No mention is made of the customary courts and the application of its laws. More so s 263 finally resolves the problem of the connecting factor as to the personal law of the parties raised earlier in this work. In other words the question of jurisdiction has been resolved in the new Code.

As to capacity to marry the Code has put a minimum age of marriage for both parties at 18 years.[34] Under the 1981 Ordinance the girl has to be at least 15 years and the boy 18 years.[35]

2   Divorce

Much has been borrowed from English Law in the new Family Code. Although no direct reference was made to the Matrimonial Causes Act 1973, the elements in s 1(2)(a)–(e) can be found in s 264 of the Code. It is also interesting to note that the Code did not adopt the spirit of no-fault divorce. Indeed the estranged couple have been encouraged to remarry even after divorce.[36] And to discourage divorce, damages may be awarded against a spouse who is responsible for the breakdown of the marriage.[37]

3   Property rights

The new Family Code recognises two types of property regimes, that is separate ownership of property and communal ownership of property. And in this connection property regime shall mean the system that shall regulate the ownership of property of the spouses at the time of the celebration of their marriage.[38] For an English trained lawyer certain sections under this heading may sound inconsistent with the contents of his textbooks. Speaking loosely, English Law knows no community of property.[39] But under the new Code separate ownership shall apply to a polygamous marriage.[40] But where the spouses opt for a monogamous marriage, they shall, at the time of the celebration of the marriage, choose one of the types of the property regime referred to in s 437 above, that is either separate ownership or communal ownership of property. But should they opt for a monogamous marriage without specifying the regime, they shall be deemed to have opted for joint ownership of property.[41] In this case English Law principles would be jettisoned to the background since English Law knows no community of property. This principle of separation of property only surfaces in polygamous marriages where the Code expressly provides that in that case the husband shall constitute with each of his wives a separate matrimonial

---

34   Section 219.
35   Section 52(1).
36   Section 265(1).
37   Section 268.
38   Section 437(1).
39   *Pettit v Pettit* (1970) AC 777 (HL).
40   Section 439.
41   Section 440.

home.[42] In this case no spouse shall be obliged to provide for the needs of her co-spouses or those of their children.[43]

The new Code is categorical as to pre-nuptial agreements. In fact it provides that a marriage settlement shall be concluded before the celebration of the marriage and shall take effect on the day of such celebration.[44]

4   Adoption

The application of English Law has been fraught with a lot of difficulty in Anglophone Cameroon. This has been especially so because the 1981 Ordinance has been laconic on the issue, and above all there is no substantive law on adoption applicable in former West Cameroon. Hence should any matter arise on this subject the High Court will be at a loss as to the applicable law. This explains why the Court of Appeal decision in the case of *Dr Bernard Fonlon v Judith Fonlon and 8 others*,[45] in which the court decided to apply the English Adoption Act 1958, has been classified as bad law.[46]

It has been argued that the slow-paced attitude to legislate on adoption in Cameroon resulted from the objection that statutory adoption runs counter to the African concept of the family where the acquisition of membership is by birth.[47] And from the economic point of view, statutory adoption could enable a 'stranger' to control family property, especially landed property. Another argument posited against the law on adoption is founded on the assumption that it is unnecessary since any member of a family is morally bound to take over and care for any child who loses his or her parents. In a sense, some form of social insurance is created to cater for such calamities in the family. This explains why a court will prefer to hand over an orphan to the relatives of the deceased parents than to a stranger in blood. This is precisely what the courts did in *Mary Lumi v Mutanga Ake*.[48]

The draft Family Code now sets the pace for a National Law on adoption. When applied the child shall sever his relationship with his family of origin and establish a new one with his adoptive family.[49] Not only does it state the procedure for adoption, but it also lays down the list of persons who can be adopted and the occasions when the consent of the child will be required.[50]

5   Guardianship and other matters

Another innovation found in the Family Code is the introduction of the issue of guardianship in cases where the person in charge of a minor is unable to

---

[42]   Section 260(1).
[43]   Section 260(2).
[44]   Section 444.
[45]   Appeal No BCA/2/75 (unreported).
[46]   E N Ngwafor *Family Law in Anglophone Cameroon* (1993) pp 240–243.
[47]   Kasunmu and Salacuse *Nigerian Family Law* (1966) p 243.
[48]   Suit No HCB/13/73 (unreported).
[49]   Section 311.
[50]   Section 314.

express his wish as a result of distance, incapacity, absence, or death of both parents.[51] The burning issues of minors,[52] succession,[53] gifts[54] and wills[55] have also been provided for.

VI CONCLUSION

The draft Family Code is a comprehensive document, which could rightly be considered historic. Having been overladen with received European Laws, Cameroon, at last, will soon be able to exploit a uniform National Law on family matters. The Code comprises 701 sections, divided up into 15 Parts. It is, however, regrettable that the drafting committee failed to consider the very topical issue of artificial insemination and the realities of surrogacy. It is high time Cameroon, like other countries, also drafted a law to cover this ever-expanding scientific method of having babies.

All in all the Family Code is salutary. Let us only hope that having suffered an unusual gestation period, the maternity is now poised to receive this beautiful baby. The promulgation of the Family Code will only go to add to the list of harmonised laws in Cameroon: the Penal Code, the Labour Code, Land Law, and most recently the Criminal Procedure Code (2005), to name but a few.

---

[51] Section 363.
[52] Part X.
[53] Part XIII.
[54] Part XIV.
[55] Part XV.

Canada

SAME-SEX MARRIAGE AND FAITH-BASED ARBITRATION OF FAMILY LAW DISPUTES

Martha Bailey[*]

Résumé

Deux questions de droit familial ont particulièrement attiré l'attention publique au cours de la dernière année. La première est celle de l'ouverture du mariage aux couples de même sexe. Depuis juin 2003 les couples de même sexe avaient la possibilité de se marier civilement dans certaines parties du Canada, à la suite de décisions de tribunaux qui en étaient arrivés à la conclusion que l'interdiction du mariage homosexuel allait à l'encontre de la garantie constitutionnelle en matière d'égalité et que, par conséquent, le certificat de mariage devait sur le champs être accordé aux couples de même sexe qui décident de se marier. Dans la foulée d'un débat public aussi vaste que musclé, le mariage entre personnes de même sexe est, depuis le mois de juillet 2005, reconnu dans une loi fédérale qui est applicable partout au pays.

La seconde question qui a considérablement retenu l'attention publique est celle de l'instauration éventuelle de tribunaux religieux en matières familiale et successorale. La controverse s'est essentiellement cristallisée autour de l'application possible de certains principes de droit personnel islamique à la situation de conjoints ayant accepté de soumettre leur litige à un tribunal arbitral religieux. À l'issue d'une vaste consultation et d'une enquête, le gouvernement de l'Ontario a proposé une réforme législative qui limiterait le choix du régime juridique que pourraient faire les parties lorsqu'elles soumettent leur différend d'ordre familial à l'arbitrage. Cette proposition a suscité de nombreuses critiques et le projet pourrait bien faire l'objet d'importants amendements en commission parlementaire. Le législateur ontarien fait ici face à un conflit bien connu opposant, d'une part, le souci de respecter l'autonomie de la volonté en matières familiales et, d'autre par, la nécessité de protéger les personnes vulnérables. De plus, le législateur est déchiré entre le souci de trouver des accommodements multiculturels et le danger d'exacerber la vulnérabilité des femmes qui peut résulter de tels accommodements réclamés pour des raisons religieuses.

Le Canada a également connu des développements importants, quoique moins publicisés, dans le domaine du droit alimentaire. La Cour suprême s'est ainsi penchée sur la délicate question de l'application des règles de fixation des

---

[*] Associate Professor, Faculty of Law, Queen's University, Kingston, Ontario.

pensions alimentaires pour enfants dans la situation particulière de la garde partagée. Quant aux aliments pour conjoints, de nouvelles lignes directrices facultatives ont été proposées. Ce projet visant à mieux encadrer l'exercice de détermination de la pension alimentaire pour conjoints, n'en est qu'à ses débuts, mais il semble déjà promis à un bel avenir.

I   INTRODUCTION

Two family law issues garnered significant public attention over the past year. The first was the opening up of civil marriage to same-sex couples. Civil marriage has been available to same-sex couples in parts of Canada since June 2003, pursuant to court rulings in some provinces that the limitation of civil marriage to opposite-sex couples violated the constitutional guarantee of equality and that marriage licenses must be issued to same-sex couples immediately.[1] Beginning in July 2005, in the context of broad public debate and some heated opposition, the option of civil marriage became available to same-sex couples across the country pursuant to a federal enactment.

The second widely publicized issue was faith-based arbitration tribunals for family and inheritance law disputes. The primary focus of this controversy was the application of Islamic personal law principles to parties in Ontario who agreed to submit to a faith-based arbitral tribunal. After extensive investigation and consultation, the Government of Ontario introduced legislation that would limit the choice of law for parties who submitted family law disputes to arbitration. This proposed resolution is attracting much criticism, and the proposed legislation may well be amended during the committee deliberations on it. Ontario legislators are struggling to resolve the longstanding conflict between support for party autonomy in family law on the one hand and the need to protect vulnerable individuals on the other. In addition, they are faced with the related conflict between the value of multicultural accommodation on the one hand and the problem of exacerbating the vulnerability of women that may result from accommodating the claims of religious communities.

There were also less widely publicized but important developments in relation to child support and spousal support. The Supreme Court of Canada dealt with the issue of how to apply Canada's Child Support Guidelines in the context of shared parenting. In the matter of spousal support, Advisory Guidelines on the quantum and duration were released. Though still in the early stages, the more structured approach to determining spousal support claims seems likely to become widely adopted.

---

[1]   The first such appellate decision was *Halpern v Canada* (2003), 225 DLR (4th) 529 (Ont CA). For a more detailed discussion of the cases see Martha Bailey 'Resuscitating the Significance of Marriage' in Andrew Bainham (ed) *The International Survey of Family Law 2004 Edition* (Jordans, 2004).

II SAME-SEX MARRIAGE

The limitation of civil marriage to opposite-sex couples was successfully challenged as a violation of the equality guarantee enshrined in the Canadian *Charter of Rights and Freedoms*[2] in the appellate courts of Ontario, British Columbia and Quebec, Canada's three most populous provinces.[3] The rulings by the British Columbia and Quebec courts were initially suspended to allow the Federal Government the opportunity to correct the *Charter* violation, but these suspensions were subsequently lifted with the consent of the Attorney General of Canada. Same-sex marriages were then taking place in three provinces. Canada's Federal Government dropped its defence of the traditional definition of marriage, and announced that it would refer to the Supreme Court of Canada a draft bill to open up civil marriage to same-sex couples.

After the initiation of the reference to the Supreme Court of Canada, the traditional definition of marriage was struck down in the Yukon,[4] Manitoba,[5] Nova Scotia[6] and Saskatchewan.[7] In each of these cases, the Attorney General of Canada conceded the *Charter* violation. Thus, by the time the Supreme Court of Canada heard and decided the reference case, same-sex marriages were taking place in most of Canada.

The Government may refer important questions of law concerning the powers of the Parliament of Canada to the Supreme Court of Canada.[8] The draft bill referred to the Supreme Court provided in relevant part:

(1) Marriage, for civil purposes, is the lawful union of two persons to the exclusion of all others.

(2) Nothing in this Act affects the freedom of officials of religious groups to refuse to perform marriages that are not in accordance with their religious beliefs.

The Supreme Court was initially asked to answer three questions:

(1) Is the draft bill within the exclusive legislative authority of the Parliament of Canada?

(2) Is the section of the draft bill that extends capacity to marry to persons of the same sex consistent with the *Charter*?

(3) Does the freedom of religion guaranteed by the *Charter* protect religious officials from being compelled to perform a marriage between two persons of the same sex that is contrary to their religious beliefs?

---

[2] *Canadian Charter of Rights and Freedoms*, Part I of the Constitution Act 1982, being Sch B of the Canada Act 1982 (UK), c 11, s 15.

[3] *Halpern v Canada* (2003) 225 DLR (4th) 529 (Ont CA); *Egale v Canada* (2003) 225 DLR (4th) 472 and (2003) 228 DLR (4th) 416 (BCCA); *Hendricks v Quebec* [2004] JQ No 2593 (CA) (QL).

[4] *Dunbar v Yukon* (2004) 8 RFL (6th) 235 (YTSC).

[5] *Vogel v Canada (Attorney General)* [2004] MJ No 418 (QL) (QB).

[6] *Boutilier v Nova Scotia (Attorney General)* [2004] NSJ No 357 (QL) (SC).

[7] *N W v Canada (Attorney General)* (2004) 11 RFL (6th) 162 (Sask QB).

[8] Such references are brought pursuant to the Supreme Court Act, RSC 1985, c S-26, s 53.

In January 2004, the Federal Government added a fourth question:

(4) Is the opposite-sex requirement for marriage for civil purposes consistent with the *Charter*?

The addition of the fourth question was problematic because it operated as a *de facto* appeal of the lower court rulings that the limitation of civil marriage to opposite-sex couples violated the *Charter*. Having announced that it would not appeal these rulings and that it supported the opening up of civil marriage to same-sex couples, this 'back-door' appeal seemed to be politically calculated to appease opponents of same-sex marriage by giving them their day in court.[9]

Another problem with the addition of the fourth question was that it delayed the hearing of the reference to October 2004. The Supreme Court, however, handed down its unanimous decision just 2 months after the arguments.[10]

The Supreme Court determined that the proposed definition of marriage for civil purposes as 'the lawful union of two persons to the exclusion of all others' was within the exclusive legislative authority of the Federal Parliament pursuant to the constitutional division of powers between the Federal Parliament and the provincial legislatures. Canada's Constitution gives exclusive jurisdiction over the capacity to marry to the Federal Parliament and exclusive jurisdiction over 'solemnization of marriage within the provision to the provincial legislatures'.[11]

The Supreme Court rejected arguments that the common law definition of marriage as it stood in 1867, the year of confederation, was constitutionally fixed and could not be changed by Parliament. Noting the definition of marriage articulated in the 1866 case *Hyde v Hyde* – 'marriage, as understood in Christendom, may for this purpose be defined as the voluntary union for life of one man and one women, to the exclusion of all others'[12] – the Supreme Court said that the notion of 'Christian' marriage was no longer relevant.

Hyde spoke to a society of shared social values where marriage and religion were thought to be inseparable. This is no longer the case. Canada is a pluralistic society. Marriage, from the perspective of the state, is a civil institution.[13]

Ann Laquer Estin has discussed the religious roots but current secular nature of marriage law in the US, and her thesis that marriage no longer carries a religious character is applicable to Canada.[14] The Supreme Court firmly

---

9   The Government admitted that this was so: Justice Canada Newsroom (28 January 2004) 'Civil Marriage and the Legal Recognition of Same-sex Unions' online at http://canada.justice.gc.ca/en/news/fs/2004/doc_31108.html.

10   *Reference re Same-sex Marriage* [2004] 3 SCR 698.

11   Constitution Act 1867 (UK), 30 & 31 Vict, c 3, ss 91(26) and 92(12).

12   *Hyde v Hyde* (1866) LR 1 P & D 130 at 133, quoted in *Reference re Same-sex Marriage*, para 21.

13   *Reference re Same-sex Marriage*, at para 22.

14   Ann Laquer Estin 'Embracing Tradition: Pluralism in American Family Law' (2004) Md L Rev 540.

rejected the 'frozen concepts' reasoning that would foreclose the possibility of changing the traditional definition of marriage, reasoning that 'our Constitution is a living tree which, by way of progressive interpretation, accommodates and addresses the realities of modern life'.[15]

In regard to whether the proposed definition of marriage was consistent with the *Charter*, the Supreme Court was dismissive of arguments that it would violate the equality rights of either religious groups that do not recognise same-sex marriage or opposite-sex married couples. 'The mere recognition of the equality rights of one group cannot, in itself, constitute a violation of the rights of another.'[16]

Section 2 of the proposed Act declared that nothing in it affected the freedom of officials of religious groups to refuse to perform marriages that are not in accordance with their religious beliefs. The reason for the attention to this issue is that in Canada religious officials are empowered by the state to solemnize marriages and there is no need to have a separate civil ceremony.[17] The Supreme Court ruled that, because legislative competence over the solemnization of marriage (including who may perform marriages) is within the exclusive legislative competence of the provinces, s 2 of the proposed Act was not within the exclusive legislative competence of the Federal Parliament. However, the Supreme Court ruled that the freedom of religion guaranteed by s 2(a) of the *Charter* protects religious officials from being compelled by the state to perform same-sex marriages.

In regard to the fourth question, whether the limitation of civil marriage to opposite-sex couples was within the *Charter*, the Supreme Court exercised its rarely used discretion to decline to answer. There were three reasons for this refusal. First, the Government stated that it would proceed with the proposed Act regardless of the answer given to the fourth question. Secondly, the parties to the successful *Charter* challenges to the traditional definition of marriage had relied on the finality of the judgments. Same-sex marriages had come to be viewed as legal and were regularly taking place in most parts of Canada. The Government had indicated that it would not appeal the lower court rulings and had conceded that the common law definition of marriage was inconsistent with the constitutional guarantee of equality. In light of all this, the Supreme Court determined that there was 'no compelling basis for jeopardizing acquired rights', which might be the result of answering the fourth question. Finally, answering the fourth question would not achieve the desired result of a uniform definition of marriage for all of Canada and had the potential to create confusion.

In the result, the Supreme Court allowed the Government to proceed with its stated intention of opening up civil marriage to same-sex couples across Canada. The legislation came to a vote in the House of Commons on 28 June

---

[15] *Reference re Same-sex Marriage*, at para 22.
[16] *Reference re Same-sex Marriage*, at para 46.
[17] See, eg, Marriage Act, RSO 1990, c M3, s 20.

2005 and was passed by a 158–133 margin.[18] The Senate voted in favour of the Bill by a 47–21 margin on 19 July 2005,[19] and on the next day Chief Justice Beverley McLachlin, acting in her role as Deputy Governor General, signed the Civil Marriage Act into law.[20]

The province of Alberta had long expressed its deep-rooted opposition to same-sex marriage. Although the capacity to marry is within the exclusive legislative competence of the Federal Government, Alberta had threatened to use whatever powers it could to avoid having to solemnize same-sex marriages. Then, on 12 July 2005, just prior to final passage of the Civil Marriage Act, Premier Klein announced that Alberta would reluctantly recognize same-sex marriage in light of the legislation that was then pending before the Senate. He said that the province would issue marriage licenses to same-sex couples but that any marriage commissioner who did not want to perform a same-sex marriage would not be forced to do so.[21]

Shortly after the first same-sex marriages were celebrated in Canada came the first dissolutions of such marriages. Ontario's Superior Court of Justice ruled that the Divorce Act definition of 'spouse' as 'either of a man or woman who are married to each other'[22] violated the *Charter* and that it must be redefined as 'either of two persons who are married to each other', so as to permit the parties, who had entered into a same-sex marriage, to obtain a divorce under the Act.[23] When the Civil Marriage Act was later passed, this new definition of 'spouse' was one of the consequential amendments that was included.

In Canada the one ground of divorce is marital breakdown, but this may be proven on the basis of one year's separation, adultery or cruelty.[24] The term 'adultery' in the Divorce Act traditionally has been interpreted as voluntary sexual intercourse between a married person and a person of the opposite sex, not the other spouse, during the subsistence of the marriage.[25] This common law definition was reconsidered in 2005 in a case involving a woman who sought a divorce on the basis of her husband's 'adultery' with another man. The court reinterpreted 'adultery' to include sexual activity with a person of the same sex. In light of the fact that same-sex marriage is now permitted in Canada, additional consideration should be given to the meaning of 'adultery' or, preferably, this outmoded 'fault' ground for divorce should be abolished.

---

18   Canada, Debates of the House of Commons, 38th Parliament, 1st Session, *Edited Hansard*, no 124 (28 June 2005).

19   Canada, Debates of the Senate, 38th Parliament, 1st Session, vol 142, issue 84 (19 July 2005).

20   Civil Marriage Act, SC 2005, c 33, available online at www.parl.gc.ca/38/1/parlbus/ chambus/house/bills/government/C-38/C-38_3/C-38-4E.html.

21   'Klein drops fight against same-sex marriage' (13 July 2005) CBC News, online at www.cbc.ca/story/canada/national/2005/07/13/klein-samesex050713.html.

22   Divorce Act, RS 1985, c 3 (2nd Supp), s 2(1).

23   *M M v J H* (2004) 73 OR (3d) 337 (Sup Ct J).

24   Divorce Act, RS 1985, c 3 (2nd Supp), s 8.

25   *Orford v Orford* (1921) 49 OLR 15 (HC); *Kahl v Kahl* [1943] OWN 558 (HC); *Gaveronski v Gaveronski* (1974) 45 DLR (3d) 317 (Sask QB); *Droit de la Famille – 1005* [1986] RDF 78 (CSQ).

III FAITH-BASED ARBITRATION OF FAMILY LAW DISPUTES

The Islamic Institute of Civil Justice (IICJ) was established in Ontario in 2003 for the purpose of conducting arbitrations according to Islamic personal law.[26] Ontario's Arbitration Act allows parties to submit private law disputes to arbitration and provides for court enforcement of arbitral awards.[27] The Act gives parties considerable freedom to choose the law and procedures that will apply. Anyone chosen by the parties may serve as an arbitrator regardless of their qualifications.

The establishment of the IICJ gave rise to considerable public discussion and alarm over the possible violation of the rights of women resulting from the application of Islamic law.[28] The Government of Ontario asked Marion Boyd, a former Attorney General of Ontario, to review the arbitration process and its impact on vulnerable people.[29] Boyd consulted widely and delivered her report in December 2004.[30] Boyd's detailed report included 45 recommendations that were primarily aimed at enhancing the protection of vulnerable parties. However, her first two recommendations were controversial. First, she recommended that arbitration should continue to be an option for family and inheritance law cases. Secondly, she recommended that the Arbitration Act continue to allow disputes to be arbitrated under religious law provided the existing and recommended safeguards were observed.

Boyd's report attracted a tremendous amount of criticism in the popular press[31] and in research papers.[32] The Ontario Government's intention to proceed with Boyd's recommendations did not withstand the public protest. On 8 September 2005, the Government issued a news release stating that it would not permit arbitration under discriminatory laws.[33]

---

[26] Judy Van Rhign 'First steps taken for Islamic arbitration board' (24 November 2003) *Law Times*.

[27] Arbitration Act 1991, SO 1991, c 17.

[28] See, eg, Natasha Fatah 'new Law for All' (1 April 2004) CBC News, online at www.cbc.ca/news/viewpoint/vp_fatah/20040401.html.

[29] Ministry of the Attorney General, News Release 'Former Attorney General and Women's Issues Minister to Review Arbitrations Processes' (25 June 2004) online at www.attorneygeneral.jus. gov.on.ca/english/news/2004/20040625-arbitrationreview-nr.asp.

[30] Marion Boyd 'Dispute Resolution in Family Law: Protecting Choice, Promoting Inclusion' (Ontario Ministry of the Attorney General, December 2004) online at www.attorneygeneral. jus.gov.on.ca/english/about/pubs/boyd/.

[31] See, eg, Peter Worthington 'Sharia has no place here' (22 December 2004) *Toronto Sun*.

[32] See, eg, Natash Bakht 'Arbitration, Religion and Family Law: Private Justice on the Backs of Women' (Law Commission of Canada, March 2005) online at www.lcc.gc.ca/research_ project/bakht_main-en.asp.

[33] Ministry of the Attorney General, News Release 'Statement by the Attorney General on the Arbitration Act, 1991' (8 September 2005) online at www.attorneygeneral.jus.gov. on.ca/english/news/2005/20050908-arb1991.asp.

In November 2005, the Ontario Government introduced Bill 27, the Family Statute Law Amendment Act.[34] Pursuant to Bill 27 the Arbitration Act would be amended to include a new clause that states that family arbitration must be 'conducted exclusively in accordance with the law of Ontario or of another Canadian jurisdiction'. It would require that arbitrations of family matters must be in writing, and that parties entering into a family arbitration have independent legal advice. Parties entering into a family arbitration could not waive their right to appeal. Family law arbitrators would be regulated and required to undergo training, including training in how to screen for family violence and power imbalances. Arbitration would be monitored through mandatory record keeping and reporting to the Ministry of the Attorney General. And parties would no longer be able to enter into advance agreements to arbitrate their family dispute. Instead, agreement to arbitrate would have to made at the time of the dispute.

Many of the provisions of Bill 27 are consistent with the recommendations for safeguards made by Boyd. Some parts of Bill 27 are problematic. Limiting the choice of law for family law arbitrations to the law of Ontario or another Canadian jurisdiction seems too drastic a limit on the freedom of the parties, particularly in light of the great emphasis on private settlement of family disputes and respect for the autonomy of the parties embodied in legislation[35] and enunciated in case-law.[36] Furthermore, Ontario's Family Law Act itself provides that the law of other jurisdictions will apply in some circumstances. For example, in regard to marital property, the law of the last common habitual residence applies.[37] It should also be noted that arbitrations of family disputes under other laws could still take place if Bill 27 is passed, but the resulting awards would no longer be enforceable under the Arbitration Act. Bill 27 does not address the problem of women being coerced into arbitration under religious laws, it simply provides that such arbitrations will not be binding. To the extent that social pressure rather than resort to the courts is used to enforce compliance with the rulings of faith-based arbitration tribunals, the inability of such tribunals to issue legally binding awards will not matter. Another problem with Bill 27 is the clause securing the right to appeal family law arbitral awards. Currently parties can waive their right to appeal, and this prevents 'sore losers' from carrying on the fight in court. Members of the family law bar have expressed concern that Bill 27 will result in increased litigation of family law disputes.[38]

---

34   Legislative Assembly of Ontario, 2nd Session, 38th Parliament, Bill 27, the Family Statute Law Amendment Act, first reading (15 November 2005) available online at www.ontla.on.ca/ documents/Bills/38_Parliament/session2/b027_e.htm.

35   See, eg, Divorce Act, RS 1985, c 3 (2nd Supp) s 9.

36   See, eg, *Miglin v Miglin* [2003] 1 SCR 303.

37   Family Law Act, RSO 1990, c F.3, s 15.

38   'Arbitration law changes could send more cases to court' (14 December 2005) CBC News, online at www.cbc.ca/toronto/story/to_arbitration20051214.html.

IV CHILD SUPPORT

Child Support Guidelines came into effect under the Divorce Act on 1 May 1997 as part of the Federal Government's child support package.[39] Prior to the introduction of the Guidelines, the quantum of child support was determined on a case-by-case basis according to the needs of the child and the respective abilities of the parents to pay. Under the Guidelines, child support quantum is in most cases determined according to the table amount, which is based on the relevant province, the number of children, and the annual income of the payor. The Guidelines were intended to address the problems of inconsistency in awards and awards that were too low.

The Child Support Guidelines were adopted by the province of Ontario effective 1 December 1997.[40] The federal rules and Ontario's rules are virtually identical. Across Canada, the provinces and territories have adopted the federal Child Support Guidelines approach (though Quebec's rules are distinctive), with the result that the rules relating to child support are pretty much the same across Canada.[41]

Section 9 has been the most conflict-ridden and inconsistently interpreted section of the Guidelines. This provision states that where a spouse exercises access to, or has physical custody of, a child for not less than 40% of the time over the course of a year, the amount of child support must be determined by taking into account:

(a) the amounts set out in the applicable tables for each of the spouses;

(b) the increased costs of shared custody arrangements; and

(c) the conditions, means, needs and other circumstances of each spouse and of any child for whom support is sought.

Some observers have expressed concern that parents are seeking shared custody for 'strategic' reasons, that is, to avoid paying the table amount rather than because they truly want shared custody. The Supreme Court of Canada resolved some of the problems with section 9 of the Guidelines in 2005 when it handed down its decision in *Contino v Leonelli-Contino*, on appeal from the province of Ontario.[42]

In this case, the child had his primary residence with his mother from the age of 3, spending alternate weekends and Thursday nights with his father. In 2000, instead of hiring a babysitter when she started a night course, the mother accepted the father's offer to have the child, then 14 years old, spend Tuesday nights with him. Relying on section 9 of the Guidelines, the father then asked a court in 2001 to reduce his child support because his son was now with him more than 40% of the time. As the case made its way to the Supreme Court of Canada, the various lower courts applied widely divergent

---

[39] Federal Child Support Guidelines, made under the Divorce Act, Can Reg 97-175, as amended.

[40] Child Support Guidelines, made under the Family Law Act, O Reg 391/97, as amended.

[41] Canada's Department of Justice Canada provides links to the legislation, guidelines, research reports and other materials, online at http://canada.justice.gc.ca/en/ps/sup/.

[42] 2005 SCC 63 ['*Contino*'].

interpretations of section 9, evincing the strong need for guidance from Canada's highest court.[43]

The Supreme Court of Canada ruled that there was no presumption in favour of the table amount, thereby disappointing the mother, but also that there was no presumption in favour of reducing child support downward, thereby disappointing the father. The Supreme Court ruled that all the factors listed in section 9 must be considered and there was no formula for determining quantum in these cases. It is important to consider any additional expenses related to shared parenting, and parties must lead evidence relating to this and other relevant circumstances.

The Supreme Court looked first at the 'set-off' amount, which was the difference between the table amount for each parent. This would have resulted in a payment by the father of $128 a month. Beyond this, the Supreme Court considered the total expenses of both parents attributed to the child and calculated each party's share in proportion to the incomes of the two parents. Applying this approach, the father would have to pay $275.33 a month. But a further consideration in this case was that the mother's expenses had not decreased as a result of the shared custody arrangement and the father's expenses had not increased. Furthermore, the mother had made financial commitments based on belief that she would be getting at least $563 a month from the father, and a reduction in this amount would cause her significant problems. In light of all these factors, the Supreme Court determined that the father should pay $500 a month in child support.

The rejection of a presumption in favour of lowering the amount of child support was a relief to many, because it is expected to reduce the problem of strategic claims for shared custody. The Supreme Court of Canada emphasized the importance of avoiding the 'cliff effect', whereby a small increase in the amount of time with the payor would result in a drastic reduction in child support. The possibility of awarding the set off amount remains open, but that is only a starting point. In many cases the set off amount will be too low. It seems likely that the alternative approach supported by the decision – sharing the total expenses attributable to the child in proportion to the parties' respective incomes – will be used in more cases. Neither approach was actually applied in *Contino*. The award of $500 a month seemed to hinge primarily on the mother's reliance on a certain level of child support.

V   SPOUSAL SUPPORT

The generally positive experience of Child Support Guidelines has given rise to calls for Spousal Support Guidelines as well. This has been particularly so since the Supreme Court of Canada's decisions in *Moge v Moge*[44] and in

---

43   *Contino v Leonelli-Contino* (2003) 232 DLR (4th) 654 (Ont CA); (2002) 62 OR (3rd) 295 (Sup Ct Div Ct).

44   [1992] 3 SCR 813.

Bracklow v Bracklow.[45] These cases articulated the various models of spousal support – compensatory, non-compensatory, and contractual, but left considerable uncertainty as to how to proceed in actual cases. As one commentator put it:

> '[A] review of post-*Moge* and most importantly, post-*Bracklow* cases reveals a relatively wide open landscape of judicial discretion, driven by a mixture of regional considerations, unarticulated assumptions and biases, pure happenstance, and at times a disjointed analysis of why support is paid in the first place. One judge's need-based reasoning is another's compensatory analysis. One judge's short-term rehabilitative plan of action is another's amelioration of long-term economic disadvantage. What is considered "over the top" in Edmonton may be quite ho-hum in Toronto. Lack of clarity and predictability in relation to spousal support orders that followed *Bracklow* led to consideration of how the guideline regimes adopted in other jurisdictions might be adapted to the Canadian context.'[46]

The Federal Department of Justice began working on Spousal Support Guidelines in 2002.[47] Draft Guidelines were developed by academics Carol Rogerson and Rollie Thompson and released early in 2005.[48]

In developing the Guidelines, Rogerson and Thompson gave careful attention to the current state of spousal support law. While the *Moge* decision had emphasized a broad approach to compensatory support that fully recognized the loss incurred by a spouse as a result of the marriage or its breakdown, the *Bracklow* decision focused on non-compensatory support. The result of *Bracklow* has been virtually to eliminate the issue of entitlement to spousal support. As one judge noted:

> '*Bracklow* has taken us to the point where any significant reduction in the standard of living of a spouse, resulting from marriage breakdown, will warrant a support order – with the quantum and/or duration of the support being used to tweak the order so as to achieve justice in each case.'[49]

Rogerson and Thompson emphasized the importance of clarifying the basis of entitlement in order to develop a sensible approach to quantum and duration. Their Advisory Guidelines are built around the 'merger over time' theory in the case of parties without dependent children. They adopted the merger over time concept from the American Law Institute, which used it in developing its Spousal Support Guidelines. The merger over time theory is that 'as a marriage lengthens, spouses more deeply merge their economic

---

[45]   [1999] 1 SCR 420.

[46]   See, eg, Marie Gordon 'Spousal Support Guidelines and the American Experience: Moving Beyond Discretion' (2002) 19 *Canadian Journal of Family Law* 247 at para 8.

[47]   Carol Rogerson 'Developing Spousal Support Guidelines in Canada: Beginning the Discussion' (Department of Justice Canada, December 2002) online at www.justice.gc.ca/en/dept/pub/spousal/; Christin Schmitz 'Ottawa secretly developing spousal support guidelines' (9 May 2003) 23:2 *Lawyers Weekly*.

[48]   Carol Rogerson and Rollie Thompson 'Spousal Support Advisory Guidelines: A Draft Proposal' (Department of Justice Canada, January 2005) online at www.justice.gc.ca/en/dept/pub/spousal/project/.

[49]   *Keller v Black* (2000) 182 DLR (4th) 690 (Ont Sup Ct) at para 22.

and non-economic lives, resulting in greater claims to the marital standard of living'.

The 'without child' formula that Rogerson and Thompson developed on the basis of the merger over time theory is an amount ranging from 1.5–2% of the difference between the spouses' gross incomes for each year of cohabitation, up to a maximum of 50%. For marriages of at least 25 years, the range is fixed at 37.5–50% of the income difference.

The duration ranges from 0.5 to 1 year for each year of marriage, but support is for an indefinite period in the case of marriages of at least 20 years or marriages of at least 5 years when years of marriage and age of the support recipient at separation added together total at least 65.

For parties with dependent children, Rogerson and Thompson developed the 'with child' formula based on the 'parental partnership' theory, which posits that the obligation for spousal support flows from parenthood rather than the marital relationship itself. The parental partnership approach looks not only at past loss but also continuing economic disadvantage that flows from ongoing child-care responsibilities. The with child formula is far more difficult to apply than the without child formula, and commercial software has been developed to do the calculations. The basic with child formula assumes that the recipient of spousal support is also the custodial parent and has the lower income. The first step is to determine the 'individual net disposable income' of each spouse. For the payor, this is the Child Support Guidelines income minus child support minus taxes and deductions. For the recipient, this is the Child Support Guidelines income minus notional child support minus taxes and deductions plus government benefits and credits. The next step is to add together the individual net disposable incomes. The final step is to determine the range of spousal support amounts that would be required to leave the lower income recipient spouse with between 40–46% of the combined individual net disposable incomes.

The Advisory Spousal Support Guidelines are still somewhat controversial but it is clear from the number of reported decisions in which they are discussed that they are being used by lawyers. Some courts have said that the Advisory Guidelines are helpful.[50] The British Columbia Court of Appeal, the first appellate court to consider the issue, commented at length on the Guidelines, first noting that their purpose is to increase certainty and predictability.[51] The Court also said that:

'[T]heir intention and general effect is to build upon the law as it exists, rather than to present an entirely new approach to the issue of spousal support. For

---

[50]   See, eg, *Carr v Carr* 2005 ABQB 265 at para 7, where the court stated: 'The Spousal Support Advisory Guidelines: A Draft Proposal is of some assistance in testing an interlocutory award of spousal support. Those guidelines will clearly benefit separating spouses, their legal advisers, and the courts by de-emphasizing the expensive and time-consuming exchange of detailed cost-of-living evidence and scrutiny of evidence on each spouse's "needs"; that sterile debate will be replaced by a focus on the spouse's entitlement to support, which entitlement is determined in situations such as this one essentially by the length of the marriage'.

[51]   *Yemchuk v Yemchuk* (2005) 257 DLR 476 (BCCA) at para 62.

that reason, like Madam Justice Martinson and many other judges, I have no hesitation in viewing the Advisory Guidelines as a useful tool to assist judges in assessing the quantum and duration of spousal support. They do not operate to displace the courts' reliance on decided authorities (to the extent that relevant authorities are forthcoming) but to supplement them. In that regard, they do not constitute evidence, but are properly considered as part of counsels' submissions.'[52]

The Advisory Guidelines are intended to reflect the law as it exists. It is expected that they will be modified as the law changes. They may also be refined in light of problems that are identified after a period of use. The response has not been universally favourable,[53] but on the whole the Advisory Guidelines seem to be enhancing certainty and simplifying the determination of spousal support.

---

[52] *Yemchuk v Yemchuk* (2005) 257 DLR 476 (BCCA) at para 64.
[53] See, eg, the criticisms canvassed in *Megyesi v Megyesi* 2005 ABQB 706.

People's Republic of China

RECENT DEVELOPMENTS IN THE MARITAL PROPERTY SYSTEM OF THE PEOPLE'S REPUBLIC OF CHINA

Chen Wei[*]

Résumé

Les règles du droit patrimonial prévues par la Loi sur le mariage de la République populaire de Chine de 1980, ont été modifiées considérablement à la suite d'une réforme législative d'Avril 1991 et de "L'Interprétation (I) de Différents Problèmes posés par cette loi", rendue par la Cour suprême en décembre 2001. Par ailleurs, "L'Interprétation (II) de Différents Problèmes posés par cette loi", est exécutoire depuis le 1 Avril 2004. Cette interprétation de la Cour suprême ajoute de nouvelles règles au système actuel de propriété matrimoniale afin de mieux encadrer les nouvelles situations de relations patrimoniales entre conjoints. Ces nouvelles dispositions reflètent l'évolution des principes dans le champ du droit patrimonial de la famille en Chine. Cet article entend, d'une part, expliquer les principaux aspects de ces dispositions, d'autre part évaluer les mérites et les écueils du nouveau système chinois en droit patrimonial de la famille et, finalement, suggérer certains changements qui pourraient améliorer la situation actuelle.

The marital property system in the Marriage Law of the PRC 1980 was amended and supplemented significantly in the Marriage Law of the PRC amended in April 2001 and the Interpretation (I) of Several Problems on the Application of the Marriage Law of the PRC, issued by the Supreme People's Court of China in December 2001. The Interpretation (II) of Several Problems on the Application of the Marriage Law of the PRC came into force on 1 April 2004. It added some new provisions to the current marital property system for the purpose of regulating new situations in relation to the marital property relationship. These new provisions embody the new developments relating to the marital property system of China. The purpose of this paper is to expound the main aspects of the new provisions,

---

[*] Professor of Law at the Southwest University of Political Science and Law, China; Director of the Center of Foreign Family Law and Theories on Women; Vice Chairwoman of the China Marriage Law Society. This item is one of the research projects sponsored by the Center of Foreign Family Law and Theories on Women of Southwest University of Political Science and Law, China.

evaluate the merits and defects of the current marital property system of China, and put forward some suggestions for the amendment and improvement of them.

I INTRODUCTION

The Marriage Law 1950 of the PRC ('the Marriage Law 1950') was the first marriage law enacted after the establishment of the PRC in 1949. However, because of the limitation of historic factors, the provisions on the marital property system were not detailed. Thirty years after the Marriage Law 1950 had been in force, the Marriage Law of the PRC 1980 ('the Marriage Law 1980') was promulgated. The provisions relating to the marital property system in the Marriage Law 1950 were amended and supplemented according to the needs of new situations. But the Marriage Law 1980 lacked explicit provisions on the scope of individual property, as well as the substance of a system of contractual property (ie the time, form and the effects of the contract), which resulted in difficulties in practice. The Supreme People's Court of China ('the Supreme People's Court') issued a series of judicial interpretations to guide judicial practice and make up for the defects of these provisions.[1] In the twenty-first century, the legislature brought the amended Marriage Law of the PRC ('the new Marriage Law') into force on 28 April 2001. Some provisions were added to guide the practice of the court in the Interpretation (I) of Several Problems on the Application of the Marriage Law of the PRC ('the Judicial Interpretation (I) of the Marriage Law') issued by the Supreme People's Court on 25 December 2001.[2] With the development of society, and the need to regulate the marital property relationship, the Interpretation (II) of Several Problems on the Application of Marriage Law of the PRC ('the Judicial Interpretation (II) of the Marriage Law') was issued by the Supreme People's Court and came into force on 1 April 2004, in which some provisions were again added.[3] This interpretation symbolises the newest development in the marital property system of China.

This paper attempts to introduce concisely the legislative developments after the establishment of the PRC and to expound the main features of the new provisions in the Judicial Interpretation (II) of the Marriage Law. Furthermore, it evaluates the merits and defects of the current marital property system of China and puts forward some suggestions on the further amendment and improvement of that system.

---

[1]   For example, Several Opinions on the Execution of Civil Policies and Law issued by the Supreme People's Court in August 1984; Several Opinions on the Disputes of Property Distribution in Divorce Cases of the People's Court issued by the Supreme People's Court in November 1993.

[2]   Sections 17–19 of the Judicial Interpretation (I) of the Marriage Law.

[3]   Sections 8–27 of the Judicial Interpretation (II) of the Marriage Law.

II   LEGISLATIVE DEVELOPMENTS RELATING TO THE MARITAL PROPERTY SYSTEM OF CHINA AFTER THE MARRIAGE LAW 1950

A marital property system is a legal system regulating the marital property relationship between spouses. Its contents include the establishment, alteration and termination of all kinds of marital property systems, the owning, managing, using, profiting from and disposing of prenuptial property or postnuptial property, the bearing of family expenses, the discharge of spouses' debts, as well as the reckoning or distribution of marital property on dissolution of marriage. Under a market economy, the property relationship between spouses not only relates to the interests of both spouses, but also to the interests of third parties trading with the husband or wife. In order to protect the equality of status between the spouses and the harmony of marriage, safeguard trade between third parties and husband or wife, maintain the social order and promote the economic development of society, the system of marital property was established in the law to regulate the marital property relationship (Chen Wei, 2000a: 175).

Section 7 of the Marriage Law 1950 provided that spouses were couples living together and their status in the family was equal. It established the equal status of spouses in the family, and in this way made historic progress. Section 10 of the law provided that both spouses should enjoy equal rights in the ownership of family property and the right to dispose of it.[4] That is, both spouses might have the ownership of prenuptial property or postnuptial property, and as well be entitled to manage children's property jointly. Under s 23 of the Marriage Law 1950 and the provisions of the judicial interpretation concerning it, we can see that the law did not distinguish between family property and marital property. The definition of marital property included the prenuptial property of both spouses, and the postnuptial property (with or without consideration) gained by one spouse or both spouses. But the prenuptial property of the wife was excluded from the joint property at the time of divorce, which was a special concession to women. That is, bearing in mind the traditional custom that most people adopted the general community system of property, the statutory property system was a 'General Joint Property System' at that time. This property system both reflects the equality of men and women and the equal status of both spouses in the family, and it is absolutely different from the feudal law which denied that women could own property and those provisions limiting the property ownership of married women in the earlier periods of several

---

[4]   See ss 10, 23(1) and 24 of the Marriage Law of 1950; the Report on the Draft Process and Grounds for the Draft of the Marriage Law by the Legal Commission of Central Government (4 May 1950). The Report pointed out that the scope of family property includes the following without exception: (1) prenuptial property of both spouses; or (2) joint property acquired during marriage, including property acquired by work of one or both spouses, bequest or gift owned exclusively by one or both spouses; or (3) property of a minor (ie the land gained in the Land Reform as well other properties). This Report pointed out further that both spouses can 'possess and dispose of the family property in Item (1), (2) and manage equally the property in Item (3)'.

western countries. In short, this law played an important role in the reform and development of the marital property system of China.

In accordance with the changed circumstances in the new China, the Marriage Law 1980 amended the basis of the marital property system in the Marriage Law 1950. The main provisions amended include two aspects: (1) the concept of 'Family Property' of the Marriage Law 1950 was substituted by the notion of 'Property Owned by both Spouses', because the definition of family property is broader than marital property; and (2) the prenuptial property owned by both spouses was excluded from marital property. The 'General Joint Property System' was replaced with the 'Community System of Postnuptial Incomes'. That made the legal concept more exact and the scope of marital property more explicit. The marital property relationship was safeguarded and the individual property of each spouse was protected somewhat to adapt to the requirements of modern times.

The Marriage Law 1980 has been in force for more than 20 years in China, and the role it has played in history should be fully acknowledged. Meanwhile, we should also bear in mind that these 20 years were the years of opening up and reform, and the new era of the institution of the market economy had been established gradually in China. Material and cultural lives have been enhanced continuously, the amounts and types of marital property have rapidly increased, transactions between third parties and spouses have been more frequent and the property relationship has become more complex. Meanwhile, the concentration on individual property has been strengthened and disputes over property on divorce have increased. Since the provisions on the marital property system in the Marriage Law 1980 were sketchy, it was unfit to deal with the new situations. For example, it only set out sketchy provisions on marital property, while the definition or detailed contents of it were not prescribed (Wu Changzhen, 2001: 30). In addition, some of these provisions fell behind the realities (Yang Dawen, 2003: 16). As a remedy, the Supreme People's Court issued several judicial interpretations before or after, especially the Several Opinions on the Disputes of Property Distribution in Divorce Cases of the People's Court issued in 1993 ('the 1993 Judicial Interpretation'). This Interpretation further elaborated on the scope of joint property and individual property, the conditions under which individual property becomes joint property, the distribution of joint property and the discharge of joint debts and individual debts. However, there were still two defects in the Marriage Law 1980: (1) it emphasised joint property and disapproved of individual property. The scope of the former was too broad while it lacked provisions on the latter; and (2) there were no detailed provisions on the contractual property system, which resulted in a lack of clarity in practice. Therefore, in order to adapt to the requirements of the new situations, amendment of the Marriage Law 1980 was necessary (Zhang Xuejun, 2002: 399–409). One of the key amendments was the improvement of the marital property system.

The new Marriage Law of 2001 still preserved the Community System of Postnuptial Incomes in the Marriage Law 1980 as the statutory property system.[5] In addition, aiming at the defects of the marital property system of the Marriage Law 1980, the new Marriage Law amended and supplemented

---

[5]   The grounds for continuing the Community System of Postnuptial Incomes in the new Marriage Law include, first, acknowledging the value of housework. According to the principle that the spouses have equal status in the family in s 13 of the new Marriage Law and the principle of equality of men and women, we must acknowledge that the contributions by one spouse who engages in housework and the other one who engages in professional work are of the same value. Hence, no matter whether they have incomes or not, or how many incomes there are, the spouses have the same right to property acquired by one spouse or both during marriage, except as otherwise provided. Secondly, respecting the traditional practices in the country, in China, we adopt the Community Property System, which was the historical custom. Nowadays, most people still adopt the Community Property System for Postnuptial Incomes after marriage as the marital property system. For example, according to surveys of cases tried in the courts located in cities such as Beijing, Haerbin and Xiamen from April 2001 to December 2002 carried out by some Chinese scholars: most couples adopted the Community System of Postnuptial Incomes after marriage; most of the divorced couples did not have an agreement on their property; 97.4% of spouses adopted the Community System of Postnuptial Incomes in Beijing; only 2% of the spouses adopted the separate property system, 3% adopted the limited community property system in Xiamen among those surveyed (Wu Changzhen, 2004: 5). The reasons are that, in reality, there are still disparities in the incomes of spouses, so adopting the Community System of Postnuptial Incomes after marriage is beneficial to encourage the spouses to share happiness and woe, give mutual support, support the old and the young and realise the functions of marriage and the family, and promote the stability of marriage and family life. Thirdly, it is consistent with the legislative spirit of the marital property system in many countries of the world. Since World War II, with the development of the International Human Rights Movement and the Women's Movement, many countries have revised their marital property systems to reflect the principle of equality between men and women and the doctrine of fairness and justice. The UN Conference adopted the Convention on the Elimination of All Forms of Discrimination against Women in December 1979. Article 2(f) of this Convention provides that all proper measures should be taken, including enacting new laws to revise or repeal current laws, regulations, customs and practices discriminating against women. Articles 15 and 16 provide that equal rights should be given to women on entering into an agreement or acquiring property. Spouses have equal rights in the owning, acquiring, operating, sharing and disposing of property, whether remunerated or not. All of these kinds of provisions offer legislative and judicial criteria for the states parties. Though legislation in many countries varies, there still exists much common content. The mixed forms of the community of property system and the separate property system have become the common characteristic of marital property systems in many countries today (Lin Xiuxiong: 2001: 98–100, 132, 142). Countries such as France and Italy adopt the system of Community of Postnuptial Incomes, Germany and Switzerland adopt a mixed form of the community property system and the separate property system – a community system of residual property or system of incomes distribution which can 'consider the economic independence of the spouses and protect the housewife without economic incomes' (Lin Xiuxiong, 2001: 37). Furthermore, even in some countries of the Anglo-American legal tradition, at the time of divorce, the property acquired by either spouse during marriage is divided justly between both spouses according to the contributions made to marriage and the children of the marriage, which can take on the character of a community property system. For example, under s 79(2), (4) of the Australian Family Law Act 1975 the court has power to divide out the property acquired during marriage, fairly and equitably, according to the contributions directly or indirectly made by either spouse to the marriage or the children of the marriage. (See *Australian Family Law Act 1975 with Regulations and Rules Consolidated to August 1 2002* (printed in Australia by McHerson's Printing Group) pp 237–238.) This means 'spouses may have claims on the property of one another as a consequence of equitable doctrines' (Patrick Parkinson, 2004: 625).

the former in the following two respects. First, it amended and improved the statutory marital property system, adding to the individual property system, excluding the property in the possession of one spouse as determined by will or by an agreement on gift from the joint property, narrowing the scope of the joint property and enumerating the scope of joint property and individual property. Secondly, it added specific provisions on a contractual property system, including the scope of contractual property, the content, the form and the effects of the agreement, which improved the marital property system of China when compared with what existed before (Chen Wei, 2003: 184–193). Thereafter, the Supreme People's Court issued the Judicial Interpretation (I) of the Marriage Law on 25 December 2001 to guide the People's Court. The Interpretation: added a right of agency over the daily family affairs of both spouses; determined the burden of proof for informing a third party when spouses entered into an agreement on their property; and provided that the individual property of either spouse could not become joint property merely because of the continuation of marriage.[6]

With the development of society, and the need to regulate new situations, the Judicial Interpretation (II) of the Marriage Law was promulgated on 26 December 2003 and came into force on 1 April 2004. This interpretation added regulations of the ownership of betrothal gifts sent by one spouse to the other before getting married; the scope of other property mutually owned by both spouses; and the method of division of some special property acquired by both spouses or one spouse during marriage. This special property includes the proceeds of intellectual property rights, the payment granted to soldiers for demobilisation or for self-determined occupational choice, the shares, bonds, and capital shares in investment, stocks, shares in partnership, assets of single-venture enterprises and the ownership of houses. The character of the donation of money given by parents on purchasing a house for both spouses before marriage or after marriage, the discharge of the individual debts on divorce, the joint and several liability for joint debts of both spouses and the effects of an agreement for property distribution on divorce were also added.[7] This interpretation not only respected the spouses' willingness to deal with their property relationship, but also protected the interests of the disadvantaged spouse without income or pension; not only acknowledged the value of housework, but maintained the Community System of Postnuptial Incomes and protected both spouses' rights to individual property; not only protected the lawful rights of both spouses, but maintained the interests of third parties and the security of transactions. All of these reforms symbolise the newest developments to the marital property system in China and another progressive piece of legislation.

---

[6]   See ss 17–19 of the Judicial Interpretation (I) of the Marriage Law.
[7]   See ss 8–27 of the Judicial Interpretation (II) of the Marriage Law.

III NEW DEVELOPMENTS TO THE MARITAL PROPERTY SYSTEM IN THE JUDICIAL INTERPRETATION (II) OF THE MARRIAGE LAW

According to the new Marriage Law and the spirit of judicial interpretation, the legislative purpose of the current marital property system is to uphold the principle of equality of men and women, safeguard the lawful rights and interests of both spouses and third parties, especially the interests of the disadvantaged. The final aim is to protect marriage and the family, promote the harmony of marriage and safeguard private transactions and the market order as well as to realise the comprehensive development of individuals. Therefore, the marital property system must reflect the legislative principles that the spouses' agreement takes precedence over statutory provisions, the principle of the equality of spouses' rights and duties in relation to their marital property, the principle of acknowledging the value of housework and protecting the interests of the disadvantaged and the principle of giving consideration to protecting the lawful property rights and interests of both spouses and those of third parties (Chen Wei, 2001: 32–33). Based on these principles, and the need to regulate the marital property relationship, broadly, the Judicial Interpretation (II) of the Marriage Law developed the marital property system of China in the following respects:

A   Defining the ownership of betrothal gifts

Section 10 states that where a spouse seeks to get back betrothal gifts sent according to custom the People's Court shall rule in his/her favour if any of the following circumstances is found:

(1) the spouses have not registered their marriage; or

(2) the spouses do not cohabit, despite having registered their marriage; or

(3) the betrothal gifts given before marriage resulted in financial hardship for the donor.

Section 10(2) states simultaneously that, items (2)–(3) of s 10(1) are to be applied when spouses are divorcing. All these provisions embody protection of the individual property of each spouse or the maintenance of communal life in marriage.

B   Supplementing the types of joint property in s 17 of the new Marriage Law

Section 11 states that the following types of property during marriage belong to both spouses. 'Other properties which should be in their joint possession' are contained in s 17 of the new Marriage Law:

(1) the proceeds of investment from the property of either spouse;

(2) the housing allowance and the housekeeping money which is actually acquired or bound to be acquired by either spouse; and

(3) the pension and settlement allowance for bankruptcy which are actually acquired or bound to be acquired by either spouse.

On the one hand, the housing allowance, the deposit for a house and pension are accumulated proportionately and deducted from the monthly salary. Under the new Marriage Law, either spouse's salary belongs to joint property. On the other hand, this provision signifies the acknowledgement of the value of housework, in that the spouse who engages in housework has the same right as the other spouse to such property as the pension, housekeeping money and other properties acquired or bound to be acquired by the other spouse for the reason that marriage is a kind of partnership which aims at a union for life. Those who get married have reason to believe that the development of either spouse is the development of the family; therefore, they should share the achievements of that development (Xia Yinlan, 2005: 48).

C   Defining the proceeds of intellectual property rights in s 17(3) of the new Marriage Law

Section 12 states that the 'proceeds of intellectual property rights' stipulated in s 17(3) of the new Marriage Law refers to the incomes that are actually acquired or are definitely to be acquired during marriage. The judge explained what is meant by proceeds that are definitely to be acquired; for example, if one spouse has entered into a publishing agreement with publishers, and the author's remuneration has been agreed, even if the author has not yet received the money, it still belongs to joint property (Huang Songyou, 2004: 123).

D   Providing for the scope of special property belonging to the soldier, the owning and the calculation of payments for demobilisation or for self-determined occupational choice

Section 13 states that the injury or death insurance for soldiers, subsidies for wounded and disabled soldiers, and their medical subsidies belong to individual property. Section 14 states that, at the time of dealing with divorce cases, where partition of a lump-sum payment granted to soldiers for demobilisation or for self-determined occupational choice is involved, the People's Court must multiply annual average payments by the years of marriage. The result should be the joint property of the spouses.

The annual average payments stipulated in the last paragraph refer to the result, where the total amount of the aforesaid payments granted to soldiers is divided by a specific period of years. The specific period of years is the gap between life expectancy (70) and the soldier's actual age at the time of joining the army. These provisions show that, on the basis of the equal status of men and women and the doctrine of fairness, the demobilisation fee or payment for self-determined occupational choice during marriage belongs to joint property like the salary of the other spouse, which must be partitioned equally between both spouses on divorce. These provisions signify equal protection of the property rights of both the soldier and his/her spouse.

E   Specifying the method of dividing bonds, shares in a company, property shares in partnership or property in single-venture enterprises possessed by both spouses

With the development of the market economy, the kinds of marital property have correspondingly increased. In order to guide the judge in a trial dealing with special property such as bonds, shares in a company and other properties possessed by both spouses, s 15 states that, on partition of securities between the spouses such as stocks, bonds, shares of investment funds and shares of an unlisted joint-stock company, if they fail to reach agreement or it is difficult to divide the assets according to the market value, the People's Court may allot this property proportionally.

With respect to the method of partitioning the stocks in a limited company, s 16 states that, in dealing with divorce cases, if only one spouse is a shareholder in the said company:

(1) where the spouses reach an agreement to transfer part or all of the investments to the spouse of this shareholder, if more than half of the shareholders consent, and the other shareholders explicitly renounce the right of pre-emption, the spouse of this shareholder may become a shareholder of the said company; or

(2) where an agreement has been reached between the spouses on such issues as the amounts and prices of the investments transfer, if more than half of the shareholders dissenting on the transfer are willing to buy these investments at an equal price, the People's Court may partition the proceeds of transforming the investments. If more than half of shareholders dissenting on the transfer are *not* willing to buy these investments, they shall be deemed to consent to the transfer, and the spouse of this shareholder may become a shareholder of the said company.

Resolutions at shareholder meetings or written statements of shareholders obtained by the spouses through other lawful means, may serve as the evidence to prove the consent of more than half of the shareholders as stipulated in the last paragraph.

As regards property shares in partnership, s 17 states that, in dealing with divorce cases, involving transfer of property shares of a partnership in the name of one spouse, where the other spouse is not a partner of the said partnership, if the spouses agree to transfer parts or all of the property shares of the partnership to the other spouse, the People's Court should deal with cases differently according to following circumstances:

(1) where all the other partners consent, the other spouse will become a partner in accordance with law; or

(2) where other partners dissent on the transfer and exercise the right of pre-emption under the equal condition, the proceeds from the transfer may be partitioned; or

(3) where other partners who neither consent on the transfer, nor exercise the right of pre-emption, agree to the retirement of the said partner or the return of parts of the investments, the property returned may be partitioned; or

(4) where other partners dissenting on the transfer do not exercise the right of pre-emption, do not agree to the retirement of the said partner or the return of parts of the investments, it shall be deemed that all the partners consent to the transfer and the other spouse shall become a partner in accordance with law.

With regard to the distribution of property in a single-venture enterprise, under s 18, the People's Court must handle cases differently according to following circumstances:

(1) where one spouse claims to manage the enterprise, after evaluating the assets of the enterprise, the spouse taking over the enterprise must reimburse the other accordingly; or

(2) where both spouses claim to manage the enterprise, on the bidding price, the spouse taking over the enterprise must reimburse the other accordingly; or

(3) where neither of the spouses is willing to manage the enterprise, it must be handled according to the Law of Single-venture Enterprises by an Individual of the PRC.

The above provisions show that the distribution of property of special character owned by both spouses on divorce must comply with the provisions in the new Marriage Law, as well as the provisions in Company Law, the Partnership Act, the Securities Act and the judicial interpretations concerning each. This fact means that special principles of distribution must be followed in the distribution of property of special character such as stock rights (Chen Wei, Xie Jingjie, 2004: 144–145).

F   Specifying the ownership and the method of dividing property rights in the home

Under ss 19–21, if a home rented by one spouse before marriage and bought with joint property after marriage is registered in the name of one spouse on the certificate of house ownership, it shall be deemed the joint property of the spouses. Where the spouses fail to reach an agreement on the value and the ownership of the house, the People's Court must handle cases differently according to following circumstances:

(1) where both spouses claim the ownership of the house and agree to acquire it at a bidding price, it shall be permitted; or

(2) where one spouse claims the ownership of the house, the house shall be valued by a valuer according to the market price, and the spouse taking

over the ownership of the house shall reimburse the other spouse accordingly; or

(3) where neither of the spouses claims ownership of the house, the house shall be auctioned on application of the spouses, and the money acquired shall be divided.

Where the spouses are in dispute over the ownership of the house and they fail to reach an agreement, it is not proper for the People's Court to make a decision on the ownership of the house. The Court shall award the use of the house in favour of one spouse based on the actual circumstances. If disputes arise later over ownership, the spouses may start another action.

As for the ownership of a home purchased with help from parents, s 22 states that, where parents contribute money to the purchase before marriage, this contribution shall be regarded as a personal gift to their own child, unless the parents explicitly say that it is intended as a gift for both spouses. Where parents contribute money to the purchase after marriage, this contribution shall be naturally regarded as a gift to both spouses, unless the parents explicitly say that it is intended as a gift for one spouse.

The above provisions show that the law pays attention to protecting the community of marriage and respecting the autonomy of both spouses, protecting the lawful ownership of housing, as well respecting the donor's right to deal with individual property freely.

G   Specifying liability for joint debts and individual debts

Sections 23–26 state that, where a creditor claims against the spouse of a debtor for his/her personal debts owned before marriage, the People's Court must not allow the claim, unless the creditor can prove that the debts were spent on family living after marriage. Where the creditor claims for the debts owned personally in the name of one spouse during marriage, it will be regarded as joint debts of the spouses with an exception where either one can prove that it was explicitly agreed that it should be an individual debt between the creditor and the debtor, or if he/she can prove that the spouses had reached an agreement that they owned property acquired during marriage separately and the third party knew the contents of the agreement.

In addition, this interpretation provides for joint and several liability for joint debts between the spouses, as well as recourse against either spouse to enforce the liability. Though the distribution of marital property has been arranged in a divorce agreement between the spouses or in the court's order, the creditor still has the right to claim against divorced spouses for joint debts owned by them. Where one spouse has already borne the burden of joint and several liability for the joint debts, he/she is entitled to recover the money from the other one under a divorce arrangement or the court's order. Where the husband or wife has died, the surviving spouse will bear joint and several liability for the joint debts owed during marriage.

These provisions show that the interpretation acknowledges the right of agency in relation to daily family affairs of both spouses. Therefore, the debts owed by either spouse are joint debts, which must be paid off jointly. In addition, either spouse is entitled to recompense from the other after shouldering joint liability, which protects the ownership of that spouse's individual property and the interests of the creditor; meanwhile, it can maintain the integrity of transactions.

H Providing for the effects of agreement on the distribution of marital property and dealing with issues arising from a property partition agreement

According to ss 8 and 9, it is those clauses on property distribution in a divorce agreement or agreement on property distribution reached by spouses on divorce which are legally binding on them. Where a spouse starts an action because of disputes arising from the carrying out of an agreement on distribution of property, the People's Court must accept and hear the case. Where either spouse seeks to alter or rescind the agreement, the People's Court shall accept and hear the case. Where no fraud or duress existed at the time of the agreement, the People's Court shall reject the litigant's claim in accordance with law after hearing. These provisions respect the autonomy of the spouses regarding their property distribution; and acknowledge the legal effects of the property distribution. Furthermore, this interpretation provides a remedy where one spouse seeks to resile from an agreement on property distribution to protect the lawful rights of both spouses.

IV DEFECTS OF THE CURRENT MARITAL PROPERTY SYSTEM IN CHINA

As stated above, the Judicial Interpretation (II) of the Marriage Law introduced many new provisions relating to the marital property system, developed and made additions to the new Marriage Law. However, there are still some defects in the marital property system which should be reformed, supplemented or improved. Principally, these defects have the following aspects. First, the structure of the marital property system is incomplete. Secondly, there are still some defects in the statutory system concerning marital property. Finally, the provisions on the contractual property system are not sufficient.

A The structure of the marital property system is incomplete

The structure of the marital property system is not complete because of its lack of general provisions. General provisions in the marital property system are general principles dealing with marital property. The Civil Codes of some foreign jurisdictions such as France, Germany and Switzerland stipulate explicitly general provisions governing the marital property system in the chapter dealing with general effects of marriage, or general principles for marital property rules, or the rights and duties between the spouses. For example, Chapter V relating to 'the General Effects of Marriage' and s 1 of

Chapter VI providing 'General Provisions' in the Civil Code of Switzerland provide general rules applicable to the marital property system. These rules include provisions relating to contractual or statutory marital property systems, the spouses' duty of maintaining the family (including bearing the expenses of the family), the proper compensation to be paid by one spouse to the other making special contributions to the family, the measures relating to the performance of duties to the family, the protection for the creditor of the husband or wife, the duty to provide information about the marital property of each other, as well as to make an inventory to guide the spouses in dealing with their property relationship during marriage. However, there are no such general provisions in the marital property system of China. This is inconvenient for the spouses in dealing with their property relationship. And it is not conducive to protecting the lawful property rights of both spouses, or upholding the interests of third parties or the integrity of transactions (Chen Wei, 2000b: 86–87).

B   Defects in the statutory system concerning marital property

The defects of the statutory system concerning marital property include the integrity of the legal structure and some substantive defects.

(a) The lack of an emergency statutory system of marital property

There is only the common statutory system of marital property (Community System of Postnuptial Incomes), but the law lacks an emergency statutory system of marital property in China. The emergency statutory system of marital property is sometimes called the Special Statutory Property System. It refers to situations where the property relationship has broken down or financial misconduct has made it unreasonable to adopt the common statutory system of marital property to regulate the marital property relationship. In those cases, the law substitutes another statutory system of marital property; this marital property system is called the emergency statutory system of marital property (Gao Fengxian, 2005: 95). In the law of certain foreign jurisdictions such as in Switzerland, according to the different situations in which the statutory systems of marital property are applied, there are the common statutory system of marital property (also called the Common Marital Property System) and the emergency statutory system of marital property (also called the Emergency System of Marital Property). The former is applied when the spouses do not reach an agreement and where the emergency system of marital property is not applied. The latter is applied in special situations, where in certain circumstances the court announces on the application of either spouse, or according to law, that the contractual or statutory property system should not apply, but the separate property system should be adopted. China has still not established this emergency system of marital property which means that the needs of spouses may not be met and that they may be forced to alter or terminate their relationship of joint property in complex and difficult circumstances.[8]

(b) The lack of spouses' rights and responsibility in relation to property

There are no provisions concerning the rights of managing, using, profiting from and disposing of the joint property, and responsibility concerning this in the statutory system of marital property. The absence of such provisions is not beneficial in guiding the spouses to exercise their rights and shoulder their responsibility.

(c) The lack of principles and the means of dividing joint property and discharging debts

The new Marriage Law continues to adopt the legal framework of the Marriage Law 1980 which places the distribution of marital property and the discharging of debts in the chapter on divorce. This is improper. Because, in reality, the need for dividing marital property may arise during marriage, and not only on divorce (Jiang Yue, 2001: 118). During marriage, if spouses terminate the statutory system of marital property and adopt the separate property system, either by court order or agreement, they will be confronted with the issues of dividing marital property and discharging the joint debts. Therefore, it is unreasonable only to put the distribution of community property or the discharging of joint debts in the chapter on divorce.

(d) The lack of compensation system relating to prenuptial property

Under s 17 of the new Marriage Law, prenuptial property is categorised as individual property. But s 16 of the 1993 Judicial Interpretation states that where the prenuptial property is damaged, consumed or lost naturally, the claim for compensating for this loss from joint property is not sustainable. This provision is not in the financial interests of the spouse who owns personal property easily consumed during marriage. It is against the doctrine of equality in the civil law.[9] Looked at from the perspective of gender equality, the consequence of applying the provision is that men and women are not equal in reality, and the law does not actually protect the married woman's prenuptial property rights (Chen Wei, Ran Qiyu, 2005: 45–46).

---

[8]   For example, during marriage, where one spouse perpetrates domestic violence against the other one and his/her property is insufficient to meet compensation for damage; or where one spouse abuses the right to joint property resulting in damage to community property, the other spouse needs to persuade the court to terminate the statutory system of community property and to adopt the separate property system.

[9]   In reality, the traditional form of marriage and living still prevails in the wider rural community in China. That is, men prepare the matrimonial home; women prepare articles for daily use and electrical appliances. During marriage, most articles for daily use and electrical appliances are usually used up in community life, leaving no value when divorce occurs. But the matrimonial home cannot be used in this way; some even increase in value. Since the current law does not acknowledge compensation for prenuptial property, if there is no other joint property distributed, divorced wives may be 'driven out of home with nothing', which is unfair to them.

(e) The provision on the proceeds of intellectual property rights is unreasonable

The Judicial Interpretation (II) of the Marriage Law interprets 'the proceeds of intellectual property rights' as 'the financial income that is actually acquired or definitely to be acquired during marriage'. For example, in relation to work that still has not been published on divorce, the judges have held that this does not meet the condition of 'incomes' contained in the new Marriage Law. The divorcing parties can only divide existing property, and where the value has not been realised the property cannot be assessed and divided. Intellectual property is joint property only when it is transformed into tangible property (Huang Songyou, 2004: 124). Section 15 of the 1993 Judicial Interpretation states that either spouse shall own his/her intellectual property gained during marriage so that no economic benefit is obtained at the time of divorce. Appropriate consideration may be given to the other spouse in the distribution of the other joint property. However, this provision requires that the other joint property already exists. If there is no joint property at all, compensation will not be given to the other spouse.[10] Hence, it may be unfair for the provision to exclude the anticipated profits from intellectual property obtained during marriage by one spouse, and this may be seen as a breach of the doctrine of equality under the civil law (Chen Wei, 2000c: 111).

(f) The lack of limits on the value of exclusive articles for daily use which are owned separately

Exclusive articles for daily use forming part of individual property refer to the property needed for the life and occupation of either spouse, for example, clothes or books used by either spouse. Section 18 of the new Marriage Law states that the exclusive articles for daily use are individual property. This provision is realistic. However, without limits on the value of exclusive articles for daily use this provision may result in unfairness. For example, where the husband is a businessman, he may own costly articles for daily use such as a car, portable computer or designer clothes. On the contrary, his wife may live a simple life; her articles for daily use are of little value. When they divorce, according to the above provision, the exclusive articles for daily use remain individual property, which is unfair to the wife. Some

---

10 For example, in one case the husband was a full-time author, while the wife was a seller working in a store. In order to support the husband in finishing the manuscript of a long story, she maintained the family with her modest income after marriage. Three years later, the husband thought that the family was doing poorly financially just because the wife was not good at managing the family. Therefore, he instituted an action for divorce on the grounds that mutual affection no longer existed. In addition, he did not submit the finished manuscript for publication for fear that the wife would claim half of the author's remuneration. Through mediation by the court, the wife agreed to divorce. But she claimed that during the past 3 years of marriage, she made large contributions to her husband's full-time writing by supporting him and maintaining the family with all her income, even though there was no existing property to be divided. Therefore, she claimed for division of the anticipated profits of the long story. The judge did not accept that the profits from the book contract were to be classified as property acquired or bound to be acquired. Finally, the judge dismissed her claim. The judgment was 'lawful'. But it appears unfair or unreasonable to the divorced wife.

foreign jurisdictions such as Russia impose limitations on the value of the exclusive articles for daily use.[11]

(g) The lack of a provision governing the ownership of the fruits of individual property acquired after marriage

Section 18 of the new Marriage Law supplemented the provision on individual property, which is some legislative progress. However, it does not provide for the ownership of the fruits of individual property after marriage. Fruits refer to the proceeds of original property, including natural fruits and legal fruits. What must be pointed out is that, before the passing of the new Marriage Law, the fruits of prenuptial property of either spouse acquired after marriage belonged to joint property according to the spirit of the general joint property system in the Marriage Law 1950 and the community system of postnuptial incomes in the Marriage Law 1980. On the contrary, after the execution of the new Marriage Law, the Legal Affairs Committee of the Standing Committee of the National People's Congress once pointed out in one publication that the prenuptial incomes of either spouse including the fruits of them acquired after marriage belonged to individual property (Legal Affairs Committee of the Standing Committee of the National People's Congress, 2001: 69). Some foreign jurisdictions provide differently in specific situations.[12]

(h) There are defects on the right of agency regarding daily family affairs

The Judicial Interpretation (II) of the Marriage Law acknowledges the right of agency in relation to the daily family affairs of both spouses. But there are some defects in relation to it. The first is that it does not use the terminology of the right of agency directly. The second is that it does not provide for limitations on the exercise of the right of agency and there are no provisions governing its effects on husband or wife or a third party. Some foreign jurisdictions have explicit provisions on this.[13]

---

[11] For example, s 36(2) of the Russian Family Code 1995 states that, except for expensive articles and luxuries, articles for personal use (clothes, shoes and other articles) are deemed to be individual property, ie even if these articles were bought during marriage with joint money. See the *Family Code of the Russian Federal Union*, translated by Yan Yimei, Beijing: CLS Research Committee of the Marriage Law, Compilation of Foreign Marriage and Family Law [Z] (Beijing: Publishing House of the Masses, 2000).

[12] For example, the Civil Code of France provides that the surplus of the fruits of individual property and the incomes of either spouse acquired during marriage belong to both spouses. Either spouse preserves the complete ownership of his or her own property. Joint property only includes the fruits acquired but which have not been consumed. Property gained in the name of the owner of the individual property as well as new securities connected with separately owned securities and other increments belong to separate property. That is to say, France deals with different things in different ways. The fruits of individual prenuptial property acquired after marriage belong to joint property, except those relating to securities. See ss 1041, 1043, 1046 of the *Civil Code of France*, translated by Luo Jiezhen (China Legal System Press, 1999).

[13] For example, the Civil Code of Germany provides that both spouses are entitled to engage in activities meeting proper needs of the family, and where their consequences have an effect on the other spouse. Both spouses share the rights and activities, except as otherwise decided. The Civil

(i) The lack of guiding principles on the distribution of stock rights owned by both spouses

With the advancement of the market economy and the development of the private sector and stock market in China, disputes over the distribution of stock rights have continually increased. In the light of the complexity of spouses' stock rights, how to divide the securities, the shares in company and the shares in partnership and property in single-venture enterprises have become difficult issues in the trial of divorce cases. Therefore, the Judicial Interpretation (II) of the Marriage Law provides for the method of dividing stock rights owned by both spouses. However, it does not introduce a guiding principle to govern the difficulties (Chen Wei, Xie Jingjie, 2004: 144–145).

C The provisions on the contractual property system are not sufficient

The new Marriage Law supplemented the scope, contents, form, application and effects of a property agreement (the effects on both spouses and third parties). But there are the following omissions.

(a) There are careless omissions regarding the content of the contractual property relationship

The new Marriage Law provides that spouses may reach an agreement on the ownership of property acquired before or after marriage. However, there are no detailed provisions on whether they can reach an agreement on the rights relating to managing, using, profiting from and disposing of marital property, the bearing of family expenses or liability for debts.

(b) There are no provisions on the formation, adjustment and termination of a contractual property relationship

Sections 8–9 provide a remedy for one spouse when the other breaks the property agreement reached by the spouses at the time of divorce. But it lacks provisions dealing with the commencement of a property contract, and the public summons for adjusting and terminating the contractual property relationship.

Code of France and the Civil Code of Japan provide that both spouses should bear joint and several liability for the debts incurred by acting in connection with family affairs. Provisions in the Civil Code in many jurisdictions usually provide that where husband or wife abuses the right of agency relating to family affairs or indicates that he/she is unable to exercise or is unfit for exercising the right, the other shall remove from him or her the right of agency. But it must not prejudice a third party. See s 1357 of the Civil Code of Germany; s 220 of the Civil Code of France; s 761 of the Civil Code of Japan; s 166 of the Civil Code of Switzerland. In addition, s 1003 of the Civil Code of China Taiwan District provides the same.

V CONCLUSION

In accordance with the realities in China and the legislative experience in other jurisdictions, I suggest supplementing and improving the marital property system of China in the following three respects.

1 **Improving the structure of the marital property system, adding general provisions on the marital property system (Chen Wei, 2000: 88–89).**

2 **Improving the structure and contents of the statutory property system by:**

(a) improving the structure of the statutory property system and supplementing the emergency statutory system relating to marital property;

(b) adding provisions dealing with the rights and liabilities of spouses for marital property, the grounds for and the consequences of terminating the marital property relationship;

(c) adding special principles on the distribution of joint stock rights;

(d) establishing a system of proper compensation in relation to prenuptial property;

(e) adding provisions dealing with the ownership of the anticipated profits of intellectual property obtained by either spouse during marriage;

(f) prescribing limits on the value of separately owned exclusive articles for daily use that are individual property;

(g) regulating the ownership of the fruits of individual property obtained during marriage;[14] and

(h) improving the content of the right of agency regarding the daily family affairs of both spouses.

3 **Improving the content of the contractual property system by:**

---

[14] That is, as for the fruits of individual property acquired during marriage, we suggest that the Chinese Legislature should make reference to the legislation in France to legislate differently for different situations. In reality, the acquisition of fruits of prenuptial property needs the investment of labour or money by one spouse or both apart from the interest from the prenuptial deposit. For example, the fruit trees planted before marriage can grow fruits only if they are cultivated and maintained after marriage. The pregnant cow bred before marriage can bear a calf only by feeding it continuously after marriage. Where the prenuptial house owned by one spouse was rented to others after marriage, the landlord still needs to perform the duty of maintaining the house (that is, the landlord needs to invest money or labour). The labour or money invested in the prenuptial property of one spouse mainly belongs to joint property (even if the costs of maintaining the house can be deducted from the rents, the incomes of letting the house belong to marital property). The increase or preservation of value of the stocks bought before marriage, as well their buying and selling involves investing much time and money during marriage. Therefore, the fruits of individual prenuptial property should be dealt with differently in different situations. It is reasonable to provide that other fruits should belong to joint property apart from the interest on the deposit. If so, it not only preserves the harmony of marriage and the family, but protects the ownership of individual property of both spouses.

(a) prescribing the time to enter into an agreement on a marital property relationship between spouses and the specific content of the contractual property system; and

(b) providing detail relating to the public summons and its effect when spouses adjust or terminate their contractual property relationship.

REFERENCES

Chen Wei, Ran Qiyu 'Gender in Public Policies – Gender Analysis of the Marriage Law of the PRC and Its Legislative Improvement [J]' (2005) Gansu: *Journal of Gansu University of Political Science and Law* vol 1

Chen Wei, Xie Jingjie 'On the Distribution of Joint Stock Rights in Divorce Cases [J]' (2004) Guangdong: *Social Science of Guangdong*

Chen Wei 'On the Amendment and Improvement of Marriage Law [J]' (2003) Chongqing: *Modern Law Science* vol 4

Chen Wei *A Study of the Legislative Principle of Marital Property System and Several Issues* [J] (Fujian: Southeast Academy, 2001) vol 2

Chen Wei *A Study of the Legislation of Marriage and Family Law in China* [M] (Beijing: Publishing House of the Masses, 2000a)

Chen Wei 'Legislative Conceptions of Perfecting the Marital Property System of China [J]' (2000b) Beijing: *China Law Science* vol 1

Chen Wei 'A Discussion on the Ownership of the anticipated profits from Intellectual Property Acquired by One Spouse During Marriage [M]' (2000c) Chongqing: *Modern Law Science* vol 4

Gao Fengxian *Theories and Practice of Kindred Law* [M] (Taiwan: Wunan Books Publishing Co Ltd, 5th edn, 2005)

Huang Songyou *On the Understanding and Application of the Interpretation (II) of Several Problems on the Application of the Marriage Law of the PRC* [M] (Beijing: People's Courts Press, 2004)

Jiang Yue *Rights and Duties of Husband and wife* [M] (Beijing: Law Press, 2001)

Lin Xiuxiong *A Study of Marital Property System* [M] (Beijing: China University of Political Science and Law Press, 2001)

Patrick Parkinson and Juliet Behrens *Australian Family Law in Context: Commentary and Materials* [M] (published in Sydney by the Law Book Co, 3rd edn, 2004)

Wu Changzhen *A Survey on the Execution of Marriage Law* [M] (Beijing: Zhongyang Wenxian Press, 2004)

Wu Changzhen *Marriage Law and I* [M] (Beijing: Law Press, 2001)

Xia Yinlan 'Examining the Method of Marital Property Distribution in China in the Framework of International Human Rights [J]' (2005) Beijing: *Global Law Review* vol 1

Yang Dawen *Law of Domestic Relations* [M] (Beijing: Law Press, 3rd edn, 2003)

Zhang Xuejun 'Amendment of the Marriage Law in China [J]' (2002) *International Journal of Law, Policy and the Family* vol 16 (published by Oxford University Press)

Legal Affairs Committee of Standing Committee of the National People's Congress (2001), *Practical Questions and Answers to the Marriage Law of the PRC* [M] (Beijing: China Wujia Press, 2001)

Costa Rica

UNDERSTANDING FAMILY LAW AND THE FAMILY COURT SYSTEM IN COSTA RICA

Diego Benavides Santos[*]

Résumé

Un magistrat du Costa Rica décrit et résume le droit de la famille et les juridictions familiales de son pays. Il propose quelques repères historiques tout en retraçant brièvement l'état du droit de la famille au cours des dernières années. Il s'intéresse particulièrement à quatre des lois internes les plus remarquables en la matière, sans oublier les traités internationaux les plus importants. Il souligne la tendance à une spécialisation des juridictions familiales. A grands traits, il brosse les procédures judiciaires costariciennes et met en lumière leurs caractéristiques principales. Après avoir isolé celles qui offrent un intérêt statistique de premier plan, il compare le contentieux familial au contentieux général, et termine sa contribution en décrivant trois domaines qui constituent un défi pour l'avenir.

I SOME INFORMATION ABOUT COSTA RICA

Costa Rica is a Central American country 50,000 sq km (19,305 sq miles) in area. It is bordered by Nicaragua to the north, Panama to the south, the Pacific Ocean to the west, and by the Caribbean Sea to the east. Its population is comprised of roughly four million Costa Rican citizens and 500,000 non-citizens. It is a unitary (non-federal) republic. There has been no standing army in Costa Rica since 1949. It has declared itself neutral vis-à-vis international conflicts. The Costa Rican Government's head of state is its President, who heads the Executive Branch and is elected to serve 4-year terms. The Legislative Branch is spearheaded by the Legislative Assembly, which is made up of 57 representatives that are referred to as deputies.

Christopher Columbus discovered the area pertaining to what is currently known as Costa Rica during his fourth trip to the Americas, and it is the one and only country with a name that can be traced back to the famous explorer.

---

[*] Judge serving on the Supreme Family Tribunal with headquarters in San José, Costa Rica. Expert in the administration of justice and arbitrator. dbenavides@poder-judicial.co.cr.

It became independent from Spain in 1821 and enjoyed renown for its consistent political stability. Its current population has its roots in waves of émigrés catalysed by the traditional customs of Spain. Its economy's mainstay was agriculture, coffee and banana production, chiefly, and it has diversified somewhat in recent decades through production of goods and services. The tourism industry has attracted visitors to the country's beautiful beaches, national parks, lush vegetation and wildlife, and its heavenly climate, making for temperatures of 68–86° F (20–30°C) year-round in the highlands and daytime highs of 95°F (35°C) on the beaches. Some readers are likely to be acquainted with these facts, having already been to the country. Its capital city is San José, and the national currency is the colón.

II   COSTA RICA'S LEGAL SYSTEM

By virtue of its Hispanic origins, Costa Rica's legal system is based on civil (continental) law. Its present-day Constitution dates back to 1949. Using simple, direct procedures, the Constitutional Court oversees the constitutionality of laws and acts, and its rulings are binding. International treaties ratified by the country take precedence over laws, and those dealing with human rights prevail even over the Constitution. Above and beyond the Constitution and ratified international treaties, the country's chief regulatory bodies of law are the Civil Code, the Commercial Code, the Penal Code, the Uniform Civil Service Law, and the Family Code. The Judicial Branch of the government is very independent, and according to the Constitution, 6% of the national budget is to be allocated to the administration of justice. The Judiciary is presided over by 20 magistrates appointed by the Legislative Assembly to serve 8-year terms that require a qualified majority to rule out renewal. Courts must be legally established, and setting up special courts for specific cases is illegal. After earning a Licentiate Degree in Law by completing an accredited university law degree programme, practising lawyers must be accepted into the Costa Rica Bar Association (*Colegio de Abogados*), which wields official authority with regard to this profession.

III COSTA RICAN FAMILY LAW

A   Historical context

While Costa Rica was one of the Kingdom of Spain's dependent territories, the prevailing law of the land and that of Spain were one and the same with the addition of the Law of the Indies. This state of affairs prevailed until 1842, with the issuance of the Uniform Code drafted to regulate, *inter alia*, matters of Family Law. This Law, obviously patriarchal, advocated male predominance and is pervaded by discrimination, including concepts such as 'natural children, products of incest and sacrilege' used to describe children born out of wedlock or whose parents were members of the clergy.

Issued in 1888 the Civil Code was a product of liberalism, an ideology that affected Catholic countries by limiting and rejecting the influence of church authorities.

Established in this regulatory body of law were divorce and a joint division system for distribution of marital property. This is considered by Comparative Law as the first of its kind to be regulated as a legal regime and regards its precedents as Hungarian Common Law and the 1825 Polish Civil Code. This regime, which presupposed full legal capacity and equality for women, is an indication of our scholars' early vocation for Family Law. This Code retained inequalities now considered rather offensive, however, such as proof of adultery as the sole requirement for a man divorcing a woman, whereas scandalous cohabitation had to be established for a woman divorcing her husband. Moreover, paternity investigation was very limited.

Special laws crucial to family law were enacted, such as the 1916 Alimony Law which was subsequently replaced by another passed in 1953. An Adoption Law was ratified in 1934.

The country's prevailing Political Constitution, containing the principles of gender and filial equality before the law, was adopted in 1949.

Reforms were made to the Civil Code to bring it in line with the Constitution. However, since these reforms were considered insufficient, a commission was formed in the 1960s to review family law regulations, culminating in ratification of the Family Code in 1973. Matters dealing with family issue-related legal and administrative procedures were, nonetheless, left unresolved. By 1960s' standards, the Family Code effectively adapted the regulations to the principles of equality among men and women and between children born both within and outside of marriage.

Practically since enactment, the Family Code has been in a state of constant flux, undergoing reforms in 1976, 1977, 1985, 1989, 1990, 1994, 1995, 1996, 1997, 2001, 2002, and 2004.

The reform of 1989 made procedural changes due to the ratification of a new Civil Code of Procedure. The reform of 1990 came about as a result of the enactment of a 'true women's equality' law. Important reforms were made in 1995 concerning adoption and declaration of abandonment of minors, which also incorporated a section on common-law (*de facto*) marriage (referred to as *unión de hecho,* in Spanish).

In 1996, adaptations dealing with disabled individuals were made. The reform of 1997 helped eliminate the consequences of 'blame' in the loss of jointly owned assets acquired during marriage. Hence, even in the event of a spouse committing adultery, the individual in question does not forfeit rights to the individual's corresponding share of such assets as part of the other spouse's patrimony. Before a landmark reform was made in 2001, the mother of a child born out of wedlock had to go to court to establish paternity, having to assume the legal fees herself initially, regardless of whether she was subsequently reimbursed or not. Currently, the mother files a statement to the examiner at the Registry Office as to the identity of the alleged father. This in turn opens an administrative proceeding summoning the suspected father either to acknowledge paternity or request a DNA test. Surprisingly for those of us in the legal profession, recent figures reveal that a high percentage of the men named in these disputes waive the DNA test and willingly register the children in question. For instance, by July 2005, DNA tests had been requested in only 5,000 cases involving 19,000 births.

Special laws have been gradually added to Family Law Regulations over the years, however. The most important of these include the Law for the Prevention of Domestic Violence (1996), the Alimony Regulation Law (1996), the Organic Law of the National Child Welfare Agency known as PANI (1996) and the Children and Adolescents Code (1998).

As explained above, several international treaties have been ratified that take precedence over domestic laws. Consequently, they exert greater influence over court decisions. Among these treaties are the following: the United Nations Convention on the Rights of the Child (20 November 1989), The Hague Convention of 25 October 1980 on the Civil Aspects of the International Child Abduction, The Hague Convention of 29 May 1993 on Protection of Children and Co-operation in respect of Intercountry Adoption, Inter-American Convention on the Prevention, Punishment and Eradication of Violence Against Women 'Convention of Belem do Para' (OAS). This has become a particularly important resource for Costa Rican Family Law over the last 15 years of binding constitutional jurisprudence.

B   Key laws governing the family in Costa Rica

1   The Family Code

The Family Code regulates issues involving marriage, annulment, legal separation, divorce, distribution of property, marital and extramarital filiation, adoption, *patria potestas*, nurturing, tutorship, guardianship and common-law marriage.

Article 2 stipulates that the fundamental principles for applying and interpreting this Code are family unity, the best interests of children and minors, and equal rights and responsibilities for both male and female parents.

Marriage ceremonies performed by notaries public, family court judges, and consuls are considered officially valid as are those performed by Catholic priests. Proscriptions applicable to marriage reflect mores prohibiting incest and espousing monogamy and heterosexuality:

'ARTICLE 14. The following are legally unacceptable conditions regarding marriages:

1) Individuals bound by prior marriages;
2) Union of forbears and descendants related by blood or kinship. This legal impediment does not expire due to dissolution of the marriage that produced the said blood or kinship relationship;
3) Union of blood siblings;
4) Union of an adopter and an adopted individual and his/her descendants; adopted persons of one and the same individual; adopted persons and the children of their adopters; adopted children and the former spouses of their adopters; and adopted persons and the former spouses of their adopters;
5) Union of the perpetrator, co-perpetrator, instigator, or accomplice of a homicide committed against one of the spouses and the surviving spouse; and
6) Union of individuals of the same gender.'[1]

Monogamy and heterosexuality are emphasised once more regarding the concepts of common-law marriage and cohabitation. Common-law marriage and cohabitation are both legally recognised in connection with stable, public, observable unions of only one man and one woman over a period of at least 3 years (Family Code, art 242). Common-law marriage rulings are made chiefly for patrimony and alimony-related purposes.

Individuals may be granted marriage annulments, legal separations, and divorces in Costa Rica.

(a) A marriage may be annulled in cases where the most egregious marriage-related prohibitions have been violated. This affects spouses that have acted in good faith to a lesser degree.

(b) Legal separation is ruled in cases of lesser breaches of marital duties and entails bodily separation, division of property, and presumption of paternity ceases, even though the spouses in question remain married, and the legally binding duties of faithfulness and mutual aid remain intact. Among the chief grounds for legal separation are abandonment of domicile, serious transgressions, actual physical separation for more than one year, unwarranted failure to carry out the duties of support/nurturing, and serious behavioural disorders. Legal separation by mutual consent is admissible when the spouses in question have been married for 2 years or more. The spouses must appear together before a notary public to come to agreement on matters dealing with custody, rearing, and education of children, property, and alimony. A judge must approve the said agreement, whereupon it must be recorded in the public records.

---

[1] A petition to declare this section unconstitutional is currently being considering by the Constitutional Court.

(c) Divorce necessarily implies terminating the bonds of matrimony. Leading grounds for divorce include adultery, brutality, attempted murder, and de facto separation for a period in excess of 3 years. Divorce by mutual consent is also admissible when spouses have been married for over 3 years.

There are two categories of filiation: marital and extramarital.

(a) *Marital filiation*: Essential to marital filiation is the basic premise that a child of the mother is also the child of the father (*presunción pater is est,* Family Code, art 69). There is a 'suit' for claiming this type of filiation on behalf of a child known as *vindicación de estado* (proof of status), which is very seldom filed in our country since it has an effective registry of vital statistics such as marriage and birth records that constitute 'proof of status' (Family Code, arts 76 and 77). Parental requests for children to be considered as born within a marriage constitute attempts at 'legitimation' (eg Family Code, art 81, final paragraph). This applies to cases of children born out of wedlock whose parents decide to marry after the fact. There are several ways to disavow marital filiation. When a husband petitions for a wife's child not to be considered as his own, it is referred to as 'contested paternity' (Family Code, arts 72–74). When the mother or child files this type of petition (Family Code, art 71), it is known as 'declaration of child born out of wedlock' (*declaratoria de extramatrimonialidad*). A biological father may also initiate a proceeding that may or may not be contested by the registered parents, as in 'acknowledgement of a married mother's child' (Family Code, art 85).

(b) *Extramarital filiation*: This type of filiation occurs outside of wedlock or when the parents are not married to each other. In these cases the child's birth is not assumed to be within the marriage; consequently, the following three mechanisms are relied upon primarily to establish the individual's paternity:

   (i) acknowledgement (Family Code, arts 84, 87–90);

   (ii) an administrative proceeding set forth in the 2001 reform of the Family Code pursuant to what is known as the Responsible Paternity Law; and

   (iii) paternity by court order (Family Code, arts 91–99).

The concept of 'open possession of status' (Family Code, arts 90, 93 and 99) is so crucial to the extramarital filiation model that acknowledgement or declaration of paternity is impossible if another filiation has already been established for a child by another open possession of status. In circumstances such as these involving extramarital filiation, the mother may decline consent even though the father is willing to acknowledge the under-age child (cf art 84), wherefore he may have to request authorisation for the said acknowledgement. Then again, the acknowledgement may very well be inconsistent with biological fact. Provisions are in place for 'contested acknowledgement' to deal with cases involving misrepresentation or error (Family Code, art 86).

The Family Code also regulates adoption, which is defined by law as a legal institution for the organisation and protection of the family, public order, and social welfare. Adoption is described as a legal process and a psycho-social process through which an adopted individual, for all intents and purposes, becomes a member of the adopter's family as a bona fide son or daughter (Family Code, art 100).

Several types of adoption bear mention:

(a) of an adult or a minor (art 109 b);

(b) of an individual or a group;

(c) by citizens residing locally or abroad (Family Code, art 112 under The Hague Convention of 29 May 1993 on Protection of Children and Co-operation in respect of Intercountry Adoption);

(d) with the parents' consent or by means of declaration of abandonment for purposes of adoption;

(e) with or without a change in the given name;

(f) of minors with or without the discernment duly to express their views or opinions;

(g) adoption of a spouse's child;

(h) married or single adopters.

Costa Rica ratified The Hague Convention of 25 October 1980 on the Civil Aspects of the International Child Abduction, and the institution wielding supreme authority with regard to this Convention is the Costa Rican Child Welfare Authority known as PANI (*Patronato Nacional de la Infancia*).

Listed below are the items in the order in which they appear in the Costa Rican Family Code.

The Costa Rican Family Code

Heading	Item regulated	Articles	Contents
Preamble	General Provisions	1–9	The Code's most important principles, ie filial equality and the equal rights and responsibilities of spouses. Deals also with important procedural issues
I	Marriage	10–68	Regulates marriage, the system of marital patrimony, divorce, legal separation and marriage annulment
II	Paternity and Filiation	69–139	Regulates marital/extramarital filiation and adoption

Heading	Item regulated	Articles	Contents
III	Parental Authority	140–163	Regulates parental authority over children, reasons for suspension, modification, and loss of *patria potestas* and declaration of abandonment
IV	Nurturing	164–174	Regulates maintenance by other members of the family
V	Tutorship	175–229	Deals with situations in which a minor has no one to take care of or represent him/her due to the death of parents or because they do not wield *patria potestas*
VI	Guardianship	230–241	Deals with the appointment of legal representatives and guardians for people who are unable to look after themselves
VII	Common-law Marriage	242–246	Deals with situations in which a man and a woman live together without the benefit of marriage

2   The Domestic Violence Prevention Law

Enacted in 1996, this law deals with safety measures that can be implemented in a summary procedure to protect victims of domestic violence, be it physical, psychological, sexual or patrimonial in nature. Examples of admissible measures would be police escorted departure from the conjugal domicile, a restraining order to limit proximity to the dwelling, place of work or study, granting of custody, upbringing, and education of the children, suspension of the said custody, upbringing, and education, alimony payments, confiscation of arms, a do-not-disturb order, etc. This is a landmark indeed in Costa Rican Family Law, especially since this very simple procedure can be invoked without the legal assistance of a lawyer.

3   The Alimony Regulation Law

Even though Family Code regulations touch on some aspects of alimony-related duties, the remainder of these matters is definitely dealt with in this law enacted in 1996 regarding issues of procedure and compulsory alimony enforcement measures. This is an extremely thorny issue for Costa Ricans in the legal profession.

4   The Children and Adolescents Code

Enacted in 1998, this law helped bring to maturity the principles of the Convention on the Rights of the Child (UN 1989) and instituted responsible, authoritative state bodies with a clear mandate prohibiting the State from alleging that its budgets are insufficient to cover matters involving children and adolescents. Child and adolescent procedural rights were enhanced and a procedure was established to request steps to protect this vulnerable population.

IV THE FAMILY COURT SYSTEM

A Legal authorities that conduct family hearings

The Costa Rican family court system centres on work in courts of first and second instance. Currently, there are 17 family courts in the country and family matters are heard and settled in eight 'civil and labour' courts. They are presided over by a judge who, as a rule, is chosen through a competitive selection process stressing family law experience. Moreover, in San José there is a Children's and Adolescents' Court (*Juzgado de Niñez y Adolescencia*), which is a family court with expertise in certain specific matters that aims to further a culture of sensitivity regarding children and adolescents, in keeping with the Convention on the Rights of the Child (UN 1989). It should be stressed here that hearings involving issues of domestic violence are held at nine courts specifically devoted to matters of this type. Moreover, where no specialised court of this type is available, these matters are heard by family court judges or by small claims courts and courts that try minor violations. The highest court in the land for family, children's and adolescents' and domestic violence-related matters (or those functioning in the same capacity) is the Supreme Family Tribunal (*Tribunal de Familia*), a professional institution whose members are authorised to hear any appeal in the country.

Appeals for the reversal of rulings handed down by the Supreme Family Tribunal are the jurisdiction of the Second Chamber of the Costa Rican Supreme Court, the highest-ranking judicial institution, whose members preside over the Costa Rican Judiciary. This Second Chamber also hears appeals to reverse decisions on matters of labour and class action suits. It bears mention that very few reversals are filed in the family court, essentially regarding marital status-related issues, liquidation of a couple's property acquired during marriage, and filiation. Roughly 80% of the cases on the Second Chamber's docket deal with labour matters.

It should be noted that issues of alimony payments are dealt with at seven special courts and at 66 misdemeanor courts (*juzgados contravencionales*). The local Family Court has jurisdiction over alimony or misdemeanour courts.

Overleaf is an illustration of how the Costa Rican family court system is organised:

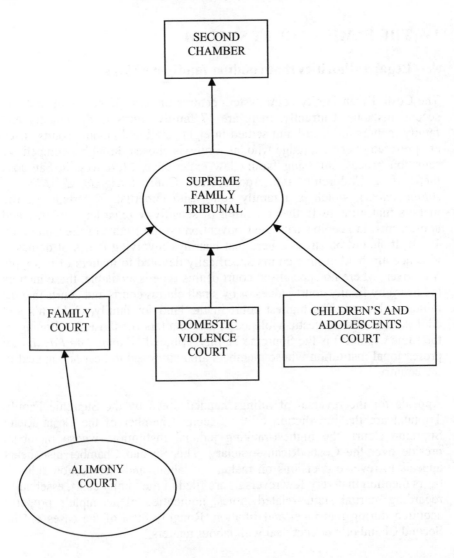

B   Description of family court processes

Overall, the design of family court procedures in Costa Rica is unsuited to certain specific prevailing strategies in this area. Some of them are documents (divorce, legal separation, marriage annulment, etc) while others are verbal in nature (filiation, declaration of abandonment, adoption, etc). Some of them require the services of a lawyer and others do not. Some are contested while others are not. The following table itemises the various types of procedures, the law regulating each one, and other significant facts:

Contested family proceedings

Procedure Type	Regulating Law	Verbal	Document	Lawyer Required	Instance	Contention
Ordinary[2]	Civil Code of Procedure		Document	X	3	X
Abbreviated[3]	Civil Code of Procedure		Document	X	3	X
Summary[4]	Civil Code of Procedure		Document	X	2	X
Filiation[5]	Family Code	Verbal		X	3	X
Conflict over *patria potestas*[6]	Family Code	Verbal			2	X
Alimony[7]	Alimony Regulation Law		Document		2	X
Instance of change in a ruling	Family Code		Document	X	2	X
Domestic violence	Domestic Violence Prevention Law	Verbal			2	X
Declaration of abandonment	Family Code	Verbal		X	2	X
Child and adolescent protection	Children and Adolescents Code	Verbal			2	X

---

[2]   Examples of this would be the liquidation in advance of property acquired during marriage and marriage annulment.

[3]   This deal with divorces, legal separations, marriage annulments, prohibitions on, suspensions of or modifications to *patria potestas*, acknowledgement of common-law marriage.

[4]   Examples of this would be visiting hours, and lifting of real estate liens against family dwellings.

[5]   These may be investigations as to paternity, contested paternity, declarations of children born out of wedlock, contested acknowledgements, legitimisations, proof of status, etc.

[6]   An example of this is minors leaving the country or other issues at which parents are at odds.

[7]   These may include procedures for settling on or adjusting figures (increases, decreases, the inclusion or exclusion of beneficiaries, exemptions, etc).

Uncontested family proceedings

Procedure Type	Regulating Law	Verbal	Document	Lawyer Required	Instance	Contention
Divorce by mutual consent	Civil Code of Procedure Family Code		Document	X	3	No[8]
Protective custody	Civil Code of Procedure Children and Adolescents Code		Document	X	2	No
Tutorship	Civil Code of Procedure Family Code		Document	X	2	No
Authorisations concerning property for gain or need	Civil Code of Procedure		Document	X	2	No
Insanity	Civil Code of Procedure		Document	X	2	No[9]
Guardianship	Civil Code of Procedure Family Code		Document	X	2	No
Marriage	Family Code	Verbal			1	No[10]
Oppositions to marriage	Civil Code of Procedure		Document	X	2	Yes[11]
Adoption	Family Code	Verbal		X	2	No[12]

---

[8]   If a dispute arises, a case is to be tried and a ruling handed down in the final determination.

[9]   If a dispute arises, an abbreviated injunction proceeding must be heard.

[10] Disputes allowed during uncontested legal proceedings are listed below.

[11] An apparent contradiction in terms, uncontested proceedings are permitted, yet they are ostensibly contested.

Summary proceedings will be conducted when a dispute is anticipated.

Procedure Type	Regulating Law	Verbal	Document	Lawyer Required	Instance	Contention
Acknowledgement of a married woman's child	Family Code		Document	X	2	No[13]

Significantly it must be borne in mind that Costa Rican family courts rely on the National Child Welfare Agency (PANI) instead of public prosecutors to defend the rights of children and adolescents. This constitutionally sanctioned administrative body must be notified of all legal proceedings involving minors. The Costa Rican Attorney-General's Office is involved to some extent with uncontested matters.

Furthermore, although art 7 of the Family Code stipulates that the State must provide legal counsel to the poor, this principle has only been applied successfully in cases involving alimony. Therefore, university programmes running legal aid offices handle a very sizeable portion of family law cases. As a result, access to justice in these situations is rather inequitable and dubious unless alimony payments or domestic violence are involved.

Expert assistance is considered an important issue and, accordingly, some Family Courts and Domestic Violence Courts are equipped with their own interdisciplinary teams of expert psychologists and social workers.

C   Statistical analysis of family court cases

The following Costa Rican judiciary graphs from the 2004 Judicial Yearbook contain annual incoming case figures by year. The statistics department makes a distinction between family cases, alimony cases, and domestic violence cases, even though the matters that they deal with are all family related. This distinction is useful, however, in accounting for specificity in courts handling alimony payment and domestic violence cases. According to the graph, in 2004, 23,754 'family' cases were opened nationwide (excluding those of alimony payment or domestic violence). In the same year, there were almost as many alimony payment cases (23,422), along with an alarming 48,073 cases of domestic violence, ie over twice the number of those considered 'family' cases.

There were over twice as many cases involving domestic violence in 2004 (48,073) compared to 1999 (20,996), as illustrated in the graph overleaf.[14]

---

[13]   An abbreviated proceeding will be conducted if a dispute arises, albeit even though a filiation proceeding may appear to be in order.

[14]   This graph and others, and their corresponding statistical interpretations are posted on the following website: www.poder-judicial.go.cr/planificacion/estadistica/judiciales/2004/33-%20Violencia%20Doméstica%202004.doc.

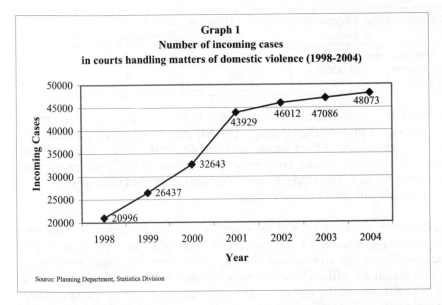

Graph 1
Number of incoming cases
in courts handling matters of domestic violence (1998-2004)

Source: Planning Department, Statistics Division

This issue of the shockingly excessive rise in these problem situations, and a likewise phenomenon regarding traffic violations, are cause of great concern to the Chief Justice of the Costa Rican Supreme Court of Justice, as expressed in his 2004 Work Report.

Rises in alimony cases have tended to be quite continual and predictable, as borne out in the following graph.[15]

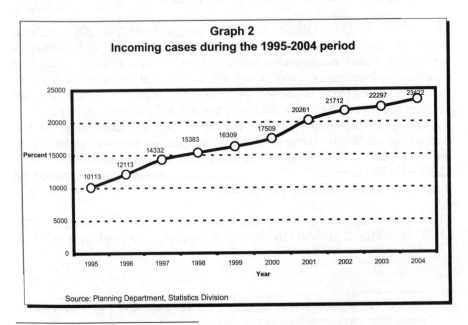

Graph 2
Incoming cases during the 1995-2004 period

Source: Planning Department, Statistics Division

---

[15]   This graph and others, and their corresponding statistical interpretations are posted on the following   website: www.poder-judicial.go.cr/planificacion/estadistica/judiciales/2004/32-%20 Pensiones%20Alimentarias.doc.

The graph below reflects the statistical performance from 1999–2004 regarding 'family' cases, ie without taking into account cases of domestic violence or alimony payment.[16]

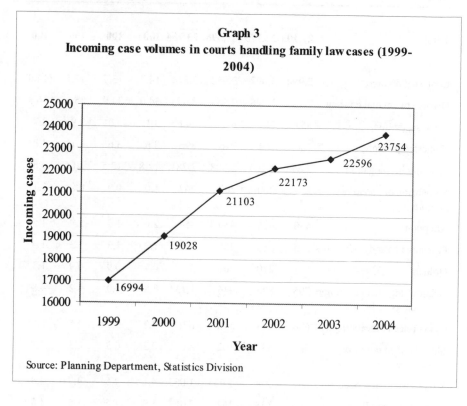

Graph 3
Incoming case volumes in courts handling family law cases (1999-2004)

Source: Planning Department, Statistics Division

It is also very interesting to observe the distribution of case types under the heading designated as 'family' cases by the Costa Rican Judiciary (which does not take domestic violence and alimony payments into account). The most common legal action is divorce by mutual consent, representing 60% of the total number of cases tried, and is followed by contested divorce, and then by paternity investigations.[17]

---

[16]   This graph and others, and their corresponding statistical interpretations are posted on the following website: www.poder-judicial.go.cr/planificacion/estadistica/judiciales/2004/31-%20Familia%202004.doc.

[17]   This graph is posted on the following website: www.poder-judicial.go.cr/planificacion/estadistica/judiciales/2004/31-%20Familia%202004.doc.

Case Type	Incoming Cases				Percentages			
	2001	2002	2003	2004	2001	2002	2003	2004
Total	21,103	22,173	22,596	23,754	100	100	100	100
Contested divorce	2,994	3,027	3,052	3,324	14.2	13.7	13.5	14.0
Divorce by mutual consent	7,175	7,748	7,963	8,633	34.0	34.9	35.2	36.3
Legal separation	653	667	655	649	3.1	3.0	2.9	2.7
Contested paternity	756	804	916	896	3.6	3.6	4.1	3.8
Paternity investigation	2,693	2,764	2,388	2,281	12.8	12.5	10.6	9.6
Suspension of *patria potestas*	221	200	207	267	1.0	0.9	0.9	1.1
Adoption	430	425	439	354	2.0	1.9	1.9	1.5
Protective custody of minors	265	286	285	327	1.3	1.3	1.3	1.4
Ordinary	151	210	206	319	0.7	0.9	0.9	1.3
Acknowledgement of minors proceedings	795	876	946	1,133	3.8	4.0	4.2	4.8
Gain or need proceedings	684	643	556	671	3.2	2.9	2.5	2.8
Shared *patria potestas* proceedings	59	63	102	82	0.3	0.3	0.5	0.3
Minor visitation proceedings	857	999	1,053	1,053	4.1	4.5	4.7	4.4
Marriage proceedings	395	338	362	310	1.9	1.5	1.6	1.3
Uncontested legal proceedings	78	109	138	171	0.4	0.5	0.6	0.7
Miscellaneous matters	2,897	3,014	3,328	3,284	13.7	13.6	14.7	13.8

The following graph reveals the ratio of resources devoted in 2002 by the Costa Rican Judiciary to settle family matters in the courts and, for statistical reasons, keeping cases involving matters of family, alimony, and domestic violence from those dealing with domestic violence:[18]

Percentage-wise distribution of workforce-related costs and variable jurisdictional expenditures, according to case type (2002)

Agriculture	2.9%
Litigation	5.3%
Constitutional	5.9%

---

[18]   This graph and others similar to it are posted on the following website: http://www.poder-judicial.go.cr/planificacion/.

Violations	6.3%
Civil	19.4%
Family	5.7%
Notarial	0.7%
Criminal	25.3%
Juvenile criminal	2.6%
Alimony	4.0%
Labour	10.2%
Traffic	4.0%
Domestic violence	7.8%

The following graph illustrates the distribution of incoming cases involving all of the different matters handled by the Judiciary, demonstrating that family cases actually do represent a considerable share.[19]

Incoming cases handled by first instance court offices listed according to case type (2000–2004)

Case Type	Year				
	2000	*2001*	*2002*	*2003*	*2004*
Total	798198	934213	996534	926940	953847
Civil[1]	76349	72797	73868	74786	78287
Agriculture[1]	-	3040	3028	3007	3027
Family	19028	21103	22173	22596	23754
Contentious-Administrative	22861	22728	22929	23032	24117
Criminal[2]	111126	116356	118667	133542	141906
Labor	24188	21257	19951	20398	20454
Violations	53304	50747	48087	46812	50845
Traffic	419545	537540	594417	507889	515037
Alimony	17509	20261	21712	22297	23433
Juvenile Criminal[3]	10837	11703	12259	12193	11494
Domestic Violence	32643	43929	46012	47086	48073
Constitutional	10808	12752	13431	13302	13420

---

[19]   This graph and others similar to it are posted on the following website: www.poder-judicial.go.cr/planificacion/estadistica/judiciales/2004/documentos/00-Resumen%20Anuario%202004_C4.pdf.

1   Cases dealing with agriculture have been considered separately since 2001.

2   Refers to cases coming into the Attorney-General's Office and crimes entered into the Criminal Courts involving private acts.

3   Refers to cases coming into the Attorney-General's Office.

Source: Planning Department, Statistics Division

V   CHALLENGES FACING FAMILY LAW AND THE COSTA RICAN FAMILY COURT SYSTEM

The challenges faced by Costa Rican Family Law include a thorough re-examination of Family Code legislation covering divorce, filiation and *patria potestas*-related issues, primarily. Despite undergoing some changes, parts of this legislation are now outdated after 30 years, given the changes that have been taking place over time.

We may conclude from this review that, on paper, Costa Rica scores high on indicators gauging specialised expertise, but in reality the system is plagued with great inconsistencies and paradoxes. As a result, it is faced with enormous strategic challenges:

(a) There is a need for the universities to offer consistently a more thorough scholarly foundation in law. Overall, the field of academic preparation plays an insufficient role in strengthening a system that has the potential for becoming tremendously specialised. Currently, no noteworthy legal research is being carried out. Reasonably expected interdisciplinary partnerships have not been formed to deal with and study family-related issues and phenomena. No postgraduate degree programmes are being offered. Doctrine studied is rather limited. As a result, a system that could become very sophisticated due to its high level of specialisation is degenerating into a field of expertise devoid of experts. The system has progressed on the strength of the instinct of a few idealists and is driven by the statistical figures as reflected in reports.

(b) There is no comprehensive procedural design to establish an implicit or explicit strategy to handle decisions in sensitive family disputes and to provide suitable tools for practitioners to deal with them. This is crucial in a continental or statute law system such as the one in place in Costa Rica, a country with a constitutional principle of doing justice 'in strict accordance with laws'. These laws governing family proceedings must provide the specific, special, satisfactory tools to allow the family judge and the general practitioner to handle reliably delicate family matters to arrive at a proper solution or ruling and enforcement.

(c) In a country where divisions among social classes are continually widening as a result of international policy pressure, and where talk is omnipresent about the existence of two separate and distinct 'Costa Ricas', the issue of having to go through lawyers to gain access to justice has been left pretty much up in the air. Even though the Family Code contains the precept of State-provided legal counsel to anyone lacking the corresponding necessary economic resources (consider the large number of husband-dependent housewives in a social fabric such as the one in Costa Rica), the truth is that this is an ineffectual precept, except for cases of alimony payments, for which more complete, specific regulations exist. Regarding lawyer intervention, another issue should likewise be stressed. These professionals are insufficiently trained, and they tend to adhere to the primitive lawyer's principle of 'wooing' clients at all costs, even with the spouse and children present.

We certainly have our work cut out for us on these fronts in our struggle to improve the system.

England and Wales

RESHAPING MARRIAGE AND THE FAMILY – THE GENDER RECOGNITION ACT 2004 AND THE CIVIL PARTNERSHIP ACT 2004

Mary Welstead[*]

Résumé

Deux législations majeures ont été adoptées en 2004. Elles reflètent la volonté du gouvernement de la Grande-Bretagne de se conformer à la Convention européenne des droits de l'Homme, à moins que ce ne soit plutôt sa crainte d'une contestation fondée précisément sur la Convention. Le *Gender Recognition Act 2004* (GRA 2004) et le *Civil Partnership Act 2004* (CPA 2004) vont, à n'en pas douter, modifier considérablement le portrait juridique de la famille. C'est la raison pour laquelle j'ai choisi cette année de dédier mon survol du droit de la famille anglais et gallois entièrement à l'analyse du contexte dans lequel ces deux lois ont été adoptées et à l'examen de leur impact sur le droit de la famille actuel.

Two major pieces of legislation, the origins of which lie in the UK Government's response to challenge, or fear of challenge, under the European Convention for the Protection of Human Rights and Fundamental Freedoms 1950 (ECHR 1950), were enacted in 2004. The Gender Recognition Act 2004 (GRA 2004)[1] and the Civil Partnership Act 2004 (CPA 2004) are likely to transform the shape of the legal family to a significant extent. For that reason, I have decided to devote this year's survey of family law in England and Wales to examining the background, and the effects on family law, of these two Acts.

---

[*]   Reader in Law, University of Buckingham.

[1]   For an interesting review of the GRA 2004 in a comparative context, see R Rains (2005) 33 Ga J Int'l & Comp L 33. See also Stephen Gilmore 'The Gender Recognition Act 2004' Fam LJ 34 (741); Julia Sohrab 'Recognising acquired gender' [2004] NLJ.

I   THE RIGHTS OF TRANSGENDERED PERSONS PRIOR TO THE GENDER RECOGNITION ACT 2004

Prior to the enactment of the GRA 2004, it was estimated that 5,000 pre-operative or post-operative transgendered persons were living in the UK in a state of legal limbo. The term transgendered (or transsexual), according to the House of Lords:

> '... is the label given, not altogether happily, to a person who has the misfortune to be born with physical characteristics which are congruent but whose self-belief is incongruent. Transsexual people are born with the anatomy of a person of one sex but with an unshakeable belief or feeling that they are persons of the opposite sex. They experience themselves as being of the opposite sex ... The aetiology of this condition remains uncertain. It is now generally recognised as a psychiatric disorder, often known as gender dysphoria or gender identity disorder. It can result in acute psychological distress.'[2]

Those with this condition could be helped (and still can) to acquire a new gender, congruent with their perceived gender, by psychiatric assessment, hormonal treatment, a supervised period of living as a member of the opposite gender and ultimately, where appropriate, by gender reassignment surgery. Because there was no legal recognition of their acquired gender status, they were at risk of public revelation of their birth gender. In particular, and rather bizarrely, given the Government's current attitude to same-sex marriage, they were only able to marry a member of the same gender as that of their acquired gender. Any attempts to marry a member of the opposite gender to that of their acquired gender would render their purported marriage void *ab initio*.[3] In *Corbett v Corbett*, in 1950, Ormrod J had taken the view that:

> '... sex is clearly an essential determinant of the relationship called marriage, because it is and always has been recognised as the union of man and woman. It is the institution on which the family is built, and in which the capacity for natural heterosexual intercourse is an essential element. It has, of course, many other characteristics, of which companionship and mutual support is an important one, but the characteristics which distinguish it from all other relationships can only be met by two persons of opposite sex ... for even the most extreme degree of transsexualism in a male or the most severe hormonal imbalance which can exist in a person with male chromosomes, male gonads and male genitalia cannot reproduce a person who is naturally capable of performing the essential role of a woman in marriage.'[4]

---

2   *Bellinger v Bellinger* [2003] 2 AC 467.
3   In accordance with the Matrimonial Causes Act 1973, s 11(c).
.   *Corbett v Corbett* [1950] at 83. See also Rebecca Probert 'How Would *Corbett v Corbett* be Decided Today?' [2005] Fam LJ 35 (382).

Ormrod J's view prevailed for many years and several futile appeals were made to the European Court of Human Rights (ECHR) by transgendered persons who maintained that the UK Government had breached Art 8, the right to respect for private and family life, or Art 12, the right to marry, of the ECHR 1950.

In 1986, Mr Rees, a female to male transgendered person who had received gender reassignment surgery in a National Health hospital, maintained that his rights had been violated. The UK Government refused to allow him to be given a new birth certificate to reflect his new gender and to permit him to marry in his new gender. He was permitted to have a passport and driving licence issued in his new identity. Mr Rees claimed that he was embarrassed and humiliated whenever he was asked to produce his birth certificate which clearly stated him to be female. The ECHR stated that there was a diversity of practices relating to birth registration of transgendered persons within member states. It accepted that the UK enjoyed a wide margin of appreciation in determining this issue and there was no obligation on it to change its practice with respect to the issue of birth certificates.

However, the ECHR made clear that

'... the Convention has always to be interpreted and applied in the light of current circumstances. The need for appropriate legal measures should therefore be kept under review having regard particularly to scientific and societal developments.'

The ECHR accepted that the right to marry under Art 12, referred to the right to marry in the traditional sense of a marriage between a male and a female. It did not include the right to marry by a transgendered person in his new gender.[5]

In 1990, Caroline Cossey, a male to female post-operative transgendered person who was a successful fashion model, complained to the ECHR that the UK Government had violated Arts 8 and 12 of the ECHR 1950. Although the ECHR rejected her complaint, the dissenting judgment of Martens J addressed clearly the dilemma facing Ms Cossey. He recognised that to deny her legal recognition in her new gender was to leave her physical and psychological treatment to acquire a new gender, which was authorised by UK law, incomplete. Martens J found difficulty in accepting Ormrod J's judgment in *Corbett* because, in his view:

'... marriage is far more than a union which legitimates sexual intercourse and aims at procreating.'

It would not be permissible for a member state to deny the right to marry to any person who was not capable of procreation. The UK Government had reduced the transgendered person's right to marry to such a significant extent

---

[5] [1987] 2 FLR 111.

that the essence of the right was seriously impaired. Martens J noted that, since the decision in *Rees*, there had been significant developments in psycho-social understanding of transgender, and now 14 member states gave legal recognition to transgendered persons compared with only five at the time of *Rees*.[6]

The decisions in *Rees* and *Cossey* were followed by two further claims by transgendered persons, the first in 1997, *X, Y and Z v The United Kingdom*,[7] and the second in 1998, in *Sheffield and Horsham v The United Kingdom*.[8] The ECHR rejected both claims that UK law was a violation of the claimants' rights under Art 8 of the ECHR 1950. However, once again, a warning was issued that the UK Government should continue to monitor social and scientific developments and keep its law under surveillance.

II THE BACKGROUND TO THE GENDER RECOGNITION ACT 2004

The Human Rights Act 1998 (HRA 1998) came into force against a background of a disproportionate number of successful claims in the ECHR, in many different fields, against the UK Government. The UK Government was under increasing pressure to remedy this unfortunate state of affairs and the new Act underlined its commitment to take human rights seriously and ensure that its law complied with the ECHR 1950. Section 3 of the HRA 1998 provides that UK law must, insofar as possible, be read and given effect in a way which is compatible with the Convention rights. Section 4 of the HRA 1998 provides that where a provision is incompatible, the court, in which the law is at issue, may make a declaration to that effect.[9]

In spite of the requests of the ECHR to the UK Government to keep its law under review in the light of any new medical and psycho-social developments relating to transgendered persons which were outlined in the previous section, the Government had only done so in a rather desultory manner. It had set up an interdepartmental working group on transgendered people, which had reported in 2000. The report was most inconclusive and the Government failed to take any further measures. In 2002, the ECHR, in *Goodwin v The United Kingdom; I v The United Kingdom*,[10] once again, criticised the UK Government for its lack of action. It found against the UK and held that the rights of two transgendered people had been breached under Arts 8 and 12 of the ECHR 1950.

---

[6]   [1991] 2 FLR 492.
[7]   [1997] 2 FLR 892.
[8]   [1998] 2 FLR 928, 30 July 1998.
      See *Ghaidan v Mendoza* [2004] UKHL 30.
      (2002) 35 EHRR 18.

The UK Government needed to respond urgently. The Government was facing not only pressure from the ECHR but also the risk of an increase in the demand for same-sex marriage. Transgendered heterosexual people, whose right to marry was so circumscribed as to be unrealistic, were likely to add their voices to those of the gay lobby which had begun to clamour for the right to marry.

The decision in *Goodwin* was swiftly followed, in 2003, by the House of Lords' judgment in *Bellinger v Bellinger*.[11] Mrs Bellinger, a transgendered female had been registered as a male at birth. She challenged the conclusions of the trial judge and the Court of Appeal that her marriage to a male, following her gender reassignment surgery, was void. She also sought a declaration that the Matrimonial Causes Act 1973, s 11(c), which requires that the parties to a marriage must be respectively male and female, was incompatible with her rights under Arts 8 and 12 of the EHCR 1950. The trial judge and the Court of Appeal had concluded, after reviewing all the case-law, that a person's sex at birth, as determined by the chromosomal, gonadal and genital tests, could not subsequently be changed to allow a person validly to marry.

Thorpe LJ, in a dissenting judgment in *Bellinger* in the Court of Appeal, had stated most lucidly that:

> 'To make the chromosomal factor conclusive, or even dominant, seems to me particularly questionable in the context of marriage. For it is an invisible feature of an individual, incapable of perception or registration other than by scientific test. It makes no contribution to the physiological or psychological self. Indeed in the context of the institution of marriage as it is today it seems to me right as a matter of principle and logic to give predominance to psychological factors just as it seems right to carry out the essential assessment of gender at or shortly before the time of marriage rather than at the time of birth.'[12]

He commented on the out-of-date approach of the UK compared with other European jurisdictions and that one of the objectives of statute law reform must be to ensure that the law reacts to and reflects such social change.

In the House of Lords, in *Bellinger*, the Lord Chancellor argued that a declaration of incompatibility in accordance with the HRA 1998, s 4 was unnecessary because the Government was already planning to legislate on gender change, although at that stage, there were no concrete proposals, nor was there a Bill in the offing. The House of Lords was unmoved by this argument and granted Mrs Bellinger's demand for a declaration of incompatibility. However, it was not prepared to go further and hold that Mrs Bellinger's marriage was valid and overrule the judgments of the trial judge and the Court of Appeal. It concluded that there was enormous

---

[11]   [2003] 2 AC 467.
[12]   [2001] 2 FLR 1048.

uncertainty surrounding the circumstances in which gender reassignment should be recognised for the purposes of marriage. It also emphasised the importance of viewing the whole question of gender recognition as part of a wider problem which should be considered in its totality by Parliament, and not dealt with in a piecemeal fashion by the judiciary.[13]

III THE GENDER RECOGNITION ACT 2004

Six months after the decision in *Bellinger*, the Government introduced the Gender Recognition Bill and after much acrimonious debate in Parliament, the GRA 2004 received the Royal Assent. Now, transgendered people who obtain a full gender recognition certificate from a Gender Recognition Panel, consisting of legal and medical experts, will be treated for all legal purposes as a member of their acquired gender rather than that of their birth gender.

A   Gender recognition certificates

In order to obtain a gender recognition certificate, a transgendered person must have attained the age of 18; must satisfy the Panel that he or she has, or has had, gender dysphoria, and must have lived in the acquired gender throughout the preceding 2 years, and intend to continue to do so until death.[14]

A claim of gender dysphoria requires evidence of a deep conviction that a person's gender identity does not match his or her appearance and/or anatomy. The claim must be evidenced either by the submission of two reports from registered medical practitioners, one of whom must be practising in the field of gender dysphoria, or one report from a chartered psychologist practising in gender dysphoria and a report from a registered medical practitioner.[15] There is no requirement for gender reassignment surgery or hormonal treatment although, clearly, they would be relevant evidence of gender dysphoria.

The requirement that an applicant must have lived in their new gender for 2 years prior to the application for a gender recognition certificate begs the question as to what it means to live in a new gender. In a world where the term unisex is commonly used to describe clothes and personal services such as manicurists and hairdressers, it is not easy to determine the essential characteristics of living in a new gender. Where the applicant has undergone gender reassignment surgery, it may seem self-evident. But is it? Jan Morris, in her book *Conundrum*, which describes her transformation from male to

---

13   Sonia Harris-Short 'Children and Young Persons, Family law and the Human Rights Act 1998: Judicial Restraint or Revolution?' [2005] CFLQ17.3 (329).
14   GRA 2004, ss 1, 2 and Sch 1.
15   GRA 2004, s 3.

female including gender reassignment surgery, regards the wearing of make-up, nail varnish and high-heeled shoes as an important part of her new female persona.[16] Not all females would share her view, and certain non-transgendered males may feel happy to indulge in such accoutrements.

B Interim gender recognition certificates

Where an applicant is married or a registered civil partner, he or she will be issued with an interim gender recognition certificate which will allow either the applicant, or his or her spouse or civil partner, to apply to annul the relationship, providing they do so within 6 months of the issue of the interim certificate.[17] A full gender recognition certificate will be issued at the time of the annulment. If within the 6-month period, a marriage or civil partnership is annulled for reasons other than the issue of an interim gender recognition certificate, or is dissolved, or the spouse or civil partner of the applicant dies, the applicant may apply to the Panel for a full gender recognition certificate.[18]

This provision is harsh. It demands that a transgendered person, who desires a full gender recognition certificate to enable him or her to lead certain aspects of his or her private life in a new gender, must first annul his or her relationship, whether or not he or she wishes to do so. The provision illustrates the Government's obsessive determination not to permit same-sex marriage. It leads to the rather bizarre situation that a transgendered person who does not require, or desire, a full gender recognition certificate may marry a same-sex partner because the partner is of the opposite gender to that of the transgendered person's birth gender.

C Effects of a full gender recognition certificate

Once a full gender recognition certificate has been granted, transgendered persons, who already have a UK registered birth entry, will be given a new birth certificate which will reflect their acquired gender. Their previous gender identity will remain unknown other than to the registration authorities; no one will have the right to inspect the separate register which will cross reference the change.[19] From the time the full gender recognition certificate is granted, transgendered persons will be treated, for most purposes, as members of their acquired gender.[20] They will be able to marry a person of the opposite gender to that of their new gender providing they do not fall within the prohibited degrees of kindred with that person. The restrictions on whom one may marry have been altered to cover those

---

16   *Conundrum* (New York: Harcourt Brace Jovanovich, 1987).
17   Matrimonial Causes Act 1973, s 12(g).
18   GRA 2004, ss 4, 5.
19   GRA 2004, s 22.
20   GRA 2004, s 9.

relationships which flow from any previous marriage in the birth gender. For instance, a female who has altered her gender to become a male may not marry his ex-husband's wife.[21]

A conscience clause is available to ensure that no member of the Anglican clergy will be forced to officiate at the marriage of a transgendered person.[22] However, because there is no obligation on a transgendered person to reveal a change of gender, the information may remain hidden from officiating clergy. It is interesting that the GRA 2004 received significant support in the House of Lords from the Anglican bishops who have given particular support to transgendered clergy.[23]

Once a person has legally changed gender and remarried or entered into a civil partnership, his or her spouse or civil partner will be able to apply for a decree of annulment if he or she was unaware of the gender change.[24] This provision is based on the assumption that such information should have been revealed prior to entering into a new relationship. It suggests some confusion in the minds of the legislators. Was it inserted because, although the transgendered person is deemed to be a member of their acquired gender, he or she is regarded as being incapable of consummating the marriage? Yet in *Cossey* the ECHR readily accepted, in contradiction to the view of Ormrod J in *Corbett*, that Caroline Cossey was capable of sexually consummating her relationship with a male.

A full gender recognition certificate will not affect the parental status of a transgendered person; a man who becomes a woman will remain a father to his children and a woman becoming a man will remain the mother of her children. Thus parental rights and responsibilities will remain unchanged.[25]

Where a person has been named as a beneficiary under a will, prior to the GRA 2004 coming into force, and the gender of the beneficiary is referred to in the will, he or she will retain his or her birth gender for the purposes of interpretation of the will. However, if the will is made after the GRA 2004 came into force, succession will take effect to reflect the new gender of the beneficiary.[26] Trustees and executors will have no duty to inquire of beneficiaries about gender change when administering the estate, but other beneficiaries will have a right to challenge the will and trace their inheritance into the hands of a transgendered beneficiary.[27] Any beneficiary who suffers the loss of an inheritance because a transgendered person benefits as a result of the gender change, may apply to the High Court for

---

[21] GRA 2004, s 11 and Sch 4.
[22] Marriage Act 1949, s 5(b).
[23] In September 2005, the Anglican Bishop of Hereford, the Rt Rev Anthony Priddis, ordained the Rev Sarah Jones who was born as Colin Jones and spent the first 33 years of her life living as a man before treatment for gender dysphoria.
[24] Matrimonial Causes Act 1973, s 12(h).
[25] GRA 2004, s 12.
[26] GRA 2004, s 15.
[27] GRA 2004, s 17.

provision from the will. The Court must take into account whether it would be just to grant the application.[28] An obvious example would be where a testator made a bequest in favour of an eldest son and the son suffered loss because his older female sibling legally changed gender prior to the death of the testator.

D   Exceptions for peers

In the House of Lords' debate on the Gender Recognition Bill, there was much discussion, some of it rather dryly amusing, about the status of transgendered hereditary peers' children. Earl Ferrer posed the question:

> 'What happens if an earl has a sex change? In order to make certain that there is no duplicity, we will call him Earl Dodger and his son Viscount Chump. If Earl Dodger has a sex change, does he become a countess, in which case there will then be two Countess Dodgers? Or does he remain as an earl although he masquerades as a woman?

> ... what happens to the title? Does Viscount Chump suddenly inherit the earldom and become an earl as the earldom is apparently vacant? That does not seem right because you would then have two earls. What happens if Countess Dodger, on the other hand, changes sex and becomes a man? ... Does she become Earl Dodger, so that there are two earls? She cannot, because she was not appointed. What does she do?

> Let us suppose that Earl Dodger has a son and a daughter. Let us suppose that the daughter is older and that she has a sex change and becomes a man. Does she then become Viscount Chump instead of her younger brother who, up till now, was Viscount Chump ... Does she inherit the title of earl instead of the proper Viscount Chump, and all the cash, if there is any? In my experience, earls do not have much cash nowadays, but they used to in the good old days. What happens to the proper Viscount Chump? There may be a trust fund under which it all goes to the holder of the earldom. Does the lady get that and, if so, will she remain friends with her brother?'[29]

Fortunately for Earl Ferrer and his peers, the Government, for once, showed favouritism toward the peerage. The peers were happy to learn that there was a major exception in the GRA 2004, relating to the descent of peerages and other honours, and to the passing of any property connected with these titles. Such honours would remain unaffected by gender change, as would any entitlement to property unless there was an express provision otherwise in a will.[30]

Since the enactment of the GRA 2004, the definitions of gender and the boundaries between gender and sexuality have become increasingly

---

28   GRA 2004, s 18.
29   *Hansard*, col 647 (3 February 2004).
30   GRA 2004, s 16.

confused and blurred. Had the Government been prepared to contemplate same-sex marriage, much of the GRA 2004 would have been otiose, as would the CPA 2004, which will be considered in the next section.

IV THE CIVIL PARTNERSHIP ACT 2004

A   Origins of the Act

The origins of the CPA 2004, like those of the GRA 2004, were based on concerns about discrimination, familial relationships,[31] and the increasing influence of human rights legislation on these matters.

The UK had lagged behind many other countries in granting legal recognition to same-sex couples. Whilst an increasing number of jurisdictions had already legislated, or were considering legislation, to allow such couples similar rights to married partners,[32] the UK Government had avoided any consideration of the matter until the House of Lords' decision in *Fitzpatrick v Stirling Housing Association* in 1999.[33]

Mr Fitzpatrick had appealed to the House of Lords and sought a declaration that he had succeeded to his deceased partner's tenancy under the Rent Act 1977, as amended. The couple had lived together in the property, for over 20 years, in a close, loving, faithful, monogamous, homosexual relationship. Eight years prior to his death, the deceased had fallen down the stairs, and sustained a blood clot to the brain. After several months in a coma, paralysed and unable to speak, he was taken home by the claimant to be totally cared for by him in a loving and dedicated way, for 24 hours a day every day, until he died.

The relevant legislation required Mr Fitzpatrick to prove that he had been living with the deceased as if a spouse, at the time of his death, to obtain a right to remain under a statutory tenancy, or as a member of his family, at the time of his death, to obtain a right to remain under an assured tenancy.[34]

The House of Lords declined to find that Mr Fitzpatrick had lived with the deceased as a spouse, but readily granted him the status of membership of the deceased's family. Lord Slynn, in a most sensitive and understanding judgment, maintained that, for the purposes of Rent Act legislation, two people of the same sex could be regarded as having established membership of a family, one of the most significant of human relationships which both

---

31   See www.parliament.uk/commons/lib/research/rp2004/rp04-064.pdf.

32   Same-sex marriage is legal in The Netherlands, Belgium, Spain and Massachusetts; civil partnerships are available in Croatia, Denmark, Finland, France, Germany, Iceland, Israel, New Zealand, Norway, Portugal, Slovenia, Sweden, Switzerland, parts of Australia and in the US in California, Connecticut, DC, Hawaii, Maine, New Jersey and Vermont.

33   [2000] Fam Law 14.

34   See Rent Act 1977, Sch 1, paras 2, 3(1).

gives benefits and imposes obligations. The hallmarks of such a relationship were that there should be a degree of mutual interdependence; sharing of lives; caring and love; commitment and support. The presence of these facts in a same-sex relationship was capable of creating membership of a tenant's family.

B   Two Civil Partnership Bills

Following the decision in *Fitzpatrick*, the Government, as noted above, was becoming increasingly concerned by human rights challenges. It realised that these challenges would soon be extended to claims of a plethora of rights for same-sex couples, including the possibility of same-sex marriage. In 2002, the Liberal Peer and Director of the Odysseus Trust, Lord Lester, had introduced a Private Member's Bill on civil partnership in the House of Lords. It was based on a joint initiative between the Trust and Stonewall, both interest groups which support, *inter alia*, the rights of gay people. The Bill did not limit itself to the rights of same-sex unmarried couples to live in a legally recognised mutually supportive partnership but extended those rights to heterosexual couples who did not wish to marry.

Lord Lester's Bill was withdrawn when the Government agreed to introduce its own Bill in 2003. This Bill provided for registration of civil partnerships but only for gay people.[35] It was an attempt to achieve a compromise between the religious right, which was vehemently opposed to same-sex marriage, and the gay lobby, which was campaigning for the right to marry.[36] The Government had hoped that by proposing to give almost identical rights to civil partners as those given to married couples, it would forestall any challenge under the ECHR 1950 that the restriction of marriage to opposite-sex partners is a breach of Arts 8 and 12 of the Convention.[37] Its hope was short lived; a British lesbian couple, who were legally married to each other whilst living in Canada, launched a challenge to the Government's refusal to recognise their marriage. The couple knew that they would be allowed to register their relationship under the proposed Civil Partnership legislation, however, they argued that civil partnership is both 'symbolically and practically a lesser substitute'. They maintained that their rights under Arts 8, 12 and 14 of the ECHR 1950 had been infringed. The hearing will take place later in 2006.

The Government refused, in the Bill, to extend the registration of civil partnership to heterosexual cohabitants. It maintained that marriage was open to this group and therefore, civil partnership was unnecessary for them. There was serious criticism of this approach by Lord Lester and by the Solicitors' Family Law Association. The latter viewed the failure to include

---

[35]   Lucy Crompton 'Civil Partnerships Bill 2004: The Illusion of Equality' [2004] Fam LJ 34 (888).
[36]   See Nicholas Bamforth 'The Role of Philosophical and Constitutional Arguments in the Same-Sex Marriage Debate: A Response to John Murphy' [2005] CFLQ 16. (245).
[37]   Murphy 'Same-Sex Marriage in England: A Role for Human Rights?' [2004] CFLQ 16.3 (245).

heterosexual couples in the ambit of the legislation as a missed opportunity to reform the law relating to cohabitation.[38]

After an abortive attempt by the House of Lords to wreck the Civil Partnership Bill by introducing amendments, which would have allowed certain groups of relatives regardless of gender to register as civil partners, provided that they were both over 30 years old and had lived together for a continuous period of 12 years, the CPA 2004 finally came into existence.

C   Government explanations of the effect of the CPA 2004

The Government explained (sic) the effect of the new Act in the following terms:

> 'Civil Partnership is a completely new legal relationship, exclusively for same-sex couples, distinct from marriage.
>
> The Government has sought to give civil partners parity of treatment with spouses, as far as is possible, in the rights and responsibilities that flow from forming a civil partnership.
>
> There are a small number of differences between civil partnership and marriage, for example, a civil partnership is formed when the second civil partner signs the relevant document, a civil marriage is formed when the couple exchange spoken words. Opposite-sex couples can opt for a religious or civil marriage ceremony as they choose, whereas formation of a civil partnership will be an exclusively civil procedure'[39]

This statement can only be described as disingenuous. The Government has attempted strongly to refute the idea that civil partnership is equivalent to same-sex marriage, yet has been unable to give any satisfactory explanation as to how it differs from marriage; the explanations given are minimalist and lack any serious credibility. The CPA 2004, except in some very minor ways, permits same-sex partners to marry in everything but name.

D   The public response

It is interesting to note that the UK media's approach, which refers to civil partnerships as 'gay weddings', has caught the imagination of the general population. The quotation marks have gradually been dropped and the word marriage has been substituted for wedding. One of the major broadsheets, for instance, printed the following news item:

---

[38]   Jane Craig 'The Civil Partnership Bill – Cohabitation Law Reform or a Missed Opportunity?' Fam LJ 34 (148). See also Stuart Bridge 'Reforming Cohabitation' Fam LJ 35 (679).
[39]   See www.womenandequalityunit.gov.uk/lgbt/faq.htm (2005). See also McK Norrie 'What the Civil Partnership Act 2004 does not do', *Scots Law Times*, 2005.

'Sir Elton John heads England's gay wedding rush
Sir Elton John and his partner David Furnish have "married" in a quiet Windsor ceremony, joining hundreds of other gay couples making legal history in England and Wales ...

... They were wed at the Windsor Guildhall, which hosted the wedding of the Prince of Wales and Duchess of Cornwall in April this year.'[40]

There has been a proliferation of new businesses which offer gay wedding services to same-sex couples. It is as if a new customary form of law – gay marriage – has come into existence by edict of the people. What the Government could not bring itself to do has, in effect, been achieved by the will of the people.

V   THE PROVISIONS OF THE CPA 2004

A   Capacity to register a civil partnership

In order to register a civil partnership, the parties must have the relevant mental and legal capacity to do so. They must, therefore, understand the nature of the relationship and its consequences. They must be of the same gender, and not in an existing civil partnership or marriage. They must have attained the age of 16 years and if they are under the age of 18, unless they have previously entered into a civil partnership or marriage which has been dissolved or annulled, they must have obtained the written consent of those who have parental responsibility for them or one of the appropriate persons listed in the CPA 2004.[41]

Transgendered persons, who have obtained gender recognition certificates from the Gender Recognition Panel, may enter into a civil partnership with a member of the same sex to that of their newly acquired gender.

B   Prohibited degrees of kindred

The couple must not be within the prohibited degrees of kindred. The prohibitions are complex and divided into absolute prohibitions and qualified prohibitions.[42] The former relate to blood relationships and relationships between an adoptive child and an adoptive parent. The latter relate to relationships of affinity.[43]

Since same-sex couples are unable biologically to reproduce with each other, all of the prohibitions are entirely connected with social mores relating to

---

[40]   Reported in *The Telegraph*, 21 December 2005.
[41]   CPA 2004, ss 3, 4 and Sch 2.
[42]   CPA 2004, Sch 1, Part 1.
[43]   CPA 2004, Sch 1, Part 1, para 2 (2).

marriage and family relationships. They appear to be rather over-extensive and, in the case of absolute prohibitions, reflect, *inter alia,* the determination of the Government not to extend the status of civil partnerships to those who are members of each other's family of origin, even where there is no question of a sexual relationship between them.

C   Formalities of civil partnership registration

The formalities for registration of a civil partnership require that notice must be given 15 days in advance, except where either party is seriously ill and may not survive. The information relating to a proposed registration must be made public by the registrar in order that anyone may object on the grounds that the couple are not eligible to register a civil partnership.[44] Gay rights groups had objected to the public nature of registration on the grounds of the right to privacy, and in order to prevent risks of discrimination towards, or homophobic attacks on, civil partners. These objections were discounted.

Registration must take place in offices provided by local authorities, or in premises licensed by them for the registration of civil partnerships, between the hours of 8 am and 6 pm. There is no provision for religious ceremonies in recognised places of worship as there is with marriage, but non-religious ceremonies may form part of the registration process. There is evidence that many local authorities are doing their utmost to provide similar facilities for ceremonies for civil partnership registration as they do for marriage in order to make registration into a meaningful and emotional ceremony. Couples are, of course, free to organise separate religious ceremonies in their own place of worship if they so wish and if they are permitted to do so. The Anglican Church is opposed to blessings of civil partnerships; however, services of thanksgiving have been used as a means of circumventing the rule.[45]

D   Nullity of civil partnerships

Just as certain purported marriages are deemed to be void or voidable, so too are certain civil partnerships.

1   Void civil partnerships

The grounds, on which a civil partnership will be void are:

(a) the parties are not of the same sex;

---

[44]   CPA 2004, ss 5–27.
[45]   An openly homosexual vicar is to have his gay 'marriage' blessed at a service of thanksgiving at which the former Bishop of Durham, the Rt Rev David Jenkins, will preach (Reported in *The Telegraph*, 9 December 2005).

(b) either of them is already a civil partner or lawfully married;

(c) either of them is under the age of 16; or

(d) they are within prohibited degrees of relationship.[46]

2   *Voidable civil partnerships*

The grounds on which a civil partnership will be voidable are:

(a) either of the parties did not validly consent to its formation (whether as a result of duress, mistake, unsoundness of mind or otherwise);

(b) at the time of its formation either of them, though capable of giving a valid consent, was suffering (whether continuously or intermittently) from mental disorder of such a kind or to such an extent as to be unfitted for civil partnership;

(c) at the time of its formation, the respondent was pregnant by some person other than the applicant;

(d) an interim gender recognition certificate under the GRA 2004 has, after the time of its formation, been issued to either civil partner;

(e) the respondent is a person whose gender at the time of its formation had become the acquired gender under the GRA 2004.[47]

It is presumed that the relevant decisions relating to voidable marriages will be followed.

3   *Non-consummation and venereal disease*

There is a notable absence of any nullity provisions relating to non-consummation of the relationship or the pre-existence of a partner's venereal disease. It would seem that the legislators were unable to come to terms with the nature of sexuality in same-sex relationships and preferred to avoid the issue completely. In November 2004, in the debate in the House of Lords on the Civil Partnership Bill, Baroness Scotland attempted to explain, with little success, that one of the major differences between marriage and civil partnership was that of consummation:

> 'In relation to marriage, for a marriage to be valid it has to be consummated by one man and one woman and there is a great deal of jurisprudence which tells you exactly what consummation amounts to, partial, impartial, penetration, no penetration ... There is no provision for consummation in the Civil Partnerships Bill. We do not look at the nature of the sexual relationship, it is totally different in nature.'

---

[46]   CPA 2004, s 49.
[47]   CPA 2004, s 50.

It may be that an application could be made for a decree of nullity of a civil partnership under the provisions for lack of valid consent in consequence of 'otherwise' (CPA 2004, s 50(1)(a)), where the respondent remained silent about an intention not to engage in a sexual relationship or withheld information about having a communicable sexual disease. It might be assumed that persons entering into a civil partnership would have discussed these matters in advance of registration.

4 Bars to relief where a civil partnership is voidable

The applicant may not obtain a decree of nullity if the respondent satisfies the court that the applicant, with knowledge that a nullity order was possible, led the respondent to believe that he or she would not seek to do so, *and* that it would be unjust to grant the respondent a decree.[48]

As with nullity of marriage, there is a time bar on applications for annulment of civil partnerships. All applications must be made within 3 years of the registration of the civil partnership.[49] Where a transgendered civil partner obtains a gender recognition certificate and wishes, or his or her partner wishes, to annul the civil partnership, the application must be made within 6 months of the issue of an interim gender recognition certificate.[50]

Leave to apply after the 3-year period has elapsed may be granted if the applicant has, at some time during the 3-year period, suffered from mental disorder, *and* in all the circumstances of the case it would be just to grant leave for the institution of proceedings.[51]

E Family home rights

Civil partners now have all the same rights as married partners under the Family Law Act 1996 relating to the family home.[52]

F Dissolution, legal separation and ancillary relief

1 Dissolution

Civil partners who wish legally to end their relationship must go through a formal process of dissolution of the civil partnership in a very similar way, and with very similar consequences, to the dissolution of a marriage.[53] Either

---

[48] CPA 2004, s 51(1)(a), (b).
[49] CPA 2004, s 51(2)(a).
[50] CPA 2004, s 51(5).
[51] CPA 2004, s 51(3), (4).
[52] CPA 2004, s 82.
[53] CPA 2004, ss 44–48.

partner may apply for the relationship to be dissolved on the ground that it has irretrievably broken down. Proof of breakdown must be evidenced by one of four facts, rather than one of the five facts available to married couples: the notable omission is that of the fact of adultery. The Government took the approach that adultery, as currently defined, could not apply to same-sex partners.[54] It declined to include extra-civil partnership same-sex sexual conduct, which might be viewed in a similar light to adultery, as one of the facts. It will, of course, be possible for a same-sex partner to plead the 'behaviour fact' and maintain that the respondent's sexual infidelity is behaviour which will lead to the conclusion that the petitioner cannot reasonably be expected to live with the respondent.

In the light of the Government's decision not to allow same-sex partners to marry, and given the discontent with the current divorce law, it must be questioned why the opportunity was not grasped to take a reforming approach to the dissolution of civil partnerships. Why should those who are denied the right to marry be forced to go through the same unsatisfactory exit hoops as married partners?

2 Separation orders

A civil partner may apply for a separation order in the same way as a spouse may apply for a decree of judicial separation.[55] Similar consequences result in that the separated civil partner may not enter into a new civil partnership or marriage but they are relieved of all other responsibilities of the relationship.

3 Financial relief

Civil partners may also apply for financial orders and property orders against each other when a nullity, separation or dissolution order is made.[56]

It is regrettable that Parliament chose to impose the current unsatisfactory law relating to financial relief for marital partners onto civil partners. How many civil partners will be aware of the vast discretion of the court to determine their financial future, without any overriding principle by which to do so on relationship breakdown? Once again, it seems that the Government missed the opportunity to look afresh at this area of law.

---

[54] In 2005, the British Columbia Supreme Court amended the definition of adultery to permit a same-sex spouse to divorce her partner who had had an extra-marital affair.

[55] CPA 2004, ss 56, 57.

[56] CPA 2004, ss 72.

G   Death

On the death of a civil partner, the surviving partner will have all the same rights as a surviving spouse with respect to testate and intestate succession, applications under the Inheritance (Provision for Family and Dependants) Act 1975, and applications under the Fatal Accidents Act 1976.[57]

One interesting consequence of the CPA 2004 is that those same-sex partners who have not registered their partnership will be able to apply under the Inheritance Act for provision for maintenance if they are deemed to be living *as if a civil partner*. It remains to be seen how the courts will determine what it means to be living as if a civil partner as there is, as yet, no *pro forma* for the relationship.

VI CONCLUSION

The GRA 2004 and the CPA 2004 have begun a dramatic reshaping of our concept of both marriage and the family. Men who were born women, and vice versa, may now marry without necessarily changing the physical characteristics of their gender. Same-sex couples can enter into a quasi-marriage and be regarded as members of each other's family. Whilst these reforms may be welcomed by both human rights and family lawyers, it must be remembered that they were primarily necessary because of the Government's implacable opposition to same-sex marriage.

If the challenge to the Government, which has been mounted by the UK couple married in Canada, is successful, not only will the reshaping of the family and marriage be complete, it may even be that the provisions in the GRA 2004 and the CPA 2004, relating to family law, may prove to be unnecessary and short lived. It will be difficult for the Government to continue to permit civil partnerships for same-sex couples, if they are given the right to marry, whilst denying the right to register civil partnerships to heterosexual couples because they have the right to marry. Reform will be inevitable. Gender will become, to a large extent, an irrelevancy; Elizabeth will be able to marry Francesca or George, regardless of her or their sexual orientation or whether any of them are in possession of a gender recognition certificate.

The traditional definition of marriage in *Hyde v Hyde*[58] which states that marriage is 'the voluntary union for life of one man to one woman to the exclusion of all others', is beginning to resemble a dinosaur.

---

[57]   CPA 2004, ss 71, 83 and Sch 4.
[58]   (1866) LR 1P&D 130.

France

EGALITÉ, VÉRITÉ, STABILITÉ: THE NEW FRENCH FILIATION LAW AFTER THE ORDONNANCE OF 4 JULY 2005

Hugues Fulchiron[*]

Résumé

L'ordonnance du 4 juillet 2005, qui entrera en vigueur le 1er juillet 2006, révolutionne le droit français de la filiation. Au nom de l'égalité, les catégories mêmes de filiation légitime et naturelle disparaissent; les règles d'établissement et de contestation de la filiation en mariage et hors mariage sont désormais unifiées. Soucieuse de vérité biologique, l'ordonnance assouplit les règles de la contestation des filiations en mariage et hors mariage. La volonté d'assurer la stabilité des filiations a cependant conduit le législateur à enfermer ces actions dans des délais raisonnables, dont la durée est liée à l'existence ou à l'absence de possession d'état.

Thirty years after the great law of 3 January 1972, the ordonnance of 4 July 2005 has revolutionised French filiation law. Symbolically, the very categories of legitimate and natural filiation disappear. The same rules henceforth govern filiation in and out of wedlock. Advance notice had been given of the reform. Some of these innovations had been anticipated in the recent reform of family names and parental authority. In addition, in its main content, it commanded wide agreement. Nonetheless, directly and indirectly, it overturns French family law.

The law of 3 January 1972, while profoundly innovative, was a balanced law. It broke away from traditional rules and proclaimed the equality of all filiation, yet with certain qualifications. The model of the legitimate family was no longer imposed, but only proposed. According to the well-known formula of Jean Carbonnier, who inspired this law, '*à chacun sa famille, à chacun son droit*'. More radically, the law of 1972 established the principle of the truth of filiation: biological truth, qualified by respect for legitimate filiation and above all by the place accorded to *possession d'état*, ie to filiation as it is personally and socially experienced (now referred to – not without ambiguity – as social reality).

---

[*] Dean of the Law Faculty, Université Jean Moulin Lyon 3, Director of the Family Law Centre. Translated by Peter Schofield.

It did not take long, however, for the desired balance to be called into question. The lightning advance of biology made paternity and non-paternity as ascertainable as maternity and non-maternity. Availability of biological truth made it more and more difficult to justify recourse to fiction and presumption. They retained their usefulness, but the precautions and barriers imposed by the law, no less than the obstacles to the triumph of a now accessible truth, most often tended to protect legitimate filiation. Now, the frequency of family separation and recomposition and of extramarital births, contributes to the ruin of the marriage model and, indirectly to the supremacy of legitimate filiation. Opinions also changed: where previously it seemed the child's interest seemed to require filiation established in relation to both parents, detestation of fictitious filiation that corresponded neither with biological truth nor with any social and affective reality, raised the question whether it was better for the child to have no filiation at all than to have one that existed only on paper.

The Legislature took action to meet these new requirements, in 1982 and in 1993, in particular to facilitate the establishment of extramarital filiation. More judicial decisions, led by a remarkably bold *Cour de cassation*, set about a process of interpretation that, while it did indeed broaden the scope for challenging fictitious legitimate filiation, also ruined the coherence of the 1972 legislation.

There had to be a complete reconstruction. This was all the more urgent as other sectors of family law were reformed, giving effect to new principles with which the law of filiation was no longer consistent.

The main lines of this general renovation of family law were set out in two reports, of the Commission chaired by Irène Théry[1] and of a working party led by Françoise Dekeuwer-Défossez.[2] From these two documents, the Legislature in 2005 drew the principal orientation of its text. The Government, for the sake of speed, chose not to follow the classic legislative route (by which it had already reformed succession, the family name, parental authority and divorce), but that of ordonnances. The 1958 Constitution allows the Government to be authorised by the Parliament to prepare legislative texts the main lines of which are fixed in advance and which are submitted for the general approval of both chambers. Until this time, the procedure had been used to pass urgently needed laws on economic or social matters when a new Government wished to give effect to its programme without delay. There was nothing about filiation that required the use of such a procedure, unless it was that the Government was anxious to avoid the difficult question of 'homoparentality' in this way, and it is a cause for concern that such an important subject, affecting the very foundations of society, should be thus denied parliamentary debate. Be that as it may, the ordonnance was promulgated on 4 July 2005. It went before

---

[1]   I Théry 'Couple, filiation et parenté aujourd'hui, le droit face aux mutations de la famille et de la vie privée' (1998) Odile Jacob (ed), *La Documentation française*.

[2]   F Dekeuwer-Défossez 'Rénover le droit de la famille' (1999) *La Documentation française*.

Parliament for approval at the end of the year 2005 and comes into force on 1 July 2006.

Obliterating the previous law, the ordonnance of 4 July 2005 rebuilds filiation law on three main principles, complementing and balancing each other. The first two, Equality (I) and Truth (II) of filiation were already part of the previous law, but now take on a new dimension. Their, at times excessive, dynamism is tempered by the wish to ensure the Stability (III) of filiation.

I EQUALITY

Under art 310 of the Civil Code:

> 'All children whose fililation is legally established have the same rights and duties in their relations with their father and mother. They are members of the family of each [parent].'

The text is based on the law of 1972. In its concern to maintain balance, the Legislature had, however, made some exceptions to the principle of equality: when the child was competing with the victims of adultery – the spouse and children born in wedlock – the child's rights of succession to the adulterer's estate were restricted. These qualifications were much criticised in France and condemned by the European Court of Human Rights.[3]

The ordonnance of 4 July 2005 takes this development to its logical conclusion. Even the categories of legitimate and natural children disappear along with legitimation. The rules relating to the establishment and challenging of filiation are henceforth the same for all children. The presumption of paternity in marriage alone still distinguishes, on the strength of the institution of marriage, between children born in and out of wedlock.

In this largely unified system, the most spectacular reversal concerns the establishment of filiation. Hitherto, its establishment in marriage – to all intents and purposes automatic – was in total contrast to the voluntary or judicial establishment of filiation out of wedlock; now the new texts of the Civil Code, however, set up a common set of rules for the establishment of filiation based on a law distinguishing between three forms of establishment: first by operation of law, secondly voluntary, and thirdly judicial.[4]

A Establishment by operation of law alone

The ordonnance of 4 July 2005 generalises the rule *mater semper certa est* and retains the presumption of the husband's paternity for children born in marriage.

---

[3] Arrêt Mazurek c France, 1er février 2000, JCP 2000, II, 10286, obs A Gouttenoire et F Sudre, JCP 2000, I, 278, obs R Le Guidec, RTD civ 2000, 429, obs J Hauser.

[4] The plan followed by the ordonnance is, in fact, less coherent. Judicial establishing of filiation is not dealt with under the heading of establishment of filiation, but under that of actions relating to filiation.

1 Generalisation of the rule mater semper certa

While maternal filiation of a child born in a marriage was established by simply naming the mother in the birth registration, this did not apply to a child born out of wedlock. The natural mother had to recognise her child, unless *possession d'état* confirmed the registration. Henceforth, art 311-25 of the Civil Code provides, in a general manner, that maternal filiation is established by identifying the mother in the child's birth registration.[5] All the same, the possibility for a woman to require, at the time of birth, secrecy as to her admission and identity is maintained (art 326), and it is thereby forbidden for the child to bring an action to discover maternity (art 325, para 1).[6]

2 Preservation of the rule pater est

The presumption of paternity, cornerstone of legitimacy, has long allowed a child to be linked to the mother's husband and thereby to give him or her a filiation. Now, the rule does not lead to legitimacy, but still bases, by operation of law alone, the husband's paternity. As before, this covers not only children conceived in marriage, but also those conceived before but born during a marriage (new art 312 which combines the two cases). After 1972, the field of operation of the presumption has been restricted to situations where the husband's paternity is likely. In particular, it does not apply in two cases: where the spouses are legally separated (art 313),[7] on the one hand, and where the birth is declared to the civil registry without naming the husband as the father and the child has no *possession d'état* in relation to him, on the other. However, in both cases, it is open to either spouse during the child's minority to call for the presumption to be restored on proof that the husband is the father (art 327). The child can also demand this during the 10 years following reaching majority (art 327 *in fine*). In case of doubt, biological evidence determines the issue.[8]

Despite its retention, the presumption of paternity is still more fragile today than it was. True, the subtle balance sought in 1972 (disavowal no longer reserved for the husband; the mother could overturn the husband's paternity on remarriage to the true father and legitimation of the child by the new

---

5   France thus comes into line, perhaps a little late, with the well-known judgment in *Marckx v Belgium* in the European Court of Human Rights (ECHR 13 juin 1979, series A, no 31, JT 1979, 513, obs F Rigaux).

6   As to 'l'accouchement sous X' (anonymity of mother), cf infra.

7   To be more precise, under art 313, the presumption does not apply where the child is born more than 300 days after the non-conciliation order authorising the spouses to live apart and less than 180 days after final rejection of the application or after reconciliation. In the case of divorce by mutual consent, it ceases to apply 300 days after judicial approval of the agreement governing the general consequences of the divorce (art 250-1). As to the automatic restoration of the presumption where the child has possession d'état in relation to both spouses, cf art 313, para 2. As to restoration of the presumption on proof that the husband is the child's father, cf art 327.

8   Previously, the law provided for restoration of the presumption in case of the parties getting together again de facto during the period of conception thus making it likely that the husband was the father. The new text is more direct.

couple)[9] had been upset by a particularly bold line of decisions in the *Cour de cassation*; while filiation could not be challenged when the entitlement (birth registration) was confirmed by *possession d'état* it could be annulled in the contrary case,[10] that is the commonest, where the child had no *possession d'état* in relation to the mother's husband.[11] The *ordonnance* of 2005 goes much further. The rules for challenging paternity in marriage are drawn up in line with the normal rules for denying filiation. Where there is *possession d'état* consistent with the registration nobody can challenge the husband's paternity, but only if this continued for more than 5 years after the birth. Failing this, the action is available to the child, to his parents (hence to the husband, who thus escapes from the short time-limits of the old action for disavowal) and to the person claiming to be the true father. The action is barred by the passing of 5 years from the day when *possession d'état* ceased. That is to say, even if the child had an embryonic *possession d'état*, filiation to the husband can be annulled. If, on the other hand, the registration is not consistent with *possession d'état*, filiation can only be challenged within 10 years from the date of the child's birth, time not running against the child during minority (cf new arts 333 and 334): here the aim of truth in filiation gives way to concern for its stability.

Redrafted in this way, the presumption of paternity survives in the shadow of marriage. There has never been any question of extending its scope to cases of stable concubinage or registered partnership (the PACS in France).

B Voluntary establishment of filiation

This is the heading under which the *ordonnance* of 4 July 2005 lists recognition and *possession d'état*. While obvious in the first case, this classification is highly arguable in the second.

1 Recognition

Under new art 316 of the Civil Code 'failing any legal establishment, filiation can be established by recognition of paternity or maternity'. This can be done in the birth registration, in a document received by the civil registration officer or in any authenticated document (eg notarised). Being a voluntary act, recognition is not subject to any control on the part of the person receiving it, or to the authority of the other parent.[12] It often happens, in practice, that such a recognition is false. There is a sort of French tradition of recognition of convenience, generally followed by marriage and legitimation to give a father to the child of the woman with whom one is living. 'Take the woman, take the child', as the saying goes.

Recognition can occur at any time in the child's life. Preserving the former practice, the *ordonnance* of 4 July 2005 specifies that it can precede the

---

[9] Cf old art 318.

[10] Interpretation a contrario of art 322 former Civil Code.

[11] Cf as to these decision Ph Malaurie et H Fulchiron *La famille* (2006, 2nd edn, forthcoming).

[12] In this French law differs from those that subject paternal recognition to the agreement of the mother. Sometimes she is not even informed of the act of recognition.

birth. It can also be posthumous. The only barriers to recognition would be that it was contrary to a filiation already established, or would be incestuous.[13] As a unilateral act, it does not normally affect the child's filiation in relation to the other parent. Although an irrevocable act, it can still be challenged, even by its own author.[14]

At first sight, then, there is no change in what has been, from the Napoleonic Code, the method of choice for establishing extramarital filiation.

In fact, the ordonnance of 4 July 2005 achieves a veritable revolution. Previously kept for extramarital filiation, it is now open to all children, born in or out of wedlock. The impact of this generalisation should be limited. It only arises in default of establishment under the law (art 316, para 1). But it could allow, for example, a married man to recognise a child before birth and 'fix' his paternity in this way without the risk of an anonymous delivery, or a husband separated from his wife to prevent the presumption of paternity from being set aside.[15] On the other hand, this extension has a considerable symbolic effect. More than anything else, this measure marks the reigning absence of differentiation between children born in and out of wedlock.

Generalised as to its scope, recognition is stabilised as to its effects. Before, filiation established by recognition could be easily challenged. Any interested party could bring the action, within a 30-year period which, for the child, was suspended during minority. The action was, however, available only to the child, the mother and the person claiming to be the true father, if the child had had a *possession d'état* consistent with the recognition (art 339). Henceforth, a challenge to recognition is based on the normal rules for actions to annul filiation which considerably restricts its availability. Thus there are three possibilities. Either during the 5 years following recognition the child has enjoyed a *possession d'état* consistent with it – in such case nobody can attack his or her filiation (art 33, para 2). Or the child has a *possession d'état* consistent with the registration, but the requirements of the previous case are not fulfilled – in this case the filiation can be attacked by the child, the parents and by the person claiming to be the true father; the time-limit is 5 years from the cessation of the *possession d'état* (art 334). Or the child has no *possession d'état* consistent with the recognition – in which case the action to challenge it can be brought by anyone with an interest within 10 years from the date on which the person has been denied the contested status (art 334).

In stabilising the child's filiation where recognition is to an extent confirmed by 5 years' *possession d'état*, the ordonnance of 4 July 2005 should have worked a fundamental change in attitudes and practices. Recognition of convenience can no longer be so easily challenged. Take the woman, take the child and keep him.

---

13 Cf infra.
14 Cf infra.
15 Cf supra.

2 *Possession d'état*

A peculiarity of French law is the place traditionally reserved for *possession d'état*. *Possession d'état* refers to the fact that the child enjoys the status of a child, in relation to a particular man or/and woman, whether or not this situation corresponds to the legal reality. Following the tradition of canon law, it is established by 'a sufficient combination of facts indicating a bond of parenthood between a person and the family to which he/she is said to belong' (art 311-1).

The most important of these facts are: 'that the child is treated as their own by those whose issue he/she is taken to be, and has treated them as father and mother'; 'that, in that capacity, they have provided for his/her education, maintenance and setting up in life'; 'that he/she is regarded as their child in society and in the family'; 'that the public authorities regard him/her as such'; 'that he/she bears the name of the person[s] whose issue he/she is taken to be' (art 311-1).[16]

In French law, *possession d'état* produces a number of effects, positive and negative. Since 1982, it has been an independent way to establish extramarital filiation. The fact of its existence establishes the bond. After the ordonnance of 4 July 2005, the rule also applies equally to the child born in marriage, and to maternal as well as paternal filiation. One still has to prove its existence. Article 317, following in its essentials the former texts, provides that 'either of the parents or the child can apply to the judge at first instance for the making of "a declaration of notoriety that will authenticate the *possession d'état* unless the contrary is proved"'. It is for the judge to assess the cogency and relevance of the facts and declarations produced. To prevent problems, new art 317, para 3 provides that 'the making of a declaration of notoriety can only be applied for within a period of five years from the cessation of the alleged *possession d'état*', because the passage of time weakens the evidence. One still has to prove the date on which *possession d'état* ceased, so the problem is only partly displaced.

Beside the simple proof of *possession d'état*, the declaration of notoriety brings into play art 317, para 4. Proof of *possession d'état* leads to the establishment of filiation, and the bond of filiation thus established is noted in the margin of the registration of the birth (art 317, para 4).

However, this filiation is fragile. For one thing, under the Civil Code, art 317, the declaration of notoriety is only evidence of *possession d'état* until the contrary appears. And, by challenging the existence of *possession d'état*, one calls the existence of the bond into question. Hence the need for stability in filiation has led the Legislature to limit the scope for disputing it. Under art 335, filiation established by *possession d'état* established in a declaration of notoriety can be challenged by any interested party producing proof to the

---

[16]   This last element has lost much of its significance with the liberalisation of the rules for attribution of the family name achieved in particular by the law of 4 March 2002.

contrary, within a 5-year period from the declaration, suspended during the child's minority.[17]

Can the filiation be challenged on the ground that the man or woman who has given the child *possession d'état*, recorded in a declaration of notoriety, is not the father or mother of the child? It is not a matter of disputing the existence of the *possession d'état*, but of denying the truth of the filiation. Even if the texts are ambiguous, such an action seems to be possible within the time-limited by art 333.

Possession d'état can also be placed on record, on application by any interested party, by judgment of a tribunal *de grande instance* (Civil Code, art 330). In this provision, the ordonnance of 4 July 2005 preserves the action to confirm filiation created by judicial decisions under the previous law. As its name shows, the sole aim of this action is to confirm the existence of *possession d'état*, from which flows the establishment of filiation. In this connection it is regrettable that the ordonnance of 4 July 2005 confusingly classifies this among the actions relating to the establishment of filiation. The purpose of the action is to place *possession d'état* on record. It is by law, not the judgment, that filiation results from this.

This is a vital distinction, as it governs the question of how such a filiation can be challenged. If the only issue is challenging the existence of *possession d'état*, once the possibility of appeal is exhausted, the decision must have the authority of *res judicata*. But that authority only concerns the existence of the *possession d'état* (on which the court has ruled), not the veracity of the filiation flowing from it. If it is the veracity itself that is in issue, it can be challenged, just as any other filiation that has not itself been judicially established. Although the drafters of the ordonnance have 'fused' (perhaps even confused) the two actions, it must be the case that a filiation must be open to challenge on its truth, according to the normal rules, ie within 10 years from the date on which the child began to enjoy the disputed status. At the very least, the obscurity of the texts on this point is a major weakness of the new law and likely to lead to some rather complicated litigation.

C   Judicial establishment of filiation

In relation to paternity and maternity actions alike, the ordonnance of 4 July 2005 removes the last obstacles that acted to restrict access.

1   The maternity action

In the absence of registration (which now establishes maternal filiation both in and out of wedlock),[18] or *possession d'état* (which similarly establishes filiation) maternity can be claimed in court (art 325, para 1). The action can only be brought by the child 'who is required to prove that he/she is the one

---

[17]   Cf infra.
[18]   Cf supra.

to whom the alleged mother gave birth'. The ordonnance of 4 July 2005 removes the need to prove serious presumptions and indications before alleging maternity in court. This requirement, though understandable at a time when biological evidence was not available, makes no sense today.

However, the action is barred if, at the time of giving birth, the mother asked for her admission and identity to be kept secret (cf arts 325 and 236).[19]

2 The paternity action

In marriage, the husband's paternity is automatically presumed. Where the law sets aside the presumption, but the husband is still claimed to be the father, it can be restored, on the application of either spouse, or of the child (during the 10 years following reaching majority) 'on proof that the husband is the father' (art 327). This can be proved by any means – primarily by expert biological evidence.[20]

The action for paternity out of wedlock has long been the subject of lively controversy. The fear of scandal, respect for the peace of families and above all the uncertainty of evidence, had led the authors of the Napoleonic Code to ban it. Not until 1912 was it finally made possible to bring the action, and then in strictly limited cases. It was still necessary to overcome a series of obstacles formed by grounds for rejection and conditions for receiving such claims. The law of 8 January 1993 removed these obstacles, but, as in the case of maternity, it required prior proof of serious presumptions and indications. The ordonnance of 4 July 2005 swept away these requirements. From now on, the action is subject to the normal time-limits of 10 years from the date of birth, not 2 years as before. Any form of evidence may be used, particularly biological expert evidence.

As we can see, the equality of filiation is closely bound to its truth.

II TRUTH

The principle of the truth of filiation is not written into the Civil Code, but it has, since 1972, formed one of its 'principal directives'. For a long time, French doctrine contrasted two aspects of the truth of filiation – biological and the so-called 'sociological' truth, that of *possession d'état*, experienced as against genetic filiation. Biological progress, that now makes it possible to be certain who is or is not the father or mother of a child, has ended a rather artificial debate. The truth of filiation is, in current French thinking, biological truth. And yet other realities, personal and familial, as well as individual and social needs, complement, moderate and sometimes run counter to the search for biological truth.

---

[19]   Cf infra.

[20]   Cf supra.

A   The advance of biological truth

Biological truth increasingly overrides the presumptions and fictions on which the law of filiation was traditionally built. This trend removes the last precautions that had surrounded the establishment of filiation and widens access to bringing challenges to filiation.

1   Biological truth and the establishment of filiation

As has been emphasised, the ordonnance of 4 July 2005 finally removes the tests an action for paternity or maternity had to pass. Knowing that the *Cour de cassation* has ruled that there is a right to a biological test,[21] it is clear that nothing stands in the way of proving biological truth. But it still has to be in the context of court proceedings. Unlike other systems, French law insists that the identification of a person by genetic markers can only be sought on the order of a judge seised of a suit directed at establishing or disputing a bond of filiation (art 16-11, réd loi of 29 July 1994). So 'private' DNA tests are forbidden, but it is well known that a parallel market is developing in countries with a more liberal regime, which threatens the balance of the French system. How long will it be possible to resist the pressure of truth scientifically proved even if such proof has been obtained without any judicial proceedings?

The favour shown by the Legislature towards the establishment of true filiation, in the biological sense of the term, can also be seen in new facilities for disputing filiation. Filiation cannot be established if the child already has one. Annulment of a false one opens the way to obtaining a true filiation.

2   Biological truth and challenging filiation

Concern for protecting marriage has for a long time led the Legislature to make it difficult to challenge filiation, particularly of a legitimate child. All that the Napoleonic Code allowed was disavowal, available only to the husband, and only within a short period. The law of 1972 enabled the mother to challenge legitimate paternity, on condition, however, that she married the true father and the new couple legitimated the child, so that one legitimate filiation was replaced by another. The pressure of manners and attitudes, as has been said, blew up this system. To bring the law into line with new aspirations, the *Cour de cassation* made use of an argument *a contrario*: art 322 provided that filiation could not be challenged if the registration coincided with the *possession d'état*, so the court deduced that a challenge would be possible if the two elements did not coincide, ie in practice, in the absence of *possession d'état*.

The ordonnance of 4 July 2005 goes one step further. Under new art 333, when *possession d'état* is in conformity with registration, the only people who can challenge filiation are the child, either parent or the person claiming to be the true parent. The text provides that the action is barred after 5 years

---

21   Civ 1ère 28 March 2000, D 731, note T Garé, JCP 2000, II, 10409, concl Petit, note Monstallier-Saint Mleux, RTD civ, 2000, 304, obs J Hauser.

from the day on which *possession d'état* ended. Thus, filiation can now be attacked in a situation where, previously it had been invulnerable, at least in marriage, as the registration was in conformity with *possession d'état*. Triumph of biological truth.

The law places certain limits on this new situation. Under art 333, para 2, nobody can challenge filiation when the *possession d'état* has lasted more than 5 years from the birth or subsequent recognition. Within the 5 years, filiation may be overthrown. Take as an example a man whose wife gave birth to a child. The child was not his, but the husband accepted it into his home. Four years later the spouses separate and the mother decides to break the bond of filiation. She can now take action to annul it. The husband, who had until then maintained the child as his own, can only hope, as a third party, for visitation rights and staying access (art 337).

There are, however, cases where access to biological truth is restricted.

B Restrictions on biological truth

In certain cases, access to truth is denied taking into account other individual or social interests.

1 The prohibition against establishing incestuous filiation

First of all, the ordonnance of 4 July 2005 reaffirms the prohibition against establishing incestuous filiation. More specifically, if the child is born of incest between ascendants and descendants, or between brother and sister and already has a filiation in relation to one parent, it is forbidden to establish filiation in relation to the other (art 310-2). Article 310-2 applies this prohibition whatever the means by which filiation was established, thus confirming the ruling of the *Cour de cassation* which forbade the establishment of incestuous filiation by means of adoption.[22]

Protecting one of the fundamental prohibitions of all societies thus overrides the principle of the truth of filiation.

2 The right to give birth under anonymity (L'accouchement sous X)

The ordonnance of 4 July 2005 likewise confirms the right of a woman giving birth to require that her admission and identity be kept secret (art 326). If she makes use of this right, no maternity action can be brought (art 325). It is known that the question of the mother's anonymity has been hotly debated and that the European Court of Human Rights held back from condemning France on this point, taking into account the adjustments that had been made to the system with a view to protecting the child's right to know his origins.[23] This does not make it any less impossible to establish maternal filiation, and often also paternal filiation, since, unable to identify

---

[22] Civ 1ère 6 January 2004, D. 2004, 362, concl J Sainte-Rose, note T Vigneau, JCP 2004, II, 10064, note C Labrusse-Riou, RTD civ 2004, 75, obs J Hauser.

[23] European Court of Human Rights, 13 February 2003, *Odièvre v France*, D 2003, 1240, note B Malet-Bricout, JCP 2003, II, 10049, note A Gouttenoire and F Sudre.

the child, the husband or partner will not be able to recognise him or her. Even if he manages to do this, he is likely to run into adoption procedures which will already have been set in motion. French courts have had to deal with these dramatic situations and their decisions have sometimes been unduly harsh in relation to the fathers.[24]

3   Medically assisted procreation

Finally, the ordonnance of 4 July 2005 does not question a somewhat paradoxical rule resulting from the law relating to medically assisted procreation. Not only can no bond of filiation be established between the third party donor and the child conceived by donor artificial insemination (art 311-19, and France remains wedded to the principle of anonymity), but more than that, consent to a medically assisted procreation 'is a bar to any action directed at disputing filiation' (art 311-20). So the husband who consents to donor artificial insemination cannot prevent his filiation being presumed. Any action to dispute this is forbidden, except under art 311-20 by proving that the child is not the result of the medical intervention, or that his consent to it was of no effect (art 311-20, para 2).

It may seem surprising that, in a field where biological science is triumphant, biological truth should be forbidden. The Legislature's reasons for taking this line are nonetheless easy to understand.

The strongest restraint on the triumph of biological truth, however, is time. As the years pass, as situations become embedded, it seems inappropriate to allow filiation to be too easily challenged. Concern for their stability overrides the search for truth.

III STABILITY

There is nothing new about concern for stability in filiation. It is rooted in the ancient principle of respect for the peace of families and the security of personal status. Changing attitudes and the increasing fragility of the bond of filiation have, however, given particular importance to the need for stability. It is worth examining the aims and the means.

A   The aims

Biological truth cannot allow the most firmly established filiations to be called into question, regardless of their duration and emotional content. To take scientific logic that far would be contrary to the interests of children, of families and of society as a whole. Such a development would be particularly harmful in a time when families are becoming fragile, couples unstable and children are shuttled from one family to another. The child, it is said, is one of the last elements of stability on which the Legislature could rebuild family law. So it is essential to give security to the bond of filiation.

---

[24]   As to these decisions cf Ph Malaurie and H Fulchiron, above note 11.

The bold interpretations delivered by the *Cour de cassation* after the law of 2 January 1972 had, in addition, shown the disastrous effects of weakening filiation, with actions to dispute it open to all interested parties, within the normal period of 30 years. True, such actions depended on inconsistency between registration and *possession d'état*, but judicial decision had shown a worrying laxity when it came to finding whether there was or was not *possession d'état*.

The Legislature in 2005 wanted to react to put an end to this drift. Actions to challenge filiation have been redesigned. If it is easier than it was to dispute filiation in a search for truth, the actions are now severely restricted.

B   The means

For the Legislature, it was a matter of combining the reality of filiation, as it is experienced by those involved, with biological reality. If more significance is given to biological truth, the actions and challenges are doubly restricted: as to the persons who can bring them, and especially in the time-limits.

The new system of actions to challenge filiation, provided for in arts 333 and 334 take account of three situations.

If the registration and *possession d'état* are consistent, filiation can still be challenged. Biological truth triumphs over *possession d'état*. However, nobody except the child, the father, the mother or the person claiming to be the true parent can act. In addition, the action is barred by the passing of 5 years from the cessation of *possession d'état*. Thus the situation is quickly stabilised.

Above all, if *possession d'état* has lasted more than 5 years from the child's birth or recognition, nobody can challenge a filiation based on registration consistent with *possession d'état*. Here again, the situation is quickly stabilised in favour of the filiation experienced by the parties.

Where registration and *possession d'état* are not mutually consistent, any interested party can bring an action to challenge filiation but only within the 10-year time-limit.[25]

So a balance has been struck between the contradictory requirements. But will the barriers set up by the law be able to withstand the pressure of biological certainty and the fascination this exerts on attitudes and opinions? It may be that, in its search for stability in filiation, the Legislature has overstepped the mark.

Thus, no new paternal filiation can be established where the child already possesses one. In other cases the false filiation can first be displaced, but if the action is barred by lapse of time, the true filiation can never be

---

[25]   Under art 32, the time runs from the day when the person loses the possession d'état that is being claimed, or begins to enjoy the status which is being disputed. Time does not run against the child during minority. As to the particular case of filiation established by possession d'état see above.

established. Are parties going to be willing to accept such an obstacle, and will courts not be tempted to try to circumvent it?

The *ordonnance* of 4 July 2005 is, in general, well crafted, despite a certain incoherence in its plan[26] and some rather obscure provisions in relation to *possession d'etat*. It remains to be seen if the balance it seeks will stand up to the force of individual claims and personal needs.

---

[26]   See above.

Germany

THE CONSTITUTIONAL COURT AS DRIVER OF REFORMS IN GERMAN FAMILY LAW

Nina Dethloff* and Kathrin Kroll**

Résumé

Il y a eu plus de réformes légales en droit allemand de la famille que dans n'importe quel autre domaine. Depuis que la Constitution allemande, la Grundgesetz (GG), est entrée en vigueur il y a plus de 50 ans, des dispositions du Code civil intéressant le droit de la famille ont été fréquemment déférées devant la Cour fédérale constitutionnelle. Les principales dispositions constitutionnelles qui ont été invoquées en matière de droit de la famille sont les suivantes: la protection particulière du mariage au regard de la famille (Art 6 para I GG), les droits et devoirs naturels des parents en matière de soin et d'éducation des enfants (Art 6 para II GG), l'égalité des enfants nés en et hors du mariage (Art 6 para IV GG), les garanties de l'égalité des droits entre homme et femme (Art 3 para II et III GG) et, enfin, les libertés individuelles telles qu'entendues par l'article 2 paragraphe I GG. Alors qu'initialement la Cour Constitutionnelle tendait à condamner les normes qui violaient gravement ces dispositions fondamentales, plus récemment – avec la diversification des nouvelles formes de famille – la question qui apparaît souvent est de savoir comment régler les conflits entre ces différentes dispositions. Dès l'origine et encore actuellement, la Cour a décelé des dispositions du droit de la famille violant la Constitution, ce qui incité à faire des réformes dans le domaine du droit de la famille. Pour autant, même là où la Cour n'avait pas décelé de violation d'un droit constitutionnel, ce contrôle a souvent conduit à des modifications législatives. Par exemple, la loi sur les partenariats enregistrés de 2001 qui a été élaborée pour mettre fin aux discriminations à l'égard des gays et des lesbiennes et qui a offert aux couples homosexuels une reconnaissance légale pour leur union avec un statut proche mais différents du mariage, n'a pas été déclarée contraire à la Constitution. Pourtant, un changement dans la législation concernant les partenariats enregistrés a suivi en 2005 (II.). De plus, la loi concernant le nom, qui était auparavant entrée en conflit avec la Constitution, a encore été soumise à la Cour et par conséquent a été réformée

---

*   Director of the Institute for German, European and International Family Law at Rheinische Friedrich-Wilhelms-Universität Bonn.

**   Assistant at the Institute for German, European and International Family Law at Rheinische Friedrich-Wilhelms-Universität Bonn.

    The authors wish to acknowledge the assistance of Thomas Spernat, who has been doing some valuable research.

(III.). Enfin, le contrôle judiciaire des accords entre époux que la Cour a demandé en 2001 a maintenant, par une décision de la Cour Suprême Fédérale en 2004, été mis en application suite à un revirement jurisprudentiel radical (IV.). En guise de conclusion, quelques autre réformes en cours seront présentées.

I INTRODUCTION

There have been more legal reforms in German family law than in any other area. Ever since the German Constitution, the *Grundgesetz* (GG), entered into force more than 50 years ago, provisions of the German Civil Code (BGB)[1] regarding family law have come under attack before the Federal Constitutional Court. The major constitutional provisions that come into play where family law is concerned are the following: the special protection of marriage and the family (Art 6, para I, GG), the natural right and duty of parents for the care and upbringing of children (Art 6, para II, GG), the equality of children born within marriage and out of wedlock (Art 6, para IV, GG), the guarantee of equal rights for men and women (Art 3, paras II and III, GG) and, finally, personal freedoms as provided for under Art 2, para I, GG. Whereas initially, the Constitutional Court tended to strike down norms blatantly in violation of such fundamental provisions, more recently – with the forms of family life having become much more diverse – the question often arises as to how conflicts between different provisions are to be resolved. Both early on and at present, the Court has found family law provisions to violate the Constitution. The effect of this has been to stimulate reforms in the field of family law. However, even where the Court did not find a violation of constitutional law, this activity has frequently led to a revision of the law: the Registered Partnership Act of 2001 that was enacted to counteract the discrimination against gays and lesbians and that offered same-sex couples a legal framework for their partnership embodying comparable though different effects to marriage, was declared not to violate the Constitution. Nevertheless, a change in the law of registered partnerships followed in 2005 (II). Furthermore, the law pertaining to marital names, which has been in conflict with the Constitution before, has yet again come under attack and consequently been reformed (III). Finally, the judicial control of marital agreements that the Constitutional Court mandated in 2001 has now, through a decision of the Federal Supreme Court in 2004, been implemented by a radical change in case-law (IV). By way of conclusion, some more reforms currently on their way will be pointed out (V).

---

[1]   'Bürgerliches Gesetzbuch', in the following cited as 'BGB'.

II REFORM OF THE REGISTERED PARTNERSHIP ACT

A Constitutionality of comparable provisions for registered partnerships and marriages

In February 2001 the German legislator passed the Act Aimed at Terminating Discrimination,[2] which in its Art 1 contained the Registered Partnership Act (LPartG).[3] By establishing a new form of registered partnership for same-sex couples, the legislator attempted to avoid any legal similarity with marriage, which is protected under Art 6, para I of the Constitution.[4] Nevertheless, three state governments filed an action before the Federal Constitutional Court, claiming the LPartG to be unconstitutional. The Court held that the creation of rules for same-sex couples that are comparable to those for marriage did not violate Art 6, para I, GG, which provides for the special protection of marriage.[5] It found that neither the constitutionally protected freedom to marry nor the guarantee of the institution of marriage, defined as a life-long union between woman and man, was violated. More importantly, the constitutionally mandated principles not to harm but to protect and further marriage are not infringed. Those principles do not bar the legislator from creating a legal instrument with the same or similar legal effects as marriage, an instrument designed exclusively for same-sex partners and which does not compete with marriage. Marriage itself can still be furthered and protected even if comparable rights and obligations are attached to alternative forms of living not open to a mixed-sex couple. Consequently, the Court upheld the law.[6]

B Revision of the Registered Partnership Act in 2005

Influenced by the stance of the Court, the German legislator passed a revised version of the LPartG in 2004 that entered into force on 1 January 2005.[7] The revised LPartG further approximates registered partnership and marriage. It contains the following modifications.

1 Impediment to marriage for registered partners

Although the original version of the LPartG included a provision[8] whereby the prospective parties to a registered partnership should not be married already, a similar provision regarding an existing registered partnership was lacking in marital law under the Civil Code. Consequently, the existence of a registered partnership did not function as an impediment to marriage. This

---

[2] 'Gesetz zur Beendigung der Diskriminierung gleichgeschlechtlicher Gemeinschaften' of 16 February 2001, entered into force on 1 August 2001 (BGBl, I, 2001, 266).

[3] See Dethloff 'The Registered Partnership Act of 2001' [2002] ISFL 171 *et seq.*

[4] For more details see Dethloff, *ibid.*

[5] Federal Constitutional Court (BVerfG), 17 July 2002, *Neue Juristische Wochenschrift* (NJW) (2002), 2543 *et seq.*

[6] *Ibid,* at 2547.

[7] 'Gesetz zur Überarbeitung des Lebenspartnerschaftsrechts' of 15 December 2004 (BGBl, I, 2004, 3396).

[8] Compare s 1, para II, No 1, LPartG.

difference could be explained by the assumption that the German legislator sought to avoid any potential conflict with the freedom to marry as provided for by the Constitution.[9] Following the Federal Constitutional Court's decision in 2002, which had declared such an impediment to marriage constitutional,[10] s 1306, BGB was amended accordingly.

2   Engagement

In its new para III, which has been added to s 1, the LPartG now provides for the possibility of registered partners to become engaged.[11] It reflects the corresponding provision in s 1297, BGB, whereby no action can be brought on the grounds of an engagement to marry. Section 1, para III, sentence 2, LPartG, further states that the respective statutory provisions in relation to civil marriages (ss 1297, para II, 1298–1302, BGB) apply accordingly. Therefore, upon the breach of an engagement a registered partner is also entitled to compensation, and upon the termination of the engagement any presents received must be returned. More importantly, however, a fiancé is privileged from testifying under the law of civil and criminal procedure.[12] Under the new version of the LPartG, those privileges are extended to same-sex partners who have become engaged.[13]

3   Marital property law and pension rights adjustment ('versorgungsausgleich')

Following the 2005 reform of the LPartG, the statutory matrimonial property regime of accrued gains ('Zugewinngemeinschaft') was extended to registered partnerships (s 6, LPartG). As the original version of the LPartG did not contain a similar provision, same-sex partners had to make a declaration concerning the property regime when establishing their relationship. In the absence of such a declaration a complete separation of property existed.[14] Despite its name, the now applicable 'Zugewinngemeinschaft' is not a true community of property, but a separation of property with a special equalisation process of the spouses' assets on termination of the marriage. During the marriage, each spouse owns and administrates independently her or his own property, being liable only for debts incurred by herself/himself. On termination of the marriage by divorce, both spouses' assets are to be compared. The gains accrued by each spouse in her/his assets are equalised. The spouse having the higher amount of 'accrued gains' must pay her/his partner half of the difference between their accrued gains as 'Zugewinnausgleich', ie compensation. This regime

---

9   The right to marry is encompassed by Art 6, para I, GG ('Marriage and family are under the special protection of the state').

10   BVerfG (note 5), at 2547.

11   For more detail see Wellenhofer 'Das neue Recht für eingetragene Lebenspartnerschaften', NJW (2005), 705; v Dickhuth-Harrach 'Das Lebenspartnerschaftsrecht Version 2005', *Familie Partnerschaft Recht* (FPR) (2005) 273, at 274.

12   Wellenhofer, *ibid*; v Dickhuth-Harrach, *ibid*.

13   Section 383, para I, No 1, German Code of Civil procedure; s 52, para I, No 1, German Code of Criminal Procedure.

14   See Dethloff (note 3), at 176.

now automatically applies to registered partners. Even though registered partners are therefore no longer obliged to make a declaration concerning their property regime, they are still free to do so (s 7, LPartG).[15]

Furthermore, the German legislator in 2005 adopted provisions for the adjustment of pension rights, which are similar in effect to the spouses' pension rights adjustment ('Versorgungsausgleich') in s 1587, BGB.[16] In the original version of the LPartG, a partner did not participate in the other partner's pension rights upon termination of their relationship.[17] Under the new law a registered partner is entitled to benefit from the other partner's entitlements, expectancies or the mere prospect of drawing old-age benefits. The partner who accumulated less pension rights during the registered partnership will have pension rights to the amount of half of the difference between the respective pensions rights transferred to him or her, thereby equalising the benefits amassed during marriage.

4 Dissolution ('Aufhebung')

The original version of the LPartG merely contained provisions for the dissolution of a registered partnership, ie the judicial dissolution for reasons arising after its conclusion, which it confusingly called *Aufhebung* (in marriage law, the term reserved for an annulment), but did not provide for the annulment of a registered partnership, ie the judicial dissolution for reasons that already existed when the relationship was entered into.[18] The law of 2005 amended this shortcoming. However, now both forms of dissolution are called *Aufhebung*. The wording still causes confusion, making it necessary, at least, to distinguish carefully both forms of termination of a civil partnership.[19] The *Aufhebung*, understood as a divorce order, may be made on one of the three grounds set out in s 15, para II, LPartG:

(1) if the registered partners have lived apart for a continuous period of at least one year and either both of them consent to the divorce or there was no reasonable expectation that the partnership could be restored;

(2) if they have been separated for 3 years;

(3) if the continuation of the registered partnership would result in unreasonable hardship for the petitioner through the action of his or her partner.

The law of registered partnerships is therefore similar to divorce law. Further declarations by the parties as provided under s 15 of the 2001 version of the LPartG are no longer required.[20]

---

[15] V Dickhuth-Harrach (note 11), at 275.

[16] For the previous legal situation compare Dethloff (note 3), at 179, 180.

[17] See the critical comment of Dethloff (note 3), at 180.

[18] With regard to the original version of the LPartG see Dethloff (note 3), at 178, 179.

[19] V Dickhuth-Harrach (note 11), at 277.

[20] Dethloff (note 11), at 179.

Moreover, the court must grant *Aufhebung*, understood in terms of an annulment order, in the case of specific grounds, such as a party's mental disorder, or the existence of error, fraud or threat when the registered partnership was entered into.[21] The provisions concerning *Aufhebung* are open to criticism for not replicating several grounds for marriage annulment included in the Civil Code. For example, a spouse's legal incapacity or the celebration of a fictitious marriage are grounds for an annulment, whereas a registered partnership – in the absence of special provisions – would automatically be void under the general rules.[22] As the provisions concerning *Aufhebung* under the LPartG do not completely mirror those that relate to marriage, they only offer a minimum standard of legal protection for registered partnerships.[23] The difference between annulment and avoidance according to the general rules lies in the fact that the latter renders a registered partnership void from the beginning (s 142, para I, BGB), whereas the first only makes a marriage voidable (ss 1313, sentence 2, 1314, BGB) with the rules on the consequences of divorce applicable (s 1318, BGB).

Finally, s 15, para III, LPartG, contains a hardship clause, which is in substance identical to the grounds set out in s 1568, BGB for marriages. The clause does not include the first alternative of s 1568, BGB, which provides that a marriage shall not be dissolved if the divorce comes into conflict with the interests of minors born out of wedlock.[24] Although the practical importance of this provision is not great, the legislator should not fail to protect children adopted by registered partners.[25]

5   Maintenance

German family law makes a clear distinction between matrimonial property and maintenance. Following the reform, the rules relating to maintenance in ss 5, 12 and 16, LPartG, are in substance identical to those relating to marriage under the Civil Code. There exist maintenance obligations both during the marriage, which may be fulfilled by keeping the house or financial contributions, as well as after separation or upon divorce.

The purpose of maintenance after divorce is to provide economic support to the dependent former spouse if he or she is unable to do so for himself/herself. To be eligible for maintenance, a spouse must establish one of the grounds set forth in ss 1569–1576, BGB. The court must find that the spouse is reasonably unable to support himself/herself through appropriate employment because, for example, of caring for children (s 1570, BGB), old age (s 1571, BGB) or sickness (s 1572, BGB). It is worth noting that the new version of the LPartG explicitly states that s 1570, BGB, applies, whereby

---

[21] Stüber 'Gesetz zur Überarbeitung des Lebenspartnerschaftsrechts', *Zeitschrift für das gesamte Familienrecht* (FamRZ) (2005) 574, at 575.

[22] Wellenhofer (note 11), at 705; for the previous application of ss 119 *et seq*, BGB, under the 2001 version of the LPartG see Muscheler *Das Recht der eingetragenen Lebenspartnerschaft* (2nd edn, 2004), at 175 *et seq*.

[23] Stüber (note 21), at 575; v Dickhuth-Harrach (note 11), at 277.

[24] V Dickhuth-Harrach (note 11), at 277; Wellenhofer (note 11), at 709.

[25] For the adoption of stepchildren according to s 9, LPartG, see below under B.6.

caring for joint children may be a ground on which a maintenance claim can be based. Therefore caring for a stepchild who was adopted by the registered partner[26] entitles the one providing care to maintenance.[27]

As far as the obligation to support following separation is concerned, the new version of the Act contains a provision[28] which mirrors s 1361, para I, BGB, whereby spouses must provide each other with appropriate financial support after separation. Unlike the situation consequent upon divorce, when the former spouse must be unable to support herself/himself for one of the grounds set out above, after separation there is generally no expectation that the non-working registered partner will gain employment. Under the 2001 version of the LPartG, on the other hand, it was the law that the non-working registered partner was obliged to support herself/himself.[29] It was therefore up to her/him to prove extraordinary circumstances preventing her/him from gaining employment.

6   Adoption of stepchildren

One of the most contested parts of the 2005 reform of the LPartG was the introduction of the adoption of stepchildren,[30] allowing a registered partner to adopt his or her partner's biological children. Before this reform, registered partners, unlike spouses, were not allowed to adopt a stepchild.[31] The registered partner, not being the parent of the child, was given only selective parental rights and duties in matters concerning daily life.[32] The reason why the German legislator eventually decided to amend s 9, LPartG, was the criticism regarding the discriminatory effect of the former version of the LPartG.[33] The law had been ignoring social reality with regard to same-sex partnerships. In Germany today, approximately 50,000 families consisting of same-sex partners and their children are in existence.[34] Several studies have shown that the fact that a child is raised by same-sex parents has no negative impact on its growing up.[35] On the contrary, it is considered to be in the child's best interest if an existing factual relationship to the non-parent partner can be legally recognised by adoption.[36] The legislative purpose was not to grant rights to registered partners, but to advance the legal status of children growing up in a same-sex relationship.[37]

As is the case with all adoptions, the parents' consent is required. Furthermore, an adoption will only be granted if it conforms to the best interest of the child. Where emotional ties to the other biological parent

---

[26]   For the adoption of stepchildren see below under B.6.

[27]   For further details compare Wellenhofer (note 11), at 707.

[28]   Section 12, LPartG.

[29]   Wellenhofer (note 11), at 707; v Dickhuth-Harrach (note 11), at 275.

[30]   Section 9, para VII, LPartG.

[31]   For the previous legal situation compare Dethloff (note 3), at 176, 177.

[32]   Dethloff (note 3), at 177.

[33]   For further details see Dethloff (note 3), at 176, 177.

[34]   Wellenhofer (note 11), at 706 with further supporting documents.

[35]   *Ibid.*

[36]   Dethloff (note 3), at 177.

[37]   Wellenhofer (note 11), at 707.

continue, it will usually not be in a child's best interest to sever those ties through an adoption. However, where this is not the case, as after an artificial insemination by donor sperm, and where there exists a parent-child relationship between the biological parent's partner and the child, adoption may be in the child's best interest. After the adoption, the child is the legal child of the stepparent: he or she has joint custody with the biological parent of the child. The parents can choose a common surname for their child.[38] More importantly, there exists a right to maintenance and mutual inheritance rights.[39] Legal ties are especially significant in case of the partners' separation or if the biological parent dies. If the registered partnership is dissolved, the child will no longer automatically and without regard to its best interest remain in the biological parent's sole custody.

Unfortunately, the German legislator failed to go a step further and allow registered partners jointly to adopt a child.[40] Under present law, a joint adoption is possible only on condition that the adoptive parents-to-be are married.[41] For this reason, a fair number of children are currently placed in foster care with same-sex partners. If the foster-care arrangement is long term and there is no chance of the child returning to his/her biological family it should be possible to recognise legally the existing factual parent-child relationship between foster parents and the child through a joint adoption.[42] Even though social constraints and prejudices still exist within society, discrimination by law should be terminated.[43] The most important purpose that the law should serve is the promotion of a child's welfare, this being best served by the securing of a relationship with two parents who love the child – whatever their gender may be.

C   What is left to reform?

With the latest reform of the LPartG, the German legislator has brought registered partnership and marriage in the area of civil law virtually into equality. The revised LPartG can therefore be said to be another step forward for registered partners in their pursuit of equal rights with married couples. However, significant points remain for reform. Of crucial importance is the fact that registered partners are still unable jointly to adopt a child. From a more technical aspect, the wording of the Act may be criticised for promoting confusion, as some of the old terms that were used to differentiate between registered partnership and marriage – such as *Aufhebung* instead of divorce and annulment – have not been replaced. Further reform is urgently needed in the area of succession and income tax law. Registered partnerships are still completely unknown under tax law, whereas marriages are highly

---

[38]   Section 9, para V, LPartG.
[39]   See also Dethloff (note 3), at 177, 178.
[40]   Stüber (note 21), at 577.
[41]   Section 1741, para II, BGB.
[42]   Dethloff 'Adoption durch gleichgeschlechtliche Paare', *Zeitschrift für Rechtspolitik* (ZRP) (2004) 195, at 199.
[43]   Dethloff, *ibid*.

privileged.[44] The assimilation of registered partnerships and marriages is obviously barred by fiscal interests of the State.[45]

III REFORM OF THE LAW PERTAINING TO FAMILY NAMES

A Unconstitutionality of limiting the choice of a common family name to birth names

Under the original version of the German Civil Code of 1896, a woman had to adopt her husband's surname upon marriage (s 1355, BGB). In 1976 the German legislator passed a new law allowing the couple to choose either the husband's or the wife's surname as a common family name.[46] However, if the spouses made no choice, the husband's name prevailed. Following a decision of the German Federal Constitutional Court in 1991,[47] which declared the priority of the husband's name unconstitutional, s 1355, para II, BGB, again had to be changed. The new law of 1993 allowed the spouses to keep their names if they did not choose the surname of either the husband or the wife as their common family name.[48] However, in practice the vast majority of women maintain the old custom of adopting their husbands' surnames upon marrying.[49]

In 2004, the Federal Constitutional Court[50] once again had to deal with the question as to whether s 1355, BGB, was constitutional. The case that came up to the Court concerned a German couple who married in the US in 1993. On their return to Germany, the spouses sought to use as their common family name the wife's name that she had acquired in a previous marriage. The German authorities rejected the applicants' request on the ground that under s 1355, para II, BGB, only one of the spouse's surnames *by birth* could be chosen as a common family name. The applicant's complaint to the German Federal Constitutional Court was based on a violation of her right to free development of her personality, protected by Art 2, para I, GG, and Art 1, para I, GG. The Court held that a person's name as part of the individual's personality is protected by Art 2, para I, GG. The right to a name as an element of personal identity and individuality includes not only one's surname by birth, but also a family name acquired by marriage.[51] The

---

44   V Dickhuth-Harrach 'Neuerungen im Erbrecht eingetragener Lebenspartner', FamRZ (2005) 1139, at 1140.

45   Kornmacher 'Eine neue Ära im Lebenspartnerschaftsrecht', *Familien-Rechts-Berater* (FamRB) (2005) 22, at 26.

46   'Erstes Gesetz zur Reform des Ehe- und Familiennamensrechts' of 14 June 1976 (BGBl I 1421).

47   Federal Constitutional Court (BVerfG), 5 March 1991, FamRZ 1991, 535 *et seq*.

48   'Gesetz zur Neuordnung des Familiennamensrechts' of 16 December 1993, entered into force on 1 April 1994 (BGBl I 2054).

49   In 2001 approximately 93% and in 2002 97% of married women chose to adopt their husband's name in Hamburg, Hanover, Frankfurt and Munich, as mentioned by the Federal Constitutional Court (BVerfG), 18 February 2004, FamRZ 2004, 515, at 516.

50   BVerfG (note 49), 515 *et seq*.

51   BVerfG (note 49), at 517.

right to such a family name does not depend on the existence of the marriage. From the time a new family name has been adopted, it replaces a person's prior surname. It becomes her or his own name and not merely a name 'borrowed' from the other spouse.

The Court stated that this constitutionally protected right to a name is violated if the choice of a common family name is limited to one of the partners' birth names, because it requires a person to give up a name acquired in a former marriage. Such a family name thus becomes a name of lesser quality. According to the Court's ruling, such violation must be justified by other prevailing interests for it to be constitutional. First, the ruling rejected the argument that the proposed choice of name could lead to a misuse of family names, especially titles of nobility.[52] Secondly, it stated that the law of names is not an appropriate means to prevent marriages being entered upon solely in the pursuit of a title of nobility.[53] Such fictitious marriages should be prohibited *per se*. However, the Court did consider the interests of a divorced partner or the surviving family of a deceased partner of a former marriage. A divorced spouse might find the use of his (or her) name by a new spouse in a subsequent marriage offensive. Moreover, such a passing on of the name to a new spouse could lead to the assumption of an existing familial relationship where there was none.

Nevertheless, the Court questioned whether these interests were of such importance that they justify an infringement upon the right to the divorced spouse's name.[54] According to the Court's reasoning, the right to a name does not entitle a person to dispose of *other* persons' names. The Constitution in Art 2 does not grant the right to an exclusive use of a name. On the contrary, the Court considered the spouse who had already abandoned her (or his) name in a first marriage as being the main party affected by s 1355, para II, BGB. When entering into a new marriage the spouse in question is being forced to give up her (or his) name once again, the Court said. It consequently found the law to be one-sided, protecting solely the interests of the partner who retains his (or her) name when getting married. The Court came to the conclusion that the law does not correspond to the constitutionally guaranteed equality of women and men. It recalled that until the 1976 law reform, the husband's name prevailed if spouses had not chosen a common family name. Moreover, the predominance of the husband's name is the established naming practice even today. Women are therefore unreasonably affected by the law.[55] Consequently, the interests of the divorced spouse of a previous marriage cannot justify the violation of the right to the individual's personality protected by Art 2, para I, GG, and

---

[52]   Manteuffel 'Zur Reform des Ehenamensrechts – quo vadis Gesetzgeber?', NJW (2004) 1773, at 1774.

[53]   BVerfG (note 49), at 517.

[54]   BVerfG (note 49), at 518.

[55]   See for an in-depth analysis of this aspect Sacksofsky 'Das Ehenamensrecht zwischen Tradition und Gleichberechtigung', FPR (2004) 371, at 374.

Art 1, para I, GG. As a result, the Court declared s 1355, para II, BGB, unconstitutional and required the German legislator to change the law.[56]

Since the reform of s 1355, para II, BGB, in February 2005,[57] spouses – as well as registered partners (s 3, para II, LPartG) – are able to choose as a common family name either one of their birth names or their currently used names, provided that they do not want to keep their own names.

B Marital agreements on the use of a common family name in a subsequent marriage

The Court's ruling and the consequent change in the law have provoked a discussion concerning how a spouse could protect himself/herself against the use of 'his' or 'her' surname by the other spouse in a subsequent marriage. The question is whether spouses are allowed to stipulate, in a premarital agreement, that the party adopting the other's surname (which then becomes the common family name) undertakes to abandon that name upon divorce or at least not to use it as a common family name in a new marriage. Considering that the parties' autonomy is protected by the Constitution,[58] such agreements will generally be permissible. Even if the legislator is not allowed to prevent a spouse from using her/his name acquired in a previous marriage as a common family name in a subsequent marriage, the parties themselves are able to do so. However, in particular cases premarital agreements are deemed unconscionable and, therefore, void.[59] First of all, an agreement would be invalid if it provided for – even indirectly – compensation of the waiving party.[60] Secondly, a premarital agreement containing a waiver of the family name should not be enforced if there is proof of duress or coercion.

Even if such agreements will in general be considered valid, this only means that they are binding on the parties themselves, but not on the registrar.[61] Whether premarital agreements should be legally enforceable or subject to judicial execution is a highly disputed point in legal literature.[62] However, it is suggested that parties stipulate a penalty in the contract in order to make sure that the waiver of a name is effective.[63]

---

56 BVerfG (note 49), at 519.
57 'Gesetz zur Änderung des Ehe- und Lebenspartnerschaftsnamensrechts' of 6 February 2005, entered into force on 12 February 2005 (BGBl I 2005, 9).
58 The parties' autonomy is encompassed by Art 2, para I, GG.
59 Everts 'Vereinbarungen über nacheheliche Namensführung', FamRZ (2005) 249, 250; v Hein 'Anmerkung zum Urteil des BVerfG', FamRZ (2004) 519, at 521.
60 Everts, *ibid*, at 250; v Hein, *ibid*, at 521.
61 Anwaltkommentar/Wellenhofer (2005) § 1355 at 15; Münchener Kommentar zum BGB/Wacke (4th edn 2000) § 1355 at 16.
62 In favour of an execution as provided under s 894, Code of Civil Procedure see Everts (note 59), at 250; v Hein (note 59), at 521; for a different view see Anwaltkommentar/Wellenhofer, *ibid*; Münchener Kommentar/Wacke, *ibid*.
63 Everts (note 59), at 253.

C   Limiting the choice of children's names and gender equality

In 2002, the Federal Constitutional Court decided another important case with regard to the choice of names.[64] The Court had to answer the question as to whether s 1617, para I, sentence 1, BGB, in disallowing parents from choosing a name consisting of both parents' surnames for their children was constitutional.[65] If spouses keep their own surnames after marriage rather than adopt a common family name, the birth name of their first child can only be either the father's or the mother's surname. The Court found no violation of Art 6, para II or Art 3, paras II and III, GG, and upheld the law. It stated that the parents' right to name a child is, in principle, encompassed by the right of care and upbringing of children as protected under Art 6 para II, GG. However, this right does not necessarily comprise the freedom of unlimited choice of names. On the contrary, the Court held that the restrictions in s 1617, para I, BGB, rationally further the State's legitimate interest in promoting the welfare of children. The legislator is free to exclude a hyphenated surname consisting of both parents' names that would over generations create the danger of 'chains of names'.[66]

The Court further noted that s 1617, para I, BGB, does not violate the principle of equality of women and men or the prohibition of discrimination in Art 3, paras II, III, GG.[67] It stated that the prohibition extends not only to provisions that openly discriminate against women, but also to provisions that are, on the face of it, gender neutral while actually affecting women for the most part on account of prevailing differences in society, in particular. It took into consideration that, in fact, the majority of couples choose the husband's surname as their common family name. Consequently, parents also tend to choose the father's name for their children. The Court therefore admitted that this predominance of the male partners' names probably reflects traditional customs regarding the roles of women and men. Hence, the Court assumed that equality in partnerships still does not exist in society. However, as the Court found the priority of the husband's name to stem from prevailing conceptions – rather than from the unfavourable situation of women in general – it did not consider it necessary to further gender equality by means of a choice of hyphenated surnames.

The Court's ruling, in terms of both the result and the reasoning, is not at all convincing.[68] If spouses can neither choose a hyphenated name as common family name, which can then become their children's surname, nor combine their respective different surnames into a hyphenated name for their children, the tradition of children bearing their father's name will continue. As a child's surname does not possess any connection with the mother's name, it makes women feel isolated within their own family. Consequently, women

---

[64]   Federal Constitutional Court (BVerfG), 30 January 2002, NJW (2002) 1256 *et seq.*
[65]   See Dethloff 'Improving the Position of Women in German Family Law: The Violence Protection Act of 2002 and Landmark Decisions in Maintenance Law' [2003] ISFL 2003, 187, at 193.
[66]   BVerfG (note 64), at 1258.
[67]   BVerfG (note 64), at 1259.
[68]   Sacksofsky 'Grundrechtsdogmatik ade – Zum neuen Doppelnamen-Urteil des Bundesverfassungs-gerichts', FPR (2002) 125.

are indirectly pressured not to keep their own name but to adopt their husbands' upon marriage.[69] As a result denying spouses and children the right to bear a hyphenated name is typically mostly at the expense of women.

IV PREMARITAL AND MARITAL SETTLEMENT AGREEMENTS

A Constitutional requirement of judicial control

It was a Federal Constitutional Court's decision of 2001[70] that obliged the German Supreme Court to overrule a consistent line of precedents concerning premarital agreements.[71] The Federal Constitutional Court dealt with a premarital agreement in which the pregnant wife-to-be had waived her right to maintenance after divorce as provided under s 1569 *et seq, BGB*. The Court examined the case in particular in the light of Art 2, para I, GG, that provides for the freedom of contract. It held that it is up to the civil courts to apply the law in order to guarantee the parties' autonomy. The parties' intention as expressed in a contract is usually assumed to reflect a fair balance of interests.[72] However, if the duties that arise out of a contract solely burden one party and if there is proof of substantially unequal bargaining power, the law must avoid allowing one party to be completely deprived of his/her self-determination. These rules also apply to marital settlement agreements. Where an agreement does not reflect the equality of the partners as protected in Art 3, para II, GG, but results from one partner's unilateral dominance, the State must limit the spouses' freedom to stipulate the economic consequences of a divorce.[73] The freedom to marry as protected by the Constitution does not authorise the parties to agree freely upon any consequences of divorce, especially if the terms are clearly disadvantageous to one party.

The Court pointed out that a premarital agreement executed by an expectant mother who is also protected by Art 6, para IV, GG, requires specific judicial control. The Court explained that such an agreement often functions as a precondition to marriage forcing a pregnant woman, who is confronted with the legal and social disadvantages attached to a birth out of wedlock, to sign the agreement in order to be married. However, the Court held that pregnancy should be only one of the factors that it ought to bear in mind when judging whether there is an inequality of bargaining power and whether one partner has the dominant position. Other factors including the parties' economic circumstances, their skills and prospects as well as the

---

[69]   Sacksofsky, *ibid.*

[70]   Federal Constitutional Court (BVerfG), 6 February 2001, FamRZ (2001) 343, and 29 March 2001. For further details with regard to that decision, compare Dethloff (note 65), at 191.

[71]   Federal Supreme Court (BGH), 11 February 2004, FamRZ (2004) 601 *et seq.*

[72]   BVerfG (note 70), at 345.

[73]   BVerfG (note 70), at 346.

intended distribution of marital duties must be taken into consideration.[74] It is eventually up to the courts to ascertain whether or not those factors exist and whether, according to the general rules set out in ss 138, para I, 242, BGB – to be interpreted in the light of the Constitution – a premarital agreement is to be upheld or not.

B   The Supreme Court's decision of 2004

Following the Constitutional Court's ruling, the Federal Supreme Court in 2004[75] overruled its prior decisions[76] concerning premarital agreements. It found that its former holding that such agreements generally should be considered valid and enforceable as a contract unless there was proof of unconscionability, including duress, coercion or conflict with the public or children's interests, did not adequately respond to a spouse's need for protection.[77] In its 2004 decision, which has been followed by several complementary judgments in 2005,[78] the Supreme Court articulated guidelines that explain when judicial control of such agreements is called for. As a starting point, it continues to hold that spouses are free in a premarital agreement to waive their statutory rights with regard to the equalisation of accrued gains, pension rights adjustments and maintenance after divorce. However, the purpose of these rules may not arbitrarily be frustrated. Where spouses enter into an obviously one-sided agreement that is not justified by the individual circumstances and is unreasonably disadvantageous to one of the spouses, the parties' autonomy should be restricted. The more the agreement by its terms violates a spouse's fundamental rights after divorce (so-called *Kernbereich*), the more it is presumed to be clearly unfair.

In order to determine which legal consequences after divorce might be defined as 'fundamental', the Court drew up the following ranking list:[79] the most fundamental and therefore at the top of the list is maintenance after divorce, which may be granted for the caring for the children of the marriage (s 1570, BGB). The Court pointed out that an agreement waiving spousal support with regard to s 1570, BGB, will not be upheld unless the parties are able to prove that the child's best interests are satisfied. Maintenance for the caring for children is, on the Court's list, followed by maintenance that may be granted in case of a spouse's illness (s 1572, BGB) or old age (s 1571, BGB), the latter being in line with the participation in pension rights ('Versorgungsausgleich'). At the end – following several other maintenance provisions – the Court ranked the marital property rights, which are broadly open to the parties' autonomy. The applicable statutory provision under

---

74   BVerfG (note 70), at 346, 347.
75   BGH (note 71), 601 *et seq.*
76   See the following precedents: Federal Supreme Court (BGH), 14 April 1985, FamRZ 1985, 788; 28 November 1990, FamRZ 1991, 306; 9 July 1992, FamRZ 1992, 1403; 2 October 1996, FamRZ 1997, 156.
77   For its prior reasoning compare BGH (note 71), at 602.
78   Federal Supreme Court (BGH), 25 May 2005, FamRZ (2005) 1444 and 1449.
79   *Ibid.*

s 1408, para I, BGB, recognises the spouses' power to reach an agreement containing terms at variance with the statutory property regime of accrued gains ('Zugewinngemeinschaft'). Taking those provisions into consideration, the Court ruled that even though the statutory matrimonial property regime presumes the participation of each spouse in the assets earned during marriage to be equal, spouses are free to agree otherwise.

On the basis of this list a two-step analysis is called for:[80] first, the judge must determine whether the agreement is valid at the moment of its execution or whether it violates s 138, para I, BGB, whereby any contract which offends good morals is void. This requires a consideration of the entire individual circumstances of the parties, in particular the economic circumstances, their income, their aims and motives and the type of relationship they lead or plan to lead. Usually only those agreements in which a party waives her or his fundamental rights – as stated in the list – after divorce without being compensated or without a justification lying in the particular circumstances of the spouses, will be found invalid. If a premarital or marital settlement agreement is void as provided under s 138, para I, BGB, it has no legal effects whatsoever. Rather, the statutory provisions will apply.

However, even if an agreement is considered to be valid when entered into, it may not be enforceable at the time of divorce because circumstances have changed. Hence, as a second step, the courts must consider if invoking a premarital agreement is improper pursuant to s 242, BGB. Under this rule, any contractual party must act in a manner consistent with good faith taking into account accepted practice. If s 242, BGB, is violated, the contract cannot be enforced. This may be the case if a spouse at the time of divorce insists on the other party's waiver of rights, even though circumstances have fundamentally changed during the marriage.[81] Consequently, an agreement waiving a spouse's rights after divorce is not enforceable if it is obviously one-sided and unreasonably disadvantages the waiving party. Again the Court's ranking list applies: the more fundamental a spouse's right, the more likely it is that a waiver will not be enforced. Where an agreement is not enforceable, it is at the Court's discretion to set up the appropriate legal consequences.

C   Back to legal certainty – or on the long road towards justice?

The Federal Constitutional Court did not specify in its decision how to apply its holding to marital agreements. Until the Supreme Court's decision in 2004, a considerable uncertainty and lack of uniformity regarding the interpretation of the Constitutional Court's ruling was evident. It was therefore generally welcome that the Supreme Court articulated guidelines for the judicial control of such agreements.[82] In future, it will be the

---

80   BGH (note 71), at 606.
81   BGH (note 71) at 606.
82   Rauscher 'Ehevereinbarungen: Rückkehr der Rechtssicherheit', *Deutsche Notar-Zeitschrift* (DNotZ) 2004, 524 *et seq*.

recording notary – preparing a premarital or marital settlement agreement – who will play an important role. In order to avoid unconscionability as provided under s 138, para I, BGB, the parties' personal and economic circumstances, including their chosen or planned-for type of marriage – be it a traditional arrangement or a 'double income no kids' style arrangement[83] – must be documented in the record.[84] Following the Court's ranking list, the notary will avoid including a waiver of maintenance for childcare.[85] Furthermore, the notary will even have to anticipate the Court's second step analysis, considering how circumstances might change between the execution of the agreement and a later separation or divorce.[86] However, it might be doubted whether the application of such general rules as s 138, para I, BGB, and s 242, BGB, rules that in fact even with the Supreme Court's guidelines may be interpreted in more than one way, will ever lead to legal certainty.[87]

Whereas the main issue in the Federal Constitutional Court's decision was to counteract inequality of bargaining power, this aspect was, surprisingly, left unaddressed by the Supreme Court.[88] On the contrary, it merely focused on the question whether an agreement by its terms clearly disadvantages one party. Inequality of bargaining power is no longer necessary to trigger judicial control of a premarital or marital settlement agreement. It seems to be sufficient that the terms of the contract are obviously one-sided and unreasonably disadvantageous to one party. However, the ranking list that the Supreme Court uses in order to determine when this is the case and an agreement is not valid or enforceable, is not altogether convincing.[89] It allows the waiver of rights whose specific purpose it is to counteract the disadvantages that a homemaking spouse suffers upon divorce. It can thus frustrate the legislative purpose of protecting that spouse. This is the case if it is possible to waive maintenance in cases where such maintenance is designed to counteract the disadvantages resulting from marriage. The same holds true in cases where the equalisation of accrued gains is waived, ie where one spouse's contribution consisted of homemaking, and no other compensation is granted.

---

[83]   For other types of marriage that may be referred to in a premarital agreement, compare Langenfeld *Handbuch der Ehe- und Scheidungsvereinbarungen* (4th edn, 2000) at 929 *et seq; idem* 'Die Ehevertragsgestaltung auf dem Prüfstand der richterlichen Inhaltskontrolle', *Zeitschrift für Erbrecht und Vermögensnachfolge* (ZEV) (2004) 311, at 315.

[84]   Langenfeld, *ibid*, at 315; Gageik 'Die aktuelle ober- und höchstrichterliche Rechtsprechung zur Inhaltskontrolle von Eheverträgen und ihre Auswirkungen auf die notarielle Praxis', *Rheinische Notar-Zeitschrift* (RNotZ) (2004) 295, at 312.

[85]   Gageik, *ibid*.

[86]   Gageik, *ibid*, at 314.

[87]   Kroll 'Rechtssicherheit oder Verwirrspiel? – Die Beurteilung vorehelicher Unterhaltsverzichte nach dem Urteil des BGH vom 11.2.2004', *Liber Amicorum Thomas Rauscher* (2005) 95, at 107.

[88]   Münch 'Inhaltskontrolle von Eheverträgen', *Zeitschrift für die Notarpraxis* (ZNotP) (2004) 122, at 128; Gageik (note 84), at 307.

[89]   For a critical view see also Goebel 'In guten, nicht in schlechten Tagen? – Sechs Thesen zur richterlichen Kontrolle von Unterhaltsverzichten', *FamRZ* (2003) 1513, at 1516; Mayer 'Zur Inhaltskontrolle von Eheverträgen', *FPR* (2004) 363, at 371.

V CONCLUSION

Law reform has again been spurred by decisions of the Constitutional Court. However, in the near future we expect more major reforms in several areas of family law that have been undertaken by the legislator but could not be completed due to the premature Federal elections in Germany and the end of the session of legislature. First, a fundamental reform of the law of family procedure is in progress.[90] A preliminary draft in its Art 1 contains a new Code of Family Procedure (FamFB)[91] that provides for uniform procedural rules regarding family matters. The following prospective improvements are worth mentioning:[92] the extension of jurisdiction of the family courts ('Großes Familiengericht'); the modification and simplification of divorce proceedings for childless spouses/registered partners who have agreed upon the consequences of divorce; the unification of legal terminology; and the establishment of procedural rights. Secondly, the law on maintenance after divorce will undergo substantial changes. The Federal Minister of Justice presented a preliminary draft regarding a modification of the law on maintenance in May 2005.[93] If the law came into force, the principle of self-sufficiency, requiring each spouse to provide for her or his support after divorce, would be intensified.[94] Furthermore, the legislature intends to include a new hardship clause (s 1578b, BGB), whereby in cases of exceptional hardship to the debtor spouse, maintenance is to be terminated or limited. Thirdly, minors will be given priority in the statutory hierarchy of maintenance creditors. Finally, there will be a revision of the law concerning the *Versorgungsausgleich*, the specific instrument for pension rights adjustment. In 2004, the Commission on Structural Changes to Pension Rights Adjustment presented its final report.[95] It proposed, for example, to deny pension rights adjustment where the duration of a marriage has been less than 3 years or to extend the options for spouses to agree upon a splitting of their pension rights upon divorce. Last but not least, we have already mentioned the legislative failure to provide for legal recognition of registered partnerships under tax law. This means that inequality still exists. Hopefully, the newly elected German Government will once again amend the LPartG, as provided for under the draft 'Lebenspartnerschaftser-gänzungsgesetz'.[96]

---

[90] Referentenentwurf zum 'Gesetz zur Reform des Verfahrens in Familiensachen und in den Angelegenheiten der Freiwilligen Gerichtsbarkeit' (FGG-Reformgesetz), published in June 2005.

[91] 'Gesetz über das Verfahren in Familiensachen und in den Angelegenheiten der Freiwilligen Gerichtsbarkeit' (FamFG).

[92] For a more detailed overview see Meyer-Seitz/Kröger/Heiter 'Auf dem Weg zu einem modernen Familienverfahrensrecht – die familienverfahrensrechtlichen Regelungen im Entwurf eines FamFB', FamRZ (2005) 1430 *et seq*.

[93] Referentenentwurf eines 'Gesetz zur Änderung des Unterhaltsrechts'; the text can be found in the 2005 Synopsis of FamRZ (2005) at 1041.

[94] For further information on the law reform see Schwab 'Zur Reform des Unterhaltsrechts', FamRZ (2005) 1417 *et seq*.

[95] The report is available at www.bmj.bund.de/enid/Familienrecht/Versorgunsgausgleich_pp.html.

[96] The draft did not become law because of the Federal Council's (Bundesrat) objection. For further information see v Dickhuth-Harrach (note 44), at 1140.

Ghana

PROGRESS AND RETROGRESSION ON DOMESTIC VIOLENCE LEGISLATION IN GHANA

Emmanuel Quansak[*]

Résumé

La question de la violence familiale, spécialement celle dont sont victimes les femmes et les enfants, est un phénomène qui ne respecte aucune frontière, qu'elle soit géographique, raciale, nationale ou culturelle. Le Ghana n'est pas une exception à cet égard. Au Ghana, la recherche empirique et les articles de journaux indiquent que la violence en général, et en particulier celle à l'encontre des femmes, a augmenté au cours des cinq dernières années sans que le droit positif parvienne à en contenir le développement. C'est dans ce contexte qu'est intervenu le projet de loi sur la violence familiale ("*Domestic Violence Act*"). L'objet de ce texte est de doter les victimes de violences familiales d'un certain nombre de recours aux fins d'obtenir des ordonnances de protection. Toutefois, le processus législatif a été retardé par des controverses ; le texte de loi a fait l'objet d'un certain nombre de critiques depuis sa publication. La principale a trait à la criminalisation du viol marital, et à la proposition de suppression des dispositions du Code pénal qui rendaient difficile la poursuite du mari ayant violé sa femme. Certains soutiennent que la poursuite et la condamnation des maris pour viol contredirait le caractère sacré du mariage. Cependant, la Coalition Nationale pour la Législation sur les Violences Familiales répond à cette critique en rappelant que 26 pays sont dotés d'une législation permettant la poursuite du mari pour viol. De plus, la Coalition ajoute que l'un des credo de la culture ghanéenne est le respect de la dignité des êtres humains. Or le projet de loi prône le respect de la personne au sein de sa famille et rejette les violences sous toutes leurs formes. Les défenseurs du texte soutiennent enfin que, selon la culture des Etats Akan, une femme mariée a le droit à la satisfaction sexuelle et peut se plaindre si son mari n'est pas à même de la lui apporter. Cet exemple démontre, selon eux que la violence sexuelle n'est pas davantage toléré dans cette culture, puisque la satisfaction sexuelle interdit nécessairement la violence sexuelle. Cette

* Lecturer in Law, University of Botswana. I must express my gratitude to Mrs Christine Dowuona-Hammond of the Faculty of Law, University of Ghana, Legon, for supplying me with most of the documents upon which I drew to write this paper, Professors Kwame Frimpong and Charles Fombad of the Department of Law, University of Botswana, for their useful comments on the paper. Any shortcoming in the paper is of course entirely mine.

disposition du projet de loi a été le point d'achoppement qui a retardé son vote. On peut cependant trouver un certain nombre d'indications laissant à penser qu'un compromis pourrait être réalisé en supprimant les dispositions litigieuses du projet pour les inscrire dans un contexte différent. Si toutes les parties prenantes acceptaient ce compromis, le projet de loi serait voté et les victimes de violences familiales trouveraient enfin un recours approprié.

I   INTRODUCTION

'Domestic violence is the systematic, ahistorical, acultural manifestation of male power. It is as immutable and enduring as patriarchy which supports and sustains it. Male violence against women is an expression of the will to power, of supremacy and domination by brute force.'[1]

The above quotation succinctly describes the problem of violence in intimate domestic relationships and serves as an appropriate starting point for a discussion of the progress, or lack of it, in addressing the problem in Ghana. The problem of violence in the domestic setting, especially against women and children, is a world-wide phenomenon which respects no boundaries whether geographical, racial, national or cultural[2] and Ghana is no exception. Central to the ever-growing global movement for human rights is the common demand for respect as an indispensable component and determinant for all human rights. The demand for respect is universal and finds expression in the cultures of different races and peoples in the various parts of the world despite the differences in traditions and styles of social organisation. The common thread running through the different social modalities and institutional practices the world over is the demand for the protection and respect of the physical and psychological integrity of each human being.[3] The cultural matrix of human rights deprivations associated with violence can be analysed at two levels. One is at the macro level and sometimes manifests itself in acts of genocide, torture and other forms of inhuman punishments and is often institutionalised, centralised, organised and systematic. The other is at the micro level and is uninstitutionalised, occasional, decentralised and unsystematic and occurs at the individual level. It is within this latter type that domestic violence takes place.

---

[1]   See S S M Edwards *Sex and Gender in the Legal Process* (Blackstone, London, 1996) pp 180–181.

[2]   See, for example, P E Andrews 'Violence against women in South Africa: The role of culture and the limitations of the law' (1999) 8 *Temple Political and Civil Rights Law Review* 425; S Tamale 'Law reform and Women's rights in Uganda' (1993) 1 *East African Journal of Peace and Human Rights* 164; A Armstrong 'Women as victims: A study of rape in Swaziland' in A Armstrong and W Ncube (eds) *Women and the Law in Southern Africa* (WLSA, 1987); P Takirambudde 'Domestic violence and the law: the case of Botswana' a paper presented at a seminar on Reform of Criminal Law and Procedure for Southern Africa (Gaborone, 8–10 October 1990) and *Report of a Study of Rape in Botswana* (Botswana Police Service, 1999).

[3]   For example, Art 15 of the Ghana Constitution 1992 provides that the dignity of all persons shall be inviolable.

International efforts have been made over the years to deal with the surge in domestic violence with some appreciable measure of success[4] and the same applies at national level.[5] In Ghana empirical research[6] and newspaper reports over the last 5 years indicate that violence in general and violence against women in particular is on the increase and the existing legal framework has become ineffective in curbing it.[7] It was reported in July 2002 that 1,831 criminal acts were perpetrated against women and children during the first half of that year.[8] Out of this figure, 679 were spousal assaults, 262 were defilement and 376 sexual assaults. In March 2003, it was reported that the police in Northern Ghana received 94 cases of assaults against women between the previous year and the time of the report.[9] Another report in August 2003 stated that a national study on violence against women revealed that one in three women is assaulted by her partner.[10] A more recent report in 2004 indicated that between January and September 2004, some 2,502 women suffered various forms of abuse in the domestic setting.[11] Of these, 837 were sexually assaulted, 130 were abducted, while 1,358 were battered. These figures may be higher since for a variety of reasons victims do not often report such cases to the appropriate authorities.[12]

The sections of the Criminal Code which deal with offences of assault and battery,[13] rape[14] and defilement of children[15] have proved woefully inadequate in addressing domestic violence.[16] This is perhaps exacerbated by

---

[4] See, for example, the UN Declaration on the Elimination of Violence against Women, General Assembly Resolution 48/104, 20 December 1993.

[5] See, for example, the South African Prevention of Family Violence Act 1993 and Domestic Violence Act 1998, and the Namibian Combating Rape Act 2000.

[6] See E Bortei-Doku Aryeetey and Akua Kuenyehia 'Violence against women in Ghana' in A Kuenyehia (ed) *Women & Law in West Africa: Situational Analysis* (WaLWA, 1998) p 272; D C Appiah and K Cusack (eds) 'Breaking the silence and challenging the myths of violence against women and children in Ghana: Report of a national study on violence' (1999) cited in C Bowman and A Kuenyehia (eds) *Women and the Law in Sub-Saharan African* (Sedco Publishing, Accra, 2003) p 331.

[7] In an attempt to address the increase in the cases of abuse against women and children, a Women and Juvenile Unit (WAJU), was created in the Ghana Police Service in 1998. The Unit currently has offices in all the ten regions of Ghana. It receives considerable donor support and funding and has made significant impact in obtaining redress for victims of domestic violence.

[8] See www.ghanaweb.com: General News, 30 July 2002.

[9] See www.ghanaweb.com: Regional News, 11 March 2003.

[10] See www.ghanaweb.com: General News, 19 August 2003.

[11] See www.ghanaweb.com: General News, 26 November 2004 quoting a statement from the National Director of the Women and Juvenile Unit (WAJU) of the Ghana Police Service as reported by the national newspaper, the *Daily Graphic*. See also www.myjoyonline.com: General News, 16 April 2005 where the Ghana News Agency (GNA) reported the conviction and jailing of an ex-husband and his accomplice for 30 years for inserting nails into the private parts of the ex-wife.

[12] For example, because of the stigma attached to the perpetrator and the victim as well as protection of the perpetrator by family members.

[13] See ss 84–88 of the Criminal Code 1960.

[14] See ss 97–100 of the Criminal Code 1960.

[15] See ss 101–111 of the Criminal Code 1960.

[16] See the call for reform of the Criminal Code by the then Attorney-General and Minister of Justice, Nana Akufo-Addo, at www.ghanaweb.com: General News, 11 November 2002.

s 42(g) of the Code which possibly encourages the use of force in a marriage by providing that the consent given by a husband or wife at marriage, for the purpose of marriage, cannot be revoked until the parties are divorced or separated by a judgment or decree of a competent court. It is against this background that the attempt over the last 5 years to enact a Domestic Violence Act is to be viewed. However, the Domestic Violence Bill has been embroiled in controversy since its publication leading to the stalling of the legislative process. This paper looks at some of the issues raised in the debate and tries to analyse the provisions of the Bill and speculate on the prospects of the Bill becoming law.

II AN OVERVIEW OF THE BILL

The genesis of the Bill can be traced to the proposals put forward by the Law Reform Commission in 1999 for legislation on domestic violence. This was followed by an initiative from the International Federation of Women Lawyers (FIDA-Ghana) who in collaboration with other Non-Governmental Organisations decided to prepare a private member's Bill in 2000. The Government subsequently took over the initiative by preparing a Bill but the prospects of this becoming law are still a long way off.

The object of the Bill is to provide victims of domestic violence with a broad set of remedies in the form of protection orders. The Bill is divided into three parts, namely, the definition of domestic relationship; what amounts to domestic violence; and redress by the courts.

A Definition of domestic violence

Clause 2 of the Bill defines domestic relationship as:

> '... a family relationship, a relationship akin to a family relationship or a relationship in a domestic situation that exists or has existed between a complainant and a respondent and includes a relationship where the complainant

(a) is or has been married to the respondent;

(b) lives with the respondent in a relationship in the nature of a marriage notwithstanding that they are not, were not married to each other or could not or cannot be married to each other;

(c) is engaged to the respondent, courting the respondent or in an actual or perceived romantic, intimate, or cordial relationship not necessarily including a sexual relationship with the respondent;

(d) and respondent are parents of a child, are expecting a child together or are foster parents of a child;

(e) and respondent are family members related by consanguinity, affinity or adoption, or would be so related if they were married or were able to be married;

(f) and respondent shares or shared the same residence or are co-tenants;

(g) is a house help in the household of the respondent; or

(h) is in a relationship determined by the court to be a domestic relationship.'

This definition seems to capture not only marriage relationships but also all other types of relationship such as that of house helps in which there is mutual dependency between the parties.

B   What amounts to domestic violence?

Clause 3 of the Bill defines what amounts to domestic violence. It states that domestic violence means:

'... engaging in the following within the context of a previous or existing domestic relationship;

(a) any act under the Criminal Code 1960 (Act 29) which constitutes a threat or harm to a person under that Act;

(b) specific acts of threats to commit, or acts likely to result in

(i)   physical abuse, namely, physical assault or any use of physical force against another including the forcible confinement or detention of another person and the deprivation of another person of access to adequate food, water, clothing, shelter or rest;

(ii) sexual abuse, namely, the forceful engagement of another person in any sexual contact whether married or not which includes sexual conduct that abuses, humiliates or degrades the other person or otherwise violates another person's sexual integrity whether married or not;

(iii) economic abuse, namely, the deprivation or threatened deprivation of economic or financial resources which a person is entitled to by law, the disposition or threatened disposition of moveable or immovable property in which another person has a material interest and hiding or hindering the use of property in which another person has a material interest.

(c) Intimidation and harassment by the induction of fear in another person.'

This definition reflects a similar definition in the United Nations' Declaration on the Elimination of Violence against Women.[17] It covers physical, sexual, emotional and psychological abuse as well as intimidation and harassment. Clause 4 defines what acts will amount to domestic violence. It provides that a single act may amount to domestic violence except in the case of harassment. Furthermore, a number of acts that form a pattern of behaviour may also amount to domestic violence even though some or all of such acts when viewed in isolation may appear minor or trivial.

C   Redress by the courts

On the redress by the courts, it is provided in clause 5 that a victim of domestic violence or any third party with information about domestic

---

[17]   See Arts 1 and 2 of the General Assembly Resolution 48/104 of 20 December 1993.

violence may file a complaint with the police at a place, for example, where the offender or the victim resides or where the violence was committed. A child may be assisted by a next-friend, which is his father or mother, to file a complaint. Furthermore, a social worker, a probation officer or a health care provider may also file a complaint where the intervention is in the interest of the victim. A family relation of the victim can also file a complaint as well as the personal representative of a deceased complainant. Clause 7 imposes a duty on a police officer to whom a complaint has been made, to respond to the plight of the victim. In doing so, he should interview the parties and in terms of clause 8 may even arrest the person alleged to have committed the offence with or without a warrant of arrest. The police officer may arrest, without a warrant, any person who commits domestic violence in his presence. Additionally, a private person may do likewise.

In terms of clause 10, all courts have jurisdiction in matters of domestic violence. However, application may be filed in such courts as are situated in the place where the applicant and/or respondent reside(s) or at such place as where the act was committed.

The Bill provides both criminal and civil remedies for breaches of its provisions. Clause 1(2) provides a penalty of a fine not exceeding 500 penalty units[18] or a term of imprisonment not exceeding 2 years or both. There are also civil remedies in the form of protection orders. In terms of clause 11 an applicant can apply for a civil protection order to prevent the respondent, a person associated with the respondent or both from carrying out a threat of domestic violence against the applicant or to prevent the respondent, an associated respondent or both from committing further acts which constitute domestic violence against the applicant. The application for the order will be heard in private in the presence of the parties, their lawyers and any other person permitted by the court to be present.[19]

The court may grant an interim order for a period not exceeding 3 months or may grant a full order for a period not exceeding 12 months in the first instance; this order may be extended, modified or rescinded on motion by a party to the proceedings if good cause is shown.[20] Protection orders may be discharged by the court on an application on notice by the applicant or respondent.[21] Any contravention of a protection order is a criminal offence for which the guilty party will be liable, on summary conviction, to a minimum fine of five penalty units and a maximum fine of 500 penalty units or to a term of imprisonment not exceeding 2 years or both.

Finally, a complaint of domestic violence may not be brought more than 2 years from the date when the last act of domestic violence occurred.[22] A

---

[18] In terms of the Fines (Penalty Units) Act 2000 (Act 572), a penalty unit is equal to the amount of cedis (the Ghanaian currency) specified in the Schedule to the Act – which is 20,000 cedis. Thus, the 500 penalty units specified in clause 1(2) will amount to 10m cedis (about US$1,117).

[19] See clause 12 of the Bill. The application is made on notice but where the circumstances warrant it may be made *ex parte*.

[20] See clauses 13, 14 and 15 of the Bill.

[21] See clause 20 of the Bill.

[22] See clause 22 of the Bill.

criminal charge brought under the provisions of clause 23 shall be in addition to and shall not affect the rights of an applicant to seek a civil protection order. Clause 28 amends s 42(g) of the Criminal Code by deleting the part that prevents husband and wife from revoking the mutual consent they exchanged on marriage during the subsistence of the marriage. As pointed out above, this is the provision which serves as a stumbling block to the prosecution of a husband for raping his wife.

III CRITIQUE OF THE BILL

The Bill has come under various criticisms since its publication. In a workshop organised in Accra on 20 January 2003 by the Legal Resources Centre, Dr Adam Nasser, of the University of Ghana, questioned whether the law should intervene in this area at all. According to him, good intentions alone may not be enough and he gave instances where legislation has been passed with good intentions but has been ignored subsequently. In his view, the content of the Bill gives the impression that it is a wholesale importation of western paradigms which have no relevance in the Ghanaian context. At the same forum, Mr Mohammed Ayariga of the Legal Resource Centre argued that the provision of both criminal and civil remedies under the Bill gives the impression that certain categories of offences under the Criminal Code 1960 should be separated from the penalties prescribed under the Bill. There is a danger, he contended, that judges and individuals are more likely to rely on the civil remedies provided under the Bill to the detriment of the punitive penalties provided under the Criminal Code thereby undermining the efficacy of the law.

Perhaps the most sustained criticism of the Bill has been its abrogation of the immunity of a husband from criminal prosecution for raping his wife.[23] The Ghanaian common law follows the English common law principle that by marriage a wife consents to intercourse with her husband and this confers on the husband a privilege which the wife cannot withdraw whenever she pleases.[24] It follows from this principle that a husband cannot be guilty as a principal in the first degree of rape on his wife.[25] However, after some 350 years of the operation of the common law immunity, the English House of

---

[23]   See generally, K Ansa-Asare 'Marital rape in Ghana? A solution in search of a problem' (July–September 2003) *Africa Legal Aid* 15 and H Combrinck 'Reforming laws on sexual violence in Africa: A new approach required' (July–September 2003) *Africa Legal Aid* 22.

[24]   See W E Ofei *Family Law in Ghana* (Sebewie Publishers, Accra, 1998) p 180. For the foundation of the English common law principle, see Sir Matthew Hale *A History of the Pleas of the Crown* (1836) 1971 at p 636 where he said 'But the husband cannot be guilty of a rape committed by himself upon his lawful wife, for by their mutual matrimonial consent and contract the wife hath given herself up in this kind unto her husband which she cannot retract'. See *R v Miller* [1954] 2 QB 282 and *R v Clarke* [1949] 2 All ER 448.

[25]   Section 42(g) of the Criminal Code 1960 provides that '... consent given by a husband or wife at marriage, for the purposes of the marriage, cannot be revoked until the parties are divorced or separated by a judgment or decree of a competent court'. On the general effect of the criminal law on marital relationship, see K Frimpong '"What God has joined together ..." and its practical implications in criminal law' (1991) 1 *Lesotho Law Journal* 49.

Lords unanimously held in *R* v *R*[26] that '... in modern times the supposed marital exemption in rape forms no part of the law of England'.[27] There is no indication as yet that the Ghanaian courts will follow the English example by jettisoning this archaic principle.

In the context of customary law, it has been stated that:

> '[T]he conceptual idea that a wife in a customary marriage can be raped by her husband does not even exist because all sex within a customary marriage is considered "consensual", whether or not the woman consents. This is true because ... marriage results in a woman's physical person and her sexuality becoming part of her husband's property. [I]t is a general rule all over Africa that a man can never be said to rape his own wife. As such, forced sex within marriage does not constitute an offense either under customary law or statutory law.'[28]

It is in the context of these principles that the Bill has been strongly criticised. Another critic, Mr F Koomson of the Ahmadiya Muslim Missions, contends that the definition of sexual abuse as contained in clause 3(1)(ii) of the Bill will enlighten and exhort women to refuse their husbands sex.[29] This, in his view, will exacerbate the incidence of divorce cases.

A corollary to the above criticism is that the prosecution, conviction and sentencing of husbands for marital rape would destroy the sanctity of marriage. The National Coalition on Domestic Violence Legislation[30] has countered this criticism by stating that experiences in 26 countries that have laws to prosecute marital rape belie this criticism.[31] Furthermore, it is the view of the Coalition that one of the basic tenets of Ghanaian culture is the respect for the dignity of the human being. The Bill advocates respect for the dignity of every person in the domestic setting and abhors abuse in every form. They point out, for example, that in Akan culture, a married woman has the right to sexual satisfaction and can complain where her husband does not provide this. They contend that this example demonstrates that sexual abuse is definitely not accepted in this culture because the presence of sexual satisfaction precludes sexual abuse.[32]

A   Prospects for the passage of the Bill

The above criticisms appear to emanate mostly from men who wish to protect and perpetuate male superiority in the face of changing perceptions of the relationship between a man and his wife. The criticisms are embedded

---

[26]   [1991] 4 All ER 481.

[27]   *Per* Lord Keith at p 489.

[28]   See F Naa-Adjeley Adjetey 'Religious and cultural rights: Reclaiming the African woman's individuality: The struggle between women's reproductive autonomy and African society and culture' (1995) 44 *American University Law Review* 1351 at pp 1359–1360.

[29]   See workshop referred to earlier.

[30]   An umbrella organisation made up of over 100 organisations and individuals set up in March 2003 to coordinate activities to ensure the smooth passage of the Bill into law.

[31]   See www.ghanaweb.com: General News, 13 January 2004.

[32]   See an undated position paper prepared by the Coalition in support of the enactment of the Bill.

in a 'cultural' norm that dictates, for example, that a man has a right, by virtue of having paid 'bride price' or dowry on his wife, to have sex with his wife whenever he wants and that it is 'untraditional' for a wife to refuse the husband sex. Thus, it has been advocated that there should be a curb on the incidence of high bride price to minimise violence against women.[33] It would also seem that undue prominence has been given to the issue of marital rape in the debates on the Bill to the detriment of the overall objective of protecting victims of domestic violence. Whilst the empirical evidence indicates a rise in violence against women it does not clearly indicate what proportion is attributable to marital rape. The evidence merely points to 'spousal assaults', 'sexual assault', 'assault against women' and the fact that 'one in three women is assaulted by her partner'. Marital rape as a form of violence against the wife or the female partner should be proscribed but should its inclusion or exclusion from the Bill be allowed to hamper, as it seems to be doing, the overall objective of protecting the victims of domestic violence? This is the question which the proponents of the Bill, as it stands now, need to answer if they wish to see accelerated progress in the passage of the Bill.

These 'cultural' obstacles and the undue prominence given to the possibility of a husband being prosecuted for raping his wife have, to a greater extent, contributed to the stalling of the passage of the Bill. In an attempt to overcome these obstacles and win public acceptance of the Bill, the then Minister of Women and Children's Affairs, Mrs Gladys Asmah, launched a national outreach programme on the Bill in November 2003[34] to explain and seek the views of various communities on the content of the Bill to ensure that the law becomes acceptable and enforceable. Since then, the debate on the Bill's provisions has been ongoing.[35] A National Coalition on the Domestic Violence Legislation has been formed to champion the passage of the Bill.[36] But despite the numerous workshops, seminars and symposia, the Bill has still not been tabled before Parliament for it to be debated. The Minister of Women and Children's Affairs reiterated in July 2004[37] that the Bill will definitely be passed although she could not give a time frame within which this would be done. Unfortunately, circumstances have conspired against her and she will not be in a position to fulfil her promise. She has been reassigned a different portfolio following the December 2004 General Election and this will adversely affect the attempt to bring the Bill before Parliament in the immediate future.[38] The new Minister for Women and Children's Affairs, Hajia Alima Mahama, will need time to settle into her Ministry and to study the work that has been done so far before she is able to

---

[33] See www.ghanaweb.com: General News, 14 December 2002.

[34] See www.ghanaweb.com: General News, 28 November 2003.

[35] See, for example, www.ghanaweb.com: General News, 18 December 2003 where it is reported that the Director of the Ghana Law School, Mr Kwaku Ansa-Asare, has called for extensive public debate and education on the Bill.

[36] See N A Afadzinu 'Towards a better future for Ghanaian women; Eradicating violence against women' (July–September 2003) *Africa Legal Aid* 27. The writer is the coordinator of the National Coalition on Domestic Violence Legislation, Ghana.

[37] See www.ghanaweb.com: General News, 27 July 2004.

[38] She has now been assigned the Fisheries portfolio.

chart the way forward. Her initial comments about the Bill during her parliamentary vetting show that she supports those who do not want marital rape to be criminalised. She is reported to have said that she understood from the debates about the Bill that people do not want marital rape to be criminalised and expressed her support for it to be expunged from the Bill to ensure its passage into law.[39] Advocates of the Bill in its present form have reacted to this report with dismay. They have argued that removing the marital rape section from the Bill would not solve the problem and that 'to say take it out of the law so that you can get it passed and live to fight it another day is not the strategy' they will support.[40] Thus, the stage is set for further polarisation between the protagonists as to the way forward and this does not augur well for the prospect of an early passage of the Bill unless a compromise is reached on the issue of criminalisation of marital rape. The new Minister responsible for shepherding the Bill through Parliament has given an indication that she is prepared to break the impasse. Time will tell whether she will have the political will to do so and be able to carry the majority of parliamentarians with her to ensure the Bill's passage into law in 2005.

IV CONCLUSION

The debate on the Bill has gone on for too long and there is grave danger that with such passage of time the Bill will fade from the public domain and be put onto the back burner of the legislative agenda. Unless the Government summons the political will and finds parliamentary time during the current session of Parliament to debate the Bill and pass it into law, all the hard work done over the years is likely to come to naught. If this happens it will be an indelible blot on the human rights record of a Government that professes, by the measures it has put into place since it came into power, to have the welfare of women at heart.[41] The Bill is a necessary first step towards eradicating domestic violence in Ghana. If passed, the Bill will provide the requisite legal protection for victims of domestic violence and will go a long way in facilitating the fulfilment of Ghana's obligations under international conventions, such as that on elimination of all forms of discrimination against women and the declaration on the elimination of violence against women to which the country is a signatory. The gestation period of the Bill has been unnecessarily prolonged. It is hoped that it will not culminate in a stillbirth.

---

[39]   See www.myjoyonline.com: Top Stories, 28 January 2005.
[40]   *Ibid.*
[41]   When elected in 2000, the Government appointed two women to oversee two new Ministries, Women and Children's Affairs and Girl-Child Education Unit within the Ministry of Education, established a Women's Endowment Fund to assist women entrepreneurs and affirmed the establishment of the Women and Juvenile Unit of the Police Service.

Republic of Ireland

ANCILLARY RELIEFS ON DIVORCE: THE EMERGING JURISPRUDENCE FROM THE SUPERIOR COURTS

Paul Ward[*]

Résumé

Pendant les quelques neuf années qui ont suivi l'introduction du divorce en Irlande, il y a eu peu de jurisprudence significative concernant la façon dont les tribunaux devraient aborder la question du partage des biens familiaux. Très récemment, un certain nombre de décisions importantes ont été par contre rendues par la Cour supérieure et par la Haute Cour de justice sur des aspects cruciaux de cette question. Comme c'est souvent le cas, ces affaires impliquent des époux jouissant de fortunes considérables. Cette jurisprudence fournit des indications précieuses sur la manière dont les biens devraient être partagés dans ce type de dossier.

I INTRODUCTION

On 24 November 1995 the Irish public voted in favour of providing for divorce laws for the first time since the foundation of the State.[1] The referendum was passed but not without first overcoming a number of obstacles, primarily the challenge to the Government's 'yes' vote campaign[2] but most notably the narrow margin of success.[3] Indeed the narrow margin of success lead to an unsuccessful challenge to the referendum result in *Hannafin v Minister for the Environment*.[4] Thus on 27 February 1997 the Family Law (Divorce) Act came into effect providing law regulating the granting of a decree of divorce.

In the near 9 years since the availability of divorce, little instructive case-law has been handed down. Admittedly, the important issue as to whether a divorce can be granted to a couple who reside in the same home but can be

---

[*]   Senior Lecturer, School of Law, University College Dublin.

[1]   See Ward 'Life, Death and Divorce' in A Bainham (ed) *The International Survey of Family Law 1995 Edition* (1995) pp 287–319.

[2]   *McKenna v An Taoiseach* [1995] 2 IR 10.

[3]   9,114 votes in favour of a total of 1,628,570 votes cast.

[4]   [1996] 2 ILRM 61.

deemed to be living apart for the purposes of the Divorce Act[5] and the Constitution[6] has been determined[7] by recognising that spouses can be living apart while still living under the same roof. Such a position is not all that surprising in the light of the fact that there is only one substantive ground for the obtaining of a divorce. The requirement is that at the date of the institution of the proceedings, the spouses have lived apart from one another for a period of, or periods amounting to, at least 4 years during the previous 5 years.[8] Once the requisite period is established the court may grant a decree of divorce provided there is no reasonable prospect of a reconciliation between the spouses[9] and such provision as the court considers proper having regard to the circumstances exists or will be made for the spouses and any dependent members of the family.[10] It is the latter of these two requirements that has generated some not insignificant case-law on how marital assets should be distributed on divorce. In particular the notion of 'proper provision' has been significant in clarifying what percentage of the total assets a spouse may acquire on divorce and whether and in what circumstances a court may direct that the ancillary relief orders granted amount to a 'clean break' in terms of ongoing and future financial and property matters arising between the parties.

II   LEGISLATIVE BACKGROUND

The Family Law (Divorce) Act 1996 provides for a considerable number of ancillary reliefs that may be ordered by the court. These can be divided into two categories. The first category provides for preliminary or pre-trial orders relating to period payments (maintenance),[11] spousal protection in the form of orders under the Domestic Violence Act 1996,[12] custody and access[13] and protection against loss of an interest in the family home.[14] In addition a *mareva* type injunction may be sought freezing assets or property in the possession or control of the other spouse,[15] where the disposition of such is intended to defeat the claim of a spouse in a divorce application. Problems with this *mareva* type injunction order have identified that a limited company cannot be the subject of such an order in terms of preventing the disposition of property owned by the company in question, but the court can prohibit a spouse form disposing of shares in any such company.[16] Also beyond the scope of this *mareva* type injunction are discretionary trusts of

---

5   Section 5(1)(a).
6   Article 43.2.1.i.
7   *M McA v X McA* [2000] 2 ILRM 48.
8   Section 5(1)(a) of the Family Law (Divorce) Act 1996.
9   Section 5(1)(b) of the Family Law (Divorce) Act 1996.
10   Section 5(1)(c) of the Family Law (Divorce) Act 1996.
11   Section 12 of the Family Law (Divorce) Act 1996.
12   Section 11(a) of the Family Law (Divorce) Act 1996.
13   Section 11(b) of the Family Law (Divorce) Act 1996.
14   Section 11(c) of the Family Law (Divorce) Act 1996 providing for an order under s 5 of the Family Home Protection Act 1976.
15   Section 36 of the Family Law (Divorce) Act 1996.
16   *L O'M v N O'M* [2002] 3 IR 237.

which either or both of the spouses are named beneficiaries.[17] However, this original position adopted by one High Court judge has been queried more recently in $M v M$[18] to the extent that a discretionary trust may be the subject of judicial consideration in the assessment of the marital assets and the power to review such trusts is not prospective in effect but also retrospective thereby enabling a court to consider a trust established prior to the enactment of the Family Law (Divorce) Act 1996.

The second category of reliefs relates to the marital assets of the parties and includes the usual assets that one would expect to find in most marriages. Orders may be made in relation to the following:

(a) periodic payments;[19]

(b) lump sum payments;[20]

(c) property adjustment;[21]

(d) orders in relation to the family home;[22]

(e) financial compensation orders;[23]

(f) pension adjustment orders;[24]

(g) extinguishing the right to apply from the estate of a divorced spouse;[25]

(h) sale of property.[26]

What, when and the amount that any of the above orders may involve is a matter for the court to determine. In determining such the court is primarily obliged to ensure that 'proper' provision is made for a dependent spouse and children. In addition there is a comprehensive check list provided for in s 20 of the Family Law (Divorce) Act 1996 to assist the court in deciding what

---

[17] *JD v DD* [1997] 3 IR 64.

[18] (Unreported) High Court, 22 June 2004, McKetchnie J.

[19] Section 13 of the Family Law (Divorce) Act 1996.

[20] Section 13 of the Family Law (Divorce) Act 1996.

[21] Section 14 of the Family Law (Divorce) Act 1996.

[22] Section 15 of the Family Law (Divorce) Act 1996 which includes such matters as providing for the right to reside in the family home for a specified period, the sale of the family home on such terms and conditions that the court directs, exclusion from the family home by use of the Domestic Violence Act 1996, protecting against loss of an interest in the family home under the Family Home Protection Act 1976, declarations as to any legal equitable interest in the family home or other property owned by the spouses, order for the partition of property under the Partition Acts 1868–1876 and order under the Guardianship of Infants Act 1964 in relation to custody and access of dependent children.

[23] Section 16 of the Family Law (Divorce) Act 1996. These relate to obliging a spouse to maintain or effect a life insurance policy for the benefit of the other spouse and are usually ordered in circumstances where it is not possible to direct a lump sum payment owing to the lack of funds available at the time of divorce hearing. Such orders are intended to provide for the future financial security of a spouse upon the death of the other spouse.

[24] Section 17 of the Family Law (Divorce) Act 1996.

[25] Section 18 of the Family Law (Divorce) Act 1996. The Succession Act 1965 provides an automatic statutory entitlement to at least one third of a deceased spouse's estate. Divorce automatically terminates the status of spouse thus removing the right to inherit. Section 18 of the Family Law (Divorce) Act 1996 allows a former spouse to apply for a share from a deceased former spouse's estate. The right to apply, however, is subject to what is known as a 'blocking order' which prohibits any such application being brought after the death of a former spouse.

[26] Section 19 of the Family Law (Divorce) Act 1996.

orders to make and the amount and value of such orders. The s 20(2) factors as they are referred to require the court to consider the following matters:

(i)   the income, earning capacity, property and other financial resources which each of the spouses concerned has or is likely to have in the foreseeable future;

(ii)   the financial needs, obligations and responsibilities which each of the spouses has or is likely to have in the foreseeable future (whether in the case of the remarriage of the spouse or otherwise);

(iii)   the standard of living enjoyed by the family concerned before the proceedings were instituted or before the spouses commenced to live apart from one another, as the case may be;

(iv)   the age of each of the spouses, the duration of their marriage and the length of time during which the spouses lived with one another;

(v)   any physical or mental disability of either of the spouses;

(vi)   the contributions which each of the spouses has made or is likely in the foreseeable future to make to the welfare of the family, including any contribution made by each of them to the income, earning capacity, property and financial resources of the other spouse and any contribution made by either of them by looking after the home or caring for the family;

(vii)   the effect on the earning capacity of each of the spouses of the marital responsibilities assumed by each during the period when they lived with one another and, in particular, the degree to which the future earning capacity of a spouse is impaired by reason of that spouse having relinquished or forgone the opportunity of remunerative activity in order to look after the home or care for the family;

(viii) any income or benefits to which either of the spouses is entitled by or under statute;

(ix)   the conduct of each of the spouses, if that conduct is such that in the opinion of the court it would in all the circumstances of the case be unjust to disregard it;

(x)   the accommodation needs of either of the spouses;

(xi)   the value to each of the spouses of any benefit (for example, a benefit under a pension scheme) which by reason of the decree of divorce concerned, that spouse will forfeit the opportunity or possibility of acquiring;

(xii)   the rights of any person other than the spouses but including a person to whom either spouse is remarried.

Section 20(3) specifically obliges a court to have regard to the terms of any separation agreement entered into between the parties. Separation agreements containing clauses prohibiting future applications have been considered by the superior courts of late. This issue is considered in more detail later on in this piece. The factors for consideration are relatively straightforward and uncomplicated as are the orders which the court may grant having considered the above factors. The most significant of the above factors are (vi) and (vii) which generally relate to what is described as the stay at home wife/mother. Prior to the introduction of the Judicial Separation and Family Law Reform Act 1989, which legislation modernised the judicial separation laws, in the context of acquiring an interest in the family home or other marital assets, Irish law did not recognise in terms of ascribing a monetary value to it, the work performed by the wife/mother who worked within the home and who had no outside independent income. Work within the home could not be valued for the purpose of making either indirect or direct contributions to the acquisition of an equitable interest most usually in the family home. The then position in Irish law was best reflected in the *BL v ML* decision.[27] The case involved a mother who had exclusively devoted her time and efforts to raising the children and providing a very comfortable home for the family. She had never earned an independent income. On the beak up of the marriage she applied for a declaration under s 12 of the Status of Married Woman's Act 1952 that she was entitled to a half share interest in the family home which share was held in trust for her by her husband in whose sole name the property was legally registered. The method of determining such disputes was resolved by recourse to the use of either a resulting or a constructive trust. Either device required the applicant to establish that they had made either a direct or indirect contribution to the acquisition of the property in question or the discharge of any loan or mortgage on the property. The High Court acknowledged that the applicant wife had made no financial contribution, direct or indirect, to the acquisition of the property but did nonetheless proceed to award her a half interest in the property based upon her constitutionally preferred status as the mother who works within the home.[28] The relevant articles of the Constitution are worth quoting in full and highlight the above point.

Article 41.2.1 provides:

'In particular, the State recognises by her life in the home, woman gives to the State a support without which the common good cannot be achieved.'

Article 41.2.2 provides:

'The State shall therefore endeavour to ensure that mothers shall not be required by economic necessity to engage in labour to the neglect of their duties in the home.'

Barr J was of the view that these Constitutional provisions entitled the applicant wife to a half share in the family home, which incidentally was a very substantial country home of considerable value. On appeal to the Supreme Court, the decision was reversed on the basis that there was nothing contained in either of the above articles which would entitle a court to conclude that a spouse was entitled to a proprietary interest in the family home.

---

[27] [1992] 2 IR 77.

[28] Article 41 of the Constitution deals with the family and affords and protects certain rights provided for therein.

The case was instrumental in the drafting of the Judicial Separation and Family Law Reform Act 1989 and in particular factors (vi) and (vii) above. These are very significant factors for a court to consider and case-law decided shortly after the introduction of the new judicial separation and divorce laws indicated that as much as 50% of the marital assets could be awarded to the stay at home wife who works exclusively within the home.[29] In *JD v DD*[30] the court emphasised the duration of the marriage which was 30 years, during which the wife devoted her efforts to the rearing of children and the maintaining of the home. Here much emphasis is placed upon the contribution made by the efforts of the wife within the home. The early cases did not place much reliance on factor (vii), namely the loss of opportunity factor. This factor, however, has featured prominently in recent case-law, particularly those cases involving extensive assets owned by the parties. These recent cases are of interest as they have identified issues not considered to be relevant to the divorce laws, namely whether a court can effect a clean break in appropriate cases, thus severing not just the legal spousal relationship but also all financial ties. The cases that have shed light on important issues all tend to fall into the same category of 'big money' cases or, as the former Chief Justice preferred to refer to these, 'ample resources' cases.[31]

III AMPLE RESOURCE CASES

DT v CT[32] is the starting point for an analysis of the contemporary approach of the Irish Superior Courts to resolution of financial property matters in cases of considerable wealth. The salient facts of this case involved a 14-year marriage which led to the parties' separation in 1994. Three children were born to the marriage. The applicant husband was a very successful solicitor who engaged in property development and in particular the purchase of an office block which he acquired after the parties separated in 1994. The acquisition of this asset was an astute one and was the most contentious aspect of this divorce case. The office block had been acquired for £4.3m and was valued at £11.5m at the hearing of the application. The total value of the marital assets at the date of trial was between £14–15m. Eighty per cent of the assets had been acquired by the husband's efforts post separation. The wife qualified as a doctor but never practiced medicine. She instead assisted her husband in his practice and maintained the children and the home they lived in. The husband's annual income was estimated at £1m whilst the wife's potential income as general medical practitioner was just over £70,000 per annum.

The primary issue for the court to determine was whether the court in making the various ancillary orders could at the same time effect a 'clean break' between the parties whereby there could be no further recourse to the

---

29 See *JD v DD* (unreported) High Court, May 1997, McGuinness J.
30 *Ibid.*
31 *DT v CT* [2002] 3 IR 334.
32 [2002] 3 IR 334.

courts by either spouse for financial or other relief in the future. The court noted that such was not possible for a number of reasons. The primary stumbling block was Art 41 of the Constitution[33] which contains the basis upon which a divorce can be granted. Article 41 expressly obliges the court to make 'proper' provision for a dependent spouse and thus it did not follow that the court could give effect to its constitutional obligation by preventing itself from hearing an application in the future for further financial relief.[34] In addition the provisions of the Family Law (Divorce) Act 1996 clearly envisage not just single applications for certain orders (for example, lump sum and property adjustment/sale orders) but multiple applications for such. In those circumstances a clean break arrangement could not be said to be provided for in the Constitution or the legislation. That said, however, the Chief Justice indicated that there was nothing in the Constitution or the legislation prohibiting a court from making 'clean break' orders in appropriate cases.[35] Appropriate cases are 'ample resources' cases and the yardstick for such is a monetary value in excess of €5m.[36] The reasons for effecting clean break orders centre on the benefits to be derived from certainty. Post divorce, which is final in terminating the marriage contract and which inevitably follows on from the factual termination of the interpersonal relationship, parties should financially provide for themselves

---

[33]   Articles 41.1.1–41.3.3 provide:

     '41.1.1.   The State recognises the Family as the natural primary and fundamental unit group of society, and as a moral institution possessing inalienable and imprescriptible rights, antecedent and superior to all positive law.

     41.1.2.   The State therefore guarantees to protect the Family in its constitution and authority, the necessary basis of social order and as indispensable to the welfare of the Nation and the State.

     41.2.1   In particular, the State recognises by her life in the home, woman gives to the State a support without which the common good cannot be achieved.

     41.2.2.   The State shall therefore endeavour to ensure that mothers shall not be required by economic necessity to engage in labour to the neglect of their duties in the home.

     41.3.1.   The State pledges itself to guard with special care the institution of marriage, on which the family is founded, and to protect against it.

     41.3.2.   No law shall be enacted providing for the dissolution of marriage.

           A court designated by law may grant dissolution of marriage where, but only where, it is satisfied that:

       i.   at the date of the institution of the proceedings, the spouses have lived apart for a period of, or periods amounting to, at least four years during the previous five years,

       ii.   there is no reasonable prospect of a reconciliation between the spouses,

       iii.   such provision as the court considers proper having regard to the circumstances exists or will be made for the spouses, any children of either or both of them and any other person prescribed by law, and

       iv.   any further conditions prescribed by law are complied with.

     41.3.3.   No person whose marriage has been dissolved under the civil law of another State but is a subsisting valid marriage under the law for the time being in force within the jurisdiction of the Government and Parliament established by this Constitution shall be capable of contracting a valid marriage within that jurisdiction during the lifetime of the other party to that marriage so dissolved.'

[34]   *Ibid*, per Keane CJ at 363.

[35]   *Ibid* at 364.

[36]   See *D v D* (unreported) 4 May 2005, McKetchnie J commenting upon specialist practitioners' opinions on such cases.

without dependence on the other former spouse. Achieving financial independence was desirable as it avoided acrimony in the future, and enabled the parties to resolve all property and financial matters. This in turn would result in the parties leaving 'the past behind' and provide a basis for a new beginning. These goals were readily achievable through the use of substantial lump sum orders.[37]

Having determined that 'clean break' orders could be made it then became necessary to assess the amount of the lump sum to be ordered that could provide for a 'clean break' position for the dependent spouse. The quantifying of the lump sum amount in turn depended upon the total value of the marital assets which in turn gave rise to the issue of what assets could be caught by court order and at what date the court should value the assets. The court had to decide on what date the court should total the assets. The husband unsuccessfully argued that the date of valuation of the marital assets should be the date upon which the parties separated in the light of the fact that the husband had here purchased an office block now worth nearly three times its original value. The husband was hoping to exclude some £11.5m from the court's calculation leaving an asset pool of between £2.5–3.5m for distribution between the spouses.

The court held that the correct date to value marital assets was the date of the trial or the date of the appeal hearing. This was so for a number of reasons. This stemmed from the wording of the legislation and the Constitution which obliges a court, before granting a divorce, to ensure that proper provision exists for the dependent spouse. The only logical date on which to value the marital assets therefore was the date of the hearing or the appeal. In addition, it would be palpably unfair to the liable spouse to value assets at a minimum 4 years in advance of a hearing[38] where there was the potential for the assets to decrease in value between the date of separation and the date of the hearing. The issue of an asset acquired by the independent efforts of one of the spouses after the separation of the parties was examined by a number of the judges with a difference in approach detectable amongst them.

Denham J indicated that the circumstances leading to the acquisition of an asset after the separation of the parties were a relevant factor in valuing the assets.[39] Murray J expressed similar sentiments in that valuable assets acquired post separation completely independently of the other spouse may be excluded from consideration by the court. He did, however, indicate that wealth brought to a short marriage may attract entirely different considerations whereby the court could ignore such assets.[40] By far the most interesting observations were those of Murphy J. He devised a formula for use in such ample resource cases, particularly those involving the acquisition of assets post separation. Once the reasonable needs of the dependent spouse have been assessed in accordance with the factors set out in s 20, and in particular in ample resource cases the standard of living enjoyed by the

---

[37]   [2002] 3 IR 382 per Denham J.
[38]   Article 41 of the Constitution requires a minimum of 4 years' separation in the previous 5 years.
[39]   [2002] 3 IR 383.
[40]   *Ibid* at 409.

spouses, any surplus once the reasonable needs have been met, could be retained by the spouse whose independent efforts acquired them.[41]

In the present case, the acquisition of the office block albeit post separation could not have been achieved without the efforts of the wife working in the home and also on a part-time basis in the husband's practice. The asset had to be included in the total assets to be assessed for distribution between the spouses.

Having identified when the assets and what assets can be distributed, the court turned its attention to devising a formula for distributing the assets. The Chief Justice clearly stated that the formula to be adopted was one of 'proper provision' and not equal 'division'. The legislation and the Constitution provides for making provision and division of assets. The Chief Justice noted that in ample resource cases a yardstick of one third of the marital assets was at the lower end of the scale. Curiously this reflects, but is not motivated by, the Succession Act 1965 which entitles a surviving spouse to a minimum of one third of the deceased spouse's estate.[42] Here a sum of £5m amounted to 38% of the total assets and such was reasonable in the circumstances. Of relevance were the efforts of the wife in the home over the course of the marriage and in particular the fact that the respondent wife had forgone a medical career, and despite being a qualified doctor, aspiring to the heights of the medical profession was not a realistic possibility.[43] Denham J agreed with the one third benchmark but added that this was subject to other factors arising such as inadequate means, forcing the sale of assets which might destroy a business, where one spouse brings wealth to the marriage or where the assets are acquired through independent endeavours.[44] Murray J felt the distribution should reflect that marriage is an 'equal partnership' and there should be no discrimination in favour of the working spouse or against the non-working spouse.[45] Fennelly J indicated the distribution should be on the basis of what is 'fair and just' and was reluctant to ascribe a specific percentage amount to the distribution.[46]

One interesting issue arose on appeal to the Supreme Court concerning the interpretation of s 20(2)(i). This relates to the conduct of the parties and whether in the court's opinion it would be repugnant to justice to disregard the conduct of the spouses in question. The High Court was of the view that the applicant husband's extramarital affair and subsequent birth of a child outside of marriage was a relevant factor to consider in the making of the ancillary orders. In particular the husband was in effect penalised by a pension adjustment order being modified form the original 49% to the husband to 45% of his pension on retirement. Denham J, for the Court, citing *Watchel v Watchel*,[47] did not equate an extramarital affair and child born

---

[41]   *Ibid* at 400.

[42]   *Ibid* at 369.

[43]   *Ibid* at 371.

[44]   *Ibid* at 384–385.

[45]   *Ibid* at 406–407.

[46]   *Ibid* at 413.

[47]   [1973] Fam 72.

thereto as conduct warranting the sanction of the court by means of imposing a financial penalty on the party in question.

The case goes some way to assisting both legal academics and professionals in providing some guidance on how marital assets are to be distributed in divorce cases albeit those involving very substantial assets. Whilst the judges differed on stating a minimum percentage entitlement where the dependent spouse has contributed to the family and the home and at the same time forgone a potential professional career, the one third yardstick has been applied subsequently. In *MK v JPK*,[48] O'Neill J divided the marital assets on a one third to two third's ratio in circumstances where the dependent spouse had contributed to the rearing of six children in a 15-year marriage. Interestingly in this case, the dependent wife's prospects of a career were not emphasised as she appeared to have met the respondent shortly after leaving school and had no third level qualification. She had in later years gained third level qualifications but it was unrealistic that she would gain employment commensurate with her qualifications at her age. In this case the husband had formed a permanent relationship with another woman after the separation.

IV SEPARATION AGREEMENTS WITH 'FULL AND FINAL SATISFACTION' CLAUSES

A separation agreement rarely omits to contain a clause binding the parties by prohibiting them from applying for any relief whatsoever under the family law legislation. Such clauses expressly refer to being entitled to obtain a decree of divorce but preclude an application for ancillary relief. Recently the High Court has considered separation agreements and their relevance in divorce applications. In July of 2000, a Circuit Court judge indicated that a separation agreement might bind the parties to the terms therein agreed in the event that a divorce was sought at a future date.[49] The agreement could be binding provided the parties obtained independent legal advice as to the consequences of agreeing the terms and that in the interim there was no significant change in the financial circumstances of the parties. The material change in this particular case was the fact that property prices in the Dublin capital had risen dramatically in the period between the entering into of the separation agreement and the application for the divorce. The court felt that property price increases were foreseeable but not at the rate that had occurred in the Dublin market.

In *MK v JPK*[50] a separation agreement entered into in 1982 was inadequate to meet the current needs of the dependent spouse. In considering the agreement, which did not contain a prohibition on applying for a divorce, the court, as it was obliged to do so, considered the agreement in accordance with s 20(3) of the Family Law (Divorce) Act 1996 and considered it inadequate to meet the needs of the wife in that it failed to make proper provision for her.

---

48 (Unreported) High Court, 24 January 2003.
49 *MG v MG*, Buckley J, 25 July 2000, *Irish Times Law.*
50 (Unreported) High Court, 24 January 2003, O'Neill J.

More significant, however, is *A v A*,[51] a case decided by a Supreme Court judge sitting on the Western Circuit of the High Court. The separation agreement in this case was extremely comprehensive in resolving the property and financial issues between the parties and also included a most detailed set of clauses dealing with the eventuality of either party instituting judicial separation proceedings or other similar type application and any claim for relief. The agreement expressly prevented either party claiming a right to the property of the other acquired after the separation of the parties. Both parties came from farming backgrounds and both brought land to the marriage. At the time of the separation the lands were divided equally between them and each owned land in current values of circa €2m. At the date of the application for the divorce, the husband, through some shrewd investments had lands and assets valued in the region of €7m, whereas the wife's fortunes declined to the extent that her lands were worth just in excess of €1.25m. On the issue of whether the agreement was binding, Hardiman J referred to *DT v CT* which as we know indicated that finality in terms of clean-break divorces was not possible and thus an agreement could not achieve what was not legally possible to achieve.[52] Hardiman J did, however, endorse the desirability of finality in such matters.[53] In addition, Hardiman J identified s 20(3) which expressly requires a court to consider the terms of a separation agreement in an application for a divorce. The court was thus statutorily prohibited or mandated as the case may be to consider the terms of the agreement and thus could not be prevented from doing so by agreement of the parties. Having considered the terms of the agreement and the factors set out in s 20, Hardiman J declined to make a relief order in favour of the respondent wife. He did so for a number of very clear and concise reasons:

(a) since the separation of the parties, the respondent wife had made no contribution to the husband's endeavours;

(b) the assets of the parties had been divided equally upon their separation which reflected their joint efforts to their acquisition prior to separation;

(c) the wife's earning capacity had not been impaired by the marriage;

(d) the wife's financial difficulties were not contributed to by the husband;

(e) the husband's good fortune had not been contributed to by the wife;

(f) the separation agreement was a fair one.

Perhaps the most telling reason given by Hardiman J is contained in s 20(5) of the Family Law (Divorce) Act 1996 which is worthy of quoting, particularly in the context of the above facts and provides:

> 'The court shall not make an order under a provision referred to in subsection (1) unless it would be in the interests of justice to do so.'

The reference to subsection (1) is to the various relief orders a court may make on the grant of a divorce. Here Hardiman J was of the view that to make an order in favour of the wife was clearly not in the interests of justice.

---

[51] (Unreported) High Court, 9 December 2004, Hardiman J.
[52] *Ibid* at 9.
[53] *Ibid*.

The decision is a good example of the circumstances in which a court having reviewed the terms of separation agreement and circumstances surrounding it will decline an application for relief in a divorce.

In *GR v GC*[54] the High Court had to consider whether judicial separation proceedings that were settled and a consent order obtained which was stated to be in full and final satisfaction of all claims arising between the parties precluded the High Court's jurisdiction to make new and further ancillary relief orders. Finlay Geoghegan J held that an attempt to exclude the court's jurisdiction was contrary to public policy and relied upon the case of *X v X*.[55] Further, a court can consider the terms of the agreement and is not obliged to ignore them but added that if the matter were a divorce settlement by consent then the agreement might bind the parties in the event of an attempt to seek financial relief in the future. Here the wife agreed a settlement of €1.7m of assets amounting to €5.3m. The court refused to make a further lump sum and did make some small increases to the maintenance payable to her and the children.

V   TAXING MATTERS AND COSTS

The case of *MP v AP*[56] taught family lawyers an important lesson in reducing to writing the terms of a settlement reached in family law proceedings. The case should have warned family lawyers of the significance of tax implications for litigants in agreeing financial settlements and the importance of precision and clarity when it comes to who should be responsible for any tax liability.

The case concerned the inclusion of the phrase 'Maintenance of £1,800 net of income tax per month. £1,400 attributable to Mrs P £200 attributable to each of the children'. The husband argued that he was obliged to deduct the relevant amount of tax payable on the sum due to the wife and remit her the balance. The wife argued that she was entitled to the sum net of any tax and the husband was liable for that amount in addition to the sum she was to receive. The Supreme Court ultimately held that the phrase used was ambiguous and remitted the matter to the High Court for the hearing of oral evidence as to what the parties intended when they settled the judicial separation proceedings. The Supreme Court hearing was a costly one for the parties concerned.

Unfortunately the lesson to be derived from the case was not learnt. In *MM v JM*[57] the High Court was faced with another relatively vague clause in a settlement of a judicial separation. The problem centred around capital gains tax liability for the wife on the sale of the family home. The agreement was silent as to who should be responsible for the capital gains liability on the sale of the family home which generated a price of just over £1m of which

---

54   (Unreported) High Court, 8 February 2005, Finlay Geoghegan J.
55   [2002] 1 FLR 508.
56   (Unreported) Supreme Court, 3 March 2000, Keane CJ.
57   (Unreported) High Court, 14 May 2003, Murphy J.

the wife received some £555,850 but with a capital gains tax liability of over £54,000 which when augmented by surcharges and interest was outstanding at over £100,000. The husband had agreed to discharge specific liabilities arising from the sale of the property and also the then payable residential property tax. From this the court inferred that, as the proceeds were to be divided on a scale agreed and that the husband had specifically agreed to discharge additional charges relating to the sale of the property from his share of the proceeds, it could not be inferred that he would be liable for both his and his wife's liability to capital gains tax.

Obviously the liability reduced the wife's lump sum considerably as did the costs of the High Court hearing. This amount, however, pales into insignificance by comparison with the case of *BD v JD*.[58] This case has been to the High Court twice and the Supreme Court once so far. The main difficulty with this case stemmed from a successful business which the husband took over when the company was in financial trouble in the 1980s. He had been an employee of the business and took the risk of rebuilding the company which he did successfully. The initial dispute before the High Court concerned the method of valuing the company. The different methods employed by the financial advisors produced a valuation ranging from €6m to €15m. The trial judge determined the correct valuation at €10m and then proceeded to direct lump sum payments in favour of the wife who was to relinquish her interest in the company. This required the husband to pay €4m over a 2-year period. If the wife retained the family home valued at €1m, then the final payment by the husband was to be halved. The sums payable to the wife were to be net of tax whereby the company or the husband would be obliged to discharge any tax liability arising therein. The tax liability arising from extracting these sums from the company ranged from between €800,000 to €1.68m.

The husband appealed the decision to the Supreme Court challenging the trial judge's approach. In particular the husband argued that the trial judge should have considered the following issues in relation to the orders made:

(i)   whether it was possible to extract the sums in question in the 2-year period provided;

(ii)   what mechanisms could be used to extract the funds;

(iii) the commercial effects of extracting the funds on the commercial viability and future of the business;

(iv)   the tax effects of extracting the funds.

Hardiman J rejected the first two issues as relevant factors for the court's consideration in the making of the various orders. He reasoned that the trial judge cannot 'stand in the shoes of a taxation adviser to the [husband] in the post litigation situation'.[59] Clearly this is correct and such a function falls entirely outside the scope of a trial judge in determining what relief orders

---

[58]   (Unreported) High Court, 5 December 2003, McKetchnie J; (unreported) Supreme Court, 8 December 2004, Hardiman J; (unreported) High Court, 4 May 2005, McKetchnie J.

[59]   (Unreported) Supreme Court, 8 December 2004, Hardiman J at 5.

should be made. The latter two issues were relevant issues and ones which the court must consider when deciding what orders should be made. The Supreme Court set aside the order directing the making of the €4m lump sum payment to the wife. The matter was remitted to the High Court for argument on these issues, the Supreme Court declining to alter the amounts ordered in the light of its decision on the relevance of these factors.

The parties resumed their dispute in the High Court in May 2005 but immediately encountered yet another application as to how the matter should proceed in the light of the Supreme Court findings. In the interim, it was claimed that the value of the companies had varied. The Court was invited to revalue the company but declined to do so.

This is perhaps one of the most expensive family law cases to have come before the courts. The High Court had ordered the husband pay a contribution of €100,000 towards the wife's legal costs. This was set aside on appeal by Hardiman J on the basis that the wife's claim that she was in effect an equal partner in a partnership failed in the High Court. Hardiman J reasoned that as she had lost her legal argument, costs should follow the result as is the general principle.[60] He also indicated that he could see no reason why one party should be responsible for the payment of the other party's costs. The seeking of a contribution from the other party in family law proceedings is very common. Family law proceedings when drafted contain many claims for relief not all of which are routinely obtained. Thus the applicant all too often fails to obtain all that was claimed. If Hardiman J's approach to the award of costs in this particular instance were to gather momentum, then it will unnerve many a family law practitioner.

On remittance to the High Court, McKetchnie J was quick to quell any fears that may arise from the quashing of the order for a contribution towards costs. He noted that Hardiman J's decision was specific to the facts of this case, namely that the applicant's case had been based squarely upon a claim of an equitable entitlement to 50% of the company. McKetchnie J specifically noted s 35 of the Judicial Separation and Family Law Reform Act 1989 which expressly provides that costs is a matter of discretion for the court.[61]

The legal costs and tax issues aside, this case also touched upon the role of the company. A limited company has separate legal identity and was a central participant in this litigation. The company (or more accurately here a group of companies) was not legally represented. There was no objection on behalf of the company as to its obligations and succumbing to the jurisdiction of the court. In essence the assets of the company were treated as those of the parties. Hardiman J expressly noted this unique feature of the case and cautioned that the decision not be seen as endorsing the authority of the court to involve a third party in family law proceedings and rendering that party liable to orders of the court.[62] No doubt a case will arise where

---

[60]   (Unreported) Supreme Court, 8 December 2004, Hardiman J at 7.
[61]   (Unreported) High Court, 4 May, McKetchnie J at 6.
[62]   (Unreported) Supreme Court, 8 December 2004, Hardiman J at 6.

objections can be made and that case will make for most interesting reading and analysis.

The Netrherlands

THE DUTCH FAMILY LAW CHRONICLES: CONTINUED PARENTHOOD NOTWITHSTANDING DIVORCE

Ian Curry-Sumner and Caroline Forder[*]

Résumé

La phrase clé, cette année, aux Pays-Bas est "la parentalité survit au divorce". Deux projets de lois qui se recoupent en partie, l'un présenté par un parlementaire et l'autre par le ministre de la Justice, sont actuellement à l'étude devant le Parlement néerlandais. Ces projets s'attaquent à la question de la procédure de divorce et aux difficultés relatives au droit de garde et d'accès, que rencontrent surtout des hommes au moment de la rupture d'une relation conjugale. Une foule de questions sont sur la table: la possibilité d'introduire le divorce administratif, la promotion de la médiation, une tentative de réponse au syndrome "divorcez et détruisez", la présomption de garde partagée, des mesures d'effectivité du droit d'accès. Un autre projet de loi concerne l'important problème de l'exécution des ordonnances alimentaires au profit des enfants et auquel sont confrontées surtout les femmes. Si ce projet devait être adopté, cela entraînerait le remplacement du processus de fixation et d'exécution des pensions alimentaires par un système beaucoup plus strict laissant peu de place aux tergiversations que permettent les règles actuelles. De nouvelles propositions législatives visent à faciliter les démarches d'adoption par les couples de même sexe, notamment en levant l'interdiction de l'adoption internationale prévue dans la loi actuelle. D'autres questions importantes de droit international privé ont été abordées par le législateur, notamment en ce qui à trait à la reconnaissance des mariages homosexuels par les autorités de l'île d'Aruba (question très controversée là-bas) et à l'entrée en vigueur de la Loi reconnaissant le partenariat enregistré. Une importante thèse de doctorat sur cette question de droit international a récemment été publiée. Finalement, ce rapport évoque également quelques autres questions: le projet de loi portant réforme du droit relatif à la garde des enfants nés de partenaires enregistrés; le projet de loi interdisant le châtiment corporel par les parents; la récente jurisprudence de la Cour suprême néerlandaise en matière de filiation et

---

[*] The first author is Lecturer and Researcher at the Molengraaff Institute for Private Law, University of Utrecht, the Netherlands. The second author is Professor of European Family Law at the University of Maastricht, the Netherlands. It is important, in connection with the progress of certain Bills discussed in the text, to note that the text was closed on 31 January 2006.

d'application du concept d'obligation naturelle en droit patrimonial de la famille.

INTRODUCTION

The key phrase this year is 'continued parenthood notwithstanding divorce'. Two partly overlapping Bills, one introduced by a private member, one by the Ministry of Justice, currently pending in Parliament address the matter of divorce procedure and the problems, mainly experienced by men following the breakdown of a personal relationship, regarding access and custody. Administrative divorce, the promotion of mediation, tackling the 'divorce and destroy' syndrome, the preference for joint custody, the strengthening of the effectiveness of the right of access are all under discussion. Another Bill is pending which purports to address the problem, largely experienced by women, of enforcement of child maintenance. If that Bill becomes law the existing procedure for establishing and enforcing child maintenance will be replaced by a much cruder instrument, allowing much less room for shilly-shallying than under the present law. Important private international law issues addressed by the Dutch legislator are the recognition of marriage between two persons of the same sex by Aruba (controversial in Aruba) and the coming into force of the Act on recognition of registered partnership. An important doctorate on this question, of international interest, has just been published. Additionally the report includes Bills to change the law of custody in cases where a child is born to registered partners, a Bill which declares corporal punishment of children by their parents to be unlawful and Dutch Supreme Court case-law on the law of descent and on the application of 'natural obligations' in matrimonial property.

I   THE LAW OF DESCENT: CASE-LAW

A   Abuse of rights by mother giving consent to recognition by another man

A man who wishes to recognise a child under the age of 16 years must obtain the prior written consent of the child's mother.[1] However, if the mother refuses to give her consent, the begetter may apply to the court for substitution of the mother's consent;[2] his request is very likely to be granted.[3] If the begetter dithers in making such an application to the court, he runs the risk of losing out if the mother meanwhile gives her consent to recognition of the child by another man. It is not a requirement of a valid recognition that the man be the child's begetter, as long as the mother gives

---

[1]   Article 1:204(1)(c) of the Dutch Civil Code.
[2]   Article 1:204(3) of the Dutch Civil Code.
[3]   Dutch Supreme Court, 16 February 2001, *Nederlandse Jurisprudentie*, 2001, 571; Dutch Supreme Court, 9 April 2004, *Nederlandse Jurisprudentie*, 2005, 565 (the begetter need not demonstrate a close personal relationship to the child in order for the court to make the order substituting the mother's consent).

her permission and the other conditions are fulfilled. The possibilities for a begetter who fails to recognise the child, and subsequently is confronted with the situation that the child has been recognised by another man, are limited. In order for the begetter to establish any legal relationship to the child, it is essential that the recognition by the other man be annulled. It is possible that a recognition, even though validly completed, can be annulled by the court if certain conditions are satisfied. However the begetter is not one of the persons entitled to apply to the court for annulment of a recognition.[4] The only remaining possibility is for the begetter to argue that the recognition should be annulled on the ground that the mother, by giving permission to recognition to another man, has abused her legal power. The doctrine of abuse of power is one of the general provisions of Dutch private law,[5] which can be invoked in a broad range of situations. It has already been held applicable in various contexts of family law (see further **II.A** below[6]). In Art 3:13 of the Dutch Civil Code it is provided:

(1) A person entitled to exercise a power is not entitled to exercise that power to the extent that such power is abused.

(2) A power can be abused, *inter alia*, by exercising it:
   - with no other purpose than to damage another person's interests;
   - for another purpose than that for which the power is granted;
   - or if, taking into account the lack of proportionality between the interest in the exercise of the power and the interest damaged by its exercise, exercise of the power cannot be considered to be reasonable (disproportionality criterium).

(3) It is possible that a power of its very nature cannot be abused.

The decision of the Dutch Supreme Court on 12 November 2004[7] concerning just such a begetter arguing that the mother, by giving consent to another man to recognise the child, had abused her power, establishes that the abuse of power argument will only succeed if the begetter can establish that the mother gave her consent *with no other purpose* than in order to spite and damage the begetter (applying the first criterium in Art 3:13(2) of the Dutch Civil Code above). Such exclusively malicious intent will normally be very difficult to establish. As long as the mother lives together with the other man and they are bringing up the child together, it will be accepted that the mother had a legitimate purpose in giving her consent to recognition by the other man. It will be of no consequence that she may additionally have malicious intent towards the begetter. However, if the begetter has not had the opportunity to make an application to the court for substitution of the mother's consent to recognition – because he was unaware of the child's birth or is reasonably unaware that he may be the begetter, De Boer has argued in his commentary under the case that the more favourable

---

[4]   Article 1:205 of the Dutch Civil Code.

[5]   The provision is found in Art 3:13 of the Dutch Civil Code.

[6]   And see, for example, Dutch Supreme Court, 31 May 2002, discussed in the Dutch report, A Bainham (ed) *The International Survey of Family Law 2003 Edition* pp 282–284.

[7]   *Nederlandse Jurisprudentie*, 2005, 248 annotation Jan de Boer.

disproportionality criterium in Art 3:13(2) of the Dutch Civil Code should be applied to determine whether the mother has abused her power.

B   International paternity

On 27 May 2005, the Dutch Supreme Court decided a case in which the central question surrounded the acquisition by a child of Dutch nationality by virtue of the recognition of the child by a Dutch citizen.[8] The facts of the case where as follows: in 2001, the child was born in Turkey. According to the birth certificate, both the father and mother were known. Although the parents were not married to each other, the father had provided a notarial instrument in which he had stated that he was the biological father of the child. In actual fact the father had, since 1973, been married to a different woman. The question brought before the court was whether the recognition, which had taken place in Turkey, could be recognised in the Netherlands, and thus lead to the acquisition of Dutch nationality.[9]

In order to answer this question, it is important to know that the Dutch private international law rules in the field of parentage have recently been codified. As of 1 April 2003, the Private International Law (Parentage) Act (*Wet Conflictenrecht Afstamming*, hereinafter WCA) applies to the recognition of foreign judicial decisions and legal facts.[10] According to Art 11 of this Act, the WCA applies to legal ties that were established or altered abroad after the entry into force of this Act and to the recognition of legal ties that were established after its entry into force. Nonetheless, both the *Rechtbank* (district court) in The Hague and the *Hoge Raad* (Dutch Supreme Court) noted that the rules laid down in the WCA were based entirely on the unwritten rules in force prior to 1 April 2003.

The answer therefore revolved around the recognition in the Netherlands of the notarial instrument drawn up by the father in 2001. According to Art 9(1)(c) in conjunction with Art 10(1) of the WCA a foreign legal fact or act whereby legal familial ties on account of parentage are established can be refused recognition in the Netherlands on the grounds of Dutch public policy. According to Art 10(2)(a) of the WCA one situation which is highlighted as being contrary to Dutch public policy is, 'if the recognition is made by a Dutch national who, according to Dutch law, would not have been entitled to recognise the child'. In order to ascertain whether or not the father was entitled to recognise the child, reference must be sought to Art 1:204(1)(e) of the Dutch Civil Code. According to this paragraph, a man who is married at the time of the recognition to another woman (other than the mother), may not recognise a child, unless the district court has held it to be plausible that (i) there is or has been a bond between the man and the

---

8   Dutch Supreme Court, 27 May 2005, *Nederlandse Jurisprudentie*, 2005, 550, National Case Law Number (LJN) AS5109. This case has also been discussed in K Boele-Woelki 'Internationaal Privaatrecht' (2005) *Ars Aequi Katern 96*, p 5312–5313.

9   The biological father had acquired Dutch nationality in 1997 by virtue of a naturalisation procedure.

10   For a translation of this Act see I Sumner and H Warendorg *European Family Law Series Volume 5: Family law legislation of the Netherlands* (Antwerp: Intersentia, 2003) pp 234–239.

mother which may be regarded sufficiently like a marriage, or (ii) that there is a close personal relationship between the man and the child. Since the biological father of the child was married at the time of the birth of the child to a woman other than the mother of the child, the recognition could only be recognised if either of the exceptions were satisfied. If the biological father was thus able to establish that there is a close personal relationship between himself and the child, then one of the grounds for exception would be satisfied.

On 14 July 2004, the district court in Leeuwaarden had decided precisely this.[11] At the request of the biological father, the district court had determined that family life existed between the father and the child. On appeal, the Court of Appeal in Leeuwaarden deferred the case until the Supreme Court had decided the case at hand.[12] On 16 December 2005, the Court of Appeal in Leeuwaarden reversed the decision of the district court, and thus it was held that the biological father did not have family life with his child.

Why is this so important? Were the court to have held that the biological father had family life with this child so that the father would therefore have been able to argue that he satisfied the exception grounds listed in Art 1:204(1)(e) of the Dutch Civil Code, then a loophole would have been created with respect to the relevant adoption provisions. This scenario would have allowed aspirant parents in the Netherlands to search for a surrogate abroad. Once a surrogate had been found and a child conceived, the biological father would have recognised the child in accordance with foreign domestic legislation, subsequently return to the Netherlands and request recognition in the Netherlands of this foreign recognition. Such action would lead to aspirant parents in the Netherlands being able to 'adopt' a child without having to satisfy the conditions of the Act on the placement of foreign children in the Netherlands (the so-called *Wobka, Wet opneming buitenlandse kinderen ter adoptie*). Nonetheless, although Art 204(1)(e), Book 1 of the Dutch Civil Code prevents a married heterosexual man from recognising the child, there is no prohibition imposed on a married homosexual man or an unmarried man. The door may therefore still be slightly ajar.[13]

II   ADOPTION: EUROPEAN COURT CASE-LAW

A   Abuse of rights by parent refusing to consent to adoption

Adoption can only take place if, *inter alia*, the condition is satisfied that neither parent objects to the adoption.[14] Under both the law applicable before

---

[11]   Rb Leeuwaarden, Case No 03-1729.

[12]   Hof Leeuwaarden, Case No 04-00289 and 04-00373.

[13]   It must, however, be remembered that the public policy exception in Art 10(1) of the WCA is not exhaustive and therefore such cases would more than likely be covered by analogy.

[14]   Article 1:228(1)(d) of the Dutch Civil Code.

and after the reforms to adoption law which came into force on 1 April 1998,[15] and even after the insertion on 1 April 2001[16] of the extra condition that the child does not have anything to expect from the parent in their capacity as parent,[17] it is possible, according to the case-law of the Dutch Supreme Court, to disregard a parental objection to adoption on the ground that the parent has abused the power to make objection given by Art 1:228(1)(d) of the Dutch Civil Code. Regarding abuse of a private law power see **I.A** above. In a case which went through all the Dutch courts[18] and was decided by the Dutch Supreme Court on 19 May 2000,[19] the mother left the matrimonial home when her daughter was 4 years old; mother and daughter did not meet any more after the daughter was 6 years old. The daughter wished, shortly before attaining her majority, to give legal force to the excellent relationship which she had with her stepmother through the instrument of adoption. However, her mother objected to the adoption. The only possibility to allow the adoption to go ahead was to establish that the mother, by objecting to the adoption, was abusing her power contrary to Art 3:13 of the Dutch Civil Code (see the text in **I.A** above). The national courts at all levels held that the mother was abusing her power and that the adoption could go ahead. The mother brought a case to the European Court of Human Rights ('the European Court') arguing that her right to respect for family life, guaranteed by Art 8 of the European Convention on Human Rights (ECHR), was violated. Her case was that she was being deprived of parenthood without good reason. On 3 March 2005 the European Court declared her application inadmissible. The European Court took into consideration the fact that the national courts had engaged the mother fully at all stages of the proceedings and that the decisions contained a motivated balancing up of the mother's interests in refusing adoption against the interests of her daughter in adoption and that the chosen priority given to the daughter's interests was understandable.[20]

---

[15] Act of 24 December 1997, Staatsblad 1997, 772; discussed in the Dutch report by Martinus Nijhoff (The Hague/Boston/London) in *The International Survey of Family Law 1997 Edition* pp 279–283. Confirming the applicability of the rule after the Act of 24 December 1997, see Dutch Supreme Court, 21 February 2003, *Nederlandse Jurisprudentie*, 2003, 214.

[16] Act of 21 December 2000, Staatsblad 2001, 10; discussed in Dutch Report in A Bainham (ed) *The International Survey of Family Law 2001 Edition* pp 312–315.

[17] Article 1:227(3) of the Dutch Civil Code; discussed in Dutch Report in A Bainham (ed) *The International Survey of Family Law 2001 Edition* pp 314–315.

[18] The case was decided according to the law pre-dating 1 April 1998: as we have just seen, the law after this date is, on this point, the same.

[19] *Nederlandse Jurisprudentie*, 2000, 455.

[20] Application 64848/01 (*Trijntje Kuijper v The Netherlands*).

III BILL REGARDING NEW PROVISIONS FOR JOINT CUSTODY AND AMENDING THE LAW ON CUSTODY ARISING FROM BIRTH OF A CHILD DURING A REGISTERED PARTNERSHIP

A New provisions regarding joint custody

The pronounced preference of the Dutch legislator and courts for joint custody is expressed in particular in the leading principle that joint custody continues even after divorce of the married parents or separation of unmarried parents.[21] In consequence of this rule it is proposed in the pending *Bill to reform registered partnership, the law of names and the acquisition of joint custody*[22] to delete the second sentence of Art 1:253o(1) of the Dutch Civil Code. The sentence to be deleted provides that a *divorced parent* who was not awarded custody in the divorce proceedings may only apply subsequently to the court for an order for joint custody if the application is made jointly with the other parent. Thus the one parent is given a position of absolute power to obstruct the application to the court for joint custody. The proposed deletion would end that situation.[23]

On 14 February 2005 the Bill was amended in order to regulate the position of *unmarried parents*. At present the Dutch Civil Code does not allow an unmarried parent (usually the father) who has never exercised, jointly with the other parent (usually the mother), custody over the child to make a sole application to the court for an order for joint custody. Article 1:253c of the Dutch Civil Code allows the unmarried parent who does not have custody to apply to the court for an order granting it: however this order means that the mother must be excluded from exercising custody. In the amendment the Bill is amended to include making such provision for a sole application for joint custody by an unmarried parent.[24] This amendment sounds very technical but has international relevance. In the opinion of the legislator and several lower courts the amendment introduced is required in order to ensure

---

[21] Dutch Supreme Court, 10 September 1999, *Nederlandse Jurisprudentie*, 2000, 20 (divorced parents); Dutch Supreme Court, 28 October 2003, *Nederlandse Jurisprudentie*, 2003, 359 (unmarried parents).

[22] Bill to reform registered partnership, the law of names and the acquisition of joint custody: *Wijziging van enige bepalingen van Boek 1 van het BW met betrekking tot het geregistreerd partnerschap, de geslachtsnaam en het verkrijgen van gezamenlijk gezag*, TK 2003/2004, 29 353, nrs 1–2, artikelen C, D, F en G. The Bill was introduced into the Second Chamber on 3 December 2003.

[23] The proposed amendment aims to give the applicant a right to make a sole application to the court whatever the original reason is for the fact that the applicant was not given custody; whether because the parent was not entitled (for example, because of mental illness) to exercise custody (Art 1:253q(5) of the Dutch Civil Code) or because parental rights were removed or suspended by court order (Art 1:277(1) of the Dutch Civil Code). It also applies to the case in which custody is exercised by the parent and another person not being a parent (Art 1:253v of the Dutch Civil Code).

[24] Including the supplementary Second Amendment Note introduced into the Second Chamber on 21 April 2005 regarding Art 1:253e of the Dutch Civil Code, which article provided that an order in favour of the applicant under Art 1:253c results in loss of custody for the other parent.

compliance with Arts 6[25] and 8[26] of the ECHR. Several courts have on this assumption already declared Art 1:253o, second sentence of the Dutch Civil Code to be of no application (as explained above),[27] and that Art 1:253c should be interpreted in accordance with the ECHR.[28] In both cases the provisions are to be dis-applied and subjected to judicial re-drafting. On 27 May 2005 the Dutch Supreme Court held that the impossibility according to the Dutch Civil Code for a never-married parent to apply to the court for an order to share custody with the other parent violated Art 6 of the ECHR: Art 1:253c(1) and 1:253e of the Dutch Civil Code should be interpreted accordingly.[29] Whatever one may think of the result, this case sits uncomfortably with case-law of the European Court regarding the matter of joint custody. In two cases the European Court has held quite clearly that the failure by a legislator to provide for joint custody in the case of never-married parents does not constitute a violation of Art 8 of the ECHR.[30] The European Court considered it reasonable, considering the uncertainties regarding the actual benefits of joint custody, for a legislator to elect not to provide for it. Accordingly it is impossible to see how there could be a violation of Art 6 of the ECHR, which guarantees procedural protection of civil rights and obligations. The Austrian cases were, moreover, on their facts stronger than the Dutch case. The Austrian couples were amicable couples who were not married to one another and who just wanted to have the legal safeguard of joint custody. In the Dutch case the couple were not in agreement.

In the same Amendment to the Bill an amendment is proposed regarding Art 1:252(1) of the Dutch Civil Code. According to this provision unmarried parents are able to acquire joint custody by jointly requesting a simple annotation on the custody register (provided for by Art 1:244 of the Dutch Civil Code). However the procedure is not available if the couple has previously held joint custody over the child and then subsequently an order

---

[25] Article 6, first sentence of the ECHR: 'In the determination of his civil rights and obligations ... everyone is entitled to a fair and public hearing within a reasonable time by an independent and partial tribunal established by law.'

[26] Article 8 of the ECHR: '1. Everyone has the right to respect for his private and family life, his home and his correspondence. 2. There shall be no interference by a public authority with the exercise of this right except such as is in accordance with law and is necessary in a democratic society in the interests of national security, public safety or the economic well-being of the country, for the prevention of disorder or crime, for the protection of health or morals, or for the protection of the rights and freedoms of others.'

[27] Leeuwaarden Appeal Court, 5 February 2003, *Nederlandse Jurisprudentie*, 2003, 352; The Hague Appeal Court, 3 September 2003, LJN-number AL8181, Arnhem Appeal Court, 8 June 2004, LJN-number AQ5059.

[28] Breda Regional Court, kanton section, 7 November 2003, LJN-number AO4091; Zwolle Regional Court, 9 February 2004, LJN-number AO3270; Utrecht Regional Court, 28 July 2004, LJN-number AQ9901; Amsterdam Appeal Court, 3 March 2005, *Tijdschrift voor familie-en jeugdrecht*, 2005, 153.

[29] Dutch Supreme Court, 27 May 2005, *Nederlandse Jurisprudentie*, 2005, 485 with annotation de Boer.

[30] *Cernecki v Austria*, Eur Court H R, 11 July 2000 (inadmissibility decision application number 31061/96) and *RW & CTG v Austria*, Eur Court HR, 22 November 2001 (inadmissibility decision application number 36222/97).

for sole custody has been made. In that case the couple are required to apply to the court for an order that they are once again entitled to joint custody. The reason for this restriction is that the child's interests require judicial scrutiny when the custody arrangements have earlier been subjected to change. However, it is necessary to make it quite clear that the restriction applies *per child*. Thus the Amendment to the *Bill to reform registered partnership, the law of names and the acquisition of joint custody* specifies that if the unmarried parents have previously had joint custody over their child, Alice, and subsequently this joint custody is changed into sole custody of the mother, a further change back into joint custody requires an application to the court. However regarding their second child, Boris, regarding whom no earlier custody arrangements have been made, the couple are free to use the simple procedure of applying for an annotation in the custody register.

B Amendment of the law on custody arising from the birth of a child during a registered partnership

In Art 1:253aa of the Dutch Civil Code it is provided:

'1. Both parents will exercise custody over a child born during the subsistence of a registered partnership.'[31]

The intention behind the provision is that Charles and Annie, who registered their partnership on 1 June 2003, will both exercise joint custody over their child, Justin, born on 1 November 2003. For this provision to apply Charles must recognise Justin before he is born; otherwise he is not regarded as a 'parent' for the purposes of Art 1:253aa of the Dutch Civil Code. The amendment which I now wish to discuss concerns an ambiguity in the wording of Art 1:253aa. The provision was capable of creating joint custody by dint of law in the following situation: Charles and Annie register their partnership on 1 June 2003. On 1 November 2003 Annie gives birth to a child who has been fathered and recognised by Sebastian. By dint of Art 1:253aa, Annie and Sebastian would exercise joint custody over Justin from the date of his birth, because Justin was born during the partnership registered by Annie and Charles. Obviously this is not the intention behind the provision, since joint custody would be granted in a situation which could potentially be very unstable for the child. The proposed amendment seeks to make it quite clear that joint custody will only arise if the child is born into a registered partnership *between the two parents*.[32]

---

[31] This provision was introduced on 1 January 2002. It was discussed in the Dutch report in A Bainham (ed) *The International Survey of Family Law 2001 Edition* pp 315–319 and the Dutch report in A Bainham (ed) *The International Survey of Family Law 2003 Edition* p 289.

[32] Bill to reform registered partnership, the law of names and the acquisition of joint custody: *Wijziging van enige bepalingen van Boek 1 van het BW met betrekking tot het geregistreerd partnerschap, de geslachtsnaam en het verkrijgen van gezamenlijk gezag*, TK 2003/2004, 29 353, nrs 1-2, artikel B. The Bill was introduced into the Second Chamber on 3 December 2003.

IV ISSUES AROUND SEPARATION AND DIVORCE: TWO PENDING BILLS

A   Introduction

Out of a total of 35,000 children per year who are affected by the divorce of their parents, approximately 25% have no contact at all with one of their parents. Furthermore, in a further 25% of cases, the access arrangements are troubled.[33] Social science research shows that a number of these children will sustain serious and permanent psychological and emotional damage as a consequence.[34] It is therefore understandable that the government is doing its best to solve the problem of access after divorce. On 3 June 2005 the *Bill to promote continuation of parenthood and responsible divorce* ('the Government Bill') was introduced into the Second Chamber of Parliament.[35] Some elements of that Bill build upon elements of a private member's Bill introduced by Mr Luchtenveld into the Second Chamber on 13 December 2004: the *Bill to end marriage without judicial intervention and to embody in legal form the continuation of parenthood after divorce* ('the Luchtenveld Bill').[36] That latter Bill was passed by the Second Chamber on 29 November 2005[37] and is now pending in the First Chamber.[38] To prevent overlap in the exposition and to facilitate comparison of the measures these two Bills will be discussed together under a number of headings.

B   Joint custody as a general rule

Both Bills aim primarily to reinforce the basic rule that joint custody should in principle continue notwithstanding divorce of the parents. However, the strategy adopted to achieve that aim in the two Bills differs considerably. One crucial issue concerns the criteria which a court must use to determine when a parent is entitled to be granted his or her application to exercise custody alone. In the Government Bill the criteria developed by the Dutch Supreme Court in its decision on 10 September 1999[39] is adopted: sole custody may be ordered (a) if the court is satisfied that there is an unacceptable risk that the child's interests are ignored or negated by the parents and that there is no prospect of improvement within a foreseeable time,[40] or (b) that the court is satisfied that change in the custody

---

33   Second Chamber 2003–2004, 29 520, nr 7, p 8.
34   E Spruijt, H Kormos, C Burggraaf and A Steenweg *Het verdeelde kind, literatuuronderzoek omgang na scheiding, Raad voor de Kinderbescherming* (Utrecht, 2002) pp 33–39.
35   *Wijziging van Boek 1 van het Burgerlijk Wetboek en het Wetboek van Burgerlijke Rechtsvorderingen in verband met het bevorderen van voortgezet ouderschap na echtscheiding en het afschaffen van de mogelijkheid tot het omzetten van een huwelijk in een geregistreerd partnerschap*, TK 2004-2005, 30 145, nrs 1–2.
36   TK 2003-2004, 29 676, nr 2.
37   Second Chamber 27-1862 (29 November 2005).
38   First Chamber 2005–2006, 29 676, A.
39   *Nederlandse Jurisprudentie*, 2000, 20. See, for an explanation, the Dutch report in A Bainham (ed) *The International Survey of Family Law 2003 Edition* p 289.
40   Government Bill, Art I, part J. I have made a rather free translation of the original, which uses colloquial terms: '*er moet sprake zijn van een onaanvaardbare risico dat het kind klem komt te*

arrangements is for other reasons necessary in the child's interests. Apart from the situation of a child born out of a marriage, the criteria are applicable to the case where joint custody has arisen by dint of birth of the child during a registered partnership between the parents (by Art 1:253aa of the Dutch Civil Code; see **III.B** above) and to the case of the birth of a child born during a registered partnership or marriage between the child's parent and a person who is not the child's parent (ie a lesbian partner), regulated by Art 1:253sa of the Dutch Civil Code.[41]

Both the Government Bill and the Luchtenveld Bill introduce a new normative rule which applies to the total packet of rights and duties which comprise 'custody rights'. Draft-Article 1:247(3) of the Dutch Civil Code provides:

> 'Parental custody includes *inter alia* the obligation on the parent to stimulate development of the bonds between the child and the other parent.'[42]

This rule applies whether there is joint or sole custody. The provision prohibits, for example, an agreement between the parents that one of the parents shall have no contact with the child. However, it does not forbid an agreement that, if the circumstances so require, contact between the parent and child may be temporarily suspended. If a longer-term interruption in contact is thought necessary, it would not be correct to do this via a parental agreement; instead the court should be asked to rule on the matter, as provided for in Draft-Art 1:253a of the Dutch Civil Code (provision for judicial adjudication of parental disputes regarding the exercise of custody).[43] This new rule, which superficially sounds attractive, carries in my view considerable hidden risks. These risks arise not so much from the rule itself, but only emerge when one reflects on what will happen when the parent with whom the child lives breaches the rule. It is already agreed that there is an arsenal of measures which can be taken against the parent who obstructs access, but invariably these measures backfire by hurting the child at least as much as the offending parent. The rule, taken together with the prospect of enforcement, underwrites the idea that contact between parent and child should be sustained whatever the price. This approach, however, is not supported by social science research which reveals that the crucial point for the child is that he or she should be freed from exposure to parental conflict; this is more important to the child's mental welfare than sustaining contact with both parents. Also the good functioning of the parent with whom the child lives is of vital importance for the child's further development.[44]

---

zitten of verloren zou raken tussen de ouders en niet te verwachten is dat hierin binnen afzienbare tijd verbetering zal komen'.

41   The Government Bill, Art I, parts L and N. See, for an explanation of Art 1:253sa of the Dutch Civil Code, the Dutch report in A Bainham (ed) *The International Survey of Family Law 2001 Edition* pp 315–319.

42   The Government Bill, Art I, part G; Luchtenveld Bill, part N.

43   Second Chamber 2004–2005, 30 145, nr 4, p 4.

44   See, for example, E Spruijt et al, above n 34.

In the present Dutch Civil Code there are separate provisions on custody and access, and two separate provisions on the adjudication of disputes between the parents regarding disputes respectively of custody (Art 1:253a) and access (Art 1:377h). In the proposals in the Government Bill these two provisions for disputes are brought together into one article: a new Art 1:253a of the Dutch Civil Code. The proposed new provision, following the scheme presently used in Art 1:377h on dispute regulation in access cases, allows the court, on request, to adjudicate disputes on the following matters:

- the division of care and upbringing tasks, including a temporary prohibition on having contact with the child;
- the establishment of the child's main place of residence;
- regarding the provision of information by the parent or third party (for example, school) to the parent with whom the child does not live.[45]

All these orders are possible under existing law: the novelty is that when parents exercise joint custody, the provisions no longer refer to custody and contact, but to the more trendy terms 'care and upbringing tasks'. The government has not reacted to the understandable comment made by the Council of State,[46] that re-naming the traditional roles of contact and custody with terms like 'tasks of care and upbringing' ignores – and indeed conflicts with – the reality that in fact the majority of these tasks are carried out by one of the parents: the mother.

In the Luchtenveld Bill the aim of reinforcing the primacy of the joint custody rule is tackled in a different way. First, in Draft-Art 1:251(2) of the Dutch Civil Code it is proposed that the parents will exercise joint custody 'in an egalitarian manner'.[47] Furthermore, the article continues:

> 'A child in respect of which the parents exercise joint custody pursuant to section (2) above, retains after divorce the right to care and upbringing by both parents.'

The idea behind this article, according to the Explanatory Notes, is to achieve a breakthrough in the present situation, namely, that the child normally lives with the mother whilst the father enjoys merely a provision for contact.[48] Under some considerable pressure in the Second Chamber Mr Luchtenveld has conceded that shared residence is not generally in the child's best interests.[49] However, it remains the case that the underlying lack of equality in sharing of contact and upbringing are influenced not only by lack of willingness of the parents but, as emerged from the Emancipation Report 2004, more profoundly by structural problems such as lack of

---

[45] Government Bill, Art I, part K.

[46] Acting in its advisory capacity in reviewing draft legislation.

[47] EK 2005–2006, 29 676, A, onderdeel O.

[48] TK 2004–2005, 29 676, nr 6, p 8.

[49] TK 6-308 (29 September 2005), reacting to criticism from MP Kalsbeek, TK 6-296 (29 September 2005).

flexibility in the workplace and fiscal disincentives in the field of tax and social security.[50]

A second instrument which is deployed in the Luchtenveld Bill is the 'fast stream dispute resolution'. The idea is that when one of the parents violates a rule concerning 'care and upbringing' (for definition, see above) which has either been agreed by them or has been established by a court adjudicating their case, the other parent should be able to bring the matter before the court by a very simple procedure, without the need for an advocate. According to the proposal, the court would be obliged to arrange a hearing of the dispute within 3 weeks,[51] unless the court decided to refer the dispute to a mediator (another 'hip' word in these two family divorce Bills). The fast stream dispute resolution is controversial but managed to gain sufficient support in the Second Chamber to be included in the Bill which is now pending before the First Chamber. The idea behind the provision is that if disputes can be dealt with swiftly, escalation can be prevented. Moreover, swift intervention in cases where one parent is being prevented by the other parent from having contact with the child prevents disturbance in the parent-child relationship caused solely by passing of time. The Minister of Justice, Mr Donner, reacted very unenthusiastically to the original idea. On 29 March he wrote to the Second Chamber expressing his concern that the provision would polarise disputes and that the basic objective of encouraging parents to take responsibility for the resolution of their own problems instead of fighting it all out in court would be undermined. Furthermore the provisions involve a considerable extra increase in work for an already greatly overburdened judiciary.[52] Further concerns were expressed in debate by MP De Pater-van der Meer (Christian Democratic faction), who proposed to require use of the usual petition procedure used in private law cases.[53] This proposal had the support of the Minister of Justice, who agreed that the courts could otherwise be flooded with ill-founded allegations and vexatious litigants unless some form of procedure was required. The use of this petition procedure implies that an advocate would have to be involved; however, the Minister of Justice pointed out that the intervention of an advocate would provide some safeguard against frivolous claims.[54] However, these objections did not carry the day and the De Pater-van der Meer amendment was rejected by the Second Chamber. In fact the very intervention of an advocate seems to have been one of the things which the fast stream procedure seeks to avoid.[55] It now remains to be seen whether the First Chamber will accept this provision. The proposal for fast stream dispute resolution seems ill researched; there has, for example, been no investigation into the effectiveness – let alone

[50]   W Portegijs, A Boelens and L Olsthoorn *Emancipatiemonitor 2004* (Sociaal en Cultureel Planbureau/CBS, Den Haag, November 2004) pp 116–131.

[51]   Fast stream dispute resolution regarding custody: Draft-Art 1:253a (EK 2005–2006, 29 676, A, onderdeel R) and fast stream dispute resolution regarding access: Draft-Art 1:377e of the Dutch Civil Code (EK 2005-2006, 29 676, A, onderdeel X).

[52]   TK 2004–2005, 29 676, nr 8, p 6–7.

[53]   TK 22-1400 (16 November 2005), amendment De Pater-van der Meer; TK 2005–2006, 29 676, nr 31.

[54]   TK 22-1406 (16 November 2005), Minister Donner.

[55]   TK 22-1402 (16 November 2005), Mr Weekers (VVD (liberal party)).

adverse side effects – of such a measure in other countries. The superficial attractions do not seem to weigh up against the important practical concerns, as well as the fear for spiralling of disputes, signalled by the Minister of Justice. Moreover, the proposal as now presented to the First Chamber provides for fast stream dispute resolution for cases in which the problem is that one parent has failed to comply with an agreement between the parties or a court order regarding custody or contact. It does not address any other problems concerning custody and contact, such as that the arrangement has proved unworkable, for example, for reasons outside the control of the parties.[56] It seems curious and inconsistent with the alleged policy behind the fast stream dispute resolution that there is in such cases no possibility to bring the matter to court under the fast procedure. These disputes will be brought under the slow procedure, which because of the queue-jumping effect of the 'fast track' cases, can be expected to become even slower in the future than they are now.

A third line of action in the Luchtenveld Bill in which the primacy of joint custody is pursued is the restriction on the parents' right to apply to the court for an order for sole custody. Mr Luchtenveld has pursued this policy with a variety of different instruments. In the original proposal it was provided that a parent would only be allowed to apply for sole custody *of the other parent* (emphasis added).[57] The Minister of Justice was very properly critical of this proposal, which reflects a failure to appreciate that in some circumstances a parent must have the possibility to protect the child's interests by requesting sole custody of him or herself. Such a case had to be decided by the Dutch Supreme Court on 18 March 2005. In the light of the very strict policy of the Supreme Court and legislator in favour of joint custody, the Leeuwarden Appeal Court had refused to award sole custody to the mother even though the father, who was addicted to drugs, led a peripatetic existence so that communication with him was impossible and who because of his psychological disturbances and aggressive behaviour constituted a persistent threat to the children. The Dutch Supreme Court held that on these facts that the Leeuwarden Appeal Court had been too cautious and that it was appropriate to award sole custody to the mother.[58] The upshot of this case is that total restriction of the possibility to apply for sole custody is unacceptable.

In a Second Amendment Memorandum Mr Luchtenveld had a second try at restricting the possibility of obtaining sole custody. This Amendment proposed that it should be possible for one parent to apply *for suspension or removal of the other parent's parental rights* if it were established that there was 'an unacceptable risk that, because of communication problems between the parents, the child's interests would be ignored or negated and that improvement in the situation is not foreseeable'. In this proposal the traditional distinction between, on the one hand, applying for a custody order

---

56   TK 22-1406 (16 November 2005), Minister van Justitie.
57   TK 2004–2005, 29 676, nr 5: Draft-Art 1:251(5) of the Dutch Civil Code; Article I, part O; Draft-Art 1:253n (1) of the Dutch Civil Code, Art I, part T.
58   Dutch Supreme Court, 18 March 2005, LJN AS8525.

in the context of a dispute between the parents and, on the other hand, an application for a child protection measure, is confounded. There are very good reasons for applying a higher threshold for intervention in the latter case, which involves a conflict between the interests of the state and those of an individual, than in the former case, which involves a conflict between two family members. This difference was accepted by the European Court of Human Rights in the case of *Soderbäck v Sweden*.[59] It is not evident that this distinction can be swept aside, certainly not without explanation. In effect the parent is being given a sledgehammer to crack a nut. Undoubtedly, considering the policy pursued by the Luchtenveld Bill, the hope was that the sledgehammer would not be used at all. These arguments did persuade Mr Luchtenveld that this measure was also not suitable to pursue his goal. So he had a third try.

In the version of the Bill which is now pending before the First Chamber the policy of restricting the application for sole custody is pursued in another way. The Bill now provides that a parent is not entitled to apply for a sole custody order during the marriage. Only in the context of the divorce proceedings or subsequent to the divorce is an application for custody possible.[60] The criteria for the grant of sole custody are the same as those used in the Government Bill, expounded at the opening of this section. This is also a strange provision. It goes against all the developments in family law in the last 15 years which separate marriage from parenthood, or the role of a person as a parent from their role as a partner. It seems that a parent who feels the need to obtain a sole order for custody must first ensure that divorce proceedings are pending. Suppose that the parent is not able to share custody with the other parent, perhaps because of mental illness or drug addiction of the latter, but still loves the other parent and does not want a divorce. A custody order may be needed in the interests of the children and because of the practicalities of everyday decisions; nevertheless perhaps the parent who is caring for the children is still ready to wait on the chance that in the future the errant partner will recover, as partner or as parent of the children. The case mentioned above decided by the Dutch Supreme Court on 18 March 2005 may be such a case. Another problem is the situation where the parent who wishes to arrange sole custody cannot file for a divorce because of conscientious objections. There are significant minority groups in the Netherlands, strict Protestant groups, and also immigrants (the new Dutchmen!), who are opposed to divorce in any form. I should think the First Chamber should be very reluctant to accept this provision.

In a fourth provision the Luchtenveld Bill seeks to uphold joint custody by restricting the possibility of appeal against decisions concerning contact and custody. In the Luchtenveld Bill such decisions are included in a list of decisions regarding which appeal and cassation is not permitted.[61] When reviewing the original proposal before it was introduced in the Second

---

59   Eur Court HR, 28 October 1998, Reports of Judgments and Decisions 1998-VII, p 3086, § 31.

60   Draft-Article 1:251a(1) of the Dutch Civil Code; EK 2005–2006, 29 676, A, onderdeel P.

61   Article 807 *Wetboek van Burgerlijke Rechtsvorderingen* (Code of Civil Procedure); EK 2005–2006, 29 676, A, Artikel IV, onderdeel C.

Chamber the Council of State had advised reconsideration of this measure. The Minister of Justice also warned against this exclusion of appeal possibilities in a letter to the Second Chamber on 18 November 2005. Considering the profound effect upon family life which decisions regarding custody and contact can have on the lives of the individuals affected, the Minister advised that the right of appeal be retained.[62] In my view it is regrettable that this advice was not followed. The restriction on appeal only applies to the types of dispute for which the fast track dispute resolution is provided; it thus applies only to disputes regarding the failure by one parent to comply with an agreement or court order regarding custody or contact. Thus, appeals regarding disputes about other matters affecting contact and custody are not excluded. Some disputes may concern partly non-compliance by one partner, partly other matters. Therefore, fine distinctions will be made as to whether the dispute is covered by the exclusion or not. This signals a further objection to the proposed exclusion; namely that fine distinctions will lead to excessive complexity.

C Procedural requirement to submit parenthood plan

In both Bills it is emphasised that primary responsibility for the continuation of parenthood following divorce lies with the parents. The objective is to ensure that both parents, in drawing up their plans for divorce and thereafter, will take account of the consequences of the divorce for the children and that regarding these matters they will make practical agreements which are susceptible to control and scrutiny. A key element in both Bills is the imposition of a requirement upon the parents to draw up a parenting plan. The desirability of such requirement had already been noted much earlier in the Second Chamber,[63] and the requirement of making a parenting plan had already been proposed by the De Ruiter Commission when conducting a review of divorce procedure some 10 years ago.[64] However, in the Bills presently under discussion, the requirement of making a parenting plan is incorporated into the divorce procedure in a totally different way. In the Government Bill the requirement is integrated into the petition procedure by which divorce proceedings are commenced. The Bill proposes the addition of two new sections to Art 815 of the Code on Civil Procedure, in which it is specified that the petition document initiating the divorce proceedings is accompanied by a parenting plan regarding the children as to which the spouses jointly, or one of them solely, hold or holds custody.[65] In order to discourage avoidance of this requirement, the requirement of a parenting plan applies to a sole petition as well as a joint one.[66] The same requirement is applied in case of an application for judicial separation and in an application to the court for termination of a registered partnership.[67]

---

62   TK 2005–2006, 29 676, nr 32.

63   Motie De Pater-van der Meer cs, TK 2002–2003, 28 600, VI, nr 112.

64   Rapport van de commissie herziening scheidingsprocedure *Anders scheiden* (Den Haag, 1996).

65   Government Bill, Art II, part A.

66   TK 2004–2005, 30 145, nr 3, p 5.

67   Article 1:80c(1)(c) of the Dutch Civil Code (application to the court by one partner requesting judicial termination of the registered partnership).

Registered partnership can also be terminated extra-judicially, by contract in a specified form. The Dutch Civil Code allows contractual termination if the partners are in agreement: the contract must declare the moment at which the partners agreed that the partnership was ended, and the contract must be signed and dated by both partners and one or more advocate or *notaris*. Accordingly, in order to apply the requirement of parenting plan also to this procedure, it is specified that if a registered partnership is terminated by agreement that agreement should include a parenting plan.[68] However, failure to include such a plan will not be a ground for having the contract annulled.[69] The parenting plan should contain appointments between the parents regarding the following matters: division of tasks of care and upbringing (Art 1:247 of the Dutch Civil Code) or, in the case of sole custody, the exercise of contact (Art 1:377a of the Dutch Civil Code); the manner of providing information to, and consultation with, the parent with whom the child does not live; and the costs of care and upbringing of the children. The document must be signed by both parents. The parenting plan can be included in the divorce covenant or in the document of petition or it can be attached as a separate document to the petition. In the light of the requirement to provide documentation in support of the petition (Art 111, third paragraph of the Code of Civil Procedure), it should be specified in the petition document as to which matters the divorcing parties have reached agreement, as to which matters agreement still has to be reached and the reasons for the failure to reach agreement on those matters. Furthermore the document of petition should record in which manner the children have been involved in drawing up the parenting plan.[70] Although the requirement of signalling the measure of involvement of the children in the drawing up of the parenting plan as such is not a bad idea, it should be borne in mind that the present practice on this score is not very promising. There is every reason to be concerned that divorcing parents are generally not very likely to consider, of their own motion, their children's interests, and that research shows that according to the present practice, mediators are also not very inclined to involve the children.[71] Extra attention needs to be given to this matter during the training of mediators and advocates specialised in family law matters.

At the present time 52.1% of all divorce petitions (in 2003) are joint. In the case of joint petitions it is not to be expected that the spouses will have great trouble in drawing up a parenting plan. Contrariwise in the case of sole petitions it is quite likely that the relationship is so disturbed that the spouses will not be able to reach agreement on any of the matters listed or draw up a parenting plan. In such cases the parent filing the divorce petition is able to

---

[68] Draft-Article 1:80d, second paragraph of the Dutch Civil Code; Government Bill, Art I, part C.

[69] In response to a comment by the Council of State in the stage of preliminary review of the Bill the government replied that the sanction of annulment would not be imposed, TK 2004–2005, 30 145, nr 4, p 2–3.

[70] Draft-Article 815, third paragraph of the Code of Civil Procedure.

[71] B E S Chin-A-Fat *Scheiden (ter)echter zonder rechter? Een onderzoek naar de meerwaarde van scheidingsbemiddeling,* sdu uitgevers (Den Haag, 2004) regarding the three propositions see, respectively, pp 287, 260 and 286.

fulfil the statutory requirements in another way, such that the divorce petition will be admissible.[72] The petitioning spouse must then give a convincing explanation as to why it has not been possible to draw up a parenting plan and thereafter indicate, from his or her point of view, how parenthood should continue in the post-divorce situation.[73]

The court must decide whether the documents produced in combination with the divorce petition satisfy the statutory formal requirements for admissibility and whether the parenting plan submitted, or the documents produced in default thereof, satisfy the substantive requirements. In a proposed Draft-Art 818 of the Code of Civil Procedure the court is empowered to inform the parties in written form prior to the hearing, or at the hearing itself, that the court refers the parties to a mediator in order to try to achieve agreement on the matters regarding which agreement has not yet been attained.[74] The referral consists of producing a list of mediators from which the parties are free to make a selection. The parties are not obliged to accept the referral. If there is no parenting plan and neither party is able to give a reasonable explanation as to why such plan has not been drawn up, and moreover taking into account the alternative material produced instead of a parenting plan, the court is entitled to declare the petition inadmissible. It should be noted, however, that the refusal by the parties to make use of a mediator is not of itself a ground for a declaration of inadmissibility.[75] In the context of the Luchtenveld Bill the Minister of Justice explained to the Second Chamber on 10 October 2005 the practical arrangements regarding payment for mediation by the less well off and also announced a universal measure to promote the use of mediation.[76] These measures are explained in **IV.E** below.

The extent to which the requirement of a parenting plan can actually be expected to be effective in achieving its goal of promoting children's interests in the divorce situation will depend upon the effectiveness of judicial scrutiny of the parenting plan. To what extent does the court have a clear view of the actual needs of children and to what extent is the court able to prick through the wall of parental interests which often obscures those of the children? The Minister of Justice insists that the child's interests are and will continue to be subject to strict judicial scrutiny, and points out that in a recent case an appeal court had rejected a joint divorce petition requesting the court to order sole custody to one of the parents.[77] However the structural situation does seem to be rather different. A study of 3,339 divorce orders granted by the 's-Hertogenbosch Regional Court in 2002 and 2003 reveals that, in cases where the petition is joint, the court conducts the barest of

---

72   Draft-Article 815(5) of the Code on Civil Procedure; Government Bill, Art II, part A.
73   TK 2004–2005, 30 145, nr 3, p 5–6 (Explanatory Memorandum accompanying Government Bill).
74   Government Bill, Art II, part B.
75   TK 2004–2005, 30 145, nr 3, p 18 (Explanatory Memorandum accompanying Government Bill).
76   TK 2005–2006, 29 676, nr 24.
77   Second Chamber 2004–2005, 30 145, nr 3, p 10; 's-Hertogenbosch Appeal Court, 15 April 2004, LJN-nummer AO7714.

scrutiny; in contrast, where the petition is sole, the court scrutiny is more thorough.[78]

What about the procedural position of children themselves? A gesture in their direction is made by the proposal in the Government Bill that the procedure for appointing a special representative in cases of serious conflict of interest between the parent and child, pursuant to Art 1:250 of the Dutch Civil Code, should be simplified. At present the court by which the main issue is pending, for example, in a custody dispute, is not empowered to appoint a special representative to represent the child. Instead, if the need for separate representation of the child becomes apparent, the proceedings have to be stayed whilst such application is made to the Kantonal court. In the Government Bill it is proposed that the court by which the matter is pending should be empowered to appoint the special representative.[79] This is a sensible proposal, but does in no respect do justice to the claim that a child who is of sufficient maturity to appreciate his or her interests, should have the right of access to court, just as an adult does.[80] In a recent judgment the Dutch Supreme Court has set out the issues which the court should consider when considering whether to exercise its power to appoint a special representative for the child.[81]

The Luchtenveld Bill also provides for a parenting plan, and does so as in the Government Bill by imposing a requirement in the petition procedure.[82] Furthermore the Luchtenveld Bill includes a normative definition of the obligations implied by joint custody as follows. According to the Luchtenveld Bill the existing paras (2) to (4) of Art 1:251 of the Dutch Civil Code are replaced by new paras (2) to (4) (highlighted by these authors in italics). According to the Luchtenveld Bill (as now pending in the First Chamber) the article reads as follows:

'1. During marriage parents exercise custody jointly.

2. *Following termination of the marriage otherwise than by death or judicial separation, parents who continue to hold custody jointly shall exercise that custody in an egalitarian manner.*

3. *A child regarding whom the parents, as provided in paragraph (2) above, exercise joint custody, following divorce retains the right to be cared for and brought up by both parents, in accordance with Article 1:247 Dutch Civil Code.*

---

78   E Beenen and P Vlaardingerbroek 'Doorlopend gezag in de praktijk' *Tijdschrift voor Familie- en Jeugdrecht* (2004) pp 36–40.

79   Draft-Article 1:250 of the Dutch Civil Code; Government Bill, Art I, part H.

80   Article 6 of the ECHR; see 'Seven steps to achieving full participation of children in the divorce process' in J C M Willems (ed) *Developmental and Autonomy Rights of Children: empowering children, care-givers and communities* (Intersentia, Antwerp/Groningen/Oxford, 2002) pp 105–140. The case for direct access to the court for children in family matters was argued in the Netherlands a few years back in a study completed in 2002, but the recommendation was not accepted by the government: see M Steketee, A Overgaag and K Lünneman 'Met een bijzondere curator of zelf naar de rechter?' *Tijdschrift voor familie- en jeugdrecht* (2004) pp 177–183.

81   Dutch Supreme Court, 4 February 2005, *Nederlandse Jurisprudentie*, 2005, 422.

82   Luchtenveld Bill in the form now pending in the First Chamber, Art IV, part F (proposed amendment to Art 815 of the Code on Civil Procedure).

4. *Parents as provided in paragraph (2) above, take account, as regards the
    form to be given to the rights provided in paragraph (3) in the agreements
    to be made in a parenting plan as provided in Article 815(2) Code on
    Civil Procedure, or by any modification thereof, of the following:*
    a. *The child's interests;*[83]
    b. *The division between the parents inter se of the tasks of care
        and upbringing during the marriage;*
    c. *Practical difficulties arising from the termination of the
        marriage or thereafter and for as long as such difficulties
        continue;*
    d. *Such division, that both parents remain to a sufficient degree in
        contact with their children.'*[84]

It has been explained above in **IV.B**, in the discussion of the third criterium,
that in the Luchtenveld Bill it was intended that the possibility of applying
for sole custody should be restricted. As explained above, an application for
sole custody is possible after the divorce order has been made. By dint of an
amendment to the Luchtenveld Bill introduced by Kalsbeek and Van der
Meer[85] and voted in by the Second Chamber[86] it is also possible for a child
of 12 years or older to make an informal contact to the court signalling that
he or she would appreciate an order for sole custody. The court is then
empowered to make an order of its own motion. A child younger than 12
years is also entitled to make such application if he or she is deemed to
understand his or her interests in the matter. This is an understandable
application of the longer standing 'informal access to court' procedure, by
which children may make their interests known to the court in matters of
access or custody.[87]

The special problems experienced by unmarried parents are recognised in
the Luchtenveld Bill in which modification of Art 1:252 of the Dutch Civil
Code is proposed. In this proposal the possibility that unmarried parents who
separate have drawn up a parenting plan is given statutory recognition.
Unmarried parents, like married parents, are both to retain parental rights
following separation,[88] and are required to make agreements regarding
parenting which are to be included in a parenting plan.[89] In a letter addressed
to the Second Chamber on 6 June 2005 the Minister of Justice, not to be
outdone, went a step further by proposing that unmarried parents should be
obliged to draw up a parenting plan whenever one of them makes an

---

[83] This phrase regarding the child's interests was not in the original Luchtenveld Bill but was
      proposed by amendment by MP Kalsbeek (TK 2005–2006, 29 676, nr 21), supported by the
      Minister of Justice during debate (TK 22-1408) and voted in by the Second Chamber on 22
      November 2005 (TK 24-1572 lk).
[84] Luchtenveld Bill, Art I, part O.
[85] TK 2005–2006, 29 676, nr 26.
[86] TK 24-1572 (22 November 2005).
[87] For explanation, C Forder, above n 80.
[88] Although this is far from clear, as the relevant provision, Draft-Art 1:252(3) of the Dutch Civil
      Code refers to 'following divorce', which seems inappropriate in the case of separation of
      unmarried parents.
[89] TK 2004–2005, 29 676, nr 5, Art I, part Q, EK 2005–2006, 29 676, A, Art I, part Q. (Bill in the
      form now pending in the First Chamber of Parliament).

application for sole custody (in accordance with Art 1:253c of the Dutch Civil Code) or an application for termination of joint custody (in accordance with Art 1:253n of the Dutch Civil Code).[90] However, the Luchtenveld Bill as currently pending in the First Chamber of Parliament retains the original proposal.[91]

The Luchtenveld Bill assumes there are to be two routes for obtaining a divorce; the presently existing route via petition to the court and a second route (explained in **IV.E** below) of administrative divorce. In the original Bill Mr Luchtenveld had envisaged that the possibility of administrative divorce would be available to all couples. However, by amendment introduced by MPs Kalsbeek and De Pater-Van der Meer[92] and accepted by vote of the Second Chamber[93] the Bill as it is now pending in the First Chamber provides that the possibility of administrative divorce is not available to spouses who exercise joint or sole custody over one or more children.[94] Furthermore, by a further amendment introduced by Kalsbeek and De Pater-Van der Meer,[95] and accepted by the Second Chamber,[96] administrative divorce is also not available to registered partners who have joint or sole custody over one or more minor children.[97] Personally, I find this exclusion from administrative divorce of spouses and registered partners with children a significant improvement, as the administrative divorce procedure seems to provide even less safeguards for the children's interests than the judicial procedure. The requirement of a parenting plan, apart from the fact that it is really not new, as many advocates already use such a plan, provides no extra safeguards for the child. As shown above, research shows that at the present time, mediators do not in general have the practice of involving children in the process of mediation. Moreover, this must be done, in any case, with great care and respect for the vulnerable position of children. A proposed amendment in the Second Chamber which would have provided for an experiment for the purposes of which administrative divorce would be provided to spouses in a limited part of the country, in order to gain some experience with administrative divorce as applied to children,[98] was rejected by vote of the Second Chamber.[99]

---

[90] TK 2004–4005, 29 676, nr 13.

[91] EK 2005–2006, 29 676, A, Art I, Part Q.

[92] TK 2005–2006, 29 676, nr 25 (10 November 2005).

[93] TK 24-1570-1571 (22 November 2005).

[94] Draft-Art 1:149a; Luchtenveld Bill, Art I, part J.

[95] TK 2005–2006, 29 676, nr 25.

[96] TK 24-1572 lk-rk (22 November 2005).

[97] In a further amendment by Kalsbeek and De Pater-Van der Meer (TK 2005–2006, 29 676, nr 27) the unsatisfactory situation caused by the inability of the court to make ancillary orders regarding children when an application to the court had been made for termination of a registered partnership was pending was addressed. The Second Chamber voted for this proposal (TK 24-1573) resulting in the introduction of Art I, onderdeel G to the Bill pending in the First Chamber.

[98] Sub-amendment by MPs Van der Laan and Weekers, TK 2005–2006, 29 676, nr 28 (16 November 2005).

[99] TK 24-1573 (22 November 2005).

D   Proposed reforms to law concerning contact

The Government Bill includes three proposed changes to the substantive law regarding contact. First, the Bill provides that a child has a right to contact with both parents or to another person with whom the child has a close personal relationship.[100] According to present law the child already has a right of contact with the parent who does not have custody. The statutory regulation of the right of contact with a parent with custody and a person who has a close personal relationship to the child is novel. However, in the light of other proposed amendments in the Bill it is unclear why this part of the Bill refers to 'contact' at all: as we have seen in **IV.B** above, the old-fashioned concepts of access and contact were to be replaced with the new terms 'tasks of care and upbringing'. Secondly, the Bill proposes that the parent who does not have custody will be obliged to have contact with the child.[101] The parent who has custody is also subjected to a new obligation to support the contact between the child and the parent without custody, as discussed in **IV.B** above, which complements the right of access of the parent who does not have custody. Article 1:247 of the Dutch Civil Code already provides that parents who have joint custody are both obliged to have contact with the child. Thirdly, the person who has a close personal relationship to the child is to have a right to contact by dint of Draft-Art 1:377a(1) of the Dutch Civil Code. This proposal is drafted in particular for the benefit of a begetter who has not recognised his child, but who has a good relationship with the child and who has had a good relationship with the child's mother. The provision could also apply to a grandparent or ex-partner of the parent with custody. According to current law such person has a right to apply to the court for a contact order pursuant to Art 1:377f of the Dutch Civil Code. The proposed change would mean that the same statutory requirements – and in particular the strictly limited possibilities which the court has to refuse an order or to exclude contact – would apply to an application to the court for an order regulating contact as presently apply to an application by a parent. This amendment was considered necessary in order to avoid discrimination between legal father and begetters.[102]

In the original Luchtenveld Bill, as has been seen in **IV.B** above, various strategies were tried out which would make it more or less impossible to obtain sole custody. Under that scheme there would be little or no scope for contact provisions as parents would exercise contact by dint of custody. There would of course remain a need for contact provisions in circumstances in which custody is suspended or terminated in consequence of state intervention. The Luchtenveld Bill originally provided that, for the rare cases in which contact would be exercised, there should be a statutory minimum amount of contact. The court should establish contact for a minimum of 2

---

[100]   Draft-Article 1:377a(1) of the Dutch Civil Code; Government Bill, Art I, part O.

[101]   Draft-Article 1:377a(1), first sentence of the Dutch Civil Code.

[102]   TK 2004–2005, 30 145, nr 3, p 16 (Explanatory Memorandum accompanying the Bill); applying, as the Bill suggests, the European Court of Human Rights' judgment in *Sahin v Germany*, 11 October 2001, *Nederlandse Jurisprudentie*, 2002, 417 and in particular the annotation by Wortmann in which the relevance for Dutch law was signalled.

days per fortnight; parents would not be allowed to contract for a lesser amount.[103] The Council of State, when conducting its review of this Bill before it was presented to the Second Chamber, quite understandably commented that this proposal takes too little account of the child's interests. In certain cases restriction of access or a lesser amount than stipulated in this proposal, is needed. Fortunately an amendment by MP Kalsbeek,[104] proposing scrapping of this proposal, was accepted by the Second Chamber.[105]

E   Abolition of speedy divorce and introduction of administrative divorce

In both Bills it is proposed that the speedy divorce procedure should be abolished. This procedure owes its existence to the possibility to convert a marriage into a registered partnership (pursuant to Art 1:77a of the Dutch Civil Code), followed by the possibility of terminating the registered partnership by mutual contract, pursuant to Art 1:80c(1)(c) of the Dutch Civil Code as explained in **IV.C** above. Both Bills propose abolition of the procedure by repealing the possibility of converting a marriage into a registered partnership.[106] But then there is the question of whether administrative divorce should be introduced in the Netherlands. As far as the Minister of Justice is concerned there is no reason to introduce administrative divorce. Not that he has any objections in principle; his reasons are rather of a practical nature. His view is that, in comparison with the present procedure the advantages of administrative divorce are rather few. In order to be sure that the divorce will be recognised by other members of the European Union, compliance with the Brussel II-bis regulation is essential. That regulation requires a constitutive decision. Furthermore, as has been noted in **IV.C** above, the Minister of Justice is firmly attached to the idea that the court should carry out a judicial scrutiny when the parties divorce, safeguarding in particular the children's interests and those of the weaker party (if there is one) to the divorce. Furthermore in the Minister's view, the court is just as efficient and speedy as the administrative instance.[107]

Contrariwise the Luchtenveld Bill provides for administrative divorce; in fact it is one of its key elements. This element is present in the version which is currently pending in the First Chamber of Parliament. As has been noted in **IV.C** above, the administrative procedure will exist next to the present possibility of judicial divorce. As has been noted, the administrative route is not open to spouses who have sole or joint custody over any children. According to the proposal the Civil Status Registrar of the place of residence of one of the divorcing spouses is authorised to make an order for an

---

[103]   Draft-Article 1:377a(1) of the Dutch Civil Code; Luchtenveld Bill, Art I, part W.
[104]   TK 2004–2005, 26 676, nr 12 (24 May 2005).
[105]   TK 24-1572 lk (22 November 2005).
[106]   Luchtenveld Bill, EK 2005–2006, 29 676, A, Art I, part F; Government Bill, TK 2004–2005, 30 145, nr 2, Art I, part B.
[107]   TK 2004–2005, 30 145, nr 3, p 9–10; TK 2004–2005, 29 676, nr 8, pp 4–5.

administrative divorce. If neither spouse has a place of residence in the Netherlands, the civil status registrar in The Hague is authorised to pronounce the divorce.[108] Before granting the divorce order the spouses must declare to the civil status registrar that their marriage has irretrievably broken down and that for this reason they wish the marriage to be terminated. They must produce a document dated and signed by both spouses and by one or more advocate, *notaris* or divorce mediator,[109] stating that they were married under Dutch law and have jointly chosen for the applicability of Dutch law and that they have signed a contract in which they have reached agreement on a number of matters specified in Draft-Art 1:150 of the Dutch Civil Code. Draft-Article 1:150 provides that the contract must deal with the following matters: maintenance of the spouse who is not able to provide for him or herself, and who cannot be expected to earn his or her own income; an agreement regarding which spouse shall be the tenant of the main matrimonial home, or, if the matrimonial home is held in ownership, which spouse shall have a right to occupy the matrimonial home and use the contents, and for which period of time; the division of any community of property or financial compensation for the value of goods as agreed by matrimonial contract; provision for the sharing or compensating for the value of any pension rights.

The advocate, *notaris* or divorce mediator is in fact the only person who can actively safeguard the spouses' interests. Accordingly it is provided in Draft-Art 1:149b of the Dutch Civil Code that the advocate, *notaris* or divorce mediator is obliged:

(a) to inform the spouses of any relevant legislation [and hopefully also any relevant case-law – CJF] as well as to advise the spouses of the consequences of ending their marriages as well as of the choices which they make in consequence thereof;

(b) to examine whether the spouses' interests are reflected in a balanced manner in the agreement concluded pursuant to Art 1:150 of the Dutch Civil Code;

(c) the advocate, *notaris* or divorce mediator shall not sign the declaration pursuant to Draft-Art 1:149a of the Dutch Civil Code if, after considering the criteria in the first paragraph, he or she is of the opinion that the minor children's interests or the spouses' interests are insufficiently reflected in the agreement.

The reference in Draft-Art 1:149b(2) is curious, since the administrative divorce is not applicable to spouses who have sole or joint custody over children. Possibly this is a mistake.

---

[108] Draft-Article 1:149a(1) and (2) of the Dutch Civil Code; Luchtenveld Bill, Art I, part J.

[109] The divorce mediator must satisfy certain professional standards, which will be specified in secondary legislation, Draft-Art 1:149a(5) the Dutch Civil Code. This provision was inserted by amendment of MP Pater-Van der Meer, TK 2005–2006, 29 676, nr 29 (16 November 2005) and voted in favour by the second Chamber on 22 November 2005 (TK 24-1572 rk).

V ADJUSTMENTS TO MAINTENANCE PROVISIONS APPLICABLE TO REGISTERED PARTNERS

There has been a lot of discussion about the maintenance provisions applicable to registered partners who terminate their relationship in mutual agreement by contract pursuant to Art 1:80c(1)(c) of the Dutch Civil Code. The problems all stem from the original assumption that, because of the assumed absence of children in the partnership, there was less need to provide for the situation that one of the partners might not be able to provide for his or her needs following breakdown of the relationship. This assumption was not based on any scientific research and, in the meantime, there are legal provisions for sharing custody of children born within a registered partnership: an admission in law that the conditions may be present from which it is generally assumed that there is a risk of inequality of earning power. The question currently at issue is: if in the agreement by which the registered partnership is terminated with mutual agreement the parties have not made any provision regarding partner maintenance, does the partner who subsequently is unable to provide for his or her own maintenance have the right to make an application to the court for maintenance provision pursuant to Art 1:157 of the Dutch Civil Code? There is a further problem: if provision has been made for maintenance in the termination contract but the parties have not specified any time-limit after which the payment of maintenance should cease (the normal statutory limit for payment of maintenance is 12 years), the question arises whether the partner liable to pay maintenance is liable to do so until the death of one of the partners. In the Government Bill the limitation in time is provided for: a link is made to Art 1:157(4) and (6) and Art 1:158 of the Dutch Civil Code (in which the statutory time-limits are regulated) by including a new third paragraph in Draft-Art 1:80d.[110] In my view this reform leads to an unbalanced result. Article 1:157 attains a fine balance between the interests of the person obliged to pay the maintenance and the person entitled to receive it. In the Bill presently under discussion, the person liable to pay maintenance is given legal protection regarding the length for which he or she can be liable to pay. However, by contrast the right to apply to court for a maintenance order is not provided for. Even less easy to appreciate is the curious omission of any application of Art 1:157(5), which provides for the possibility of modification of the statutory limitation period if unmodified application should, in the light of the principles of reasonableness and fairness, not be expected of the person entitled to receive maintenance. Again, due to this omission, the person entitled to maintenance is under-protected. There seems no good reason for this.

---

[110] Government Bill, Art I, part C.

VI BILL TO REFORM THE SYSTEM FOR ESTABLISHING LIABILITY FOR AND ADJUSTMENT OF CHILD MAINTENANCE

There is no doubt that the present system of child maintenance is in urgent need of reform. Only 43–65% of mothers bringing up their children alone in the post-divorce situation receive child maintenance in respect of children under the age of 18. Furthermore, the lengthy procedures for establishing the liability to pay maintenance and the amount, followed by frequent adjustment procedures, have the unfavourable effect that a divorced couple remains, for a long period after the divorce, emotionally and materially tied to one another. Furthermore, the burden on the judiciary with all this disputation about child maintenance is considerable. How should these problems be dealt with? A Bill to reform the system of establishing child maintenance was introduced into the Second Chamber on 18 March 2004, and is now in an advanced stage of preparation.[111] The Bill is drafted with the intention that the present system, according to which a detailed investigation into the ability to pay of the person liable to pay maintenance is the pivotal element, should be replaced by the establishment of a flat-rate sum, the level of which will be fixed according to tables laid down in secondary legislation. The reason for this proposal lies in the conclusion of an interdepartmental investigation into the policy behind the maintenance system,[112] namely that the present child maintenance system causes an unequal division between the residential parent and the non-residential parent of the burden of bringing up children. The concern to protect the income of the person liable to pay maintenance in combination with the poor rate of enforcement lead in practice to the full load of the cost of the children's upbringing being borne by the residential parent. If the latter is dependent upon social security, the real costs are borne by the community. The drafters of the Bill purport to create a simple, transparent system for determining the level of child maintenance, by which it is hoped that parents will be facilitated to make clear and firm agreements, and that there will be little incentive to enter into discussion about the amount to be paid. The Bill has not had an easy path through the Second Chamber. When the Bill was introduced, it met opposition from all the factions on the left and centre[113] that there was too little scope for taking account of the circumstances of the person liable to pay maintenance, and that the system was too inflexible because of the restricted opportunities to ask for subsequent adjustment. In an Amendment Memorandum on 22 November 2004,[114] the government tried to meet these objections with three new measures.

---

[111] Wijziging van Boek 1 van het Burgerlijk Wetboek alsmede van enige andere wetten in verband met de vaststelling van kinderalimentaties, TK 2004–2005, 29 480, nr 13.

[112] *Het kind centraal: verantwoordelijkheid blijft* (Children first: responsibility stays) kabinetsstandpunt op 10 februari 2003, TK 2002–2003, 28 795, nr 1.

[113] *Partij van de Arbeid* (Social Democratic Party), *VVD partij* (Liberal Party) *D66 partij* (Liberal Party, more towards the centre than the *VVD partij*) and *Groenlinks* (Green Party).

[114] TK 2004–2005, 29 480, nr 10.

First, an effort was made to improve the opportunities to take account of the individual circumstances of the person liable to pay maintenance. The original Bill already provided for the possibility of adjustment of a level of maintenance which had already been fixed[115] whenever there was such a profound change of circumstances that a failure to change the level of maintenance would be unacceptable in the light of the principles of reasonableness and fairness. It had already been agreed that such profound circumstances were established whenever the income of the person liable to pay maintenance would, in consequence of making the maintenance payment, drop to 70% of the net minimum earnings or lower. In a new third paragraph to Art 1:406ab of the Dutch Civil Code the Amendment Memorandum made special provision for the situation in which the income of the person liable to pay maintenance would drop below 70% of the net minimum earnings in consequence of the fact that he is liable to pay maintenance to more than one child. In these circumstances the Bill, in consequence of the Amendment Memorandum, now provides that the National Office for Recovery of Maintenance (*Landelijk Bureau Inning Onderhoudsbijdragen*) can, at the request of the person liable to pay maintenance, change the amount originally established, such that the amount available is spread over all the children who depend upon the person liable to pay. This rule is in accordance with a rule already established in a recent decision of the Dutch Supreme Court.[116]

Secondly, in order to meet the objection that the system created by the Bill offers too little opportunity for applying for adjustment of the level of maintenance in consequence of an increase or decrease in earnings of the person liable to pay maintenance, the Amendment Memorandum introduced the possibility, in Draft-Art 1:406ab, paras (5) and (6) of the Dutch Civil Code, of requesting a review every 5 years. This possibility is additional to the possibility, mentioned above, of applying for a revision of the amount on the grounds of profound change of circumstances.

Thirdly, in a draft statutory instrument a number of specific provisions were introduced to deal with the situation of co-parenting. For such circumstances the fixed rates set out in tables are adjusted proportionate to the extent to which the parents have achieved a factual division of the upbringing of the child. This measure allows for each parent to make his or her contribution to maintenance of the children either with money or in kind. Furthermore, to make this construction more attractive from a fiscal point of view, the level of contribution in case of co-parenting is determined in relation to income received in the fiscal year just completed, and not, as is the normal case, the income received in the fiscal year 2 years earlier.[117] In my view this amendment opens the door to some very complex and time-consuming discussions, about the exact division of money and provision in kind.

---

[115]   Draft-Art 1:406ab of the Dutch Civil Code: Bill, Art I, part G.
[116]   Dutch Supreme Court, 22 April 2005, Rechtspraak van de Week 2005, 59.
[117]   TK 2004–2005, 29 480, nr 12, p 9–10.

The Bill is now in its final phase in the Second Chamber. Since the amendments the objections to the Bill are less fierce than they were. In the light of the objectives of the Bill, namely, to simplify the system and relieve the burden on the judiciary, the proposed flat-rate system is attractive. The problems of non-payment in the present system and the very serious consequences that this has on the earning-power and thus on the lives of women and children in the post-divorce situation, are very serious. However, there is still very strong support, especially from the judiciary, for retention of the old system, with some adjustment as it is agreed that the present system over-protects the interests of the person liable to pay maintenance.[118]

VII PRIVATE INTERNATIONAL LAW RULES IN THE FIELD OF REGISTERED PARTNERSHIP

The introduction in 1998 of a new formalised institution, namely registered partnership, alongside marriage, created a great deal of attention not only in family law circles, but also in Dutch (and of course foreign) private international law circles.[119] How were international cases to be dealt with? Was this family form to be governed by the same rules as those on marriages, or according to the rules on contractual agreements? Were foreign nationals allowed to register their partnership in the Netherlands? These and many other questions were answered in a report published by the *Staatscommissie* (State Commission) in May 1998. Although the *Staatscommissie* published explicit proposals for legislation, these proposals lay virtually untouched for more than 5 years, before eventually being enacted on 6 July 2004, and coming into force on 1 January 2005.[120] The influential nature of the *Staatscommissie* report is to be found in the Explanatory Notes to the Private International Law (Registered Partnerships) Act (*Wet conflictenrecht geregistreerd partnerschap*, hereinafter abbreviated to WCGP). Save for a few minor amendments, the text of the Explanatory Notes is more or less identical to the 1998 *Staatscommissie* report.[121] This section will thus deal with the three separate parts of this piece of legislation, namely the establishment of the relationship (**VII.A**), the rights and duties attributed to the parties (**VII.B**) and the dissolution of the relationship (**VII.C**)

A   Establishment of the relationship

One can ask one of two main questions when parties wish to register a partnership. First, if the partnership is to be registered in the Netherlands,

---

[118]   P van Teeffelen 'Kinderalimentatie op drift' *Tijdschrift voor familie- en jeugdrecht* (2005) pp 122–125.

[119]   For an overview of the situation in 1999, see Dutch report in A Bainham (ed) *The International Survey of Family Law 2000 Edition* pp 242–247.

[120]   Nonetheless, even before these rules become effective, they were being referred to by courts and Registrars. See, for example, Rb Roermond, 29 March 2001, *Tijdschrift voor Nederlands Internationaal Privaatrecht* (2001) p 188.

[121]   *Dutch Second Chamber*, 2002–2003, 28 924, No 3 (Explanatory Notes).

which law will be applicable to this registration (**VII.A.1**)? Secondly, if the partnership has already been registered abroad, then will this be afforded recognition in the Netherlands (**VII.A.2**)? The answer to the first question can be found by researching the relevant choice of law rules applicable to the registration of partnerships in the Netherlands, whilst the answer to the second question can be found in the rules on the recognition of partnerships registered abroad.

A.1 Choice of law rules

The choice of law rules governing the celebration of a marriage in the Netherlands stem from the 1978 Hague Convention on the Celebration and Recognition of the Validity of Marriages.[122] This Convention, currently in force in the Netherlands, Luxembourg and Australia, entered into force on 1 May 1991. The Convention has entered into force in the Netherlands by virtue of the Private International Law (Marriage) Act (*Wet conflictenrecht huwelijk*, hereinafter WCH). As the *Staatscommissie* had already pointed out in May 1998,[123] registered partnerships do not fall within the ambit of the 1978 Hague Marriage Convention or the WCH. Therefore, new choice of law rules needed to be formulated to deal with such relationships. In so doing, the Dutch Government opted to maintain a distinction between the formal and essential validity of the relationship. Although this distinction has been made, the end result is unsurprisingly uniform. According to Art 1(1) and (2) of the WCGP questions related to the formal and essential validity of partnerships registered in the Netherlands will be governed by Dutch law. This therefore means that all partnerships registered in the Netherlands will need to be registered in accordance with Art 1:80a *et seq* of the Dutch Civil Code. The alternative choice of law rule applicable to (same-sex) marriages is therefore not replicated with respect to registered partnerships.[124] The absence of such an alternative is easy to explain when one realises that the institution of registered partnership is not widely accepted. Both the *Staatscommissie* and the Dutch Government therefore felt that it was not unreasonable to require couples wishing to register their partnership in the Netherlands to comply with Dutch law.

A.2 Recognition of foreign relationships

When dealing with the recognition of relationships registered abroad, one must first address the preliminary issue of characterisation. Before one can determine whether a particular form of 'registered partnership' will be recognised in the Netherlands, the question must first be answered whether the registration can even be considered to be a form of 'registered partnership'. This legal issue can, however, be approached from two different perspectives. On the one hand, one can emphasise the contractual

---

[122] *Tractatenblad* 1987, No 137.

[123] Staatscommissie voor het Internationaal Privaatrecht *Advies van de Staatscommissie voor het Internationaal Privaatrecht inzake geregistreerd partnerschap* (The Hague: Staatscommissie, 1998).

[124] See Art 2(b) of the WCH.

nature of the relationship. The parties to a non-marital registered relationship agree upon certain legal effects pursuant to a mutual agreement; the moment the relationship is registered the contract becomes enforceable.[125] Alternatively, one could place more emphasis on the effect on the parties' personal status. Upon registering the relationship, the parties acquire a status as registered partners, with certain rights and duties, capacities and incapacities attendant upon that status.[126] Accordingly, one is confronted with a choice between two traditional private international law legal categories: personal status and contract.[127] Although this dilemma has been important in other jurisdictions, in the Netherlands a clear choice has been made for the latter of these two approaches.

In terms of the issue of characterisation, the legislation passed by the Dutch Parliament differs markedly from the recommendations of the *Staatscommissie*. Unlike the *Staatscommissie*, which left the question of characterisation open-ended, Art 2(5) of the WCGP provides for a list of criteria in order to determine whether a foreign relationship can be characterised as a 'registered partnership' for the purposes of the WCGP.[128] Article 2(5), in conjunction with Art 2(4), ordains the following criteria:

– the registration was completed before a competent authority in the place where it was entered into;[129]

– the institution is exclusive, ie that a registered partnership cannot be concluded alongside another registered partnership or marriage;[130]

– the partnership must only be concluded between two persons;[131]

– the solemnisation of the registered partnership creates obligations between the partners that, in essence, correspond with those in connection to marriage;[132]

– the partnership must be based on a legally regulated form of cohabitation.[133]

---

[125] See I Curry-Sumner *EFL Series: Volume 11. All's well that ends registered? The substantive and private international law aspects of non-marital registered relationships in Europe* (Antwerp: Intersentia, 2005) pp 46, 86–89, 125–127, 171–173, 217–221 and 265–266.

[126] C Allen 'Status and capacity' (1930) *Law Quarterly Review* 277–310 at 288. He comments on the fact that a status is the state of being from which a number of capacities and incapacities flow. A status is thus, according to him, 'the condition of belonging to a particular class of persons to whom the law assigns certain peculiar legal capacities or incapacities or both'.

[127] Some authors believe one should distinguish between the category of marriage and the category of contract: S Henneron 'New forms of cohabitation: private international law aspects of registered partnerships' in K Boele-Woelki (ed) *EFL Series: Volume 4. Perspectives for the harmonisation and unification of family law in Europe* (Antwerp: Intersentia, 2004) pp 464–468 and G Kessler *Les partenariats enregistrés en droit international privé* (Paris: LGDJ, 2004) pp 69–76.

[128] On the interaction of Art 2(1) and (5) of the WCGP see I Sumner 'Private international law aspects of registered partnership: Great Britain and The Netherlands compared' in A Bonomi and B Cottier (eds) *Aspects de droit international privé des partenariats enregistrés en Europe* (Zurich: Schultess, 2004) Vol No 49, pp 29–59 at 55–57.

[129] Article 2(4) and (5)(a) of the WCGP.

[130] Article 2(5)(b) of the WCGP.

[131] Article 2(5)(b) of the WCGP.

[132] Article 2(5)(c) of the WCGP.

[133] Article 2(5) of the WCGP.

The dearth of a characterisation provision in the original proposals by the *Staatscommissie* and in the current work on the codification of Dutch private international law has, fortunately, not been followed by the legislator.[134] Nonetheless, although these criteria appear clear and workable, a certain degree of confusion surrounds the precise application of Art 2(5)(c) of the WCGP. According to the wording of the article, the obligations which the partners owe to each other should correspond with those in connection to marriage. However, in the Explanatory Notes to the Act it is stated:

> 'The proposed rules also lend themselves to application on legal institutions which do not have the name "registered partnership", but still possess the key characteristics thereof, even if not completely. Examples are the Belgian statutory cohabitation, the PACS in France and the statutory regulated cohabitation forms in Catalonia and Aragon.'[135]

It is, therefore, not entirely clear how these criteria will be interpreted. Although the Explanatory Notes refer to the subsequent promulgation of information on these criteria, no such information has been released. Which foreign relationships satisfy these criteria is thus still an unanswered question. A better solution would have been if certain 'registered partnerships' would have been *a priori* listed as having fulfilled such criteria, leaving the criteria to be applied on an *ad hoc* basis for new forms of 'registered partnership'.[136]

Nonetheless, once it has been determined that a foreign relationship can be characterised as a 'registered partnership' for the purposes of the WCGP, the question is whether such a relationship will then be recognised. The starting point for both the Dutch Government and the *Staatscommissie* was that the recognition rules on registered partnership should correspond to the equivalent recognition rules for marriage.[137] As a result, Art 2(1) of the WCGP is a replica of Art 5(1) of the WCH, subject to the standard public policy exception.[138]

The distinction thus created between registered partnership and marriage in terms of foreign relationships is a very difficult one and will thus often turn on semantics. For example, a Swedish registered partnership, which in

---

[134] On the lack of a provision dealing with characterisation in the proposals for the codification of Dutch private international law, see H U Jessurun D'Oliveira 'Autonome kwalificatie in het internationaal privaatrecht: geregistreerde niet-huwelijkse relaties' in K Boele-Woelki, C H Brants and G J W Steenhoff (eds) *Het plezier van de rechtsvergelijking. Opstellen over unificatie en harmonisatie van het recht in Europa, aangeboden aan prof. mr. E.H. Hondius bij gelegenheid van zijn afscheid als voorzitter en bestuurslid van de Nederlandse Vereniging voor Rechtsvergelijking* (Deventer: Kluwer, 2003) pp 141–154 at 1-4 and P Vlas 'De Algemene Bepalingen als sluitstuk van de codificatie van het Nederlandse IPR' *Weekblad voor Privaatrecht, Notariaat en Registratie* (2003) pp 443–449 at 443.

[135] *Dutch Second Chamber*, 2002–2003, 28 924, No 3, p 3.

[136] Such a solution has, for example, been adopted in the UK. See further I Curry-Sumner *EFL Series: Volume 11. All's well that ends registered? The substantive and private international law aspects of non-marital registered relationships in Europe* (Antwerp: Intersentia, 2005) pp 341–343.

[137] Article 18, Staatscommissie voor het Internationaal Privaatrect *Geregistreerd partnerschap* (The Hague: Staatscommissie, 1998) p 29 and *Dutch Second Chamber*, 2002–2003, 28924, No 3, p 10.

[138] Article 3 of the WCGP.

Sweden is virtually identical to marriage, will more than likely be recognised in the Netherlands in accordance with the rules laid down by the WCGP and not under the WCH.[139] Although in the majority of cases this will not lead to differences in the legal rights offered to same-sex couples, this may be of importance should the parties have children. Take the following example:

Lotta and Janik, both Swedish nationals, register their partnership in Stockholm. They subsequently use the possibilities for artificial insemination and Lotta conceives a child. According to Swedish law both Lotta and Janik are the legal parents of the child. The following year the parties decide to move to Almere, the Netherlands.

Two questions arise: the first in relation to the recognition of the parties' relationship and the second in relation to the mother-child relationship created between the partner of the birth mother and the child. Lotta and Janik's relationship would satisfy the characterisation criteria laid down in Art 2(5) of the WCGP.[140] As such they would be determined to have validly registered a partnership according to Swedish law. The question arises whether their relationship could be regarded as a marriage, and would thus fall within the scope of the WCH. However, it is unlikely that a Dutch court or registrar would characterise a Swedish registered partnership as a marriage, even though according to Swedish law there is no difference between a registered partnership between same-sex couples and a marriage between different-sex couples. Especially in light of the fact that the Swedish Government is now reviewing the registered partnership legislation and investigating the possibility to open marriage to same-sex couples, it would seem highly unlikely that a Dutch competent authority would characterise a Swedish registered partnership as a marriage.

However, the second question then relates to the issue of parentage. The couple would arrive in the Netherlands requesting the determination of the legal status of the birth mother's partner in respect of the child; namely is Janik the legal mother of the child? The question depends upon whether the Dutch competent authority would regard the question as requiring the application of the Dutch choice of law rules or the Dutch recognition rules. If the parties are asking for the determination *in the Netherlands* of Janik's legal parentage, then one could argue that resort would need to be made to Chapter 1 of the WCA. According to Art 1(1) of the WCA the parentage of the birth mother and her 'husband' will be determined according to the law of the parties' common nationality, or in the absence thereof of their common habitual residence, or in the absence thereof according to the habitual residence of the child. Two issues arise on the basis of this article. First, the article is phrased in gender-specific terminology, causing problems for the recognition of joint legal parentage of same-sex couples. Secondly, if

---

[139] This solution would thus follow the approach adopted by the European Court of Justice in the case of *D and Sweden v Council* where a Swedish registered partnership was held not to be considered as equivalent to a marriage in determining eligibility to spousal housing allowance.

[140] For further information on the application of these criteria, see I Curry-Sumner *EFL Series: Volume 11. All's well that ends registered? The substantive and private international law aspects of non-marital registered relationships in Europe* (Antwerp: Intersentia, 2005) pp 337–338.

the parties have already been determined to have registered a partnership and not celebrated a marriage, this article would more than likely be deemed not to be applicable. Further analysis of the WCA also indicates no rule which would allow Janik to have her legal parentage recognised. Obviously there appears to have been little thought paid to the ensuing consequences of characterisation of a particular relationship as a marriage or a registered partnership. It will thus have to be seen whether these distinctions are able to stand the test of time.

Alternatively the Dutch competent authority could decide that the question posed by Janik centres on the recognition of a legal familial tie established abroad. This approach would centre on the question of whether the Dutch authorities could regard the 'by operation of law' presumption as a legal fact (*rechtsfeit*) in the sense of Art 10 of the WCA. If this could be done, then there are possibilities for this form of same-sex parentage to be recognised in the Netherlands, as long as it is not contrary to Dutch public policy. In the light of the fact that Dutch law allows for two persons of the same sex to adopt a child, and thus become joint legal parents of a child, it would seem strange for a Dutch judge to argue that the recognition of joint parentage rights created in this manner would be contrary to Dutch public policy. With proposals having been made in England and Wales to introduce a similar presumption,[141] and such moves having already been made in California, it would appear that the time is right for the Dutch legislature to solve these inconsistencies in the field of private international law.

B   Rights and duties incumbent on the parties in the relationship

Space unfortunately limits the amount of time which can be dedicated to the complicated issues surrounding the rights and duties attributed to the parties by virtue of their registered partnership. In this section, light will only be shed on the issue of the law applicable to the partnership property regime (**VII.B.1**) and matters in relation to inheritance and children (**VII.B.2**).[142]

B.1 Partnership property regime

Although a new set of private international law rules applicable to the property law aspects of registered partners has been created in the Netherlands, these rules are based entirely on those rules laid down in the 1978 Hague Convention on the law applicable to matrimonial property regimes (1978 Hague MPR).[143] Although, as with spouses,[144] parties to a

---

[141]   Response by the Human Fertilisation and Embryology Authority to the Department of Health's consultation on the Review of the Human Fertilisation and Embryology Act, 24 November 2005, p 37, Question 55. See further www.hfea.gov.uk/AboutHFEA/HFEAPolicy/ReviewoftheHFEAct.

[142]   For further information on the other rights and duties, see I Curry-Sumner *EFL Series: Volume 11. All's well that ends registered? The substantive and private international law aspects of non-marital registered relationships in Europe* (Antwerp: Intersentia, 2005) Chapter XII.

[143]   I S Joppe 'Het geregistreerd partnerschap in het Nederlands IPR (II)' (Weekblad voor het Privaatrecht, Notariaat en Rgistratie, 2000) pp 391–395 at 392–393; E N Frohn 'De Wet conflictenrecht geregistreerd partnerschap' *tijdschrift voor familie- en jeugdrecht* (2004) pp 292–293.

[144]   Article 3 of the 1978 Hague MPR.

non-marital registered relationship have the freedom to choose the law applicable to their property regime regardless of where the relationship was registered,[145] a substantial difference in approach is apparent. Spouses are restricted in their choice of legal systems to the national law of the parties, the law of the habitual residence of the parties, the law of the first matrimonial habitual residence or the law of the place where immovable property is situated, for as far as this choice affects such immovable property.[146]

Registered partners, on the other hand, are totally free to choose any legal system to govern their property issues, as long as the chosen system recognises a form of non-marital registered relationship in the sense of the WCGP.[147] The parties need not have any connection with the chosen jurisdiction at all. However, it was probably not the intention of the Dutch legislature to grant registered partners such a wide freedom to choose their applicable law. When the *Staatscommissie* published its proposals outlining a set of private international law rules for registered partnerships,[148] the freedom to choose any country was enormously restricted by the need to choose a country which recognised a form of non-marital registered relationship.[149] By the time the proposals were eventually enacted, this freedom had grown substantially and should thus have been restricted in a similar manner to the restriction imposed on spouses.

B.2 Matters in relation to inheritance and children

Many private international law rules should be analysed within the broader context of their fields of operation, instead of being dealt with independently in relation to registered partnerships. Many private international law rules with respect to children, for example, do not focus solely on the parent's relationship. Instead the primary concern in the fields of parentage, parental responsibilities or adoption is normally the protection of children and the aspiration that decisions are taken in their best interests. In this way, both the jurisdiction and choice of law rules often reflect a greater degree of physical proximity than is perhaps evident in other areas of private international

---

[145]   Article 6(1) of the Neth PIL(RP)A. See further I S Joppe 'Het geregistreerd partnerschap in het Nederlands IPR (II)' (Weekblad voor het Privaatrecht, Notariaat en Rgistratie, 2000) pp 391–395 at 392.

[146]   Article 3 of the 1978 Hague MPR. Prior to 1978, spouses were entitled to a total freedom in their choice of jurisdiction, HR, 10 December 1976, *Nederlands Jurisprudence,* 1977, 275 (*Chelouche-Van Leer*). See further L Strikwerda *Inleiding tot het Nederlands Internationaal Privaatrecht* (Deventer: Kluwer, 8th edn, 2005) pp 137–140, 142–143.

[147]   Article 6(2) of the Neth PIL(RP)A. See further G J Steenhoff 'Nieuwe IPR-regels voor het partnersvermogensrecht in de WCGP' *Juridische Berichten voor het Notariaat* (2005) pp 9–11 at 9.

[148]   Staatscommissie voor het Internationaal Privaatrect *Geregistreerd partnerschap* (The Hague: Staatscommissie, 1998) p 21.

[149]   At that time, there were only four other countries with similar schemes (Denmark, Norway, Iceland and Sweden). G J Steenhoff 'Nieuwe IPR-regels voor het partnersvermogensrecht in de WCGP' *Juridische Berichten voor het Notariaat* (2005) pp 9–11 at 10.

law.[150] The physical presence of the child is often determinative for jurisdiction, ie the child's habitual residence, and the *lex fori* is usually applied automatically by virtue of child law being rooted in a country's public policy.[151] These aims are no different if the child is born in or brought into a registered partnership. Therefore, registered partnerships should simply be taken into account in the cornucopia of instruments already dealing with issues relating to children.

A rationale similar to that applied in the field of child law is also pertinent in the field of inheritance law. The private international law rules with respect to inheritance only become operational upon a person's death. The existence of a registered partnership or marriage only plays a subsidiary or incidental role in determining the overall form of such private international law rules. Consequently, any private international law rules relating to registered partners and their inheritance rights should be incorporated within the range of current and future inheritance law rules. Although any such rules must also be in conformity with the principles laid down with respect to the private international law aspects of registered partnerships, it is crucially important to ensure constancy of principle within the field of inheritance law. However, one cannot close one's eyes to the fact that, should a choice of law rule indicate that the law of a state is applicable which does not recognise registered partnerships then an alternative solution must be found.[152] As a result, instead of tampering with the existing private international law rules in inheritance, the Dutch Government has committed itself to investing more time and money in advising aspirant registered partners of the complications that may arise as a result of not drawing up a will.[153]

C   Dissolution of the relationship

C.1 Jurisdictional issues

In crafting international jurisdictional rules for the dissolution of registered partnerships the Netherlands has striven for simplicity. By virtue of Art 4(4) of the Dutch Code of Civil Procedure, the Brussels II-bis regime is *mutatis mutandis* applicable to all questions of international jurisdiction with respect to the dissolution of registered partnerships. In this way the Netherlands endorses one set of international jurisdictional rules applicable in all situations; the same grounds apply whether the case falls inside or outside

---

[150] See, for example, Recital 12, Brussels II-bis. This is furthermore underlined in allowing a *forum non conveniens* exception with respect to parental responsibility proceedings (Art 15 of the Brussels II-bis) and not in the field of divorce.

[151] See, for example, the decision of *Johnstone v Beattie* (1843) 10 Cl & Fin 42 at 120, where Lord Copley, Lord Chancellor stated that: 'The Lord Chancellor, representing the Sovereign as *parens patriae*, has a clear right to interpose the authority of the court for the protection of the person and property of all infants resident in England ...' and later, at 122: 'the benefit of the infant, which is the foundation of the jurisdiction, must be the test of its right exercise'.

[152] Staatscommissie voor het Internationaal Privaatrecht *Geregistreerd partnerschap* (The Hague: Staatscommissie, 1998) pp 9–12.

[153] *Dutch Second Chamber*, 2002–2003, 28 924, No 3, p 7.

the material scope of Brussels II-bis and whether the case involves the dissolution of a marriage or registered partnership. Alongside these rules, Dutch law also provides for the residuary jurisdiction of Dutch courts if the relationship was registered in the Netherlands.[154] In this way, Dutch law recognises the need for a *forum necessitatis*.[155]

When the Dutch *Staatscommissie* published its proposals in 1998, there were in fact only four countries besides the Netherlands that had introduced equivalent legislation, namely Denmark, Norway, Sweden and Iceland. It was thus deemed suitable to provide an unconditional forum for all those couples who had registered their partnership in the Netherlands. However, by the time the government eventually enacted legislation in this field, the number of jurisdictions to have introduced a form of registered partnership had increased dramatically. It would therefore have been advisable for the government to restrict this *forum necessitatis* to those couples who are unable to dissolve their relationship outside of the Netherlands.[156]

Furthermore, as a result of the passing of the WCGP, Art 1:80c of the Dutch Civil Code has also been amended so as to provide a general rule of competency for the Dutch Registrar of Births, Deaths, Marriages and Registered Partnerships with respect to the administrative dissolution of non-marital registered relationships. Article 1:80c(2) of the Dutch Civil Code now provides that the Dutch Registrar is competent on identical grounds to those laid down in Brussels II-bis,[157] thus furthering the simplicity in jurisdictional grounds for relationship breakdown in the Netherlands.

C.2 Choice of law rules

Despite the apparent complexity of the Dutch choice of law rules laid down in the WCGP, the ultimate scheme is based on a simple distinction. It is assumed that Dutch law will apply in all cases unless certain conditions are present.[158] As a result, three categories must be distinguished, namely:

---

154   Last sentence, Art 4(4) of the Dutch Code of Civil Procedure.

155   *Dutch Second Chamber*, 1999–2000, 26855, No 3, p 33 and thus following the advice of the Dutch Staatscommissie, see Staatscommissie voor het Internationaal Privaatrect *Geregistreerd partnerschap* (The Hague: Staatscommissie, 1998) p 35. Such a solution has also found academic support, for example, I S Joppe 'Het geregistreerd partnerschap in het Nederlandse IPR (II)' *Weekblad voor Privaatrecht, Notariaat en Registratie* (2000) pp 391–395 at 393–394 and P M M Mostermans 'Nieuw Europese scheidingsprocesrecht onder de loep: de rechtsmacht bij echtscheiding' *Nederlands Internationaal Privaatrecht* (2001) pp 293–305 at 304.

156   This solution has, for example, been followed in Switzerland (Art 65b of the Swiss Code of Private International Law) and England and Wales (Civil Partnership Act 2004, s 221(1)(c)(iii) (dissolution), s 221(2)(c)(iii) (nullity) and s 222(c) (presumption of death)), Scotland (Civil Partnership Act 2004, s 225(1)(c)(iii) (dissolution), s 225(3)(c)(iii) (nullity) and s 1(3)(c) of the Presumption of Death (Scotland) Act 1977, as amended by s 44, Sch 28 to the Civil Partnership Act 2004 (presumption of death)) and Northern Ireland (Civil Partnership Act 2004, s 229(1)(c)(iii) (dissolution), s 229(2)(c)(iii) (nullity) and s 230(c) (presumption of death)).

157   Article 1:80c(2) of the Dutch Civil Code refers to Art 4(4) of the Dutch Code of Civil Procedure, which in turn refers to Art 4(1) of the Dutch Code of Civil Procedure and thus to the application of the jurisdictional grounds stated in Brussels II-bis.

158   I S Joppe 'Het geregistreerd partnerschap in het Nederlands IPR (II)' *Weekblad voor Privaatrecht, Notariaat en Registratie* (2000) pp 391–395 at 393; L Frohn 'De Wet conflictenrecht geregistreerd

- registered partnerships registered in the Netherlands;
- registered partnerships registered abroad where dissolution is sought on the grounds of mutual consent; and
- registered partnerships registered abroad where dissolution is sought on the grounds of a sole petition.

In the first category, Dutch law, as both *lex fori* and *lex loci registrationis*, will be applied in all cases.[159] In the second category, Dutch law will be applied,[160] unless the parties have made a choice for the *lex loci registrationis*.[161] In the third category, Dutch law will also be applied,[162] unless either of the parties have jointly chosen for the *lex loci registrationis* or this choice has been made by one party and is not contested by the other,[163] or one party has made a choice of law for the place where the relationship was registered and both parties have close ties with that country.[164] The choice is, however, restricted to the substantive requirements of the dissolution; the form and manner in which the dissolution takes place will be determined according to Dutch law.[165] This approach is therefore based on the choice of law rules in the field of divorce as proposed by the Dutch *Staatscommissie*, save for the replacement of the choice for the *lex patriae* with the *lex loci registrationis*.

C.3 Recognition of dissolution orders obtained abroad

In drafting rules dealing with the recognition in the Netherlands of dissolutions obtained abroad a distinction has been drawn between those relationships terminated with mutual consent and those dissolved upon the request of one of the parties. Although this distinction has been made, the requirements therefore are identical. Four minimum conditions must therefore be satisfied, namely:

(1) A foreign relationship dissolution must have been obtained by a competent authority.[166] Whether the authority was competent is to be judged according to 'international standards' and not the jurisdictional rules of the issuing country or Dutch law.[167] However, if the Dutch authorities would have been competent on identical grounds, then it

---

partnerschap' *Tijdschrift voor familie- en jeugdrecht* (2004) pp 290–294 at 293; B E Reinhartz 'Het wetsvoorstel Wet conflictenrecht geregistreerd partnerschap' *Weekblad voor Privaatrecht, Notariaat en Registratie* (2004) pp 491–498 at 495–496.

[159] Article 22 of the WCGP.

[160] Article 23(1) of the WCGP.

[161] Article 23(2) of the WCGP.

[162] Article 23(1) of the WCGP.

[163] Article 23(3), first sentence of the WCGP.

[164] Article 23(3), second sentence of the WCGP.

[165] Article 23(4) of the WCGP.

[166] With respect to registered partnerships, administrative decisions have been expressly included: P M M Mostermans *Echtscheiding. Praktijkreeks IPR. Deel 5* (Deventer: Kluwer, 2nd edn, 2003) pp 112–113, §328–329.

[167] L Strikwerda *Inleiding tot het Nederlands Internationaal Privaatrecht,* (Deventer: Kluwer, 8th edn, 2005) p 289, §270; P M M Mostermans *Echtscheiding. Praktijkreeks IPR. Deel 5,* (Deventer: Kluwer, 2nd edn, 2003) pp 99–100, §279–282.

would appear somewhat hypocritical to refuse recognition on the basis that jurisdiction was assumed on grounds not in accordance with international standards. This could thus be important in cases where a foreign judge assumes jurisdiction on the basis of an unconditional *forum necessitatis.*[168]

(2) If the dissolution was obtained as a result of a unilateral petition, it will only be recognised if it was obtained as the result of a proper legal process (*behoorlijke rechtspleging*).[169] Nonetheless, even if either of these first two criteria is not met, the dissolution may still be recognised if the other party either expressly or implicitly consented to the procedure.[170]

(3) A foreign decision may also not be contrary to Dutch public policy.

(4) Finally, a decision will not be recognised, even if it complies with the aforementioned criteria, if it is not in conformity with a previous decision.[171]

VIII   SAME-SEX MARRIAGE IN ARUBA AND THE NETHERLANDS ANTILLES

Although in 2001 it was unclear whether a same-sex marriage celebrated in the Netherlands would be recognised in the other parts of the Kingdom of the Netherlands,[172] this has now been affirmatively answered by the Joint

---

[168] An unconditional *forum necessitatis* is not an internationally recognised standard of jurisdiction and would thus, under normal circumstances, not be recognised. However, such a ground is also recognised in Dutch internal procedural law, and it would therefore be rather hypocritical to refuse to grant recognition to a foreign dissolution on this basis, if a Dutch court would be able to grant a dissolution having declared itself competent on identical grounds. For more on this ground of jurisdiction, see I Curry-Sumner *EFL Series: Volume 11. All's well that ends registered? The substantive and private international law aspects of non-marital registered relationships in Europe* (Antwerp: Intersentia, 2005) pp 436–437 and the evaluation of such criteria in I Curry-Sumner *EFL Series: Volume 11. All's well that ends registered? The substantive and private international law aspects of non-marital registered relationships in Europe* (Antwerp: Intersentia, 2005) pp 438–445.

[169] Article 24(2) of the WCGP. P M M Mostermans *Echtscheiding. Praktijkreeks IPR. Deel 5* (Deventer: Kluwer, 2nd edn, 2003) pp 97–98, §275–278; L Strikwerda *Inleiding tot het Nederlands Internationaal Privaatrecht* (Deventer: Kluwer, 8th edn, 2002) pp 289–290, §270.

[170] Article 24(2) of the WCGP. This is another example of the *favor divortii* and *favor dissolutionis* principles explained in I Curry-Sumner *EFL Series: Volume 11. All's well that ends registered? The substantive and private international law aspects of non-marital registered relationships in Europe* (Antwerp: Intersentia, 2005) pp 446–463.

[171] P M M Mostermans *Echtscheiding. Praktijkreeks IPR. Deel 5* (Deventer: Kluwer, 2nd edn, 2003) pp 102–103, §289–293.

[172] Staatscommissie voor het Internationaal Privaatrecht *Advies van de Staatscommissie voor het Internationaal Privaatrecht inzake het internationaal privaatrecht in verband met de openstelling van het huwelijk voor personen van hetzelfde geslacht* (The Hague: Staatscommissie, 2001) p 42. See also J De Boer 'Homohuwelijk en adoptie in het Koninkrijk' (2001) *Nederlands Juristenblad* pp 764–765 and H U Jessurun D'Oliveira 'Het Nederlandse huwelijk en het Koninkrijk' (2001) NJB pp 807–808, met naschrift van J De Boer.

Court of Appeal of the Netherlands Antilles and Aruba.[173] The case concerned a lesbian couple, one Dutch and one Aruban, married in the Netherlands. The couple sought recognition of their marriage in Aruba, which was initially refused by the Registrar. The Joint Court of Appeal held that the marriage must be recognised on the basis of Art 40 of the Charter for the Kingdom of the Netherlands (*Statuut voor het Koninkrijk der Nederlanden*), and thus should be registered in the Population Register, but not in the Registers of Civil Status. According to Art 1:26 of the Aruban Civil Code, only marriages celebrated in Aruba can be registered in these registers. In terms of the legal consequences for the couple themselves, this difference is insignificant.[174]

IX MATRIMONIAL PROPERTY LAW: CASE-LAW

The Dutch Supreme Court gave an interesting judgment on 1 October 2004.[175] The case concerned the application of the 'natural obligation' (an obligation which applies, if the circumstances so require, by dint of common law) to the situation of a married couple who had excluded by matrimonial covenant the statutory community of property which would normally be imposed by Book 1 of the Dutch Civil Code (the so-called 'cold exclusion').[176] The case reveals the ability of the Dutch 'common law' to respond to situations in which one individual to the marriage has failed properly to protect his or her interests. It also reveals that the 'common law' is capable of differentiating between situations in which the parties are at arm's length and situations where there is a complex intermingling of interests. The couple married in 1971. Nine years later (1980) the husband bought some building land, half of which he then sold, for the price of 100,000 Guilders, to the wife. The wife never paid the purchase price for her half-share. Subsequently, a matrimonial home with office was built on the land. The building was financed by two mortgages. Before the first mortgage was paid off, the husband converted it into a redemption-free personal loan. To increase the security on this loan, the husband opened a saving insurance with himself as the beneficiary. In 1998 the marriage was dissolved and the house was sold for 1,400,000 Guilders. Because the wife was co-owner of the house, in consequence of the transaction in 1980, the wife was entitled to half of the profits of sale. However, the husband did not agree. In his view the wife was obliged to compensate him, at least to the tune of the value of the purchase price which the wife had never paid, for half of the value of the building works (paid for by the husband) and half of the value of the building work which the husband had carried out himself. However, the wife had a powerful defence: all the payments and works carried out by the

---

[173] *Gemeenschappelijk Hof van Justitie van de Nederlandse Antillen en Aruba*, 23 August 2005, Case No EJ 2101/04 – H12/05.

[174] K Boele-Woelki 'Editorial: Erkenning van het homohuwelijk op de Nederlandse Antillen en Aruba' *Tijdschrift voor Familie – en Jeugdrecht* (2005) p 221.

[175] *Nederlandse Jurisprudentie*, 2005, 1 with annotation Kleijn.

[176] For explanation see the Dutch report in A Bainham (ed) *The International Survey of Family Law 2004 Edition* pp 339–361.

husband could be regarded as the satisfaction of a natural obligation, more specifically, the obligation that the husband should ensure, in the event of termination of the marriage, that the wife is in a position to provide for her material needs. This principle had already been established in earlier case-law. A novelty in comparison with earlier case-law is the character of the property upon which the obligation 'bites'. The natural obligation did not only 'bite' on the price of the building land, but also the cost of building operations, the value of the work carried out by the man himself, and, most surprising of all, the entire value of the saving insurance which the husband had taken out in his own name. The parties' actual intentions do not play any role. Whether a particular obligation is to be regarded as fulfilment of a natural obligation depends ultimately entirely on the particular circumstances of the case, including the relative wealth and needs of the parties concerned. The Dutch Supreme Court attached particular weight to the following circumstances: the circumstance that the wife ended her paid employment in 1980; that she had worked for a considerable time, unpaid, in the man's business; that she had two children of the marriage to care for and that the parties did not keep separate documentation of their income and outgoings. The Dutch Supreme Court did not exclude the possibility that, in exceptional circumstances, it would be possible to show that the natural obligation does not apply or has already been discharged, for instance, if the parties had expressly agreed in 1980 that the wife was being given a loan by the husband, or if the parties had been able to demonstrate that they kept their financial matters entirely separate.

X   BILL PROHIBITING USE OF CORPORAL PUNISHMENT IN THE UPBRINGING OF CHILDREN

On 28 September 2005 the Bill to contribute to the prevention of emotional and physical abuse of children or any other humiliating treatment of children in care and upbringing was introduced into the Second Chamber.[177] The Bill proposes the amendment of one paragraph of one article of the Dutch Civil Code: Art 1:247. The provision is set out below. The new words are in italics.

'Article 1:247 Dutch Civil Code:

1. Parental authority includes the obligation and the right of the parent to care for and bring up his or her minor child.
2. Care and upbringing includes the care and responsibility for the child's emotional and physical welfare *and his or her safety as well as* the facilitation of the development of his or her personality. *In that care and upbringing of the child the parents should not use emotional or physical violence or any other humiliating treatment.*'

As the title of the Bill makes clear, the Bill aims to contribute to prevention of child abuse. According to estimates, some 50,000 to 80,000 children are

---

the victim of child abuse each year. A number of them die in consequence. The government expects at the beginning of 2006 to provide more specific details regarding child abuse. Obviously the proposed reform is a very minor measure. The idea is that it is impossible to tackle child abuse as long as the legal system permits parents to use physical force and humiliation as part of the upbringing. In imposing this restriction on parental power, the government aims to strike a balance between respecting the freedom of parents to bring up their children as they think fit (protected by the right to private and family life in Art 8 of the ECHR), and complying with the obligation to protect children from abuse in Art 19 of the United Nations Convention on the Rights of the Child. Furthermore the rights of the children themselves are at issue, such as the following: the right to bodily integrity, protected by the prohibition on degrading treatment in Art 3 of the ECHR, and the child's right to private life protected by Art 8 of the ECHR and Art 17 of the International Covenant on Civil and Political Rights.[178] The measure is a reaction to an explicit recommendation by the Committee on the Rights of the Child in its concluding report regarding the Netherlands in 2004. In that report the Committee advised the Netherlands to 'explicitly prohibit corporal punishment in law throughout the state party and carry out public education campaigns about the negative consequences of ill-treatment of children, and promote positive, non-violent forms of discipline as an alternative to corporal punishment'.[179] Furthermore, the European Committee on Social Rights, the expert committee which scrutinises compliance of the member states with the European Social Charter, has signalled that the Netherlands is not at this moment in compliance with the obligations to secure the protection of children as laid down in Art 17 of European Social Charter (ESC).[180] According to that committee, Art 17 of the ESC requires legal prohibition of all forms of violence against children, at school, in other institutions, home and elsewhere. Finally, the Parliamentary Assembly of the Council of Europe has recommended on 23 April 2004 a Europe-wide ban on corporal punishment of children.[181]

The Bill is intended to put an end to the 'corrective slap' or any other parental right to use force by way of discipline. Any form of deliberately inflicted pain on a child is to be a prohibited exercise of violence.[182] The proposed amendment to the Civil Code should have the consequential effect that any use of violence on a child will be more readily qualified as assault and thus in violation of the criminal law, than is the case at present. In 2000 the Den Haag Appeal Court had acquitted a father of the criminal charge of assault of his child, accepting his defence of parental chastisement. The Dutch Supreme Court overturned the judgment, however, on technical grounds.[183] It is intended that the defence of parental chastisement will never

---

[178] TK 2005–2006, 30 316, nr 3 (Explanatory Memorandum) pp 1–2.
[179] CRC/C/15/Add 227, 30 January 2004, recommendation 44, sub d.
[180] European Social Charter, European Committee of Social Rights, Conclusions XVII-2; published on the European Social Charter website at http://www.coe.int/T/E/Human_Rights/Esc/.
[181] Recommendation 1666 (2004).
[182] TK 2005–2006, 30 316, nr 3, p 2.
[183] Dutch Supreme Court, 10 October 2000, *Nederlandse Jurisprudentie*, 2000, 656.

be run with success anymore. The Dutch Supreme Court on 4 October 2005 held that a charge of criminal assault brought against a man who slapped his 15-year-old daughter in the face, could not be defended in law with a defence of chastisement in the course of upbringing.[184] However, according to the Explanatory Memorandum, preventative action involving the use of force should be distinguished from the application of force in order to punish:

> 'At the same time it cannot be stated that every slap which is done with the intention of correction, constitutes violence. A slap on the fingers to prevent plunder of the sweet-pot is not a violation of the prohibition. Also taking a child in a firm grip in order to prevent the child from doing something dangerous does not fall under the prohibition; the central element in such cases is not punishment but prevention. However, it can be stated that every deliberate infliction of pain on another person is a form of exercise of violence within the meaning of this Bill. Every type of physical punishment of a child after the event is for that reason therefore not compatible with the prohibition.'[185]

Through the application of Art 1:247 of the Dutch Civil Code to other persons acting *in loco parentis*, for example, guardians or other persons caring for the child who do not have custody of him or her,[186] the provision is also applicable to them.

It is expected that the provision will bring about a significant change in attitude to the use of violence on children. By introducing this measure, the use of violence is in all circumstances made questionable. Furthermore, the grey line between corrective measures and child abuse becomes sharper. It should become easier for professionals to take action in situations in which the parents engage in physical and emotional forms of punishment. The Minister of Justice has undertaken to ensure that specific criteria are developed to determine with greater certainty than is the case at present, the circumstances in which a child protection measure should be applied.[187] Civil law prohibitions on the use of violence against children are already in force in Sweden, Denmark, Germany and Austria. According to an investigation carried out by the Dutch Institute for Care and Welfare (*Nederlands Instituut voor Zorg en Welzijn*), the introduction of this measure had a significant effect in all the countries mentioned.[188]

It is acknowledged in the Explanatory Memorandum that this measure alone will not be sufficient to tackle the very serious problem of child abuse. It stands alongside other measures initiated by the Ministries of Health, Welfare and Sport and of Justice. These are: the development and legislative

---

[184] Nieuwsbrief strafrecht, 10 November 2005, zaaknr 411.
[185] TK 2005–2006, 30 316, nr 3, p 3.
[186] Article 1:248 of the Dutch Civil Code.
[187] TK 2005–2006, 30 316, nr 3, p 5; TK 2003–2004, 28 606 en 29 200 VI, nr 19, p 3 (letter of 30 June 2004).
[188] K Kooijman, I J ten Berge and A M Oostveen *Fysieke bestraffing van kinderen. Een inventarisatie van wettelijke verboden in vier landen*, uitgevoerd in opdracht van het Wetenschappelijk Onderzoek-en Documentatiecentrum van het Ministerie van Justitie, 2003.

provision of the Child Abuse Reporting Centres;[189] the support of the RAAK group, which emphasises the importance of measures which support the parents as well as keeping an eye on them; the setting up of a group (INVENT) to investigate and give advice regarding early warning of situations where child abuse may be anticipated; the introduction of a reporting code for child abuse; and the organisation of various publicity campaigns aimed at raising public awareness of child abuse. Furthermore, the Ministry of Justice initiated an investigation into the nature and extent of child abuse; the report of which is expected imminently.

XI TRANSLATION OF DUTCH INHERITANCE LAW

In 2003 the first ever English translation of Dutch family law legislation was published in the fifth volume of the *European Family Law* series.[190] This publication takes that process one step further by providing a translation of the new inheritance law legislation of the Netherlands, as in effect since 1 January 2003.[191] Although at first glance the law, enacted as Book 4 of the Dutch Civil Code, may seem modern and innovative, the legislative process leading to this enactment commenced in 1947 when Professor E M Meijers was commissioned to draft a new Civil Code. The crucial element of discussion in the years before agreement on the text of the inheritance law was finally reached centred around the position of the surviving spouse in relation to any children of the deceased. Should the surviving spouse and the children be protected from disinheritance and, if so, in what form and to what extent? Although having taken more than 50 years to see the light of day, the new Book 4 has been met with enthusiasm in the Netherlands.

Although, our task as translators was somewhat eased by the use of modern terminology, we encountered many difficulties. Take, for example, the term *erflater,* which refers to the deceased regardless of whether he or she died testate or intestate, its closest translation, *testator,* only refers to the situation where the deceased had died testate. We have resolved this by using the term *deceased,* which in Dutch is often translated as *overledene* (although this term is not used in legal terminology). We have refrained from using the term *de cuius* due to its archaic reference, despite its use in academic publications. Further choices have also had to be made, for example, with reference to the *Register of Deceased's Estates* as a translation for *boedelregister.*

Moreover, difficulties were encountered with translating words such as *notaris* and *executeur.* In both cases, although a seemingly comparable translation has been found, it must be borne in mind that the meaning of these words can differ enormously between various legal systems. In order

---

189   See Dutch report in A Bainham (ed) *The International Survey of Family Law 2003 Edition* pp 308–315.

190   I Sumner and H Warendorf *European Family Law Series Volume 5: Family law legislation of the Netherlands* (Antwerp: Intersentia, 2003).

191   See further the Dutch report in A Bainham (ed) *The International Survey of Family Law 2004 Edition* pp 338–339.

to gain a more complete understanding of Dutch inheritance law it is essential to refer to commentaries and explanatory texts. At present the only commentary in English on the new Dutch inheritance law is Professor Nuytinck's *A short introduction to the new Dutch succession law* (Deventer: Kluwer, 2002), which deals with salient issues. In this translation *erfrecht* has, however, been translated as inheritance law.

New Zealand

LANDMARK FAMILY LEGISLATION

Bill Atkin[*]

Résumé

En Nouvelle Zélande, des modifications législatives importantes en droit de la famille ont marqué l'année 2004. La loi sur la tutelle de 1968 (*Guardianship Act 1968*), qui réglemente les questions de garde et de droit de visite, a été complètement remaniée par la loi de 2004 sur les soins des enfants (*Care of Children Act 2004*). Bien que sous un certain nombre de ses aspects, la loi nouvelle procède à de simples mises à jour, elle contient des dispositions nouvelles. En particulier, elle inclut une liste de principes pour clarifier le concept de bien être et de meilleur intérêt de l'enfant. De même, des amendements ont été apportés aux règles sur l'état des personnes, le plus controversé étant celui autorisant des partenaires lesbiennes à devenir juridiquement les parents d'un enfant. Une autre modification législative majeure est l'*Human Assisted Reproductive Technology Act 2004* qui pose un nouveau cadre règlementaire en matière de procréations médicalement assistées reproduction. Enfin, la loi sur l'union civile de 2004 (*Civil Union Act 2004*) autorise à la fois les couples de même sexe et ceux de sexe différent à enregistrer leur union, alignant ainsi, pour l'essentiel, leur statut sur celui des couples mariés.

I LANDMARK YEAR

Every so often a year stands out as a landmark year in the development of a country's laws. In the history of family law in New Zealand, 1980 was monumental not only because there were major changes to the substantive law including no fault divorce but also because the Family Court was established. A smaller revolution occurred in 2001 when a raft of laws placed de facto relationships on virtually the same basis as married couples for the purposes of property division and succession rights.

Now, there has been significant legislation that will see 2004 go down as another of those landmark years almost on a par with 1980. First of all, the rules relating to custody and access have been comprehensively rewritten,

---

* Reader in Law, Victoria University of Wellington.

with the new Care of Children Act 2004 replacing the Guardianship Act 1968. Secondly, rules relating to the status of children have been revised largely because of new reproductive technologies. These technologies have inspired a third piece of legislation which sets in place a broad framework for tackling the ethical and policy issues arising increasingly from developments in human biotechnology. The Human Assisted Reproductive Technology Act 2004 also sets up an information system that gives relatively free access to information about donor parents and donor children. Finally, reflecting the growth in unmarried heterosexual and homosexual partnerships, the Civil Union Act was passed, with an accompanying package of amendments to a large number of statutes that was finally legislated in the early part of 2005.

In many ways, none of the topics is novel. They will be familiar to readers around the world and some may consider that New Zealand, often in the past a leader in family law matters, is just catching up. Further, while some particular policy choices may have a radical tint to them, overall many of the reforms are modest and echo patterns that can be discerned elsewhere. For example, unlike Canada, Belgium, the Netherlands, Spain and Massachusetts, New Zealand has eschewed gay marriage and opted for the arguably less satisfactory but easy to sell civil union approach to same-sex relationships. All of this has happened when the country has had a centre-left government, which might have been expected to take a more radical line. On the other hand, some approaches such as cementing parental rights, especially of fathers, have been advanced by right-wing parties and, while there are odd signals in the new law which resonate with these approaches, by and large they have not been promoted.

II CARE OF CHILDREN ACT

A Role of family and culture

The Care of Children Act is a misnomer. It does not deal with childcare issues in their entirety. Most notably, questions of child abuse and children 'in need of care and protection' are dealt with under the Children, Young Persons and Their Families Act 1989 ('the 1989 Act'). The Care of Children Act deals primarily with the consequences of the breakdown of the relationship between parents and embraces rules and procedures that tend to suit the classic European nuclear family. The 1989 Act on the other hand was passed at a time when new right ideologies were being implemented and coincidentally a renaissance in the traditional mores and values of the indigenous Maori emerged. Centre-stage in the 1989 Act is not the Family Court nor counsellors nor professional advisors but the so-called 'family group conference'. This locates core decision making in the family group as distinct from the parents or any other body. The family group is defined to include the broader family network, in Maori the *whanau*. It is not, however, limited to those with blood ties as people with whom the child has significant psychological bonds, such as long-term foster parents, may be part of the family group.[1]

As Maori culture places a high value on the communal rather than the individual, it should be apparent how the model just outlined sits comfortably with a Maori perspective. How does it compare with the new Care of Children Act? While there is the occasional acknowledgement of cultural diversity, overall the new Act is a world away from the 1989 Act.

One of the express purposes of the Care of Children Act is to acknowledge 'the role that other family members may have in the care of children'.[2] As widely accepted internationally, the welfare and best interests of the child are the first and paramount consideration[3] but new principles relevant to this inquiry have been inserted. These include the following: '... the child's relationships with his or her family, family group, whanau, hapu, or iwi, should be stable and ongoing', 'relationships between the child and members of his or her family, family group, whanau, hapu, or iwi should be preserved and strengthened, and those members should be encouraged to participate in the child's care, development, and upbringing', and 'the child's identity ... should be preserved and strengthened'.[4]

Just how these principles will affect outcomes of disputes remains to be seen. To assist in their decision making, the courts will in future be able to order a 'cultural report' although this may include religious practices, not merely ethnicity.[5] These reports are to be written but, recognising that Maori is historically an oral tradition, there is also provision for the courts to hear someone on the child's cultural background.[6] In the past, the courts have been careful to see cultural ties and family heritage as being an important part of the assessment of a child's welfare. However, blood ties have not prevailed over the ultimate welfare and best interests of the child. Arguably, the new principles may lead to greater weight being given to family connections but not at the expense of other factors such as the child's safety and the child's own views. The principles relevant to the welfare and best interests of the child are inclusive, not exclusive, which means that all the circumstances relating to the particular child must still be considered.

The family is expressly recognised in one other context. Under the new Act 'parenting orders' replace custody and access orders. The terminology of 'role of providing day-to-day care', though hopelessly long-winded, is substituted for the unfashionable 'custody' and 'contact' for 'access'. Some may apply for parenting orders as of right. These are parents, including step-parents, and guardians.[7] Members of 'the child's family, whanau, or other culturally recognised family group' may also apply but they need leave of the court. Furthermore, 'any other person' may also apply with leave, so that

---

[1] Section 2(1), as explained in *CMP v D-GSW* [1997] NZFLR 1.
[2] Section 3(2)(b).
[3] Section 4.
[4] Section 5(b), (d) and (e). Hapu and iwi roughly translate as sub-tribe and tribe.
[5] Section 133.
[6] Section 136.
[7] Section 47.

the family group is not in any privileged position at all. Leave is doubtless a filter to weed out vexatious or hopeless applications and in appropriate cases leave is likely to be given without great difficulty. The point remains nevertheless that the role of the family group is weak compared with its position under the 1989 Act.

Interestingly, no attempt at all has been made in the Care of Children Act to replicate family group conferences. In some respects this is understandable. Where two parents separate, ideally they should be able to work out suitable arrangements for the children themselves. If matters become fraught, then the assistance of a counsellor or a mediator may help to resolve matters. Many couples may find it oppressive to have other members of the family in on the act. However, will this always be true, especially for Maori and other ethnic groups? It is rather surprising that the high-profile conference procedures for child protection have not been incorporated into the Act even as an option for those who desire it.

B   Role of parents

Underlying the question just discussed of the place of family members and culture in child cases is the question of the role of parents. While some people rhetorically promote the cause of parents' rights, their position can be problematic. Should we always presume that the parents are the ones who have the controlling powers in relation to children?

According to the 1989 Act, 'the primary role in caring for and protecting a child or young person lies with the child's or young person's family, whanau, hapu, iwi and family group'.[8] Under the Care of Children Act 2004, 'the child's parents and guardians should have the primary responsibility ... for the child's care, development, and upbringing'.[9] Again we see the sharp contrast between the two children's statutes. However, the Care of Children Act is in some respects the more equivocal of the two. The New Zealand law has, mercifully in the writer's opinion, retained the language of 'guardianship'. Under s 15 it is guardians who have duties, powers, rights and responsibilities in relation to a child's upbringing. This includes day-to-day care unless a parenting order distributes care and contact differently. While parents are usually also a child's guardians, this is not always the case and further, other people may also be appointed guardians. Thus while in practice it will usually not matter, there is not only an inconsistency with the 1989 Act, there is also an internal inconsistency in the 2004 Act itself.

There is a further curiosity in the new Act which suggests that Parliament was somewhat schizophrenic in its policy objectives. The principle that a child's relationships with the family, whanau, etc, should be stable and ongoing has already been cited. Strangely tacked on in parentheses at the end of the principle is the phrase 'in particular, the child should have continuing relationships with both of his or her parents'. What is a court to make of all

---

8   Section 13(b).
9   Section 5(a).

this when a case reaches it involving a dispute between parents, guardians, family members and non-family members? Despite the conflicting signals, guardians surely have priority under the Care of Children Act but subject to the overall paramountcy of the welfare and best interests of the child.

This is illustrated by a high-profile case that reached the High Court, *K v G*.[10] In earlier related proceedings,[11] a prominent right-wing Member of Parliament had been found guilty of contempt for trying to pervert the course of justice and improperly influence a witness. The case concerned a 7-year-old boy who, because of serious matrimonial problems between the parents, had been placed with a cousin in another part of the country and had lived there for 6 years. The parents claimed that they had sorted out their difficulties and wanted the boy back. Unfortunately the proceedings were protracted but the Family Court eventually granted custody to the cousin with access to the parents. This decision was upheld on appeal. The Family Court judge had said that the evidence strongly suggested that to give the parents custody 'would, not could, cause serious trauma' to the boy and 'seriously affect his development emotionally and socially. The risk is simply too great at this time'.[12]

In the High Court the two-judge bench grappled with these issues. Wisely they located the decisive factors with the child rather than with the adults:[13]

> 'The focus has to return always to the welfare of the individual child and the attributes and qualities of their parents are of course relevant but they are only part of the total mix. So too is the question of blood ties of biological parents ... it is not correct to regard parents as having a pre-eminent position or having an exclusive "right" to the custody of the child when the future of that child is being considered by the Court. The words "rights of parents" appear to have assumed some prominence from the correspondence of the parents, or their supporters, in this case. That may be understandable from their point of view, but it misses the true focus. Parents have obligations and duties towards their children. They do not have "rights" in the sense that they can enforce or pursue them, unless such a course corresponds with promoting the welfare of the child.'

K v G was an inter-family struggle, a Maori family as well. For this reason, some of the references in the Care of Children Act to the wider family may in future scenarios assist a person such as the cousin in that case. However, what if the caregiver had not been a relative but a genuine third party? The parents would doubtless invoke the new provisions that talk about parents and families and for this reason may be on stronger ground than under the Guardianship Act 1968. The caregiver would therefore be much more reliant on the underlying concept of welfare and best interests as outweighing the

---

[10]   [2004] NZFLR 1105.

[11]   *Solicitor-General v Smith* [2004] 2 NZLR 540 (conviction) and [2004] 2 NZLR 570 (sentence). This is discussed in the review of family law in New Zealand in 2003: Andrew Bainham (ed) *The International Survey of Family Law 2005 Edition* (Jordan Publishing, Bristol, 2005).

[12]   *K v G* [2004] NZFLR 1105, para 4, quoted in the High Court judgment.

[13]   Paragraphs 22 and 23.

parental and family considerations: there should still be no talk of
presumptions – the paramountcy principle must still prevail.

C   Guardians

The role played by guardians in a child's life is spelt out in greater detail in
the Care of Children Act than it was in the previous law. For example,
guardians are to contribute 'to the child's intellectual, emotional, physical,
social, cultural, and other personal development' and to determine or help
the child determine 'important matters'.[14] These important matters are name,
residence, medical treatment, culture, language and religion. These broad
guardianship tasks are part of the role whether or not the child is living with
the guardian. This is significant when a potentially significant new provision
is borne in mind. Guardians must act jointly, although this does not apply to
day-to-day matters if the guardians are not living together. There is also
potential confusion with respect to medical decisions as a separate section
permits 'a' guardian to consent to treatment.[15] That aside, the clear statement
that guardianship is a joint responsibility is a partial recognition of the
arguments put forward by those who favour a presumption of shared or joint
custody or parenting, designed primarily to assist the cause of aggrieved
fathers.[16] However, New Zealand law has long distinguished between
guardianship and custody, now 'day-to-day care'. The promoters of the
fathers' cause seek parenting orders that presume that both parents share
day-to-day care in near equal portions. While there is nothing to stop a court
making an order to this effect, there is certainly no presumption built into the
new law. Furthermore, the Court of Appeal has in the past confirmed that
'the equal and shared legal right to exercise guardianship' is not the starting
point for custody disputes.[17] Thus, the express statement in the Care of
Children Act about joint guardianship does not spill over into the
determination of day-to-day care and contact disputes.

A footnote to the last paragraph is necessary in relation to relocation cases,
where one parent wishes to shift with the children to another part of the
country or to a different country, sometimes the other side of the world.
There is older Court of Appeal authority that this was a custody issue[18] but
nevertheless a relocation dispute was not to be determined according to any
presumptions or by giving great weight to the reasonable proposals of the
custodial parent.[19] Under the Care of Children Act, 'changes to the child's
place of residence' is expressly a guardianship matter,[20] going surely beyond
day-to-day care. Couple this with the requirement that guardians act jointly

---

14   Section 16.
15   Section 36(3)(a).
16   For example, right-wing MP Muriel Newman attempted unsuccessfully to introduce a Bill to this
      effect into Parliament: Family Courts (Openness of Proceedings) Amendment Bill 2004.
17   *D v S* [2003] NZFLR 81, para 17 (the Court of Appeal's second judgment in these proceedings).
18   *Wright v Wright* [1984] 1 NZLR 366, 371.
19   *Stadniczenko v Stadniczenko* [1995] NZFLR 493 and *D v S* [2002] NZFLR 116 (the first Court of
      Appeal judgment in these proceedings where the English decision of *Payne v Payne* [2001] 2 WLR
      1826 was not followed).
20   Section 16(2)(b).

and the argument against relocation begins to look stronger. Whether this will in fact make any difference to the outcome of cases remains to be seen: welfare and best interests must still ultimately govern.

Who is a guardian? Supporters of fathers' rights may take a little more comfort from changes here, as unpartnered fathers are now much more likely to be guardians automatically. If the father is married to the mother or in a de facto relationship with her at any time after conception, then he will be a guardian. Previously, the unmarried father had to be living with the mother at the time of birth. Further, a new provision means that in most situations where the father is named on the child's birth certificate he will be a guardian. If a father is not a guardian under one of these rules, he can apply to the court to be appointed one and the court must grant the application 'unless to do so would be contrary to the child's welfare and best interests'.[21]

As under the previous law, the court can appoint other persons as guardians,[22] a process that can be very useful for giving relatives and other carers some legal authority with respect to a child. Likewise the new law continues testamentary guardianship whereby a parent can appoint someone to be a guardian in the event of the parent's death but with no automatic day-to-day care rights.[23] A variation on this theme is a new provision whereby a child's parents can appoint a step-parent as an extra guardian without a formal court order.[24] This is a somewhat controversial move because there is no judicial assessment of whether the appointment is in the child's interests. However, it relies on the parents, who have likely been in a relationship that broke down, to be on sufficiently amicable terms to agree. One may wonder how often this will be so.

III STATUS

A Challenges from assisted human reproduction and sexuality

The rules in the Care of Children Act depend in many respects on the determination of who are legally the child's legal parents. Conventional wisdom tells us that a child has one mother and one father, the father sometimes not being identified. When there is an adoption, typically the biological parents are replaced for legal purposes by the adoptive parents. Many jurisdictions including New Zealand have modified their rules to take account of new assisted human reproduction procedures with the result that the donor of gametes is excluded from legal parenthood. In New Zealand the conventional wisdom is being challenged in several ways.

The challenge has tended to arise in the situation where a lesbian couple uses a gay friend to help them have a child. For sexual preference reasons, they will use an assisted means of conception but there is no reason why

---

21   Section 19(4)(a).
22   Section 27.
23   Section 26.
24   Sections 21–25.

heterosexual parties might not be involved in a similar arrangement using either assisted or natural means of reproduction. In the scenario under examination the parties intend that the donor will maintain links with the child, indeed be treated openly as a parent.

Until recent changes, the law treated the assisted reproduction donor as a 'shell father' ostensibly with no rights or responsibilities.[25] However, despite the apparent effect of the legislation to exclude the donor, case-law found a back-door method of giving the donor legal standing. In *P v K*,[26] the High Court held that the donor, although being unable to apply for custody as 'the father', could apply as 'any other person' with the court's leave. The Court slid over the apparent logical implication of the word 'other' and reached a pragmatic solution to the question. In follow-up judgments, the Family Court and the High Court on appeal[27] granted custody to the mother and her partner on condition that the donor had reasonable access, spelt out in some detail by the Family Court judge. That case involved an initially amicable arrangement between a lesbian couple and a gay couple that turned sour. They used assisted means: had they used natural means, the biological father would have been the legal father with usual rights and responsibilities.

The law dealing with the situation just outlined has been changed in several respects. By an amendment in 2004, the provisions dealing with assisted reproduction in the Status of Children Amendment Act 1987 have been revised and incorporated into the principal Act. The first significant change affects the lesbian couple. Under s 18, where a partnered woman gives birth as a result of semen donation, the partner is one of the child's legal parents so long as the partner consented. In other words, the birth mother's lesbian partner is the other legal parent. This of course challenges the conventional notion that a child has one mother and one father (if identified). It also means that, if we can think of a child as having two legal mothers, we may be able to contemplate a child's having more than two legal parents. It is this notion that has been seriously advanced in a report by the Law Commission, ie that not only would the two women be legal parents but so also would be a known donor where all agree on this outcome.[28]

Section 14(2) of the Status of Children Act 1969 (as amended) provides that a lesbian partner who is a parent as just discussed must 'be treated so far as practicable in the same manner as the father of, or as the other parent of, the child'. Although not expressly stated, the implication of this provision is that the rules on fathers as guardians will apply with the result that the cohabiting partner will automatically be a guardian.

The third significant change relates to the donor. The non-partner man whose semen was used 'is not, for any purpose, a parent of any child of the

---

25   Status of Children Amendment Act 1987.
26   [2003] 2 NZLR 787.
27   *P v K and M* [2004] NZFLR 752 (FC), *P v K* [2004] 2 NZLR 421 (HC) (rather unhelpfully, this is not reported as *P v K (No 2)*).
28   Law Commission *New Issues in Legal Parenthood* (Report 88, Law Commission, Wellington, 2005) 68 ff.

pregnancy' (s 21(2) of the Status of Children Act 1969). Thus, the donor in a *P v K* type situation is not even a 'shell father'. What does this do to the donor's chances of obtaining contact rights through a parenting order under the Care of Children Act 2004? Henaghan has said it is 'a moot point whether ... a donor can apply as "any other person" for a parenting order', ie under s 47(1)(e).[29] Doubtless the reason for this is that the courts should be very wary of giving someone what Parliament has demonstrably taken away, ie parental rights. An application may be seen as just a device to get round the effect of Status of Children Act as amended. On the other hand, arguably a donor is in a better position than the applicant in *P v K*. In *P v K*, the applicant was a parent, even if only a shell father. It is odd then to say that he could also be any *other* person, ie other than what he is. Nevertheless the High Court allowed his claim to proceed. Now that the donor is not even a parent, the semantic difficulty does not arise.

Perhaps the point is more telling with respect to the granting of leave. Although the statute gives no guidance on the granting of leave, one can surmise that it is designed to filter out frivolous and hopeless cases. If the merits favour the application, then leave is likely to be readily granted. But if a donor is a legal outsider, perhaps there is an argument that he should be denied leave.

There is an argument that a donor can apply for a parenting order under s 47(1)(d) as a member of the 'family, whanau, or other culturally recognised family group'. The outcome may depend on how these words and phrases are interpreted. Arguably, while the donor is not a legal father or parent, he may be seen as a member of the child's family, whanau or family group in a wider sense. The words in s 47(1)(d) are not defined. Could the biological parent be included or is this again distorting the rules in the Status of Children Act as now amended? In any event, leave is needed under (d) and it is unclear whether a court will be more influenced by the desirability of upholding the ostensible purpose of the amendments or whether other values will prevail. Possibly of assistance under the new law are the s 5 principles in the Care of Children Act which relate to the preservation and strengthening of family and family group links, and also the importance of identity (see above). The problematic meaning of family, whanau and family group has already been touched on. However, identity is surely not limited to legal relationships. That this is so is supported by the Adult Adoption Information Act 1985, which provides a mechanism for people to find out about biological reality despite the intervention of an adoption. Likewise, the Human Assisted Reproductive Technology Act 2004 (see later) has an information system to cover the situation where donation has occurred in the context of reproduction.

Assuming leave is granted, would a parenting order be made? This also depends on an assessment of the child's welfare and best interests. The judges in *P v K* decided in the donor father's favour for a number of reasons including the donor's commitment to the child and the child's right to know

---

[29]   M Henaghan *Care of Children* (LexisNexis, Wellington, 2005) 48.

his parents under art 8 of the United Nations Convention on the Rights of the Child. Yet, under s 4 we must consider the *particular* child in the *particular* circumstances. In other words, generalisations in the end are subservient to an overall assessment of welfare and best interests. The legal parents would likely argue that the child is being well cared for, that there are no problems in the upbringing, that the child has bonded well, and to introduce an outsider will upset the existing arrangements and may cause stress and confusion for the child. Further, where there is considerable conflict between the parties, the child should not be exposed to this.

These points have been explored in the context of parenting orders. Many of them are also relevant to an application to appoint the donor as an additional guardian. In *P v K*, the parties lived in different countries, Australia and New Zealand. Because of this, making joint guardianship decisions could be very difficult and the source of more friction.

B   Status and agreements

In *P v K*, the parties had entered into a fairly detailed agreement on the upbringing of the child and the part the various adults were to play. It even recorded the intention to have the child baptised in a sympathetic church in Sydney. The agreement was unenforceable as such but nevertheless influenced the judges' assessment of the various issues at stake.

Largely in response to *P v K*, Parliament added a new provision into the Care of Children Act that will strengthen such agreements. Section 41 addresses agreements entered into between donors and parents which relate to contact and the donor's role in upbringing. The parties may take the agreement to a court which may in turn embody it wholly or partly in a consent order. It can then be enforced as if it were an ordinary parenting order and, if there is a dispute, the parties may also seek directions from the court.

Section 41 is a pragmatic solution to the *P v K* situation. It is somewhat logically inconsistent with the removal of parental status from the donor, a problem that would be avoided if the Law Commission's three-parent proposal were adopted. The latter is unlikely to happen immediately given that Parliament has only just given its attention to status and parenting matters. In the meantime, it will be interesting to see to what extent the half-way house in s 41 is utilised.

C   Other status changes

The 2004 package of reforms made a couple of other subtle changes. Jurisdiction to grant a paternity 'declaration' has been extended to the Family Court. Up until now, the Family Court has been able to grant paternity 'orders' on the application of the mother (under the Family Proceedings Act 1980). This has usually been for the purpose of obtaining financial support. However, a paternity order could be trumped by a paternity declaration from the High Court, often sought for inheritance purposes (under the Status of Children Act 1969). This is a rather confusing situation, largely the result of the higher respect given to the superior courts in the judicial ladder. Given the inferior place of the Family Court in the system and the discrete nature of family cases, it was somewhat anomalous that the High Court should have an exclusive role to fulfil a task that the Family Court has proven perfectly capable of doing under other legislation. What is now of interest is to see whether the change in jurisdiction will gradually render paternity orders redundant. There is increasingly little logic in retaining two separate statutory regimes, especially when DNA testing can usually resolve the dispute.

Such evidence as DNA tests has been the subject of another modest reform. The law has in the past provided for blood tests to take place but this has now been extended to buccal samples for DNA purposes and the reference to 'blood tests' has been replaced with 'parentage tests'.[30] In some situations, samples from other sources may be useful and it is a little surprising that the amendment did not provide for this. However, case-law suggests that evidence that falls outside the express statutory parameters may nevertheless be admissible: the Court of Appeal in *T v S*[31] happily dealt with buccal swabs before the amendment was passed. That case also faced the question of obtaining samples from a child against the mother's wishes. It was a situation where the putative father was trying to establish his paternity but was having trouble obtaining evidence. While there is power for the court to recommend tests,[32] there is no express power to order tests. The question was whether this could be done indirectly by placing the child under the guardianship of the court and the court in effect consenting instead of the mother. While an earlier authority had considered that this undermined the rights of the mother,[33] the Court of Appeal thought that the desirability of the child's knowing who his father is should take priority. The fact that under new technology a sample from the mother was not needed and that a buccal sample was less intrusive than a needle for the extraction of blood helped sway the Court.

The final reform measure sounds insignificant but previous case-law has found it annoying that there has been no ability to declare that a man is not the father of a child.[34] That power has now been expressly provided for.[35]

---

[30] Sections 54–59 of the Family Proceedings Act 1980, as amended by provisions contained in Sch 3 to the Care of Children Act 2004.

[31] [2005] NZFLR 466.

[32] Section 54 of the Family Proceedings Act 1980. This applies whether proceedings are initiated under that Act or the Status of Children Act 1969.

[33] *Cairns v James* [1992] NZFLR 353 (Temm J).

[34] *Roguski v Marsh* (unreported, New Plymouth High Court, M 24/00, 26 June 2001).

[35] Section 51(1)(b) of the Family Proceedings Act 1980 (as amended by Status of Children Amendment Act 2004, s 17) and s 10(3) (as inserted by the 2004 amendment).

IV ASSISTED HUMAN REPRODUCTION – THE BROADER PICTURE

The question of status is just one aspect of the broader picture of the law and policy relating to assisted human reproduction. The issues have evoked widely different responses around the world and form one of the most controversial topics in bioethics. Until recently, apart from the question of status, New Zealand law has been largely silent on assisted reproduction. Finally in 2004 a major piece of legislation was enacted.

The path to legislation has been slow. In 1994 the Ministerial Committee on Assisted Reproductive Technologies submitted a report which advanced a number of options for law reform, including the creation of a new Council on Assisted Human Reproduction, the main object of which was to address policy issues, develop codes and guidelines and advise the government.[36] Already existing was an ethics committee handling approvals for new treatments and research. This function would continue but the new system would not go as far as the kinds of licensing regimes that exist in other countries such as Britain. It was thought that this was unnecessarily bureaucratic in a small nation such as New Zealand.

The next major step in the process was the introduction of two Bills into Parliament. One was by an Opposition Member of Parliament, Dianne Yates, the Human Assisted Reproductive Technology Bill 1996. Shortly afterwards the then Minister of Justice introduced a government Bill entitled the Assisted Human Reproduction Bill 1998. A change of government in 1999 might well have heralded some fresh momentum on the legislation, both Bills remaining before Parliament despite the dissolution. However, it was not until 2004 that finally the Human Assisted Reproductive Technology Act was passed. While the name is the same as the Yates' Bill rather than the previous government's Bill, the Yates' Bill was effectively rewritten and little is left of the original.

The Act bans certain activities. These include cloning for reproductive purposes, the creation and implantation of hybrid embryos, the development, export or import of embryos after the fourteenth day, sex selection other than for genetic disorder or disease reasons, using children as donors, trading in gametes and embryos, and using surrogacy for profit.[37] Reproductive treatment and research must receive ethics approval from the ethics committee, but this does not apply to 'established procedures'.[38] The latter are declared to be 'established' by Order in Council and will certainly include those common procedures and treatments that have been practised for some time or become so in the future.

---

[36] *Assisted Human Reproduction Navigating Our Future* (Report of the Ministerial Committee on Assisted Reproductive Technologies, Wellington, 1994). The author was one of the two members of the Committee.

[37] Sections 8–15 and Sch 1 to the Human Assisted Reproductive Technology Act 2004.

[38] Sections 5 and 16–23 of the Human Assisted Reproductive Technology Act 2004.

One of the novel centrepieces of the Act is the creation of an Advisory Committee, very similar to the Council that the Ministerial Committee advocated.[39] The adjective 'advisory' may be misleading because the Committee will have power to issue guidelines that the ethics committee must follow. Further, the advice that it gives especially on contentious issues will doubtless be highly influential and given various public consultation requirements laid out in the Act the Committee's procedures may not infrequently be in the public spotlight. The combined approach of advisory committee and ethics committee is an interesting one because it ensures a degree of day-to-day control over reproductive activities but is also flexible enough to cope with new technologies and practices, rich with ethical dilemmas, as they emerge.

The final part of the new Act that is worth mentioning is the provisions which ensure that there will be openness when donated gametes or embryos have been used. This again is in line with the recommendations of the 1994 Ministerial Committee. Openness is especially important for the Maori population in New Zealand, for whom whakapapa or genealogy is a major factor for identity and social interactions. Practice in New Zealand had already shifted heavily towards an open approach even before the 2004 Act. The legislation is in some respects catching up but it does ensure that clinics keep appropriate records and that the Registrar-General of Births, Deaths and Marriages keeps a central database of relevant information. Generally speaking, donor offspring will have access to this information on reaching 18 and their parents before that. Donors may receive information about the offspring with the latter's consent. The new regime applies only from the date when the Act comes into force (22 August 2005) and is not retrospective.

V   CIVIL UNIONS

In common with other western nations, New Zealand has been grappling with the best way of providing some legal recognition for same-sex couples. Decriminalisation of the law took place with legislation passed in 1985 and in 1993 human rights legislation was revised to include sexual orientation in its anti-discrimination provisions. More recently, beginning with the Domestic Violence Act 1995 and more significantly with revision of matrimonial property division and inheritance laws in 2001, unmarried couples including same-sex ones have been treated on much the same basis as married couples. With most of the practical issues affecting unmarried couples having been addressed, why bother with anything more?

For some time, some sections but certainly not all of the gay and lesbian community have been seeking a change in the law to allow them to marry. When this was tested in the Court of Appeal, it was staunchly rebuffed.[40] There have been no serious proposals to amend the marriage laws. Instead,

---

[39]   Sections 32–42 of the Human Assisted Reproductive Technology Act 2004.

[40]   *Quilter v Attorney-General* [1998] 1 NZLR 523.

advocates for gay and lesbian causes prepared draft legislation for civil unions or partnerships. Latterly this cause was taken up by the government which sponsored legislation that was passed by 65 votes to 55 in 2004 and came into force on 26 April 2005. It was decided on a 'personal' or 'conscience' vote of Members of Parliament rather than on strict party lines. Nevertheless, there was some virulent opposition, primarily from right-wing Members and also a high-profile conservative church, the Destiny Church, which also has a political arm.

The New Zealand version of civil unions is available to both heterosexual and homosexual parties. In broad terms, the civil union law mirrors that for marriage. Thus, there are similar rules for invalidity. For example, there must be consent, the parties must not be within the prohibited degrees and neither party can be in a still-existing marriage or civil union. The rules for dissolution of marriage in New Zealand, 2 years living apart, are extended to civil unions. There is a new exception of relevance here, however. Section 18 smoothes the path for a couple which wants to convert from marriage into a civil union or vice versa (if heterosexual). Without s 18 the parties would have to have had their marriage or civil union dissolved, which would in turn have required living apart for 2 years, hardly their intention. Section 18 allows the parties to convert their relationship into the alternative status within having to go through a dissolution process. Just how many people will take advantage of this is unclear. Perhaps some married people who are no longer convinced of the traditional trappings may decide to make some sort of ideological point. And if at some stage in the future marriage is opened to same-sex couples, then one can imagine some civil union partners wanting, again for symbolic reasons, to alter their status.

While civil unions largely mirror marriages, there are one or two differences. Minors under 18 must get parental permission to marry or enter a civil union. While breach of this rule does not render a marriage invalid, it does have this effect for civil unions. Likewise, a person under 16 cannot marry or enter a civil union but such a marriage unlike a civil union will be valid. The Marriage Act 1955 contains certain provisions for the celebration of a marriage outside New Zealand, for example, for servicemen and women. These rules are not extended to civil unions but the parliamentary select committee added a provision which enables regulations to be made 'prescribing types of overseas relationships that are recognised in New Zealand as civil unions'.[41] At the time of writing, no regulations have been made. Marriages may be celebrated by marriage celebrants as well as registrars. One of the major subgroups is officiating ministers provided by the churches. There is no equivalent for civil unions and marriage celebrants are not automatically civil union celebrants. A separate application must be made for appointment as a civil union celebrant.[42]

At the same time as the Civil Union Bill was before Parliament, there was a companion 'omnibus' Bill which made consequential amendments to a vast

---

41   Section 35(1)(a) of the Civil Union Act 2004.
42   Section 26 of the Civil Union Act 2004.

array of statutes. In most instances, this was for the purpose of extending to civil unions the same provisions that related to marriages but in some instances the amendments also considered de facto relationships. This Relationships (Statutory References) Bill was large, detailed and in many respects very technical. The select committee decided that it needed more time to consider it, so, while the Civil Union Bill was passed in 2004, the omnibus Bill was not passed until March 2005. While it treated civil union similarly to marriage, in some instances the select committee saw fit to delete provisions that extended to de facto relationships. However, two matters relating to civil unions are worth mentioning.

First, a provision relating to revocation of wills on entering a civil union, designed to reflect the rule that relates to marriage, was consciously dropped by the select committee in the hope that the issue would be handed over to the Law Commission for consideration. One thought was that the rule might be abolished entirely. Does it today serve the same purpose that it did historically? Most people entering civil unions will already have been cohabiting, probably for many years. They are highly likely to have made wills on the basis of that cohabitation and so, to have them automatically revoked on getting the relationship officially recognised through a civil union simply upsets established patterns. It might be argued that such wills might have been made 'in contemplation of' the civil union but that is stretching concepts somewhat when civil unions did not exist until the 2004 Act came into force. Similar thinking could apply to marriages, except of course that the institution of marriage has not newly come into existence. Nevertheless most people getting married today have been cohabiting prior to the marriage and may well have made wills, not necessarily planning at the time to get married.

Secondly, there is a curious omission relating to the property division rules. Under the Property (Relationships) Act 1976, relationship property is divided equally subject to some exceptions. One of these is where there is a marriage of short duration, ie one where the parties have cohabited for less than 3 years.[43] There is also an exception for de facto relationships of short duration but the details differ.[44] In calculating the 3-year period, a prior period of unmarried cohabitation is included.[45] Thus, 2 years of de facto relationship followed by 2 years of marriage counts as 4 years, not 2. Civil unions have been treated largely the same way as marriages for the purposes of the exception. Section 2BA has been added to the Act to make it clear that a prior period of marriage is included in calculating the 3-year period for a civil union, and likewise vice versa. Thus, where a couple convert the status of their relationship as discussed above, time does not start running again for the purposes of the 1976 Act. However, what is not provided for is the situation where a civil union is preceded by a period of unmarried cohabitation, a highly likely scenario. Ministry of Justice officials have told

---

[43] Sections 2E and 14 of the Property (Relationships) Act 1976.
[44] Sections 2E and 14A of the Property (Relationships) Act 1976.
[45] Section 2B of the Property (Relationships) Act 1976.

the author that this is an oversight that will have to be remedied by an amendment Bill.

The creation of civil unions takes some of the pressure off the call for same-sex marriage. It gives official endorsement to those same-sex couples who opt to enter a union and provides an alternative for heterosexuals. On the other hand, from a legal point of view it creates a new institution that appears to serve the same contemporary function as marriage, yet is not marriage. Is it worth the candle? It has led to a raft of amendments, with some subtle distinctions that will trip up the unwary. It also fails to remove the different treatment of people under the marriage laws which many, despite the Court of Appeal's ruling, regard as discriminatory. It is predicted that there will be changes to the Marriage Act within the next 10 years.

Norway

CHANGING PATERNITY

Peter Lødrup[*]

Résumé

Dans l'édition 2003 du *International Survey of Family Law*, j'ai présenté les changements fondamentaux qui ont été apportés au chapitre de la paternité dans la Loi norvégienne de 1981 sur les enfants et les parents. Les réformes de 1997 et de 2002 concernaient les possibilités de modifier un lien de paternité existant, notamment par la réouverture du jugement établissant ou niant un lien de paternité à l'égard d'un enfant né d'une mère non mariée ou d'une mère mariée.

Ces réformes ont levé tous les obstacles qui jusqu'alors interdisaient au tribunaux de modifier un lien de paternité existant. Ces obstacles ont fait l'objet de mon analyse en 2003 que je ne reprendrai pas ici. Dans cet article je présentais également les discussions qui ont mené à la réforme d'alors. En bref, le législateur estimait que la reconnaissance de la paternité biologique devait prévaloir, dès lors que la paternité existante est contestée par l'enfant, la mère, le père ou un tiers qui se prétend le père biologique.

L'objet du présent texte est de montrer comment ces réformes se sont concrétisées en pratique.

I   THE BASIC ISSUES

In the 2003 edition of *The International Survey of Family Law* I presented the far-reaching changes in the 1981 Norwegian Act on Children and Parents regarding paternity issues. Reforms in 1997 and 2002 concerned the possibilities for changing an existing fatherhood, including the reopening of a judgment which either established paternity in a case of a child born to an unmarried mother, or failed to establish the paternity of the alleged father.

These reforms abolished all the barriers which up until then could prevent the courts from changing an existing fatherhood. These barriers were discussed in the 2003 article, and I will not repeat them here.[1] In that article I

---

[*]   Professor of Law, University of Oslo.
[1]   See p 354.

also presented the discussion that led up to the changes in those years. In brief, the legislator found that establishing the biological fatherhood should be the aim of the law if an existing paternity was contested by the child, the mother, the father or a third person claiming to be the biological father of the child.

My aim with these remarks is to add some information about how these reforms have worked out in practice.

After the amendments, the Act on Children and Parents, s 6 now reads:

> 'The child, each of the parents, and a third party claiming to be the father of a child who already has a father, may institute paternity proceedings when the existing paternity is based upon marriage or acknowledgement ... If special grounds so indicate, proceedings may be instituted by the county office of the National Insurance Service.'

It follows from the wording of this paragraph, that there are no time-limits and no need for new information or evidence which may prevent new proceedings.

We see that this paragraph deals with cases where paternity is established:

(a) according to the 'pater est' rule, which applies to children born in wedlock during the marriage and before the parents have obtained a decree of separation or divorce, and

(b) where paternity is established by the acknowledgement of paternity in relation to a child born to an unmarried mother.

When the proceedings are instituted, the court will normally order a blood test to be taken in order to get a DNA analysis. The result of the analysis will be decisive for the court's decision. If the analysis shows that the plaintiff is not the biological father, the court will relieve him from the status of legal fatherhood. A formal hearing in the court is not necessary. As will be seen, such a case will be decided quickly, and it is inexpensive. According to s 9 of the Children and Parents Act the result of the DNA analysis must be followed and the court has no discretionary power to reach a judgment which is in contradiction with the DNA result.

Previously, that is before a DNA analysis was mandatory in all cases where the child of an unmarried mother did not get a legal father by acknowledgement, fatherhood had to be decided by the courts. Up until 1990 the Norwegian courts decided thousands of such cases between the years 1950–1990. It is of interest to note that about 100 of these cases went to the Supreme Court, and in these cases the defendant became the father in a 3 to 2 vote in 13 cases. The blood tests used during this period varied, and could in many cases not provide a satisfactory answer whether or not the defendant was the biological father. Many cases ended without sufficient proof to establish any paternity.

With a DNA test the means to get a correct answer to the question of biological fatherhood in these cases is at hand. But could the result of such a test be used to reopen these cases? If the parties voluntarily obtained a DNA analysis which showed that the former judgment was wrong, one had the proof necessary to get the former case reopened. If the test showed that the judgment was wrong, that is if the existing legal father was not the biological father, he was relieved of the status of fatherhood.

But if only the legal father wanted the case reopened and the mother and/or child did not want to give material for a DNA analysis, this route was closed. The mere possibility that the result of such an analysis might conclude that the judgment was wrong could not be the basis for reopening the previous case. This was decided in 1998 by the Supreme Court in plenary session on a 9 to 8 majority vote.

This result was, however, not accepted by the Minister for Children and Family Affairs. After a hearing, a bill was presented to the Norwegian Parliament, with the result that the rules for reopening paternity cases were removed from the general rules in the Civil Procedure Act to the Children and Parent Act in a new s 28a, which reads:

> 'A final judgement can be demanded to be reopened without regard to the conditions of the Civil Procedure Act, §§ 405–408 if there was no DNA test available in the case. If a reopening is agreed to, the court should request a blood test to be taken together with a DNA analysis.'

It is quite evident that these new provisions and the goal of discovering the correct biological fatherhood would be impossible without the availability of DNA testing. Since the DNA test both confirms fatherhood and excludes fatherhood, a judgment can be made shortly after the tests have been analysed. Consequently, the case as such is no burden to the parties.

II THE USE OF THE REFORMS

The first statistical information is now available. From 1 April 2003 to 20 April 2004, there were 237 persons who wanted paternity reviewed, and in 211 cases the DNA analyses were finished in that period.

Our first question is: Who wanted to the have the DNA tests taken? The information in 129 out of the 211 cases shows the following:

Table 1. Who took the initiative?

The mother	4 cases
The child	12 cases
The legal father	109 cases
A third party	4 cases

It may be noted that in four cases the third party took the initiative, and his paternity was confirmed in two cases.

Table 2. Result of the tests

Fatherhood established by:	Number	Fatherhood confirmed	Fatherhood not confirmed
Judgment by the court	40	27	13
Acknowledgement	105	71	34
By marriage (pater est)	66	38	28
Total	211	136	75

Table 3 illustrates the percentage of the two alternatives:

Table 3. Result of the DNA analysis in cases reviewed in the period 1 April 2003 to 20 April 2004 (210 cases)

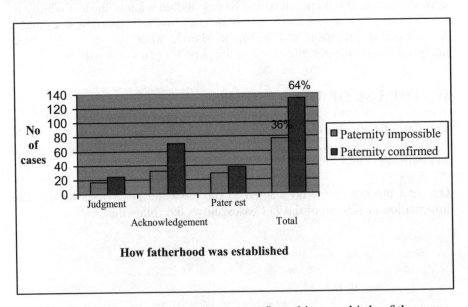

We see that the existing fatherhood was confirmed in two-thirds of the cases, while it was biologically wrong in one third of the cases. It is interesting to note that there were so many men who had acknowledged fatherhood who years later doubted its correctness. A little less than half of them found their doubt well founded and they were relieved of the status of fatherhood.

One may ask: Are the figures high? My answer is 'no'. This was the first year under the new regime, and the number will obviously go down in the future. It may be added that these figures cover the whole country, which has about 4.5 million inhabitants.

The next question is: How old were the children involved in these cases?

Table 4. The age of the child

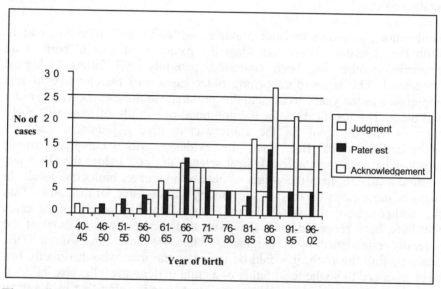

These figures give us some clear conclusions. A few children were old people; the majority were between 20 and 50 years old. What is important is that no child involved was born after 1990 as regards paternity by judgment. This shows that DNA tests have largely eliminated cases as regarding paternity of a child born to an unmarried mother.

III FINAL REMARKS

The present position in Norwegian law on the possibilities for changing paternity which is not biologically correct are based on views that merit a discussion. I find them basically sound, even if a third person's right to institute proceedings which may cause the breakdown of an existing and good relationship may be doubted.[2] On the other hand, such a third person,

---

[2] It should be noted that such a right for a third party to contest the paternity of the father is not unknown in European jurisdictions: see Marie-Therese Meulders-Klein 'The position of the father in European legislation' (1990) *International Journal of Law and the Family* p 139.

with whom a wife has had an affair, may at any time unveil the secret to the husband and/or child with the consequences that may have for future relationships. Generally, it may be argued that factors other than biology should constitute paternity; such as the social relationship between the parties. And can it be said making biology the crucial factor always yields a result that is in the best interest of the child? The answer to this question is obviously 'no'. But it was submitted when there reforms were drafted, that children, generally, would benefit from fatherhood being based on pure biological criteria. One may add that, even if the best interest of the child concept is of greatest importance, in these cases the interests of the man who believed in the mother's evidence that he was the only man she had been together with, along with the feelings of a betrayed husband, cannot be totally neglected.

Furthermore, as shown in Table 3 above, the 'child' will often be an adult. With the obligatory DNA test when the paternity of a child born to an unmarried mother has been contested, paternity will follow biological fatherhood. The issue of reopening older cases will therefore be of less importance as the years go by, and the 'children' in these cases will be older and older. The justification for the unlimited possibility of reopening these cases is that the goal for the court was to give a judgment that was biologically correct. But when the evidence was incomplete, wrong conclusions were inevitable. Medical science did not, before the DNA test became available, help the courts to obtain the correct biological result. In many of those cases the mother's testimony was decisive for the courts. That the mother did not always tell the truth is confirmed by several of the cases that have been reopened, with the result that the man was relieved of the paternity established by a judgment. When we now can, with a DNA analysis, find the truth, it would be unjust to the men who incorrectly had been adjudged to be the legal father of a child to deny them the possibility of obtaining a correct decision. Here one must bear in mind that in the great majority of the cases there has been little or no contact between the child and the father and, as said above, the child will be an adult. If the alleged man was found not to be the father, the mother and the child may now have an opportunity to present a new case where the DNA test may lead to another conclusion, and the fatherless child will finally get a father. With this background, I see no reason why a biological father should be protected by the law barring the reopening of the case.

As will be seen from s 6 quoted above, the county office of the National Insurance Service may also institute a paternity proceeding if 'special grounds' may justify it. Is this a provision of practical importance, and what may constitute 'special grounds'? The answer is 'yes'; the provision is of importance, and a 'special ground' may be that a man who is not the biological father has acknowledged paternity of a child. A recent case is illustrative.[3] The man with whom the unmarried mother lived acknowledged paternity of a boy after the mother had given his name as the boy's father.

---

[3]   Judgment of Kongsberg County Court, 25 August 2004.

The county office of the National Insurance Service, however, instituted proceedings against the father, and the DNA test showed that he could not be the biological father of the boy. The court then gave a judgment concluding that the man was not the father of the boy. The court referred to guidelines given by the National Insurance Service[4] governing when the county office should institute proceedings. In these guidelines it is stated that where fatherhood is based on an acknowledgement, but by a man other than the biological father, proceedings should be instituted. This will also apply when the man lives together with the mother and he wishes to be the legal father of the child. We see how these guidelines stress the importance of identity in legal and biological fatherhood. In cases of this kind, adoption would seem to be a better alternative than acceptance of fatherhood established by acknowledgement from a man who is not the biological father of the child.

---

[4] Runskriv 51 – 2000, amended 25 March 2003.

Scotland

CASES FROM THE TRENCHES BUT ONLY MODEST LEGISLATIVE RESPONSES

Alastair Bissett-Johnson[*]

Résumé

L'Ecosse dispose d'un système juridique distinct de celui de l'Angleterre, y compris en matière de droit de la famille et a son propre Parlement qui est compétent pour les matières qui lui sont dévolues. Ce chapitre traite des évolutions les plus significatives en droit de la famille jusqu'au 1er juillet 2005. L'une des plus importantes est la nouvelle loi (*Family Law (Scotland) Bill*) qui réforme la loi sur le divorce, la loi concernant la cohabitation et un certains nombre d'autres domaines. Un paragraphe est consacré à la jurisprudence la plus significative pour illustrer à la fois les difficultés qui ont conduit à l'intervention législative et le contexte dans lequel la loi a été élaborée.

Scotland has a separate system of law, including family law, than England and has its own Parliament which has responsibility for devolved matters. This chapter deals with the more significant developments in family law during the period until 1 July 2005. Chief amongst these is a new Family Law (Scotland) Bill which deals with reform of the law of divorce, the law affecting cohabitants and a number of other matters. A section on the more important cases has been included both to illustrate the problems which have led to legislative intervention in the Bill and to provide some context for it.

I   INTRODUCTION

Although there have been case-law developments in the time frame concerned (up until 15 September 2005) some of them highlight the need for some major legislative reform, much of it in an omnibus Family Law (Scotland) Bill which the Scottish Executive has introduced and which had reached its Stage 1 in the Scottish Parliament by 15 September. The legislation not merely attempts to reform some of the problems identified in

[*]   Professor of Private Law, Dundee University. I gratefully acknowledge the assistance of my colleague, David Brand of Dundee University, and David Lessels of Aberdeen University in preparing this article.

the case-law but also introduces reforms, albeit rather modest ones compared with other jurisdictions, in the area of divorce and cohabitation to reflect the changes in contemporary Scottish society. Accordingly these legislative developments have been the main focus in preparing this survey.

II   CASE-LAW

A   ECHR and the Children's Hearing system

Children in Scotland, whether they have committed an offence or are in need of protection, may be referred to a Children's Hearing.[1] This system of trained lay members provides an informal, largely civil procedure,[2] by which the 'panel' may determine whether a child should be subjected to 'compulsory measures'[3] once 'specified grounds of referral' are accepted by the child and parents. If the child or parents object to the grounds of referral the facts alleged to constitute the ground must be referred to a sheriff for a determination. In *Martin v N*[4] a 15-year-old girl was already subject to a supervision order from the Children's Hearing for some years. She was supposed to attend a review meeting against a background that she was getting out of control and had a potential for offending. She was then apprehended by the police on a Friday and held in a place of safety over the weekend in order to be brought before a hearing on the Monday. At this hearing neither she nor her parents were legally represented because her assigned legal representative had other commitments which precluded his acting for her. The outcome was that a warrant was issued by which she was to be held in secure accommodation for a further period of 21 days until a review hearing was held. Before that date she obtained legal representation and appealed to the sheriff who allowed the appeal and revoked the warrant for her apprehension. The sheriff held that granting a warrant to hold an unrepresented child in secure accommodation infringed her rights under the European Convention on Human Rights and the matter was further appealed to the Inner House of the Court of Session (First Division) as raising issues of general importance. The Inner House held that the mere fact that the child's apprehension was ordered by a Children's Hearing did not take the matter outside the protection of Art 5(4) of the Convention for a person to

---

[1]   See B Kearney *Children's Hearings and the Sheriff Court* (Butterworths, 2nd edn, 2000). See also A Griffiths and L Edwards *Family Law* (Greens, 1997) chapter 7 and Bissett-Johnson's chapter 4 in G Miller (ed) *Frontiers of Family Law* (Ashgate, 2003).

[2]   Legal Aid is only available in a narrow range of cases dealt with by Children's Hearings. As a result of the decision in *S v Miller* 2001 SLT 531 (analysed by Edwards 'S v. Miller: The End of the Children's Hearings System as We Know It' 2001 SLT (News) 187) legal aid is only now available in cases involving: (i) complex legal issues; (ii) cases involving children with limited communication skills; and (iii) cases where the making of a secure accommodation order is likely.

[3]   Eg to live at home under the supervision of a social worker with whom the child meets periodically, to live with foster parents, or to live in secure accommodation provided by the local authority.

[4]   2004 SLT 249.

have the lawfulness of *his or her* detention reviewed speedily by a court. Even if the detention was not ordered by a court it was enough that a detained child had a right of appeal to the courts. The right of appeal to a sheriff under s 51 of the Children (Scotland) Act 1995 and the right of a children's hearing to review the warrant might have saved the legality of the detention under the Convention. However, it was the potential length of the detention (21 days) that posed the real problem. The Scottish Office Advice to Panel Members of January 2002 had advised that an unrepresented child could be held in secure accommodation but an early review was to be held once representation had been secured. The Inner House held that the period of detention here breached good practice but did not constitute a fundamental procedural irregularity as the sheriff had held. Looked at as a whole, there was no breach of the right to a fair and public trial as required by Art 6 of the Convention. The better course might have been for the sheriff to have issued a new warrant. After the decision in *S v Miller*[5] the Children's Hearings (Legal Representation) (Scotland) Regulations 2001, SSI 2001/478, were passed to allow children facing complex or serious cases before a children's hearing to be represented by legally qualified safeguarders and curators *ad litem*. Lawyers not on the panel can act but will not be paid from public funds. Edwards[6] has suggested that the interim solution provided by the Regulations should be replaced by a broader strategy if children are to participate effectively in the Children's Hearing system. The decision in *Martin* suggests that the Courts are mindful of the cost implications of securing speedy legal representation for children involved in complex or serious cases before the Children Hearings system.

B   Contact and residence

In *D v H*[7] a 15-year-old boy brought proceedings under s 11 of the Children (Scotland) Act 1995 seeking contact with his sister who had been adopted some time earlier. The Sheriff held, and was upheld by the Sheriff Principal on appeal, that the action under s 11(2) of the Act was one that was for a parental right. As the brother's action could not be so categorised, it failed. It was held that contact under s 11(2) was expressly linked with application for parental responsibilities and rights under s 11(1) and that the suggestion by Wilkinson and Norrie[8] that s 11(2) was 'free standing' *was erroneous.*[9] A contrary view was reached in *E v Mr and Mrs E.*[10] Here a 14-year-old raised an action against her parent and step-parent seeking contact with her half siblings who had lived in the same house as her until 18 months previously. At this time undisclosed difficulties had arisen and the children were placed with foster parents. Sheriff Crowe took a different view from the Sheriff

---

5   2001 SLT 531 and 1304, discussed by Bissett-Johnson, op cit note 1.

6   Edwards 'Legal Representation Arrives at the Children's Hearing – But at What Cost' 2002 *Green's Family Law Bulletin* [57] p 2.

7   2004 SLT (Sh Ct) 73.

8   *Parent and Child* (SULI/ W Green, Edinburgh, 2nd edn) para 9.11.

9   A view adopted in the case of *W v W* (unreported, 25 April 2001) mentioned in *D v H*.

10   2004 *Green's Family Law Bulletin* [71] 5.

Principal in *D v H*[11] and held that he did have the power to make the contact order sought and that the provisions of the Human Rights Act 1998, Art 8, on the family militated against a narrow construction of s 11 of the Children (Scotland) Act 1995. Sheriff Crowe asserted that he had power to make a contact order supervised by the Social Work Department. It is submitted that a proper reading of the legislation should attempt to concentrate on the alleged benefit to the child, and whether restoration of contact would be a benefit to child after so long a period.[12] If Sheriff Crowe and Wilkinson and Norrie's views are wrong in suggesting that contact between a child and sibling can be granted independently of an action for parental rights, then it is submitted that it may be appropriate to amend the Children (Scotland) Act 1995 in promised legislation on Adoption and Children to create a 'freestanding' right for applicants in this type of case. Whether or not the application would be successful, is, of course, a separate matter to be determined in the light of the best interests of the child with whom contact is sought.

C   Hague Convention on international child abduction cases[13]

The thrust of the Hague Convention is that it is generally in the best interests of children to return them to the jurisdiction in which they were habitually resident before the abduction or wrongful retention.[14] The best interest of particular older children is respected by Art 12 which prevents a child being returned to his habitual residence if they run a 'grave risk of physical or psychological harm' there, and Art 13 which allows a court to decline to

---

11   *Supra.*

12   And possibly whether the brother's application for contact was a 'Trojan horse' for *de facto* contact by a birth parent.

13   Different considerations apply in non-Convention cases. See *Re J (a child) (return to foreign jurisdiction: convention rights)* [2005] 3 All ER 291. In such cases the concentration is on the best interest of the individual child. If there was a genuine issue about whether it was better for the matter to be determined in the UK or elsewhere, it was relevant to ask whether the other court was capable of determining the best interest of the child without having to give effect to the wishes of the father who seemed to have a particularly strong position in the forum concerned.

14   For more detail see Beaumont and McEleavy *The Hague Convention on International Child Abduction* (OUP, 1999) chapter 4. The Convention was regarded by Lady Paton in *AJ Petitioner* 2004 *Green's Family Law Bulletin* [71] 4 as a careful compromise of rights which had to be procedurally followed to the letter. Thus in *AJ Petitioner*, supra, the fact that a declarator of wrongful removal was sought in Scotland by the wife's attorney, rather than by the judicial or administrative authorities of a Contracting State as required by Art 15 of the Hague Convention, led to the declarator which had been sought in aid of proceedings in Texas being refused. The case was reversed by the Inner House of the Court of Session (2nd Division) sub nom *AJ v FJ* (2005 *Green's Family Law Bulletin* [75] 2). The Inner House held that under the Child Abduction and Custody Act 1985, 'any person appearing to the court to have an interest in the matter' could raise an issue under Art 15 of the Convention. This included the mother. On the substantive issue it had originally been held that the mother had failed to exercise her rights of custody. The Inner House held that the mother had not failed to exercise her rights but rather had difficulty in exercising them because her older son refused to see her, and illness overtook her when she had only a limited contact with her younger son. The Inner House also endorsed the view of Professor Norrie expressed in Hague Convention Rights and s 2(3) and (6) of the Children (Scotland) Act 1995 that rights of custody for the purpose of the Convention included rights of contact.

return a child to its habitual residence on the basis of the objections of a child of sufficient age and maturity for their views to be taken into account. The period concerned has thrown up a number of cases. In *M Petitioner*[15] the proceedings concerned a boy, then 12, whose parents had moved to Ireland. They had sold their business in Scotland in order to further the father's business. After living in rented accommodation, they bought a property to renovate and live in. After 2 years the mother took her son to Scotland for the usual family holiday with relatives, as she had done previously, but then declined to return. The mother asserted that she had never changed her habitual residence from Scotland, citing by way of support her retention of a Scottish bank account, her continued registration of her car in Scotland and the fact that furniture had been kept in store in Scotland. Lady Smith held that these facts had to be set against the wife having acquired a home in joint names in Ireland, having sent her son to school there and the context of the husband's attempt to establish a new business in Ireland. All these factors pointed to her having satisfied the definition of a habitual residence in Ireland. The mother voluntarily moved there as part of her regular way of life and for a settled purpose. The mere fact that it had been for a trial period and she was disappointed and unhappy there did not preclude her having acquired a habitual residence in Ireland.[16] Nor could she unilaterally change the habitual residence of her son without the permission of her husband. However, this still left the issue of whether the boy's reluctance to return to Ireland, where he had been bullied and teased, and where he lacked the friends he had in Scotland, would be sufficient for the Court to decline to return the child to Ireland[17] on the basis that the child had become 'settled' in his new home. Her Ladyship stated that the proper analysis of Art 13 involved:

(i) deciding as a matter of fact whether the child 'objects' to being returned (with 'objects to being returned' being defined according to its ordinary meaning);

(ii) asking whether the child has attained the age and degree of maturity at which it was appropriate to take their views into account.

Only if these two questions are answered in the affirmative does judicial discretion come into play[18] as a third stage.

---

[15] 2005 SLT 2 and commented on in 2005 *Green's Family Law Bulletin* [73] 5.

[16] The period can be quite short, perhaps as little as a month or two, but a habitual residence cannot be acquired immediately (*Nessa v Chief Immigration Officer* [1998] 2 All ER 728) except in cases involving EC residents. For instance, to refuse the reacquisition of a UK habitual residence in the UK by a former UK resident who had resided in and worked in the EC, would prevent his being eligible for UK social security benefits and thus inhibit freedom of movement within the European Community (*Swadling v Chief Immigration Officer* [1999] 2 FLR 184).

[17] Relying on Art 13 of the Hague Convention.

[18] This contrasted with the earlier case of *W v W* 2003 SLT 1253 in which the Inner House suggested that the strength of the child's views and reasons for objection should be assessed prior to reaching the discretion stage. Lady Smith held that this approach was inconsistent with the weight of authority and the structure of Art 13.

However, since the boy did object to being returned to Ireland, *and* was mature and above average intelligence, it was necessary to consider the exercise of judicial discretion, even though such discretion should only be used in exceptional cases. It was at this stage that the welfare of the child became relevant. Having regard to the possible disruption in the boy's present secondary school which he had just started, his unhappiness in his Irish school and his own substantial objections to returning to Ireland, which were not influenced by his mother, no return order was made. The fact that the child and mother were both independently represented may have had an affect on the outcome.

It is noteworthy that this case antedated the coming into force of Brussels II-bis in March 2005 which affects intra EC cases[19] by making it more difficult for a member state to which a child has been wrongfully removed to make a 'non-return' order. Had it been in force, although the possibility of making a 'non-return' order under Art 13 still exists, such an order may be ineffective. It now has to be made within a 6-week period, save where there are exceptional circumstances, and the 'left behind' parent and the child[20] *have* to have an opportunity to be heard. Crucially, where a 'non-return' order is made based on Art 13 of the Hague Convention, the order and a transcript of the proceedings must be forwarded to the court of the child's habitual residence.[21] Crucially that court may, after hearing the parties, override the 'non return' order by 'trumping it' and in such a case the child must be returned to the jurisdiction of its habitual residence under a new 'fast track recognition' procedure.

D Financial provision in divorce cases

When it comes to making awards of financial provision on divorce, the level of judicial discretion is less in Scotland than that found in other jurisdictions such as England, Canada or Australia. What constitutes matrimonial property and how it is to be shared is specified in some detail in the Family Law (Scotland) Act 1985. It may be of interest, therefore, to show how in a system with a lesser degree of judicial discretion than operates elsewhere, case-law continues to show where the system pinches 20 years after the enactment of the statute.

---

[19]   Under the Treaty of Amsterdam the European Commission acquired the right to regulate conflict of laws matters within the EC and exercised that right in Regulation 2201/2003. For more detail on this see P McEleavy 'Brussels II bis: Matrimonial Matters, Parental Responsibility, Child Abduction etc' 2004 53 ICLQ 503 and 'Communitarization of Divorce Rules: What Impact for English and Scottish Law' 2004 ICLQ 605. The exercise of power by the Commission seems to owe something to the fact that some countries were alleged to invoke the 'non-return' orders under Art 13 of the Hague Convention more readily than the UK Courts.

[20]   Article 11(7). Hearing the child is mandatory save where this is inappropriate having regard to the child's age or maturity.

[21]   Article 11(4), Brussels II bis.

E The Wallis 'trap'

The present law of Scotland relating to financial provision on divorce starts from a proposition that, with exceptions such as inherited property and gifts from third parties, most property acquired during marriage until the relevant date[22] (usually the date of separation),[23] is matrimonial property.[24] Generally the value of 'matrimonial property' at the relevant date is to be equally divided provided the result, taken together with the other orders the court is asked to make, is 'reasonable' within s 8 of the 1985 Act.[25] However, as the Policy Memorandum accompanying the Family Law (Scotland) Bill 2005 recognised[26] this 'formula' can create problems if the parties are separated for a long period[27] before the value of the matrimonial property is shared. In *Wallis v Wallis* this served to create what has become known as the *Wallis Trap*.[28] This deprived a wife of her right as a joint owner of the family home where she had agreed to transfer it to her husband and it increased in value by over £20,000 between separation (the relevant date) and the date of proceedings.

---

[22] *Stuart v Stuart No 2* 2004 SLT (Sh Ct) 44 is an example of how property can have no value at the relevant date. The parties had acquired a council house in joint names at a discount. The discount had to be repaid if the property was sold within a specified period. At the relevant date the discount would still have had to be repaid and the equity in the house at that time had a 'nil' valuation. Thereafter, the husband stayed in the home and repaid all the mortgage payments on it. He then sought to recover half the mortgage repayments made after separation from the wife on the basis of the obligations of the joint title. It was held that action was time barred. It was also suggested (contrary to the suggestion of the sheriff in earlier proceedings) that the wife had no right to share in the increase in the value of the property after the relevant date since this was covered by the decision in *Wallis*, post.

[23] Section 10(3) of the Family Law (Scotland) Act 1985. This is the most usual of the relevant dates specified in s 10(3).

[24] As specified in s 10(4) of the Family Law (Scotland) Act 1985.

[25] Bissett-Johnson and Barton 'Financial Provision on Divorce in Scots Law' 2000 JR 265. The usual stages in dealing with financial provision on divorce in Scotland are: (i) all property is defined as 'matrimonial' or 'excluded' under the Act; (ii) the matrimonial property has to be valued at the 'relevant date' (usually the date of separation); (iii) current ownership of the matrimonial property is established; (iv) the court then sees whether there are 'special circumstances' as defined in a non-exhaustive list in s 10(6) of the 1985 Act which would warrant an unequal division of the matrimonial assets; (v) the court transfers from the richer to the poorer spouse a sum that represents an equal division of the matrimonial assets or an unequal division to give effect to s 10(6). Finally, other claims to cover any financial benefit one spouse has conferred on the other or any detriment a spouse has suffered on behalf of the other or the children are dealt with (s 9(1)(b)) or childcare costs (s 9(1)(c)) are dealt with. Only exceptionally are periodical allowances dealt with under s 9(1)(d) or (e) since the aim of the legislation is to achieve a 'clean break' between the parties.

[26] Paragraph 88. The Bill is described in more detail later.

[27] Such as 5 years' separation, one of the proofs of divorce discussed later.

[28] *Wallis v Wallis* 1992 SLT 676, 1993 SLT 1348 discussed and criticised in Sutherland *Child and Family Law* (T & T Clark, Edinburgh, 1999) chapter 14. The property in question had increased in value by over £20,000 in a very short period of time, and the husband was able to take the benefit of the whole of this windfall notwithstanding that the property had been acquired in the joint names of the spouses.

More often than not it is the wife who remains in the home and gets the benefit of the post-separation increase in value,[29] but in the cases of pensions it is more likely that the husband, who is likely to have the larger pension, will benefit from the exclusion of any post-separation increase in value. The problem is particularly acute in 'the uniformed forces' cases.[30] Moreover, if a spouse retires between the date of separation and retirement, the pension may be better regarded as an income stream rather than a capital asset. The problem has continued to bedevil practitioners[31] and judges[32] during the period in question and they have been only too well aware of the unfairness flowing from the decision in *Wallis*. The case casts 'a long and baleful shadow'[33] even 12 years after its publication, even though most specialist family law practitioners will not agree to the transfer of a house from, say, the husband's name to that of the wife, without it being at *current value* rather than at the value at the date of separation (the 'relevant date').[34] Failing that, a sale of the property would be sought. This was very much the background to *McCaskill v McCaskill*[35] in which a husband sought the transfer of his wife's share in the jointly owned family home in return for £20,000. The house had gone up from a value of £45,000 at the relevant date to £100,000 at the time of trial. For her part the wife sought a sum of £80,000, plus an order for sale of the home. (The only other matrimonial property was the husband's pension which had a value of £21,640.) The Sheriff divided the pension equally and gave the wife an extra sum for future child caring expenses and then ordered the home to be sold. The husband appealed to the Sheriff Principal who rejected the husband's claim on the basis that the husband was seeking a share in property worth £50,000 for a mere £20,000: an order that would be 'so inequitable that no reasonable sheriff, properly exercising his discretion, could conceivably make such an order'.

---

[29]   See *Little v Little* 1990 SLT 785 for an example.

[30]   See eg Buchanan 'Pension: Valuation and Sharing Issues' 2005 *Green's Family Law Bulletin* [75] 3. The uniformed services would include (inter alia) the armed forces, the police and the fire service.

[31]   See Thomson *Family Law in Scotland* (Butterworths, 3rd edn, 2002) p 151, fn 2 for the assertion that practitioners will resist settlements involving transfer of property orders. This view is shared by K B Lockhart 'Wallis v Wallis Again' 2004 *Green's Family Law Bulletin* [72] 2 who adds that a party seeking a property order should either be met with a request from the other side that it be at current value or alternatively that the property should be sold and the proceeds evenly divided.

[32]   See *Kennedy v K* [2004] SCLR 777 where a Sheriff Principal had to reverse a Sheriff who tried to invoke s 9(1)(b) of the Act to compensate a husband who had agreed to his wife remaining in a matrimonial home which increased in value after the date of separation, and which was transferred into her name in the course of the divorce settlement. The right of a court to give a capital sum to compensate a spouse for suffering an economic disadvantage in the interest of the other spouse or the family was not to be used to subvert the rule that property was *prima facie* to be equally divided at its value at the date of separation. The Sheriff Principal was unwilling to consider awarding interest to the husband for the transfer of his share in the home from the date of separation. In doing so he apparently overlooked the important Inner House decision in *Geddes v Geddes* 1993 SLT 494.

[33]   To use the words of the Editors of 2004 *Green's Family Law Bulletin* 68 at p 1.

[34]   See note 25 ante.

[35]   See 2004 *Green's Family Law Bulletin* [72] 3.

One way of mitigating the problem is to allow the party who would lose by a substantial increase in value after the relevant date but before the trial, to claim interest backdated to the time of separation.[36] *Coyle v Coyle*[37] shows other ways in which judicial ingenuity can be used to prevent a spouse getting an unfair benefit from the *Wallis Trap*. In *Coyle* the wife, a cabin-crew member with British Airways, had given up work after the birth of her first child in order to look after the home and family. When the marriage broke down she sought an order for payment of a £20,000 capital sum for the benefit she had conferred on her husband and family whilst giving up her job at her husband's request.[38] The sum represented half the increase in the husband's business during the marriage. Lady Smith declined to grant the additional sum sought because she said that the court was required to balance the economic advantages and disadvantages suffered by each party[39] and then to see whether any resulting imbalance had been corrected by an equal sharing of the matrimonial property. In the present case the wife had benefited from a transfer of the family home which had gone up in value from £270,000 at the relevant time (separation) to £500,000 at trial. This benefit to the wife more than corrected any economic disadvantage that *she* had suffered in giving up her job. This is not to say that in the absence of the large increase in value of the house the wife would not have been entitled to compensation for giving up her job for the benefit of the family – which left the husband free to pursue his business interests. The case also contains a warning about the failure to disclose property. The husband had failed to include a Ferrari car in his list of assets. It had been listed in his firm's books as having a value of £185,000 at about the relevant date, although he sold it sometime later for only £50,000. Its value as a matrimonial asset was based on its higher value at the 'relevant date'.

F   Reasonableness of awards and s 8(2) of the Act

Following the steps set out earlier,[40] the end point of any calculation of family provision is that the result must be justified by the principles set out in s 9 of the Act and be reasonable having regard to the resources of the parties. The importance of the 'reasonableness' of the award emerged in *Fraser v Fraser*.[41] The husband was 69 whilst the wife was 65. They had been married for over 40 years and had four grown-up children. The matrimonial property at separation in 1997 was valued at £800,000, consisting of the family home and various pension schemes of the husband. From a pension sum available when the husband retired shortly after the parties separated, the husband gave the wife £106,000 to buy a new home.

---

[36]   See *Geddes v Geddes* 1993 SLT 494 (IH).

[37]   See 2004 *Green's Family Law Bulletin* [67] 6.

[38]   Section 9(1)(b) of the Family Law (Scotland) Act 1985 allows the court to take 'fair account of any economic advantage derived by either party from contributions by the other, and of any economic disadvantage suffered by either party in the interests of the other or of the family'.

[39]   See s 11(2) the 1985 Act.

[40]   See note 25 ante.

[41]   2004 *Green's Family Law Bulletin* [68] 2.

(The marriage had irretrievably broken down at least in part because the husband was cohabiting with a younger woman and her small son.) The wife had not worked during the marriage and could not work after separation due to illness. She was living off aliment (maintenance) of £1,000 per month provided by the husband. Equal sharing of the matrimonial property would have given the wife a right to an additional £274,000 over and above the money she had already received to buy a house. Sheriff Evans invoked s 8(2) of the 1985 Act to hold that the former family home (worth £135,000) should be left out of the calculation since it was needed for the foreseeable future by the husband and his partner and her son. Any other result would have been unreasonable. Nor could the husband raise money on it, since a loan was not available to someone of his age. Instead the wife received a capital sum of £150,000 payable by a lump sum of £10,200, plus monthly instalments of £1,165. This approach, as the commentary to the case suggests,[42] differs from that suggested by Lord Jauncey in *Wallis v Wallis*[43] that under s 8(2) awards had to be (a) justified by the principles of the Act and (b) reasonable having regard to the parties resources. Heads (a) and (b) were cumulative and Lord Jauncey suggested that a court either had to make a 'justified' award or no award at all. Instead here the Sheriff chose to scale down the order to make a 'reasonable' one rather than make no order at all.

G Valuation of company shares in a private company

In *AM or W v JW*[44] the main issue was how to value a husband's minority (37%) share in a car dealership of which the husband was a director, and which had an agreed value of £1,600,000. It was a private company in which the directors controlled the transfer of shares. The wife's valuer suggested that a discount of 40% was appropriate since one or other of the other two directors could acquire a controlling interest, and the Companies Acts protected the husband against 'oppressive' conduct. The husband's valuer proposed a 60% discount to reflect the fact that the husband was a trusted employee who had no management role in the company. The current controlling shareholder had no intention of selling the company and any thought of his buying out the husband's shares was well down his list of priorities. The 60% discount was accepted by Lord Clarke and was supported by the authors of the commentary of this case on the basis that the husband could easily have been replaced as an employee with very little effect on the business. This was not a case where a break up of the company on a sale at market value was imminent nor one in which the company was run like a partnership with each partner having a management role as in other cases.[45]

---

42   Ante note 41.
43   Ante. See also the discussion of *Stuart v Stuart No 2*, ante note 22.
44   2004 *Green's Family Law Bulletin* [68] 4, together with a helpful annotation.
45   See *Larsen v Larsen* 2003 GWD 25-715 and *Jackson v Jackson* 2000 SCLR 81.

H   Valuation problems and tax

The problem of what is the appropriate value of matrimonial assets such as shares which increase in value between the date of marriage and the date of separation, but which are subject to a contingent tax liability, arose in *Sweeney v Sweeney*.[46] On appeal the Extra Division of the Inner House held that as a matter of statutory construction the shares' value should be based on what a hypothetical purchaser would pay for the property, and this did not include a deduction for tax. One might add that any apparent unfairness is mitigated by the fact that the legal owner of the shares has the opportunity to minimise the tax liability by choosing an appropriate time to sell or by taking advantage of rules such as the rule that in any given year a capital gain of approximately £8,200 could be taken free of tax.[47]

III   STATUTE LAW REFORM

A   The Vulnerable Witnesses (Scotland) Act 2004

Scots law has increasingly recognised the views of mature children as an important factor to be taken into account in making decisions involving them.[48] A series of procedures have emerged by which courts ascertain the views of children.[49] However, when it comes to giving evidence in court the same willingness to accommodate children's special position has been less apparent. The Vulnerable Witnesses (Scotland) Act 2004, aims at making it easier and, as Sheriff Kearney says,[50] 'less daunting' for children and other vulnerable witnesses to give evidence in criminal and civil proceedings. Detailed provisions are given for defining 'vulnerable witnesses' before they give evidence and enabling them to give evidence by what are termed 'special measures'.[51] The Commencement Order[52] brought most of the provisions relating to children into force on 1 April 2005.

Generally vulnerable witnesses include children who are under 16 at the date of commencement of proceedings, together with other persons not being

---

[46]   2004 SCLR 256.

[47]   Taxation of Chargeable Gains Act 1992, s 3, as amended.

[48]   Section 6 of the Children (Scotland) Act 1995 makes the views of the child an important factor which parents should take into account when exercising any major decision based on a parental responsibility or right. The child is presumed to be mature enough to have a view on reaching 12, though he may be mature under that age. The only provisos mentioned are where the child (i) does not wish to express his views; (ii) or his being too young or immature to have them taken into account. Similar rules bind courts (s 11) and local authorities and children's hearings (s 16).

[49]   See Raitt 'Judicial discretion and methods of ascertaining the views of the child' (2004) 16 C & F LQ 151.

[50]   See his commentary 'Child and Other Vulnerable Witnesses' in 2005 *Green's Family Law Bulletin* [75] 2.

[51]   Section 18.

[52]   Vulnerable Witnesses (Scotland) Act 2004 Commencement Order 2005, SSI 2005/168.

child witnesses, where there is a significant risk that the quality of evidence to be given by a person will be diminished by reason of mental disorder or fear or distress in connection with giving evidence at trial.[53]

The use of special measures include:

(a) taking evidence by commissioner;

(b) use of a live television link;

(c) screening of the witness from an accused or other similar party; and

(d) allowing the child to have a 'supporter' with him or her;[54] or (e) further measures which may be added by the Scottish Ministers by statutory instrument.

Such measures are mandatory in most cases. The only exception to this is where the child does not want them, or where there is a risk of prejudicing the fairness of the proceedings and that risk outweighs the risk to the child. This creates a need for any party wishing to cite a child to lodge with the court a 'child witness notice' in accordance with existing Scots *delegated legislation* specifying the special measures thought appropriate, or stating why such measures might be unnecessary. Transfer of proceedings from a court not possessing the requisite technology to another possessing it is required under the Act. The court must then make either an order specifying which is the appropriate special measure or, alternatively, order that the child can give evidence without special measures. The considerations relevant to which (if any) special measures are required are specified[55] and include the best interest of the child witness, his or her age and maturity and the views of their parent. Following the practice of the Children (Scotland) Act 1995 children are presumed to be mature at 12.

The provisions relating to taking evidence by commissioner under s 19 have yet to be brought into force. The commissioner is presumably to be a judge or qualified lawyer appointed by the court. A party to the proceedings is only to be allowed to be present with the permission of the court, but is entitled to have access by live television link or other means to the proceedings; and the proceedings will be recorded on video.

In cases involving offences containing a significant sexual content the Act introduces two new provisions[56] to protect child witnesses from questioning on their prior sexual activity in child protection or sexual offence

---

[53]   Section 11(1)(a). A similar definition is provided for criminal proceedings by s 1. For reasons of brevity concentration has been placed on civil proceedings, since most of the provisions affecting criminal proceedings are in similar terms to those applicable to civil proceedings.

[54]   Defined by s 22 as 'a person who is not a witness, nominated by or on behalf of the child to sit alongside the child whilst he gives evidence, though without prompting or influencing the child'. Sheriff Kearney comments (*op cit*) on problems of ensuring compliance with the latter requirement.

[55]   Section 15.

[56]   Sections 68A and 68B to the Children (Scotland) Act 1995.

proceedings. Section 68B aims to protect the right of a party to question witnesses where the interest of justice so requires. An application must be made to the sheriff to allow such questioning of the child witness and the sheriff is empowered to permit such questioning on specific matters relevant to the proceedings where their probative value is likely to outweigh any risk of prejudice to the administration of justice, including appropriate protection for their dignity and privacy.

Previously[57] the evidence of a child or other vulnerable witness in both criminal and civil proceedings was subject to a test of competency. This required the judge to talk to the child, to see whether he or she understood the need to tell the truth and knew the difference between the truth and a lie.[58] If the judge decided the child had sufficient understanding then either the oath to tell the truth or an admonition to tell the truth was administered, leaving the jury to determine the weight to attach to the child's evidence: though Sutherland[59] questioned whether the child's evidence might be devalued in the eyes of the jury by this process. The common law test of competency was abolished by s 24 from 24 April 2005. Sheriff Kearney suggests, however, that children under 12 should still be admonished to tell the truth whereas for children aged 12 to 14, judicial inquiry into whether or not the child understands the nature of an oath to tell the truth will still be necessary.[60]

B The Family Law (Scotland) Bill 2005

Two major statutory sources of Scots family law affecting adults (the Divorce Act (Scotland) 1976 and the Family Law (Scotland) Act 1985) are increasingly showing their age. Over the last 15 years or more reform has been promised but has only recently shown signs of being implemented with the Family Law (Scotland) Bill 2005 which is the major reform in the period concerned. In addition, the patchy statutory treatment of opposite-sex cohabitation has been tackled in the 2005 Bill, along with certain matters relating to children that were not dealt with in the Children (Scotland) Act 1995. Also, notice has been given of a foreshadowed Adoption Bill which will make amendments in adoption law, which will bring Scots law into line with the Adoption and Children Act 2002, and was largely confined to English law, and in some cases went beyond it.[61] Although the Family Law

---

[57] See Sutherland *Child and Family Law* (T & T Clark, Edinburgh, 1999) p 95 for more detail.

[58] A splendid verbatim account of the judge's examination of a 5-year-old boy to see whether he could give 'an intelligent account' of his evidence can be found in Spencer and Flin *The Evidence of Children* (Blackstone Press, 2nd edn, 1993). However, it cannot be said that the examination of the 5-year-old seems searching.

[59] *Op cit*.

[60] Kearney, *op cit*, p 4.

[61] On 10 June 2005 the Deputy Minister of Education and Young Children announced in Dundee at the AGM of the British Association for Adoption and Fostering (Scotland) meeting that a new adoption statute would be introduced in 2006 to allow same-sex and unmarried couples to apply jointly to adopt children. Currently only one of a cohabiting pair can be the legal adopter with their

Bill 2005 has been referred to as an omnibus Bill, there are still other long-standing reforms of Scottish Family Law awaiting implementation such as the Scottish Law Commission's Report on the Law of Succession,[62] which is needed to prevent hardship to surviving spouses by allowing them to claim 'legal rights' in the family home (and other heritable property) which the present law does not allow.[63]

C   Divorce

1   Background

The existing Scots divorce law[64] is similar to the unhappy amalgam of 'fault'[65] and 'no fault'[66] proofs found in English law,[67] which masquerades as 'irretrievable breakdown' of marriage, the only ground for divorce. In practice, adultery and (unreasonable) behaviour, the two major fault-based proofs can lead to a divorce in under 2 months (depending on the region in which the court concerned operates). Where the parties have no dependent children, the proofs invoked tend to be the separation proofs, but, more worryingly, where there are dependent children, resort is often made to the fault based proofs which can bypass the need for at least a 2-year period of separation. In *Improving Scottish Family Law*[68] pie charts showed that in cases involving children in 1997, 70% of divorces relied on fault-based proofs and only 30% on non-fault separation proofs.[69] In contrast, in the same year, in cases where no children were involved, 78% were based on the separation proofs (predominantly 2 years' separation with consent) and only 22% involved fault-based proofs. The figures for 1998 are a little less clear-cut with reliance being made on the fault-based grounds in 54% of cases where there are children and on the separation proofs in the remaining 46% where there were children. Where no children were involved, 77% involved the separation proofs and 23% the fault-based proofs.[70] Since actions based

---

partner being obliged to seek parental rights under s 11 of the Children (Scotland) Act 1995. A new 'permanency order' will also be introduced to give (usually) older children the security of a new home without severing all legal ties to their birth family. 'Severance' is a feature of existing Scottish Adoption law.

62   Scottish Law Report 124, 1990 (Edinburgh).
63   Legal rights exist as a restraint on testamentary freedom, probably as a result of an old form of 'community property': see D R Macdonald *Succession* (2nd edn, 1994) 4.34 and the author's comments in 2004 JR at 153 for an amplification of the problems in Scots law.
64   Divorce (Scotland) Act 1976.
65   Adultery (s 1(2)(a)); behaviour (s 1(2)(b)); and the rarely used desertion proof (s 1(2)(c)).
66   Two years' separation with the consent of the defender (s 1(2)(d)) and 5 years' separation in other cases (s 1(2)(e)).
67   Currently found in the Matrimonial Causes Act 1973, but based on the Divorce Reform Act 1969.
68   A Scottish Office Consultation Paper 1999.
69   *Ibid*, p 4.
70   *Parents and Children*: White Paper on Scottish Family Law, Scottish Executive, Edinburgh, 2000, p 16. After 2000 the more detailed breakdown of divorce statistics referred to in the text appears to have been discontinued and the figures quoted by the Scottish Executive in their Explanatory Notes to the Family Law (Scotland) Bill at p 5, although more up to date, eg the figures for 2003 show

on the fault-based proofs are rarely defended, relatively little evidence is necessary to obtain a divorce.[71] In undefended cases the procedure can, unless the court otherwise directs, be based on affidavit rather than parole evidence. Sadly the Scottish simplified ('do-it-yourself')[72] procedure is much more restricted than its English counterpart.[73] The main limitations being to restrict cases to those involving the two separation proofs previously mentioned and to cases where there were no children of the marriage under 16. Some of the reforms in the Bill on divorce date back to 1989,[74] and seem less radical now than when they were introduced.

2 The Bill's proposals (cls 10–15)

The Bill follows the proposals in the Scottish Law Commission Report on Divorce.[75] This proposed to abolish the rarely used proof of desertion[76] and to reduce the periods of divorce on the basis of separation. The 2 years' separation with the consent of the other party will be reduced to one year and the 5-year period of separation will be reduced to 2 years. Whether the shortening of the periods of separation in the Bill will reduce the use of 'fault grounds' or of the 'leverage' of the party asked to consent to the divorce on the basis of separation for one year is open to question. This is particularly the case if, on refusal of the consent, the defender, usually the husband, decides to 'trump' the pursuer by proceeding with an action for divorce on a 'fault'-based proof, a not unlikely effect given the relative ease of proof of (unreasonable) behaviour. Moreover the use of consent as leverage to secure more advantageous financial provision or other ancillary terms[77] is recognised in the case-law as being exercisable without regard to motive, even where there is a withdrawing of a consent previously given.[78] It is arguable that some of the reasons advanced for the retention of 'fault-based' proofs no longer hold good. Is the need for some parties to have

---

that 82% of the cases where brought on the basis of the separation proofs, do not break the figures down between cases where there are or there are not children involved.

[71] For a not untypical case see *Meikle v Meikle* 1987 GWD 26-1005. The short account of this case can be read as revealing a clash of cultures, a wife from an urban background who married a hill farmer who spent long hours working to produce a limited income. The wife complained about being 'kept short' financially and sought a divorce. After an unsuccessful attempt at counselling the undefended proceedings resulted in a divorce. It would be a reasonable inference that the court decided to 'bury' a dead marriage.

[72] Found in Rules of Court based on SI 1982/1679.

[73] See Herring *Family Law* (OUP, 2nd edn, 2004) p 86.

[74] *Report on the Ground for Divorce*, Scottish Law Commission Report 116 (1989).

[75] *Supra*. The more radical proposal of the Scottish Law Commission's Discussion Paper No 76 of the same name dated February 1989 seems consigned to history. It had proposed divorce after the passage of a given period of time after a notice of intention to divorce had been served on the other party during which in all probability the parties would have separated. The period notice was not stated but widely assumed to be a year.

[76] Used in only 1% or so of cases according to *Parents and Children*, Scottish Executive, Edinburgh, 2000, p 16.

[77] Save for questions of parenting which are subject to the best interests of the child.

[78] *Boyle v Boyle* 1977 SLT (Notes) 69. The point is reinforced by the exchange between Charles McNair and Nicholas Mostyn in *The Report to the Lord Chancellor by the Ancillary Relief Advisory Group*, July 1998, Appendix 3, p 56.

access to a speedy divorce still so pressing? This reason adduced by the Scottish Law Commission, in Report 116, seems influenced by the view that the police were more likely to become involved in suppressing cases of family violence once the parties were no longer married and issues of marital privacy were not involved. However, with the passage of the Protection from Abuse (Scotland) Act 2001[79] and the amendments proposed in this Bill to the Matrimonial Homes (Family Protection) (Scotland) Act 1981, aimed at providing better remedies against domestic violence regardless of whether the parties are married, this approach seems questionable.

The abolition of 'fault-based proofs' might have enabled the Scottish Executive to meet the argument that the reforms make divorce easier in the sense of being obtained more quickly whilst doing nothing to minimise the bitterness attendant on 'fault'-based proofs. The abolition of 'fault' has been the approach in Australia ever since the Family Law Act 1975 and has given rise to no significant problems.[80] The reduction of the regrettably high divorce rate in Scotland, one of the highest in Europe, is more likely to be successful by an approach of providing sufficient funding to organisations such as Couples Counselling, Scotland. This would enable the parties to seek an early first interview, coupled with a series of reconciliation meetings thereafter, in an attempt to see whether the marriage can be saved.

If the Executive implements legislation as presently framed, then it might be preferable to introduce it in the first place in a limited area of Scotland, ie one or two sheriffdoms in urban and rural areas. This would enable monitoring of whether:

(i) the number of 'fault'-based proofs will fall, as hoped, under the new statutory regime; and

(ii) more importantly, whether the 'fault'-based proofs decline in number in cases in which there are dependent children.

D   Parental responsibilities and rights (cl 17)

The existing Scots law is that, though 'unmarried fathers' do not have parental responsibilities and rights, other than of support, little or no evidence is needed to support an unmarried father's claim for contact particularly where the father has had contact with the child during the relationship prior to it breaking down. It is generally assumed[81] that contact in such circumstances will be conducive to the child's welfare.[82] However, where the father has had no prior contact with the child, then different

---

[79]   The 'anti-stalking' provisions of the Protection from Harassment Act 1997 seem to have been relatively little used, possibly because of the statutory requirement of 'a course of conduct'.

[80]   The decision of the Canadian Government to combine one year's separation with fault-based proofs was the subject of strenuous debate on the Canadian Bar Committee's Family Law Sub-Committee on which the author served at the time of the passage of the Divorce Act 1985.

[81]   The Court declined to raise this to a presumption.

[82]   See *White v White* 2001 SC 689.

considerations come into play and the court may be unwilling to make a contact order in favour of the father in such circumstances. In *McKerrow v Crawford*[83] a mother and the father of the child had a brief relationship which the mother broke off soon after becoming pregnant saying that she wanted nothing more to do with the father. Sheriff Principal Bowen declined to make a contact order requested by the father. The Bill proposes to give parental responsibilities and rights to unmarried fathers who have registered the birth of their child jointly with the mother. This reform, which is already in force in England under the Adoption and Children Act 2002, will not operate retrospectively. It might be appropriate to monitor the operation of the reform to see whether there is any reduction in the number of joint registrations of the birth of children born outside marriage. The laudable aim of the legislation is to increase the involvement of some fathers with their children, and to prevent the 40% of fathers who almost immediately lose touch with their children on relationship breakdown.[84] Given this aim, it would be unfortunate if mothers became reluctant to join in joint registrations of the birth of their child. One provision on children which had been envisaged in the earlier Scottish Executive and Discussion Papers[85] was to introduce step-parent agreements, by which a step-parent could acquire parental rights over their child by virtue of the agreement rather than a court order.[86] The British Agencies for Adoption and Fostering regretted the omission of this provision when they gave evidence to the Justice Committee. Such agreements would give the child an additional parent rather than replacing the birth father (as it would usually be) by the stepfather. Some of the difficulties associated with such agreements could be cured by requiring the agreement of the child of 12 or more acting on his own behalf, or if a child was under 12, by someone acting on the child's behalf, who could confirm that the matter has been discussed with the child and the child was in agreement.[87]

E   Cohabitants

The provisions giving increased rights to cohabitants, have to be seen in a context in which rights analogous to marriage have been given to registered

[83]   2004 *Green's Family Law Bulletin* [67] 5.

[84]   *Children Come First – a new approach to child support* 1998, Cm 3992, HMSO.

[85]   See *Family Matters* Scottish Executive, Edinburgh, 2004, p 12; *Parents and Children* Scottish Executive, 2000, Edinburgh, p 9; and *Improving Scottish Family Law*, Scottish Executive, Edinburgh, 1999, p 28.

[86]   Currently this can only be done by a court order, which is expensive for the parties, or by making an irrevocable parental rights agreement in prescribed form. This agreement has to be lodged in the Books of Council and Session, Scotland's official register for such documents (s 4 of the Children (Scotland) Act 1995). The need for, and availability of, the latter seems to have been unknown to many unmarried fathers, and they are rare. Just as one might expect of a procedure which seems unnecessary and expensive when the relationship is working well, but an unnecessary watering down of the mother's rights when the relationship is failing.

[87]   The failure of the Adoption and Children Act to deal with this was criticised by BAAF in their evidence to the Scottish Executive's Justice No 1 Committee.

same-sex partners,[88] whilst the growing number of heterosexual cohabitants[89] and, *a fortiori*, unregistered same-sex cohabitants, have only been given limited rights. The provisions in the Bill inevitably have a dated feel about them since things have moved on from the publication of the Scottish Law Commission Report No 53 on Family Law in 1992, on which most of the proposals are based. The law in other jurisdictions, as the Scottish Executive's Social Research Paper of 2005 demonstrates only too clearly,[90] has moved on substantially. The belief that the parties to such an agreement could marry if they chose to, ignores the need for consensus in a situation in which the economically stronger partner may well choose not to act against their own selfish interests. The danger lies in creating a new 'under class' for whom the safety net provided by these proposals, is appreciably weaker than might be required, not merely when judged against recent developments in jurisdictions such as Australasia, Canada and parts of the European Union which have introduced provisions which give cohabitants rights on break-up of the relationship similar to those of married couples. The rights created by the Bill are modest when judged against existing English law. Currently English common law allows remedies such as the constructive trust and equitable estoppel to be deployed by English claimants against a wide variety of assets including land.[91] These are supplemented by the statutory amendments in 1995,[92] allowing claims for discretionary relief to be made out of a deceased's estate by a person living with the deceased:

> '... during the whole period of two years ending immediately before the date when the deceased died ... in the same household as the deceased, and as the husband or wife of the deceased.'

In addition more radical promises of statutory reform have been promised in England.[93]

There is likely to be significant opposition to giving too many rights to cohabitants, because many Church groups would regard this as inconsistent with protecting the sanctity of marriage, a relationship which is beneficial to

---

[88] Civil Partnership Act 2004 – applicable to Scotland by virtue of a Sewel motion conferring legislative power on the Westminster Parliament for predominantly devolved matters of Scots family law.

[89] See Table 7, p 22 of the Explanatory Notes accompanying the Bill.

[90] See S Bulloch and D Headrick *Cross-jurisdictional Comparison of Legal Provisions for Unmarried Cohabiting Couples,* Scottish Executive Social Research, Legal Studies, Research Findings No 55/2005. See also Barlow and Bissett-Johnson 'Cohabitation and the Reform of Scots Law' 2003 JR 105.

[91] The reason for this seems, particularly in the case of heritage, to involve a reluctance on the part of Scots law to create interests which do not appear on either of the Scottish Land Registers. In addition it creates problems in bankruptcy situations, but is also open to criticism for a lack of precision in defining constructive trusts. See Gretton 'Constructive Trusts' (1996–97) 1 ELR 281 and 408, who argues that the constructive trust exists only to a limited extent in Scots law, provides an unsatisfactory remedy and would be better replaced by a statute.

[92] Law Reform (Succession) Act 1995, reforming the Inheritance (Provision for Family and Dependants) Act 1975 by adding new ss 1(1)(ba) and 1A.

[93] See 'Cohabitation Reform' (2005) *Family Law* 344.

the State[94] and to the children of the marriage. However, it must be doubted whether it is appropriate for the law to collude passively in the financial exploitation of the weaker party, usually the women and their children, on the ending of a cohabitation relationship. Nor does the fact that cohabitants could choose to marry, meet the consideration that often the financially more secure cohabitant will simply decline to marry, as a way of selfishly avoiding a loss of economic benefits. Whilst accepting that many cohabitation relationships break down quickly, it would be possible to give increased rights to cohabitants in relationships which are of longer duration, eg 2 years, as is done in Australia. Simply sloughing off the changes in the law made in jurisdictions similar to Scotland, such as Australasia and Canada, as unsuitable for transplanting into Scotland is a parochial view. The weaker partner (and their children) in a failed long-term cohabitation relationship is left with an inadequate safety net – one that will often lead them to becoming a charge on the public purse. It would be preferable if more significant remedies had been made available to Scottish cohabitants, especially in the light of the proposed reforms foreshadowed by the Westminster Parliament, which is alleged to be considering more significant changes in English law than those prepared by the Executive.[95]

The rights introduced by the Bill are quite limited. The presumption of a right to share in the value of household goods acquired during cohabitation conferred by cl 19 of the Bill, is based on s 26 of the Family Law (Scotland) Act 1985. The exclusion of homes, which are not by definition 'household goods', money (excluded by para (a)), securities (excluded by para (b)) and motor vehicles (excluded by para (c)), operates to exclude most things of value that cohabitants might wish to share on the breakdown of the relationship. What is left is likely to be a share in the value of potentially rapidly depreciating assets such as furniture and electrical goods, or assets of limited value such as second-hand bedding, china and crockery. There is nothing wrong with the proposal provided that its limitations in practice are appreciated. That seems doubtful from para 65 of the Explanatory Notes and Other Accompanying Documents.

An illustration may assist with the argument (all items are assumed to have been acquired during cohabitation until the relationship failed):

Equity in house of richer cohabitant	£25,000 not shareable
Car of richer cohabitant	£2,500 not shareable
Pension, insurance, bank account, savings/shares of richer cohabitant	£7,500 not shareable
Second-hand value of furniture and plenishings of richer cohabitant	£5,000 shareable
TOTAL	£35,000

---

[94] Eg the duty of mutual financial support serves to keep many spouses off social security.
[95] See *The Guardian* 14 March 2005 and 'Cohabitation Reform' (2005) *Family Law* 344.

Poorer cohabitant only acquires 50% of furniture	£2,500
Richer cohabitant keeps	£32,500

The new right to share in property or money derived from a housekeeping allowance is based on the Married Women's Property Act 1964, a statutory provision in favour of spouses described by a leading English author as based on an 'outdated' scenario of family finances.[96] The provision harks back to a time when 'housekeeping' allowances and non-working mothers were more common. Clearly there is nothing wrong in presuming that cohabitants wish to share windfall lottery or similar profits, but for cohabitants operating with limited financial resources it would be wrong to see this provision as having a significant contribution towards resolving the finances on the breakdown of a relationship.

Clause 21 gives an applicant a new right to a capital sum for any economic disadvantage that they have suffered in the interests of the defender, or any child of the cohabitants, or for any advantage they have conferred on the defender and is modelled on s 9(1)(b) of the Family Law (Scotland) Act 1985. Unfortunately, a present Scottish Law Commissioner and former Regius Professor of Law has pointed out the limited use that has been made of s 9(1)(b).[97] If its use to spouses is limited, it is open to question how much it will benefit a cohabitant. The reported case-law shows that, in the main, it has been of use in cases where spouses have substantial resources[98] and is a way of permitting a remedy where assets would not be shareable matrimonial assets under s 10 of the 1985 Act, but where a spouse has (i) inherited assets during the marriage or (ii) where assets owned prior to marriage have appreciated substantially during the marriage.[99] The value of these two items would not be shareable on divorce. In the context of cohabitation between spouses of limited resources, the court under the 1985 Act must consider whether the economic disadvantages suffered by the applicant have been balanced by the advantages conferred on the applicant by the defender, usually the man.[100] Assuming the process applicable to *cohabitants* under cl 20 is similar, it may be that the applicant's claim will, at best, be a fairly limited one.

---

[96]   Herring *Family Law* (Pearson/Longmans, 2nd edn, 2004) p 129.
[97]   J Thomson *Family Law in Scotland* (6th edn) p 159.
[98]   See eg *De Winton v De Winton* 1996 Fam LB 23-6 and *Wilson v Wilson* 1999 249. For a discussion of these and related cases and a broader discussion of whether such claims, particularly for lost careers, are best dealt with by an award of a capital sum or periodical allowances see Bissett-Johnson 1999 SLT (News) 37.
[99]   Interestingly this problem is addressed by cl 14 of the Bill.
[100] See s 11(2) of the 1985 Act.

F Miscellaneous sections

1 *Clause 1 (Marriage to the parent of the former spouse)*

The Marriage (Scotland) Act 1977 restricts certain people from marrying. In addition to forbidding persons related by blood ties from intermarrying, a group of people who were related by 'affinity' were also forbidden to intermarry, unless certain other conditions were met – these conditions aimed at protecting roles within the family.[101] Although there might be thought to be few people who would wish to marry the in-law of a former spouse whom they had divorced, they were included in this group unless certain conditions were satisfied. Currently such persons can only intermarry after the death of both the former spouse and in-law. The assumption being that by this stage the 'affront' to family roles will have disappeared. However, these restrictions are removed by c 1 of the Bill. This reflects the suggestion of the Scottish Law Commission in their Report 135 that they gave rise to unnecessary, odd and unreasonable consequences.[102] They cited one case where a woman had divorced her husband and obtained custody[103] of her children. Her husband's parents were a great support in raising the children and the woman in turn helped with caring for her ex-mother-in-law until the mother-in-law died. Some time later she and her ex-father-in-law decided that they would like to marry, but were told that they could not because the woman's former husband was still alive.[104] The matter has recently come to the fore in a case involving 'L' and 'B' who successfully argued before the European Court of Human Rights[105] that whilst the corresponding English provision[106] had the legitimate aim of protecting family integrity, in the absence of criminal sanctions it did not prevent extramarital relations between couples caught by the statutory provision. The mere fact that the parties could avoid the problem by seeking a Private Act of Parliament to exempt themselves from the statutory ban on marriage was insufficient to save the ban and the parties were awarded costs of £12,000 plus expenses.

G Consent and void marriages

It is not uncommon for parties to *enter* a valid civil ceremony of marriage and then to argue that the marriage is invalid because the parties (or one of them) believed that a religious ceremony was required in addition to the earlier civil ceremony. Such a marriage in Scots law,[107] unlike English

---

[101] See SLC Report 135, *ante*, para 811.
[102] *Ibid*, para 8.8.
[103] The term has since been replaced by residence.
[104] See SLC Report 135, *ante*, paras 8.8 and 8.9.
[105] See *B an L v United Kingdom* (Application No 36536/02) (2005) *The Times*, October 5.
[106] Marriage Act 1949, s 1, Sch 1, Part 3.
[107] See Thomson *Family Law in Scotland* (Butterworths, 4th edn, 2002) p 40 *et seq* and cases like *Orlandi v Castelli* 1961 SC 113 and *Mahmud v Mahmud* 1977 SLT (Notes) 17.

law,[108] may be void for lack of true consent. Despite some reservations by the judiciary, this also applies where the parties' ulterior motive for a marriage was to secure a collateral advantage such as to evade the UK immigration rules.[109] The Bill alters the law in a way first suggested by the Scottish Law Commission,[110] that where it can be established that a party was aware of the nature of the ceremony to which they ostensibly consented, such a marriage will be valid. The statutory modification has the beneficial effect of making the law on 'sham marriages' for a collateral advantage, eg immigration benefits, the same in Scotland as in England.

H   Amendments to the law of financial provision[111]

The Bill, as originally drafted, attempts to solve the problem by giving a court the power, on the application of one of the parties, but not by the court *ex proprio motu*, a discretion by which it can take into account a change in net value, not merely between marriage and the relevant date (usually the date of separation), but also later dates such as those agreed on by the parties or the date on which the court makes the determination or such other date as the court determines. Unfortunately it does not deal with the problem of inherited property or property such as a home which one party owned before the parties married and which became the family home and then substantially increased in value during the marriage – not an unusual case in a marriage of any significant length. Such property is not part of the matrimonial property to be shared under s 10(4)(b) of the 1985 Act. The author has advocated[112] the need to do something with such cases by way of an addition to the proposed cl 14 as a way of enabling the court to deal with cases such as *Maclellan v Maclellan*,[113] without regard to subtle arguments about whether property has 'changed character' from 'inherited property' (excluded from being 'a matrimonial asset'), to being a 'matrimonial asset' and therefore shareable.[114] There is probably equally a case for widening cl 14 to cover other assets, which would normally be matrimonial assets but

---

108   See Herring *Family Law* (Longman, 2nd edn, 2004) p 56.
109   See Lord Dunpark's comments in *Akram v Akram* 1979 SLT (Notes) 87.
110   See *Report on Family Law* HMSO (1992) p 72 *et seq*.
111   For some assets such as farms the exemption is larger and no capital gain is payable in respect of the increase in value of a party's family home.
112   See Bissett-Johnson and Barton 'Financial Provision in Scots Law – Does it Need Reform' (2000) JR 265 at 270–272.
113   1988 SCLR 399. The case involved a woman who married a crofter only to find after the breakdown of a marriage of 26 years that she had no claim to the croft since the husband had bought it prior to their marriage. In other cases s 9(i)(b) of the Act has sometimes mitigated the harshness of this problem but cases like *De Winton* and *Wilson* mentioned above in note 98 suggest that this cannot be regarded as a totally adequate solution. Indeed the restriction on s 9(1)(b) by s 9(2) to compensation for 'economic advantages and disadvantages' suffered or benefits in the interest of the other party or of the family 'whether before or during the marriage', poses difficulties for a woman who faces future post-separation career losses. See the comments of Sheriff Morrison in *Dougan v Dougan* 1998 SLT (Sh Ct) 27, though the need to take a longer-term future view of career losses was suggested by Sheriff Principal Bowen in *Cahill v Cahill* 1998 SLT (Sh Ct) 96.
114   See the case of *Latter v Latter* 1990 SLT 426.

where their exclusion from the matrimonial 'pot' leads to a risk of an unfair division. There is a case for consideration being given to:

(i) including within the matrimonial assets 'any family home used by both the parties during the marriage' irrespective of whether it had been acquired for use by them;

(ii) to allow an application in circumstances where property excluded from sharing such as inherited property or property acquired by way of gift had increased substantially during any marriage other than a short one;[115]

(iii) in the case of jointly owned property such as the matrimonial home, using a current valuation at the time of trial rather than a valuation at the 'relevant' date;[116]

(iv) in the cases of pensions, especially those of the 'uniformed forces', for allowing a current valuation at trial rather than the relevant date, where there has been a significant rise in value of the pension between the two dates.

1 Clause 16 (Domicil of a minor)

This clause had been advocated by the Scottish Law Commission as a means of removing the last *vestige* of illegitimacy in Scots law. The existing Scots law attributed a different domicil of origin to a child depending on whether they were born in wedlock or not.[117] Clause 16(3) contains a series of rebuttable presumptions about the domicil[118] of a child. Whilst both parents are alive and a child has a home with one or both parents who are domiciled in the same country the child will be domiciled in that country. Where both parents are alive and the child lives with only one parent and the parents are domiciled in different countries then the child's domicil is that of the country in which the parent with whom he or she resides. In the case of the death of one of the parents with whom the child resided, the relevant domicil is that of the country in which the parent with whom the child resided, unless the child has resided with the surviving parent, in which case the child takes his domicil from that parent. Further presumptions are provided to cover all contingencies which lead to the child being domiciled in the country with which he or she is most closely connected. It is regrettable, however, that the wider reforms of the law of domicil advocated by the English and Scottish Law Commissions' Domicil Reports[119] have not been implemented. The time for review of doctrines such as the revival of the domicil of choice and

---

[115] Mentioned earlier in the text to note 22 *et seq*. This attracted considerable criticism from members of the 'Lord Chancellor's Advisory Relief Committee' July 1998, Appendix 3, p 13 and even from some of the Scottish lawyers who addressed the Committee (see the remarks of McNair, *ibid*, at p 14 *et seq*).

[116] See the discussion of the *Wallis Trap* earlier.

[117] See Anton *Private International Law* (SULI/W Greens, Edinburgh, 2nd edn, 1990) p 130 *et seq*.

[118] Both domicil of origin and dependence.

[119] English Law Com No 168 (1987) and Scottish Law Com No 107 (1987) discussed by Anton *Private International Law* (SULI/W Greens, Edinburgh, 2nd edn, 1990) p 135 *et seq*.

the undue emphasis on intention in determining domicil of choice, are long overdue. It would have been better to have had a comprehensive Domicil Bill rather than dealing only with limited aspects of the problem.[120]

2   Clause 28–30 (Private international law)

The common law rules relating to capacity to marry, consent to marry, and formalities of marriage, have been the subject of the debate in the existing case-law. The more orthodox view is that capacity to marry is governed by the *lex domicilii* of the party concerned at the time of marriage,[121] but other views can be found.[122] The orthodox views receive statutory recognition[123] along with cl 28(4) which states that a failure to obtain a parental consent on the part of a party domiciled outside Scotland will only invalidate the marriage if the failure to obtain the parental consent would make the marriage void. This appears to confirm the decision in *Bliersback v McEwan*,[124] that a failure on the part of a Dutch lady to obtain her father's consent to her marriage in Scotland would merely make the marriage voidable rather than void *ab initio*. The father's objection which had been lodged with the marriage registrar was therefore rejected. The clause also makes clear that marriages valid by the *lex loci celebrationis*, are to be recognised in Scotland subject to the special rules contained in the Foreign Marriages Acts 1892, 1947 and 1988.

Clause 29 introduces into Scots law, for the first time, rules about the applicable law to questions of matrimonial property. These are, however, of only limited application since cl 29(6) specifically excludes financial provision on divorce or cases where the spouses have made their own contract. What are left are largely questions of express or implied marriage contracts, a comparative and relatively rare phenomenon in the UK. Unsurprisingly the questions governing immoveable property are governed by the *lex situs*, together with issues involving the use or occupation of the matrimonial home and its contents.[125] In the case of moveable property where the parties are domiciled in the same area the general rule is that the law of the common domicil is to apply,[126] subject to a rule that rights in moveable property which have vested in a spouse cannot be lost by a change of domicil.[127] Where the parties are domiciled in different areas, any issues about the rights of parties in each other's moveable property arising by virtue of marriage are to be decided on the basis of such property as they had

---

[120]   I acknowledge the assistance of my colleague Prof McEleavy in formulating these views.

[121]   See Anton, *op cit*, pp 428 *et seq* and 442 *et seq*.

[122]   See Anton, *op cit* pp 428 and 442.

[123]   Clause 28(2), though where a foreign divorce is recognised in Scotland, a party can remarry in Scotland even if the divorce is not recognised in the place where a party was domiciled immediately before the marriage.

[124]   1959 SC 43.

[125]   Clause 29(1) and (4).

[126]   Clause 29(3), though this is subject to cl 29(4) and (5).

[127]   Thus codifying the result of *De Nichols v Curlier* [1900] AC 21 and *De Nichols v Curlier No 2* [1900] 2 Ch 410.

before the marriage. This still leaves open complicated issues where rights in property arise by virtue of cohabitation under one or both of the parties' domiciliary law.

IV MATRIMONIAL HOMES AND MATRIMONIAL INTERDICTS (CLS 4–8)

In Scotland a spouse whose name does not appear on the title of a matrimonial home, the 'non-entitled-spouse', acquires rights of occupation[128] in the matrimonial home by virtue of marriage. Such rights of occupation can bind third parties, unless they have taken the precaution, when buying a house of obtaining an affidavit from the seller, that the house was not a matrimonial home at the relevant time or of obtaining the 'non-entitled-spouse's' consent to the disposition. Alternatively a court order may be obtained to dispense with the need for the consent of the 'unentitled spouse'. In order to provide an effective remedy for victims of domestic abuse, orders may be obtained from the court requiring to restrain or prohibit an entitled spouse from harassing the other, or to exclude the entitled spouse from the matrimonial home. Although such orders are civil in nature, they can be enforced by the police via the expedient of attaching powers of arrest to them.[129] More limited remedies are available to *'non* entitled' cohabitants.[130] One of the sad anomalies of the present Matrimonial Homes (Family Protection) (Scotland) Act 1981, arises from the wording of the Act that it is only the *non-entitled* partner who can take advantage of the occupancy order provisions of the Act. Thus, in *Clarke v Hatten*,[131] a woman, who was the entitled partner under s 18 of the 1981 Act, was unable to obtain an interdict against her violent non-entitled partner. It was held that she could avail herself of a remedy under the 1981 Act only in the unlikely circumstances of her violent partner bringing proceedings under that Act against her. She was left to her common law remedies rather than the more extensive ones under the 1981 Act. It seems a pity that this anomaly was not removed in the Bill either in cl 4 or 24 and the Act made as comprehensive as possible, notwithstanding that a remedy may arise under the Protection from Abuse Act 2002. The Bill does, however, make some changes to the 1981 Act. The range of interdicts available to prevent domestic violence are renamed 'domestic interdicts' and extended to cover, not merely opposite-sex cohabitants, but also same-sex ones.[132] Such interdicts cover not merely

128 Ie to continue to live in the matrimonial home, or, if not living there, a right to occupy it.
129 Matrimonial Homes (Family Protection) (Scotland) Act 1981, discussed in more detail by Thomson *Family Law in Scotland* (Butterworths, 4th edn, 2002) p 85 *et seq.*
130 The rights only arise by court order, which last only for 6 months unless renewed, and do not bind third parties.
131 1987 SCLR 527.
132 Clause 26. Giving effect to the Civil Partnership Act 2004 which, though largely governing devolved matters of Scots family law, was passed by the Westminster Parliament pursuant to a Sewel motion. This empowered the Westminster Parliament to legislate in respect of matters devolved to the Scottish Parliament.

the matrimonial home but are extended to cover any other home occupied by the applicant and their place of work, or of any school attended by a child in the care of the applicant.[133]

The Bill also makes minor changes to the 1981 Act to deal with conveyancing problems which may arise in relation to homes subject to occupation rights. Clause 4 introduces a time bar on the assertion of rights by a 'non-entitled' spouse. Where there has been no cohabitation between a married couple for 2 years during which the 'non-entitled spouse' has not occupied the matrimonial home, the occupancy rights of the 'non-entitled spouse' will cease. To cover the case where a third party buys a house from another third party in a chain of dealings initiated by the 'entitled spouse' but where the third party is unaware of the existence of a 'non-entitled spouse', then after 2 years[134] in which the 'non-entitled' spouse has not occupied the home then the 'non-entitled spouse' will lose their rights of occupation.

V   FAMILY LEGISLATION STILL REQUIRING ATTENTION

As the Bill has been referred to as an omnibus Family Law Bill consideration will be given either to adding clauses to deal with the following matters, or, in the case of adoption and succession, to bringing forward the promised bills dealing with these topics at an early date.

A   Succession

Although there is nothing in the Act which goes towards implementation of the Scottish Law Commission's Report on Reform of Succession Law[135] the failure to implement it throws up cases of severe hardship within family law. A spouse only acquires legal rights in the moveable property of their deceased spouse; thus in one tragic but memorable case known to the author,[136] a husband and wife who had been married for many years and who had one daughter, became embroiled in a bitter divorce. The main asset was the family home which stood in the husband's name. Just before the conclusion of the divorce action, the husband transferred the family home to his daughter and then took the drastic step of committing suicide. This had the effect of halting the divorce proceedings and the claim for financial provision that went with it; the wife was no longer a spouse for the purposes of the Matrimonial Homes (Family Protection) (Scotland) Act 1981, as amended, and was left without any effective remedy in respect of the main asset.

---

[133]   Clause 8(2).
[134]   Rather than 5 years as at present.
[135]   Report 124 (1990).
[136]   See Bissett-Johnson, *op cit*, note 25.

B Marriages by cohabitation with habit and repute

Whilst many would have preferred to accept the Law Commission's proposal in Report 135 for the abolition of this rare form of marriage, the same people would urge that, even if these marriages are retained, the ability of the Court of Session to backdate such a marriage to a date prior to a later formally valid marriage, should be abolished. It cannot be right for a declarator of this nature to put in jeopardy a prior formally valid Scottish marriage which met all the requirements for a valid marriage when it was celebrated. This possibility was envisaged by the Scottish Law Commission in Report 135 at para 7.3, p 64 and a case illustrating this problem has recently been reported.[137] Although action was promised on this in *Family Matters* – the Scottish Executive's 2004 White Paper at p 56 – the chance of solving this problem seems to have been missed.

---

[137] *Sheikh v Sheikh* 2005 *Green's Family Law Bulletin* [74] 8.

Serbia and Montenegro

THE NEW FAMILY ACT OF SERBIA

Marija Draškić* and Gordana Kovaček Stanić**

Résumé

La Loi serbe sur la famille fut adoptée par le Parlement en février 2005 et est entrée en vigueur huit jours après sa publication. En réalité, sa mise en œuvre n'est effective que depuis le 1ᵉʳ juillet 2005.

Cet article comporte deux parties. La première explique les raisons qui ont conduit la Serbie à se doter d'une nouvelle loi sur la famille et la seconde présente les principaux aspects de celle-ci. La présentation des plus importants concepts contenus dans la loi est divisée elle-même en deux parties: la première fait état de principes nouveaux et la seconde explique les changements apportés aux principes existants. Les principales nouveautés sont les suivantes: la reconnaissance des droits de l'enfant, l'exercice conjoint des droits parentaux, la protection contre la violence familiale, la mise en place d'une procédure de médiation, la spécialisation des juges, la création du contrat nuptial et du contrat de donation, le droit d'habitation, l'émancipation, la protection du droit au nom. Les domaines qui ont subi d'importants changements sont les suivants: l'adoption, la cohabitation hors mariage, le divorce, les actions d'état , les règles de filiation en matière de procréation médicalement assistée, l'obligation alimentaire, les régimes matrimoniaux et la capacité des mineurs en matière contractuelle.

The Serbian Family Act was adopted in Parliament in February 2005 and entered into force 8 days after being published. However, its implementation began on 1 July 2005.[1] The Draft Family Act was prepared by a Draft team with Professor Marija Draškić as a coordinator and Professor Gordana Kovaček Stanić as one of the members. In Montenegro, the Family Act entered into force in 1989.[2]

1   WHY DID SERBIA NEED THE NEW FAMILY ACT?

Family law matters are very important in a catalogue of issues pertaining to legal policy in general. Family structure and family relations affect society in

---

*   Faculty of Law, University of Belgrade.
**   Faculty of Law, University of Novi Sad. Translated by Mirna Rakić.
1   *Official Journal of the Republic of Serbia*, no 18/2005.
2   *Official Journal of the Republic of Montenegro*, no 7/1989.

several different ways: economically, educationally, socially, psychologically and emotionally. Human beings live in families in order to satisfy essential needs in the life of every individual – the need for human touch and the development of a person. These cannot be imagined without a family. In that respect, the family provides a connection between society and an individual, stronger and better than any other social group – the universality of the human need for a family and the individuality of the family's significance in the life of every individual. On the other hand, the development of civilization and common social transformations arising from that development, including innovations in medical accomplishments and new technologies, inevitably affect the role of the family in society, but also influence changes within the family itself.

Many important international legal acts have been adopted during the last two decades of the twentieth century, following changes under the auspices of the United Nations and Council of Europe, which have established new standards in family law and practice. One should bear in mind that the Serbian Law on Marriage and Family Relations was adopted a long time ago, in 1980;[3] thus it is clear that this law did not contain references to some of the most important international legal documents which in the meantime have become the source of domestic law (they are listed in chronological order according to the time of ratification):

- Convention on the Rights of the Child;[4]
- Convention on the Civil Aspects of International Child Abduction;[5]
- European Convention on Recognition and Enforcement of Decisions concerning Custody of Children and on Restoration of Custody of Children;[6]

---

[3]   See *Official Journal of the Socialist Republic of Serbia*, no 22/1980. This Law entered into force 8 days after being published, but has been effective since 1 January 1981 pursuant to Art 419. This Law has been changed and amended several times. See Law Amending the Law on Marriage and Family Relations (*Official Journal of the Socialist Republic of Serbia*, no 11/1988) and Law Amending and Supplementing the Law on Marriage and Family Relations (*Official Journal of the Republic of Serbia*, nos 22/1993, 35/1994 and 29/2001).

[4]   It was adopted by the Resolution of the United Nations General Assembly of 20 November 1989, and was ratified by Yugoslavia in 1990, *Official Gazette of the Socialist Federal Republic of Yugoslavia-International Contracts*, no 15/1990. The following acts have been ratified later: the Optional Protocol to the Convention on the Rights of the Child on Involvement of Children in Armed Conflicts, which forbids the compulsory conscription and direct participation of persons who have not yet attained the age of 18 in armed conflicts and the Optional Protocol to the Convention on the Rights of the Child on the Sale of Children, Child Prostitution, and Child Pornography, by which the member states undertook to punish child trafficking, child prostitution and child pornography by the operation of the criminal law. See *Official Gazette of the Federal Republic of Yugoslavia-International Contracts*, no 7/2002.

[5]   It was adopted within the Hague Academy of Private International Law on 25 October 1980, ratified by Yugoslavia in 1991, *Official Gazette of the Socialist Federal Republic of Yugoslavia-International Contracts*, no 7/1991.

[6]   It was adopted in Luxembourg, on 20 May 1980, ratified by Yugoslavia in 2001, *Official Gazette of the Federal Republic of Yugoslavia-International Contracts*, no 1/2001.

- Convention No 182 on the Worst Forms of Child Labour;[7]
- European Convention for Protection of Human Rights and Fundamental Freedoms amended according to the Protocol number 11.[8]

However, some important changes happened in the country after the adoption of the Law on Marriage and Family Relations. At the time of the adoption its application was limited only to the territory of Serbia without the provinces, except for the General Principles (Arts 26–39), which had uniform application in the entire territory of the Republic of Serbia according to Art 300, para 1, item 5 of the Constitution of the Socialist Republic of Serbia. Amendment 33 to the Constitution of the Socialist Republic of Serbia exceeded the number of family matters that became uniformly regulated by the Republic of Serbia for the entire territory. Meanwhile, a new Constitution of the Republic of Serbia was adopted in 1990 and it created preconditions for regulating family matters in a uniform way in the territory of the Republic of Serbia. However, adoption of the Constitution of the Federal Republic of Yugoslavia in 1992 once again raised the issue of division of legislative power in the field of family law between the federal state and member states. The uniform application of the Law on Marriage and Family Relations in the territory of the Republic of Serbia was accomplished by the adoption of the Constitutional Act on Changes and Supplements to the Constitutional Law for the Enforcement of the Constitution of the Republic of Serbia.[9] Finally, the previous dilemma

---

[7] It was adopted by the General Conference of the International Labor Organization in Geneva on 1 June 1999, ratified by Yugoslavia in 2003, *Official Gazette of the Federal Republic of Yugoslavia-International Contracts,* no 2/2003. The Convention contains also the Recommendation of the International Labor Organization number 190 Concerning the Prohibition and Immediate Action for the Elimination of the Worst Forms of Child Labor, which was also subject to ratification.

[8] It was ratified by Serbia and Montenegro in 2003, *Official Gazette of Serbia and Montenegro-International Contracts,* no 9/2003. At the same time, the State Union of Serbia and Montenegro ratified several Protocols to the European Convention for the Protection of Human Rights and Fundamental Freedoms, namely: The First Protocol of 20 March 1952, Protocol no 4 which provides for certain rights and freedoms that have not been included in the Convention and the First Protocol to the Convention of 16 September 1963, Protocol no 6 Concerning the Abolition of Capital Punishment of 28 April 1983, Protocol no 7, Protocol no 12, Protocol no 13 on Abolition of Capital Punishment in all circumstances. See *Official Gazette of Serbia and Montenegro-International Contracts,* no 9/2003. Up to the present time, several international covenants on human rights have been adopted under the auspices of the Council of Europe, which will also be open for execution and ratification by Serbia and Montenegro in the next few years and are particularly important for family law. The most important are the following: European Convention on the Adoption of Children, 24 April 1967, European Convention on the Status of Children Born Out of Wedlock, 15 October 1975, European Convention on the Exercise of Children Rights, 25 January 1996, Convention for the Protection of Human Rights and Dignity of the Human Being with regard to the Application of Biology and Medicine (Convention on Human Rights and Biomedicine), 4 April 1997; European Convention on Nationality, 6 November 1997 and the Convention on Contact Concerning Children, adopted on 15 May 2003.

[9] Since 10 March 1993 the Serbian Law on Marriage and Family Relations has been effective in the territory of the Autonomous Province of Vojvodina and Autonomous Province of Kosovo and Metohija since all the provincial laws ceased to apply that day. See Constitutional Act on Changes and Supplements of the Constitutional Law for the Enforcement of the Constitution of the Republic of Serbia, *Official Journal of the Republic of Serbia,* no 20/1993.

As far as Vojvodina is concerned, such a situation exists today as well, since solving the issues concerning family law rights in the second instance is in the competence of the province

concerning the division of legislative power was definitively resolved by the adoption of the Constitutional Charter of the State Union of Serbia and Montenegro on 4 February 2003.[10] It also made it possible to regulate the issues which were in the exclusive competence of the federal state and which related to the special court and administrative proceedings for rendering decisions in family matters and also to regulate an issue pertaining to the field of private international law (the right of a foreign citizen to adopt a child) by the operation of republic laws.

The main purpose of the amendment was, thus, to establish a normative system in the field of family matters that would be compatible with modern European legislation and practice, while paying full respect to the new character of family relations and modern concept of human rights, especially the rights of the child. If one takes into consideration the experience of the 20-year application of the Law on Marriage and Family Relations, one may conclude that the solutions presented in the new Family Act will provide for better legal protection of the family. Special attention has been paid to the right of the child to obtain the best possible living and health conditions for harmonious and full development and to the establishment of mechanisms for the efficient enforcement of the rights of the child, which have been recognised by the ratified conventions. In addition, Art 6/1 states:

'(1) Everyone is under the obligation to act in the best interest of the child in all activities related to the child.'

When proposing solutions, the Draft team kept in mind that family law should primarily regulate internal family relations, and that intervention from outside should take place only when necessary.

2   THE MOST IMPORTANT LEGAL CONCEPTS

The Family Act has 12 sections, namely: General Provisions, Marriage, Child-Parent Relationship, Adoption, Foster Care, Guardianship, Support, Property Relations, Protection from Violence within the Family, Proceedings in Family Matters, Personal Name and Transitional and Final Provisions.

In order to make this paper simple and concise, the presentation of the most important legal concepts in the new Family Act will be divided in two parts: the new legal concepts and the legal concepts which were subject to major changes.

---

administration in charge of family protection according to the Law on Establishment of Certain Competences of the Autonomous Province, *Official Journal of the Republic of Serbia*, no 6/2002.

As far as Kosovo is concerned, although Resolution 1244 of the United Nations Security Council of 19 June 1999 and a constitutional framework for the provisional local self-government on Kosovo of 15 May 2001 (ss 5.1 (k) and 9.1.26) entitle the Kosovo Assembly to adopt laws that regulate, among other issues, the family, gender and juvenile issues, the Kosovo Assembly never used this power. Therefore, the previous Kosovo's Law on Marriage and Family Relations 1984 has been effective in Kosovo since 10 June 1999.

10   See *Official Gazette of Serbia and Montenegro*, no 1/2003.

2.1 The new legal concepts

2.1.1 Rights of the child

For the first time, this Law has set out the rights of the child (Arts 59–66), as well as the special civil procedure which guarantees that those rights will be enforced (Arts 261–273).[11] Thus, for example, the child has a right to live with the parents and a right to be taken care of by his or her parents in preference to all others (Art 60, para 1); the child has a right to maintain personal contacts not only with a parent he or she does not live with, but also with the relatives and other persons he or she is particularly close to (Art 61, para 5); the child who is capable of having his or her own opinion, has a right to express freely this opinion and a right to file a request to the court or administrative authority, alone or represented by another person or authority, and to require assistance in the exercise of his or her right to free expression of opinion; the court or the administrative authority must determine the child's opinion in co-operation with a school psychologist, guardianship authority, family counselling and the authority specialised in family mediation, in the presence of a person chosen by the child (Art 65); the court must take care that the child be promptly informed of all relevant matters and must allow the child to express his or her opinion and must pay attention to the child's opinion taking into account the child's age and maturity (Art 266), etc. It is also very important to mention that this law has created for the first time some new special legal capacities for the child, such as the right of a child who has attained the age of 15 and who is capable of reasoning to decide on which parent he or she wants to live with (Art 60, para 4), what will be the means of maintaining personal contact with a parent he or she does not live with (Art 61, para 4), which school he or she is going to attend (Art 63, para 2) or to what medical intervention he or she will agree (Art 62, para 2), as well as the right of a child who has reached the age of 10 and who is capable of reasoning to require, alone or through a representative, the guardianship authority to appoint a guardian, or to ask the court to appoint a temporary attorney because of the conflict of interests between him or her and his or her legal representative (Art 265, paras 2 and 3), etc.

On the other hand, the Family Act has preserved the term 'parental right', to confirm the right of a child to have a parent taking care of him or her – prior to anybody else – but it has been underlined that the parental right is derived from the parent's duty and that it exists only to the extent to which it is necessary to protect the personality, rights and interests of the minor child (Art 67).[12] In addition to that, the term 'parental right' was preserved partly

---

11 For further discussion of the rights of the child in different laws see: Gordana Kovaček Stanić 'Legal reforms concerning the family' in A Bainham (ed) *The International Survey of Family Law 1996 Edition* pp 533–542; Marija Draškić 'The Rights of the Child: Yugoslavia and the United Nations Convention on the Rights of the Child', *Belgrade Center for Human Rights* (Belgrade, 1977) pp 45–60.

12 The entirety of parents' rights and duties to take care of their minor child's personality, rights and duties is generally defined as a parental right in domestic law. In comparative law we may find terms such as 'parental responsibility' in English law, 'parental rights and responsibilities' in Irish law, 'parental authority' (*autorité parentale*) in French law, 'parental care' (*elterliche Sorge*) in

due to the fact that in Serbian language the term 'parental responsibility' could create confusion in relation to the parents' liability for damage caused by the child to third parties.[13]

2.1.2   Joint exercise of the parental right

A provision stating that parents may continue to exercise jointly the parental right even after they stop living together, provided that they make an agreement on joint custody and provided that the court is satisfied that this agreement is in the best interest of the child (Arts 75–76),[14] has been introduced in the domestic legal system for the first time. This kind of parental agreement will enable the parents to exercise all the rights and duties comprised within the parental right after they stop living together as spouses or cohabitees and is intended to avoid the hostility and antagonism caused by court decisions granting the exercise of the parental right to one of them. The concept of joint exercise of the parental right (joint custody) has been recognised in a number of European laws (Swedish, Norwegian, Finnish, Danish, English, French, Italian, German, Belgian, Dutch, Swiss, Hungarian, Czech, Croatian, etc) and by US law and Australian law, as well.

The wording of the provision on joint exercise of the parental right confers great freedom upon the parents since it enables them to agree on the matters related to their child in a manner which is the most appropriate for their own particular situation. The only limitation is the parents' duty to reach an agreement on the issue of the child's domicile (Art 75/2). The domicile, followed by the child's address, must be established for the sake of legal certainty, and especially for the sake of facilitating legal acts (communication of legal documents, notification, etc). In the opinion of the Commission which produced the Draft, this limitation does not necessarily mean that the parents cannot agree on so-called 'factual joint custody'. Factual joint custody implies that the child lives with both parents and it is one of the components of joint custody in comparative law.

German law, 'parental authority' in Italian law (*potesta dei genitori*), in Portuguese law (*poder paternal*), in Spanish law (*patria potestas*), etc.

[13]   Since the parent's duties constitute the cornerstone of the parental right and its main purpose, some legal documents in comparative law have substituted the term 'parental right' with the term 'parental responsibility'. See, for example, ss 2–4 of the English Children Act 1989 and Art 163, para 1 of the German Civil Code. The Convention on the Rights of the Child took over the concept of responsibility (Art 18, para 1). Nevertheless, we want to underline that the term 'parental responsibility' as a family law concept is different from the concept of liability in English language, which is used in the field of civil law. On the contrary, in Serbian language the same term is used for responsibility and liability.

Parental responsibility is a legal concept, which will, together with the concepts of 'rights of the child' and 'child's best interest' determine the parent-child relationship in a more contemporary way. The main feature of this legal concept is that it suggests the creation of a new system of legal and ethical valorisation of a child as a legal entity and parents' special role in the harmonious development and upbringing of a child.

[14]   See further on the exercise of parental rights before 2005: Gordana Kovaček Stanić 'Legal Status of Non-custodial/Non-residential Parent in Yugoslav Family Law' in A Bainham (ed) *The International Survey of Family Law 2001 Edition* pp 449–456.

2.1.3 Protection from family violence

Family violence is a phenomenon that can be manifested in different forms, and it is very common not only abroad but also in Serbia. Unfortunately, it is difficult to assess the actual incidence of family violence for many reasons, but it is probably more widespread and more serious than any statistical records can show. Since family violence creates severe physical and psychological pain for mainly women and children and since such behaviour is especially repulsive and traumatic for the victim – like incest, for example – provisions on protection from family violence have been included in the text of the Family Act. At this point we must underline that this is civil law protection from family violence and it must be differentiated from the legal protection provided by the criminal law for the victims of the violence, in the form of the new criminal offence in the Serbian Criminal Code called 'Family Violence'. Measures such as: prohibition from approaching a family member, prohibition from entering the area close to the family member's place of residence or place of work, prohibition of further harassment and an order for entering or leaving the family apartment or house (Art 198) are designed to prevent the offender from repeating the act of violence and to protect the physical integrity, moral health and tranquility of family members.[15] Due to the fact that this is a completely new phenomenon in our law, a special civil procedure has been introduced for the protection from family violence and for keeping the records and evidence of family violence (Arts 283–289). The proposed provisions amending and supplementing the Law on Executive Procedure are also on the agenda, in order to enforce such protection more efficiently.

2.1.4 Mediation procedure

Mediation is an alternative method of dispute resolution as compared with judicial or administrative procedures. Instead of these procedures – which usually last too long or cost too much both in financial and emotional terms – the impartial and analytical judgment of the mediator creates the opportunity to settle a dispute through a compromise, while maintaining the parties' dignity. In comparative law, dispute settlement by way of mediation has shown significant results (95% success rate in the US, 20–30% in Germany, 5–10% in Slovenia).[16]

Mediation is particularly important in family law since divorce is usually a traumatic experience both for the parents and for the child. Thus, the procedure of mediation has been introduced into the new Family Act as a constituent part of the proceedings in family matters (Arts 229–246) in

---

[15]   The Draft team intended to include two more measures in the scope of measures for protection from family violence: compulsory treatment of alcoholism and drug addiction and compulsory counselling and psychiatric treatment. Unfortunately, the Secretariat in charge of Legislation of the Government of the Republic of Serbia omitted these measures from the Draft law, unaware of the fact that these two measures are very important for the protection from violence and that the greater number of offenders suffer from alcoholism and/or other addictions.

[16]   See Marija Draškić 'Mediation in Family Matters', A Tempus Project 'European Space of Justice', www.uniadrion.unibo.it/judge.

accordance with the Council of Europe Recommendation on Mediation in Family Matters. The mediation procedure consists of two stages: first, there is a procedure for reconciliation attempts, which has as its purpose to settle incompatible relations between the spouses without a divorce and the other is a procedure for reaching a settlement by which the spouses whose marriage has been terminated by a divorce or has been declared null and void endeavour to agree on the issue of custody and division of joint property. In any case, mediation will take place only if both parents agree to it, which is one of the basic principles of mediation in family matters (Art 230, para 2, item 1).[17]

2.1.5   Specialisation of judges

The Family Act has introduced a specialisation for judges for proceedings in family matters (Art 203). Thus, judges must have special knowledge in the field of the rights of the child, and lay judges must have experience in working with children and juveniles. The Minister in charge of Family Protection and the Minister of Justice must jointly establish the programme and determine the way this special knowledge is to be attained.[18] This innovation is extremely important; the specialisation of judges is necessary in order to make the trial in family matters fair, since family matters are dealing with personal relationships and therefore require sensitivity and special skills, not only legal ones. Serbian family law is finally recognising court specialisation in family matters like the majority of European laws. The following solutions exist in comparative law: special panels, which are currently present in domestic law, special divisions within a court, and specialised courts (for example, for juveniles).

2.1.6   Nuptial contract

According to the legal solutions that existed in the domestic law before, the regime of joint property was a binding legal regime, which means that the spouses were free to conclude only those agreements which would not change that legal regime. Contrary to this strict legal provision, which does not correspond to the economic realities of the market economy, the Family Act allows the spouses, or future spouses, to regulate their property relations in relation to existing or future property in a different way provided that they make a nuptial agreement. This type of agreement is not particularly regulated by the law, as in some foreign laws, and the spouses are free to draft it themselves or with the help of their legal counsellor (for example, they may stipulate that everything that each of them acquires through work during a marriage constitutes his or her own property and to eliminate fully

---

17   The other principles of family mediation are the requirements which must be fulfilled by the mediator: impartiality, neutrality, a duty to respect the opinion of each party and to maintain the equality of their bargaining power, not to impose solutions on the parties to a dispute, to guarantee privacy and confidentiality of the negotiations, to observe what is in the best interest of the child, to consider whether there was violence; the mediator can furnish legal information, but not legal advice, etc. See further the Council of Europe Recommendation on Mediation in Family Matters, no R (98) 1 of the Council of Europe.

18   The application of this Article is postponed until 1 July 2006.

the regime of joint property in such a manner). However, the nuptial agreement must be in writing and must be certified by a judge, who will read the agreement to the spouses before its certification and warn them that the agreement excludes the legal regime of joint property (Art 188). Such a strict procedure (written form, certification, warning of a judge) is prescribed for, we would say, two reasons. The first reason is the significance of these agreements for spouses' property relations, since they are modifying the regime established by law. The second reason is that this contract is a novelty; thus the spouses should be informed of its terms and its effect. A nuptial agreement concerning real estate must be entered into the land register to provide for publicity for third parties.

However, a nuptial agreement cannot regulate all the issues relating to property. In the provisions which relate to support it has been stated that withdrawal of the right to support is not valid (Art 2). This provision has a protective character, its role being to protect the economically weaker spouse from remaining without means of support on the basis of the contract. It is legally binding and the parties cannot change it according to their will.

Speaking of occupation, the occupational right that belongs to a child and to a parent who exercises the parental right, in relation to the apartment which is owned by the other parent, provided that the conditions prescribed by law are met, is also a means of protection mainly for a child but also for a parent who exercises the parental right. This provision also cannot be excluded by an agreement.

2.1.7 Gift contract

There was a legal vacuum in Serbian family law until now concerning the deed of gift, since there was no legal provision concerning this legal concept in domestic law. According to the new Family Act, it has been expressly acknowledged that the spouses are free to conclude a gift contract (Art 190, para 1). However, if they divorce or their marriage is declared null and void, the usual gifts made by the spouses while living together in a marriage are not to be returned, but the gifts made by the spouses while living together in a marriage whose value is disproportionately large comparing it to the value of the spouses' joint property, must be returned (Art 190, para 2).

2.1.8 The right of residence

The Serbian Family Act has regulated for the first time the right to reside (*habitatio*), in favour of a minor child and a parent who exercises the parental right, in the apartment owned by the other parent, provided that the child and parent who exercises the parental right do not possess a vacant apartment and provided that such a decision would not constitute an obvious injustice for the parent who is the owner of the apartment (Art 194). The reason for drafting such a provision is an obligation to provide the child with such protection and care which is necessary for his or her welfare (Art 3, para 2 of the Convention on the Rights of the Child); this solution was inspired by many similar provisions in comparative law.[19]

In Serbia, habitation is regulated by the Habitation Act 1992. However, the previously adopted law, the Habitation Act 1990, amended the habitation regime.[20] This law provided the possibility to purchase an apartment which was socially owned, and therefore the habitation right was substituted by the ownership title on the apartment. (The regime of habitation right on the socially owned apartment, which was predominant until 1990, paid full respect to family needs since these were one of the preconditions to determine who was going to be awarded the right of habitation.) The Habitation Act does not regulate any special right in the family home in the situation of termination of marriage. Thus, the spouse who lives with the children can find herself in an inconvenient situation when the apartment is the property of the other spouse or when both parents are the owners of the apartment but the apartment is not big enough to satisfy the needs of the parents and children, either through the sale or through the division of the apartment. After 1990 a right to a permanent lease has substituted the right of habitation in the socially owned apartment. The provisions concerning the lease do offer sufficient protection to a family. It has been prescribed that after a divorce, the spouses may agree on the issue of who is going to continue to use the apartment in the capacity of the lessee and, if they do not reach an agreement, the court is to decide in a non-contentious procedure. The court must take into consideration the following criteria when rendering a decision: habitation needs of the divorced spouses and their children, which of the spouses is the apartment lessee, the financial state and state of health of the spouses, etc (Art 35/4).

What is the aim of the provision concerning the right to reside? It is to solve an inconvenient living situation in which the child and parent who exercises the parental right may be in, especially after a divorce. In a discussion before the Serbian Parliament, at the time when this law was on the agenda, there was an objection to this solution, stating that it was constitutionally unacceptable being a limitation of the ownership right. However, on the one hand, the law recognises other cases of the limitation of ownership and, on the other hand, if we analyse the solutions that exist in comparative law, we may conclude that the family home has a specific legal regime in many foreign legal systems. This is especially so in capitalist countries, in which ownership is an untouchable legal concept, one might say.

2.1.9   *Emancipation*

The Family Act establishes one more basis for acquiring legal capacity before reaching the legal age (emancipation), where the minor child reached

---

[19]   In English law, the judge has a right of discretion to regulate property rights of the spouses after a divorce and to transfer the ownership of a family home in favour of the spouse who remains living with the children, and does not have other accommodation. See ss 24 and 24A of the Matrimonial Causes Act 1973.

[20]   Habitation Act, *Official Journal of Serbia*, no 50/92; Habitation Act, *Official Journal of Serbia*, no 12/90.

the age of 16, became a parent and became physically and psychologically mature enough to provide independently for his or her own personal rights and interests (Art 11, para 3). The Family Act provides for a special non-contentious procedure to acquire legal capacity on this basis, and the draft law amending and supplementing the Law on Non-Contentious Procedure will be on the agenda. Meanwhile, the Family Act has established that the provisions concerning the procedure for granting permission to conclude marriage will accordingly apply, which means that full legal capacity can be acquired by getting married with court permission before reaching the legal age (Art 360).

The other form of emancipation that exists in Serbian law is by concluding a marriage with court permission before reaching the age of majority. The court may permit a minor, who has reached the age of 16, and who has attained the physical and emotional maturity necessary to exercise rights and duties in a marriage to get married for justifiable reasons (Art 11/2). Unlike foreign laws (English and French, for example), our law does not require the parents' consent in the case of a marriage between minors; their opinion will be taken into consideration but is not a precondition for a marriage.

2.1.10 Protection of the right to a personal name

The right to a personal name is one of the fundamental human rights; however, the detailed provisions on protection of the right to a personal name were legally defined for the first time in the new Family Act of Serbia. The Family Act has established by enumeration, *exempli causa*, that the right to a personal name may be violated by stopping or preventing in any way a person from using his or her personal name, by attributing a different personal name or part of the name to a person, by stating that person's name in a distorted, abbreviated or expanded way, and by unauthorised usage of somebody's personal name (Art 351). The holder of the right to a personal name can approve usage of his or her personal name for justifiable reasons and even for a reward (Art 352). Where the right to a personal name has been violated, one can require the court to issue different protective measures, including the right to compensation for material and non-material damage (Art 355).

2.2 Legal concepts that were subject to major changes

2.2.1 Adoption

Instead of partial and full adoption, which existed in the previous Law on Marriage and Family Relations, the Family Act recognises only one form of adoption. Practice showed that partial adoption did not happen very often, and that the adopter's motives in this type of adoption were usually not very positive or desirable. The concept of adoption which has been created in the new Serbian Family Act is full adoption, in terms of the conditions for the adoption and its effects. The only significant difference when compared with the previous full adoption is the fact that children can be adopted regardless of their age, which means that they can be adopted before reaching the legal age or acquiring full legal capacity before the legal age (Art 90); the second difference relates to the family status of the adopted child. Unlike the previous legal solution, which was applicable to full adoption, now a child can be adopted even if he or she has both parents alive, provided that they have agreed to the adoption (Art 91, para 5).

On the other hand, this solution has resolved a direct collision between the provision of the Law on Marriage and Family Relations, which authorised a limitation or exclusion of the adoptee's inheritance rights toward the adopter,[21] with the provision of the European Convention on the Adoption of Children, stating that the status of the adopted child cannot be different from the status of the child born in a marriage.[22] The European Court of Human Rights has concluded several times that every form of discrimination between children born in a marriage and adopted children constitutes a violation of the right to respect for family life, established by Art 8 of the European Convention on Human Rights.[23]

Finally, the new law provides for a special administrative adoption procedure (Arts 311–327), which introduced the most important innovation, namely a centralisation of the data on potential adopters and potential adoptees in the Unified Personal Register of Adoptions, kept by the Ministry in charge of family protection (Art 316). In that respect, the transfer of information and efficiency in finding adopters or adoptees who are suitable for adoption will be much better.

Both the child and the adopters of the child have the right to inspect the Birth Register. A child has this right if he or she has reached the age of 15 and is capable of reasoning, and this relates to all cases and not only to adoption (Art 59/3). Psychosocial counselling for a child has been introduced as an innovation, which has a role in preparing the child to learn the facts about his or her biological parents, and which may be stressful, and even traumatic. Before allowing the child to inspect the Birth Register, the registrar must send the child to psychosocial counselling (Art 326), which may be conducted by the guardianship authority, family counselling or other institution specialising in family mediation.

A innovation which relates to adoption is the establishment of an age difference between the adopter and adoptee which cannot be less than 18 or more than 45 years. Adoption mirrors the child-parent relationship and therefore the age difference should be similar to the age difference which exists between the child and natural parents. However, exceptionally, adoption can be granted to a person who is less than 18 years older or to the person who is more than 45 years older than the child if such an adoption is in the best interest of the child. A permit will be issued by the Minister in charge of family protection.

---

21   See Art 176, para 1 of the Law on Marriage and Family Relations.
22   See Art 10 of the European Convention on the Adoption of Children.
23   See, for example, *Case of Pla and Puncernau v Andora*, No 69498/01 of 13 July 2004.

2.2.2 Nonmarital cohabitation

The effects of nonmarital cohabitation were regulated for the first time by the Law on Marriage and Family Relations 1980 in Serbia and by the Family Act 1989 in Montenegro. Until then, the opinion on the admissibility of such a union was different. The laws of the Kingdom of Yugoslavia did not contain provisions on nonmarital cohabitation, nor was this union socially accepted at that time. Soon after the Second World War, case-law gave certain significance to nonmarital cohabitation, owing to the war and the impossibility of marrying during the war. In the subsequent period, up to the 1980s, the law did not protect nonmarital cohabitation, and when a cohabitation union ended, the rules of the civil law were applied to solve disputes.

In the Family Act, nonmarital cohabitation has been defined as a sustained cohabitation of a woman and a man, which does not necessarily mean that it was a long-term relationship but that the intention of the partners was to make it long term. On the other hand, if one compares this solution with the solution of the former Law on Marriage and Family Relations, it may be noticed that the major innovation relates to the fact that marriage impediments which can prevent recognition of the legal effects of nonmarital cohabitation have been extended to all marriage impediments, and that nonmarital cohabitation is now comparable with marriage in this respect as well (Art 4). Since nonmarital cohabitation produces family law effects only if it satisfies the preconditions that are set by the law, in practice some nonmarital cohabitations could lack family law protection.

The family law effects of nonmarital cohabitation are partially equalised with the effects of a marriage, although the law regulates support and property relations separately. A novelty is that the cohabitees can use the assistance of biomedicine for conception, since in that case the Family Act establishes a presumption of the partner's paternity similar to the presumption of a spouse's paternity in a marriage. Apart from that, the Family Act has introduced a possibility for the partners to adopt a child together, or a possibility for a partner to adopt a child of his or her partner. The partner is also to be considered as a family member in the case of family violence.

Cohabitees do not inherit from each other by virtue of law according to the domestic legal system.[24] The new concept of family law, which considers nonmarital cohabitation equal to the marriage, should affect other branches of law, and therefore we should revise the provisions not only of the inheritance law but also of the other branches of law.

2.2.3 Divorce

The family law of the former Yugoslavia, which was effective in the 1970s and 1980s, introduced a no-fault divorce and abandoned guilt for a divorce.

---

[24]   Inheritance Law of Serbia, *Official Journal*, no 46/1995.

The special causes for a divorce ceased to exist; actually they were preserved only at random (long separation, absence of a person).[25]

The Family Act provides two main causes for divorce. One is divorce by mutual consent (Art 40), and the other is irretrievable breakdown of a marriage (Art 41). The Family Act pays no attention to guilt in case of divorce either. Only in the case of support is special attention paid to certain subjective elements. It has been established that a spouse does not have a right to support where his request for support would constitute an obvious injustice to the other spouse. The legal standard 'obvious injustice' encompasses different situations and circumstances.

The new Family Act has limited divorce by mutual consent prescribing one extra condition. In addition to the written agreement on exercise of the parental right which used to apply before the Family Act was adopted, the spouses must now also make a written agreement on division of joint property (Art 40, para 2). The intent was to motivate the spouses to settle the two most important issues in their relationship after the divorce amicably, in order to have a right to divorce by mutual consent. Long-lasting and expensive court trials for division of the joint property of the spouses would be inconsistent with the concept of divorce by mutual consent, since they would indirectly hinder the best interest of the child and the child's right to have the best living conditions for full and harmonious development (Art 62). Therefore, divorce by mutual consent was defined with the intention to 'discipline' gently the parents to invest more efforts to make their divorce a result of agreement concerning the most important issues in their future relationship.

2.2.4 Establishing and contesting maternity and paternity

The most important innovation in the new Family Act is a provision stating that a woman who gives birth to a child is to be considered as the child's mother (Art 42) unlike the solution prescribed by the previous Law on Marriage and Family Relations, which provided for different procedures for establishment of maternity in the case of child born in a marriage and child born outside of marriage.[26] The similar provision of the Belgian law – which prescribed that the maternity of the illegitimate child was not to be established by the child's birth but by the mother's acknowledgement – the European Court of Human Rights evaluated as an infringement of the right

---

25   Marriage Act of Serbia, *Official Journal*, no 52/74, Marriage Act of Vojvodina, *Official Journal*, no 2/75, Marriage Act of Kosovo, *Official Journal*, no 43/74, Marriage Act of Montenegro, *Official Journal*, no 17/73, Marriage Act of Macedonia, *Official Journal*, no 35/73, Law on Marriage and Family Relations: of Serbia, *Official Journal*, no 22/80, of Kosovo, *Official Journal*, no 10/84, of Slovenia, *Official Journal*, no 15/76, of Croatia, *Official Journal*, no 11/78, 45/89, Family Act of Montenegro, *Official Journal*, no 7/89 and of Bosnia and Herzegovina, *Official Journal*, no 21/79, 44/89.

26   See further on this issue before 2005: Gordana Kovaček Stanić 'The Significance of Biological Parentage in Yugoslav Family Law', *California Western Law Journal*, Vol 31, 2000, p 101 at www.uniadrion.unibo.it/judge114.

to respect for family life.[27] Maternity can also be established by court decision. This appears where a woman who gave a birth to a child was not entered into the Birth Register as the child's mother. Maternity can be contested too. This procedure is necessary in cases where the wrong data of a child's mother have been entered into the Register, in case of default or even misuse (for example, accidental or deliberate substitution of children or use of somebody else's health identification card in a delivery hospital).

As far as paternity is concerned, the new rule is that the presumption of paternity of the mother's husband has been limited. In a situation in which the child has been born after the termination of a marriage (within 300 days) the husband of the child's mother is to be considered the child's father only if the marriage ended by the husband's death and if the mother did not get married in that period. Marital paternity can be contested.

Paternity of the child born out of wedlock can be established in two ways: by the father's voluntary acknowledgement or by court judgment. Acknowledgement is not a unilateral act, the consent of the mother and of the child is required if the child has reached the age of 16.

The main novelties introduced by the Family Act concerning the family status of the child are: the right of a child to know who are his or her parents, which is explicitly prescribed (Art 59); for that reason, the deadline within which the child can bring a legal action in maternity and paternity lawsuits has been abandoned (Arts 249, para 1, 250, para 1, 251, para 1 and 252, para 1). Therefore, the right of a child to learn about his or her origin, which is guaranteed by Art 7, para 1 of the Convention on the Rights of the Child, has been directly implemented in such a manner. The other novelty consists of the fact that the deadlines for other persons have been synchronised. When adopting the Family Act the legislator decided to synchronise the deadlines in all maternity and paternity disputes by providing all the parties, except for the child, with a subjective deadline of one year from learning the relevant facts and an objective deadline of 10 years from the child's birth. This kind of synchronisation has cut the deadline for some of the parties. This does not mean that options to initiate the procedure after the deadline are exhausted. In other words, the deadline for the child is unlimited, so if it is in the interest of the child to initiate the procedure before he or she reaches majority, the procedure will then be initiated by his or her legal representative and after reaching the legal age – by the child himself. If the child's interests conflict with the interests of his legal representative, the guardianship authority will appoint a so-called collision guardian for the child (according to Art 132/2, item 3 and Art 265).

---

[27] See *Case of Paula and Alexandra Marckx v Belgium*, No 6833/74, 24 October 1978. It is interesting to mention that the Law on Marriage and Family Relations was adopted after this decision of the European Court of Human Rights but unfortunately the legislator did not refer to the international standards on the recognition of human rights which were already effective back then.

2.2.5 Establishing and contesting maternity and paternity in the case of biomedically assisted conception

The Family Act has regulated the issues concerning establishment and contesting the maternity and paternity of a child who is conceived with biomedical assistance in a more elaborate and detailed manner and according to the prevailing opinions in comparative law. This means that a woman who gives birth to a child is always considered the child's mother (Art 57, paras 1 and 2) which implicitly discourages surrogate motherhood, and that a mother's husband or her cohabiting partner who has given written consent to the biomedically assisted conception is considered the child's father (Art 58, paras 1 and 2) and that the maternity of a woman who donated the ovum or paternity of a man who donated the semen cells cannot be established (Art 57, para 2 and Art 58, para 5).

2.2.6 Support

The major innovations in the matters of support are the following: introduction of the legal standard of 'obvious injustice' in all the circumstances for the support debtor when there are justifiable reasons to reject the exercise of the right of a support creditor (Arts 151, para 3, 153, para 2, 155, para 4, etc), and a legal standard for 'minimal amount of support' (Art 160, paras 1 and 4); limitation of the spouse's right of support to 5 years at most (Art 163, para 2), conferring a right upon the support creditor to choose whether he or she will request support in a fixed monthly amount or in a percentage from the monthly incomes of the support debtor (Art 162, para 1).[28]

2.2.7 Legal regime of the spouses' property

The normal regime is a regime of joint property, consisting of property that was acquired by working and living together in a marriage (Art 171), and the spouse's separate property.[29] A division of joint property has been established as a determination of the joint ownership or co-ownership share of each spouse in the joint property (Art 177). The Family Act establishes a presumption of equal shares for the spouses in joint property. However, one spouse can get a larger share in joint property, which depends on his or her earnings during the marriage, managing the household, taking care of children, managing the property and other circumstances important for maintaining and increasing the value of joint property (Art 180).

A rule that relates to the child's property has been changed too. Thus, those items belong to the exclusive property of the spouse who is exercising the parental right, and if the parents exercise the parental right jointly, they have joint ownership of the items intended for the child's use (Art 183).

---

[28] See further on maintenance before 2005: Olga Cvejic-Jancic 'Maintenance Duties of Parents towards Children' in A Bainham (ed) *The International Survey of Family Law 2003 Edition* pp 453–460.

[29] See further on these issues before 2005: Olga Cvejic-Jancic 'Property relations between spouses' in A Bainham (ed) *The International Survey of Family Law 1996 Edition*, pp 506–516.

Separate property is property acquired by a spouse before the marriage and property that was acquired by the spouse during the marriage by division of property or by inheritance, gift or other legal transfer (Art 168). A new provision, which was introduced by the Family Act, relates to the increase in the value of the separate property of one of the spouses while living together in a marriage. If there is a major increase in value of the spouse's separate property, the other spouse has a right to a share in this property proportionally to his or her contribution. If this increase is insignificant, the other spouse has a right to require compensation in money proportionally to his or her contribution (Art 170). This provision provides for the better protection of the spouse who contributed to the increase in the value of separate property of the other spouse, since he or she can get a share in this property, which means that he or she may become a co-owner, for example. This is a better position compared with the situation in which he or she has only a right to an adequate sum of money.

2.2.8 Personal contacts between the child and other persons

The Family Act provides for a right of a child to maintain personal contacts with a parent he or she does not live with, which means that a child is established as a holder of that right (Art 61). However, it has been prescribed that a parent who does not exercise the parental right has a right and a duty to maintain personal contacts with a child (Art 78/3). This means that a holder of this right is not only the child but also the parent, although for a parent maintaining personal contact constitutes a duty as well. In order to maintain personal contact, it is usually necessary to enable the parent who does not live with a child to maintain personal contacts (for example, if it is a small child, personal contacts are impossible without the active participation of the parent who lives with a child). A parent who avoids maintaining personal contact with a child or a parent who prevents maintaining personal contact between the child and other parent may be charged with the most severe legal punishment imposed on parents which is full deprivation of the parental right. Therefore, the Family Act has made parents' duty of maintaining personal contact with a child stricter in this manner because this right is a very important right of the child.

The Family Act prescribes that the court has jurisdiction to decide on the limitation of personal contact and the court can render such a decision only if it is in the best interest of a child and if there are justifiable reasons to deprive a parent wholly or partially of the parental right, or in case of family violence. The Family Act has extended the list of the child's rights of maintaining personal contacts by stating that a child who has reached the age of 15 and who is capable of reasoning can decide on maintaining personal contact with a parent with whom he or she does not live. Another novelty that relates to personal contacts is the right of a child to maintain personal contacts with relatives and other persons with whom he is close. This right can be limited only by court decision. The Family Act has established the persons with whom a child can maintain personal contacts in the widest possible manner, which means that they are not only relatives but also all other close persons. As far as the relatives are concerned, it is important to mention that if brothers and sisters do not live together, they should maintain personal contact, the same applies to grandparents and their grandchildren. It may happen that a parent, for example, does not allow the child to maintain personal contact with a grandmother and grandfather after the death of the other parent or after a divorce. On the basis of this provision one may initiate the court proceedings. A foster family which took care of a child can be considered as another person especially close to the child.[30]

---

[30] See further: Gordana Kovaček Stanić 'The Serbian Law on Family 2005 and European Perspective', *International Family Law*, June 2005, pp 99–104.

Singapore

A COMMUNITARIAN EFFORT IN GUARDIANSHIP AND CUSTODY OF CHILDREN AFTER PARENTS' DIVORCE

Wai Kum Leong[*]

Résumé

Comme tous les pays, Singapour adhère résolument au principe de la nécessaire protection des enfants contre les effets néfastes du divorce de leurs parents. Cet article démontre comment la législation de Singapour en matière d'autorité parentale et de droit de garde a évolué à la lumière de ce principe. Il fait également état des différents services sociaux et judiciaires mis en place par la communauté dans ce même esprit.

SUMMARY

Singapore is as committed as any other country to the ideal that children should be shielded from any traumatic fall-out from their parents' divorce. This article examines how the law in Singapore of guardianship and custody of children has developed motivated by this ideal. It also examines the social and legal services offered by the community that supplement her legal efforts to achieve this ideal.

I   LAW OF CUSTODY OF CHILDREN AFTER PARENTS' DIVORCE RELATED WITH THE CONCEPT OF PARENTAL RESPONSIBILITY

The law of guardianship and custody in Singapore is still largely based on that which she received from England on the establishment of her legal system in 1826.[1] Of the part of the law that relates to the situation after the

---

[*]   Professor, Faculty of Law, National University of Singapore, lawlwk@nus.edu.sg.
[1]   The Second Charter of Justice 1826 extended the Court of Judicature of the then Prince of Wales' Island (now Penang in the neighbouring Federation of Malaysia) to Singapore with the direction that it should dispense justice 'so far as the several Religions, Manners, and Customs of the said Settlement and Places will admit'. For discussion of the establishment of the Singapore legal system and how the courts' interpretation of the direction in the Second Charter of Justice affected

parents of a child have terminated their marital relationship through divorce, the law allows either parent to apply to the courts in Singapore for an order of 'custody'[2] over the child.[3] As litigation in Singapore, including that of family proceedings for applications for an order of custody, continues to be based on the adversarial process, it had become a common outcome of such applications for one of the parents to be awarded 'custody' of the child. Such a court order is thus of 'sole custody' in favour of a parent.

As will be discussed in the following paragraphs, the inappropriateness of an order granting sole custody to one parent, at the expense of the other parent who is thus denied 'custody' to his or her child, has received attention in academic writings for several years. The courts in Singapore are beginning to heed the call of the academics not to allow the law of guardianship and custody to undermine the continued discharge of parental responsibilities by divorced parents. The key to the discussion is the modern idea of parental responsibility. This article begins with how this concept has become the cornerstone of child law in Singapore.

A   Origins of the law on guardianship and custody

Child law in Singapore originated in the common law where, within the guardianship and custody of infants, the father held almost absolute authority over his legitimate children.[4] Over time this one-sidedness became tempered, one, by the equalisation of the legal privileges and capacity of husbands with their wives[5] and, two, with greater concern for the well-being of the child. The legal expression of greater concern for the child developed, first, through equity tempering the harshness of the common law and, secondly, through the modern notion of parental responsibility owed to a child that now substitutes for the former notion of parental rights over a child.

---

the development of family law, see Leong Wai Kum *The Family Law Library of Singapore* (a CD-ROM) (Singapore, Butterworths, 1999) pp 69–130.

[2]   While the term 'custody' is not defined in any of the statutes, academic opinion has described it as 'the bundle of rights, duties, obligations and responsibilities' that a parent or, if another person were appointed the child's guardian, the guardian possesses over the child as representing the parent or guardian's authority over the child, see Leong Wai Kum *The Family Law Library of Singapore, ibid*, p 536.

[3]   The non-Muslim marriage statute, the Women's Charter, Cap 353, 1997 Revised Edition of the Statutes of the Republic of Singapore, in s 124 that is headlined as a provision on 'Custody of children' allows a court, upon the pronouncement of a decree of divorce, to 'make such orders as it thinks fit with respect to the welfare of any child'. The substantive law of guardianship and custody consists of the principles of the common law and equity as these have been moderated or substituted by the provisions in two statutes, *viz*, the Women's Charter and the Guardianship of Infants Act, Cap 122, 1985 Revised Edition of the Statutes of the Republic of Singapore.

[4]   The writer observed in Leong Wai Kum *The Family Law Library of Singapore*, above note 1, pp 529–530, that Singapore in 1826 would have started with the common law rule that the father's authority over his legitimate child was nearly absolute. This principle was retained in the first Civil Procedure Code of 1907 and continued in the first Guardianship of Infants Ordinance of 1934.

[5]   The discussion of this influence lies beyond the interest of this article but see Leong Wai Kum *The Family Law Library of Singapore*, above note 1, pp 424–431.

B Influence of equity

Even before the enactment of Guardianship of Infants Act[6] that facilitates the appointment of guardians by a court, the Straits Settlements Supreme Court in Penang[7] had, in 1888, entertained an application by the paternal uncle of orphaned infants to be appointed their guardian where Justice Pellereau observed:[8]

'I have come to the conclusion ... that in the selection of such guardians the Court should apply the law of England, and in doing so, should consider the ... welfare of the infants, their treatment, their sex, their education, the religion of their parents and the rules which, according to that religion, regulate their domestic customs and relations.'

The influence of equity culminated in the principle that whenever a court had to decide an issue pertaining to the upbringing of a child, the court should make the 'welfare of the child' its first and paramount consideration. This has been encapsulated in a statutory principle that continues to apply today.

C Influence of parental responsibility substituting parental rights

The next major influence on the law of guardianship and custody was the enactment of what continues today as the non-Muslim marriage statute in Singapore, *viz*, the Women's Charter.[9] Section 46 of the Women's Charter exhorts parents to be 'mutually bound to co-operate with each other ... in caring and providing for the children'.[10] Of this provision the writer has said:[11]

---

[6] The original facilitative provision was in the Straits Settlements Civil Procedure Code 1907, which provisions on guardianship and custody were later extracted and enacted as the Straits Settlements Guardianship of Infants Ordinance 1934.

[7] After Singapore was 'founded' in 1819 by officials acting on behalf of the British East India Company, from 1825 through the end of the Second World War in 1946, she was one component of three units (Penang and Malacca, in what is today the neighbouring Federation of Malaysia, were the others) of the Straits Settlements. For discussion of Singapore's political history, see Leong Wai Kum *The Family Law Library of Singapore*, above note 1, pp 2–4.

[8] *In re Sinyak Rayoon* (1888) 4 Kyshe 329.

[9] The original Women's Charter was enacted as Ordinance 18 of 1961, Cap 353, while the current version is the 1997 Revised Edition, see above note 3. For a discussion of its enactment and amendments to date, see Leong Wai Kum *The Family Law Library of Singapore*, above note 1, at pp 38–61.

[10] Although the provision, read literally, only applies to 'the husband and the wife' '[u]pon the solemnization of marriage', the writer has observed that it should optimally apply to all parents of a child whether validly married to each other or not married at all. To some extent this broader reading is supported by other provisions within the same statute, for example, by s 68 a parent is under a duty to maintain his or her child 'whether they are legitimate or illegitimate' and the provisions in Part X, Chapter 5 on 'Welfare of children' allow the courts to make orders of parents regarding their responsibilities where the parents were married by the time of the children's births.

[11] See *Halsbury's Laws of Singapore* Vol 11 Family (Singapore, Butterworths, 2001) contributed by Leong Wai Kum at para 130.358.

'Thus, parenting is as much the equal co-operative partnership of efforts of the spouses as their obligations to each other.[12] Indeed, it could be considered the pinnacle of co-operation by any two persons. When spouses engage in parenting, the Women's Charter creates expectations of them as parents in the same way it creates expectations of them as spouses. The Women's Charter exhorts parents to adopt a moral view of their parenthood.'

The promulgation of this modern idea of a parent owing responsibility towards his or her child necessarily rendered obsolete the old common law idea of a parent having rights over the child since applications for orders of custody under the Guardianship of Infants Act[13] became resolved according to this modern view of the relationship between parent and child. Decisions are single-mindedly focused on pursuing what is in the welfare of the child. The critical provision reads:

'Where in any proceedings before any court the custody or upbringing of an infant or the administration of any property belonging to or held in trust for an infant or the application of the income thereof is in question, the court, in deciding that question, shall regard the welfare of the infant as the first and paramount consideration and save in so far as such welfare otherwise requires the father of an infant shall not be deemed to have any right superior to that of the mother in respect of such custody, administration or application nor shall the mother be deemed to have any claim superior to that of the father.'

Parental authority and any surviving notion of parental rights over the child had been subjected, from the ascendance of the idea of parental responsibility, to the courts' paramount concern for the well-being of the child.

The general provision in s 46 of the Women's Charter is bolstered by more specific provisions on the responsibilities of parents that are enforceable in the courts. Section 69 allows a court to order a parent to provide reasonable maintenance 'for his child who is unable to maintain himself', which s 68 elaborates is a duty imposed on the parent 'whether [the child is] in his or her custody ... and whether ... legitimate or illegitimate'. The court may even order such payment after the child 'has attained the age of 21 years' provided 'the provision of maintenance is necessary because of a mental or physical disability; the child is or will be serving full-time national service;[14] the child is or will be ... receiving instruction at an educational establishment or undergoing training ...; or special circumstances ... exist which justify the making of the order'. Indeed an order can only be made by the court under s 70 that a non-parent should provide maintenance for the child where 'the father or the mother of the child fails to do so' and this non-

---

[12] For a discussion of this see Leong Wai Kum 'Supporting marriage through description as an equal partnership of efforts' in A Bainham (ed) *The International Survey of Family Law 2002 Edition* p 379.

[13] At the enactment of the Women's Charter, it was still the original Ordinance of 1934, above note 6, but this was amended by Act 17 of 1965. The current statute is Cap 122, 1985 Revised Edition, see above note 3, and the paramountcy of the child is encapsulated in its s 3.

[14] Every able-bodied male Singaporean resident is expected to serve almost 2 years' military service.

parent's duty 'shall cease if the child is taken away by his father or mother' and in any case 'any sums expended by a person maintaining that child shall be recoverable as a debt from the father or mother of the child'. There are, of course, a slew of provisions to protect the child from the incidence of family violence.[15] One of the latest enactments designed to keep the child secure in his or her current living arrangements is the provision of a minor offence if a 'person' whether or not a parent 'shall take a child who is subject of the custody order out of Singapore except with the written consent of both parents or the leave of the court' although the offence is not committed if the taking is 'for a period of less than one month'.

A comprehensive survey of the duties and responsibilities of parents reveals a fairly stringent regime. Parental responsibility is tenacious and not subject to the parents' agreeing between themselves that either should relinquish it in favour of the other.[16] Where circumstances so justify, a parent may be ordered by the court to continue to discharge his or her responsibility for the life of the child. It should come as no surprise, then, that judges in Singapore have continually made observations on the high legal expectations of parents in their conduct towards their children. In a memorable comment Chief Justice Yong Pung How said to two couples, neither of whom had any biological relationship with the young girl they were hoping to adopt, who had injudiciously involved her in a bewildering number of applications in court:[17]

> 'Little Esther has been subject to too many upheavals, and faced too many emotional trials for an infant of her age ... A child is not a thing ... one can simply take for granted and discard at one's convenience, to pick up again when circumstances become pressing. A child is a living being, dependent on adults from birth and must be cherished with genuine love from the outset ... In any case ... the very least the court must do is to advocate the underlying premise that parents, natural or potential, must care for the children.'[18]

---

[15] See the whole of Part VII of the Women's Charter, above note 3, which supplements the provision of the major offences in the Penal Code, Cap 224, 1998 Revised Edition of the Statutes of the Republic of Singapore and the minor offences in the Children and Young Persons Act, Cap 38, 2001 Revised Edition of the Statutes of the Republic of Singapore.

[16] The interminability of parental responsibility, as a common law idea, stands in sharp contrast with that prevalent in most European countries from the civil law tradition where, either by agreement or court order, one parent may relinquish his or her responsibility in favour of the other; see the individual country reports to the Commission on European Family Law Questionnaire on Parental Responsibilities at www.law.uu.nl/priv/cefl.

[17] *Lim Chin Huat Francis v Lim Kok Chye Ivan* [1999] 2 SLR 38 at [91]; see discussion of the case in Leong Wai Kum 'Restatement of the Law of Guardianship and Custody in Singapore' [1999] Sing JLS 432.

[18] Following that approach the Chief Justice in the highest Court of Appeal in Singapore dismissed this latest application between the two couples for the girl to be ordered returned to the physical possession of one of them from the other. His Honour noted that the parties' petitions for adoption had already been filed by that time and that it would be the outcome of those petitions that should settle the matter of who between them should have the honour of being the caregivers of the girl, so that the optimal decision in this application was simply to refuse to make any order that would require the girl to be moved one more time from her present home.

In a comment on his Honour's words, the writer said:[19]

> 'These are strong, timely words. The moral view underlies all aspects of child law [in Singapore]. The Chief Justice emphasised that the responsibility the law holds a parent to with regard to his or her child is equally true of adults who want to become adoptive parents. They too must demonstrate readiness to discharge their moral commitment to the well being of the child.'

The commitment to the idea that the court should make its paramount concern the well-being of the child, including ensuring that the discharge of parental responsibility is similarly driven, has had a major influence on the shape of the law of guardianship and custody after parents divorce. The developments are traced below.

II   POSSIBLE TO MAKE NO CUSTODY ORDER

A   Sole custody to one parent inappropriate

It has been noted that a sole custody order, given that 'custody' consists of the responsibilities, duties and authority a parent naturally possesses over his or her child, theoretically places all these on one parent alone. In theory, for as long as an order of sole custody operates, the parent who was not awarded custody is cut off from his or her responsibilities, duties and authority over the child. The child, in theory, is denied parenting by this parent. The parental responsibility of this parent is, in theory, suspended.

Fortunately, a brilliant decision of the High Court in Singapore in 1992[20] set the stage for the trend that is now more clearly discernible, ie the courts forbearing from choosing one of the parents on whom to bestow sole custody over their child.[21] In other words, the court chooses to use the law of guardianship and custody in such a way that it continues to support parental responsibility instead of undermining it. To this extent this decision may be said to have begun the task of appropriately relating the law of guardianship and custody of children after their parents' divorce with that of parenthood and the legal expectations of parents.

---

[19]   Leong Wai Kum 'Restatement of the Law of Guardianship and Custody in Singapore', above note 17 at 481.

[20]   The jurisdiction in the courts over the guardianship and custody of children used to lie with the High Court in Singapore. In 1996 this jurisdiction, together with that over the hearing of petitions for divorce and eventually over all family proceedings, was transferred to the Family Court in Singapore *vide* Supreme Court of Judicature (Transfer of Matrimonial, Divorce and Guardianship of Infants Proceedings to District Court) Order of 1996 (generally simply called the 1996 Transfer Order). By a like Transfer Order 2003, one part of the jurisdiction thus transferred was returned to the High Court of Singapore, *viz*, to hear an ancillary application for an order of division of matrimonial assets where the alleged value of the asset is at least Singapore $1.5m.

[21]   *Re Aliya Aziz Tayabali* [2000] 1 SLR 754. Although reported only in the year 2000 Judicial Commissioner Michael Hwang had decided this custody application by December 1992. For discussion of this case see Leong Wai Kum *The Family Law Library of Singapore*, above note 1, pp 334–337.

B Possible to make no custody order between parents

In *Re Aliya Aziz Tayabali* the parents of an infant girl of about 30 months old, both Muslim, agreed that, upon their divorce, the mother should have care and control. When 'care and control' is extracted from 'custody' it refers to the child actually living with this parent. The parent with care and control of the child would necessarily also decide the mundane day-to-day issues such as when she should eat, what and how much, etc. The major decisions, however, do not fall within 'care and control' and unless ordered differently, parental responsibility for making the major decisions concerning the child continues to be regulated by the Women's Charter requirement that the parents should co-operate in discharging it towards the girl.[22] In this application, the mother sought an order of sole custody while the father counterclaimed for an order of joint custody.

Then Judicial Commissioner Michael Hwang observed that he could either make the order for sole custody the mother wanted, the order of joint custody the father wanted or 'no order as to custody, leaving only the orders for care and control and access'. His Honour observed favourably of both parents thus:[23]

'... the father is a devoted and conscientious parent. In time, he will no doubt improve his care-giving skills, but I have no reason to doubt his genuine love and concern for the child. My impression of the mother is in similar terms except that there is no reason to doubt her parenting skills. I consider that there will be a reasonable amount of cooperation between the parties in the daily life of the child, but there will inevitably be disagreements about her long-term upbringing.'

The parents were thus not facing any immediate difficulties in making major decisions over their child.

In these circumstances his Honour made the perfectly reasonable decision of dismissing the applications for an order of custody. That this decision appeared very bold at the time can be explained only by the fact that such a result is seldom chosen within the adversarial system of litigation where the parties have come to expect one of them to emerge 'victorious'.

On why his Honour rejected sole custody, he said:[24]

'It would not be right at this stage to give one parent the absolute right to determine any decisions with long-term implications without hearing the other parent ...'

On why even he also rejected joint custody, he said:[25]

'A joint custody order would only be useful if it indicated symbolically that the father had an equal say in these long term decisions relating to the child.

---

22 See discussion corresponding to above note 10.
23 Above note 21, at [13].
24 Above note 21, at [13].
25 Above note 21, at [13] and [14].

However, the symbolism could be abused if the father decided to use the joint custody order to impinge on matters which might properly or more appropriately be left to the decision of the mother having care and control ... I do not wish to encourage unnecessary dissension between the parties. I am concerned about the psychological effect of a joint custody order ...'

On why the best decision was 'no order of custody', he said:[26]

'I believe that the appropriate decision is to make no order as to custody, thereby leaving neither party the prima facie advantage of deciding any serious matters relating to the child's upbringing. Hopefully, the parties will have enough sense to resolve important matters affecting the child by mutual agreement.'

C   Subtle differences between making no order and making an order of joint custody between parents

While the practical effect of making no court order of custody and thus leaving the parents to be regulated by law as to their joint parental responsibility towards their daughter may appear no different from making the order of joint custody that the father had sought, it is submitted that there are significant, if subtle, differences. His Honour was astute in choosing the option that leaves neither parent 'victorious' in this litigation. The psychological effect of making an order of custody that one party had sought so that he or she can claim 'victory' is best avoided where this is possible. Parents upon divorce and in the midst of a custody suit are possibly at the lowest point in their capability of joint co-operative parenting. The last thing they need is for one to feel the sense of having won and the other of having lost this suit. Instead, as his Honour rightly achieved by his decision, parents should be reminded of the law's expectation that they continue as best as they can to co-operate in their parenting of their child. The most a court can do is not pressure their difficult relationship further at this time. We will have simply to wait for the parents to find their equanimity upon which most parents should be able to resume joint parenting.

As the writer commented of this decision:[27]

'In not making either of the orders sought, his Honour achieved two [laudable] objectives. First, from the infant's perspective, his Honour required both parents to continue to discharge their responsibility and authority over [their daughter]. Second, his Honour affirmed the proper role of the court to intervene only when it can do some real good [for the child].'

There is no additional advantage in making an order for joint custody between parents. The law already mandates joint co-operative parenting so that an order for joint custody to parents is truly superfluous.

---

26   Above note 21, at [14].
27   Leong Wai Kum *The Family Law Library of Singapore*, above note 1, p 540.

Such a decision also acknowledges how little a court order of custody to her parents achieves for the infant involved. The writer has said:[28]

> '[T]his result reinforces how temporary a court order is as "resolution" of the disagreement between the adults over the upbringing of the child. The relationship between the child and the adults on whom the child is dependent, primarily his or her parents, is truly dynamic. All that any order made by court achieves is temporarily to assuage a pressing point of disagreement. No order, however well and deeply considered, can truly resolve parental disagreement with finality. It behoves the court to remind parties that it is painfully aware of the real limits of its powers. The adults must be cajoled to rise above their petty concerns to give the child under their care the best they are capable of.'

III EVEN PARENT DENIED CUSTODY RETAINS RESIDUAL DECISION-MAKING AUTHORITY

In 1996 the highest court in Singapore, the Court of Appeal, delivered a significant judgment in *L v L*[29] that emphasised the equalisation of the rights and responsibilities of father and mother under the law. In the result, despite the mother of the 2-year-old girl having sole custody over her, the court found her unilateral act of changing the girl's surname to be unlawful and ordered her to reverse it. By this decision the court affirmed that even the parent who is not awarded custody of his or her child retains residual decision-making authority over the very most important matters affecting the child and the court extended the list of these most important matters.

A Parent with sole custody cannot unilaterally change child's surname

The father in *L v L* was, as one would hope most parents in Singapore are wont to be, loving and responsible towards his young daughter. Justice Goh Joon Seng observed that he[30] 'had been providing for [her] ... been taking an active interest in and regularly enjoying his generous access to [her]'. When the father discovered that his daughter's surname had been unilaterally changed by her mother from his surname to that of the mother's lover he applied to the courts alleging the unlawfulness of her unilateral action and asking for an order from the court to her to reverse it.

His Honour began by noting that by the current law of guardianship and custody in Singapore[31] 'while both parents of an infant are alive, they are both natural guardians with equal rights on the question of custody of the infant before the court'. The question, then, was what extent of change to the

---

[28]   Leong Wai Kum 'Restatement of the Law of Guardianship and Custody in Singapore', above note 17, at 487. See similar academic call for the courts to desist from making orders of sole custody between the parents by Debbie Ong Siew Ling 'Parents and custody orders – A new approach' [1999] Sing JLS 205.

[29]   [1997] 1 SLR 222; for discussion of the case see Leong Wai Kum *The Family Law Library of Singapore*, above note 1, at pp 366–371.

[30]   *Ibid* at [23].

[31]   Above note 29, at [17].

legal norm of joint parental responsibility an order granting her sole custody made and, in particular, if it allowed her unilaterally to change their daughter's surname without giving him prior knowledge of this or considering his opinion. His Honour agreed with the view expressed by the Law Commission of England and Wales of the significance of a child's surname:[32]

> 'The child's surname is an important symbol of his identity and his relationship with his parents. While it may be in his interest for it to be changed, it is clearly not a matter on which the parent with whom he lives should be able to take unilateral action.'

His Honour continued[33] to say that '[t]here was also no suggestion that ... it was in any way undesirable for [the daughter] to continue to be known by [her own father's surname]'. For this reason the Court of Appeal decided that the mother was not empowered, even by the order of sole custody in her favour, to change this unilaterally. This was a matter so very important to the child's interest that the mother had to co-operate with the father in order lawfully to effect a change.

B   Other matters in relation to which parent denied custody retains residual authority

The writer has commented on the decision thus:[34]

> 'Justice Goh Joon Seng decided that [the mother's] authority as sole custodian did not extend to unilaterally changing the girl's surname as this was one matter exceptionally important to her well being. There appears to be at least two more matters where [Singapore] statute demands that the custodian must consult with the parent or obtain the leave of the court. ... [T]he Adoption of Children Act[35] [from its original enactment][36] requires that the consent of "every person ... who is a parent or guardian of the infant" and [by an amending enactment in 1996] the Women's Charter[37] prohibits the removal of a child out of Singapore for longer than one month "except with the written consent of both parents".'

Of the residual decision-making authority that a parent who is denied custody of his or her child continues to retain the writer has said:[38]

---

32   See above note 29, at [17] quoting the Law Commission of England and Wales' Report No 172 (Review of Child Law, Guardianship and Custody) para 4.14.

33   See above note 29, at [23].

34   Leong Wai Kum 'Restatement of the Law of Guardianship and Custody in Singapore', above note 17, at 488. See also Leong Wai Kum *The Family Law Library of Singapore*, above note 1, at pp 453–457.

35   Cap 4, 1985 Revised Edition of the Statutes of the Republic of Singapore, s 4(4).

36   As the Straits Settlements, see above note 7, Adoption of Children Ordinance No 18 of 1939 where s 3(4) was substantially similar to the current version's, see *ibid*, s 4(4).

37   See above note 8, s 126(3).

38   Leong Wai Kum 'Restatement of the Law of Guardianship and Custody in Singapore', above note 17, at 489 repeating Leong Wai Kum *The Family Law Library of Singapore*, above note 1, p 541.

'[A] fair suggestion ... may be said to be as follows. A parent, despite not given custody, continues to retain decision-making authority over [the most] serious matters concerning his or her child. The less serious have been left to the sole discretion of the parent given sole custody. Serious matters, however, are set aside and both parents continue to retain decision-making authority over them. [This may be the optimal] balance of authority between the parent granted sole custody and the other.'

IV GUARDIANSHIP AND CUSTODY SHOULD SUPPORT PARENTAL RESPONSIBILITY

In *L v L* Justice Goh Joon Seng went so far as to remark that[39] '[a] custody order ... would only empower the custodial parent to decide on the day to day matters relating to the child'. It is submitted that one can disagree with this statement as it undervalues the effect of an award of custody in such a way that it becomes indistinguishable from the acknowledged lesser award of 'care and control'. The writer has commented:[40]

'[C]ustody can be divided into two smaller bundles, *viz*, "care and control" and the residual "custody" ... The child must stay with one parent so he or she has the daily "care and control" of the child ... This care and control will also include the small decisions which are made on a daily basis by the adult having the care of the child. The other rights outside daily care and control make up the "custody" where "care and control" have been excluded. Although Justice Goh Joon Seng ... suggested that the authority of the parent granted custody may be no different from one granted mere care and control, it is submitted that the better view is that the terms are different. The parent given sole custody receives the court's sanction for making decisions beyond the day to day matters although, as the case rightly decides, this authority is not *carte blanche*.'

The writer has further commented that there could have been an ulterior reason for his Honour's statement that the parent who is awarded custody *vis-à-vis* the other parent receives no greater authority than to decide the mundane daily matters affecting the child:[41]

'[His Honour's statement] reflects an underlying dissatisfaction with an order of sole custody. This is not unreasonable. To the extent an order of sole custody appears to cut off the other parent, it is unduly disruptive of the relationship between the infant and his or her parents ... The authority of parents should, as far as possible, not be completely undermined by an order of custody. An order giving one parent sole custody is unattractive precisely because it undermines the authority of the other parent.'

---

39 Above note 29, at [21].
40 See Leong Wai Kum *The Family Law Library of Singapore*, above note 1, pp 536–537.
41 See Leong Wai Kum *The Family Law Library of Singapore*, above note 1, pp 541–542. See also Leong Wai Kum 'Restatement of the Law of Guardianship and Custody in Singapore', above note 17, at 481–492.

Academic writings continued to encourage the better use of the courts' power to award guardianship and custody so that the order supports the continued discharge of parental responsibility. The writer has said:[42]

> '[G]uardianship and parenthood overlap in that a parent is a natural guardian and a parent is the most likely appointee by the court as guardian of a child at the end of litigation between the parents over this matter. [Further] the law and courts view guardians, just as a parent and a potential adoptive parent, to owe responsibility to the child ... It is right that the law exhorts parents to continue their responsibilities to their child even though their marriage has ceased functioning. A lesser exhortation will be poor legal regulation of the relationship between parent and child. [It follows that it] is clearly better for guardianship to support the continuance of parental responsibility. This means where the guardian of a child is appointed at the end of guardianship proceedings, the responsibility of the parent who is not appointed the guardian should not be eclipsed to any greater extent than absolutely necessary.'

Of how this can be achieved, the writer has suggested:[43]

> 'An order of "care and control" ... is a necessary evil when two parents separate ... It is now generally expected that the parent who does not have "care and control" of the child should get generous access ... An order of custody is not as necessary ... The High Court in *Re Aliya Aziz Tayabali*[44] has shown the way. Not making an order of custody upholds the exhortation in section 46(1) of the Women's Charter[45] at a crucial time in the parents' relationship with their child. It provides a timely reminder to them of their continuing responsibility ... The need to make a custody order, therefore, really only arises in the exceptional situation where the court is asked to consider appointing a non-parent as guardian ... [so as to acquire] parental authority over the child that [the non-parent] would not otherwise possess. Where a custody order must be made ... in the normal guardianship application between the two parents, a custody order appointing both parents guardians is preferred over an order of sole custody. While there are [some] situations where joint custody is not recommended [it] has been suggested that the fear that the parents cannot co-operate to make such joint custody order practicable may be overstated.'[46]

---

[42]   Leong Wai Kum 'Restatement of the Law of Guardianship and Custody in Singapore', above note 17, at 481 and 483 and see also Debbie Ong Siew Ling 'Parents and custody orders – A new approach', above note 28.

[43]   Leong Wai Kum 'Restatement of the Law of Guardianship and Custody in Singapore', above note 17, at 490–492.

[44]   See above note 22 and accompanying text.

[45]   See above note 10 and accompanying text.

[46]   Debbie Ong Siew Ling 'Parents and custody orders – A new approach', above note 28, at 223–227.

V COMPARING 'NO ORDER OF CUSTODY' AND 'JOINT ORDER OF CUSTODY' BETWEEN PARENTS

A No order of custody

The High Court in Singapore has, in 2003, given a decision that supports the academic suggestion that making no order of custody between parents may be preferred over making an order of joint custody and this may be possible more often than not. In *Re G (guardianship of an infant)*,[47] on fairly unexceptional facts, the Family Court had ordered that the mother should have sole custody. The father appealed against this order to the High Court, on appeal, seeking an order of joint custody instead. Justice Tan Lee Meng began by citing academic writing and agreeing[48] 'it is preferable that joint parental responsibility for a child's welfare be maintained' and that 'an order for sole custody is losing favour'.

His Honour then continued:[49]

'While it is true that a joint custody order may be unrealistic where the parents of a child have an acrimonious relationship, it does not always follow that the alternative in such a situation is to grant sole custody of the child to one parent. Where there is no immediate or pressing need for the question of custody to be settled, one should seriously consider whether an order for sole custody is in the best interest of a child ... At the moment neither [parent] face serious problems relating to the upbringing of [the child]. All that is presently required is an order for care and control of the child ... Hopefully, the parents will realise in due course that it is best if they can cooperate in matters in relation to their child's upbringing.'

His Honour cited *Re Aliya Aziz Tayabali*[50] and agreed with Michael Hwang JC that an order of joint custody may have subtle psychological effects on the parties and not necessarily encourage the preservation of amicable relationships between parents and their child. By *Re G (guardianship of an infant)*, then, the High Court has repeated its earlier decision that brilliantly relates the law of guardianship and custody to parental responsibility to support rather than undermine the idea that has become the cornerstone of child law in Singapore.

My colleague has commented thus of this 'outstanding decision':[51]

'It is expected that when this *ratio decidendi* is followed in future cases, sole custody orders in custody suits between parents will only be made in exceptional circumstances such as where one parent has been demonstrated to

---

47   [2004] 1 SLR 229 noted in Debbie Ong Siew Ling 'Making no custody order: *Re G (guardianship of an infant)*' [2003] Sing JLS 583.

48   *Ibid*, at [6].

49   Above note 47, at [8] and [9].

50   See above note 21.

51   Debbie Ong Siew Ling 'Making no custody order: *Re G (guardianship of an infant)*', above note 47, at 586.

be "bad" for the child where he or she has physically, sexually or emotionally abused the child.'

B   Order of joint custody

Perhaps it was too much to expect that the notion of making no order of custody would find favour with every judge operating as he or she must, in Singapore, within the adversarial system of litigation. In the latest as yet unreported High Court, on appeal, decision in *CX v CY*[52] the Family Court judge had cited *Re Aliya Aziz Tayabali* and *Re G (guardianship of an infant)* to support the decision not to make a custody order. The High Court, however, on the appeal of both parents, the father seeking an order of joint custody and the mother an order of sole custody, reversed this decision and substituted it with an order of joint custody instead.

Justice Kan Ting Chiu clearly disapproved of the decision not to make an order describing it as 'passivity' and gave these reasons for reversing the lower court decision:[53]

> 'Passivity is not necessarily the best course. One may ask whether a custody order should be deferred because there is no immediate or pressing need for the question of custody to be settled. If there is some apprehension that the parents may not be able or prepared to exercise custody rights together, the making of an order would allow them (and the court) to know if they can work together, and to make the necessary changes if they cannot. There is no advantage in keeping the matter in suspension and then making an order when there is an immediate or pressing need for an order without the benefit of a "trial" period
> ...
>
> It is desirable that someone be vested with the authority to make important decisions for the child's welfare, eg the schooling and religious education the child is to receive. When no custody order is made, does it mean that neither parent has the authority? That is a most unsatisfactory state of affairs. Who is to make those decisions for the boy? Alternatively, does it mean that such decisions are to be taken by both parents, effectively putting them in joint custody?'

C   Critique

With all due respect, the best that can be said of his Honour's remarks in *CX v CY* is that they show how difficult it is to appreciate the optimal way of relating the law of guardianship and custody with that of parenthood. Despite the strenuous efforts of Michael Hwang JC in *Re Aliya Aziz Tayabali* and Tan Lee Meng J in *Re G (guardianship of an infant)* which, to academics, read as brilliant expositions of the right way to relate these areas

---

52   See judgment on LawNet, the website that carries, *inter alia*, all the latest judgments in Singapore, at http://lwb.lawnet.com.sg as [2005] SGHC 17.
53   *Ibid*, at [14] and [17].

of the law, there continues to be grave suspicion about making no order of custody in the application by parents.

The key may be Kan Ting Chiu J's fear that, if no order awarding custody to one or both parents were to emerge from the application between them, 'does it mean that neither parent has the authority?'. The answer of course is that, if no custody is awarded, the court is leaving the regulation of the parents' relationship with their child to the general law of parenthood rather than superimposing the law of guardianship and custody. By the general law of parenthood, encapsulated in s 46 of the Women's Charter,[54] both parents owe parental responsibility to their child and they are expected to co-operate in their exercise of their joint authority always pursuing the objective of the welfare of their child. This expression of parental responsibility under the general law of parenthood is as close to perfect as any can get. Focusing on it and holding parents to their joint co-operative responsibility is the most the court can do for the child whose parents are pursuing a custody suit against each other. There is nothing in the law of guardianship and custody that improves on this idea. Superimposing the law of guardianship and custody on that of the general law of parenthood to regulate parents in their relationship with their child can, instead, throw confusion at the parties.

His Honour may have accorded greater worth to an order of joint custody than is warranted. As Michael Hwang JC and Tan Lee Meng J have noted, there are psychological effects to deciding the way one parent (in this case the father) sought custody and thus making him the 'victor' in this appeal. How does it help the child for one of his parents to emerge from court infused with the idea that he won this round? The only real way to help the child is to remind both parents that the law expects them to contain their unhappiness with each other, forget about winning and losing regarding their child and continue to work together for his or her welfare. Rather than being inert, making the decision not to make an order of custody between parents is the thoughtful choice.

What indeed is settled by an order of joint custody? Would the parents, with the order of joint custody the father sought, now find it easier to co-operate in their parenting? It is submitted that perhaps Michael Hwang JC and Tan Lee Meng J understood the human condition more sensitively. They also appreciated the ephemeral character of any custody order. Nothing the court orders settles definitively the delicate and dynamic relationship between a dependent child and his or her parents. Whether they make themselves the best parents they can be and resume their co-operation in joint parenting are never settled even by the most ambitious court order. By choosing the law of guardianship and custody over the general law of parenthood his Honour has passed up the opportunity to remind the parents that their joint co-operative responsibility towards their child has not been affected in any way by the failure of their marital relationship.

It would appear that the contest between whether the outcome of a custody suit between parents should be the court making no order of custody or the

---

[54] See text corresponding to above note 10.

court making an order of joint custody remains live. There was an appeal from his Honour's decision in *CX v CY* and, although it is not yet clear what was sought by the appellant, it appears that the Court of Appeal, whose judgment is eagerly awaited, was content with the order of joint custody that his Honour had made.[55]

On a brighter note, it appears that the old practice of making orders of sole custody has rightly lost favour in Singapore. Making an order that appoints one parent, somewhat at the expense of the other, is the worst outcome of a custody suit between parents. While an order of joint custody is preferable as it at least mirrors the legal norm at parenthood, it is hoped that more judges will consider simply leaving the parents to their parental responsibility at law by making no order of custody between them.

VI COMMUNITARIAN EFFORTS

If the discussion above has shown anything, it is the fact that the law on its own cannot help parents be the best parents they can be. The courts can only keep reminding parents of their responsibility but it is through social services that the community can help parents in their joint parenting so that their children will be the beneficiaries thereof. In this regard Singapore can claim to have lived up to its commitment to her children to help their parents become and remain the best they can be through the ups and downs of their own marital relationship.

A   Government-led

The Ministry of Community Development, Youth and Sports in Singapore heads the provision of public services to this end and helps coordinate the provision of private services by charitable and non-governmental organisations. The public social services most relevant to supporting and enhancing parenting come within the 'Family Life Education' programme of the Ministry that regularly runs parenting courses for members of the public. Among the newer programmes is the 'Family & Community Development Town' that is a[56] 'one-stop portal that presents a generous serving of information and e-services on family and community development matters in Singapore' including information on 'Care for your children, experience youth, parenting teenagers and nurturing and protecting the young'.

B   Family court

While education in parenting is necessary at all times, the Family Court in Singapore recognises the particular need to so educate and assist parents in their joint parenting after the parents have become divorced. The court's

---

55   As a keynote speaker at a recent conference held in Singapore, one of the judges who sat on the appeal revealed that the appeal was dismissed.

56   This appears on the Ministry's website at www.mcys.gov.sg.

website[57] informs of the impressive range of social services it makes readily accessible to children and parents at this difficult time in their relationships. These programmes are part of the 'Family and Juvenile Justice Centre' that is one arm of the court.

Counselling is always available both to parents and their children. This is readily and affordably offered by counsellors and psychologists working at the Centre. Once care and control and access orders have been ordered, there are programmes directed to the needs of parents and children new to this way of living. Courses and workshops are offered 'to give insights to divorcing parents on how to cope with issues arising from divorce or separation, such as dealing with their own or their children's grief, the re-adjustment of lifestyles after divorce, new financial situations, and the balancing of work and home responsibilities'. Parents either attend these sessions voluntarily or may be ordered by the court to do so.

There are also programmes that assist the transfer of the children from one parent to the other. Counsellors help and supervise the actual handover to ensure it is done as ordered and without as much of the tension as may be expected in the beginning of this great change to the parents' and child's lives. The Centre also works with non-governmental service centres to widen the pool so that such assistance in handovers is offered all over the island Republic.

To a respectable degree Singapore can claim to live up to the adage that 'it takes a village to raise a child'. The need for concern and assistance from the whole community is no greater than in the distressing situation of divorce that involves young dependent children. A caring community appreciates that good legal regulation plays only one part.

VII REFORM OF LAW OF GUARDIANSHIP AND CUSTODY

The writer has said before that, as long as the law of guardianship and custody as it affects parents is re-aligned with the cornerstone idea of joint co-operative parental responsibility to their child, there is no real need to abolish the concept of child custody by parents.[58] As long as our courts do not make orders of sole custody that, in theory, dispossess the other parent except in highly exceptional circumstances where the parent has abused the child or otherwise shown himself or herself to be seriously unfit, Singapore can continue with the current law. The only choice is whether to favour making a no custody order between the parents.

It may nevertheless be inevitable for Singapore to consider reform. If, as has been advocated above, the optimal outcome of a custody suit between parents (and it should be remembered that custody suits are invariably brought between parents) is for the court not to make a custody order then

---

57   At www.familycourtofsingapore.gov.sg.

58   Leong Wai Kum 'Restatement of the Law of Guardianship and Custody in Singapore', above note 17, at 490.

why not abolish the concept of parental custody of their child altogether? There has recently been a call for review of the law in Singapore with the goals of abolishing parental custody and emphasising joint parental responsibility.[59]

Any such review will no doubt begin with the Children Act that was enacted for England and Wales in 1989. This statute has since been acknowledged as the foremost statute of its kind in the common law world. This Act abolishes the idea of a court order of custody and substitutes, instead, lesser court orders of the nature of 'residence order',[60] 'contact order',[61] 'specific issue order'[62] and 'prohibited steps order'.[63] By such change in the law, then, the courts avoid altogether the inappropriate sole custody order in favour of one parent and also avoid the superfluous joint parental custody order. One can appreciate, however, that it is just as possible to achieve these aims without necessarily abolishing parental custody of the child.[64]

To an enviable extent the (English) Children Act 1989 has served as a model in other common law and related jurisdictions although, as may be expected, each jurisdiction would have made its own adjustments to the content of the statute. The Children (Scotland) Act was enacted in 1995 to adopt its ideals, the (Australian) Family Law Act 1975 was amended in 1995[65] to entrench joint parental responsibility within the court's jurisdiction to make 'parenting orders', the (New Zealand) Care of Children Act 2004[66] also substitutes 'parenting orders' for 'custody' and 'access' which parenting orders will aim at 'ensuring a stronger focus on the rights of the child; and recognising the diversity of family arrangements that exist for the care of the child; and improving New Zealand's compliance with international obligations'. In March 2005 the Law Reform Commission of Hong Kong completed its

---

[59] By Justice Lai Siu Chiu of the Supreme Court of Singapore in her keynote address at the Law Asia Conference on 'Children and the Law' in Singapore on 27 May 2005. Her Honour's speech is expected to be published in the forthcoming July issue of the *Law Gazette*, the journal of The Law Society of Singapore which was the organiser of the conference.

[60] An order settling the arrangements to be made as to the person with whom a child is to live that is, in substance, akin to the order for 'care and control' that a Singapore court might make.

[61] An order requiring the person with whom a child lives, or is to live, to allow the child to visit or stay with the person named in the order, or for that person and the child otherwise to have contact with each other that is, in substance, akin to an 'access order' a Singapore court may make.

[62] An order giving directions for the purpose of determining a specific question which has arisen, or which may arise, in connection with any aspect of parental responsibility for a child that is similar to the situation where a court in Singapore gives directions with regard to any matter relating to the upbringing of a child.

[63] An order that no step which could be taken by a parent in meeting his parental responsibility for a child, and which is of a kind specified in the order, shall be taken by any person without the consent of the court. This should be regarded merely as an order that is more specifically worded but one which is clearly also within the wide powers available to a court in Singapore whenever its guardianship jurisdiction is attracted.

[64] This is not to suggest, of course, that a review of the law would not also allow other timely changes, for example, that address who may be allowed to apply to court for orders relating to the upbringing of a child and the relationship between guardianship and custody and the power of the court to make a child its 'ward'. It is simply to say that a review of the guardianship and custody as it affects parents will not be of any greater significance.

[65] *Vide* the (Australian) Family Law Reform Act 1995 effective June 1996.

[66] That came into effect on 1 July 2005.

review of its law and substantially recommends following the changes brought by the (English) Children Act 1989.[67]

VIII CONCLUSION

In form the law in Singapore of guardianship and custody, especially as it relates to the child and his or her parents, appears to be more old-fashioned than that prevailing among its common law friends. Despite this, however, there have been forward-looking decisions from the courts in Singapore motivated to relate optimally the law with the cornerstone idea of joint co-operative parental responsibility to their child as has been advocated in academic writings. At the same time it has been shown that Singapore offers parents and children in need an impressive array of social services to help them, in particular, just after the parents have terminated their marital relationship. Whether Singapore decides to reform her law to the model set by the (English) Children Act 1989, it remains true that a communitarian effort supplements good legal regulation with accessible social services. Parents and children always live oblivious of legal regulation of their relationships until the parents terminate their own marital relationship. Then it is reassuring that the legal regulation in Singapore of the relationship between parents and children may be as good as it can be and it is supplemented by the provision of social services to educate and to assist.

---

[67] See the Law Reform Commission of Hong Kong *Report on Child Custody and Access*, available at www.hkreform.gov.hk.

Slovenia

LEGAL REGULATION OF ADOPTION IN SLOVENIA – DO WE NEED CHANGES?

Suzana Kraljić*

Résumé

Cet article porte sur l'adoption en droit slovène. Dans un premier temps, il fait état des caractéristiques essentielles de l'adoption, des conditions légales de celle-ci en regard de l'enfant et des candidats adoptants, des étapes de la procédure, des effets de l'adoption et des fondements d'une éventuelle annulation d'une décision d'adoption.

Dans sa deuxième partie, ce texte s'intéresse à l'adoption internationale en Slovénie, avec une attention particulière pour la récente entente bilatérale entre la Slovénie et la Macédoine. L'article se termine en mettant en lumière quelques aspects importants du projet de Code familial touchant à l'adoption.

1 INTRODUCTION

Life plays its games frequently. In spite of the fact that a child is wanted and lives with parents who are offering everything to that child, destiny often interferes and deprives the child of its world – eg the parents die in an accident. What is going to happen to the child? And then there is the other side of childhood – the child living in surroundings where there is continuous conflict between the parents, physical, psychological and sexual violence – is that a 'healthy' environment where he or she can develop an independent personality? What should happen to this child? These are two different situations with one consequence – the child cannot live with its biological parents. And, international conventions, constitutions and laws guarantee special care for children who cannot live with their parents, due to different circumstances, by the state. Thus, children who cannot live with their parents are given to foster parents, tutorship, adoption and institutional custody. Therefore, adoption is just one of the forms of custody[1], but we can positively state that it is the most complete and best measure of care for a child who is not able to live with his or her parents. Does the legal regulation of adoption in 1976 by the Marriage and Family Relations Act[1] (valid since 1

---

*   Faculty of Law, University of Maribor.
1   Marriage and Family Relations Act (MFRA) – Ur l SRS, no 15/76, 30/86, 1/89, 14/89; Ur l RS, no 13/94, 82/94, 29/95, 26/99, 70/00, 64/01, 110/02, 42/03, 16/04.

January 1977) (MFRA), after 30 years, still measure up to modern circumstances, or is it necessary to implement changes?

2   ESSENTIAL CHARACTERISTICS OF ADOPTION

Of course, what is best for the child is life with its own family, ie the community to which it belongs. If this is not possible, adoption should be the last resort, since before adoption all possibilities for preservation of the child's original family should be explored. Adoption is the replacement for the original birth family and should not be considered before it is totally clear that the original family will not be able to satisfy the needs of the child and fulfil all obligations towards the child.[2] Thus, there is the assumption that the original family of the child, the biological family, is the best environment in which to take care of a child. If the situation occurs where the circumstances do not live up to this assumption, the state is obliged to guarantee and provide the resources and activity to enable the upbringing of the child and the protection of its best interests in its original family. If that is not possible, the child should be adopted by another family, as soon as possible.

The basic principles of adoption derive from the Constitution of the Republic of Slovenia (CRS)[3] from 1991, stressing in its art 56, s 3, that *children and minors, for whom the parents do not take care, who do not have parents or are without proper family care, enjoy special protection by the state.* The state protects the minor child always, when its healthy development is endangered or when other needs of the child demand it, and that is the case with adoption, since, as a special form of protection of minor children, the same relations as between parents and children are to be established between the adopter and the adoptee.

The MFRA recognises only one sort of adoption, ie *full adoption.*[4] The fundamental characteristics of full adoption are as follows:

- exactly the same relationship as between natural parents and their children is to be created between the adopter and the adoptee;
- exactly the same relationship as between the adoptee and its natural relatives is to be created between the relatives of the adopter and the adoptee;
- full adoption cannot be revoked.

---

[2]   P Ropoša Tanjšek et al Organizacija in standardi na področju posvojitve (Visoka šola za socialno delo Univerze v Ljubljani, Ljubljana 1999) p 8.

[3]   Constitution of the RS (CRS) – Ur l RS, no 33/91-I, 42/97, 66/00, 24/03, 69/04.

[4]   The Basic Act on Adoption from 1965 regulating adoption in the territory of the former SFRJ knew only incomplete adoption which could be terminated by an agreement between the parties ex officio or on demand by the adopter or the adoptee, if there were reasonable grounds for doing so.

3 CONDITIONS FOR ADOPTION

The MFRA demands the fulfilment of certain conditions by the adopter, as well as the adoptee, in order that adoption may be valid.

3.1 Adopter (active capacity for adoption)

The MFRA states for the adopter the following conditions:

(a) *The adopter must be a mature person* (art 137, s 1, sent 1).

(b) *The adopter must be at least 18 years older than the adoptee* – only in extraordinary cases may the centre for social work allow adoption in the case of an adopter who is not 18 years older than the adoptee. The allowance in this case is given only when all circumstances of the case are studied and it is established that adoption is in the best interest of the adoptee (art 137, s 1, sent 2). The reason for the disparity of 18 years in age between the adopter and the adoptee is based on the fact that at 18 years full legal capacity is reached – this is necessary for independent action in legal affairs; further it is about the biological difference in age being the basis for the relationship of parents and children (a 23-year-old woman will not be able to adopt the 17-year-old child of her husband – in the case of adoption by a single person); also the adopter should have an age considered normal for natural parenthood.[5]

(c) *The child must be adopted by both spouses* – an exception applies only when one of them adopts the child of his or her spouse (art 138).

(d) Since the institution of adoption is intended for the best interests of minor children, the MFRA contains further conditions for the adopter of a negative nature. Thus, *the adopter cannot be*:

– a person deprived of the parental right;

– a person for whom it is rightfully assumed that adoption would be abused and would cause damage to the child;

– a person who does not guarantee that he or she will ensure the stable personal development of the adoptee and prepare him or her for independent living and work;

– a person deprived of business capacity or being mentally disordered or ill, so that he or she might endanger the life and health of the adoptee (art 139, s 2).

(e) *The adopter cannot be a direct relative or kin or brother or sister* (art 136, s 1).

---

[5]   A similar solution is found in the Act governing infertility treatment and procedures of biomedically assisted procreation (ITPBAPA – Ur l RS, no 70/2000), determining in its art 6:

'(1) Spouses and cohabitants of full age, sound judgment and appropriate age for the carrying out of parental duties and in such psychological shape that gives reason to expect that they will be capable of carrying out parental duties for the best interest of the child, are entitled to procedures for fertilization with biomedical assistance. (2) The woman has to be of an age appropriate for giving birth.'

(f) *The adopter cannot be the tutor of the child or ward*, as long as this tutorship lasts (art 136, s 2). This provision is very important and has a preventive purpose, since the tutor might abuse his or her position in a way that he or she would not file a report on his or her work which he or she would be obliged to produce at the end of his or her tutorship. From the report of the tutor, it has to be determined how he or she took care of the ward, the data on the management of the property of the ward, on the disposal of his or her property and on the status of his or her property.[6]

(g) *In principle, a Slovenian child should be adopted by a Slovenian citizen* (art 140, s 2) – the adopter may be a foreign citizen, as an exception where the centre for social work could not find an adopter among the Slovenian population. This allowance is not required where the adopter is the spouse of the child's parent.

3.2 Adoptee (passive capacity for adoption)

In the same way, the MFRA determines the conditions to be fulfilled in relation to the child, ie the future adoptee. These are as follows:

(a) *An adoptee can only be a minor* (art 134). A nasciturus cannot be adopted. When couples decide on adoption, some of them imagine the child they wish to have. The majority wish to have a baby, since in the first months of a child's life he or she is still a 'blank sheet of paper'. But such cases are very rare, since the 'adoption market' also contains older children who have been 'marked' by their past lives, habits and experience. If these children have been exposed to physical, psychological or sexual violence, or if they lost their parents tragically, a lot of professional work is needed with the future adopters during the preparation period, as well as with the child who needs to regain trust in the first place, especially in cases of abuse, towards people and their surroundings.

(b) The MFRA, in its art 141, s 1, determines that the following children may be adopted:

– *children whose parents are unknown*;

– *children whose parents have not had a known residence for a year*;

– *children of parents who have agreed before the competent authority, to give the child up for adoption.* The agreement of the parents is not necessary if the parent was deprived of the parental right or if they are permanently not capable of expressing their will.

In all these cases, adoption is possible only after one year has expired from the fulfilment of the necessary conditions (art 141, s 2). Adoption is, as an exception, possible within the limitation period of one year if the centre of social work establishes that this would be in the best

---

[6]   M Geč-Korošec and S Kraljić Družinsko pravo, II altered and completed edition (Faculty of Law of the University of Maribor, Maribor 1997) p 207.

interest of the child (art 141, s 3). A child without living parents is also available to be adopted.

(c) *Adoption has to be for the best interest of the adoptee* – whilst the best interest of the child is the guiding principle in adoptions, the Slovenian MFRA is in accordance with the basic principle of the UN Convention on the Rights of the Child.

(d) The conditions mentioned above for the adopter are also valid for the adoptee:

– *the adoptee cannot be a direct relative and also not the brother or sister of the adopter* (art 136, s 1);

– *the adoptee cannot be adopted by its tutor* (art 136, s 2);

– *the adoptee cannot be adopted by more than one person, except where the adopters are spouses* (art 138);

– *the adoptee is at least 18 years younger than the adopter* with some exceptions;

– *the adoptee over the age of 10 years has to give his or her consent to the adoption* – the MFRA uses a set age limit as the start of the child's right to express its opinion, which is not in accordance with arts 3 and 6 of the European Convention on the Exercise of Children's Rights[7] and art 12 of the Convention on the Rights of the Child. The Slovenian legislator has already followed the regulation of EKUOP and KOP in several other Acts such that the fixed limit for taking into account the child's opinion was abolished, and this means that the child's capability to express its opinion is judged in each individual case and is no longer tied to age.

(e) The MFRA has no special provision providing that the adoptee can be a foreign citizen, but this is not excluded (see more on this in section 7 of this chapter).

4 PROCEEDINGS FOR ADOPTION

The proceedings for adoption may be started ex officio by the centre for social work or based on the proposal by the future adopter. The centre for social work (CSW) has local competence in all cases within the competence of the CSW and is in general determined by the residence of the person in need of support and custody. If that person has no residence, local competence is determined by the place where he or she is living, or, if the person does not have that, either by the last residence or the last place of living, respectively. If local competence cannot be determined under these provisions, it is determined by the place where the adoption proceedings are commenced. Local competence for a minor (also for the adoptee) is determined by the residence or the place of living of both parents, respectively. For a minor whose parents do not live together local competence is determined by the residence or the place of living of the

---

[7] European Convention on the Exercise of Children's Rights (ECECR) – Ur l RS – MP, no 26/99.

parent with whom the minor lives or to whom they were given. If neither of the parents of the minor is known, local competence is determined by the place where proceedings were commenced.

Adoption proceedings can be divided into the so-called preliminary proceedings and the act of conclusion of adoption:

(a) Preliminary proceedings involve the acts of the CSW. In the adoption proceedings, several documents have to be produced. They are:

- curriculum vitae of the adopters;
- copies of the register of births;
- confirmation of citizenship;
- medical report;
- confirmation of personal income;
- confirmation from the criminal register;
- confirmation from the court of justice that there is no investigation and that no claim has been filed;
- confirmation that the future adopter was not deprived of the parental right or business capacity;
- the expertise of the competent CSW encompassing data on the personality of the person applying for adoption, an assessment of the character of the individual, their suitability for raising a child, and, most importantly, establishing the motive for adoption. A visit to the home is obligatory, since people are more relaxed, honest and open at home than in official environments. In the same way, the insight into the private lives of the adopters is also important, since through this it is possible to get an idea of the cultural surroundings of the adopters.

All these documents should not be prepared more than 3 months before the commencement of adoption proceedings. For the adopters, the expertise of the competent CSW demanded ex officio by the body carrying out the adoption proceedings is very important. From this expertise the personality of the future adopter, his or her emotional maturity, family relations of the future adopters, their suitability for raising a child and motive for adoption should be made clear. This decision should be made by a team of experts (psychologist, medical doctor, teacher and social worker).

The preliminary proceedings also include the collection and establishing of data on the child or the future adoptee. The competent CSW has to hear the mature brothers and sisters, the grand-parents, or if they are not living, the uncles and aunts of the child, whose parents do not have a known place of residence or are not alive, before deciding on adoption. From all available data and with the further help of a psychologist and a paediatrician, the complete social situation and psycho-social status of the child has to be established. Only in this way can adopters who will be the most appropriate for the child's development and his needs be chosen.[8]

(b) The future adoptee spends time in the family of the adopter before the decision on adoption is taken. The duration of this time is not determined by law, but it is needed to establish whether the adoptee and adopter will get along in the new situation and whether adoption will be beneficial for the adoptee.

(c) The act of adoption is the decision on adoption made in administrative proceedings and within the competence of the CSW if it establishes that all conditions provided for adoption have been satisfied and that adoption will be beneficial for the adoptee. With the decision on adoption the name and surname of the adoptee are determined by the adopter. Therefore, adoption takes place when the decision on adoption becomes valid. The decision on adoption is sent by the CSW to the competent registrar in order to enter adoption into the register. In the register the adopters are entered as parents of the adoptee. When the competent CSW establishes that the conditions provided for adoption are not fulfilled, or that adoption would not be beneficial for the child, it rejects the proposal for adoption or stops the adoption proceedings. In spite of the fact that the Act does not have special provisions on this, in practice the decision on adoption is handed to the adopters in a solemn manner.

5   LEGAL CONSEQUENCES OF ADOPTION

Since adoption is a special form of protection of minor children the same relation is established between the adopter and the adoptee as between parents and children. At full adoption, all rights and duties of the adoptee towards its parents and other relatives end, and in the same way the rights and duties of the parents and the relatives towards the adoptee. Thus, by full adoption the legal right to inheritance is lost.[9]

The adopter determines the personal name of the adoptee, where the parents are not known. If the child – the future adoptee – already has a personal name, the adopter can determine his or her last name or a new personal name for the adoptee at the moment of adoption (art 7 of the Personal Name Act (PNA)).[10] The change of the personal name is possible if the adoptee is less than 4 years old (art 7, s 2, PNA). For the change of the personal name of the adoptee older than 10 years his or her consent is needed for the change.

By full adoption the adopter and the adoptee have the same relationship as natural parents and children. The adopted child is received totally and permanently into the family of the adopter and obtains the position of a birth

---

[8]   M Geč-Korošec and S Kraljić, p 210.

[9]   After the Basic Act on Adoption in 1965 the adoptee retained his or her right to inheritance from parents and relatives.

[10]   Personal Name Act (PNA) – Ur l SRS, no 2/87, RS 5/91, 29/95.

child. Everything which applies to relations between parents and their children also applies to the relations between the adopter and the adoptee.

The same relations as between relatives appear between the adoptee and his or her successors and the adopter and his or her relatives, except where the law provides otherwise.

At adoption, the adopters are entered into the register as parents of the adoptee.

6   ENDING OF ADOPTION?

The MFRA knows only one form of adoption, full adoption, which is established by the decision in administrative proceedings of the centre for social work. The decision on adoption means that the adoptive relation cannot be broken, but the decision can be annulled. The annulment of adoption is sought in administrative proceedings. The following grounds exist:

– the adoptee was not a minor;
– the adoptee was adopted by more than one person who were not spouses;
– the adoptee and the adopter are direct relatives or brother or sister;
– the adopter and the adoptee are still in the relationship of tutorship;
– the adopter is not 18 years older than the adoptee and the competent CSW did not waive this condition;
– the adoptee who is more than 10 years old did not give consent to adoption;
– the adopter is a person:
    – who was deprived of the parental right;
    – who, it is suspected, would abuse adoption to the disadvantage of the adoptee;
    – who does not ensure a stable personal development for the child;
– the adopter was deprived of business capacity or was mentally disordered or ill, so that he or she might endanger the health and life of the adoptee;
– the provisions of art 140 of MFRA setting out the conditions when a foreign citizen adopts a Slovenian child have been violated;
– the provisions of art 141 of MFRA determining which child is allowed to be adopted and that adoption is possible only after the end of one year from the fulfilment of these conditions are violated.

The annulment of the decision on adoption can be sought by the adoptee, his or her parents and the adopter. The proceedings for annulment take place before the CSW which can also start the proceedings ex officio.

The legal consequences of adoption end from the date of the annulment of the adoption (ex nunc).

7 INTERNATIONAL ADOPTIONS IN SLOVENIA – DESCRIPTION OF THE STATUS QUO

As mentioned, in Slovenia there are a lot more potential adopters than children available. This situation existed before in former Yugoslavia but owing to poor regulation in the other Yugoslav republics, Slovenian couples mainly adopted children from Macedonia, Kosovo and Bosnia and Herzegovina. From independence, these internal adoptions became international.

Even today, when in Slovenia there is an interest in the adoption of foreign children, the interest is directed towards children coming from the countries of former Yugoslavia, mainly Macedonia and Bosnia and Herzegovina. However, none of these countries has signed the Hague Convention on Inter-Country Adoption, neither has Slovenia signed any bilateral agreement with a foreign country, in spite of the attempts made over the years. Yet countries being economically and socially weaker are reluctant to enter such agreements, since every country protects its own citizens. However, Slovenia and Macedonia signed a letter of intent in February 2005 by which they expressed their readiness to start negotiations on the conclusion of an agreement on international adoptions. The draft agreement was prepared on the Slovenian side and will determine the conditions and proceedings for introducing international adoptions and guarantee that adoption will be carried out in the best interest of the child and that the rights of the child will be respected in accordance with recognised international law.[11] The agreement between Slovenia and Macedonia is the first agreement of this sort to determine the proceedings of adoption. The Ministry of Labor, Family and Social Affairs planned the signing of this agreement for Autumn 2005, and the first children from Macedonia will be adopted by Slovenian couples after the signing of the agreement on international adoptions at the beginning of 2006.[12] In spite of the agreement, we do not expect a significant rise in the number of adoptions in Slovenia, since the preparations for international adoption will demand readiness for children from a different cultural, religious and national surrounding than that of the adopters.

At the CSW in Maribor, being the largest[13] in Slovenia, there have already been two single adoptions (where one of the spouses adopted the child of his or her partner) where the children were foreign citizens, ie citizens of White Russia and Ukraine, living in Slovenia. In this case, the proceedings were carried out through the Ministry of Labor, Family and Social Affairs.

The question of international adoptions became especially pertinent at the end of 2004, when some Asian countries were hit by the tsunami. Immediately 'market offers of orphan children' for adoption emerged. But, because countries avoid international adoptions in such cases, especially

---

[11] Source: Ministry of Labor, Family and Social Affairs (Media centre), Letter of Intent for the Preparation of the Agreement on International Adoptions with Macedonia, 2005.

[12] See www.arnes.si.

[13] CSW Maribor has the largest number of employees, bearing in mind the number of inhabitants in its territory, as well as its area of operation.

when the primary principle in adoption is the principle of the best interest of the child, in the affected countries a moratorium on international adoptions was put in place. It is the task of the state to find the closest relatives of the child. That could not have been done since the first offers were made on the second day after the tsunami. Tracing relatives under those conditions can take years. But, because in cases of adoption, internal as well as international, time runs against the children, it is known that adopters are much easier to find for younger children. On the other hand, the possibility of finding the child's parents reduces from year to year. In addition these children, who usually live their childhood in different institutions or fall into the hands of people using them for prostitution, slave labor or as 'organ donors', have to be considered as well.

8   ADOPTION – DE LEGE FERENDA REGULATION FOLLOWING THE PROPOSAL UNDER THE FAMILY CODE

The legal regulation of adoption in Slovenia, as mentioned, is almost 30 years old. Today, a fundamental reform of family law is being prepared, since the Family Code (FC), which is supposed to regulate adoption, is being reformed. More important innovations introduced by the FC regarding adoption are as follows:

(a) the present MFRA does not provide for adoption by cohabitants, whilst the proposal of the FC expressly mentions that cohabitants have the possibility to adopt;

(b) the provision of the MFRA, under which it is impossible to adopt any direct relative or brother or sister, is most frequently not for the best interest of the child. Under the draft, grandparents – and all relatives in a horizontal line – have capacity to obtain all rights and duties as between parents and children;[14]

(c) for the child's consent to adoption, there is no longer the limitation of age to 10 years. The child's right to state its opinion in the proceedings of adoption will be judged in each case especially regarding its degree of understanding. This means that the child will give its opinion on adoption when it is capable of understanding the meaning of the adoption and its consequences;

(d) the consent of one of the parents to adoption is sufficient where the residence of the other has been unknown for one year;

(e) the child can be placed for adoption in cases where both parents are deprived of parental responsibility, ie immediately, when the decision on the deprivation of the parental right takes effect;

---

[14]   In the US, in 1970, more than half of the adopters were relatives, in Ireland there were 10% of adoptions of this kind – G Shannon *Child Law* (Thomson Round Hall, 2005) p 272.

(f) the draft FC also states that the parents cannot consent to adoption before the child has reached the age of 8 weeks, since the birth of the child may influence the mother's decision on adoption;

(g) adoption proceedings are usually started ex officio by the CSW. An exception is where it is a single adoption or adoption by relatives. Here, proceedings may be started on the application of the future adopter;

(h) the draft FC suggests the establishment of a central register of children available for adoption and persons wanting to adopt;

(i) if the child is entrusted to the potential adopter (period of trial), for this placement of the child the provisions on the carrying out of foster activities are not applicable. Here, the provisions of the Act Concerning the Pursuit of Foster Care,[15] setting special conditions for the foster parent, cannot apply to the potential adopter. In addition, adoption has to be supported, because in the case of a child in foster care it is moved from one family to another.[16] We can never speak of the child's best interest here.[17]

9 CONCLUSION

In Slovenia, in economic terms, demand still exceeds supply. This means that there are many more potential adopters waiting to adopt a child than there are potential children available. In spite of Slovenia being a signatory of the Hague Convention on Inter-Country Adoption, there are practically no international adoptions. In Slovenia, soon, the first bilateral agreement, ie with Macedonia, will be signed, opening the path for Slovenian adopters to adopt Macedonian children, but here the question arises whether the number of adoptions will really rise. In the case of international adoptions even more preparations relating to future adopters will be necessary because different cultural, religious and national circumstances will be brought together.

In the same way, it is necessary to mention that between internal and international adoptions there are essential differences of which potential adopters should be informed. Couples deciding for international adoption go abroad and look for the child by themselves, while for internal adoptions the CSW looks for the child. In international adoptions the adopters also make contact in the country from which they wish to adopt a child by themselves with the institution there and send in an application for adoption. International adoption will demand much more personal, as well as financial, investment from the would-be adopters.

---

[15] Act Concerning the Pursuit of Foster Care (ACPFC) – Ur l RS, no 110/02.

[16] In the US, in 1980, the Adoption Assistance and Child Welfare Act was created, of which the fundamental goal was to avoid an unnecessary placement of a child in foster care and to support the reunion of families, where this is possible. The goal of this Act was also the limitation of time that a child should live in foster care and that adoption should be supported when the return of the child to its original family was not possible. But, the Act did not achieve the set goals – see J Hauguard and R Avery in B Bottoms, M Bull Kovera and B McAulif (eds) *Children, Social Science and the Law* (Cambridge University Press, 2000) p 133.

[17] The Draft of the Slovenian Family Code.

However, internal adoptions also reveal certain problems. Frequently, the children remain in foster families or move from one family to another for too long a time, which results in negative consequences for the child's whole life. In cases where it is obvious that the child will not be able to return to the original family, proceedings for adoption have to be advanced.

The South Pacific

LIVING IN SIN IN PARADISE –
COHABITATION IN THE SOUTH PACIFIC

Sue Farran[*]

Résumé

Depuis de nombreuses années, les conséquences de la cohabitation non-maritale ou "mariage de fait" ont été inscrites au programme législatif de nombreux pays développés. En effet, dans un certain nombre de pays, les préoccupations liées aux relations homosexuelles ont dépassé celles qui concernaient la cohabitation hétérosexuelle. Bien que souvent décrite pour son mode de vie érotique et exotique, la région des îles du Pacifique Sud n'est pas un havre idyllique pour ses "cohabitants". C'est un peu le contraire, en raison de l'influence toujours présente de la morale protestante, d'une législation coloniale surannée, de magistrats conservateurs, de traditions familiales enracinées et de ressources insuffisantes pour promouvoir une réforme de fond. Cependant, ces pays se développent et la société change sous l'influence des échanges internationaux, des médias, et un nombre croissant de personnes cohabitent de fait. Cette contribution offre un tour d'horizon du cadre juridique de la région et des défis sociaux qu'affrontent ces micro-Etats où la coutume, le christianisme, et le droit, se battent pour prendre en compte ces nouvelles revendications.

I   INTRODUCTION

It might be thought that the relatively undeveloped state of many Pacific islands would tolerate or even encourage cohabitation and informal 'de facto' unions. This would be a mistake. The region of the Pacific islands is some 50 years or more – legally – behind in either recognising or tolerating the range of personal relationships which might be found elsewhere in the more developed world. While Australia can offer cohabitees the De Facto Relationship Act 1999 in Tasmania;[1] the De Facto Relationships Act 1984 in New South Wales; the De Facto Relationship Act 1996 in South Australia; and the De Facto Relationships Act 2004 in the Northern Territory, and in New Zealand cohabitees may be able to sort out their property problems

---

[*]   Senior Lecturer, University of Dundee, Scotland; Visiting Lecturer School of Law, University of the South Pacific.
[1]   No 93 of 1999.

under the Property (Relationship) Act 2001,[2] in most of the island countries of the South Pacific cohabitation continues to lie outside the law, particularly for the adults involved, less so, in some instances for their children. In some circumstances indigenous persons who cohabit may be able to rely on modified versions of customary law to assist them – although this is not always the case as will be seen. Conversely they may imagine themselves to be married in custom and then find that this is not so.[3] However, although customary law is, to a degree, flexible and able to modify with the times, non-indigenous persons may fall outside the scope of customary law altogether and therefore be subject to legal regimes which for the greater part are firmly anchored in the English common law of the 1970s and earlier.[4] This article reviews the legal environment which applies to cohabitees in that part of the South Pacific region which came predominantly under the influence of the English common law.[5]

This region includes Micronesian countries such as the Federated States of Micronesia and Marshall Islands; Melanesian countries such as Papua New Guinea, Solomon Islands and Vanuatu; Polynesian countries such as Tonga and Samoa and countries such as Fiji, which are partly Polynesian and partly Melanesian. It excludes, however, French Polynesia and the islands of Wallis and Fortuna, New Caledonia and Palau. It also excludes those parts of the region which have been brought under US control such as American Samoa and Hawaii.

Cohabitation for the purposes of this article means couples living together outside marriage in the type of relationship that is characterised by many of the same features as marriage.[6] Although such relationships may be homosexual as opposed to heterosexual, the former are likely to receive even less legal sympathy than the latter. Not only is homosexuality still a crime in much of the region, but strong religious adherence in most island countries of the region means that homophobia is widespread.[7] While legal reform

---

2   See B Atkin and W Parker *Relationship Property in New Zealand* (Butterworth's, Wellington, 2000) and Hughes 'Recent legislative changes affecting succession law in New Zealand – The Property (Relationship) Act 2001' (2001) 5 *JSPL* at www.paclii.org/vu/journals/JSPL/2001?13.html.

3   O Jessop suggests that one of the reasons for the difficulty in ascertaining the incidence of cohabitation in Papua New Guinea is that sometimes couples do not realise that they are 'merely' cohabitees. 'De Facto Relationships and the Law in Papua New Guinea' (1992) 41 *ICLQ* 460.

4   Non-indigenous may include Pacific islanders from another country, for example, a Samoan cohabiting with a ni-Vanuatu in Vanuatu, or an 'ex-patriate' (white) person cohabiting with an indigenous person, or a non-indigenous person born and domiciled in the country (possible of mixed parentage) cohabiting with an indigenous person.

5   This excludes that part of the Pacific known as French Polynesia, but includes Vanuatu – formerly the New Hebrides – which prior to independence came under the condominium rule of France and Great Britain and therefore under the influence of both French law and English law.

6   The Fiji Family Law Reform Commission paper on De Facto Relationships (Discussion paper 4-1997, p 1) defines a de facto relationship as 'a non-secretive relationship between a man and a woman who live with each other as spouses on a genuine domestic basis even though they are not legally married'.

7   See A Jowitt 'Reconstructing Custom: The politics of homophobia in Vanuatu' (2005) 30(1) *Alternative Law Journal* 10; and T McIntosh 'Words and Worlds of Difference: Homosexualities

might eventually encompass unmarried heterosexual couples, this is unlikely to encompass same-sex couples in the foreseeable future.[8] The focus of the article is, therefore, the regional law on unmarried heterosexual cohabiting couples and some of the problems likely to be encountered in a range of island jurisdictions.

II   THE LEGAL CONTEXT AND LIKELY LEGAL ISSUES

A   Constitutions and human rights

A glance at a selection of the written constitutions of the region indicates that the cornerstones of the law and the society which it governs are religion, the family and the customs or traditions of indigenous people. For example, the preamble to the Constitution Amendment Act 1997 of Fiji states:

'(R)eaffirming our recognition of the human rights and fundamental freedoms of all individuals and groups, safeguarded by adherence to the rule of law, and our respect for human dignity and for the importance of the family ...'

while the preamble to the Samoa Constitution opens with the words:

'(W)hereas sovereignty over the Universe belongs to the Omnipresent God alone, and the authority to be exercised by the people of Western Samoa within the limits prescribed by His commandments is a sacred heritage;

Whereas the Leaders of Western Samoa have declared that Western Samoa should be an independent State based on Christian principles and Samoan custom and tradition ...'[9]

and that of Vanuatu declares:

'(W)e the people of Vanuatu, proud of our struggle for freedom, determined to safeguard the achievements of this struggle, cherishing our ethnic, linguistic and cultural diversity, mindful at the same time of our common destiny, hereby proclaim the establishment of the united and free Republic of Vanuatu founded on traditional Melanesian values, faith in God, and Christian principles, and for this purpose give ourselves this Constitution.'[10]

Although all the constitutions of the region – with the exception of Niue – include some form of a bill of rights,[11] only in Nauru is there specific

---

8   in the Pacific' Working Papers on Sociology and Social Policy, University of the South Pacific, 1999.

8   Section 42 – which is the interpretation section – of the Family Law Act 2003 (Fiji) defines a de facto relationship as 'the relationship between a man and a woman who live with each other as spouses on a genuine domestic basis although not legally married to each other'.

9   Samoan Constitution 1960.

10   Constitution of the Republic of Vanuatu 1980.

11   In the Cook Islands and Vanuatu these provisions are modelled on the Canadian Bill of Rights, whereas those of Fiji, Kiribati, Nauru, Samoa, Solomon Islands and Tuvalu are modelled on the Universal Declaration of Human Rights and the European Convention on Human Rights. For comment on the interpretation of such rights see J Corrin Care, T Newton and D Paterson *Introduction to South Pacific Law* (Cavendish, London, 1999) pp 85–88.

provision for respect for 'private and family life' listed among the fundamental rights and freedoms safeguarded to individuals,[12] and only the Constitution of the Marshall Islands prohibits discrimination on the grounds of 'family status or descent'.[13] Consequently, cohabitees may be hard pressed to support claims to various rights on the grounds of discrimination even where there may be a general right to equality before the law.

Alternatively international human rights conventions may be of some assistance, for example, the Convention on the Elimination of All Discrimination Against Women (CEDAW),[14] or the Convention on the Rights of the Child (CRC) particularly where legislation remains in place which discriminates between legitimate and illegitimate children. However, although a number of countries in the region have signed up to these international instruments, not all of them have incorporated them into domestic law,[15] and in some instances the constitution or other legislation specifically allows differential treatment.[16]

B   Introduced laws and ideas

The law relating to private or domestic relationships is a mix of custom and statutes and legal principles – including those of equity – introduced into the region from an era which has long passed in the country of origin. The reason for this is that on independence – and much of the region is relatively young – transitional provisions were incorporated into the constitutions providing that until the national legislative bodies of the newly independent states made their own laws, those in force would continue to apply except where they were inconsistent with the new political status of the country or repugnant in some way to local circumstances. Most island countries have what is referred to colloquially as a 'cut-off' date, after which new legislation from the previous colonial power is inapplicable. This cut-off date varies from one Pacific island country to another and there may be a different date applicable to statutes and general principles of common law and equity.[17] A consequence of this limitation on applicable statutes is that much of the written law left in place at independence has been replaced by

---

12   Section 3.

13   Section 12.

14   18 December 1979. Article 16 of CEDAW declares: 'States Parties shall take all appropriate measures to eliminate discrimination against women in all matters relating to marriage and family relations …'

15   For example, most of the countries of the region are signatories to the CEDAW. The latest Pacific region countries to accede were Kiribati on 17 March 2004 and Federated States of Micronesia on 1 September 2004. Only Tonga, Nauru and Marshall Islands are not parties to this Convention. Many are also signatories to the CRC: Fiji, Papua New Guinea, Samoa and Vanuatu, or have acceded to the Convention: Cook Islands, Kiribati, Federated States of Micronesia, Nauru, Niue, Solomon Islands, Tonga and Tuvalu.

16   For example, in the case of land rights or the acquisition of citizenship.

17   For a detailed review of the range of 'cut-off' dates and the variations which apply see J Corrin Care 'Colonial legacies? A study of received and adopted legislation applying in the University of the South Pacific region' (1997) 21 *The Journal of Pacific Studies* 33.

more modern laws in the country of origin but this process of modernisation has not occurred in Pacific island countries.

In some countries developments have taken place post independence which have reduced the applicability of introduced colonial law. For example, in Samoa, although on independence in 1962 imperial laws continued in force,[18] these were abolished in 1972 by the Reprint of Statutes Act 1972,[19] as were those New Zealand Acts of Parliament which had continued in force after independence.[20] Similarly, in Kiribati, the Western Pacific (Courts) Order 1961,[21] which was applied by the British to a number of Pacific countries, has been repealed. However, it still applies in Tuvalu and Vanuatu.[22]

The one country which does not have a cut-off date is Tonga, where in principle the most contemporary statutes of English law might apply,[23] provided they are 'statutes of general application in force in England'.[24] This latter phrase has no clear meaning but seems to encompass Acts of Parliament which are not based upon politics or circumstances peculiar to England.[25] Logically one might have thought this excluded most Acts of Parliament which invariably reflect a certain political agenda and, in a democratic system, should meet the specific needs of the electorate or a targeted group thereof. Nevertheless courts of the region seem to have accepted that there are such Acts which apply in the region although their categorisation as 'general' or not may vary from one jurisdiction to another.[26] What is required is that the legislation is of the kind that applies to mankind in general.[27] In the case of family law, however, it might be argued that the later the cut-off date the less likely it is that legislation emanating from outside the region will be compatible with the local context because of the rapid changes which have taken place in society in countries such as the

---

[18]   Article 114 of the Constitution.

[19]   The only exception was the Wills Act 1837, which has now been replaced by the Samoan Wills Act 1975.

[20]   The only New Zealand Acts which appear to have remained in force after 1977 were the Bankruptcy Act 1908; Companies Act 1955, Property Law Act 1952, Samoa Act 1921 and the Estates and Gift Duties Act 1955 (now replaced by a National Act of 1977); see Corrin Care, note 17.

[21]   This included, *inter alia*, a provision that 'the civil and criminal jurisdiction of the High Court (of the Western Pacific) shall, so far as circumstances admit, be exercised upon the principles of and in conformity with: (a) the statutes of general application in force in England on the 1st day of January 1961, and (b) the substance of the English common law and doctrines of equity'.

[22]   Repealed by s 14 of the Laws of Kiribati Act 1979.

[23]   Civil Law Act 1966, s 3.

[24]   Civil Law Act 1966, s 4(b).

[25]   K Roberts-Wray *Commonwealth and Colonial Law* (Stevens & Sons, London, 1966) p 556.

[26]   For example, in *Freddy Harrisen v John Patrick Holloway* (1980–88) 1 Van LR 147 it was held that the differences in the structure and organisation of the police force found in the UK compared to that in Vanuatu meant the Police Act 1964 (UK) could not be regarded as one of general application.

[27]   For example, the Fatal Accidents Act (UK) has been held to apply in Vanuatu – *Boe and Taga v Thomas* (1980–1994) Van LR 293 – and in Fiji it has been held that the Forfeiture Act 1870 (UK) was a statute of general application – *Mohammed Isaac v Abdul Kadir* (1962) 9 Fiji LR 152.

UK, Australia and New Zealand, and their impact on the legal construction of 'the family'.

In fact since independence, unless a colonial statute has been adopted by the national Parliament[28] or the courts have recognised its application, it may be unclear whether a law remains one of general application.[29] Even if the courts accept an introduced law they may choose to interpret or apply it in a way which they feel best suits the local context.[30]

Understandably for most newly independent countries, private law matters were not high on the political agenda – and indeed have remained a fairly low priority – so that it is not unusual to find dated statutes introduced from England, New Zealand or Australia still in force. For example, the Matrimonial Causes Act 1950 (UK) still applies in Solomon Islands and Kiribati, while in Cook Islands the Matrimonial Proceedings Act 1963 of New Zealand applies.[31]

In some countries of the region, former colonial and distinct laws still apply to foreigners or non-indigenous people. For example, in Kiribati divorce of non-Kiribati is regulated by the Matrimonial Causes Act 1950 (UK) and a similar situation applies to non-Solomon Islanders in the Solomon Islands.[32]

Even in those countries where domestic legislation has been passed post independence this may be modelled on earlier English law statutes.[33] For example, the Matrimonial Causes Act 1986 of Vanuatu has been held to be similar to the UK 1950 or 1965 Act,[34] while even in Fiji, where there is a new Family Law Act 2003, this is modelled on the Australian law.

One consequence of this is that frequently such legislation is seen as reflecting alien values and of being out of touch with customary forms of family regulation. This is an ongoing problem with the drafting of new laws in the region due to the tendency to bring in external, aid-funded consultants to undertake the task, many of whom have little acquaintance with the culture or social organisation of the society to which those laws will apply. Where countries can afford to engage in extended public consultation – as

---

[28]   As happened in the Cook Islands under the Cook Islands Act 1915.

[29]   For more detailed discussion of the question of whether a law is one of general application or not see Corrin Care, note 17.

[30]   For example, the Married Women's Property Act 1882 (UK) has been accepted as applicable in the Solomon Islands and applied in a liberal fashion to arrive at an equitable division of property on divorce – see below. See comment by K Brown and J Corrin Care 'Putting Asunder: Divorce and Financial Relief in Solomon Islands' (2005) 5 (1) *Oxford University Commonwealth Law Journal* 85 at 104.

[31]   Other examples are the Wills Act 1837 (UK) which applies in Kiribati, Fiji, Cook Islands, Niue, Nauru and Solomon Islands; the Adoption Act 1958 (UK) which applies in Kiribati and Vanuatu; the Matrimonial Homes Act 1967 (UK) which applies in Nauru.

[32]   Although the term 'islander' was used to replace that of 'native' by the Statutes Revision Act 1974 it has been held to cover any person domiciled in the Solomon Islands: *Mahlon v Mahlon* (1984) SILR 86.

[33]   Either directly from England or the English common law as applied in countries such as Australia and New Zealand.

[34]   *Banga v Waiwo* [1996] VUSC 5. Similarly the Marriage Act (Cap 50) in Fiji.

occurred with the Fiji Family Law Act[35] – then new laws may have a greater chance of success but even here key forces behind reform may be strongly driven by external influences and the aspirations manifested in the legislation may be impossible or difficult to deliver.[36]

C   Customary laws and traditions

As indicated by the extracts from selected constitutions above, independence marked a revival in traditional or customary law especially in the private law sphere, where the personal law of individuals might vary considerably from country to country, island to island or even within single islands. Lack of homogeneity in customary law together with lack of legislative activity in this area has meant that for many, family life is primarily determined by customary law and in many cases issues are decided and resolved outside the formal legal structure. In some respects this could be a positive benefit to cohabitees. Custom is not inflexible. It adapts and changes over time and can in some circumstances accommodate cohabitees either by relaxing the requirements for customary marriage,[37] or by accommodating the consequences of cohabitation – such as the birth of children – within the customary structure.[38] Lack of certainty or homogeneity in custom may, however, result in confusion as to the legal status of couples.[39] Indeed that status may change over a period or time or due to certain events.[40]

Custom, however, will not extend to couples, both of whom are not indigenous, and indeed may stop short of extending to couples where one is not indigenous and the other is, although this is not always the case.[41] Even

---

35   See, for example, the summary of the Family Law Bill by Fiji Law Reform Commissioner P Jalal at www.vanuatu.usp.ac.fj.

36   The Fiji Family Law Act 2003 is one such example. It has not yet come into force because the sheer logistics of setting up dedicated family courts with sufficient trained personnel is delaying its implementation. See comments by S Rabuka 'Innovative features and challenges of the Family Law Act' *Legal Lali* December 2004.

37   So, for example, even where bride price is not paid, acceptance by the immediate family and the community of the relationship may, over time, bring it to be recognised as a customary marriage – as in two Solomon Island cases: *Rebitai v Chow* [2002] SBHC 85 (24 years' cohabitation), and *Koru v Official Administrator of Unrepresented Estates* (unreported) 6 November 1985, Civil Case number 83 (10 years' cohabitation). Alternatively a reduced payment of bride price may be accepted as evidence of a customary marriage, as in *Hepworth v Sikela* [1994] SBHC 2, where only $60 of the $500 requested was actually paid.

38   For example, by naming ceremonies; by the payment and acceptance of customary payments for the child, and/or the mother's fertility; by customary adoption of the child into the family; or by general recognition and the assimilation of the cohabiting couple into the family either formally or informally.

39   For example, in Papua New Guinea, Solomon Islands and Vanuatu, if a person has been married in custom then they can only be divorced in custom. However, the moment at which a custom divorce is finalised is obscure and that person may enter into a subsequent relationship which turns out to be bigamous, or polygamous – where that is allowed – or merely one of cohabitation. See Jessop, note 3, and Brown and Corrin Care, note 30.

40   For example, betrothal may or may not confer marital status, similarly the birth of a child, or the building of a house.

41   See the Samoan case of the *Samoan Public Trustee v Annie Collins and Others* [1960–69] WSLR 52 – where an American had entered into what was recognised as a customary (polygamous)

the cohabitation of indigenous couples may not be accepted as marriage if the requisite formalities have not been observed.[42] These couples may find themselves outside the law on two counts. They do not fall within custom and the written law makes no provision for them. A further factor is that while customary law may be resorted to on a daily basis in the courts at village or local level, this is much less likely to happen in the more formal court structure of magistrates' and higher courts, where custom may have to be proved as a matter of fact, rather than accepted as a matter of law. Thus the forum for hearing disputes may determine what laws are taken into account. Non-indigenous persons, or those who have become urbanised, are more likely to access the formal court structure.

D   General equitable principles

Where this is the case the only law which may be available to cohabitees is that deriving from the principles of common law and equity which have been introduced into the countries of the region prior to independence and since independence have been built on by national courts.[43] Most of the constitutions of the region include reference to a residual source of law described variously as 'the general principles of English common law'. For example, the Constitution of Solomon Islands 1978, states:

> '(T)he principles and rules of the common law and equity shall have effect as part of the law of the Solomon Islands ...'[44]

while that of Fiji continues to enforce the provisions of the Supreme Court Ordinance 1875 which refers to 'the common law, the rules of equity and the statutes of general application which were in force in England ... on the second day of January 1875'.[45] In Cook Islands the Cook Islands Act 1915 (NZ) states:

> '(T)he law of England as existing on the fourteenth day of January in the year eighteen hundred and forty ... shall be in force in the Cook Islands ...'[46]

which is interpreted to include the principles of common law and equity as established through English case-law, as well as statute law. However 'English' need not be limited to the law of England but has been taken to

---

marriage with a Samoan; the Solomon Island case of *Rebitai v Chow* [2001] SBHC 85 where a man of Chinese nationality had entered into a customary marriage with a Solomon Islander; and the Solomon Island case of *Hepworth v Sikela* [1994] SBHC 2 where it was held that there was nothing in principle to prevent an indigenous Solomon Islander and a non-indigenous Solomon Islander entering into a customary marriage.

42   As was held in *Application of Thesia Maip* [1991] PNGLR 80.

43   For a comprehensive overview see D Paterson 'The application of the common law and equity in countries of the South Pacific' (1997) 21 *Journal of Pacific Studies* 1.

44   Paragraph 2 of Sch 3.

45   The Constitution of the Republic of Fiji Islands 1897. It is not in fact clear if the 1875 date only refers to legislation or the common law and rules of equity as well. Fiji courts also refer from time to time to the case-law of Australia and New Zealand.

46   Section 615.

include general principles of common law and equity found in those systems which derive from the English common law.[47]

Recourse to general principles of equity may be of assistance not only to disputes between cohabitees – especially as regards property – but also where there is no legislative provision for married couples. For example, in the case of *Elisara v Elisara*,[48] Chief Justice Sapolu stated:

'(T)here is no legislative or judicial guidance so far as to how to deal with matrimonial property disputes between married couples. No legal principles have been laid down on how to deal with such a situation ... the case law on property disputes between married and unmarried couples has come to the point where the constructive trust device is now broadly applied to achieve a just result ...'

Indeed, the constructive trust has been used throughout the region to determine property interests on the dissolution of marriage,[49] or to assist the courts in making a determination under matrimonial causes legislation.[50] In fact, in a number of cases concerning the division of property between married couples the courts have had to be proactive owing to the lack of direction provided by legislation.[51] It might therefore be hoped that the courts would be similarly inventive in deciding the property rights of cohabitees. However, there is indication in the case of *Maharaj v Chand* of reluctance to engage in judicial law making in the case of property claims by cohabitees.[52]

Further, or alternatively, there may be reference to a broader jurisprudential touchstone such as 'substantial justice'. For example, in Vanuatu the Constitution, art 47(1), states:

'(T)he administration of justice is vested in the judiciary, who are subject only to the constitution and the law. The function of the judiciary is to resolve proceedings according to the law. If there is no rule of law applicable to a matter before it a Court shall determine the matter according to substantial justice and whenever possible in conformity with custom.'

---

[47] This was expressed to be the case by the Chief Justice of Samoa in the case of *Opeloge Olo v Police* (unreported) m5092/80 and Paterson (note 43: 6–7) suggests that the same approach may be used in Tuvalu and Vanuatu where the term 'English' is used as an adjective. See also the case of *Official Administrator for Deceased Estates v Allardyce Lumber Company Ltd* [1980/81] SILR 66.

[48] [1994] WSCC 14. The case concerned a married couple but there was a lacuna in the law.

[49] See *Philip v Tuponia* (1977) Fiji Civil Action 92/1997 (unreported); *Me Folau v Tevita Folau* (1923–1962) 2 TLR 208.

[50] See, for example, the Fiji case of *Pratima Devi v Rajeshwar Singh* (1985)31 FLR 109, where the court held that it has clear powers under the constructive trust principle and under the powers vested in it by s 86 of the Matrimonial Causes Act to make a division of matrimonial property.

[51] See, for example, in Vanuatu the case of *Joli v Joli* [2003] VUCA 27 – comment by S Farran 'The Joli Way to Resolving Legal Problems: A New Vanuatu Approach?' (2003) 7(2) *JSPL* at http://law.vanuatu.usp.ac.fj/jspl; in Solomon Islands *Kuper v Kuper* (unreported) High Court of the Solomon Islands, 18 November 1988 – comment by Corrin Care and Brown, note 30 at 104.

[52] [1986] AC 898. Here the Privy Council drew the line at creating property rights for cohabitees, preferring instead to find an occupational licence.

This provision has been relied on to determine the outcome of a dispute over the custody of children to a de facto relationship where there was no applicable law.[53] Indeed such considerations may – implicitly – lie behind those decisions where the courts have been prepared to hold that long-standing cohabitation confers rights similar to those of marriage. However, the failure to articulate the rationale for such decisions sets no reliable precedents for cohabitees.

III CHILDREN

Unlike the lack of law relating to adult cohabitees there is much greater legal provision for the children of such unions, especially as regards rights to economic support – usually from their fathers once affiliation or paternity is established.

For example, in Vanuatu illegitimate children are entitled to maintenance under the Maintenance and Affiliation Act, Cap 52, and also under customary law, provided paternity is established.[54] This legislative approach is common throughout the Pacific region,[55] but the amount to which an illegitimate child is entitled may be differently assessed from the way in which maintenance for a legitimate child is assessed,[56] or the consequences for failure to maintain may be distinguishable.[57]

In Vanuatu, constitutionally, parents of children – whether those children are legitimate or illegitimate – have the duty 'to support, assist and educate all (his) children'[58] and although this is a non-justiciable duty and therefore perhaps weak, given the fact that Vanuatu is also a signatory to the CRC and has given this effect in its domestic legislation,[59] there is scope and foundation for development through case-law to support and indeed strengthen the claims of illegitimate children. In Fiji, positive measures to treat all children, regardless of status, on an equal footing is evident in the Family Law Act 2003 which has extensive provisions relating to the care

---

[53]   *Pandosy v Thuha* [1997] VUSC 49.

[54]   See the Custom Policy of the Malvatumauri (Council of Chiefs), art 14.

[55]   See Maintenance and Affiliation Act (Cap 52) Part 111 Fiji read with Division 8, ss 100–159 of the Family Law Act 2003; Maintenance of Illegitimate Children Act (Cap 30) Tonga; Maintenance (Miscellaneous Provisions) Ordinance (Cap 4) Tuvalu read with Custody of Children Ordinance (Cap 20) Tuvalu.

[56]   For example, in Vanuatu an order of maintenance against an unmarried father where paternity is established is payable in money or its equivalent not exceeding Vt1,000 (about £5) weekly – Maintenance of Children Act (Cap 46) – whereas in the case of a failure to maintain legitimate children there is no ceiling indicated in the Maintenance of Family Act (Cap 42), so that the courts may assess what would be reasonable in the circumstances – see *Public Prosecutor v Benson* [2002] VUSC 44.

[57]   In Vanuatu under the Maintenance of Family Act (Cap 42) it is an offence for a man to fail to maintain the woman to whom he is legally married or his legitimate children under the age of 18 years (s 1), but for a woman it is an offence to desert her children for any period exceeding a month, whether they are legitimate or illegitimate.

[58]   Article 7(h).

[59]   Act No 26 of 1992. Article 2 of the CRC states that there should be no discrimination against children on the grounds of status at birth.

and welfare of children and makes no distinction between married and unmarried parents regarding the obligations of parental responsibility and support.[60]

Moreover it is not unusual to find that custom will be extended to recognise children and bring them within the family even though the union of their parents remains outside the law. For example, in Tuvalu where paternity of an illegitimate male child is acknowledged, that child may be claimed by the father and taken to reside in the father's village in order to establish – through residence – land claims.[61]

Alternatively, once there are children of the union, compensation payments to the mother's parents or naming ceremonies may integrate the child within the extended family.[62] It is also not unusual to find cases of infant and adult adoption, whereby illegitimate children may be integrated into the family by formal or custom adoption.

IV CUSTODY OF CHILDREN

Some countries have specific legislation dealing with the custody of children,[63] others deal with such matters alongside maintenance orders or as part of divorce orders where the parents are married.[64] The trend throughout the region in recent years has been to focus on the 'best interests' or 'welfare' of the child in custody of children disputes due to the influence of introduced law,[65] and international law, notably the CRC.[66]

The welfare principle may apply whether the child's parents are married or not. For example, in the case of *Pandosy v Thuha*,[67] the parents were unmarried. The father was claiming custody of the two children of the relationship. At first the court held it had no jurisdiction to determine the matter because it fell outside the law. However, because the courts are required under the Constitution to determine matters for which there is no rule of law 'according to substantial justice' the court would hear the matter. In doing so the court held that it would be wrong to suggest that the natural

---

[60] See, for example, the provisions of Division 2 of the Act.

[61] This is under the Native Lands Ordinance, s 20(1) and (2). See *Tepulolo v Pou* [2005] TVHC 1.

[62] The writer is aware of situations among students where there has been cohabitation and subsequent pregnancy, where family disapproval has been ameliorated by compensation payments to the girls' parents. There are also cases where the child of such unions is maintained by the parents of one or other of them – often in a different country – so that the students can complete their studies.

[63] See, for example, Kiribati – Custody of Children Ordinance, and Tuvalu – Custody of Children Act (Cap 20).

[64] For example, Samoa – Divorce and Matrimonial Causes Ordinance 1961, No 20, Part 111 – and Tonga – Divorce Act (Cap 19), s 15.

[65] For example, the Custody of Infants Act 1873 (UK) and the Guardianship of Infants Act 1886 and 1925 (UK) – the latter act being widely applied in the region.

[66] An example of the CRC being resorted to can be found in the Vanuatu case of *Molu v Molu* [1998] VUSC 15, where the court used the provisions of Art 3(1) of the CRC as guidance on what matters should be taken into account in exercising its child custody powers under the Matrimonial Causes Act of Vanuatu.

[67] [1997] VUSC 49.

father had no rights at all, but the paramount consideration was the child's welfare and for this reason custody was awarded to the mother. Conversely, in Fiji it has been held that in the case of children from de facto relationships only the mother has the right to custody unless she has been certified as insane, or has abandoned the child or is considered to be unfit, or has conducted herself in such a way as to indicate that leaving the child with her is not in the child's best interests.[68]

Sometimes the application of the welfare principle will coincide with customary approaches to custody, sometimes it will run contrary to customary approaches.[69] An example can be found in the Solomon Islands case of *K v T and KU, In re Custody Application*.[70] Here it was argued that the welfare principle was an alien concept which should give way to customary law which would have automatically awarded custody of the child to the father.[71] While it was accepted that customary law was part of the law of the Solomon Islands the court held that until such time as Parliament ruled that custody questions were to be governed by customary law the welfare principle would prevail, even if, as in this case, bride price had been paid. Given the relegation of custom to secondary place in determining custody of the child it might be thought that the unmarried parent will be in no different position from the married parent. The obstacle, especially for fathers, is to establish that they are the person best placed to care for the child. In the Papua New Guinea case of *VZ v JK* the court, while rejecting the automatic claim of a mother of a young child unless she was still breast-feeding the baby, held that unless there is a danger to the child's health or welfare, the mother is in the best position to apply for custody. The father could, however, be granted access or visitation rights.[72]

In Fiji under the Family Law Act 2003 there is now a more liberal and egalitarian approach. Parental responsibility for children applies to both parents regardless of whether they are married or not, and it would seem to allow the courts greater freedom to consider the claim of a father to custody either on the grounds of parenting arrangements made under a court approved parenting plan, or by an order of the court made in the child's best interests. It will remain to be seen, however, to what extent courts are prepared to award unmarried fathers in particular custody of their children.[73]

Unfortunately, whether the child is legitimate or not, there are very limited resources for facilitating a process whereby the child's views are taken into account.[74] There are no separate children's courts and although Fiji is in the

---

68   Fiji Family Law Reform De Facto Relationships discussion paper 18 December 1997. Under the Maintenance and Affiliation Act (Cap 52), s 2, it is possible for a person other than the mother or putative father of an illegitimate child to be awarded custody.

69   For comment see K Brown 'Customary rules and the welfare principle: post-independence custody cases in Solomon Islands and Vanuatu' (1997) 21 *Journal of Pacific Studies* 83.

70   [1985/86] SILR 49.

71   A custom which was confirmed in the case of *Re B* [1983] SILR 223.

72   *VZ v JK* [1994] PGNC 17.

73   Married fathers may be in a stronger position due to the continuing patriarchal structure of society.

74   See comment on this in S Farran 'Approaches to Child Custody in the Pacific Region' Occasional Paper No 3, 2003, University of the South Pacific 14–15.

process of establishing family courts these have yet to be finalised. However, there are reported cases in which the views of the child have been acknowledged and taken into account and there is no reason to suppose that this would not happen in the case of unmarried couples contesting custody.[75]

One point that should be noted is that many of the countries of the region are not parties to the Hague Convention 1980, which governs the abduction of children. This was a matter which arose in the case of *Gorce v Miller*,[76] in which former cohabitees were disputing custody of their child who had been removed by the mother from Australia to Tonga. The Supreme Court of Tonga had jurisdiction by virtue of residence of the mother. As Tonga is not a party to the Hague Convention the court had to apply the common law legal principles which would have applied in the UK before 1985 – which was the date the UK ratified the Convention – notably the welfare of the child in dispute. In this case the court did not find that it would be against the child's best interests to be taken back to Australia where the Australian Family Court could complete its assessment of the custody dispute which had originated in that country.

In much of the region inheritance to customary land is patrilinially based and recognition by the father will be essential to secure land rights. This may be done by the payment of 'child price', by adoption of the (illegitimate) child into the family under custom or formal adoption, or by residence. A number of countries have laws in place which safeguard the land rights of illegitimate children. For example, in Tuvalu, the Native Lands Ordinance[77] states:

'If the father being a native accepts the child as being his, such child shall after reaching the age of 2 reside with the father or his relations and shall in accordance with native customary law inherit land and property from his father in the same way as the father's legitimate children.'

This allows a court to order a child to be placed in the custody of the father (or his family) even if this appears to be contrary to the welfare principle.[78]

In Fiji, children of Fijian parents, or where one parent is Fijian, must be entered in the register of native land titles in order to benefit from land held by the Native Lands Trust Board.[79] For this to happen the child – whether illegitimate, adopted or legitimate – must be accepted by a land-owning unit, which may require that the child resides within the area owned by that unit and as he or she gets older observes family obligations. Elsewhere an illegitimate child may acquire rights to land through his or her mother but often women only have temporary use rights of their parents' land on the

---

75   See, for example, *Bulekuli v Saksak* [2000] VUSC 61.

76   [2003] TOSC 50.

77   Cap 22 (1978 Revised Laws).

78   As happened in the case of *Tepulolo v Pou* [2005] TVHC 1.

79   This is the *Vola ni Kawa Bula* which records the names and personal details of all members of the land-owning unit (*bito*). This register is kept at the office of the Native Land Commission. S Takilai 'Women's Rights to Land in Fiji: A Fijian Perspective' unpublished LLM thesis, University of the South Pacific, 2004.

premise that they will marry and move to the land of their husband.[80] The retention and exercise of these may depend on physical presence.

V PROPERTY

While most of the legal systems of the region have little to say about property rights during a relationship, here as elsewhere, cohabitees fall outside the law relating to divorce, so that when their relationship breaks up the law which determines property rights tends to be that which would apply to strangers as the courts lack the power they might have to determine the allocation of property on divorce.[81] There are no provisions such as those which might be found under specific legislation in Australia.[82]

The consequence is that unless there is a clear contractual arrangement relating to property or the rights of both parties are evident from documents of title – as where both are parties to a lease, for example – then the only recourse is either to the application of introduced notions of equity and trusts, or a liberal interpretation of legislation such as the Married Women's Property Act 1882,[83] or its local equivalent.[84]

One of the leading cases in this area is the Privy Council decision in the Fiji case of *Maharaj v Chand*.[85] Here there was cohabitation over a 12-year period together with assertions, for the purpose of obtaining a favourable loan, that the plaintiff was the defendant's wife. An action to evict the plaintiff female cohabitee from the formerly shared home was defeated by the court recognising that the circumstances gave rise to an estoppel, whereby an occupational licence granted by the defendant to the plaintiff became irrevocable for the lifetime of the plaintiff. What the court was not prepared to do was to confer beneficial interests in the property on the female cohabitee.

Nevertheless, the use of the constructive trust is found in a number of jurisdictions although different approaches may be adopted. For example, the Samoan courts appear to adopt the tests of unjust enrichment and reasonable expectation,[86] whereas in Fiji the emphasis has been on common – but unexpressed – intention, usually evidenced by some kind of monetary

80   See, for example, the rationale in the Vanuatu case of *John Noel v Obed Toto* [1995] VUSC 3.

81   Even in the case of divorce some systems lack clear legislation regarding the division of matrimonial property – as opposed to payment of alimony or provision of maintenance and support for children. Vanuatu is a case in point – see S Farran 'What is the Matrimonial Property Regime in Vanuatu?' (2001) 5 *JSPL* Working Paper No 4, and 'The *Joli* Way to Resolving Legal Problems: A New Vanuatu Approach?' (2004) 1 *JSPL* (at www.vanuatu.usp.ac.fj refereed papers).

82   See, for example, s 9 of the De Facto Relationship Act South Australia 1996 which states 'after a de facto relationship ends, either of the de facto partners may apply to a court for the division of property'.

83   This piece of UK legislation has been applied as a statute of general application in much of the region despite the fact that its original context was a far cry from that found in much of the region.

84   Such as the Fiji Married Women's Property Act (Cap 37).

85   [1986] FJ-UKPC 1.

86   See *Elisara v Elisara* [1994] WSSC 14.

contribution either directly or indirectly.[87] Similarly in the Cook Islands the courts seem to have favoured the common intention test.[88] The use of the constructive trust to arrive at a fair distribution of property when de facto relationships breaks down relies on the courts' adopting a proactive equitable approach. In particular the courts need to move away from a focus on the 'solid tug of money' (that is financial contribution directly or indirectly to the acquisition of property) given the fact that many women, whether married or not, do not have access to financial resources or that if they do these are frequently absorbed by daily costs of living. It is much more likely in cases of marriage and de facto relationships that women, in particular, are in a position of dependency and that their contribution lies in homemaking, domestic services and childcare.[89]

Also, as has been experienced elsewhere, the stronger the patriarchal nature of society the less likely it is that women, especially married or cohabiting women, will have their name on documents of title – even supposing there are such documents and in the case of customary land tenure there frequently are not. While there are examples of the courts applying equitable principles to uphold claims of equitable estoppel or to find a constructive trust, these cases are rare. There is moreover a reluctance among some judges to appear too liberal in conferring rights on those who shun marriage.[90]

As regards the Married Women's Property Act 1882, it might be thought that this piece of introduced legislation could have no application to unmarried couples, and strictly speaking that is so. The Act enables a court to decide who is the original owner of property in a marriage. The Act marked a radical change in English law insofar as it allowed married women to retain their own separate property on marriage thereby doing away with the notion that on marriage not only did husband and wife become one but that their property merged. In essence therefore a single woman has the same property rights as a married woman during the course of the marriage. However, the courts of the region had demonstrated a remarkable ability to use this legislation not only to determine existing property interests but also to allocate property where there is no other way of doing so. For example, in the Solomon Island case of *Kuper v Kuper* where the Islander's Divorce Act gave no guidance on how the distribution of property was to be determined, the Chief Justice interpreted the 1882 Act as conferring the power on the court to achieve an equitable solution.[91] Although cases to date have been concerned with married women, the enlarged application of this legislation could be applied to de facto couples, particularly where to all intents and purposes the couple are regarded as 'married' in the eyes of the community.

---

[87] See *Nisha v Munif* [1999] 45 FLR 246.

[88] *Sandilands v Carlaw* (unreported) High Court of the Cook Islands, 4 June 1982.

[89] This problem applies in marriage as well. See *Tavake v Tavake* (unreported) High Court of Solomon Islands, 19 August 1998.

[90] For example, the Fiji courts have indicated that they will not apply constructive trust principles to de facto relationships: Fiji Law Reform Commission Discussion Paper 4, 1997.

[91] (Unreported) High Court of Solomon Islands, 18 November 1988. See also *Pusau v Pusau* [2001] SBHC 86.

The second property aspect which is of concern to married and unmarried couples is the question of support, both during the relationship and on its termination. Generally unmarried cohabitees have no financial claims on each other unless they have entered into some form of contract.[92] This issue arose in a Papua New Guinea case of *Bulage v Casey Ben*,[93] in which a de facto husband sought to be reimbursed by his de facto wife for money expended on her. The court found that without some kind of contract there was no cause of action. In fact it is questionable even if there were some form of agreement or contract entered into between the cohabitees that it would be enforceable. Certainly in English law this has proved difficult either because of the lack of evident intention to be contractually bound,[94] or because such contracts are considered to be contrary to sound public morals.[95] Given the strong Christian ethos which prevails in the region concern about undermining the institution of marriage might lead judges to refuse to recognise cohabitation contracts.

However, there are some provisions found in the region which could encompass a de facto partner. In Tuvalu the Native Lands Act (Cap 22) provides that in cases where a man denies paternity but the court nevertheless is satisfied that he is the father of the child, and if he has no land which can be utilised to provide for the child, then the court can order him to pay money or its equivalent in foodstuffs to the mother or whoever is raising the child, until the child reaches the age of 21 or the father acquires land which can be transferred to the child.[96] In Kiribati an order of maintenance can be made under the Magistrates Court Act (Cap 52) and the Maintenance (Miscellaneous Provisions) Ordinance (Cap 53) the long title of which is '(A)n Ordinance to provide for the maintenance of neglected persons ...'. Under s 3 of this Ordinance the court has liberal powers to make orders:

> '... on application by or on behalf of any person ... that another person or other persons shall be liable to maintain that person where it is satisfied that there is a legal or customary obligation to do so.'

In deciding whether or not to exercise its powers the court can take into account the age of the person for whom the application is made and all the surrounding personal circumstances, and can call for any evidence or information which it considers necessary in the interests of substantial justice. Potentially this would allow a neglected de facto partner to sue for maintenance or to apply for maintenance for any children. It also opens up the possibility of adult children applying on behalf of a parent.

---

[92]   For example, in the Solomon Islands, where the Affiliation, Separation and Maintenance Act 1992 makes no provision for unmarried persons living together.

[93]   [1990] PNGLR 473.

[94]   See *Balfour v Balfour* [1919] 2 KB 571, CA.

[95]   *Fender v St John Mildmay* [1938] AC 1. See comments by J L Dwyer 'Immoral Contracts' (1977) 93 *LQR* 386; S Poulter 'Cohabitation contracts and public policy' (1974) 124 *NLJ* 1034; E Kingdom 'Cohabitation contracts and equality' (1990) 8 *International Journal of the Sociology of Law* 287.

[96]   Section 20(2)(iii).

VI DOMESTIC VIOLENCE

Domestic violence is not limited to married couples. Indeed cohabiting couples, especially female partners, may be more vulnerable to domestic violence and less able to call on the support of the family because of the very nature of their informal union. While victims of domestic violence, whether married or not, will be able to resort to the criminal law, police in the region – as elsewhere – are notoriously reluctant to get involved in domestic matters. While domestic violence is increasingly on the legal and political agenda, thanks mainly to non-governmental organisations bringing the matter to the public's attention,[97] it is still the case that domestic violence – in which women are the main victims – is rarely prosecuted and if it is, those in a de facto relationship may be in a worse position than spouses.[98]

Some countries of the region now have legislation which applies regardless of marital status. In the Cook Islands, the Cook Islands Amendment Act 1994 now includes provision for obtaining non-molestation orders in respect of de facto couples either to protect the applicant man or woman or any children in his or her custody.[99] Although the duration of the relationship may be a consideration taken into account by the court this is not a determining factor.

In Fiji, in 2003, the Cabinet approved the inclusion of consideration of laws relating to domestic violence in the work of the Fiji Law Reform Commission. At present domestic violence orders are limited in scope to married couples and children – whether the children are living in marital or non-marital households. However, the Law Reform Commission began to review the law in July 2004 under broad terms of reference which hopefully will lead to more extensive provision in the not too distant future. In the meantime under s 123 of the Family Law Act 2003, when it comes into force, a family violence order can apply to de facto parents through the broader interpretation of family given in s 42 of the same Act.

Elsewhere lack of confidence in the legislative process or the political will to bring about change has led to alternative approaches. For instance, in Vanuatu the Family Protection Bill has been repeatedly knocked back since being first mooted in 1999. Consequently, the problem of domestic violence has been addressed through reform of civil procedure rules. Here, new Civil Procedure Rules[100] create a broadly applicable regime of *ex parte* interim injunctions to protect victims of domestic violence whether married or not. In some countries however it remains the case that only the spouses are covered by domestic violence protection measures.[101]

---

[97] See, for example, the work of Mapusaga o Aiga in Samoa, the Vanuatu Women's Centre, and the Fiji Women's Crisis Centre.

[98] For example the *Fiji Times*, 16 September 1999, reported the case of *State v Croker* (unreported) in which the Fiji High Court sentenced a man who beat his de facto wife to death to only 18 months' imprisonment.

[99] Section 523J.

[100] No 49 of 2002.

[101] For example, Solomon Islands: The Affiliation Separation and Maintenance Act 1992.

VII DEATH AND INHERITANCE

In the Pacific region the devolution of a deceased's estate may be governed by a mixture of laws including introduced laws relating to testate and intestate succession and customary law.[102] The matter is complicated by the fact that in much of the region land held under customary land tenure – that is the majority of all land – cannot be alienated and so that even if there is a testamentary disposition of such land this may be void as being contrary to restrictions on alienation and the operation in custom that land devolves according to traditional patterns – for example, matrilineally or patrilineally, often, but not always by primogeniture. However, as economies develop and people acquire more material wealth and perhaps alternative forms of land tenure, such as leases and sub-leases, it is likely that the potential for conflicting claims to succeed to a deceased's estate will arise. It is also likely to be the case that the mobility of people may see an increase in those having both spouses and cohabiting partners,[103] or conflicting claims between blood relatives and a de facto partner.

In some countries of the region there is an obligation for a deceased person to make proper provision for members of their family,[104] but whether this includes a cohabitee will often depend on the discretion of the court. For example, in the Nauru case of *Harris v Hedmon* a deceased had made provision in his will for his eight illegitimate children and their mother.[105] The will made no reference to his two legitimate children but the court held that unless the latter were expressly excluded the will should be interpreted as including the legitimate children as equal beneficiaries of the deceased's estate. The justification for the court's approach – despite the clear wording of the will – was that in Nauru it is extremely unusual for a person to disinherit his legitimate children and usually these will inherit on intestacy and illegitimate children will not. In the Solomon Island case of *Koro v Official Administrator*,[106] the court held that where there had been cohabitation in a de facto relationship for a number of years the child of the de facto wife had the right to inherit from the deceased father on the grounds that the long-term relationship involved the same degree of commitment as marriage and should therefore be treated no differently. It may be that the courts will look more favourably on the rights of the children than on the surviving partner, or arrive at a compromise. For example, in the Vanuatu case of *In Re the Estate of Wilson Hansal*,[107] the de facto wife of the

---

102   In most of the region the Wills Act 1837 (UK) and the Wills Act 1963 (UK) or legislation modelled on this, applies to testate succession, although in fact the use of wills is rare. See R Hughes *Succession Law in the South Pacific* (IJALS, Fiji, 1999).

103   This is not uncommon when there is movement from rural to urban areas within a country or where a person relocates for work or further education. Often there will be a spouse left at home and new relations commenced in the town or new place of work.

104   See, for example, the case of *In Re Hugh Maclean* [1976] PNGLR 360. This can extend to restrictions on inter vivos dispositions: see s 4 of the Gilbert and Ellice Islands Lands Code which applies in Kiribati, and the same section in the Tuvalu Land Code.

105   [1982] NRSC 1, Land Appeal No 06 of 1981, Supreme Court of Nauru.

106   (1985) SILR 132.

107   [2001] VUSC 14.

deceased was granted letters of administration of the deceased to hold the deceased's property on trust for the four (illegitimate) children. Elsewhere, however, it may be essential to establish that the children are legitimate in order to inherit.[108]

Where a person dies testate, provision may be made for both a de facto partner and illegitimate children in the will. Where no provision is made the right of a surviving de facto partner or illegitimate child to challenge the will is very limited, partly because there has been very little legislative action on family provision schemes.[109] In the Solomon Islands where there is a will or partial intestacy, a Magistrates' Court has jurisdiction to make an order for the proper maintenance and support of the deceased's spouse and children.[110] Clearly this excludes a surviving de facto partner but could extend to illegitimate children. In Fiji, the Inheritance (Family Provision) Act (Cap 61) enables the Supreme Court to make an order for family provision to a limited class of applicants.[111] These include 'a daughter who has not been married' which could include a daughter who has lived in a de facto relationship; 'an infant son', which could include an illegitimate son but would exclude an adult son – whether married or not, unless that son was 'incapable of maintaining himself' due to some mental or physical disability.[112] It also includes 'a parent who is on account of old age or by reason of some mental or physical disability incapable of maintaining himself or herself'. Hence the will of deceased offspring of de facto couples could be challenged if children pre-decease parents. In Samoa, the Administration Act 1975 includes among possible applicants for family provision a parent, child or grandchild of the deceased, so that again illegitimate children and the parents of such child may potentially be covered.[113] The person who will not usually be included, however, is the surviving de facto partner because of the emphasis on spouse or widow/widower rather than dependant. Such a state of affairs does little to provide for the bereaved de facto partner who may have cohabited with the deceased for a number of years either intentionally choosing a de facto relationship or unknowingly in the mistaken belief that there was a marriage.

Apart from rights of inheritance, surviving cohabiting partners and their children are generally excluded from any benefits which may be provided by compensation for wrongful death, unless insurance policies have been assigned in their favour. For example, where a cohabiting partner dies as a result of an accident, the surviving cohabitee is unlikely to find him or herself covered by the largely introduced Fatal Accident legislation of the

---

[108]   See the Samoan case of *Public Trustee v Annie Collins and Others* [1961] WSLR 52, where the successful claim to inheritance hinged on the question of the validity of a customary marriage and thus the legitimacy of the children.

[109]   See, for example, the Family Provision Act 1982 (NSW) and the Inheritance (Provision for Family and Dependants) Act 1975 (UK).

[110]   Wills, Probate and Administration Act 1987, Part VII.

[111]   Hughes suggests that this Act extends to testate and partially testate succession. Note 102, p 201.

[112]   Similarly a daughter suffering from a physical or mental incapacity who is unable to maintain herself due to this – whether married or not, may apply: s 3(1).

[113]   Part IV.

region,[114] nor are they likely to be eligible for life insurance payments under provident fund legislation, although one area where cohabitees may be inadvertently provided for is under Workmen's Compensations Acts, if there is provision for 'dependants' without indication of specific status.[115]

One of the difficulties that can arise where there is death is that the deceased may leave both a lawful spouse and legitimate children and a de facto partner and illegitimate children. The extent to which the latter will be provided for either by law or by custom will depend on the moral approval of such relationships and the social ranking of claims. In some respects the Pacific region may be more forgiving than western countries insofar as there is greater focus on the extended family, rather than the nuclear family.[116] While the law falls short, custom may provide, so that, for example, if a surviving de facto partner is left unprovided for and has been accepted over a number of years as part of the extended family then the family may continue to provide support. Alternatively if the de facto partner has not been approved of or the relationship has been frowned on by the family the de facto partner may be ostracized or excluded.[117]

VIII CONCLUSION

While most countries which have formerly had colonial links with the islands of the Pacific have increasingly extended legal provisions to cohabitees – including same-sex couples – this has not been the case in the majority of Pacific island countries. This is partly due to the strong Christian principles which were introduced under colonial influence and the legacy of laws left in place at independence which reflect a time and a moral code long abandoned in most of the countries from which they originated.

There are of course many forms of de facto relationships. Some may be the result of a rejection of marriage or as a trial prior to marriage. Some may be short lived and others endure for many years. Some may be entered intentionally others mistakenly – especially where there is confusion about the validity or not of customary marriages and divorces. At different points in the relationship there are issues which arise which raise legal questions: the birth of children; the acquisition of property; domestic violence; the breakdown of the relationship and the fragmentation of the family unit, or death. At any point there may be dependency or domination. But reservations about the legal recognition of de facto relationships are not just

---

[114] See, for example, Fatal Accidents Acts 1846–1959 introduced into the Solomon Islands.

[115] For example, under the Workmen's Compensation Act (Cap 78) Solomon Islands a cohabitee may fall within the definition of dependant. Similarly in Papua New Guinea under the Workers' Compensation Act (Ch 179).

[116] Jessop points to the interesting conundrum facing the Papua New Guinea Law Reform Commission. In 1990 it made the recommendation that polygamy should not be encouraged but restricted and prohibited. However if de facto relationships are to be recognised there could be inconstancy as a man may have both a lawful wife and a de facto partner. Note 3, at 471.

[117] In Fiji, for example, Indo-Fijian women may be particularly harshly treated both by their own families and by society.

the concern of the middle-aged and the old. Young people too have doubts and fear that radical legal reform would undermine the institution of marriage and its central importance to Pacific societies.[118] Men are concerned that it would lead to multiple claims for maintenance and that casual liaisons would have unanticipated consequences. At the same time, however, there is an awareness that the current legal position can be unfair to the children of the relationship and to dependent partners – usually women – who may have committed themselves to relationships without marriage for a number of years.[119] It is also generally acknowledged that an increasing number of Pacific islanders themselves – especially young people – are living together outside marriage, or in 'quasi-marital' situations – sometimes bigamously.[120] The purchase of second homes, holiday apartments and timeshares in Pacific islands by those coming from Australia and New Zealand in particular – although not solely – has also seen an increase in non-Pacific islanders taking up residence – sometimes in de facto relationships, while there is also the large number of Pacific islanders currently living abroad or moving around the region who may return to their islands at some point.[121]

The lack of legal provisions for unmarried cohabitees raises a number of questions for Pacific island states. The first is: to what extent these island countries might be expected to 'keep in line' with legal developments occurring elsewhere, especially among their nearest neighbours? Clearly there is scope to develop the law so as to extend its application to cohabitees through reference to fundamental rights provisions, international conventions and the general principles of law and equity referred to in national constitutions. However, the moral and social environment of Pacific islanders cannot be discounted. It should also be pointed out that there are still major lacunae and inequalities in the law relating to married couples, women and children in general, and it might be considered appropriate to address these first.[122]

If the needs of de facto couples are to be addressed, there is the possibility of adopting models from countries such as Australia, New Zealand and the UK, either in a piecemeal fashion – for example, by amending the laws relating to

---

[118] I am grateful to the 80 or so members of the Family Law Class of 2004 at the University of the South Pacific who contributed their views on these matters.

[119] One of the views that students expressed was that there should be recognition of enduring and committed relationships and indeed some thought that in custom these relationships were often accepted and assimilated into society.

[120] Population statistics for countries of the region do not reflect the numbers of non-married cohabiting couples, and even if they did they might not be accurate due to the various perceptions that individuals may have of their own status.

[121] Students at the University of the South Pacific are an example. With three residential campuses for the 12 member countries which have students at the university it is highly likely that at some point in his or her studies a young Pacific islander is going to be living with and socialising with people from other islands away from home.

[122] For example, in Samoa there is no legislation which addresses the question of occupational rights of the matrimonial home – *L v L* [1994] WSCA 3; in Tonga women cannot inherit land – Land Act (Cap 132); and in Vanuatu there is no domestic legislation to deal with the allocation of property on divorce – *Joli v Joli* [2003] VUCA 27.

succession – or by modifying de facto legislation so as to indicate not only what rights de facto couples may have but also to indicate which ones they do not have.

The second point is the question of the capacity of Pacific island countries to develop a strong regional jurisprudence especially an equitable jurisprudence. With little political will or parliamentary time to encourage widespread legislation in the area of domestic relations, there is, it is suggested, a real opportunity for the courts actively to develop a strong Pacific equitable jurisdiction. In a number of countries there is provision for recourse to broad principles of 'substantial justice' – or a similar provision – where there is a gap in the existing legal provision. Potentially this could enable courts to react in a creative way to new situations such as the claims of cohabitees. However, although the courts of the region have never known anything except a fusion between common law and equity – to which may be added customary law except where that is reserved for separate courts – there has been a noted reluctance to use equity in a vigorous way to achieve just and fair outcomes when the law falls short. There is also the problem that frequently judges are very poor at articulating their reasoning in dealing with difficult cases with the consequence that the law appears to develop on an ad hoc and unclear basis, which is of little help to those who might be called on to advise de facto couples.

Alternatively where custom is a recognised source of law it might be adapted to meet new cohabitation situations. Indeed this may happen informally.[123] In some cases, however, custom is very conservative and will not accommodate de facto relationships or will result in the punishment or ostracism of perceived offenders.[124] There is also the danger that the manipulation of custom to cover cohabitees will result in the undermining of custom values, bearing in mind that marriage in custom is a complex inter-familial arrangement which is fundamental to the cohesion of society.[125] By and large custom operates so as to provide for the majority and ensure stability. It cannot pander to the non-conformist behaviour of a minority.

The third concern is the extent to which continuing strong Christian affiliation will stand in the way of any recognition of the rights of cohabitees not to be discriminated against. This is no mean obstacle. In Fiji, part of the consultation process preceding the Family Law Act involved a discussion paper issued by the Fiji Law Reform Commission on De Facto Relationships. The paper drew attention to Fiji's obligations under the CEDAW and CRC to remove discrimination in the law and indicated that in a number of respects Fijian laws were out of step with many other countries.

---

[123]   The author is aware of situations where custom payments have been made for the illegitimate children of cohabitees to the female partner's family in order to ensure their acceptance by the family and to compensate for the loss of their daughter's virginity.

[124]   The author is aware of a situation in which the cohabitee and child of a married man returned to their homeland after his sudden demise and were met by death threats from the man's family and his lawful spouse – now widow. The cohabitee also faced ostracism from her own family.

[125]   This is particularly so where there is little or no social welfare provision. See S Farran 'Pigs Mats and Feathers: Customary Marriage in Vanuatu' (2004) 27 (2) *Journal of Pacific Studies* 245.

Reaction to the discussion paper was such that any proposals to ameliorate the position of cohabitees were effectively dropped from the Family Law Bill. The consequence is that the Act – as it now is – makes little provision for cohabitees, although the consequences for their children are somewhat improved.

To conclude, in the Pacific region there is a considerable distance to travel before cohabitees can be said to enjoy anything like equality of rights under the law. In some respects this is not particularly discriminatory as women and children also have a long way to go. There are, however, some promising reforms and certainly there are some concerns which transcend the boundaries of the marriage vow, such as domestic violence and the rights of children to a safe, secure and nurturing environment. Nevertheless the law remains piecemeal in its approach and cohabitees should proceed with caution, aware that for the most part they remain outside the law in the Pacific region.

Spain

FAMILY LAW REFORM IN DIFFERING DIRECTIONS

Gabriel García Cantero[*]

Résumé

La contribution espagnole s'intéresse à la récente législation sur la protection des personnes inaptes, les procédures de séparation et de divorce, ainsi que le mariage des personnes de même sexe.

La Loi du 18 novembre 2003 aborde les questions relatives au patrimoine des personnes inaptes et met en place des mécanismes de protection, de traitement, de réhabilitation et d'intégration des personnes atteintes d'un handicap physique, sensoriel ou mental. Elle apporte également quelques changements mineurs aux règles relatives aux relations entre grands-parents et petits-enfants, garantissant une meilleure protection du droit d'accès. La suite de l'article traite d'une loi de 2005 qui vient simplifier les procédures en matière de séparation et de divorce mais qui crée également la controverse en permettant le mariage des couples de même sexe.

I INTRODUCTION

In this report I shall deal with the final family law reform legislation of the Aznar (centre right) Government, together with the more significant changes brought about in the first 18 months of the socialist Government of Rodriguez Zapatero, which came to power in the elections that followed the tragic terrorist outrage of 11 March 2004 in Atocha Station. The latest changes take a profoundly innovative and, to some extent, revolutionary direction when seen alongside the laws promulgated since the Constitution of 1978.

The Law of 18 November 2003 mainly deals with protecting the patrimony of persons under incapacity, and with changes to certain provisions of the Civil Code, and to primary and subordinate legislation relating to the same matters. The new law is based on art 49 of the Spanish Constitution (CE),

---

[*]   Emeritus Professor of Civil Law at the University of Zaragoza. Translated by Peter Schofield.

requiring public authorities to establish a system of protection, treatment, rehabilitation and integration for the physically, sensorily or mentally disabled. It creates a specially protected patrimony for the benefit of such persons, closely and directly tied to meeting their vital needs, and lays down rules to assist in its establishment, and in the free granting of assets and rights. Unlike the normal personal property rights of the person entitled to them, these new rights are subject to a special regime of administration and supervision. It is a patrimony dedicated to a particular purpose (*patrimonio de destino*). The proprietor must be subject to incapacity within the degrees of handicap administratively declared, whether he has or has not been judicially declared incapable. Rules are laid down for supervising the administration of this patrimony, determined by the assets of which it consists, by the Ministerio Fiscal, by an administrative Commission for the protection of the patrimony of persons under disability. This law follows the modern direction of certain European legislation (eg German or Italian) in keeping judicially declared incapacity distinct from purely administratively declared incapacity. Among the reforms introduced into the Civil Code, we should note particularly the important provision that allows appointment of a tutor for oneself (persistently demanded over recent years) (Civil Code, art 223, para 2), which consequently implies changes in the grounds for termination of authority by supervening incapacity (Civil Code, art 1732-3, para 2).[1]

The Law of 21 November 2003 also includes rather minor changes to family relations between grandparents and grandchildren. This focuses on an improved regulation of the right of contact with minor children, and of relations with their grandparents and other friends and relations (Civil Code, art 160, para 2), which had already been recognised in the Code and in decisions of the courts. The new law seeks to reassert the role of grandparents in the modern family, creating a special procedure for applying for contact rights when the parents are engaged in dispute in court, allowing the judgment to lay down the terms of the exercise of the grandparents' contact rights.

The socialist Government, on taking power, put forward a package of fundamental reform of family law, in three directions: to simplify the procedures of separation and divorce as far as possible; to permit same-sex marriage; to regulate de facto unions. Legislation on the first two points was passed in July 2005, after a great national debate, in which critical contributions were made by a large number of independent jurists, and advice not to proceed was given by several high-ranking bodies, including the Council of State, the General Council of the Judicial Power, the Royal Academy of Jurisprudence and Legislation; similar opposition was

---

[1]   In effect, previously, if the person granting the authority was subsequently declared incapable, this automatically terminated the authority of the person he had himself nominated as tutor to act for him precisely in that event. Now, if the person granting the authority specifically so provides, or if the authority is granted for a situation of incapacity established by him, such termination no longer occurs.

expressed by the principal religious denominations (Catholics, Protestants, Orthodox, Muslims and Jews) in the form of a joint statement. About 1.5 million people, from all parts of Spain, demonstrated in Madrid on 18 June 2005 in defence of marriage and against same-sex marriages. The law on same-sex marriage was also rejected by the Senate, having first been approved in the Congress, which eventually passed it on a second reading. The Socialist Party was able to amass sufficient support, among the various nationalist and minority parties, to bring its projects to completion.

II   TRUE DIVORCE, WITHOUT THE NEED FOR GROUNDS

The reform of separation and divorce shows an astonishing simplification of its juridical regime built round favouring divorce, and not consistent with the Constitution. The justification for this appears to rest on the absence of direct access to divorce under the system established by the Law of 7 July 1981, part of the first package of family law reform introduced in Spain after the Constitution of 1978. Under that Law, following traditional Spanish law, judicial separation freed spouses from the duty to live together, but did not allow them to enter into a new union. Separation could be consensual (on the application of both spouses, by agreement, not less than a year after their marriage was celebrated, accompanied by a proposal for terms of separation). Or it could be for cause (based on non-performance of the duties arising from marriage or from common parenthood). Divorce was effectively based on objective grounds (divorce for breakdown). It almost always required a prior judgment of separation and the passage of a certain period of time thereafter (1, 2 or 5 years according to the circumstances). The new Law retains the distinction between separation and divorce, while making the two independent of each other, so as to give spouses direct access to divorce. Mutual agreement to separate is retained as a ground for separation and becomes a ground for divorce. There is no longer a requirement to rely on, and prove to a judge, a statutory ground for divorce. Instead, the spouses, or one of them, after at least 3 months have passed since celebration of the marriage, can apply for separation or divorce, presenting with the petition proposed terms for dealing with the personal and matrimonial consequences. The Statement of Reasons for the Law justifies the new system by reference to the principle of the spouses' freedom to break the marriage bond, and to the ancient Roman law concept of marriage.[2] It is not clear that such a general principle suffices to derogate from art 32.2 of the Constitution,

---

[2]   This appears to follow from the paragraph in the Statement of Reasons that runs: 'It is proposed to reinforce the principle of the freedom of the spouses in marriage, since the continuation of their living together depends on their continuing consent no less than its initial establishment does.' Can we now say concubitus, non consensus facit nuptias?

which remits the regulation of the causes of separation and of dissolution of marriage to the ordinary law.[3]

As a result arts 82 and 86 of the Civil Code, both relating to the grounds for separation and divorce, are repealed.

One of the most fiercely debated issues, among practitioners and in Parliament, has been the ability of judges to award the joint or shared custody of children to separated or divorced parents. The Government has finally managed to realise its initial, if somewhat exceptional, proposal.[4]

The basic text is art 92, newly drawn up in more technical terms than that which it replaces. It should be quoted in its entirety:

'**Art. 92**. 1. Separation, nullity and divorce do not relieve parents of their obligations with regard to children. 2. The judge, when he has to make an order as to custody, care and education of minor children, is to take account of their right to be heard. 3. The judgment may terminate parental authority when there are grounds for this. 4. Parents can make an agreement, or a judge may order in the interest of children, that parental authority is to be exercised, wholly or in part, by one of the parents. 5. Shared exercise of care or custody of children will be ordered when parents so request in their proposed arrangement or when they reach agreement to that effect in the course of proceedings. When ordering joint custody, and in reaching that decision, the judge will take appropriate steps to ensure the proper operation of the care arrangements ordered, seeking not to separate siblings. 6. In every case, before making arrangements for care and custody, the judge must receive the report of the Ministerio Fiscal and, if they have enough understanding, hear the children, whenever he considers it necessary ex officio or on the petition of the Ministerio Fiscal, of the members of the Equipo Técnico Judicial, or of the minor himself, assess the allegations made by the parties in the hearing and their evidence presented there, and the state of relationships between the parents, to determine their suitability for such arrangements. 7. Joint custody will not be ordered when either parent is involved in criminal proceedings for an offence against the physical integrity, liberty, psychological wellbeing or the liberty or sexual integrity of the other spouse or of children living with them. Nor will it be ordered when, from the parties' allegations and the evidence before him, the judge sees well-founded signs of domestic violence.

---

[3]   Regulating the grounds of separation and divorce is not the same as abolishing them. Article 32.2, CE clearly provides that both separation and divorce must have legal grounds; any Spanish court could call the constitutionality of the new law into question on this point.

[4]   The Statement of Reasons for the Law appears to blame the influence of the fault principle in separation and divorce for the fact that, under the previous system, the regular practice has developed in such a way that children are often prevented from maintaining a flexible relationship with both parents. In my view, the reality is more complex: on the one hand, a real or supposed feminism of Spanish judges, tending to marginalise fathers with regard to custody of their children; on the other, the machinations of mothers to obstruct the fathers (eg dragging out proceedings to such an extent that before a final judgment can be arrived at the child has already come of age). There is no certainty that a change in the law will stop such abuses.

8. In exceptional cases, even when the conditions in paragraph five of this article are not satisfied, the judge, at the instance of one of the parties, with favourable advice of the Ministerio Fiscal, may order sharing of care and custody on the grounds that this is the only way to sufficiently protect the paramount interest of the minor. 9. Before taking any of the decisions referred to in the preceding paragraphs, the judge may, ex officio or at the instance of a party, call for reports from duly qualified specialists as to the suitability of the manner of exercising parental authority and of the arrangements for the custody of the minors.'

This, one of the longest provisions of Title IV, Book I, of the Civil Code, governs one of the most fought-over aspects of divorce settlements, where the children are made into bargaining chips or conscripted allies in the battles of one parent against the other. Feminist groups are, in principle, opposed to shared custody, while associations of fathers support it in the belief that it will help fathers to retain custody of their children for a longer time. It is surprising that the judicial decision to share custody is hedged about by such a surprising number of reservations and precautions, and that the basic question of the fundamental test of the paramount interest of the minor does not appear at the head of the article, as was the case in the former article, which referred to the children's welfare in para 2, but rather the principle that should inspire the decisions of the judges appears only in paras 4 and 9 of art 92.

A   Other changes in the law

* A strange additional rule on the duties arising from marriage: '[Spouses] must also share the domestic responsibility and in giving care and attention to ascendants and descendants and others in their charge' (art 68).[5]

* The creation of a guarantee fund for unpaid maintenance: 'The State will guarantee the payment of support required and unpaid, in favour of minor children, in agreements judicially approved or ordered by a judge, by means of specific legislation which will concretise the system of covering such payments' (sole additional provision), a promise of future legislation for the effect of which we must wait until it appears in concrete terms.

* Introduction and generalisation of matrimonial mediation: 'The Government will present to the Legislature a project for a law on mediation based on the principles set out in the provisions of the

---

[5]   The contents of this addition are repetitive: in effect, the duty of sharing domestic responsibilities is taken up, in other words, in Civil Code, art 1318; care and attention for descendants in arts 143-2 and 154; care and attention for ascendants in the already mentioned art 143-2; all that remains is that related to other persons in their charge (presumably a reference to minors they have taken in, or under their tutorship).

European Union, and in any event, on those of voluntariness, impartiality and confidentiality in relation to the mediation services set up by the Autonomous Communities' (third final provision). This is an attempt to fill a gap in State legislation.

- The fourth final provision fixes its coming into force on the day after it is published in the State Official Bulletin.

III SO-CALLED 'HOMOSEXUAL MARRIAGE'

The legalisation of homosexual marriage appears to follow strong pre-electoral commitments made by the President of the Government to Gay and Lesbian associations, even though there was no authentic social demand for this. (The National Institute of Statistics gives the number of homosexual couples more or less formally existing in Spain at 10,000.) The Government project was both technically primitive and drawn up under great pressure. This led to a lack of parliamentary debate with those who were willing to accept some regulation of homosexual unions, outside the scope of Title IV, Book I, of the Civil Code, and without calling it marriage. The reform effectively consists of a new paragraph added to art 44 of the Civil Code, under which marriage will be subject to the same requirements and have the same effects whether the parties are of the same or of different sex,[6] replacement of references to father and mother by spouses in arts 66 and 67 of the Civil Code, and in art 154, para 1 (in relation to parental authority) by progenitors.[7]

This legislative technique is, in my view, the worst of all those recently followed in the Netherlands, Scandinavian countries and finally Germany, Switzerland and the UK. The Spanish Legislature has vacillated on a concrete point in the process of equalisation, namely when it came to applying the presumption of the husband's paternity to a homosexual union, and in the final version of the Statement of Reasons for the law it is concluded that the presumption could not be applied to homosexual

---

[6]   At first sight this addition looks like a mere clarification. In fact it completely redefines marriage, with implications right across Spanish law. Additional Provision 1 is an important rule for defining and interpreting 'marriage': 'Provisions in laws and regulations containing any reference to marriage are to be read as applicable regardless of the sex of the partners.' Henceforth, as a result, the opposite sex factor disappears from the notion of marriage. We can say that the concept of a union of persons of opposite sex has disappeared, for all purposes of Spanish law, to be replaced by a single category applicable to same-sex unions. However, it turns out to be very hard to achieve the equalising of effects that the new rule pronounces. The familiar system is thought out, based and reliant on the spouses being of opposite sex, so that the Legislature will have no small difficulty in removing this (short of drawing up a new Law of the Family specifically based on homosexuality, a thing the new law clearly does not do).

[7]   A reform that seems to contradict the purpose of the law, since the word progenitor means the person who engenders or procreates, a metaphysical impossibility when applied to a homosexual couple. One member of such a couple could be the biological procreator of the minor, but could never have procreated jointly with the other member. Adoption by homosexuals is yet another controversial topic which I shall come to later.

marriage; yet the text of the law enunciates the principle of equality without restrictions – which interpretation will prevail? A deeper analysis of this supposed equality shows that it cannot be applicable, for instance, to matrimonial filiation (see the presumption of paternity under art 116 ff of the Civil Code), nor in the determining of family relationships (art 915 ff), nor in relation to succession, and so on.

Chercher l'enfant seems to be the cynosure of associations of Gays and Lesbians, given that such unions are, by their nature, infertile. It may, of course, be that one or both members of the homosexual couple have been married and have biological children of that union, whose custody has been given to one of them; also recourse may be had to assisted procreation, or even the law allows both members of the couple to apply to adopt minors.[8] It would seem that children living in a homosexual household in the Netherlands can be in up to five different situations in relation to the couple, with different rights and duties applying in each case.[9] It seems clear that homosexual marriage destroys the unity of filiation. We may well ask whether it is reasonable, in order to meet the claims of a small group of citizens, to risk breaking the principle of legal equality of all forms of filiation, recognising various different forms of the status it confers, or, worse still bringing in situations of triple parenthood, totally foreign to the legal beliefs of the citizens.

On the other hand, the much-vaunted voluntariness that the President of the Government has made so much of in the production of this law leads to causing collateral harm to third parties. In particular international adoptions

---

[8]   The possibility that homosexuals might legally adopt has raised passionate argument in Spain. We should really define the terms of the debate. Adoption calls for a double procedure – administrative (to declare the suitability of the adopters and select possible adoptees) and judicial, since adoption is subject to requirements of a civil nature (capacity of adopters and adoptees, age of each, difference of age between them, etc) – and creates the civil status of an adopted person. Previous legislation did not allow a homosexual couple to adopt, though individually each member could receive a child in adoption (probably more easily if the fact was concealed). Relying on the autonomous legislation of Navarre, three adoption orders have recently been made in favour of lesbian couples. However, not much notice has been taken in Spain of the recent judgment of the Human Rights Court in Strasbourg, directly confronting the situation of a French homosexual who applied to the competent court for adoption, openly declaring his homosexuality. As we know, the Human Rights Court upheld the unanimous refusal at every judicial level in France, affirming that it did not violate the European Convention of 1950. Now, indeed, since the passing of this law, in future, homosexual couples can apply to adopt minors. But they must still submit to the competent administrative decision as to suitability, and, in addition, the court has to declare that adoption by the homosexual couple Z would be appropriate and would be right for minor X, taking account of expert advice if it saw fit (art 176.1). In general, there are few Spanish children available for adoption. Nor do we know what judicial criteria will be applied in each case, when it comes to allowing homosexual couples to adopt (significantly, most judges belong to the Professional Association of the Magistrature – conservative in nature). Some authors draw attention to the usefulness of a clause in a parent's will forbidding the eventual adoption of his orphan children by homosexuals. Recourse to international adoption would seem to be impossible in practice. It is not, therefore, likely that there will be many adoptions by Spanish homosexuals.

[9]   See in more detail W Schrama 'The Netherlands: Reforms in Dutch Family law during the course of 2001: Increased Pluriformity and Complexity' in A Bainham (ed) *The International Survey of Family Law 2002 Edition* p 277 ff, in particular p 298 ff (with at-a-glance diagrams).

– the majority of adoptions judicially approved in Spain – may suffer a reduction in numbers, since most of them come from countries radically opposed to letting homosexual households adopt children (as is the case in China, Russia, Romania, India and a number of Latin American countries).

To sum up: not a model to be followed by other European countries. It is likely that the law will be challenged in the Constitutional Tribunal,[10] and, eventually, in the Human Rights Court in Strasbourg, and it is not impossible that, when there is a change of parties in the Government, it will be repealed on account of the serious problems that may arise from its implementation.[11]

The new law also makes simple terminological changes in various articles (160, para 1; 178, cl 2; 637, para 2; 1323; 1344; 1348; 1351; 1361; 1365, para 2; 1404; 1458) of an exclusively cosmetic or aesthetic nature, the aim of which is to eliminate the existence of the status of husband and wife from the Spanish Civil Code. A proposal that, in my view, experience will show to be impossible.

---

[10]   The Advice of the Council of State (principal governmental advisory body), of the General Council of the Judicial Power and notably of the Royal Academy of Legislation and Jurisprudence, all drew attention to the risk of running into unconstitutionality. In my view, recourse on that ground would be well founded. In fact, art 32.1 of the Constitution declares that a man and a woman have the right to contract marriage with full legal equality. The Spanish Constitution in force has followed the example of the Constitutions of Bonn and of the Italian Republic, making the jus connubii into a constitutional norm. That means heterosexual marriage is enshrined as the only legal form of union between the sexes. Altering the reference to heterosexuality in this institution is not within the ordinary legislative competence, but calls for a constitutional reform.

[11]   I have dealt with the distortion that homosexual marriage introduces in the law of filiation in general in García Cantero *Unidad o pluralidad de modelos matrimoniales?* (Zaragoza, 2003), particularly p 54 ff.

Sweden

LEGISLATION ON FORCED MARRIAGE AND INTERCOUNTRY ADOPTION

Åke Saldeen[*]

Résumé

La contribution suédoise s'intéresse à deux législations adoptées par le Riksdag (le parlement de Suède). La première, la Loi suédoise concernant certaines relations juridiques internationales en rapport avec le mariage et l'autorité parentale, concerne les conflits de lois en matière de mariage et de reconnaissance des mariages étrangers. La seconde, la Loi sur l'adoption internationale, modifie les procédures de l'adoption internationale en Suède en mettant l'accent sur le respect des droits de l'enfant. Cet article évoque également la récente législation adoptée par le Riksdag concernant le droit des conjoints de même sexe de bénéficier de l'insémination artificielle.

I INTRODUCTION

In my report on the development of Swedish family law during 2003, I mentioned that it would be appropriate to say something in the report for 2004 about the legislation that entered into force on 1 May 2004. This legislation is aimed at improving protection for the individual against compelled and premature marriage. In addition, there is new legislation aimed at improving the rights of the child in the adoption procedure as regards intercountry adoptions. I will deal with the first issue under II and the second issue under III.

In my previous report, I also mentioned that legislative work was in progress concerning the right to gain access to artificial insemination for lesbian women who are registered partners, according to the Registered Partnership Act (1994:1117), or who co-habit with another woman. Such legislation has now been passed during 2005 and there is consequently cause to report on this legislation in the 2005 report.

---

[*]   Professor of Private Law, Faculty of Law, Uppsala University. Translated by James Hurst.

II PROTECTION FOR THE INDIVIDUAL AGAINST COMPELLED AND PREMATURE MARRIAGE

The Swedish Act on Certain International Legal Relationships relating to Marriage and Guardianship (1904:26, p 1) contains provisions on which the country's law shall apply when considering impediments to marriage and the recognition of foreign marriage. In the spring of 2002, the Riksdag (Swedish Parliament) stated that legislative measures should immediately be passed with the aim of preventing child marriage and compelled marriage. Subsequently, a memorandum was prepared by the Ministry of Justice entitled 'Swedish and Foreign Marriage' (Ministry Report – Ds 2002:54), which, after it had undergone the consultative procedure, formed the basis for the Government Bill 2003/04:48, Measures Against Child Marriage and Compelled Marriage. The Government Bill was passed by the Riksdag and this new legislation, which as mentioned above entered into force on 1 May 2004, briefly entails the following.

It may be mentioned, as a background to the report on this reform, that certain impediments to marriage are prescribed by Chapter 2 of the Marriage Code. Consequently, those who are under the age of 18 may not get married without the permission of the county administrative board (s 1). Those who are related in a directly ascending or descending line or who are brothers/sisters of whole blood may not enter into marriage (s 3, first paragraph). Brothers/sisters of half blood may only marry each other with the permission of the Government or the authority appointed by the Government (s 3, second paragraph). A person who is already married, or is a partner in a registered partnership, may not get married (s 4). The corresponding impediments for the registration of partnership are prescribed by the Registered Partnership Act (1994:1117), though with the difference that a person under the age of 18 cannot get a relaxation from the age requirement (see Chapter 1, s 3 of the Act).

If there is an international link, the authority that conducts the consideration of impediments to marriage (now the Swedish Tax Agency) determines which country's law should apply. The main rule for this choice of law has been that the decision should be made according to the law of the country of nationality (*lex patriæ*).

According to a Government statement contained in Government Bill 2003/04:48 it was necessary to adapt the present rules on choice of law relating to consideration of impediments to marriage to changed values within the area. On the basis of the Government Bill, which was passed by the Riksdag, the rules have now been changed in such a way that the consideration of impediments to marriage before a Swedish authority must *always* be conducted applying Swedish law. If neither of the parties has any link to Sweden through nationality or residence, the law of the country of nationality or the law of the country of residence (*lex domicilii*) must also be applied for each individual. However, if there are special reasons, the consideration of impediments to marriage may be conducted applying only Swedish law also in a case where there is only a weak link to Sweden. One consequence of this statutory amendment is that no one under the age of 18 can now enter into a marriage before a Swedish authority without a special permit. Moreover, through this statutory amendment, the conditions for such a permit have been made more stringent. Permits for marriage prior to the age of 18 may thus, according to the new legislation, only be granted if there are special reasons (Chapter 2, s 1, Marriage Code). A new rule has also been introduced through this legislation clarifying and improving the power to refuse recognition of a foreign marriage that has been entered into under compulsion or which would not have been allowed upon consideration of impediments to marriage in Sweden. Thus, a marriage that has been entered into according to a foreign law, will not be recognised in Sweden if, at the time that the marriage was entered into, there would have been an impediment according to Swedish law and at least one of the parties was a Swedish national or was resident in Sweden, or if it is probable that the marriage had been entered into under compulsion. However, this does not apply if there are special reasons to recognise the marriage (Chapter 1, s 8 a of the Act on Certain International Legal Relationships relating to Marriage and Guardianship (1904:26, p 1)). The new legislation also means that the control of, among other things, persons authorised to officiate at weddings has been improved. If it is discovered that a consideration of impediments has not been conducted, this may entail, for example, disciplinary liability, dismissal and, in the worst case, notification to the public prosecutor. Finally, it may be mentioned that the legislation in question provides that the possibility to get a divorce without a preceding period for reconsideration is also extended to apply in cases where the marriage has been entered into under compulsion or in violation of the age requirement. In such cases, the public prosecutor may now bring an action for divorce.

III RIGHTS OF THE CHILD IN INTERCOUNTRY ADOPTIONS

There are about 43,000 people in Sweden today who were adopted through intercountry adoption and came to this country during the years 1969–2003. Approximately 1,000 children born abroad are adopted in Sweden each year, of which the primary countries of origin are currently China, South Korea and Colombia.

In April 2004, the Government submitted to the Riksdag the Intercountry Adoption Affairs Bill 2003/04:131 aimed at, in various ways, improving the rights of the child in the adoption procedure. This Government Bill was passed by the Riksdag and the new legislation entered into force on 1 January 2005. First, regarding this legislation, it may be mentioned that it not only covered intercountry adoption operations but, among other things, also introduced a provision into the Marriage Code (Chapter 2, s 3, third paragraph, Marriage Code) prohibiting marriage between adoptive parent and adoptive child. Prior to this statutory amendment such marriage was allowed. In the Government Bill (2003/04:131, p 73), the Government concluded:

'... that developments that have occurred in the field of adoption mean that an adoptive relationship has come to be equated with a biological relationship in the vast majority of areas. The principle of equality has strong roots in public legal awareness. With this perspective, which nowadays predominates on a broad front, the possibility of an adoptive parent and adoptive child entering into marriage seems almost offensive. Even if there is no biological bond, social and ethical reasons strongly suggest that marriage between an adoptive child and adoptive parent should not be allowed.'

Marriage or partnership between adoptive child and adoptive parents' biological children may be entered into with permission, and the same also applies to marriage and partnership between two adoptive siblings.

It is, among other things, mentioned in Government Bill (2003/04:131, p 21 ff) that adoption of foreign children started in Sweden during the 1950s and that intermediation operations were initially conducted by individual people. From the middle of the 1950s up to 1965, it was the function of the National Board of Health and Welfare to arrange contact between adoption applicants and foreign bodies. In order to get a firmer grip on adoption operations, the National Board of Health and Welfare established an advisory board in 1971, which was subsequently reformed and became the Swedish Council for Intercountry Adoptions (NIA). After 1979, and through the introduction of the Act on Intercountry Adoption Assistance (1979:552), intercountry adoption intermediation in Sweden has been dealt with by a number of (currently six) authorised organisations over which NIA had supervisory functions. In conjunction with the reorganisation in 1981 of the National Board of Health and Welfare, NIA became an independent authority known as the National Board for Intercountry Adoptions, which continues to use the abbreviation NIA.

Through the 2004 legislation, NIA has been wound up and reformed as the Swedish Intercountry Adoptions Authority (MIA). This new authority has taken over NIA's functions as supervisory authority, among other things, but has also been given extended responsibility with new functions regarding the exercise of supervision over intercountry adoption operations. (MIA, and formerly NIA, is the central agency according to the act passed as a result of Sweden's accession to the 1993 Hague Convention on Protection of Children and Co-operation in Respect of Intercountry Adoption.) The legislation in question also means that the requirements for an organisation or association to be granted authorisation to intermediate intercountry adoption have been made more stringent. Authorisation is to be granted in two steps. Consequently, in order to be able to authorise an adoption agency, MIA must first consider the agency's or association's basic capacity to function as an intermediator of intercountry adoptions. In addition to this, MIA must investigate if the prevailing situation in the particular country for which authorisation is applied is such that co-operation is appropriate. Authorisation according to the first step is granted for a maximum of 5 years and in accordance with the second step, for a maximum of 2 years. Through the 2004 legislation, the applicable conditions for an association to be granted authorisation to work with intercountry adoption intermediation *in*

Sweden have been supplemented with the requirement that, if an association also conducts other operations than intercountry adoption intermediation (for example, foreign assistance operations, public relief work, church or mission operations), such other operation must not jeopardise confidence in the adoption operation. In the Government Bill (2003/04:131, p 36) it was concluded that Sweden is – both on the basis of the UN Convention on the Rights of the Child (CRC) and the 1993 Hague Convention on Protection of Children and Co-operation in Respect of Intercountry Adoption – liable to prevent such a situation arising. In order to obtain authorisation to work with intercountry adoption intermediation *in Sweden* it is also, according to the new legislation, required that the association has a board, auditors and by-laws whereby the association is open to everybody. In order for an association that has been granted authorisation to work with intercountry adoption intermediation in Sweden to be granted authorisation to be allowed to work with intercountry adoption intermediation in *another country,* it is also required, according to the new legislation, that the country with which it wishes to collaborate has acceptable adoption legislation; the country has a functional administration concerning adoption operations; the association reports its costs abroad and how these are broken down; and also that, considering the cost profile, balance between the Swedish associations and the circumstances generally, it is considered appropriate for the association to co-operate with the other country.

In Swedish law, the conditions for adoption are governed by Chapter 4 of the Code on Parents, Children and Guardians. Besides the provisions contained in this Chapter, it has already been prescribed that children may not, without the consent of the social welfare committee, be received for permanent care and upbringing in a private home that does not belong to one of the parents or any other person who has custody of him or her (Chapter 6, s 6, first paragraph, Social Services Act (2001:453)). According to s 12 of the same Act, certain conditions for the consent of the social welfare committee are imposed, which must be satisfied if the matter involves the receipt of a child resident abroad with the purpose of adopting the child. Through the 2004 legislation, the conditions that should be satisfied for consent by the social welfare committee in such cases have been stipulated in a more detailed way. The rule contained in Chapter 6, s 12, of the Social Services Act is, following the statutory amendment, worded as follows:

> 'A child domiciled abroad may not be received for purposes of adoption by a person who is not the child's parent or guardian without the consent of the social welfare committee. Consent must be obtained before the child leaves the country of domicile.
>
> Consent may only be given if the applicant is suitable to adopt a child. The assessment of suitability must pay particular attention to the applicant's knowledge and insight concerning adopted children and their needs and the implications of the planned adoption, as well as to the applicant's age, state of health, personal qualities and social network. Moreover, prior to adoption the applicant must have taken part in a parenting course commissioned by the municipality.

If the applicant has previously adopted a child from abroad, consent may be given even if he or she has not taken part in a parenting course.

The consent will lapse if the child has not been received into the home within two years of consent being given.'

Finally, it may be mentioned that in the Government Bill (2003/04:131, p 52) it was concluded that for a properly functional intercountry adoption operation it is necessary, besides having clear internal legislation and stringent supervision, to enhance international co-operation. This co-operation should, according to the Government as expressed in the Government Bill, aim 'to secure both an ethical and transparent adoption operation, which proceeds in the best interests of the child and to formulate development cooperation which in the long term improves social and economic conditions in the countries of origin. The ultimate goal should be that intercountry adoption becomes unnecessary'.

Tanzania

THE CONSTITUTIONALISATION OF
FAMILY LAW IN TANZANIA

Bart Rwezaura[*] and Ulrike Wanitzek[**]

Résumé

Cette présentation met l'accent sur ce que ses auteurs appellent la *constitutionnalisation* du droit de la famille tanzanien. Depuis l'introduction en 1984 d'une charte des droits dans la constitution de la Tanzanie, un certain nombre de juges seniors ont fait preuve d'un remarquable courage et d'une inébranlable volonté d'utiliser cette charte des droits, ainsi que les plus importants traités et déclarations en matière de droit international de la personne, pour introduire des réformes qui s'imposaient depuis longtemps dans plusieurs domaines du droit de la famille et du droit successoral. Par exemple, l'interdiction de la discrimination fondée sur le sexe a permis une interprétation de dispositions en matière de mariage et de divorce de manière à protéger les droits patrimoniaux des veuves et des épouses divorcées; elle a également permis de régler le contentieux concernant la désignation de la personne autorisée à régler les funérailles des époux. Les juges ont également appliqué le principe du meilleur intérêt de l'enfant aux enfants nés hors mariage, permettant désormais aux tribunaux de trancher des questions relatives à la garde et à la protection, sans égard au statut légal des enfants. Les auteurs avancent que la constitutionnalisation du droit de la famille en Tanzanie, loin d'être un phénomène isolé, participe d'un vaste mouvement de libéralisation politique et économique qui caractérise la société civile en Tanzanie.

This *Survey* focuses on what the authors describe as the constitutionalisation of family law in Tanzania. Following the enactment in 1984 of a Bill of Rights in the Tanzania Constitution a number of senior judges have shown remarkable courage and willingness to use the Bill of Rights and a number of major international human rights treaties and declarations to effect overdue reforms in the various areas of family and succession laws. For example, the prohibition against gender discrimination has been combined with existing provisions in the law of marriage and divorce to protect the property rights of widows and divorced women; and to decide disputes over who has the right to arrange a burial for a deceased spouse. Judges have also extended the principle of best interests of the child to non-marital children

---

[*] Associate Professor, Faculty of Law, University of Hong Kong.
[**] Associate Professor (Privatdozentin), Institute of African Studies, Faculty of Law and Economics, University of Bayreuth, Germany.

thus enabling courts to rule on custody and childcare issues without being constrained by the illegitimate status of the child. The authors argue that the constitutionalisation of family law in Tanzania is not an isolated phenomenon but is part of a wider process of political and economic liberalisation taking place in the country and affecting other aspects of civil society.

1   INTRODUCTION[1]

The last *Survey* on Tanzania focused on the proposed reforms to the Law of Marriage Act 1971 (No 5 of 1971, 'LMA'), the integration and reform of the law of succession and the law relating to children.[2] It was noted in that *Survey* that these proposed reforms had been driven largely by wider concern within Tanzania for gender justice and the rights of children. The *Survey* also noted that the social movement for such reforms had greatly benefited from the incorporation in 1984 of the Bill of Rights into the Constitution of Tanzania.[3] In the words of Justice Raymond Mwaikasu, then Chairman of the Law Reform Commission, the underlying policy of the new succession law was to 'promote unity, equality and justice among our people in accordance with the Universal Declaration of Human Rights and the Bill of Rights, as enshrined under our 1977 Constitution'.[4] It is significant to note that the Law Reform Commission began its work on the reform of the laws of succession, marriage and children more than 19 years ago in January 1987. In July 2004, the Minister of Justice and Constitutional Affairs announced for the third time in Parliament that the recommendations of the

---

[1]   We wish to acknowledge the assistance of Kennedy Gastorn, Naelijwa Mrutu, Mohamed Nassoro, Eliamani Mbise, Tumaini Silaa, Grace Bingileki, Clement Rutaihwa, John Kahyoza, Justice Augustine Shangwa and Vivian Mbando in the collection of materials used in this *Survey*.

[2]   See Bart Rwezaura 'Gender Justice and Children's Rights: A Banner for Family Law Reform in Tanzania' in A Bainham (ed) *The International Survey of Family Law 1997* (Martinus Nijhoff Publishers, The Hague, 1999) pp 413–443.

[3]   Fifth Constitutional Amendment Act 1984 (No 15 of 1984). The Bill of Rights came into force on 1 March 1988, see s 5 (2) of the Constitution (Consequential, Transitional and Temporary Provisions) Act 1984 (No 16 of 1984). On the impact of the Bill of Rights in other fields of the law see Justice K S K Lugakingira 'Personal Liberty and Judicial Attitude: The Tanzanian Case' (1990) *Eastern Africa Law Review* 17, 107–133; Chris Maina Peter *Human Rights in Tanzania: Selected Cases and Materials* (Rüdiger Köppe Verlag, Köln, 1997); Florens D A M Luoga 'The Tanzanian Bill of Rights' in Chris Maina Peter and Ibrahim Hamisi Juma (eds) *Fundamental Rights and Freedoms in Tanzania* (Mkuki na Nyota Publishers, Dar es Salaam, 1998) pp 37–46 at 43 note 37; and Chris Maina Peter 'The Enforcement of Fundamental Rights and Freedoms in Tanzania: Matching Theory and Practice' in Chris Maina Peter and Ibrahim Hamisi Juma (eds) *Fundamental Rights and Freedoms in Tanzania* (Mkuki na Nyota Publishers, Dar es Salaam, 1998) pp 47–61 at 51 *et seq*.

[4]   R J A Mwaikasu 'The Law Reform Project on the Law of Succession in Tanzania Mainland', Speech to the Members of the Bar at Arusha, Tanzania (2.2.1993) at p 3. See also Bart Rwezaura 'Tanzania: Building a New Family Law out of a Plural Legal System' (1995) *University of Louisville Journal of Family Law* 33, 523–540 at 538.

Law Reform Commission had now been forwarded to the government for further consideration.[5]

Given this background of protracted delay it is difficult to predict when exactly the proposed reforms will be enacted into law. Nonetheless, and despite the delay, the people of Tanzania have not patiently waited for the formal legislation to bring home the promised 'equality and justice'. During the period under review there has been what might be described as a form of individual self-help whereby some litigants, assisted by their legal representatives, have seemingly twisted the arm of the judiciary forcing it to deliver on the promises made by the government. It is this spontaneous social movement that we refer to in this *Survey* as the trigger for the constitutionalisation of family law in Tanzania.

The object of this *Survey* is to analyse the above process by showing how litigants have used the Tanzania Bill of Rights and the various United Nations Conventions and Declarations to alter the landscape of family and succession laws. In some cases, especially where parties are not legally represented, superior court judges have sought guidance from the Constitution and from international human rights norms without being specifically prompted to do so by litigants.[6] Also to be noted at the outset is that in many cases the litigation has not taken the form of a direct challenge to existing general statutory provisions.[7] Rather, the attack has focused on the provisions and practices of certain African customary laws and religious laws.[8] In this sense the reform process which has been initiated through the courts, albeit piecemeal and unstructured, ought to be seen as ultimately leading to the integration of the various systems of personal laws within the national legal system.

This *Survey* is divided into five parts including this introduction. The second part examines cases in which married women and widows have sought the assistance of courts in their effort to protect their property rights. Their efforts can be divided into two main categories. The first relates to cases involving division of matrimonial assets on divorce and judicial separation.[9] The second category concerns cases where a widow seeks a share from the estate of her deceased husband, sometimes in competition with her late husband's lineage, her own children or the former co-wives and their children.

The third part of this *Survey* examines a somewhat novel topic in Tanzania relating to disputes over the right to bury one's deceased spouse. The relevance of burial disputes to our theme is that they highlight the problem

---

[5]   See United Republic of Tanzania, *Budget Speech of the Minister for Justice and Constitutional Affairs to the Parliament* (Government Printer, Dar es Salaam, July 1997) at 7–8; July 2002, at 19; July 2004, at 15–16.

[6]   See *Elizabeth Mtawa* (note 34 below).

[7]   As was the case in other areas of the law, see Chris Maina Peter (1998) (note 3 above) at 51–52.

[8]   An earlier example of such focus is the case of *Bernardo Ephraim v Holaria Pastory and Gervazi Kaizilege* [1990] LRC (Const) 757 (per Mwalusanya J); also reproduced in Chris Maina Peter (1997) (note 3 above) at 387–398.

[9]   Within this category are claims by *de facto* cohabitants on the termination of their relationship.

that certain African customary laws and religious practices exclude a widow from determining the place of burial of her deceased husband. Indirectly, the disputes also underline a wider conflict between the ethos of the lineage and extended family, on the one hand, and the emerging ideas based on individualistic values of the nuclear family and the rights of married women, on the other.

The fourth part of this *Survey* relates to issues of children and children's rights. Of particular importance is the problem of status of children born out of wedlock and their right not to be discriminated against. To some extent this problem arises from the delayed reform of child law to eliminate the distinction between children born in wedlock and non-marital children including the children of cohabitants. Custody decisions also appear to underline the values of the nuclear family at the expense of the extended family.

This *Survey* is concluded, in the fifth part, by noting that although it is widely agreed that court decisions are rarely a true reflection of the major social processes in a given society, there is a sense in which the cases discussed in this *Survey* reflect wider social reality and political trends in Tanzania. These cases demonstrate a persistent demand for gender justice not only in the family law field but also in other spheres of Tanzanian society. They also highlight the political direction towards which the country is moving. These changes involve a movement away from a one-party system underpinned by a poorly managed socialist economy with minimal concern for individual rights to an emerging multi-party system. The latter system seeks to rely on the ethos of liberalism and the market economy. Indeed the recent reforms in the land tenure system,[10] the establishment, for the first time, of the Commission for Human Rights and Good Governance[11] and a separate Commercial Division and Land Division of the High Court[12] demonstrate Tanzania's genuine aspiration towards political liberalism and the market economy. It is in this context that we must place the growing willingness of the senior members of the judiciary to support individual family members' rights and liberties.

---

[10]   See the Land Act 1999 (No 4 of 1999); the Village Land Act 1999 (No 5 of 1999); the Courts (Land Disputes Settlements) Act 2002 (No 2 of 2002); and the Land (Amendment) Act 2004 (No 2 of 2004).

[11]   See Thirteenth Constitutional Amendment Act 2000 (No 3 of 2000); Commission for Human Rights and Good Governance Act 2001 (No 7 of 2001); and Commission for Human Rights and Good Governance (Amendment) Act 2001 (No 16 of 2001). See also the Basic Rights and Duties Enforcement Act 1994 (No 33 of 1994). For comments on Acts No 33 of 1994 and No 7 of 2001 see C K Mtaki 'The Quest for Rule of Law in a Free Market Economy: The Tanzania Experience' (2002) *Recht in Afrika* 165–182 at 175–177; and Chris Maina Peter (1998) (note 3 above) at 54–55.

[12]   The Commercial Division of the High Court was established in 1999 by Government Notice (GN) No 141 of 1999, amending the High Court Registry Rules 1984 (GN No 23 of 1984) by s 5A. It was set up as a specialised commercial court to improve the efficacy of commercial dispute resolution in Tanzania. The Land Division of the High Court was established in 2002 under s 3 of the Courts (Land Disputes Settlements) Act 2002 and is vested with jurisdiction in land matters by s 167 of the Land Act 1999, s 62 of the Village Land Act 1999 and ss 37 and 38 of the Courts (Land Disputes Settlements) Act 2002.

2 PROTECTING THE PROPERTY RIGHTS OF DIVORCED WIVES AND WIDOWS

During the period under review courts have decided several cases which, for convenience, are discussed under the sub-title of judicial protection of the property rights of divorced wives and widows. There are three features common to these cases. The first feature is that although all levels of courts in Tanzania are bound to apply the same law in relation to division of matrimonial assets on divorce or separation, there is a significant difference between the approach taken by the lower courts and that taken by the High Court and Court of Appeal.[13] Such difference of approach is more noticeable in probate and administration cases where rules as to choice of law are somewhat uncertain and therefore provide room for dispute and manipulation by litigants.[14]

The second feature is that the majority of appellants in these cases are women who are aggrieved by the orders of the lower courts on division of matrimonial assets. [15] In probate and administration cases widows' grievances relate to the appointment of the administrator of the deceased's intestate estate.[16] The most frequent grievance relates to widows who are unhappy about their exclusion from a share of their deceased husband's estate.[17] The third and final feature, and this is clearly a new trend, is the way in which the High Court and the Court of Appeal have consistently relied on the Tanzania Bill of Rights as well as on international human rights instruments and the general human rights norms to support their decisions.[18] As the cases below show, there is an emerging jurisprudence in the superior courts of Tanzania which is described in this *Survey* as the constitutionalisation of Tanzania family law.

2.1 Division of property on marriage breakdown

The High Court decision in *Mwajuma Mohamed Njopeka v Juma Said Mkorogoro*[19] ('*Mwajuma*') contains all the three elements noted above. The parties married in 1989 in accordance with Islamic rites. The couple lived together until 1998 when the husband, Juma Mkorogoro, purported to divorce his wife by issuing her the Islamic *talaq*. The wife in turn applied for

---

13 Eg *Mwajuma* (note 19 below); *Paul Msilu v Rahema Chiponde*, Dar es Salaam High Court (PC) Civil Appeal No. 12 of 2000 (per Manento J, 28.3.2001, unreported); *Latifa* (note 83 below).

14 Eg *Elizabeth Mtawa* (note 34 below).

15 Eg *Mwajuma* (note 19 below); *Crencensia Raphael Ulomi v Lucas Osmund Mwalonga*, Dar es Salaam High Court Civil Appeal No 12 of 2000 (per Kimaro J, 3.4. 2001, unreported); *Stella Arbogast v Charles John Mwankenja*, Mwanza High Court Matrimonial Civil Appeal No 2 of 2000 (per Nchalla J, 22.10.2002, unreported).

16 Eg *Sekunda Mbwambo v Rose Ramadhani*, Moshi High Court (PC) Civil Appeal No 11 of 2002 (per Rutakangwa J, 23.2.2004, unreported); *Latifa* (note 83 below).

17 Eg *Elizabeth Mtawa* (note 34 below); *In the Matter of an Intended Appeal between Hawa Mgelwa v Hassan Nsubuga*, Court of Appeal Civil Application No 31 of 2003 (per Mroso JA, 10.6.2003, unreported).

18 Eg *Mwajuma* (note 19 below); *Elizabeth Mtawa* (note 34 below); *Marandu* (note 53 below).

19 Dar es Salaam High Court (PC) Civil Appeal No 6 of 2001 (per Kimaro J, 13.7.2001, unreported).

judicial divorce at a local primary court and further claimed division of matrimonial assets consisting of the couple's two houses. The parties had no children. The Primary Court granted divorce and ordered the husband to pay the petitioner Tshs 500,000.[20] The wife appealed to the District Court stating that the award of Tshs 500,000 was inadequate as it did not reflect her contribution during the 9 years of marriage.

When the District Court dismissed the wife's appeal (on account of insufficient grounds), she appealed again to the High Court. In a well-reasoned judgment, the appellate judge, Kimaro J, upheld the decree of divorce granted by the lower court, set aside the orders of the two lower courts awarding the wife Tshs 500,000, and further held that the wife was entitled to one of the two houses being her share of the matrimonial assets. The husband was allowed to keep the other house. Both parties appeared in person throughout the entire litigation.

What marks this case out from previous cases on division of family assets is the way the appellate judge used the Tanzania Bill of Rights as well as international human rights norms to decide this appeal. The judge first outlined the legal principles which she deemed to be applicable. She cited art 13(1) of the Tanzania Constitution of 1977 (as amended)[21] which provides for equality before the law and equal protection of the law. Next the judge referred to the fundamental objectives and directive principles of state policy contained in Part II of the Tanzania Constitution. In particular, the judge cited art 9(f) which requires 'state authority and all its agencies ... to direct their policies and programmes towards ensuring that human dignity is preserved and upheld in accordance with the spirit of the Universal Declaration of Human Rights'.[22]

Finally the appellate judge cited the United Nations Convention on the Elimination of All Forms of Discrimination Against Women ('CEDAW')[23] which Tanzania ratified on 17 July 1980 and stressed in particular the provisions of art 2 which require states parties to 'condemn discrimination against women in all its forms [and] to pursue by all appropriate means and without delay a policy of eliminating discrimination against women ...'. Article 2(a) of CEDAW requires states parties to 'embody the principle of equality of men and women in their national constitutions or other appropriate legislation ... and to ensure, through law and other appropriate means, the practical realization of this principle'.

Having built up such an awesome arsenal of applicable law, the appellate judge proceeded to apply it to the case. She reasoned that the decisions of the

---

[20]   This sum had been offered by the husband as a 'parting gift' in accordance with Islamic practices. However, the husband had reneged on this promise which partly accounts for the wife's decision to take the matter to court. The exchange rate (as at June 2005) is 1,120 Tanzania shillings to one US dollar.

[21]   See art 13(5) of the Tanzania Constitution, as amended by the Thirteenth Constitutional Amendment Act 2000 (No 3 of 2000), which specifically prohibits gender discrimination.

[22]   The judge further noted that art 7 of the Universal Declaration of Human Rights was similar to art 13(1) of the Tanzania Constitution.

[23]   Of 18 December 1979 (GAOR 34th Sess, Res 180; UNTS Vol 1249, p 13).

two lower courts contravened the appellant's right to the equal protection of the law. According to s 114 of LMA the court, when granting divorce or judicial separation, has power 'to order the division between the parties of any assets acquired by them during the marriage by their joint efforts'. In 1983 the Tanzania Court of Appeal held that domestic services, including childcare, constituted a contribution towards the acquisition of matrimonial assets within the meaning of s 114 of LMA.[24] In the instant case, the appellate judge held that the lower courts had failed to apply properly s 114 of LMA because they allowed the former husband to keep the two houses acquired during the subsistence of the marriage. They had thus not given due weight to the contribution of the appellant for 9 years and this had resulted in leaving the appellant without shelter. Moreover, according to the appellate judge the lower courts' decision was discriminatory and in contravention of art 13(1) of the Tanzania Constitution. It did not 'put into consideration the right to equal protection [of] and [equality] before the law'.

In her conclusion Kimaro J reminded the lower courts always to abide by their judicial oath which requires them to 'protect the Constitution and to do justice without fear or favour'. The implication of this timely admonition from the High Court is that judicial officers at all levels of courts are expected to be guided by the state Constitution as well as the spirit of international human rights norms, where applicable, even if parties or their legal representatives do not specifically plead or seek to rely on those provisions. Similar judicial thinking is evident in claims by widows to a share of their late husband's estate. It is to these cases that this *Survey* will now turn.

2.2 Protection of widows' property rights

The death of a husband in many communities in Tanzania triggers what has become known in sub-Saharan Africa as 'property grabbing' committed mostly by the relatives of the deceased husband.[25] Whether such 'grabbing' takes the literal form or is launched through the clan leadership, it will invariably lead to the widow (and sometimes her minor children) losing her property to some clan members. This is the context in which widows are driven to the courts to seek redress.

The common features to these court disputes include the lack of a testament to speak after the husband's death. The absence of a will often leads to disputes as to the law applicable. The deceased man's clan members tend to

---

[24] See *Bi Hawa Mohamed v Ally Sefu* [1983] TLR 32 (per Nyalali CJ, Makame and Kisanga JJA); also reproduced in Chris Maina Peter (1997) (note 3 above) at 398–407.

[25] See Chuma Himonga 'Protecting the Minor Child's Inheritance Rights' in A Bainham (ed) *The International Survey of Family Law 2001 Edition* (Jordans, Bristol, 2001) pp 457–473; and Bart Rwezaura '"This is not my Child": The Task of Integrating Orphans into the Mainstream of Society in Tanzania' in A Bainham (ed) *The International Survey of Family Law 2001 Edition*, (Jordans, Bristol, 2001) pp 411–435. In *Ndewawiosia d/o Ndeamtizo v Imanuel Malasi* (1968) HCD 127 Saidi J held, *inter alia*: 'The age of discrimination based on sex is long gone and the world is now in the stage of full equality of all human beings irrespective of their sex, creed, race or colour.'

prefer the application of customary law of succession which is more favourable to them.[26] Where the deceased is a Muslim, similar disputes will emerge, with some relatives seeking the application of customary law while others, Islamic law.[27] And where the deceased is a Christian who has worked and resided outside his home village and possibly married from outside his ethnic group, there will be a dispute as to whether customary law or the general law of succession applies to the administration of his intestate estate.[28] Where the widow was not formally married to the deceased, the deceased's relatives will challenge her married status including the status of her children born in that relationship.[29]

It has been noted above that Tanzanian law of succession is widely acknowledged to be pluralistic, complex and highly unsatisfactory. It is also out of date compared with the law of marriage and divorce which was reformed in 1971. This situation has led judges to improvise by applying the principles of property division on divorce to intestate succession, arguing that it was 'inequitable to dispossess a widow of almost all her husband's

---

[26] According to s 11(1) of the Judicature and Application of Laws Act (Cap 358, Laws of Tanzania, Revised Edition 2002):

> 'Customary law shall be applicable to, and courts shall exercise their jurisdiction in accordance therewith, in matters of a civil nature (a) between members of a community in which rules of customary law relevant to the matter are established and accepted ... (b) relating to any matter of status of, or succession to, a person who is or was a member of a community in which rules of customary law relevant to the matter are established and accepted ... except in any case where it is apparent, from the nature of any relevant act or transaction, manner of life or business, that the matter is or was to be regulated otherwise than by customary law ...'

> For the customary law of succession of the majority of the patrilineal communities in Tanzania see *Sheria ya Urithi*, Local Customary Law (Declaration) (No 4) Order, 2nd Schedule, GN No 436 of 1963; *Sheria za Wosia*, Local Customary Law (Declaration) (No 4) Order, 3rd Schedule, GN No 436 of 1963; *Sheria Zinazohusu Hali ya Watu*, Local Customary Law (Declaration) Order, GN No 279 of 1963, esp rule 77.

[27] Section 11(1)(ii) of the Judicature and Application of Laws Act states that 'nothing in this subsection shall preclude any court from applying the rules of Islamic law in matters of marriage, divorce, guardianship, inheritance, *wakf* and similar matters in relation to members of a community which follows that law'. Section 11(4) of the same Act provides however that '[n]otwithstanding the provisions of this Act, the rules of customary law and the rules of Islamic law shall not apply in regard to any matter provided for in the Law of Marriage Act'. On Islamic law in Tanzania see: J N D Anderson *Islamic Law in Africa* (Frank Cass, London, 1970) pp 122–147; Robert V Makaramba 'The Status and Application of Islamic Law in Tanzania' (1991) *Eastern Africa Law Review* 18, at 277–310, on the law of succession at 294–299; Ibrahim Juma 'Unsystematic Growth of Islamic Jurisprudence in Tanzania – An Overview' (2004) *Recht in Afrika*, 177–193. According to M K Rwebangira and M C Mukoyogo (eds), there are fixed and unfixed shares of inheritance which are gender based and according to which widows are entitled to one eighth of the total estate of the deceased husband irrespective of their number or contribution, see *id*, *The Law of Inheritance in Tanzania* (Women and Law in East Africa, Nairobi, 1995) at 17.

[28] Section 11(2) of the of the Judicature and Application of Laws Act provides that '[i]t is hereby declared for the avoidance of doubt that ... (b) a person may cease to be a member of a community by reason of his adoption of the way of life of some other community (whether or not any customary law is established or accepted in such other community) ...'. See M K Rwebangira and M C Mukoyogo (note 27 above) at 12–15 both on 'the mode of life' test (noted above) and 'the intention of the deceased' test applicable in the cases of Muslims under s 19(1)(a) of the Administration (Small Estates) Ordinance, Cap 30.

[29] See *Elizabeth Mtawa* (note 34 below).

property, which the spouses obtained through their joint efforts, simply because the marriage had ended as a result of the husband's death instead of divorce'.[30] That sense of injustice felt by some judges has now found a robust remedy in the form of the Bill of Rights and international human rights norms. It is within the above context that the following cases must be located.

In the Matter of the late Rabiuzima Matiro Mboro and in the Matter of an Application for Letters of Administration by Adeline Rabiuzima[31] (*'Rabiuz-ima'*) the widow applied to the High Court, seeking to be appointed the administrator of her deceased husband's intestate estate. Her application was opposed by the deceased husband's brother on the ground that he was the one appointed by the clan to act as the administrator.[32] The clan had previously decided to disinherit the widow and her two sons on the erroneous ground that they had murdered the deceased. One of the issues before the High Court was whether the clan had acted lawfully in disinheriting the deceased's widow and her two sons. Justice Mchome held that the clan's decision to disinherit the widow was illegal because it was made in her absence. According to Mchome J, the clan's decision, which condemned the widow unheard, had contravened the rules of natural justice and could not stand. The judge further held that the clan had also acted illegally in purporting to disinherit the widow and her two sons based on the erroneous ground that they had murdered the deceased husband. The judge noted that the sons had been acquitted and their mother, the widow, had never been charged with the murder of her husband. In his final judgment Justice Mchome held that the widow, rather than the deceased husband's brother, was the person entitled to be appointed administrator. The judge also held that both the widow and her two sons were entitled to inherit from the deceased's estate, adding that the widow was in fact 'a co-owner of the matrimonial property which is the deceased's estate'.[33]

Justice Mchome's final observation is very significant because it establishes a principle that *prima facie* the widow has separate and independent ownership rights or entitlement in her husband's estate which do not depend

---

[30] See *Asha Mbulayambele v William Shibungi*, High Court Civil Appeal No 56 of 1986 (per Chipeta J, 13.6.1988, unreported); and Bart Rwezaura (note 4 above) at 533.

[31] Moshi High Court Probate and Administration Cause No 2 of 1998 (per Mchome J, 17.10.2001, unreported).

[32] In *Sekunda Mbwambo v Rose Ramadhani*, Moshi High Court (PC) Civil Appeal No 11 of 2002 (per Rutakangwa J, 23.2.2004, unreported), the judge quotes at length, and commends the District Court magistrate's excellent grasp and explanation of the role of the administrator of the estate who may be selected from amongst the beneficiaries of the estate, but who has to be very careful and impartial in the way he/she distributes the estate. Such an administrator must have been close to the deceased to be able to identify easily the deceased's properties and must have the confidence of all the beneficiaries or dependants of the deceased. The administrator is obliged to collect all the properties of the deceased, pay his/her debts, ensure that the children whom the deceased left behind and other dependants of the deceased are properly taken care of, and distribute fairly the properties forming the estate to the beneficiaries. It is evident that the administrator is not supposed to use the deceased's properties as his/her own or dissipate them as he/she wishes.

[33] At p 7 of the judgment.

on the provisions of the deceased's will nor on the good will of the deceased husband's clan.

The principle that a widow has separate and independent property rights in the estate of the deceased husband was endorsed and further elaborated upon by another High Court judge in *Elizabeth Mtawa v Hassan Mfaume Risasi*[34] ('*Elizabeth Mtawa*'). In this case the appellant, a widow, appealed against the decision of the District Court which set aside the trial Primary Court's order permitting her to continue to reside in the matrimonial home, until her death or remarriage, as provided in r 77 (3) of the Local Customary Law (Declaration) Order (GN No 279/1963). Upon reviewing the provisions of r 77,[35] Justice Kileo noted that r 77(3) and (4) did not provide for the 'possibility of a married woman asserting ownership rights over real property [as] she is given only usufruct rights'. This, according to the judge, discriminated against the woman on the basis of her sex and thus contravened arts 2 and 17 of the Universal Declaration of Human Rights[36] and the Tanzania Constitution.[37] It was also contrary to s 3(2) of the Land Act 1999 which provides that every woman has legal capacity to acquire, hold, use and deal with land to the same extent and subject to the same restrictions as any man.[38]

The appellate judge then noted that 'women contribute a lot to matrimonial assets though their contribution most often is not easily ascertainable in monetary terms'.[39] But according to the landmark case of *Bi Hawa Mohamed v Ally Sefu*,[40] such non-monetary contributions have been held by the Court of Appeal, in the context of divorce, to amount to contribution to

---

[34]   Dodoma High Court Civil Appeal No 12 of 2001 (per Kileo J, n d, unreported).

[35]   An English translation (from Kiswahili) of r 77 of GN 279/1963 states that:

> '(1) All movable and immovable properties which were acquired during the subsistence of the marriage shall be divided into two equal shares after paying all debts of the deceased. The widow shall get 1/20 of one half for each year of marriage. For the immovable property the widow shall get a portion of land in the same proportion and she shall have the right to use the land in a diligent manner all the time until her remarriage or her death. (2) In the case of permanent crops she shall get her share in the same proportion and may get its interest till she remarries or dies. (3) The widow should be allowed to stay in the house till she remarries or dies. (4) All immovable property shall revert to the deceased's relatives immediately upon the widow's remarriage.'

[36]   Article 2 of the Universal Declaration of Human Rights of 10 December 1948 (GAOR 3rd Sess, Res 217 A) reads:

> 'Everyone is entitled to all the rights and freedoms set forth in this Declaration, without distinction of any kind, such as race, colour, sex, language, religion, political or other opinion, national or social origin, property, birth or other status ...'

> Article 17 of the same Declaration states:

> '(1) Everyone has the right to own property alone as well as in association with others. (2) No one shall be arbitrarily deprived of his property.'

[37]   See art 13(5) of the Tanzania Constitution, as amended (see note 21 above), which expressly prohibits gender discrimination.

[38]   At p 8 of the judgment. Section 3(2) of the Land Act 1999 provides:

> 'The right of every woman to acquire, hold, use, and deal with land shall to the same extent and subject to the same restrictions be treated as a right of any man.'

[39]   At p 9 of the judgment.

[40]   See note 24 above.

the welfare of the family thus entitling a wife to a share in the matrimonial assets on divorce. Relying on the above case Justice Kileo reasoned that although *Bi Hawa* concerned division of matrimonial assets on divorce, the principle in that case is also relevant 'when considering distribution of a deceased's estate where he is survived by a widow'.[41] According to the appellate judge, it was unjust for a rule of customary law to make provision that the widow was entitled only to a specific portion of the property in the estate for each year of marriage 'without first ascertaining her contribution and setting it aside because obviously her contribution cannot be said to form part of the estate of her deceased husband'.[42] Stressing the same point the judge concluded that it was wrong to mix the widow's contribution 'with the estate because by so doing it amounts to saying that she has no right to own property alone'.[43]

Based on the above two cases it is clear that judges have raised the legal status of the widow beyond anything customary law would have contemplated. Now the widow has a higher claim in her late husband's intestate estate than the clan members. She now owns part of the estate which must be ascertained first and set aside before the distribution of the deceased's estate can begin.[44] *Elizabeth Mtawa* is also important in that it struck down the entire r 77 of GN 279 as being discriminatory on the ground that it treats a man and woman differently, prescribing and limiting the property rights of a widow but not that of a widower. Rule 77 was also judged as contravening the widow's right to privacy, home and family life under art 16(1) of the Constitution of Tanzania.[45] According to Justice Kimaro, r 77 requires the widow to stay unmarried and not cohabit with any man as a condition for continuing to reside in the matrimonial home. Finally, the appellate judge made orders that Elizabeth was entitled to a half share of the disputed matrimonial home 'by virtue of her contribution to the welfare of the family'. That half share was not subject to distribution and Elizabeth had the 'right to do with her share as she please[d]'.[46] The judge granted the other half to the children of the deceased.

In concluding this section it is essential to stress that disputes between widows like Elizabeth and her deceased husband's clan over inheritance reflect a deeper and more enduring conflict between, on the one hand, ideas of kinship and patriarchal power encapsulated in some provisions of

---

[41] At p 10 of the judgment. As noted above, the same reasoning was adopted by Chipeta J in *Asha Mbulayambele* (note 30).

[42] The principle that a widow has a separate and independent right to a share in the estate of her deceased husband is considered above (note 33).

[43] At p 9 of the judgment.

[44] This case goes further than the Law Reform Commission which recommended that a 'surviving spouse should be entitled to inherit the immovable property of the deceased, including the matrimonial home, until his or her death at which point such property should revert to the children of the couple or the trustee if the children are minors', see Bart Rwezaura (note 2 above) at 433.

[45] Article 16(1) of the Constitution states:

'Every person is entitled to respect and protection of his person, the privacy of his own person, his family and of his matrimonial life, and respect and protection of his residence and private communications.'

[46] At p 12 of the judgment.

customary law such as r 77. On the other hand, there are emerging values expressed in concepts such as the nuclear family and ideas about individual autonomy which see the Tanzania Bill of Rights and international human rights norms as a source of support and political legitimacy. This wider theme is also expressed in the burial cases to which this *Survey* now turns.

3 WHO IS TO BURY THE DEAD: NEW SITE FOR OLD CONFLICT?

On 29 December 1986, 9 days after the death of her husband, a Kenyan widow, Virginia Edith Wambui Otieno, supported by her two adult sons, went to court to demand her right to determine where to bury the remains of her deceased husband. Virginia was a member of the politically powerful Kikuyu ethnic group while her late husband, a prominent legal practitioner in Nairobi, was from the equally powerful Luo ethnic group. The application was strongly opposed by the deceased's clan which demanded the right to bury Otieno's remains in his home village alongside his ancestors. The High Court held that both the widow and the Luo clan had a right to bury the remains of Otieno and further ordered that the body be buried in the village of Otieno's ancestry. Virginia's appeal to the Court of Appeal was dismissed on 15 May 1987, nearly 6 months after Otieno's death.[47]

It will be recalled that *Otieno* sparked off several political controversies within the Kenyan society and beyond.[48] Some observers argued that the case represented a clash between two famous ethnic groups. [49] Others believed the real clash was between tradition and change, with change represented by the English common law and tradition by African customary law.[50] Still others considered *Otieno* to have provided an excuse for airing the women's rights issues.[51] In this section three cases from Tanzania are discussed. It must be noted at the outset that despite their lack of *Otieno's*

---

[47] *Virginia Edith Wambui Otieno v Joash Ochieng Ougo and Omolo Siranga*, Kenya Court of Appeal Civil Appeal No 31 of 1987 [1982–88] 1 KAR 1060 (per Nyarangi, Platt and Gachuhi JJA, 13.2.1987); also reproduced in: Eugene Cotran (ed) *Casebook on Kenya Customary Law* (Professional Books Limited and Nairobi University Press, Nairobi, 1987) pp 331–345 ('*Otieno*').

[48] See eg Sean Egan (ed) *S.M. Otieno. Kenya's Unique Burial Saga* (Nation Newspapers, Nairobi, 1987).

[49] See Paul Tiyambe Zeleza, a review of: David William Cohen and E S Atieno-Odhiambo *Burying S.M.: The Politics of Knowledge and the Sociology of Power in Africa* (Heinemann, Portsmouth, New Hampshire, 1992) in *CJAS/RCEA* 29 (1995), 139–141; see also Patricia Stamp 'Burying Otieno: The Politics of Gender and Ethnicity in Kenya' (1991) *Signs: Journal of Women in Culture and Society* 16, 807–845 at 835–840.

[50] J B Ojwang and J N K Mugambi (eds) *The S.M. Otieno Case. Death and Burial in Modern Kenya* (Nairobi University Press, Nairobi, 1989); John W van Doren 'Death African Style: The Case of S.M. Otieno' (1988) *American Journal of Comparative Law* 36, 329–350; Ralph Schumann 'Interne Kollisionsnorm und traditionelles Recht im Spannungsfeld kulturellen Wandels: "The Case" S.M. Otieno' (1991) *Verfassung und Recht in Übersee* 24, 245–270.

[51] Marsha A Freeman 'Measuring Equality: A Comparative Perspective on Women's Legal Capacity and Constitutional Rights in Five Commonwealth Countries' (1989–90) *Berkeley Women's Law Journal* 5, 110–138 at 121; Patricia Stamp (above note 49) at 807–845.

dramatic grip, they also raise similar legal issues and are driven by comparable social forces.

3.1 Marandu

The case of *Cecilia Dismas Marandu; Thomas Sawaki Marandu (Chairman, Marandu Clan) v Lucresia Donasian Marandu*[52] (*'Marandu'*) is to some extent Tanzania's *Otieno*.[53] However, unlike *Otieno*, the *Marandu* decision was decided by a lower court and took a shorter time to decide.[54] Furthermore, the trial court in *Marandu* rejected the reasoning in *Otieno* on the ground that society had moved on since *Otieno* and it was no longer the case that 'a woman should sit by and wait for men to decide on what to do with her husband's body'.[55]

The main question in *Marandu* was who of the two disputing parties had a right to bury the remains of Donasian Dismas Marandu who died on 19 July 2003. The widow Lucresia, supported by her children, wanted her husband's remains to be buried at Katanini Karanga near Moshi town where the family had settled. The Marandu clan, supported by the deceased's mother, Cecilia Marandu, argued the opposite case that the only burial place for the deceased had to be his ancestral home at Keryo village in Rombo District, Kilimanjaro.

The case for the clan can be summed up as primarily grounded in the patrilineal customs and traditions of the Marandu clan supported by a mild form of ancestor worship. As the magistrate noted in her judgment, the case for the Marandu clan was mounted on three pillars, namely, that (i) the deceased was the heir to the ancestral land; (ii) his umbilical cord was buried at the ancestral land; (iii) he was still a traditional Marandu; and therefore, it was mandatory under the deceased's 'tribal' customs for his remains to be buried at his ancestral home 'where his grave shall also be a shrine for his mother Cecilia'.[56]

The case for the widow began by challenging the clan's assertion that the deceased was still a traditional Marandu. She stated that the deceased was a Catholic who had broken away from traditional beliefs, customs and norms. Then she argued that the deceased was not the first male child of the family.[57] And even if he was obliged to have his remains buried there by

---

52   Moshi District Court Civil Case No 33 of 2003 (per Kitusi RM, 10.10.2003, unreported).

53   This was one of the arguments made by Counsel for the Marandu clan who urged the court to follow *Otieno* because Tanzania did not have a case on the point.

54   The judgment was given on 10 October 2003, that is, less than 3 months after the deceased's death.

55   At p 14 of the judgment.

56   At p 4 of the judgment. In case of contravention, it is feared that the Marandu clan could be haunted by their ancestral spirits and its members might become mentally ill from the curse of the ancestors.

57   It was further submitted that if there was a custom which binds first male children to be buried on their ancestral land, such custom was discriminatory and inconsistent because it discriminated against male children who were not the eldest and was not applied to all the eldest children. The question of unfair discrimination between male and female children within the same family is discussed in *Bhe & Others v The Magistrate, Khayelitsha and Others; Shibi v Sithole & Others;*

reason of inheriting the ancestral land, the deceased had a right to change his mind which he had exercised during his lifetime by expressing the wish to be buried at Katanini. The widow informed the court that before her father-in-law died, he had instructed that her husband should change his permanent place of abode and stay permanently at Katanini. As the magistrate noted, Lucresia's case was 'that she wants to bury her husband at Katanini in fulfilment of his expressed wish and in fulfilment of her father-in-law's instruction'.[58]

Having heard the parties the magistrate framed the issues for decision and proceeded as follows. First, the court considered whether the deceased had a right to decide where his remains should be buried upon his death and held that he had such right. The question whether the deceased had expressed the wish to have his remains buried in a place other than his ancestral home was answered by the court in the affirmative. The court held that the deceased had communicated that wish to his family and overruled the submission by counsel for the clan that the testimony of the widow and her daughter required to be corroborated. The magistrate noted that there was 'no justification for subjecting to external test matters which a man decides to tell his wife and children in exclusion of his brothers'.[59]

Next the court considered whether the deceased was still bound by the local customary law of his clan and held that he was not. The resident magistrate rejected the submission by counsel that the court should follow *Otieno* where it was held that the deceased's remains should be buried in his ancestral home on the ground that he had not abandoned his traditions despite having worked and lived in Nairobi. The court preferred the submission of counsel for the widow to the effect that the deceased's belief as a Catholic was such that it left no room for other beliefs. The magistrate agreed that there was sufficient evidence to show that the deceased 'had gone so deep into Christianity that he was considering himself capable of healing the sick through prayers'.[60]

The final issue, and arguably the more interesting, was whether or not the local customary law of the Marandu clan concerning burial was discriminatory and therefore in breach of the Constitution of Tanzania including major international human rights treaties to which Tanzania was a party. Counsel for the clan argued that according to Keryo's customs 'it was

---

South African Human Rights Commission and Another v President of the Republic of South Africa & Another, Constitutional Court of South Africa, Cases CCT 49/03, 69/03, 50/03 (15.10.2004), www.concourt.gov.za. In this case the Constitutional Court of South Africa declared that the rule of male primogeniture under customary law was unconstitutional and invalid because it discriminated unfairly against women and illegitimate children. According to Langa DCJ, the effect of changing circumstances was that the 'customary law rules of succession [nowadays] simply determine succession to the deceased's estate without the accompanying social implications which they traditionally had' (at para 80 of the judgment). The court, however, did not have to determine the question of unfair discrimination of younger male children, as implied in the rule of male primogeniture (para 94 of the judgment).

58   At p 7 of the judgment.
59   At p 14 of the judgment.
60   At p 14 of the judgment.

unthinkable for a woman to arrange burials [or] make decisions regarding where to bury' and therefore again urged the court to follow *Otieno*.

Counsel for the widow responded with an impressive array of authorities beginning with art 13(4) of the Constitution of Tanzania which prohibits discrimination on the ground of sex.[61] He followed this up with reference to art 7 of the Universal Declaration of Human Rights;[62] art 26 of the International Covenant on Civil and Political Rights;[63] art 2 of CEDAW;[64] and s 68 of LMA.[65] He also cited three decisions of the High Court in which it has been held that discrimination based on sex was prohibited by the Constitution of Tanzania and major international human rights treaties and instruments.[66]

After commending counsel for his 'research and able submissions' the magistrate considered the above authorities and their relevance to the issue of discrimination on the ground of sex. She proceeded to dismiss the application by the Marandu clan holding that it was 'based on principles which are forbidden by the law' and could not be granted.[67] That ruling effectively cleared the way for Lucresia and her children to arrange the burial of her deceased husband at their home in Katanini. Before concluding this part, two more cases are discussed. In the first case the magistrate decided to follow *Otieno*. In the second it was the surviving husband rather than the widow who claimed the right to bury the remains of his deceased wife.

---

[61] See note 21 above.

[62] Article 7 of the said Declaration states that all human beings 'are equal before the law and are entitled without any discrimination to equal protection of the law. All are entitled to equal protection against any discrimination in violation of this Declaration and against any incitement to such discrimination.'

[63] Of 16 December 1966 (GAOR 21st Sess, Res 2200 A; UNTS Vol 999, p 171). Article 26 states that:

> 'All persons are equal before the law and are entitled without any discrimination to equal protection of the law. In this respect, the law shall prohibit any discrimination and guarantee to all persons equal and effective protection against discrimination on any ground such as race, colour, sex, language, religion, political or other opinion, national or social origin, property, birth or other status.'

[64] Article 2 of CEDAW states that:

> 'States Parties condemn discrimination against women in all its forms, agree to pursue by all appropriate means and without delay a policy of eliminating discrimination against women ...'

[65] Section 68 of LMA states that:

> 'Notwithstanding any custom to the contrary, a woman whose husband has died shall be free – (a) to reside wherever she may please; and (b) to remain unmarried or, subject to the provisions of s 17, to marry again any man of her own choosing ...'

[66] *Ndewawiosia* (note 25 above); *David Deogratias Makene & William Mugurusi v Jonia Makene* Dar es Salaam High Court Civil Case No 341 of 1999 (per Kimaro J); *Elizabeth Mtawa* (note 34 above).

[67] At p 16 of the judgment.

3.2 Ayugi and Nevele

In *Joseph Odungo Elijah Ayugi, Samson Nondo and Peter Lanya v Esterziah Ayugi*[68] (*'Ayugi'*) three relatives of the late Elijah Yongo Ayugi applied to the court of the resident magistrate seeking a declaratory order that the applicants have an overriding right to bury the deceased in his home village of Buturi in Tarime District, Mara Region. The widow, Esterziah Ayugi, and her four children opposed the application. They urged the court to allow them to bury the remains of the deceased at his new home in Dar es Salaam, in accordance with Christian rites. Having decided that the Magistrate's Court had jurisdiction to hear the dispute,[69] the court held in favour of the Ayugi clan and ordered that the body of the deceased be handed over to the applicants 'to be taken for burial at his home village'. The court noted that the deceased had left no will instructing his family as to where he should be interred after his demise. Furthermore, no one, not even the wife, had informed the court as to where the deceased wanted to be buried. In the circumstances, the court opted to follow *Otieno* which decision the magistrate found to be persuasive.

A notable aspect of this case is that although its facts are comparable with the facts in *Marandu*, and the parties in this case were also legally represented, one does not see much vigour and enthusiasm in the manner the case was argued. One possible reason for this low-key approach is that the respondent widow was still ill and remained in hospital recovering from injuries suffered in the same motor accident that had claimed her husband's life. Moreover, the four children who supported their mother remained in the US where they were studying.

In contrast to *Ayugi* above is the case of *Anjelina Samira, Beatus Nevele and John Samila v Abdul Salum and Director of Muhimbili Medical Centre*[70] (*'Nevele'*) which, coincidentally, was also decided by the same Dar es Salaam Resident Magistrate's Court by a different magistrate. The mother of the deceased and two paternal uncles of the deceased acted as plaintiffs. The defendants were Abdul Salum, the deceased's husband, and the Director of Muhimbili Medical Centre, where the deceased's body was preserved after her death on 29 November 2003 at 32 years of age. All the parties were legally represented.

---

[68]	Dar es Salaam Resident Magistrate's Court (Kisutu) Misc Cause No 205 of 2002 (per Magere RM, 16.12.2002, unreported).

[69]	Counsel for the respondent raised a preliminary objection grounded in the court's lack of jurisdiction and the law applicable. The resident magistrate in overruling the objection correctly pointed out that the line between customary law and the written law could not be drawn sharply and that in any case the courts were mandated to decide all such cases according to substantial justice without undue regard to legal technicalities and without undue delay. The court's ruling is based on s 95 of the Civil Procedure Code 1966 (No 49 of 1966) ('CPC'), cited by Counsel for the applicants. It provides that '[n]othing in this Code shall be deemed to limit or otherwise affect the inherent power of the court to make such orders as may be necessary for the ends of justice or to prevent abuse of the process of the court'. The CPC is applicable to proceedings in the courts of a resident magistrate by virtue of s 2 of CPC.

[70]	Dar es Salaam Resident Magistrate's Court (Kisutu) Civil Case No 427 of 2003 (per Mgetta SRM, 27.01.2004, unreported).

Four main issues were identified for decision as follows:

(i) whether the deceased, Stella Modestus Nevele alias Mariam Modestus Nevele, had converted from Christianity to Islam;

(ii) whether the change of religion had the effect of alienating the deceased from her paternal relatives;

(iii) whether the deceased contracted a valid marriage with the first defendant, Abdul Salum; and finally

(iv) whether by reason of the deceased's marriage, the plaintiffs had lost their right to bury the deceased's body.

The court considered each of the four issues and held first that there was sufficient evidence that the deceased had converted from Christianity to Islam on 15 November 2001. The court noted that the deceased being an adult of sound mind had a constitutional right to change her religion without the consent of her parents or guardians.[71] The magistrate referred to art 19(1) of the Constitution of Tanzania which guarantees freedom of thought including the right to change one's religion and concluded that the deceased had correctly exercised her constitutional right.[72]

The court then considered the second issue and concluded that there was insufficient evidence to show that the change of religion had alienated the deceased from her kinship group. As for the third question concerning the validity of the deceased's marriage to the defendant Abdul Salum, the court considered this issue at length and held that a valid marriage had been contracted in accordance with s 25(3)(a) of LMA. This provision recognises marriages in accordance with Islamic rites.[73] The court also held in relation to the final issue that the marriage of the deceased had not taken away the right of the deceased's relatives to bury her body in the event of her death. However, according to the magistrate, since the deceased had converted to Islam, it was proper that her remains be buried in accordance with Islamic rites and further that since the deceased had married a Moslem in accordance with Islamic rites, her husband's right to bury the deceased took priority over that of the plaintiffs. The court entered judgment in favour of the defendants with costs.

The significance of *Nevele* is that it stresses that an adult, irrespective of gender, has a constitutional right to change his or her religion without the intervention of the kinship group or wider family.[74] *Nevele* is also interesting because the decision as to who has the right to bury the deceased and what

---

71 The deceased was 30 years old when she converted from Christianity to Islam.

72 Article 19(1) of the Constitution provides that 'Every person has the right to the freedom of thought or conscience, belief or faith, and choice in matters of religion, including the freedom to change his religion or faith'.

73 Section 25(1)(c) of LMA provides that 'A marriage may, subject to the provisions of this Act, be contracted in Tanganyika – ... (c) if the intended husband is a Muslim, in civil form or in Islamic form'; and s 25(3)(a) of LMA provides that 'For the purposes of this Act – (a) a marriage in Islamic form means a marriage contracted in the manner recognized by Islam or by any school or sect of that faith'.

74 In other words, an adult woman, whether married or single, has the same legal capacity as men to do anything lawful. See Marsha Freeman (note 51 above).

funeral rites were to be followed was derived not from the deceased's wishes or lack of them, but from the Holy Koran which, according to the court, provides that a man is responsible to protect and guard a woman including conducting a proper burial when she dies.[75] Thus *Nevele* differs from *Marandu* and *Ayugi* which respectively relied on the deceased's express wishes and the absence of such wishes. It should be noted that a submission in *Ayugi* that the deceased's remains should be buried in Dar es Salaam in accordance with Seventh Day Adventist rites was not accepted by the court.

At another level all three burial cases have a number of similarities. They all reveal what some might view as a conflict between tradition and change. In all three cases the deceased lived and worked in the urban centre while also maintaining a home in his respective village of origin. The rural relatives founded their claims on tradition and customs while the deceased's urban-based family argued for the deceased's right to choose where he wanted to be buried except in *Nevele*. In all three cases there were arguments tending to show that the deceased had abandoned tradition in favour of modernity or a new religion. In *Marandu* and *Nevele* there was great reliance on individual liberty, and ideas consistent with the nuclear family. Indeed in *Marandu* the magistrate noted that she understood 'the feeling of senior citizens … and their fear [of] change'.[76] Quoting from an earlier decision where Samatta J (now Chief Justice) quoted Lord Denning, the magistrate stressed the point that '[i]f we never do anything which has never been done before, we shall never get anywhere'.[77]

As this *Survey* has shown many litigants have indeed succeeded in doing what they have never done before. This is true not only in relation to claims by married women to a fair share of the matrimonial assets on divorce or separation, their rights as widows to a separate interest in the estate of their deceased husbands, but also, and ultimately, their right to decide where to bury the remains of their husbands. The fourth section of this *Survey* draws from the above theme to show that new ideas such as equality between children and the concept of best interest of the child have been relied upon either to override existing personal laws (including religious laws) which make contrary provisions or to make up for any gaps where the law has not marched with the changing times. The need to fill in the gaps, as noted above, arises largely because of the delay in the harmonisation and reform of the law relating to children.

4   BEST INTERESTS AND EQUAL PROTECTION OF THE LAW

We discuss in this part two types of cases in which judges have applied the principle of best interests of the child to achieve two main objectives. In the

---

[75]   See pp 21–22 of the judgment.

[76]   At p 14 of the judgment.

[77]   At pp 14–15 of the judgment. In *Mwasegile Samuli v Makanika Katatula* [1980] TLR 152 at 153, Samatta J quoted from Lord Denning's judgment in *Packer v Packer* [1953] 2 All ER 127 at 129.

first group of cases judges have extended the best interests principle to disputes over child custody to children born out of wedlock.[78] In this way, judges have extended equal protection of the law to all children notwithstanding contrary legal provisions which draw a clear distinction between marital and non-marital children.[79] In the second group of cases, the best interest principle has been applied to underline the policy that parental responsibilities may not be delegated to other relatives except under exceptional circumstances.[80] Here again these cases seem to support the ideals of the nuclear family by stressing that the obligation to care for children is placed primarily upon the child's parents.

4.1 The principle of non-discrimination

The law relating to children draws a distinction between children born during wedlock and children born to unmarried parents.[81] One of the effects of the present law is that a father of a child born out of wedlock is free of any legal obligation to maintain his child unless ordered to do so by a court of law under s 5 of the Affiliation Ordinance. This statute, which dates back to the British colonial era, remains in force. Moreover even where the child's parents subsequently marry one another, their marriage does not change the illegitimate status of their child.[82] The law relating to the status of the child has also not been unified such that Islamic law and various customary laws still apply.

The case of *Latifa Lukio Mashayo v Bushiri Hassan*[83] ('*Latifa*') is an example of the poor state of the law and how judges try their best to mitigate

---

[78] *Latifa* (note 83 below); *Hamisi* (note 85 below).

[79] The primary object of the Affiliation Ordinance is 'to provide for the maintenance of children born out of wedlock' (No 42 of 1949, Cap 278 of the Laws of Tanzania), while the object of the LMA, Part VI Matrimonial Proceedings, is to make 'provisions on custody and maintenance of children' under ss 125–137 of the LMA, and to 'regulate the law relating to marriage, personal and property rights as between husband and wife, separation, divorce and other matrimonial reliefs and other matters connected therewith and incidental thereto' (No 5 of 1971).

[80] *Mabagala* (note 89 below). Section 125 of LMA reads:

'(1) The court may, at any time, by order, place an infant in the custody of his or her father or his or her mother, or where there are exceptional circumstances making it undesirable that the infant be entrusted to either parent, of any other relative of the infant or of any association the objects of which include child welfare. (2) In deciding in whose custody an infant child should be placed the paramount consideration shall be the welfare of the infant and, subject to this, the court shall have regard – (a) to the wishes of the parents of the infant; and (b) to the wishes of the infant, where he or she is of an age to express an independent opinion; and (c) to the customs of the community to which the parties belong. (3) There shall be a rebuttable presumption that it is for the good of an infant below the age of seven years to be with his or her mother but in deciding whether that presumption applies to the facts of any particular case, the court shall have regard to the undesirability of disturbing the life of an infant by changes of custody.'

[81] See note 79 above.

[82] Unlike several common law jurisdictions Tanzania does not have a law which provides for legitimation of a child by the subsequent marriage of that child's parents. Such a child may, however, be legitimated under the parties' customary laws but not under Islamic law or the general law.

[83] Arusha High Court Civil Appeal No 25 of 2002 (per Shangwa J, 25.6.2004, unreported).

its negative effect. In this case the couple contracted an Islamic marriage in May 1992. They had previously cohabited and had a daughter before marriage in May 1991. In March 2002 the wife petitioned for divorce including orders for custody and maintenance for their only child. The resident magistrate granted divorce and custody in favour of the mother but refused to order maintenance in favour of the child on the ground that under Islamic law the father had no obligation to maintain a child who was born out of wedlock.

The mother successfully appealed to the High Court where the appellate judge held that it was not proper for the lower court to apply Islamic law in respect of a matter which is supposed to be governed by the LMA. According to Shangwa J, s 129 of LMA imposed a duty upon the father to maintain his child 'whether such child is legitimate or illegitimate [and] even if such child is not under his custody'.[84]

The decision in *Hamisi Shabani v Amina Mohamed*[85] (*'Hamisi'*) concerns an unmarried mother of twins who sued the children's father for their custody and maintenance. The said twins who were about 7 years old were residing with their father at the time. The resident magistrate granted custody to the mother and ordered the father to pay maintenance for the two children. The father appealed to the High Court where Chipeta J set aside the lower court's decision, holding that the father was a much better-suited person to have custody of the two children. In making this order the judge did not follow the rule that a mother has a right to the custody of a non-marital child.[86]

The two cases demonstrate a practice observed in Tanzania over a decade ago when it was reported that judges were applying the principle of best interest of the child contained in s 125 of LMA[87] to all children irrespective of whether they were born in or out of wedlock.[88] At the time it was greatly anticipated that the reforms in the law relating to the child would make such judicial improvisations unnecessary. But with further delay of the said reforms this practice is likely to continue for some years.

4.2 Parents have primary responsibility for children

The principle that parents have primary responsibility for the care and upbringing of their children is contained in s 125 of LMA. Only in exceptional circumstances may a person other than a parent be entrusted with the custody of a child. Although this principle is widely accepted in most western jurisdictions its application in practice can lead to serious

---

84 At p 6 of the judgment. This decision would appear either to make obsolete s 5 of the Affiliation Ordinance or, at least, to offer an alternative remedy. It is also arguable that the Affiliation Ordinance contravenes the anti-discrimination provisions of the Constitution and of several international human rights treaties and instruments. It is probably a matter of time before the courts declare this law unconstitutional and therefore invalid.

85 Dar es Salaam High Court Civil Appeal No 53 of 2000 (per Chipeta J, 17.10.2000, unreported).

86 See rr 178–189 of GN No 279 of 1963 (above note 26).

87 See above note 80.

88 See Bart Rwezaura (above note 4) at 535–536.

difficulties especially for mothers whose economic status is weaker than that of their husbands.

The case of *Rosemary Mabagala v Robert Mabagala and Batuli Yusuf Tupa*[89] ('*Mabagala*') is a recent example of how this principle is applied. In the course of their divorce proceedings at the High Court in Dar es Salaam, the husband filed a chamber summons under a certificate of urgency applying for an interim custody order in respect of two children of the marriage. At the time of the application the two daughters were respectively 7.5 and 8.5 years old, enrolled at a primary school in Dodoma, central Tanzania, and living with their maternal grandparents.

The father informed the court that his wife had left the matrimonial home with the children in April 1998 without his permission, and that she had subsequently 'abandoned the children at her parents' residence at Dodoma without his consent and came to live ... in Dar es Salaam where she is working'.[90] The father wished to have the children back as he was now making arrangements for them to join what he described as one of the best primary schools in the country.[91] He pointed out that he had also recently installed at home modern facilities for the children's education including two training computers and various books.

The wife, who was also legally represented, strongly opposed the chamber summons on the ground that she had left the matrimonial home with the two children because she was frequently assaulted and abused by her husband. She informed the court that the children were well looked after by her parents, adding that her father was a retired High Court judge who understood the importance of education for his grandchildren. She produced the children's academic records showing that both children had scored an average of 90% in their 1999 school assessment. The wife also stated that her husband being a university professor did travel widely attending seminars, workshops and doing research outside his home. That consequently he would not be able personally to look after the children. The wife further informed the court that her husband was currently living with another woman who had moved into the former matrimonial home with her three children by an earlier marriage. She pointed out that if the husband was granted custody there would be a total of five children in the household and she feared her two children would not be properly looked after by their stepmother. Finally, the mother stated that she had now secured a suitable house in Dar es Salaam where she could live with the two children provided that her husband maintained them.

---

[89] Dar es Salaam High Court Matrimonial Cause No 6 of 2000 (per Manento J, 3.1.2001, unreported).

[90] At p 2 of the judgment.

[91] The husband applied for interim custody on the ground that he wanted to have the children transferred to the new school in time for the new academic year beginning on 1 January 2001. He feared that by the time the divorce proceedings were finalised, it would be too late for the children to join the new school. In our opinion such an interim application for custody was misconceived. It should have been rejected because, first, the children's welfare was not at risk and, second, the application, if granted, would have had the effect of pre-empting the final decision on child custody.

After considering the above submissions the trial judge dismissed the mother's objection and held in favour of the children's father. The judge considered the strong economic position of the father, his academic achievements, and the arrangements he had made for the children's education. He contrasted this with the lack of suitable accommodation by the mother which the judge believed was the main reason why the mother preferred the children to stay with their grandparents. The judge noted that 'one can be short-sighted in seeing the two children happily playing with their grandparents, but that is a very temporary life. Their good future is to be built today'.[92] It is clear from the entire judgment that the judge based his decision on s 125 of LMA which provides that a court may grant custody to a person other than the parent 'where there are exceptional circumstances making it undesirable that the infant be entrusted to either parent'. Having referred to the above provisions, the trial judge concluded, noting that while the mother had entrusted the children with their maternal grandparents, the father of the infants was 'able and not only willing to take the children, but has urgently applied for their education ... where he lives and works'.[93]

Although in the end the judge's order was stayed by another High Court judge[94] upon the mother's application, the principle underlying the judge's decision appears to strike hard at the old African custom where certain grandparents are viewed at least as equally competent to act as guardians of their grandchildren.[95] The decision also exposes the vulnerability of mothers whose economic standing is often weaker than that of their husbands. Mothers stand to lose custody of their children if they decide to return to the job market when their marriage has broken down. Moreover, the law relating to spousal maintenance is not friendly to former wives[96] while orders for child maintenance are rarely ever sufficient to maintain a child to an adequate standard.[97]

---

[92] At p 5 of the judgment.

[93] *Ibid.*

[94] *Rosemary Mabagala v Robert Mabagala and Batuli Yusuf Tupa*, Dar es Salaam High Court Matrimonial Cause No 6 of 2000 (per Muro J, 6.6.2001, unreported).

[95] The general principle that parents are primarily responsible for the care of their children cannot be faulted. However, it needs to be applied with flexibility in specific cases bearing in mind 'the customs of the community to which the parties belong' (s 125(2)(c) of LMA). Moreover, the court has discretion under s 126 of LMA to impose conditions on custody including stipulating the place where the infant is to reside, the manner of his or her education and as to the religion in which the child is to be brought up. These powers provide flexibility to the court to apply the principle of best interests of the child in making custody orders and orders for the upbringing of the child.

[96] See s 115 of LMA:

> '(1) The court may order a man to pay maintenance to his ... former wife ... (e) when granting or subsequent to the grant of a decree of divorce ... Provided that where the marriage has been dissolved, the wife shall not, unless the court for special reason so directs, be entitled to maintenance for herself for any period following the date when the dissolution takes effect.'

[97] See Bart Rwezaura and Ulrike Wanitzek 'Family Law Reform in Tanzania: A Socio-Legal Report' (1988) *International Journal of Law and the Family* 2, 1–26 at 22.

5 CONCLUSION

This *Survey* has concentrated on the decisions of superior courts[98] and shown how judges have played a significant role in the transformation of Tanzanian family law during the last 5 years. This change, which remains incomplete, has taken place during the protracted delay in the enactment of a unified law of succession and the reform of the law relating to children. At the same time wider changes in the political and social structures of Tanzania have given birth to a market-oriented economy and an emerging liberal political system underpinned by the Bill of Rights. The shift towards political liberalism, albeit remaining incomplete and fragile, has created ideal conditions and a willingness on the part of the senior members of the judiciary to deliver on the promises contained in the state Constitution and in a number of international human rights treaties to which Tanzania is a signatory. In their effort to mitigate some of the more obvious shortcomings in the existing law, certain judges have also extended existing statutory provisions to cover new situations. For example, the principle governing distribution of matrimonial assets on separation or divorce has been extended to cases of intestate succession thus enabling the courts to provide economic protection to widows. Furthermore, the principle of best interests of the child has been widened to cover non-marital children.

More generally, courts deserve credit for having done more than merely delivering justice between individual litigants. They have also in the process taken part in the larger project of integration of the various systems of customary laws and religious laws into the national legal system. In this connection, some analysts might think that judges have pre-empted the long-awaited formal process of reform and integration; and, furthermore, that judicial law reform is nonetheless unsystematic and not comprehensive. Indeed, others might view the constitutionalisation of family and succession laws as an even more radical programme of reform than what the government had previously intended. This is true to some extent because some of the reforms proposed by the government would not pass the constitutional test if they were subsequently challenged in court.

The implication of this assertion could be far reaching for the government. Perhaps there is a case, after all, for further reconsideration of the delayed reforms by the government. Paradoxically, what we may have viewed initially as a negative outcome of a delayed process of reform has emerged looking like a positive consequence of the delay. Thus the optimist among us could conclude this *Survey* by predicting yet a longer period of delayed reforms but this time for good reasons and hopefully, at the end of the day, for a better product.

---

[98] With the exception of the cases relating to burial all of which were decided by the Court of the Resident Magistrate.

THE STORY OF ADULTERY IN TURKEY

Esin Örücü[*]

Résumé

Jusqu'en 1915 dans l'empire ottoman il n'existait pas, de causes de divorces spécifiques, dès lors que le mari n'avait pas à justifier sa décision de prononcer le divorce. Selon l'Islam, l'adultère était une infraction pénale qui s'appliquait tant à l'homme qu'à la femme (*Coran*, 24:2) : "Frappez la fornicatrice et le fornicateur... de cent coups de fouet" le règne du Calife Omar (634-644), la lapidation à mort de la femme fut ajoutée à la peine prévue pour l'adultère, mais elle fut rarement mise en œuvre et fut bannie par le Sultan au 17ème siècle. Le Code pénal ottoman de 1858 s'inspirait du Code français de 1810. Une femme adultère était punie par un emprisonnement de trois mois à deux ans, de même que son complice. En revanche, le mari ne commettait l'adultère que s'il vivait avec une autre femme dans la maison qu'il partageait avec son épouse légitime. Ce Code est demeuré en vigueur jusqu'en 1926.

Le Code pénal de 1926 de la République turque, inspiré du Code italien, considérait également l'adultère comme une infraction punissable. Bien que la peine fût de 6 mois à trois ans dans tous les cas, l'adultère d'un homme était défini comme le fait de vivre, en tant que mari et femme, avec une femme non mariée, dans la maison conjugale partagée avec l'épouse légitime, ou à un autre endroit connu du public (article 441). Au contraire, pour la femme, toute relation sexuelle avec un homme autre que son mari constituait un adultère, et une seule relation sexuelle était suffisante pour encourir la condamnation (article 440).

En 1996, la Cour Constitutionnelle a annulé l'article 441 sans pour autant porter de jugement sur le sens et la place de l'adultère dans la société. Elle a considéré que la différence de traitement entre l'adultère de l'homme et celui de la femme violait l'article 10 de la Constitution sur l'égalité. La Cour a suggéré que le pouvoir législatif supprime l'adultère des infractions punissables pour les deux époux, ou qu'il le maintienne avec des conditions nouvelles ne distinguant pas entre les époux. Le pouvoir législatif a choisi de ne pas réglementer la question. Aussi, en 1999, l'article 440 a-t-il également été annulé par la Cour Constitutionnelle. Cette question a encore été évoquée sous l'angle de l'égalité

[*] Professor of Comparative Law, University of Glasgow and Emeritus Professor of Comparative Law, Erasmus University Rotterdam.

entre hommes et femmes, la Cour faisant remarquer qu'il existait maintenant une nouvelle inégalité dès lors que le mari avait acquis une position privilégiée.

Pendant les discussions de 2005 sur le nouveau Code pénal, la question de l'adultère a été un sujet vivement débattu. Bien que la version originale du projet ne mentionnât pas l'adultère, des membres du gouvernement ont souhaité, à la dernière minute, en faire mention dans le Code, ce qui n'a pas manqué de provoquer des réactions tant à l'étranger qu'à l'intérieur du pays. Les défenseurs de l'adultère se fondaient sur les deux décisions de la Cour Constitutionnelle, lesquelles en annulant l'adultère sur le fondement de l'égalité n'avaient pas émis un jugement de valeur. La motivation immédiate de ce camp était la sauvegarde de la morale de la société turque. Au contraire, les détracteurs de la criminalisation de l'adultère estimaient que la morale était préservée dans la mesure où l'adultère était déjà une cause légitime de divorce. Ils jugeaient la criminalisation de l'adultère comme l'expression d'un parti pris conservateur, voire religieux, et qu'elle constituait un obstacle à l'adhésion de la Turquie à l'Union européenne. Ils avançaient également un argument technique : si l'adultère était réintroduit dans le Code pénal, un homme marié officiellement à une femme selon un mariage séculier – c'est-à-dire le mariage reconnu par le Code civil et la Constitution – et avec une ou plusieurs femmes avec lesquelles il aurait contracté seulement un mariage religieux, serait considéré comme entretenant une relation adultère et pourrait être emprisonné, tout comme les autres femmes ! Dans le nouveau Code pénal du 1er juin 2005, aucune mention n'a été faite de l'adultère.

Aujourd'hui, l'adultère est une cause fréquente de divorce en Turquie (article 161 du Code civil de 2002) dans le respect du principe d'égalité entre époux. L'adultère présente également des conséquences en matière de dommage moral, de pension alimentaire, lors de décès et du régime matrimonial. Depuis que la Cour Constitutionnelle a annulé, en 1991, la disposition du Code civil interdisant la reconnaissance d'enfant naturel, au motif que tous les enfants devaient être traités sur un pied d'égalité, un père peut reconnaître un enfant né d'une relation adultère.

I　INTRODUCTION

The Turkish Republic rose from the ashes of the Ottoman Empire in 1924. In the Ottoman Empire the Holy Law of Islam, the *Şeriat* (*sharia*) applied to the Moslem population both in family law and criminal law. This remained the case in family law until the time of the Republic, when in 1926 a Civil Code based on the Swiss Civil Code was adopted, and in criminal law until 1858 when a Penal Code was promulgated based on the French Napoleonic Penal Code of 1810. This Code survived until the Republic was established and a new Code was prepared in 1926 based on the Italian Code.

The first thing to note is that prior to 1915, when an imperial edict was promulgated granting women the right to sue for divorce in case of desertion or the husband's contagious disease making married life dangerous, and the more extensive 1917 Ottoman Law of Family Rights – the first such Law in the Islamic world – there were no specific grounds for divorce, since the husband did not have to show cause when he pronounced divorce (repudiation). Therefore, adultery was not mentioned as a ground for divorce. Only in one type of divorce, divorce by judicial process, do we see adultery being mentioned in the primary source of the Şeriat, the Quran. If the husband alleges, without legal proof, that the wife has committed adultery, she is entitled to file a suit to bring about a retraction of this statement or the swearing of an oath by her husband that she is guilty of adultery. If he had accused her falsely, his insistence under oath on her guilt would bring the wrath of Allah upon him. Intercourse with the husband becomes unlawful once the wife has filed the suit, unless he retracts his claim (Quran 24:6–9). After the oaths of both husband and wife, the husband can divorce his wife. If he refuses to do so, and if the parties do not agree to forgive each other, the Şeriat court must dissolve the marriage.[1]

The Quran regulated adultery mainly as a criminal offence to be applied equally to both men and women. According to the Quran (24:2), the punishment for adultery is as follows:

'Flog the adulteress and the adulterer, each one of them, with a hundred stripes, and let not pity for them restrain you from executing the judgment of Allah, if you believe in Allah, and the last day.'

In addition there is a ban on marrying an adulterous person unless the consorting party is also an adulterous person. Later, during the rule of Caliph Omer (634–644) 'stoning to death' of the woman (recim or rejm) was added as a punishment for adultery, though not cited in the Quran. For recim, the offender may or may not be married at the time of the adulterous act. What is important is that one should have been married at some time. Those who have never been married are to be punished by flogging. Recim was rarely used in the Ottoman Empire and was last seen in the seventeenth century. The Sultan who was watching the execution of this punishment in Sultanahmet Square ended this punishment by saying: 'From now on, I do not want such disgrace in the Ottoman lands.'[2] In fact, for either punishment to be meted out, the act must have either been seen by four male witnesses or the offenders must have confessed four times individually and under oath to their action; thus this offence was very difficult to prove.

In 1840 a Penal Law came into force for the first time. It was influenced by French Law but remained mainly within the framework of the Şeriat, as was a second Penal Law in 1851. The 1858 Penal Code, however, was based on the French Napoleonic Penal Code of 1810. Adultery as an offence and the punishment for it were regulated in a paragraph added to Section 201. According to this paragraph, an adulterous woman was to be punished by 3

---

[1]   For types of divorce in Islam see J L Esposito *Women in Muslim Family Law* (Syracuse, Syracuse University Press, 1982) pp 30–36.

[2]   B Toprak 'Türk Modeli Laikliğin 21. Yüzyılda Geleceği' in *Devlet ve Din İlişkileri – Farklı Modeller Konseptler ve Tecrübeler* (Ankara, Konrad Adenaver Vakfı yay, 2003) p 118.

months' to 2 years' imprisonment upon the petition of her husband or her guardian, unless her husband accepted her back. The accomplice would also be imprisoned for between 3 months and 2 years. In addition he would be fined between 5 and 100 gold *mecidiye*. However, a husband would only be considered adulterous if he lived with another woman in the house he shared with his wife, upon the petition of the wife, on the proof of which he would be fined between 5 and 100 gold *mecidiye*.[3] As stated above, this Code remained in force until 1926. The 1926 Code based on the Italian Penal Code also regarded adultery as a punishable offence.

Thus, in the period prior to the founding of the Republic of Turkey, adultery was not cited as a ground for divorce but was a punishable offence. In the primary source of law, the *Quran*, the punishment was equally applied to men and women. However, later, an additional and very harsh punishment was introduced for women by *sünnet* (*Sunna*). In 1858 a Penal Code was promulgated and the offence of adultery was added to the source French Penal Code as a punishable offence to fit the presumed mores of Moslem society, whereby the treatment of men and women differed.

In Turkey today, adultery is an important and frequently used ground for divorce. Seen as a breach of the marital duty of fidelity, it is a specific and absolute ground for divorce, which can be used within 6 months of the act of adultery coming to the knowledge of the other spouse and within 5 years of the act. The court has no discretion to take into consideration the circumstances or assess whether adultery constitutes a serious violation of marital duties in a particular case.

Until 1999, adultery was a criminal offence in the Penal Code, though in divorce cases civil courts were not obliged to await the judgment of the criminal court. Two Sections (440 and 441) in a Chapter of the Penal Code entitled 'Offences Against General Morality and Family Order' regulated adultery and regarded it as a violation of the duty of sexual fidelity of the spouses and a threat to the purity of the blood line.

However, although the Civil Code of 1926,[4] viewed adultery within the principle of equality of the spouses, as does the 2002 Civil Code, the 1926 Penal Code did not. It distinguished between the adultery of the wife and that of the husband (Sections 440–441).

---

3   A Gökçen *Tanzimat Dönemi Osmanlı Ceza Kanunları ve Bu Kanunlardaki Ceza Müeyyideleri* (Istanbul, 1989) p 152.
4   See E Örücü 'Turkey: Reconciling Traditional Society and Secular Demands' (1987–88) 26 *J Fam L* 221–236 at 230.

II WHAT IS SAUCE FOR THE GOOSE IS NOT SAUCE FOR THE GANDER

The 1926 Penal Code regulated adultery in five sections (Sections 440–444). The punishment for adultery was 6 months' to 3 years' imprisonment in all cases.

For the husband, adultery was defined as living with an unmarried woman as man and wife either in his house of residence with his lawful wife, or in another place known to the public (Section 441). The condition was continuous cohabitation with the same unmarried woman in the same house. He would not be guilty if he cohabited with a different woman at different times, or even with the same woman, but in different places. This meant, for example, that a one-off affair of the husband, for example, while, on a business trip, would not count as adultery and neither would a liaison without sexual intercourse. This last exception was developed by the High Court of Appeal (the *Yargıtay*). In addition, according to the High Court of Appeal, during the course of a divorce or an alimony case, the mention of the fact that the husband had established an emotional tie with another woman could not in itself constitute proof of adultery.[5] However, if the husband kept an unmarried woman as if they were married, then one instance of sexual intercourse was enough for the establishment of adultery.[6]

For the wife, however, any sexual intercourse with a man other than her husband constituted adultery, thus one voluntary sexual act was enough for punishment. The interesting twist for a husband was that if he cohabited with a married woman other than his wife even once, he would be guilty of adultery as an accomplice to the offence of adultery committed by a married woman. The punishment would be 6 months' to 3 years' imprisonment.

Section 442 stated that if the spouses, though still married, were separated by a court decision or if one deserted the other, then the period of punishment would be reduced to between 3 months and one year. In all cases, the other party to the act would be subject to the same sanction if he/she knew of the marriage when involved in the sexual act.

The punishment for the offence of adultery was petitioned by a private claim by the aggrieved spouse to the public prosecutor. Then the public prosecutor would initiate criminal proceedings (Section 443). The death of one of the spouses abated the action (Section 444). The petitioning spouse could renounce the case and this would have effect even after judgment had been made. In such a case punishment would be set aside (Section 444).

---

5   *Yargıtay* 5, CD, 25/9/1980, *İlmi ve Kazai İçtihatlar Dergisi*, 1981, 9.
6   *Yargıtay* 5, CD, 1/7/1980, *Yargıtay Kararlar Dergisi*, 1981, 369.

III THE CONSTITUTIONAL COURT TAKES FIRM ACTION

In 1996, the Constitutional Court (*Anayasa Mahkemesi*), upon referral from a
Criminal Court of General Jurisdiction (*Asliye Ceza Mahkemesi*), annulled
Section 441 of the then Penal Code regulating the adultery of the husband,
finding the differences between the adultery of the husband and of the wife to
be in violation of Article 10 on equality of the Constitution.[7] Section 440 of the
same Code regulated adultery of the wife stating that the penalty for a wife's
adultery was 6 months' to 3 years' imprisonment. The same applied to a man
who had sexual intercourse with a woman knowing that she was married. Here
there was obvious equality. However, the annulled Section 441 had additional
conditions for a husband's adultery. As stated above, a single instance of sexual
intercourse, which was sufficient in the case of a wife's adultery, was not
deemed to be sufficient in the case of a husband's. According to Section 441 as
it then stood, the man must have been living with an unmarried woman as if she
was his wife either in his marital home or another place known to others. Only
in this case would he be imprisoned for between 6 months and 3 years and the
woman also if she knew that he was married. The Constitutional Court opined
that since for the establishment of adultery different conditions applied to the
man and the woman, the husband was granted a legal position of superiority to
the wife; there was no legitimate reason to justify this, spouses being under the
same obligation to be faithful to each other. This was a unanimous decision. In
the reasoning an extensive discussion of the concept and the rule of equality is
to be found. Though the decision was based solely on Article 10 of the Turkish
Constitution of 1982, there are references to the International Covenant on Civil
and Political Rights, the European Convention on Human Rights and the
Convention on the Prevention of All Forms of Discrimination Against Women.
During its deliberations, the Constitutional Court briefly said: 'International
documents on human rights to which we are a party also negate discrimination
based on sex.' This reference is only to the provisions of these documents
however, rather than to the cases of the European Court of Human Rights; that
is, the Court adopted a purely 'legalistic approach'. In addition, there was no
extensive discussion of adultery as a criminal offence, its meaning and place in
society.

Usually, decisions of the Constitutional Court come into force upon
publication. However, this decision taken in December 1996 came into force in
December 1997, as the Court regarded the gap in the Code to be created by the
annulment as a threat to public policy and against public interest. In such cases
the Court can decide on a future date at which a decision comes into force. Here
a period of one year was set so that the legislature could take appropriate
measures to close the gap and make the necessary regulations.

The Court suggested that the legislature could either remove adultery from
among punishable offences altogether for both spouses or keep adultery as a
criminal offence with new conditions, but could not create any distinction

---

[7]   *Anayasa Mahkemesi,* 1996/15; 1996/34; 23.9.1996; *Resmi Gazete* No: 22860; 27 December 1996; 246.

between them. Thus, Section 441 ceased to exist but the legislature took no steps to regulate this area although extensive debate did take place in the academic world. So after 27 December 1997 a wife's adultery remained a punishable offence, whereas a husband's adultery did not. There was still inequality and, what was worse, the wife was now totally penalised for being unfaithful while the husband was free to do what he liked outside the marriage. Until the legislature could make up its mind, there was this new anomaly and new inequality. In addition, the message was seen to be that men were entirely at liberty to enter other relationships at will.

At the time it did not seem feasible that adultery would be abolished as a punishable offence in Turkey as this would be against the public mores of the vast majority of Turks.

Feminists and the progressive legal camp were carrying out comparative work pointing out that in the last two decades even those countries which considered adultery a criminal offence had changed their tune and that Turkey should follow suit. The legislature did not, but the Constitutional Court did.

In 1999, Section 440 of the then Penal Code was also annulled upon referral from another Criminal Court of General Jurisdiction.[8] Again the issue was dealt with entirely within the context of equality of the sexes. This time the arguments centred on the fact that now there was a new inequality as the husband had acquired a privileged position, adultery no longer being an offence for the husband. This time there was a dissenting opinion signed by two justices. This opinion claimed that adultery was a criminal offence in most legal systems; that sexual activities of married couples should be confined within marriage; that adultery harmed the innocent spouse and public order; that considering adultery as an offence is not only for the purpose of satisfying the feelings of the innocent spouse but for the protection of the institution of marriage itself; and that the annulment of Section 441 had already created more harm in society than the correction of violation of equality. According to this opinion, different conditions for the two sexes in the name of public interest and other considerations could not be considered a violation of the Constitutional Article 10 on equality.

In 1997 another case had reached the Constitutional Court.[9] This involved a claim that Section 462 of the then Penal Code was in violation of four Articles of the Constitution: Articles 5 (the State is under an obligation to remove all obstacles limiting fundamental rights and freedoms), 10 (Equality), 12 (Everyone has inalienable and non-transferable fundamental rights and freedoms), 17 (Everyone has the right to life, to protect and develop his/her material and moral being) and 19 (Everyone has individual freedom and security).The application was made to the Constitutional Court by an Aggravated Felony Court dealing with an accused who was convinced beyond doubt that his sister was in an illegitimate sexual relationship and had tried to

---

8 *Anayasa Mahkemesi*, 1998/3; 1998/28; 23.6.1998; *Resmi Gazete* No: 23638; 13 March 1999.
9 *Anayasa Mahkemesi*, 1997/45; 1998/48; 16.7.1998; *Resmi Gazete* No: 25297; 22 November 2003; 311.

kill both her and her lover. Section 462 introduced a reduction of up to one-eighth of the sentence of an accused if he/she was a spouse, an ascendant, a sister or brother of the husband, wife, sister or descendant of the victim. The accused should have no doubt that that person had been adulterous or in an illegitimate sexual relationship, caught in the act or about to perform the act or been a party to the act. The killing or maiming of both parties to the act fell into this Section. Life was converted to between 4 and 8 years' imprisonment and the death penalty (in force at the time) was converted to between 5 and 10 years' imprisonment.

The reasoning of the Felony Court and the Constitutional Court gives insight into the attitudes towards illegitimate sexual activity, including adultery, in Turkey. The Aggravated Felony Court stated that everyone has the right to life and to the protection and development of life and can freely choose his/her lifestyle; that this Section finds its base in a person's claim to ownership of and domination of another, the egoism in not allowing that other to be happy with another, and the belief in cleansing the name and honour (*namus*), and therefore is repugnant to the general principles of law. To reduce the sentence of someone without any inquiry into whether that person cared for the other, showed any interest in his/her life, work and happiness, and whether there was a loving relationship is not in keeping with the feelings of justice.

The Constitutional Court, however, limited its inquiry to the killing or maiming of a sister by her brother, considered it within the ambit of serious provocation and did not find Section 462 to be unconstitutional, stating that the legislature is free to decide which actions are to be considered as offences in society, what kind of and what length of sentence is appropriate and what are to be regarded as provocation and aggravating or mitigating circumstances. According to the Court, in using this discretion the legislature keeps in mind the sentencing policy, the social and cultural structure, and the ethical values of the country.

The dissenting opinion was critical of the Court's decision in that the reduction in the sentence is related to who the victim is and therefore serious provocation seems to be the basis of the decision. The dissenting opinion regarded Section 462 as creating a privilege for the accused by accepting higher levels of reduction of the sentence than provided for generally by the Penal Code. It stated that the personality of the victim is an issue to be taken into consideration during sentencing by the judge and cannot form the basis for granting privileges to certain individuals; such a serious reduction sends a message that such an assault on the right to life is condoned in the name of protecting the name and honour of another. The opinion stated that when principles expressed in the Preamble of the Constitution, the priority given to the individual and developments in penal law are taken into consideration, it becomes obvious that such a Section in the Penal Code is unconstitutional in a pluralist, freedom-loving and participatory democracy which has reached levels of contemporary civilization.[10] It is worthwhile noting that this time, the decision of the

---

[10]   Today, neither this Section nor Sections related to adultery have a place in the new Penal Code of 1 June 2005.

Constitutional Court was only published in November 2003, a full 4 years after the decision had been reached. This delay tells us a lot about the ambivalent attitude of Turks, the Turkish judiciary and the Turkish legal system towards adulterous or illegitimate relationships.

IV THE TREATMENT OF ADULTERY IN THE NEW 2002 CIVIL CODE

A new Civil Code came into effect on 1 January 2002.[11] There have been no further changes to the divorce grounds beyond the amendments of 1988 introducing divorce by mutual consent upon irretrievable breakdown.[12] The mixed-grounds system with the same grounds still exists: adultery (Section 161 – old 129); threat to life, extreme cruelty and serious insult (Section 162 – old 130); committing a humiliating crime, leading a dishonourable life (Section 163 – old 131); desertion (Section 164 – old 132); incurable mental illness (Section 165 – old 133); and irretrievable breakdown (Section 166 – old 134).

Adultery was not defined in the Civil Code of 1926, neither is it defined in the Civil Code of 2002 which states in Section 161 that:

> 'If one spouse commits adultery, the other can sue for divorce. This ground must be used within six months of knowledge of adultery and in any case within five years of the adulterous act. A spouse who condones (pursuer forgives the defendant's adultery) has no right to sue for adultery.'

We see that the adulterous party cannot bring a divorce suit to court based on that ground, and neither can a spouse who forgives the other's adultery. Collusion can be used as a defence. The proof of adultery is binding on the judge, there being no need to prove that life in common has become intolerable. This is an absolute ground to be used within 6 months of having knowledge of the adultery and within 5 years of the adulterous act itself.

What is regarded as adultery by the courts is voluntary sexual intercourse between a married person and a person of the opposite sex, not being the marriage partner. Thus pre-marital sex cannot be adultery, neither can sex that is not voluntary or if consent cannot be given due to mental incapacity at the time of the sexual act. For the purposes of establishing adultery, for which a single act suffices, sexual intercourse must involve some degree of physical penetration of the vagina by the penis. Penetration elsewhere, by other means or oral sex, for example, do not amount to adultery. Artificial insemination of the wife with the sperm of someone other than the husband, even if without the husband's consent or knowledge, cannot be considered as adultery.

---

[11] See E Örücü 'Family Law Enters the New Century' in A Bainham (ed) *The International Survey of Family Law 2004 Edition* pp 469–482.

[12] See the report by E Örücü 'Turkish Family Law: A New Phase' (1991–92) 30 *J Fam L* 431.

In addition to being a ground for divorce, adultery has consequences in the 2002 Civil Code in moral damages (Section 174), alimony (Section 175), upon death (Section 176) and related to matrimonial property (Section 236).

Upon divorce, material damages are awarded for existing or expected interests. Moral damages are awarded if the spouse is faultless or less faulty or if his/her personality rights are damaged (Section 174). An adulterous spouse therefore cannot ask for moral damages.

Alimony for an unlimited period can be granted if one of the divorced spouses falls destitute, on condition that he/she is not the more faulty party (Section 175). This means that an adulterous spouse cannot ask for alimony.

Section 176 states that alimony ends upon death, marriage to another, living with another as if married, or leading a dishonourable life. Adulterous relationships would also fall into this category. An important amendment indicating a change in social policy is that if death occurs while the divorce suit is pending, the heirs to the pursuer can continue the suit and if they can prove that the defendant was at fault, then the defendant cannot inherit from the deceased pursuer. Earlier, as the lawsuit fell upon death, the defendant always inherited.

Section 236 relating to the matrimonial property regime of participation in acquisitions, states that a spouse has rights in half the added value of the other's possessions. However, upon divorce based either on adultery or threat to life, the judge may decide to reduce or remove this right in keeping with the principle of fairness.

Another area where adultery had consequences in the 1926 Civil Code was for children born into adulterous relationships, both as to their acknowledgement and their inheritance rights. This is no more. Turkey now follows the European principle of 'the best interest of the child'. The first thing to note is that prior to 1981, the paternity of a child born into an adulterous relationship could not be decided by a court except as 'paternity for financial support only'. This provision was found to be unconstitutional by the Constitutional Court in 1981.[13] Thus a court can now declare paternity for a child whose father was already married to a woman other than his mother at the time of the sexual intercourse.

However, as far as the right to succession was concerned there remained a distinction between legitimate and illegitimate children. Even if they were acknowledged or their paternity was established by a court decision, these children could inherit from their fathers only half as much as their legitimate children. Thus the status of the child was still determined by the father's relationship with the mother. This was the case until the Constitutional Court

---

13   21.5.1981; E. 1980/29; K. 1981/22. See E Örücü 'Turkey: Reconciling Traditional Society and Secular Demands' (1987–88) 26 *J Fam L* (Annual Survey of Family Law, 1986, Vol 10) p 228.

annulled this provision in 1987 with effect from 1988.[14] In 1990, the Civil Code was amended to read that illegitimate and legitimate relatives had the same rights of inheritance. Though in the best interest of children, some regarded this as the condoning of religious marriages in Turkey and a concession to societal practices and values. It is now established that the natural child of a father is also regarded as illegitimate and therefore, has the same rights as a legitimate child. This position is the one taken by the High Court of Appeal since 1997.

It is also important to note that since 1991 it has been possible for a father to acknowledge a child born into an adulterous relationship, as the Constitutional Court held in 1991 that the provision of the Civil Code which stated that a married man could not acknowledge his child from an adulterous relationship was unconstitutional and all children should be treated equally, whether born into illicit relationships or not.[15] However, though a child born from an adulterous relationship of the father can be acknowledged, one born from the adulterous relationship of the mother cannot.

The final change in this field came with the new Civil Code in January 2002. Today, the Civil Code deals with relatives in the Book on Law of Succession (Sections 495–682). There is no mention of legitimacy or illegitimacy in this Book. The only Section dealing with this issue is Section 498, which states that those born out of wedlock become heirs to their father in the same way as those born into wedlock if their blood ties are established by acknowledgement or by a court decision.

V THE NEW 2005 PENAL CODE AND CONCLUDING REMARKS

Whether the removal of adultery as a criminal offence would be condoned in Turkey, where not only is adultery still a ground of divorce, but also is a widely used one, remained an open question until the passing of the new Penal Code in 2005. During the deliberations this issue became a hotly debated contentious problem. In the original Draft there was no mention of adultery. The last-minute efforts of some members of the government to put adultery back into the Code attracted immediate attention both at home and abroad. The issue received especially extensive coverage in the foreign media. It was presented in these debates as being a conservative or even a religious step, an obstruction in the way of Turkey's European Union membership. After a week of intensive exchange of opinions the final shape of the Code was agreed upon. In the New

---

14   See E Örücü 'Turkish Family Law: A New Phase' (1991–92) 30 *J Fam L* (Annual Survey of Family Law, 1990, Vol 14) p 437; E Örücü 'Diverse Issues, Continuing Debates' in A Bainham (ed) *The International Survey of Family Law 1996 Edition* pp 452–454.

15   *Anayasa Mahkemesi*, 90/15; 91/5; 28.2.1991, *Resmi Gazete*; 27 March 1992. For a discussion of the cases both at the Constitutional Court and the High Court of Appeal, see, E Örücü 'Improving the Lot of Women and Children' in A Bainham (ed) *The International Survey of Family Law 1999 Edition* pp 473–477.

Penal Code, which came into effect on 1 June 2005, there is no mention of adultery.

In this context, a paradox was also highlighted.

The anti-adultery camp relied on arguments of modernity and current developments in the civilised world. Their concern was also related to their prospective membership of the European Union. They relied on domestic facts and said that there had been no increase in the number of adulterous relationships since 1999 when adultery was no longer held to be a criminal offence. In addition they pointed out that since adultery was still a divorce ground, this should suffice to satisfy the moral position that was taken in this field.

The pro-adultery camp stemmed from the decisions of the Constitutional Court saying that at no stage in the two decisions of 1996 and 1999 annulling adultery in the Penal Code, could one see an assessment of adultery or a value-judgment, the cases being decided solely on the grounds of equality and that the Constitutional Court showed the way on how to legislate in this field constitutionally. This camp's immediate concern was the mores of Turkish society. The proponents of the proposal to re-introduce adultery into the Penal Code were mostly members of the pro-Islamic and conservative ruling Party, the AKP.

However a bizarre argument was put forward by the anti-adultery camp, which had an immediate impact on the others. The argument ran thus: If adultery is to be re-introduced into the Penal Code, a man who has a wife to whom he is officially married – and this is a secular marriage, the only kind of marriage officially recognised in secular Turkey as appears in the Civil Code and protected by the Constitution – but then has one or two other 'wives' with whom he only has a religious marriage, would be deemed to be in an adulterous relationship and might end up in prison; as would the other women! This obviously had always been a possibility but had not come to light in open discussion. At this point the proposal was dropped.

Unless Turkey one day opts to accept law reform in the field of family law along the lines of the Principles of European Family Law as proposed by the Commission on European Family Law[16] and goes for the ground 'divorce by mutual consent' or 'divorce without consent', the conditions of which are that 'the divorce should be permitted without consent of one of the spouses if they have been factually separated for one year', adultery will remain as a ground for divorce in Turkey. However, it will not re-enter the Penal Code.

---

[16]   *Principles of European Family Law Regarding Divorce and Maintenance Between Former Spouses* (prepared by K Boele-Woelki, F Ferrand, C Gonzalez Beilfuss, M Jantera-Jareborg, N Lowe, D Martiny and W Pintens) (Intersentia, Antwerp-Oxford, 2004).

The United States

DEVELOPMENTS IN THE US – THE STRUGGLE OVER THE CREATION OF A STATUS FOR SAME-SEX PARTNERS

J Thomas Oldham[*]

Résumé

C'est avec un certain retard sur de nombreux pays occidentaux que les Etats-Unis ont été confrontés à la controverse relative au statut juridique des couples de même sexe. Jusque récemment aucun État n'avait créé pour ceux-là un statut qui se rapprochât du mariage, même si quelques rares États permettaient aux couples homosexuels de se donner un statut leur accordant quelques maigres droits. Le mariage leur était, bien entendu, inaccessible.

Lorsque la Cour suprême du Vermont décréta que la constitution de cet État obligeait le gouvernement du Vermont à créer pour les couples homosexuels une institution similaire au mariage, cela eut l'effet d'une onde de choc sur le droit de la famille américain. Avec pour résultat qu'en l'an 2000 le Vermont devint le premier État à mettre en place un mécanisme de partenariat semblable au mariage et appelé "union civile". Depuis le 1er janvier 2005, la Californie a emboîté le pas en modifiant sa législation relative au partenariat domestique afin de rendre ce statut, pour l'essentiel, similaire au mariage. Pour sa part, le Connecticut a adopté une loi sur l'union civile, calquée sur celle du Vermont, et entrée en vigueur le 1er octobre 2005.

Le développement le plus remarquable dans ce domaine fut très certainement la décision historique de la Cour judiciaire suprême du Massachussets de 2004 (décision dont on ne se surprendra pas qu'elle fut rendue par 4 voix contre 3).

I   INTRODUCTION

The United States became embroiled in the controversy about committed same-sex relationships somewhat later than many western countries. Until a few years ago, although a few states permitted a same-sex couple to opt into a status with

---

[*]   John H Freeman Professor of Law, University of Houston Law School.

few attributes, none had created a status anything like marriage for such couples. And, of course, marriage itself was not possible.

When the Vermont Supreme Court determined that the Vermont Constitution required that the state provide a marriage-like status for same-sex couples, this was a sea change in American family law.[1] As a result, in 2000, Vermont became the first state to provide a marriage-like opt-in option for same-sex couples, called a 'civil union'. Effective 1 January 2005, California followed suit, revising its 'domestic partner' statutes so the status became in almost all respects like marriage.[2] Connecticut has enacted a 'civil union' scheme that is very similar to that of Vermont, effective 1 October 2005.[3]

The most sweeping development to date has been the determination by the Massachusetts Supreme Judicial Court in 2004 (perhaps not surprisingly, by a 4-3 vote) that the state Constitution mandated a right to marry for same-sex couples.[4] At about the same time, a number of provincial courts in Canada were reaching the same conclusion, based on the Canadian Charter of Rights and Freedoms.[5] While Canadian developments are not technically relevant in the US, they may have enhanced the sense that gay marriage might become much more accepted in the US.

In addition, in 2003, the US Supreme Court struck down a Texas statute that criminalized same-sex sodomy.[6] Although on first blush it would appear that striking down a statute that criminalized sexual behavior in private would indicate little about whether a constitutional right to same-sex marriage existed, one justice predicted in his dissent that the decision would lead to that result.[7]

Finally, in a surprising display of civil disobedience, in 2004, state officials in a few states began to issue marriage licences to same-sex couples, even though state law clearly barred doing so. While these marriages were eventually held to be void by the California and Oregon Supreme Courts,[8] these actions by state

---

[1]   *Baker v State*, 744 A 2d 864 (Vt 1999).

[2]   California Assembly Bill 2005 [2003 AB 2005, adding Cal Fam Code §§ 297.5 and 298.5]. This law was held not to be inconsistent with a recently enacted statute barring same-sex marriage in *Knight v Superior Court*, 31 *Fam L Rep* (BNA) 1256 (Cal App 2005).

[3]   2005 Conn S B 963.

[4]   *Goodridge v Dept of Public Health*, 798 NE 2d 941 (Mass 2003); *Opinion of the Justices to the Senate*, 802 NE 2d 565 (Mass 2004). This ruling withstood constitutional attack in *Largesse v Supreme Judicial Court of Massachusetts*, 373 F 3d 219 (1st Cir 2004). Opponents of this development are attempting to amend the state constitution to reverse this rule. See Belluck 'A New Challenge to Same-Sex Marriages' *N Y Times*, 17 June 2005 at A11; Emery 'Massachusetts Governor Backs Gay Marriage Ban' *S F Chronicle*, 17 June 2005, at A4.

[5]   By late 2004, same-sex partners could marry in six Provinces and the Yukon Territory. *W v Canadian Atty Gen*, 31 *Fam L Rep* (BNA) 1018 (Sask Ct QB 2004). In summer 2005, Canada adopted same-sex marriage for the whole country.

[6]   *Lawrence v Texas*, 539 US 558 (2003).

[7]   *Id* at 605 (Scalia, J, dissenting). Cf *Bronson v Swenson*, 31 *Fam L Rep* (BNA) 1232 (D Utah 2005) (finding the Utah ban on polygamous relationships remained constitutional, despite *Lawrence*).

[8]   See *Lockyer v City and County of San Francisco*, 95 P 3d 459 (Cal 2004); *Li v Oregon*, 31 *Fam L Rep* (BNA) 1267 (Ore 2005).

employees undoubtedly exacerbated the fears that gay marriage was becoming increasingly accepted.

In any event, all these developments caused conservative activists to be concerned that courts in other states might determine that same-sex couples had the right to marry or establish some equivalent relationship, or that residents of their state would go to Massachusetts, California, or Vermont, marry (or form a civil union), and return to the state of domicile and demand that the relationship established elsewhere be accepted. As a result of these concerns, a number of states recently have adopted laws or amendments to their state Constitutions providing that marriage is for heterosexuals only, and that the state should not recognize any marriage entered into by same-sex partners elsewhere.[9] As of early 2005, 40 states had adopted a provision of this type.[10]

These developments in US family law present novel issues. This chapter will outline the rules applicable to marrying in Massachusetts, as well as for establishing a civil union or domestic partnership in Vermont, Connecticut, or California. In addition, I will discuss whether other states will recognize a status entered into elsewhere.

II HISTORY OF THE REGULATION OF UNMARRIED PARTNERS IN THE US

Unmarried partners certainly have a long history in the US. During the nineteenth century, their numbers were reduced pursuant to the acceptance of common-law marriage by many states.[11] In recent times, common-law marriage has been abolished in most states.[12] Same-sex couples, of course, never were included in this scheme because only heterosexuals were considered eligible for common-law marriage.

US family law generally continues to be based on state rules.[13] Not surprisingly, the rules in the 50 states frequently vary in some respects. However, rules applicable to unmarried partners are fairly uniform.[14] Under US law, if a couple does not marry they are largely considered unrelated third parties, for purposes of determining their mutual rights and responsibilities (other than those relating to any children of the relationship). This is true both for heterosexual couples

---

9   For example, 11 states amended their respective constitutions in 2004 (31 *Fam L Rep* (BNA) 1022 (2004)). One court to date has found that an amendment of this type violated the US Constitution and was void. *Citizens for Equal Protection v Bruning*, 31 *Fam L Rep* (BNA) 1315 (D Neb 2005).

10   See Koppelman 'Interstate Recognition of Same-Sex Marriages and Civil Unions: A Handbook for Judges' 153 *Pa L Rev* 2143, 2165 (2005).

11   Bowman 'A Feminist Proposal to Bring Back Common Law Marriage' 75 *Oregon L Rev* 709 (1996).

12   *Id.*

13   See Krause, Elrod, Garrison and Oldham *Family Law* (5th edn, 2003).

14   Oldham *Divorce, Separation and the Distribution of Property* § 1.02 (2005).

and gay couples.[15] Upon dissolution of any such relationship, a remedy exists only if a remedy generally accepted between unrelated third parties can be established, such as contract or partnership.

Although a few states will not enforce contracts between unmarried partners, almost all will. Of those that do enforce contracts, a few states require unmarried partners to have a written agreement to qualify for a remedy when a relationship breaks down.[16] Most states have rejected this requirement. Still, few unmarried partners in the US enter into written agreements; courts must try to determine from the parties' behaviour whether an oral agreement existed or whether some other ground for recovery exists. US courts have not been as creative in developing remedies for unmarried partners using equitable doctrines as have courts in other common-law countries. As a result, unmarried partners often have no remedy when a relationship dissolves.

Unmarried partners could create via contract many of the rights that otherwise would exist *inter se* by operation of law upon dissolution of a marriage (such as marital property rights, etc). Some rights could also be created by doing something like signing a power of attorney for health care. In contrast, parties cannot create by contract other rights that flow to spouses in the US, such as the right to file a joint tax return, the right to social security benefits or survivor rights of various kinds, or the right to inherit property free of estate tax.

III STATES THAT HAVE CREATED A STATUS FOR SAME-SEX COUPLES

A The development of a constitutional right of access to a status for same-sex partners

Historically, only heterosexuals have been permitted to marry in the US. This restriction has been challenged a number of times, until recently always unsuccessfully.[17] After the US Supreme Court held in 1986 that same-sex couples did not enjoy the same constitutional protections as heterosexuals,[18] these challenges have been based on state constitutional law, not federal law.[19]

Recent results have been more mixed. State Supreme Courts in Vermont and Massachusetts have determined that a marriage-like status must be provided for gay couples.[20] Of course, not all recent decisions have been in agreement; a

---

[15] *Id.* Cases involving gay couples include *Whorton v Dillingham*, 248 Cal Rptr 405 (Cal App 1988); *Estate of Reaves v Owen*, 25 *Fam L Rep* (BNA) 1193 (Miss App 1999).

[16] See Minn Stat Ann § 513.075; Tex Fam Code §1.108.

[17] *Baker v Nelson*, 191 NW 2d 185 (Minn 1971), appeal dismissed, 409 US 810 (1972); *Singer v Hara*, 522 P 2d 1187 (Wash App 1974); *Dean v District of Columbia*, 653 A 2d 307 (DC 1995).

[18] *Bowers v Hardwick*, 478 US 186 (1986).

[19] The more recent opinion in *Lawrence*, supra note 6, reflects a more lenient attitude toward gay rights.

[20] See supra notes 1 and 4.

number of courts have reiterated the previous consensus view that same-sex marriage (or some equivalent status) was not constitutionally required.[21] The recent amendments to a number of state Constitutions may significantly affect how this issue will be resolved in the future.

B States that have created a status for same-sex partners

Section II above sets forth a summary of the limited rights of unmarried partners in most US states. Some states have created a status for same-sex partners that, if established, results in significantly different rights both while the relationship continues and upon relationship breakdown.

New Jersey and Hawaii have created an opt-in status for same-sex partners. In New Jersey, it is 'domestic partnership';[22] in Hawaii, such partners are called 'reciprocal beneficiaries'.[23] These laws create a status with rights much less expansive than those granted spouses, so will not be discussed in detail.

A status for same-sex couples much like marriage has been created in Vermont, Connecticut, California and Washington; in Massachusetts, such couples are permitted to marry. These systems will be explored in more detail below.

1 Entering into a Vermont civil union

A couple may enter into a civil union only if they are of the same sex.[24] Parties to a civil union have all the rights and benefits of marriage.[25] It is entered into in a manner similar to a ceremonial marriage, with a license and a ceremony.[26] A civil union must be certified by a judge or a member of the clergy.[27] A civil union is dissolved pursuant to rules analogous to those applicable in a divorce action.[28] There appear to be no residency requirements for establishing one.

2 Entering into a Connecticut civil union

The Connecticut scheme is very similar to the one adopted in Vermont. Only same-sex couples may enter into a civil union.[29] Parties to a civil union have all the rights and responsibilities that spouses do.[30] It is entered into in a procedure

---

21   See *Stanhardt v Superior Court*, 77 P 3d 451 (Ariz App 2003); *Morrison v Sadler*, 821 NE 2d 15, 31 *Fam L Rep* (BNA) 1135 (Ind App 2005); *Lewis v Harris*, 31 *Fam L Rep* (BNA) 1375 (NJ App Div 2005).

22   New Jersey Domestic Partnership Act, P L 2003; NJ Stat § 26:8A-4.

23   Haw Rev Stat § 572C-l.

24   15 Vt Stats Ann § 1202.

25   *Id* at § 1204.

26   18 Vt Stats Ann §§ 5160–62.

27   18 Vt Stats Ann § 5164.

28   15 Vt Stats Ann § 1206.

29   Conn Civil Union Law § 2.

30   *Id* § 14.

analogous to that established for marriage, with a licence and a ceremony,[31] and only judges and clergy can join people in a civil union.[32] Civil unions are to be dissolved by rules similar to those governing dissolution of a marriage. There appear to be no residency requirements for creating a civil union.

3   Entering into a California domestic partnership

A domestic partnership is formed by signing a 'Declaration of Domestic Partnership' and filing it with the Secretary of State.[33] To enter into such a partnership, the parties must either be (i) of the same sex, or (ii) be a heterosexual couple with at least one member over the age of 62.[34] A 'registered domestic partner' has the same rights as a spouse.[35] There appear to be no residency requirements for establishing such a partnership. A domestic partnership is dissolved by filing a proceeding to dissolve a domestic partnership.

4   Establishing a meretricious relationship in Washington

In Vermont, Connecticut, and California, a status is created by affirmatively opting into it. This scheme resembles those that have been established for same-sex couples in Scandinavia, Germany and England.[36] Parties must take some affirmative joint action to establish their status. In Vermont, Connecticut and California (and, indeed, in Massachusetts) if parties do not elect to opt into the status provided, their rights would be as summarized in Section II above, regardless of the duration of the relationship.

This is not the sole model found internationally for schemes to regulate the rights of same-sex couples. In some jurisdictions, the rights of parties are not determined by whether they formally have opted into a status, but the inquiry instead is whether the relationship satisfied certain specific characteristics. If the parties are found to have met these characteristics, a status relationship of some sort is created. In some jurisdictions, such as some Canadian provinces[37] and New Zealand,[38] if the characteristics are met, the parties are treated as if they were married. In other jurisdictions, such unmarried partners are given some rights, but not as may as a married couple.[39]

---

[31]   *Id* §§ 7–11.
[32]   *Id* § 4.
[33]   Cal Fam Code § 298.5.
[34]   *Id* at § 297(b)(5).
[35]   Cal Fam Code § 297.5(a).
[36]   See Krause et al, supra note 13, at 247.
[37]   Hovias 'Property Division for Unmarried Cohabitees in the Common Law Provinces' 21 *Can F L Q* 175 (2003).
[38]   Grainer 'What's Yours Is Mine: Reform of the Property Division Regime for Unmarried Couples in New Zealand' 11 *Pac Rim L & Pol J* 285 (2002).
[39]   See Krause et al, supra note 13, at 247.

The State of Washington has created such a status for unmarried partners. In Washington, parties may establish what is known as a 'meretricious relationship' if it is a 'stable, marriage-like relationship'.[40] Relevant factors considered by courts in making this determination include whether the cohabitation was continuous, its duration and purpose, whether resources were pooled, and the intent of the parties. In reversing a Court of Appeal's decision, the Washington Supreme Court held in 2001 that same-sex partners could establish such a relationship.[41] If a couple is found to have established such a relationship, at dissolution the court treats all property accumulated as if the parties had a community of acquests regime; no right to post-dissolution support exists.[42]

5   Marrying in Massachusetts

After the Massachusetts Supreme Court decided that gay couples had the right to marry, Massachusetts has permitted same-sex marriage.[43] Massachusetts has long had a law that forbade non-residents from marrying if they would not be permitted to marry under the laws of their state of residence.[44] As a result, the governor has taken the position that American non-resident gay couples should not be permitted to marry in the state (because gay marriage is not permitted in any other state).[45]

IV   RECOGNITION OF SAME-SEX RELATIONSHIPS BY OTHER STATES

In the US, certain rights that flow from marriage, such as marital property rights and post-divorce support obligations, flow from whether the parties are considered married for purposes of state law. The discussion below pertains to whether other states will recognize the same-sex status relationships discussed above, for purposes of rights governed by state law.

Other rights, such as the right to file a joint federal tax return or inherit property free of federal inheritance taxes, are based on whether parties are considered married for purposes of federal law. Congress has passed a statute clarifying that a same-sex couple may not be considered married for purposes of federal law.[46]

---

40   *Connell v Francisco*, 898 P 2d 831 (Wash 1995).
41   *Vasquez v Hawthorne*, 33 P 3d 735 (Wash 2001); *Gormley v Robertson*, 83 P 2d 1042 (Wash App 2004).
42   See *Connell v Francisco*, supra note 40.
43   Waldman 'Hundreds of Same-Sex Couples Wed in Massachusetts' *N Y Times*, 18 May 2004, at A1.
44   Mass Gen Laws, ch 207, § 11.
45   Belluck 'Romney Won't Let Gay Outsiders Wed in Massachusetts' *N Y Times*, 25 April 2004, at A1.
46   1 USC, § 7. A gay couple considered 'married' under Massachusetts law would not be considered married for purposes of federal law. So, for example, such a couple could not file a joint federal income tax return. D C Office of Tax & Revenue, 31 *Fam L Rep* (BNA) 1347 (2005). The federal

A   Residents who attempt to create a status elsewhere

1   Recognition in the state of residence

When the right of same-sex couples to marry was adopted in the Netherlands and Belgium, both countries severely restricted the ability of non-residents to marry. Similarly, the Scandinavian countries also limited the ability of non-residents to enter into a registered partnership, the alternative status for same-sex couples available there. So, these countries have largely been able to avoid problems that would result if non-residents attempted to opt into a status under their law. In contrast, residency restrictions have not been put in place by California, Connecticut, Canada or Vermont for entering into the status for same-sex partners offered in each jurisdiction. Same-sex partners residing elsewhere therefore can go to Canada or one of these states and attempt to create such a status.[47] Evidence from Vermont suggests that about 85% of those creating civil unions there are non-residents.[48] Such marriages by non-residents, attempting thereby to avoid a marriage restriction in the law of their domicile, have been termed 'evasive' marriages.[49] Would such a status be recognized in the state of residence?

In the US, the validity of a marriage generally is governed by the law of the place of celebration.[50] However, this is not required if the law of the place of celebration violates an important public policy of the forum.[51] The Restatement (Second) of the Conflict of Laws provides that the validity of a marriage generally should be governed by the law of the state that has the most significant relationship with the parties at the time of celebration.[52] It appears that a significant majority of Americans reject gay marriage.[53] This is reflected in the significant number of states that have enacted laws against gay marriage. In addition, many recent constitutional amendments regarding gay marriages were submitted to the electorate in a number of states, all of which passed these amendments with significant majorities.[54]

---

restriction relating to who can be considered 'married' has to date survived constitutional challenge. See Egelko 'Judge Calls DOMA Legally Sound' *S F Chronicle*, 17 June 2005, at A4.

[47]   Krause 'A Few Gay Americans Tie the Knot in Canada' *N Y Times*, 28 June 2003, at A2.

[48]   Gallanis 'Inheritance Rights for Domestic Partners' 79 *Tulane L Rev* 55, 67 (2004) (stating that 6,014 of 7,029 civil unions had involved non-residents); Baker 'Current Controversies in the Marriage Debate' 18 *BYU J Pub L* 569, 609 n 336 (2003).

[49]   See Koppelman, supra note 10, at 2145.

[50]   See Weintraub *Commentaries on the Conflict of Laws* (4th edn, 2001) pp 289–291; 'Symposium on International Marriage and Divorce Regulation and Recognition' 29 *Fam L Q* 495 (1995); Koppelman 'Same-Sex Marriage and Public Policy' 16 *Quinnipiac L Rev* 105 (1996); 'Developments in the Law of Marriage and the Family' 116 *Harv L Rev* 1997, 2035–36 (2003).

[51]   *Id*. See, for example, Utah Code Ann § 30-1-4; Idaho Code § 32-209; La Civ Code, art 3520. See generally Hogue 'State Common-Law Choice-of-Law Doctrine and Same-Sex Marriage: How Will States Enforce the Public Policy Exception?' 32 *Creighton L Rev* 29 (1998).

[52]   Restatement, Second, Conflict of Laws, 2d (1971) § 283(1).

[53]   See Silberman 'Same-Sex Marriage: Refining the Conflicts of Laws Analysis' 153 *Pa L Rev* 2195, 2209 n 60 (2005) (citing surveys).

[54]   Gootman 'For the President, Some Easy Victories, and a Crucial Close One in Florida' *N Y Times*, 3 Nov 2004, at 12.

So, if a gay couple went from their state of residence elsewhere to attempt to marry, it seems likely that the status would not be recognized by the state of residence, either under the theory that it violates an important policy of the forum or on the theory that the state of residence had the most significant relationship with the parties at that time (and the law of that state does not accept gay marriage). Another reason for predicting this result is that some states have enacted 'marriage evasion laws' which provide that parties may not go elsewhere to marry if the marriage would be barred by the law of the forum.[55] Finally, a number of states have enacted laws which provide that the state should not recognize a same-sex marriage, even if the marriage was valid where celebrated.[56]

The US Constitution does contain a provision requiring states to give 'full faith and credit' to the laws and judgments of other states.[57] This provision has been construed so that one state must honor final *judgments* from other states; it has not been construed as requiring the recognition of the *laws* of other states.[58] So, if gay Massachusetts domiciliaries married and divorced there, courts in all other states would have to enforce the resulting judgment. However, if no judgment exists, it seems fairly clear that a state of residence that does not recognize a status for gay couples does not have to honor a same-sex marriage entered into by its residents elsewhere.[59]

The 'full faith and credit' clause does require states to give full faith and credit to 'acts, records and judicial proceedings' of other states. One commentator has argued that a marriage licence or a civil union licence would constitute a 'record' which would need to be recognized by other states.[60] This argument has not been addressed by any court relating to recognition of gay relationships.

A recent New Jersey case involved New Jersey residents who had married in Canada. The court held that, because New Jersey did not accept same-sex marriage, it would not recognize the Canadian marriage.[61]

A Connecticut case considered the effect of a purported 'marriage' in Massachusetts by two women who were Connecticut residents. One of the women sued in Connecticut to annul the marriage. The judge concluded that Connecticut law does not permit non-residents to marry, so the marriage was

---

[55]   Scoles, Hay, Borchers and Simeonides *Conflict of Laws* §13.13 at 564 (3rd edn, 2000). See, for example, 15 Vt Stat Ann § 5; W Va Code § 48-2-602.

[56]   See, for example, Colo Rev Stat § 14-2-104; Fla Stat Ann § 741.212; Ohio Rev Code § 3101.01.

[57]   US Constitution, art IV, § 1.

[58]   *Baker v Gen Motors Corp*, 522 US 222, 232 (1998); Borchers '*Baker v General Motors*: Implications for Interjurisdictional Recognition of Non-Traditional Marriages' 32 *Creighton L Rev* 147 (1998); Silberman 'Can the Island of Hawaii Bind the World?' 16 *Quinnipiac L Rev* 191 (1996); Opinion of the Oklahoma Atty General, 2004 WL 5574 73 (2004).

[59]   Graham 'Same-Sex Unions and the Conflicts of Law' 3 *Whittier J Child & Fam Advocacy* 231 (2004). This issue was presented in *Wilson v Ake*, 354 F Supp 1298, 31 *Fam L Rep* (BNA) 1171 (MD Fla 2005), where the court analyzed the question as predicted above. Cf *Langan*, infra note 67.

[60]   Reppy 'The Framework of Full Faith and Credit and Interstate Recognition of Same Sex Marriages' 3 *Ave Maria L Rev* (2005).

[61]   *Hennefeld & O'Dell v Montclair*, 22 NJ Tax 166 (15 March 2005).

void.[62] (This case was decided before the civil union statute was passed in 2005.)

A recent bankruptcy case involved two Washington residents who went to British Columbia, 'married', and then returned to Washington and filed a joint petition for bankruptcy. A joint petition may only be filed by a debtor and a spouse. The court held that, pursuant to federal law,[63] two members of the same sex could not be spouses.[64] The joint petition therefore was rejected.

So, it seems quite unlikely that states not accepting some gay status will recognize an evasive gay marriage entered into elsewhere. The probability of recognition of 'evasive' civil unions or registered partnerships is a bit less clear. Compared with gay marriages, these alternate status forms seem somewhat less objectionable to the US public. Also, many of the state laws that have been enacted expressly disapprove of recognition of a gay marriage, but are silent regarding any other status for gay couples.

A Virginia case involved Virginia residents who travelled to Vermont to establish a civil union. In the case, which was a custody dispute, the effect of the civil union under Virginia law arguably was relevant. The judge ruled the civil union was void in Virginia.[65]

In a Georgia case, a woman had agreed in her divorce decree that, when exercising her visitation rights, she would not spend the night with an unrelated adult to whom she was not married. She entered into a civil union and spent the night with her partner when exercising her visitation rights. When her former husband challenged this, the court agreed with the husband that a civil union was not the same as a marriage; the court added that it would not recognize a same-sex marriage entered into elsewhere.[66]

A New York case took a different approach. In this case, a person who had entered into a Vermont civil union had died and the partner filed a wrongful death action. Under US law, only spouses of the decedent (and not de facto partners) may bring such an action. The court permitted the partner to bring the wrongful death action.[67] The opinion emphasized that it was not holding members of civil unions should be treated as spouses for all purposes. It was also noted that, unlike many states, New York had not passed any law disapproving of gay unions.

---

[62] *Lane v Albanese*, 31 *Fam L Rep* (BNA) 1243 (Conn Super 2005).
[63] Bankruptcy law is a federal law in the US, so the definition of marriage in federal law (as limited to a man and a woman) governs. See supra note 46.
[64] *In re Kandu*, 315 BR 123 (Bankr W D Wash 2004).
[65] *Miller-Jenkins v Miller-Jenkins*, 31 *Fam L Rep* (BNA) 1051 (Va Cir Ct 2004).
[66] *Burns v Burns*, 560 SE 2d 47 (Ga App 2002).
[67] *Langan v St Vincent's Hospital*, 765 NYS 2d 411 (NY Sup 2003).

New Jersey has adopted a rule that a civil union established elsewhere should be recognized if it was valid where established.[68] California has adopted a similar rule.[69]

Statutes like the New Jersey statute could create significant confusion, however. The statute provides that New Jersey should 'recognize' a Vermont civil union. But what does this mean? For Vermont, a civil union status is the equivalent of marriage. In New Jersey, a domestic partnership is more limited. In a recent New Jersey case, the court suggests that a Vermont civil union would be recognized, but as a more limited New Jersey domestic partnership.[70]

2   Dissolving the status

Interestingly, although Connecticut and Vermont do not have residency requirements for establishing a domestic partnership or civil union, they do have residency requirements for dissolving the status.[71] So, non-residents who establish the status could find it difficult to dissolve it. They would not satisfy the residency requirements of Connecticut or Vermont, and their state of residence may well not recognize the status to let them dissolve it there.

This happened in a Connecticut case, when the court barred a Connecticut resident from obtaining a dissolution of a civil union entered into in Vermont. The court noted that Connecticut law did not favour the recognition of civil unions or the right to dissolve them.[72] (This case was decided before Connecticut adopted its civil union law.) Courts in Florida and Texas have rejected such dissolution actions for similar reasons.[73] In contrast, an Iowa court reacted differently to an Iowa gay couple who had established a civil union in Vermont. When they later petitioned an Iowa court for a divorce, the court granted it, even though Iowa accepts no gay status.[74]

In a case decided after Massachusetts accepted gay marriage, a Massachusetts court did let a resident dissolve a civil union established in Vermont.[75]

California does not have a residency requirement for dissolving a domestic partnership, thereby avoiding the problems outlined above.[76]

---

[68]   N J Domestic Partnership Act, Pub L 2003, Ch 246, § 6(c).

[69]   Cal Fam Code § 299.2.

[70]   *Henefeld & O'Dell v Montclair*, 22 NJ Tax 166 (2005).

[71]   For example, the residency requirement for Vermont is 6 months. 15 Vt Stats Ann §§ 592, 1206.

[72]   *Rosengarten v Downes*, 802 A 2d 170, 179 (Conn App 2002).

[73]   Baker, supra note 48, at 615 n 274.

[74]   *Brown v Perez*, 30 *Fam L Rep* (BNA) 1094 (2003).

[75]   *Salucco v Alldredge*, 2004 WL 864459 (Mass Super Ct 2004).

[76]   Cal Fam Code §299(d).

B   Residents who establish a status in their state of residence and later move

A somewhat more difficult issue would be presented if a same-sex couple established a status permitted under the law in the state of residence and later moved. Such a status (sometimes referred to as a 'migratory' status[77]) would be valid under the law of the state of celebration, and that state would also be the state that had the most significant relationship with the parties at that time.

There is some precedent which would support the argument that this situation should be handled differently from an evasive marriage. Professor Koppelman looked at cases involving interracial marriages in the US. Some time ago, a number of states barred such marriages and these statutes presumably would be considered ones that reflected important state policies. Indeed, in a number of states establishing an interracial marriage was a felony.[78] Professor Koppelman found that if the parties left their common domicile which barred such marriages to marry in another state that did not bar interracial marriage (an 'evasive' marriage), such marriages were almost never upheld in the state where they lived. However, in those instances where parties had validly married in their state of common domicile and later moved to a state that barred mixed-race marriages, the results were much more mixed.[79]

Still, it appears that most US courts will not uphold a status for same-sex couples even if valid where celebrated and that state was the common domicile of the parties at the time, if the parties later move, and the new domicile does not recognize any gay status.[80] When similar issues have been presented, courts have applied US law to invalidate a marriage (or divorce), even though the parties had no contact with the forum at the time of the marriage (or divorce).

In a Texas case, an Indian national was married to another Indian national, living in India. He went with his girlfriend to Kuwait, where he participated in a talak, an Islamic divorce procedure. He then married his girlfriend (also an Indian national) in Kuwait. They later emigrated to the US. Some years later, the wife filed for divorce. The husband challenged the validity of their marriage, urging the court not to recognize the Kuwait talak as a divorce. The court decided that, although at the time the talak occurred the parties had no contacts with the US, because the parties had lived in the US for a number of years that gave Texas a significant interest in the controversy. The court applied

---

[77]   Koppelman, supra note 10, at 2145.

[78]   Koppelman 'Interstate Recognition of Same-Sex Civil Unions' 65 *Ohio St L J* 1265, 1270 (2004).

[79]   Koppelman 'Same-Sex Marriage, Choice of Law, and Public Policy' 76 *Texas L Rev* 921, 949–961 (1998). Compare, for example, *State v Kennedy*, 75 NC 251 (1877) (not recognizing an evasive interracial marriage) with *State v Ross*, 76 NC 242 (1877) (recognizing an interracial marriage between residents of another state who later moved to North Carolina).

[80]   Professor Koppelman has been quite critical of such a result, where a party's marital status might 'wink out of existence when a party enters a state (and wink back into existence when he leaves?)'. Koppelman, supra note 10, at 2156. Professor Silberman is also critical of such a result. See Silberman, supra note 53, at 2214.

Texas law to invalidate the talak; therefore the subsequent 'marriage' was void.[81]

A recent Arizona divorce case involved the question of whether a marriage between first cousins was valid. The parties had married in Virginia while Virginia residents. Under Virginia law, first cousins could marry. The parties later moved to Arizona, which barred such marriages. When the parties moved to Arizona, Arizona applied a 'place of celebration' choice of law rule to determine marriage validity. Arizona law was later amended so that certain types of marriages, including first cousin marriages, were invalid even if valid where celebrated. The appellate court noted that Arizona generally followed the 'place of celebration' choice of law rule. However, the legislature retains the power, the court stated, to invalidate certain marriages, even if valid where celebrated, and even if that state had a more significant relationship with the parties.[82]

Here the court therefore applied Arizona law to determine whether the marriage was valid. If current law was applied, the marriage would be invalid. However, when the parties first moved to Arizona, the marriage was valid under Arizona law (under the place of celebration approach). The court concluded that to apply the new Arizona statute retroactively to the parties here would deprive the parties of rights that had previously vested. The court determined that the change in the law should be not be applied to parties who had moved to Arizona before the law changed.[83]

Although the Arizona court did not apply Arizona law to invalidate a marriage that was valid under the law of the place of celebration which was also the common domicile of the parties at the time of celebration, the court strongly suggests this would be the result for those people who move to Arizona after the effective date of the law. In addition to proscribing marriage between first cousins, the Arizona law invalidates gay marriages celebrated elsewhere.

Under US law, a state may apply its law to a dispute only if the state had at least a minimum level of contact with the dispute and the parties at a time considered relevant.[84] One commentator has argued that, in situations where parties have established a gay status where they live, and later move to another state that does not accept this status, this contact with the second state would be too late to permit the state constitutionally to apply its law.[85] This argument has not yet been considered by courts.

It was mentioned above that many US states have adopted statutes or amended their respective constitutions to provide that only a marriage between a man and a woman should be recognized. Any question involving whether a court will

---

81   *Seth v Seth*, 694 S W 2d 459 (Tex App 1985).
82   *Cook v Cook*, 104 P 3d 857, 31 *Fam L Rep* (BNA) 1136 (Ariz App 2005).
83   *Id.*
84   *Allstate Ins Co v Hague*, 449 US 302, 308 n 10 (1981).
85   Reppy, supra note 60.

recognize a same-sex relationship established elsewhere could be affected by the language of the particular statute.

A number of these state provisions refer only to gay 'marriages'. Alternate status forms such as civil unions or partnerships are mentioned in a relatively small number.[86] It is unclear whether this difference will make states any more likely to recognize gay civil unions or partnerships, as opposed to marriages, in those states where only gay 'marriage' is expressly disapproved. Some commentators have suggested that one compromise relating to issues pertaining to both recognition of gay marriage as well as civil unions would be for states to recognize some but not all incidents of the relationship, based on the policies involved.[87]

The choice of law issue that would be presented if a Washington gay couple moved would be similar to the other questions presented. It would seem to present another type of choice of law issue regarding status. Still, the rules are potentially very complex and surprisingly not well developed.[88] To date, it has not been uncommon for a couple first to live in one state, move to another and then break up. In the subsequent litigation in the state of the last domicile, the court generally has applied forum law, but it appears the choice of law issue has not been considered in depth.[89] If a same-sex couple established what would be considered a meretricious relationship under Washington law, moved elsewhere, and then broke up, it is quite conceivable that the forum would apply its law, not Washington law, either due to its being the last common domicile or due to public policy concerns.

C   Those who establish a status in their state of residence, do not move, but need the status recognized elsewhere

It is conceivable that in some instances residents of Massachusetts, California, Connecticut or Vermont might need their status recognized elsewhere even if they never move. For example, a Massachusetts couple might travel to another state and have a car accident. In the US, only a spouse can bring a loss of consortium claim or a wrongful death claim. So, it could be important in connection with a legal action stemming from the accident, for example, whether the state where the accident occurred would recognize the status. (This has been characterized as a situation where the parties were never residents, but were 'visitors'.)[90]

---

[86]   A few do mention other status relationships. Va Code Ann § 20-45.3; Neb Rev St Const Art I, § 29; Ohio Const Art XV, § 11; Tex Fam Code § 6.204. For a complete list, see Koppelman, supra note 10, at 2165 (Appendix).

[87]   Silberman, supra note 58, at 203.

[88]   For a detailed commentary, see Reppy 'Choice of Law Problems Arising When Unmarried Cohabitants Change Domicile' 55 *SMU L Rev* 273 (2002).

[89]   For example, this happened in *Connell v Francisco*, supra note 40; *Alderson v Alderson*, 225 Cal Rptr 610 (Cal App 1986); *Western States Construction v Michoff*, 840 P 2d 1220 (Nev 1992).

[90]   See Koppelman, supra note 10, at 2145.

Similarly, a couple who had married or established a civil union might own property in another state. When one party died, for inheritance purposes it might be important whether that state would recognize the status. For example, this could impact whether the surviving partner is an intestate heir, or whether the property would pass to the partner free of state taxes.

Would the state where the accident occurred or the property is located recognize the status in such situations? Professor Koppelman, in his review of cases involving interracial marriage, found that states were more likely to recognize an interracial marriage, even if barred under its law, if the parties never lived in the state.[91] Under this line of cases, a state might be more willing to recognize a gay marriage or civil union by a non-resident, even if barred under its local law, if recognized under the law of the state of residence.

This seems understandable. Presumably what violates a state's norms would be situations where *residents* engaged in relationships considered offensive. Forum policies would seem much less offended by temporary visitors or those who were never physically in the state.

For example, Professor Koppelman notes the case of *Ex Parte Kinney*,[92] where a Virginia couple travelled to the District of Columbia to marry in order to circumvent the miscegenation laws of Virginia (an evasive marriage). When they returned to Virginia they were imprisoned. In *Kinney*, the man unsuccessfully challenged his imprisonment. The court did note, however, that an interracial couple from the District of Columbia would have the 'right of transit', through Virginia, and of 'temporary stoppage'.[93]

Similarly, a party to a mixed-race marriage who resided elsewhere sued in Mississippi to be recognized as the intestate heir of her spouse. The parties had never resided in the state. The court recognized the marriage for this purpose, noting that the policy of Mississippi was to prevent interracial couples from living together in Mississippi as husband and wife. Because the parties did not violate this policy, the marriage was recognized.[94]

A more recent California case also supports this distinction. In this case, an Indian national had married two women in India. He moved to California with one wife and there died intestate. Both wives sued as intestate heirs. The court permitted both women to make a claim, noting that the husband had never cohabited with both women in California.[95]

---

91   Koppelman, supra note 79, at 961.
92   14 F Cas 602 (CCED Va 1879).
93   Koppelman, supra note 10, at 2161–2162.
94   Koppelman, supra note 10, at 2163 (citing the case of *Miller v Lucks*, 36 So 2d 140 (Miss 1948)).
95   *Dalip Singh Bir's Estate v Boyes*, 188 P 2d 499 (Cal App 1948).

V CONCLUSION

A few US states have created a status for same-sex partners that closely resembles marriage. One permits gays to marry; three others, California, Connecticut and Vermont, provide a status much like marriage. Washington also provides significant rights for certain same-sex partners.

Still, same-sex relationships remain very controversial in the US. A number of states have amended their laws or their Constitutions to clarify that gays may not marry and that such marriages entered into elsewhere should not be recognized. Because California, Connecticut and Vermont do not bar non-residents from creating a domestic partnership or a civil union, non-residents can ostensibly establish such relationships, thereby creating some confusion about the validity of the status. In addition, it is conceivable that residents of Massachusetts, California, Connecticut or Vermont might create such a status and then later move elsewhere.

It appears fairly clear that most states will not recognize any status relationship between gay partners, even if the partners attempt to create such a relationship in Massachusetts, California, Connecticut or Vermont, and even if the parties resided in one of those states at the time the status was initially created, if the parties later move to a state that does not recognize the status. This result would be particularly likely in those states that have passed laws which direct a court not to recognize gay unions established elsewhere. And, of course, even if Massachusetts partners are considered married for various purposes of state law, the parties will not be considered married for purposes of US federal law, due to the definition of marriage in the federal Defense of Marriage Act. In contrast, if the couple has never lived in the state, it is more likely the forum will recognize a gay status established elsewhere.

It must be recognized that US law in this area is in quite a turbulent phase. In 2004, New Jersey adopted a status for gay couples that was not a marriage equivalent. During the past few years, two courts have ruled that their respective state Constitutions require a status for gay couples that approximates marriage. Litigation in other states continues. In 2005, California and Connecticut established a status for gay couples that closely resembles marriage. In neither of these instances was the legislature forced to adopt such laws by the state Supreme Court. It seems likely that a few more states, possibly prodded by their respective highest court, will soon adopt a status that is the equivalent of marriage for gay couples. As the number of states that accept a significant gay status increases, this will increase the number of states that will recognize gay status relationships established elsewhere.